Microsoft® SQL Server™ 2008

A BEGINNER'S GUIDE

Dušan Petković

McGraw Hill

New York Chicago San Francisco Lisbon
London Madrid Mexico City Milan
New Delhi San Juan Seoul Singapore
Sydney Toronto

The McGraw·Hill Companies

Library of Congress Cataloging-in-Publication Data

Petković, Dušan.
  Microsoft SQL server 2008 : a beginner's guide / Dusan Petkovic.
     p. cm.
  Includes index.
  ISBN 978-0-07-154638-6 (alk. paper)
  1. SQL server. 2. Relational databases 3. SQL (Computer program language) I. Title.
QA76.9.D3P495145 2008
005.75'85—dc22

                                                                    2008024965

Microsoft® SQL Server™ 2008: A Beginner's Guide

1234567890   DOC DOC   0198

ISBN   978-0-07-154638-6
MHID   0-07-154638-3

Sponsoring Editor Wendy Rinaldi	**Proofreader** Divya Kapoor
Editorial Supervisor Janet Walden	**Indexer** Broccoli Information Management
Project Manager Aparna Shukla	**Production Supervisor** Jean Bodeaux
Acquisitions Coordinator Mandy Canales	**Composition** International Typesetting and Composition
Technical Editor Todd Meister	**Illustration** International Typesetting and Composition
Copy Editor Bill McManus	**Art Director, Cover** Jeff Weeks

Contents at a Glance

Contents

Part II   Transact-SQL Language

Part III   SQL Server: System Administration

Acknowledgments

First, I would like to thank my sponsoring editor, Wendy Rinaldi. Since 1998, Wendy has been in charge of all four books that I have published with McGraw-Hill. I appreciate very much her extraordinary support over all these years. Also, I would like to acknowledge the important contributions of Mandy Canales and Todd Meister.

Introduction

There are a couple of reasons why SQL Server, the system that comprises Database Engine, Analysis Services, Reporting Services and Integration Services is the best choice for a broad spectrum of end users and database programmers building business applications:

► SQL Server is certainly the best system for Windows operating systems, because of its tight integration (and low pricing). Because the number of installed Windows systems is enormous and still increasing rapidly, SQL Server is a widely used system.

► Database Engine, as the relational database system component, is the easiest database system to use. In addition to the well-known user interface, Microsoft offers several different tools to help you create database objects, tune your database applications, and manage system administration tasks.

Generally, SQL Server isn't only a database system. It is a platform that not only manages structured, semistructured, and unstructured data but also offers comprehensive, integrated operational and analysis software that enables organizations to reliably manage mission-critical information.

Goals of the Book

Microsoft SQL Server 2008: A Beginner's Guide follows three previous editions that covered SQL Server 7, 2000, and 2005.

Generally, all SQL Server users who want to get a good understanding of this database system and to work successfully with it will find this book very helpful. (If you are a new SQL Server user but understand SQL, read the section "Differences Between SQL and Transact-SQL Syntax" later in this introduction.)

This book addresses users of all components of the SQL Server system. For this reason, it is divided into several parts: users who want to learn more about the relational database component called Database Engine will find the first three parts of the book the most useful. The fourth part of the book is dedicated to business intelligence users who use either Analysis Services or relational extensions concerning BI. The last part of the book provides insight for users who want to use XML data and/or spatial data.

SQL Server 2008 New Features Described in the Book

SQL Server 2008 has a lot of new features, and almost all of them are discussed in this book. For each feature, at least one running example is provided to enable you to understand that feature better. The following table lists the chapters that describe new features and provides a brief summary of the new features introduced in each chapter.

Chapter 3	The IntelliSense functionality of SQL Server Management Studio's Query Editor is described in this chapter. IntelliSense provides a list of options that make language references easily accessible. In SQL Server 2008, frequently used Transact-SQL elements are supported.
Chapter 4	This chapter describes several new features, the most important of which is the support for the new temporal data types DATE, TIME, DATETIME2, and DATETIMEOFFSET. Two other new data types, FILESTREAM and HIERARCHYID, are also explained. The VARDECIMAL storage format is discussed in detail, too. (This storage format was introduced with Service Pack 2 of SQL Server 2005.)
Chapter 5	The creation of user-defined table types is shown in this chapter. Their practical use in relation to table-valued parameters can be found in Chapter 8.
Chapter 6	In this chapter you can find the syntax and examples for the enhanced form of the GROUP BY clause: GROUP BY().
Chapter 7	This chapter describes the MERGE statement as well as the row-value constructor of the INSERT statement. The MERGE statement combines the sequence of conditional INSERT and UPDATE commands in a single atomic statement, depending on the existence of a record. The row-value constructor allows you to simplify the way you write INSERT statements.
Chapter 8	Table-valued parameters, which allow you to simplify the task of sending many parameters to a routine, are described in this chapter.
Chapter 12	This chapter describes Extensible Key Management and Transparent Data Encryption, which enhance the data encryption capabilities of the previous version. Also, the new tracking mechanism called CDC (change data capture) is introduced and its practical use is shown.
Chapter 13	Enhancements in relation to lock escalation are described in this chapter.
Chapter 16	This chapter describes two tools, of which Declarative Management Framework (DMF) is new. DMF is a framework for managing instances of Database Engine. It allows you to create policies, which are then valid for the whole instance or part of it.
Chapter 17	This chapter describes how you can compress the content of a backup, and introduces several enhancements related to database mirroring.
Chapter 19	The peer-to-peer transactional replication supports the new form of conflict detection, which is explained in this chapter.
Chapter 20	The new hint called FORCESEEK and the new dynamic management view (sys.dm_exec_procedure_stats) are described here. Also, the new form of user-friendly display for execution plans is shown.
Chapter 21	This chapter discusses, among other things, two new and very important performance tools, Performance Data Collection and Resource Governor.

Chapter 24	SQL Server 2008 implements the ROLLUP and CUBE functions with standardized syntax, which are described here. (Both the functions existed in the previous versions, but have supported only the proprietary syntax.) The chapter also discusses a new function called GROUPING SETS.
Chapter 26	The first part of this chapter describes parallelism for data partitioning. The second part of this chapter is entirely new and describes star schema query optimization.
Chapter 28	At the end of this chapter, the minor enhancements in relation to XML schema and the XML data type are described.
Chapter 29	This is an entirely new chapter describing spatial data and two new data types, GEOMETRY and GEOGRAPHY.

Organization of the Book

The book has 29 chapters and is divided into five parts.

Part I, "Basic Concepts and Installation," describes the notion of database systems in general and Database Engine (SQL Server's relational database system) in particular, as well as the installation process. It includes the following chapters:

▶ Chapter 1, "Relational Database Systems—An Introduction," discusses databases in general and Database Engine in particular. The notion of normal forms and the **sample** database are presented here. The chapter also introduces the syntax conventions that are used in the rest of the book.

▶ Chapter 2, "Planning the Installation and Installing SQL Server," describes the first system administration task: the installation of the overall system. Although the installation of SQL Server is a straightforward task, there are certain steps that warrant explanation.

▶ Chapter 3, "SQL Server Management Studio," describes the component called SQL Server Management Studio. This component is presented early in the book in case you want to create database objects and query data without knowledge of SQL.

Part II, "Transact-SQL Language," is intended for end users and application programmers of Database Engine. It comprises the following chapters:

▶ Chapter 4, "SQL Components," describes the fundamentals of the most important part of a relational database system: a database language. For all such systems, there is only one language that counts: SQL. In this chapter, all components of SQL Server's own database language, called Transact-SQL, are described. You can also find the basic language concepts and data types in this chapter. Finally, system functions and operators of Transact-SQL are described.

▶ Chapter 5, "Data Definition Language," describes all data definition language (DDL) statements of Transact-SQL. The DDL statements are presented in three groups, depending on their purpose. The first group contains all forms of the CREATE statement, which is used to create database objects. The second group contains all forms of the ALTER statement, which is used to modify the structure of some database objects. The third group contains all forms of the DROP statement, which is used to remove different database objects.

▶ Chapter 6, "Queries," discusses the most important Transact-SQL statement: SELECT. This chapter introduces you to database data retrieval and describes the use of simple and complex queries. Each SELECT clause is separately defined and explained with reference to the **sample** database.

▶ Chapter 7, "Modification of a Table's Contents," discusses the four Transact-SQL statements used for updating data: INSERT, UPDATE, DELETE, and MERGE. Each of these statements is explained through numerous examples.

▶ Chapter 8, "Stored Procedures and User-Defined Functions," describes procedural extensions, which can be used to create powerful programs called stored procedures and user-defined functions (UDFs), programs that are stored on the server and can be reused. Because Transact-SQL is a complete computational language, all procedural extensions are inseparable parts of the language. Some stored procedures are written by users; others are provided by Microsoft and are referred to as system stored procedures. The implementation of stored procedures and UDFs using the Common Language Runtime (CLR) is also discussed in this chapter.

▶ Chapter 9, "System Catalog," describes one of the most important parts of a database system. The system catalog contains system tables that are used to store the information concerning database objects and their relationships. The main characteristic of system tables of Database Engine is that they cannot be accessed directly. Database Engine supports several interfaces that you can use to query the system catalog.

▶ Chapter 10, "Indices," covers the first and most powerful method that every user (especially database application programmers) can use to tune their applications to get better system response and therefore better performance. This chapter describes the role of indices and gives you guidelines for how to create and use them. The end of the chapter introduces the special types of indices supported by Database Engine.

▶ Chapter 11, "Views," explains how you create views, discusses the practical use of views (using numerous examples), and explains a special form of views called indexed views.

► Chapter 12, "Security System of Database Engine," provides answers to all your questions concerning security of data in the database. It addresses questions about authorization (which user has been granted legitimate access to the database system) and authentication (which access privileges are valid for a particular user). Three Transact-SQL statements are discussed in this chapter, GRANT, DENY, and REVOKE, which provide the access privileges of database objects against unauthorized access. The end of the chapter explains a new feature of SQL Server 2008, tracking data changes.

► Chapter 13, "Concurrency Control," describes concurrency control in depth. The beginning of the chapter discusses the two different concurrency models supported by Database Engine. All Transact-SQL statements related to transactions are also explained. Locking as a method to solve concurrency control problems is discussed further. At the end of the chapter, you will learn what isolation levels and deadlocks are.

► Chapter 14, "Triggers," describes the implementation of procedural integrity constraints using triggers. Each example in this chapter concerns an integrity problem that you may face in your everyday life as a database application programmer. The implementation of managed code for triggers using CLR is also shown in the chapter.

Part III, "SQL Server: System Administration," describes all objectives of Database Engine system administration. It comprises the following chapters:

► Chapter 15, "System Environment of Database Engine," discusses some internal issues concerning Database Engine. It provides a detailed description of the Database Engine disk storage elements, system databases, and utilities.

► Chapter 16, "Managing Instances and Maintaining Databases," describes two important components of Database Engine, Declarative Management Framework and Maintenance Plan Wizard, which are used to manage server instances and databases, respectively.

► Chapter 17, "Backup and Recovery," provides an overview of the fault-tolerance methods used to implement a backup strategy using either SQL Server Management Studio or corresponding Transact-SQL statements. The first part of the chapter specifies the different methods used to implement a backup strategy. The second part of the chapter discusses the restoration of databases. This chapters also describes how to ensure the availability of database systems and databases.

▶ Chapter 18, "Automating System Administration Tasks," describes the Database Engine component, SQL Server Agent, that enables you to automate certain system administration jobs, such as backing up data and using the scheduling and alert features to notify operators. This chapter also explains how to create jobs, operators, and alerts.

▶ Chapter 19, "Data Replication," provides an introduction to data replication, including concepts such as the publisher and subscriber. It introduces the different models of replication, and serves as a tutorial for how to configure publications and subscriptions using the existing wizards.

▶ Chapter 20, "Query Optimizer," describes the role and the work of the query optimizer. It explains in detail all the Database Engine tools (the SET statement, SQL Server Management Studio, and various dynamic management views) that can be used to edit execution plans of the optimizer. The end of the chapter provides optimization hints.

▶ Chapter 21, "Performance Tuning," discusses performance issues and the tools for tuning Database Engine that are relevant to daily administration of the system. After introductory notes concerning the measurements of performance, this chapter describes the factors that affect performance and presents the tools for monitoring SQL Server.

Part IV, "SQL Server and Business Intelligence," discusses business intelligence (BI) and all related topics. These chapters introduce Microsoft Analysis Services and Microsoft Reporting Services. SQL/OLAP and existing optimization techniques in relation to BI are described in detail too. This part includes the following chapters:

▶ Chapter 22, "Business Intelligence—An Introduction," introduces the notion of data warehousing. The first part of the chapter explains the differences between online transaction processing and data warehousing. The data store for a data warehousing process can be either a data warehouse or a data mart. Both types of data stores are discussed, and their differences are listed, in the second part of the chapter. The data warehouse design is explained at the end of the chapter.

▶ Chapter 23, "Microsoft Analysis Services," discusses the architecture of Analysis Services and the main component of Analysis Services, Business Intelligence Development Studio.

▶ Chapter 24, "Business Intelligence and Transact-SQL," explains how you can use Transact-SQL to solve business intelligence problems. This chapter discusses all SQL extensions, such as CUBE and ROLLUP operators, rank functions, the TOP *n* clause, and the PIVOT relational operator.

- ▶ Chapter 25, "Microsoft Reporting Services," describes the Microsoft enterprise reporting solution. This component is used to design and deploy reports. This chapter discusses the development environment that you use to design and create reports, and shows you different ways to deliver a designed and deployed report.

- ▶ Chapter 26, "Optimizing Techniques for Business Intelligence," describes two of several specific optimization techniques that can be used especially in the area of business intelligence: data partitioning and star schema join optimization. The data partitioning technique called range partitioning is described. (This partitioning type is entirely transparent to the application.) In relation to star schema join optimization, the role of bitmap filters in the optimization of schema joins is explained.

Part V, "Beyond Relational Data," is dedicated to two "nonrelational" topics, XML and spatial data, because SQL Server, as a data platform, doesn't have to handle only relational data. The following chapters are included in this part:

- ▶ Chapter 27, "Overview of XML," gives you an overview of XML documents, DTDs, and XML Schema. A running example is used to demonstrate how XML documents can be validated using either a DTD or XML Schema.

- ▶ Chapter 28, "SQL Server and XML," discusses SQLXML, Microsoft's set of data types and functions that supports XML in SQL Server 2008, bridging the gap between XML and relational data. The beginning of the chapter introduces the standardized data type XML and explains how stored XML documents can be retrieved. After that, the presentation of relational data as XML documents is discussed in detail.

- ▶ Chapter 29, "Introduction to Spatial Data," discusses spatial data and two different data types (GEOMETRY and GEOGRAPHY) that can be used to create such data. Several different standardized functions in relation to spatial data are also shown.

Almost all chapters include at their end numerous exercises that you can use to improve your knowledge concerning the chapter's content. All solutions to the given exercises can be found either at McGraw-Hill Professional's web site (www .mhprofessional.com) or my own home page (www.fh-rosenheim.de/~petkovic).

Changes from the Previous Edition

If you are familiar with the previous edition of this book, *Microsoft SQL Server 2005: A Beginner's Guide*, you should be aware that I have made significant changes in this edition. To make the book easier to use, I separated some topics and described them in totally new chapters. (For instance, Chapter 20 is an entirely new chapter and describes the query optimizer in depth. In the previous edition, this topic was described lightly, together with indices, in Chapter 9.) The following table gives you an outline of *significant* structural changes in the book (minor changes aren't listed).

Chapter 2	The entire chapter concerning all facets of SQL Server installation (previously Chapter 17) has been moved to the beginning of the book.
Chapter 6	The description of the SELECT statement is now streamlined and described in one chapter. (The number of examples is reduced, but there are still 77 examples and 30 exercises.)
Chapter 9	The system catalog is described earlier in this edition than in the prior edition (previously Chapter 11). The reason is that the general discussion of dynamic management views (DMVs) is given in Chapter 9, while the description of specific DMVs starts in Chapter 10 and continues throughout the rest of the book.
Chapter 10	This chapter is now exclusively dedicated to indices.
Chapter 13	Chapter 13 doesn't describe transactions only, as in the prior edition, but handles the entire topic of concurrency control. (For example, the section "Concurrency Models" explains in detail both models supported by Database Engine.)
Chapter 14	Triggers are now described after concurrency control because they use a mechanism, row versioning, that is related to the latter topic and thus described in Chapter 13.
Chapter 16	This chapter is entirely new and describes two components related to management of server instances and maintenance of databases.
Chapter 20	This chapter is entirely new and describes in detail the query optimizer of Database Engine. (This component was described in the previous book in Chapter 9 together with indices.)
Chapter 26	This chapter is partly new, and describes data partitioning and star schema join optimization.
Chapter 29	This is an entirely new chapter, with spatial data as the topic.

Differences Between SQL and Transact-SQL Syntax

Transact-SQL, SQL Server's relational database language, has several nonstandardized properties that generally are not known to people who are familiar with SQL only:

▶ Whereas the semicolon (;) is used in SQL to separate two SQL statements in a statement group (and you will generally get an error message if you do not include the semicolon), in Transact-SQL, use of semicolons is optional.

► Transact-SQL uses the GO statement. This nonstandardized statement is generally used to separate statement groups from each other, whereas some Transact-SQL statements (such as CREATE TABLE, CREATE INDEX, and so on) must be the only statement in the group. The extended syntax of this statement, GO n (where n = 1, 2, 3,…), means that the corresponding statement group will be executed n times.

► The USE statement, which is used very often in this book, changes the database context to the specified database. For example, the statement USE **sample** means that the statements that follow are related to the **sample** database.

Working with the Sample Databases

In contrast to its predecessor, this edition uses several sample databases:

► This book's own **sample** database

► Microsoft's **AdventureWorks** database

► Microsoft's **AdventureWorksDW** database

An introductory book like this requires a sample database that can be easily understood by each reader. For this reason, I used a very simple concept for my own **sample** database: it has only four tables with several rows each. On the other hand, its logic is complex enough to demonstrate the hundreds of examples included in the text of the book. The **sample** database that you will use in this book represents a company with departments and employees. Each employee belongs to exactly one department, which itself has one or more employees. Jobs of employees center around projects: each employee works at the same time for one or more projects, and each project engages one or more employees.

The tables of the **sample** database are shown here.

The **department** table:

dept_no	dept_name	location
d1	Research	Dallas
d2	Accounting	Seattle
d3	Marketing	Dallas

The **employee** table:

emp_no	emp_fname	emp_lname	dept_no
25348	Matthew	Smith	d3
10102	Ann	Jones	d3
18316	John	Barrimore	d1
29346	James	James	d2
9031	Elsa	Bertoni	d2
2581	Elke	Hansel	d2
28559	Sybill	Moser	d1

The **project** table:

project_no	Project_name	budget
p1	Apollo	120000
p2	Gemini	95000
p3	Mercury	185600

The **works_on** table:

emp_no	project_no	job	enter_date
10102	p1	Analyst	2006.10.1
10102	p3	Manager	2008.1.1
25348	p2	Clerk	2007.2.15
18316	p2	NULL	2007.6.1
29346	p2	NULL	2006.12.15
2581	p3	Analyst	2007.10.15
9031	p1	Manager	2007.4.15
28559	p1	NULL	2007.8.1
28559	p2	Clerk	2008.2.1
9031	p3	Clerk	2006.11.15
29346	p1	Clerk	2007.1.4

You can download the **sample** database from McGraw-Hill Professional's web site (www.mhprofessional.com) or my own home page (www.fh-rosenheim.de/~petkovic). Also, you can download all the examples in the book from my home page.

Although the sample database can be used for many of the examples in this book, for some examples, tables with lot of rows are necessary (to show optimization features, for instance). For this reason, two Microsoft sample databases—AdventureWorks and AdventureWorksDW—are also used. Both of them can be found at the Microsoft CodePlex web site www.codeplex.com/MSFTDBProdSamples.

Part I

Basic Concepts
and Installation

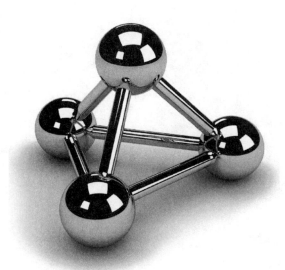

Chapter 1

Relational Database Systems—An Introduction

In This Chapter

- ▶ Database Systems: An Overview
- ▶ Relational Database Systems
- ▶ Database Design
- ▶ Syntax Conventions

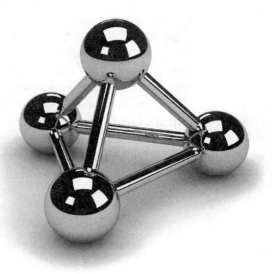

This chapter describes database systems in general. First, it discusses what a database system is, and which components it contains. Each component is described briefly, with a reference to the chapter in which it is described in detail. The second major section of the chapter is dedicated to relational database systems. It discusses the properties of relational database systems and the corresponding language used in such systems—Structured Query Language (SQL).

Generally, before you implement a database, you have to design it, with all its objects. The third major section of the chapter explains how you can use normal forms to enhance the design of your database, and also introduces the entity-relationship model, which you can use to conceptualize all entities and their relationships. The final section presents the syntax conventions used throughout the book.

Database Systems: An Overview

A database system is an overall collection of different database software components and databases containing the following parts:

- Database application programs
- Client components
- Database server(s)
- Databases

A database application program is special-purpose software that is designed and implemented by users or implemented by third-party software companies. In contrast, client components are general-purpose database software designed and implemented by a database company. By using client components, users can access data stored on the same or a remote computer.

The task of a database server is to manage data stored in a database. Each client communicates with a database server by sending user queries to it. The server processes each query and sends the result back to the client.

In general, a database can be viewed from two perspectives, the users' and the database system's. Users view a database as a collection of data that logically belong together. For a database system, a database is simply a series of bytes, usually stored on a disk. Although these two views of a database are totally different, they do have something in common: the database system needs to provide not only interfaces that enable users to create databases and retrieve or modify data, but also system components to manage the stored data. Hence, a database system must provide the following features:

- ▶ Variety of user interfaces
- ▶ Physical data independence
- ▶ Logical data independence
- ▶ Query optimization
- ▶ Data integrity
- ▶ Concurrency control
- ▶ Backup and recovery
- ▶ Database security

The following sections briefly describe these features.

Variety of User Interfaces

Most databases are designed and implemented for use by many different types of users with varied levels of knowledge. For this reason, a database system should offer many distinct user interfaces. These interfaces include, among others, menus and forms for end users, and an interactive query language for experienced users.

Physical Data Independence

Physical data independence means that the database application programs do not depend on the physical structure of the stored data in a database. This important feature enables you to make changes to the stored data without having to make any changes to database application programs. For example, if the stored data is previously ordered using one criterion, and this order is changed using another criterion, the modification of the physical data should not affect the existing database applications or the existing database *schema* (a description of a database generated by the data definition language of the database system).

Logical Data Independence

In file processing (using traditional programming languages), the declaration of a file is done in application programs, so any change to the structure of that file usually requires the modification of all programs using it. Database systems provide logical data independence—in other words, it is possible to make changes to the logical structure of the database without having to make any changes to the database application programs. For example, if the structure of an object named PERSON exists in the database system and you want to add an attribute to PERSON (say the address), you have to modify only the logical structure of the database, and not the existing application programs.

Query Optimization

Every database system contains a subcomponent called an *optimizer* that considers a variety of possible execution strategies for querying the data and then selects the most efficient one. The selected strategy is called the *execution plan* of the query. The optimizer makes its decisions using considerations such as how big the tables are that are involved in the query, what indices exist, and what Boolean operator (AND, OR, or NOT) is used in the WHERE clause. (This topic is discussed in detail in Chapter 20.)

Data Integrity

One of the tasks of a database system is to identify logically inconsistent data and reject its storage in a database. (The date February 30 and the time 5:77:00 P.M. are two examples of such data.) Additionally, most real-life problems that are implemented using database systems have *integrity constraints* that must hold true for the data. (One example of an integrity constraint might be the company's employee number, which must be a five-digit integer.) The task of maintaining integrity can be handled by the user in application programs or by the DBMS. As much as possible, this task should be handled by the DBMS. (Data integrity is discussed in two chapters of this book: declarative integrity in Chapter 5 and procedural integrity in Chapter 14.)

Concurrency Control

A database system is a multiuser software system, meaning that many user applications access a database at the same time. Therefore, each database system must have some kind of control mechanism to ensure that several applications that are trying to update the same data do so in some controlled way. The following is an example of a problem that can arise if a database system does not contain such control mechanisms:

1. The owners of bank account 4711 at bank X have an account balance of $2,000.
2. The two joint owners of this bank account, Mrs. A and Mr. B, go to two different bank tellers, and each withdraws $1,000 *at the same time*.
3. After these transactions, the amount of money in bank account 4711 should be $0 and not $1,000.

   All database systems have the necessary mechanisms to handle cases like this example. Concurrency control is discussed in detail in Chapter 13.

Backup and Recovery

A database system must have a subsystem that is responsible for recovery from hardware or software errors. For example, if a failure occurs while a database application updates 100 rows of a table, the recovery subsystem must roll back all previously executed updates to ensure that the corresponding data is consistent after the error occurs. (See Chapter 17 for further discussion on backup and recovery.)

Database Security

The most important database security concepts are authentication and authorization. *Authentication* is the process of validating user credentials to prevent unauthorized users from using a system. Authentication is most commonly enforced by requiring the user to enter a (user) name and a password. This information is evaluated by the system to determine whether the user is allowed to access the system. This process can be strengthened by using encryption.

Authorization is the process that is applied after the identity of a user is authenticated. During this process, the system determines what resources the particular user can use. In other words, structural and system catalog information about a particular entity is now available only to principals that have permission to access that entity. (Chapter 12 discusses these concepts in detail.)

Relational Database Systems

The component of Microsoft SQL Server called Database Engine is a relational database system. The notion of relational database systems was first introduced by E. F. Codd in his article "A Relational Model of Data for Large Shared Data Banks" in 1970. In contrast to earlier database systems (network and hierarchical), *relational database systems* are based upon the relational data model, which has a strong mathematical background.

NOTE

A data model is a collection of concepts, their relationships, and their constraints that are used to represent data of a real-world problem.

The central concept of the relational data model is a relation—that is, a table. Therefore, from the user's point of view, a relational database contains tables and nothing but tables. In a table, there are one or more columns and zero or more rows. At every row and column position in a table there is always exactly one data value.

Working with the Book's Sample Database

The sample database used in this book represents a company with departments and employees. Each employee in the example belongs to exactly one department, which itself has one or more employees. Jobs of employees center on projects: each employee works at the same time on one or more projects, and each project engages one or more employees.

The data of the **sample** database can be represented using four tables:

▶ department
▶ employee
▶ project
▶ works_on

Tables 1-1 through 1-4 show all the tables of the **sample** database.

The **department** table represents all departments of the company. Each department has the following attributes:

department (dept_no, dept_name, location)

dept_no represents the unique number of each department. **dept_name** is its name, and **location** is the location of the corresponding department.

The **employee** table represents all employees working for a company. Each employee has the following attributes:

employee (emp_no, emp_fname, emp_lname, dept_no)

emp_no represents the unique number of each employee. **emp_fname** and **emp_lname** are the first and last name of each employee, respectively. Finally, **dept_no** is the number of the department to which the employee belongs.

dept_no	dept_name	location
d1	Research	Dallas
d2	Accounting	Seattle
d3	Marketing	Dallas

Table 1-1   *The Department Table*

emp_no	emp_fname	emp_lname	dept_no
25348	Matthew	Smith	d3
10102	Ann	Jones	d3
18316	John	Barrimore	d1
29346	James	James	d2
9031	Elke	Hansel	d2
2581	Elsa	Bertoni	d2
28559	Sybill	Moser	d1

Table 1-2   *The Employee Table*

project_no	project_name	budget
p1	Apollo	120000
p2	Gemini	95000
p3	Mercury	186500

Table 1-3   *The Project Table*

emp_no	project_no	job	enter_date
10102	p1	Analyst	2006.10.1
10102	p3	Manager	2008.1.1
25348	p2	Clerk	2007.2.15
18316	p2	NULL	2007.6.1
29346	p2	NULL	2006.12.15
2581	p3	Analyst	2007.10.15
9031	p1	Manager	2007.4.15
28559	p1	NULL	2007.8.1
28559	p2	Clerk	2008.2.1
9031	p3	Clerk	2006.11.15
29346	p1	Clerk	2007.1.4

Table 1-4   *The works_on Table*

Each project of a company is represented in the **project** table. This table has the following columns:

project (project_no, project_name, budget)

project_no represents the unique number of each project. **project_name** and **budget** specify the name and the budget of each project, respectively.

The **works_on** table specifies the relationship between employees and projects. It has the following columns:

works_on (emp_no, project_no, job, enter_date)

emp_no specifies the employee number and **project_no** specifies the number of the project on which the employee works. The combination of data values belonging to these two columns is always unique. **job** and **enter_date** specify the task and the starting date of an employee in the corresponding project, respectively.

Using the **sample** database, it is possible to describe some general properties of relational database systems:

▶ Rows in a table do not have any particular order.

▶ Columns in a table do not have any particular order.

▶ Every column must have a unique name within a table. On the other hand, columns from different tables may have the same name. (For example, the **sample** database has a **dept_no** column in the **department** table and a column with the same name in the **employee** table.)

▶ Every single data item in the table must be single valued. This means that in every row and column position of a table there is never a set of multiple data values.

▶ For every table, there is at least one column (i.e., a combination of columns) with the property that no two rows have the same combination of data values for these columns). In the relational data model, such an identifier is called a *candidate key*. If there is more than one candidate key within a table, the database designer designates one of them as the *primary key* of the table. For example, the column **dept_no** is the primary key of the **department** table; the columns **emp_no** and **project_no** are the primary keys of the tables **employee** and **project**, respectively. Finally, the primary key for the **works_on** table is the combination of the columns **emp_no**, **project_no**.

▶ In a table, there are never two identical rows. (This property is only theoretical; Database Engine and all other relational database systems generally allow the existence of identical rows within a table.)

SQL: A Relational Database Language

The SQL Server relational database language is called Transact-SQL. It is a dialect of the most important database language today: Structured Query Language (SQL). The origin of SQL is closely connected with the project called System R, which was designed and implemented by IBM in the early 1980s. This project showed that it is possible, using the theoretical foundations of the work of E. F. Codd, to build a relational database system.

In contrast to traditional languages like C, C++, and Java, SQL is a set-oriented language. (The former are also called record-oriented languages.) This means that SQL can query many rows from one or more tables using just one statement. This feature is one of the most important advantages of SQL, allowing the use of this language at a logically higher level than the level at which traditional languages can be used.

Another important property of SQL is its nonprocedurality. Every program written in a procedural language (C, C++, Java) describes *how* a task is accomplished, step by step. In contrast to this, SQL, as any other nonprocedural language, describes *what* it is that the user wants. Thus, the system is responsible for finding the appropriate way to solve users' requests.

SQL contains two sublanguages: a data definition language (DDL) and a data manipulation language (DML). DDL statements are used to describe the schema of database tables. The DDL contains three generic SQL statements: CREATE object, ALTER object, and DROP object. These statements create, alter, and remove database objects, such as databases, tables, columns, and indexes. (These statements are discussed in detail in Chapter 5.)

In contrast to the DDL, the DML encompasses all operations that manipulate the data. There are always four generic operations for manipulating the database: retrieval, insertion, deletion, and modification. The retrieval statement SELECT is described in Chapters 6, while the INSERT, DELETE, and UPDATE statements are discussed in detail in Chapter 7.

Database Design

Designing a database is a very important phase in the database life cycle, which precedes all other phases except the requirements collection and the analysis. If the database design is created merely intuitively and without any plan, the resulting database will most likely not meet the user requirements concerning performance. Another consequence of a bad database design is superfluous data redundancy, which in itself has two disadvantages: the existence of data anomalies and the use of an unnecessary amount of disk space.

Normalization of data is a process during which the existing tables of a database are tested to find certain dependencies between the columns of a table. If such dependencies exist, the table is restructured into multiple (usually two) tables, which eliminates any column dependencies. If one of these generated tables still contains data dependencies, the process of normalization must be repeated until all dependencies are resolved.

The process of eliminating data redundancy in a table is based upon the theory of functional dependencies. A *functional dependency* means that by using the known value of one column, the corresponding value of another column can always be uniquely determined. (The same is true for column groups.) The functional dependencies between columns A and B is denoted by A → B, specifying that a value of column A can always be used to determine the corresponding value of column B. ("B is functionally dependent on A.")

The following example shows the functional dependency between two attributes of the table **employee** in the sample database.

EXAMPLE 1.1

emp_no → emp_lname

By having a unique value for the employee number, the corresponding last name of the employee (and all other corresponding attributes) can be determined. (This kind of functional dependency, where a column is dependent upon the primary key of a table, is called *trivial* functional dependency.)

Another kind of functional dependency is called *multivalued dependency*. In contrast to the functional dependency just described, the multivalued dependency is specified for multivalued attributes. This means that by using the known value of one attribute (column), the corresponding *set of values* of another multivalued attribute can be uniquely determined. The multivalued dependency is denoted by →→.

The next example shows the multivalued dependency that holds for two attributes of the object BOOK.

EXAMPLE 1.2

ISBN →→ Authors

The ISBN of a book always determines all of its authors. Therefore, the **Authors** attribute is multivalued dependent on the **ISBN** attribute.

Normal Forms

Normal forms are used for the process of normalization of data and therefore for the database design. In theory, there are at least five different normal forms, of which the first three are the most important for practical use. The third normal form for a table can be achieved by testing the first and second normal forms at the intermediate states, and as such, the goal of good database design can usually be fulfilled if all tables of a database are in the third normal form.

NOTE
The multivalued dependency is used to test the fourth normal form of a table. Therefore, this kind of dependency will not be used further in this book.

First Normal Form

First normal form (1NF) means that a table has no multivalued attributes or composite attributes. (A composite attribute contains other attributes and can therefore be divided into smaller parts.) All relational tables are by definition in 1NF, because the value of any column in a row must be *atomic*—that is, single valued.

Table 1-5 demonstrates 1NF using part of the **works_on** table from the sample database. The rows of the **works_on** table could be grouped together, using the employee number. The resulting Table 1-6 is not in 1NF because the column **project_no** contains a set of values (p1, p3).

Second Normal Form

A table is in second normal form (2NF) if it is in 1NF and there is no nonkey column dependent on a partial primary key of that table. This means if (A,B) is a combination of two table columns building the key, then there is no column of the table depending either on only A or only B.

emp_no	project_no	....
10102	p1	....
10102	p3	....
....	....	. . ..

Table 1-5   *Part of the works_on Table*

emp_no	project_no	....
10102	(p1, p3)	....
....	....	....

Table 1-6   *This "Table" Is Not in 1NF*

For example, Table 1-7 shows the **works_on1** table, which is identical to the **works_on** table except for the additional column, **dept_no**. The primary key of this table is the combination of columns **emp_no** and **project_no**. The column **dept_no** is dependent on the partial key **emp_no** (and is independent of **project_no**), so this table is not in 2NF. (The original table, **works_on**, is in 2NF.)

NOTE

Every table with a one-column primary key is always in 2NF.

Third Normal Form

A table is in third normal form (3NF) if it is in 2NF and there are no functional dependencies between nonkey columns. For example, the **employee1** table (see Table 1-8), which is identical to the **employee** table except for the additional column, **dept_name**, is not in 3NF, because for every known value of the column **dept_no** the corresponding value of the column **dept_name** can be uniquely determined. (The original table, **employee**, as well as all other tables of the **sample** database are in 3NF.)

emp_no	project_no	job	enter_date	dept_no
10102	p1	Analyst	2006.10.1	d3
10102	p3	Manager	2008.1.1	d3
25348	p2	Clerk	2007.2.15	d3
18316	p2	NULL	2007.6.1	d1
....	....	....		....

Table 1-7   *The works_on1 Table*

emp_no	emp_fname	emp_lname	dept_no	dept_name
25348	Matthew	Smith	d3	Marketing
10102	Ann	Jones	d3	Marketing
18316	John	Barrimore	d1	Research
29346	James	James	d2	Accounting
....	....	....	....	....

Table 1-8 *The employee1 Table*

Entity-Relationship Model

The data in a database could easily be designed using only one table that contains all data. The main disadvantage of such a database design is its high redundancy of data. For example, if your database contains data concerning employees and their projects (assuming each employee works at the same time on one or more projects, and each project engages one or more employees), the data stored in a single table contains many columns and rows. The main disadvantage of such a table is that data is difficult to keep consistent because of its redundancy.

The *entity-relationship (ER) model* is used to design relational databases by removing all existing redundancy in the data. The basic object of the ER model is an *entity*—that is, a real-world object. Each entity has several *attributes*, which are properties of the entity and therefore describe it. Based on its type, an attribute can be

- ▶ **Atomic (or single valued)**   An atomic attribute is always represented by a single value for a particular entity. For example, a person's marital status is always an atomic attribute. Most attributes are atomic attributes.

- ▶ **Multivalued**   A multivalued attribute may have one or more values for a particular entity. For example, **Location** as the attribute of an entity called ENTERPRISE is multivalued, because each enterprise can have one or more locations.

- ▶ **Composite**   Composite attributes are not atomic because they are assembled using some other atomic attributes. A typical example of a composite attribute is a person's address, which is composed of atomic attributes, such as **City**, **Zip**, and **Street**.

The entity PERSON in Example 1.3 has several atomic attributes, one composite attribute, **Address**, and a multivalued attribute, **College_degree**.

EXAMPLE 1.3

PERSON (Personal_no, F_name, L_name, Address(City,Zip,Street),{College_degree})

Each entity has one or more key attributes that are attributes (or a combination of two or more attributes) whose values are unique for each particular entity. In Example 1.3, the attribute **Personal_no** is the key attribute of the entity PERSON.

Besides entity and attribute, *relationship* is another basic concept of the ER model. A relationship exists when an entity refers to one (or more) other entities. The number of participating entities defines the degree of a relationship. For example, the relationship **works_on** between entities EMPLOYEE and PROJECT has degree two.

Every existing relationship between two entities must be one of the following three types: 1:1, 1:N, or M:N. (This property of a relationship is also called *cardinality ratio*.) For example, the relationship between the entities DEPARTMENT and EMPLOYEE is 1:N, because each employee belongs to exactly one department, which itself has one or more employees. Also, the relationship between the entities PROJECT and EMPLOYEE is M:N, because each project engages one or more employees and each employee works at the same time on one or more projects.

A relationship can also have its own attributes. Figure 1-1 shows an example of an ER diagram. (The ER diagram is the graphical notation used to describe the ER model.)

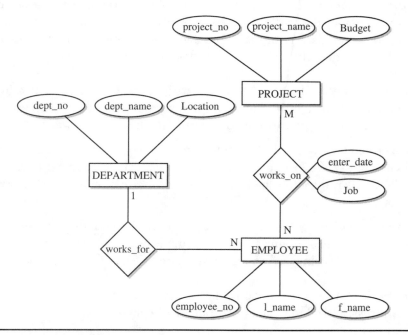

Figure 1-1   *Example of an ER Diagram*

Using this notation, entities are modeled using rectangular boxes, with the entity name written inside the box. Attributes are shown in ovals, and each attribute is attached to a particular entity (or relationship) using a straight line. Finally, relationships are modeled using diamonds, and entities participating in the relationship are attached to it using straight lines. The cardinality ratio of each entity is written on the corresponding line.

Syntax Conventions

This book uses the conventions shown in Table 1-9 for the syntax of the Transact-SQL statements and for the indication of the text.

NOTE

In contrast to brackets and braces, which belong to syntax conventions, parentheses, ( ), belong to the syntax of a statement and must always be typed!

Convention	Indication
Italics	New terms or items of emphasis.
UPPERCASE	Transact-SQL keywords—for example, CREATE TABLE. Additional information about the keywords of the Transact-SQL language can be found in Chapter 5.
lowercase	Variables in Transact-SQL statements—for example, CREATE TABLE tablename. (The user must replace "tablename" with the actual name of the table.)
var1 | var2	Alternative use of the items var1 and var2. (You may choose only one of the items separated by the vertical bar.)
{ }	Alternative use of more items. Example: { expression | USER | NULL }
[]	Optional item(s). Example: [FOR LOAD]
{ } ...	Item(s) that can be repeated any number of times. Example: {, @param1 typ1} ...
bold	Name of database object (database itself, tables, columns) in the text.
Default	The default value is always underlined. Example: ALL | DISTINCT

Table 1-9   *Syntax Conventions*

Conclusion

All database systems provide the following features:

- ► Variety of user interfaces
- ► Physical data independence
- ► Logical data independence
- ► Query optimization
- ► Data integrity
- ► Concurrency control
- ► Backup and recovery
- ► Database security

The next chapter shows you how to install SQL Server 2008.

Exercises

E.1.1

What does "data independence" mean and which two forms of data independence exist?

E.1.2

Which is the main concept of the relational model?

E.1.3

What does the **employee** table represent in the real world? And what does the row in this table with the data for Ann Jones represent?

E.1.4

What does the **works_on** table represent in the real world (and in relation to the other tables of the **sample** database)?

E.1.5

Let **book** be a table with two columns: **isbn** and **title**. Assuming that **isbn** is unique and there are no identical titles, answer the following questions:

    a. Is **title** a key of the table?

    b. Does **isbn** functionally depend on **title**?

    c. Is the **book** table in 3NF?

E.1.6

Let **order** be a table with the following columns: **order_no, customer_no, discount**. If the column **customer_no** is functionally dependent on **order_no** and the column **discount** is functionally dependent on **customer_no**, answer the following questions and explain in detail your answers:

    a. Is **order_no** a key of the table?

    b. Is **customer_no** a key of the table?

E.1.7

Let **company** be a table with the following columns: **company_no, location**. Each company has one or more locations. In which normal form is the **company** table?

E.1.8

Let **supplier** be a table with the following columns: **supplier_no, article, city**. The key of the table is the combination of the first two columns. Each supplier delivers several articles, and each article is delivered by several suppliers. There is only one supplier in each city. Answer the following questions:

    a. In which normal form is the **supplier** table?

    b. How can you resolve the existing functional dependencies?

E.1.9

Let $R(\underline{A}, \underline{B}, C)$ be a relation with the functional dependency: $B \rightarrow C$. (The attributes A and B build the composite key, and the attribute C is functionally dependent on B.) In which normal form is the relation R?

E.1.10

Let $R(\underline{A}, \underline{B}, C)$ be a relation with the functional dependency: $C \rightarrow B$. (The attributes A and B build the composite key, and the attribute B is functionally dependent on C.) In which normal form is the relation R?

Chapter 2

Planning the Installation and Installing SQL Server

In This Chapter

- ► **Planning the Installation**
- ► **Installing SQL Server**
- ► **Starting and Stopping an Instance of Database Engine**
- ► **Dedicated Connection to an Instance of Database Engine**

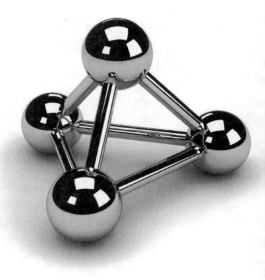

T his chapter describes all tasks involved in the installation of the SQL Server system. First, the necessary steps in planning the installation are covered. This is followed by discussion of the actual installation of the database server. Toward the end of the chapter, you will learn how to install, start, use, and stop instances of Database Engine. You will also be introduced to the dedicated administration connection, which can be used to connect to an instance of Database Engine.

Planning the Installation

The specification of an installation plan should always precede the actual installation of the SQL Server system. Careful planning is absolutely necessary because several decisions have to be made before the installation of the system is started. The system administrator should have clear answers to the following questions before beginning the installation process:

▶   What is the purpose of the SQL Server system?

▶   What are the hardware and network requirements?

▶   How many users will be active at the same time?

NOTE

As you already know, "SQL Server" is an umbrella name for several different components, such as Database Engine, Analysis Services, Reporting Services, and Integration Services. During the installation process, you can decide which of these components you want to install on your computer. In this chapter, "SQL Server" refers to all components of that system that are installed on your computer.

Purpose of the SQL Server System

The purpose of the SQL Server system can be manifold. For example, your system may be used exclusively for education, or it may be a production system. In the case of production systems, you need to make decisions concerning the number of users and the amount of stored data, because these systems differ widely. Another decision concerning modern database systems is whether the system is used for operational or analytical tasks.

If yours is a large database with a few hundred users, or if your system carries a heavy transaction load, performance of database operations will be an issue. In both cases, the use of multiprocessor computers will be a general requirement to guarantee scalability and good response times of the system. If you have a huge database, insufficient disk storage could be an issue. In this case, the system will usually perform better if you use several smaller disks instead of one or two large disks.

You must differentiate between systems used for operational tasks (that is, systems that require fast access and short transactions) and systems used for analytical tasks (systems that use complex retrieval operations on huge databases), because both tasks cannot be optimally achieved using one database server. For this reason, Database Engine is used for operational tasks and Analysis Services is used for analytical tasks. (For more information on Analysis Services, see Part IV of the book.)

Hardware and Network Requirements

The fact that the SQL Server system runs only on Microsoft operating systems simplifies decisions concerning hardware and network requirements. The system administrator has to be concerned only about the hardware and network requirements.

Hardware Requirements

Windows operating systems are supported on the Intel and compatible system hardware platforms. Processor speed should be at a minimum 1 GHz.

NOTE
Generally, two SQL Server edition groups exist: 32-bit and 64-bit. The requirements for these two groups differ. Therefore, the values listed in this section are general values. For exact requirements for each edition, refer to the SQL Server 2008 Books Online article "Hardware and Software Requirements for Installing SQL Server 2008," which you can find at http://msdn2.microsoft.com/en-us/library/ms143506(SQL.100).aspx.

Officially, the minimum requirement for main memory is 512MB. However, almost everybody recognizes that such a minimal configuration will not perform very well, and as a general guideline, main memory of your computer should be at least 1GB or more.

Hard disk space requirements depend on your system configuration and the applications you choose to install.

Network Requirements

To connect to any SQL Server components, you must have a network protocol enabled. The SQL Server system can serve requests on several protocols at once. Clients connect to the system using a single protocol. If the client program does not know which protocol the system is listening on, configure the client to sequentially attempt multiple protocols.

As a client/server system, SQL Server allows clients to use different network protocols to communicate with the server, and vice versa. During connectivity installation, the system administrator must decide which network protocols (as libraries) should be available to give clients access to the system. The following network protocols can be selected on the server side:

- ▶ Shared memory
- ▶ Transmission Control Protocol/Internet Protocol (TCP/IP)
- ▶ Named Pipes
- ▶ Virtual Interface Adapter (VIA) protocol

Connections to the system from a client running on the same computer use the shared memory protocol. Shared memory has no configurable properties, and this protocol is always tried first.

Named Pipes is an alternative network protocol on the Windows platforms. After the installation process, you can drop the support for Named Pipes and use another network protocol for communication between the server and clients.

The TCP/IP network protocol allows the system to communicate using standard Windows Sockets as the Internet protocol communication (IPC) method across the TCP/IP protocol.

Virtual Interface Adapter (VIA) protocol works with VIA hardware. For information about how to use VIA, contact your hardware vendor.

NOTE

Shared memory is not supported on failover clusters.

SQL Server Editions

As you plan your installation, you need to know which kind of SQL Server editions exist. Besides the 32-bit and 64-bit edition groups, Microsoft supports the following editions of SQL Server 2008:

- ▶ **Express Edition**   The lightweight version of SQL Server 2008. This product should be used by application developers. For this reason, the product includes the basic Express Manager (XM) program and supports CLR integration and native XML. Also, you can download SQL Server Management Express for SQL Server Express, to easily manage a database. SQL Server Express is available as a free download at http://msdn.microsoft.com/express.

▶ **Workgroup Edition**   Designed for small businesses and should also be used at the department level. This edition provides relational database support without the business intelligence (BI) and high-availability capabilities. This edition supports up to two processors and a maximum of 2GB of RAM.

▶ **Standard Edition**   Provides a 32-bit version and 64-bit support for both x64- and Itanium-based systems. It also supports up to four processors and includes the full range of BI functionality.

▶ **Enterprise Edition**   The special form of the SQL Server system that is intended for time-critical applications with a huge number of users. In contrast to Standard Edition, this edition contains additional features that can be useful for very high-end installations with symmetrical multiprocessors or clusters. The most important additional features of Enterprise Edition are data partitioning, database snapshots, and online database maintenance.

▶ **Developer Edition**   Allows developers to build and test any type of application with SQL Server on 32- and 64-bit platforms. It includes all the functionality of Enterprise Edition, but is licensed only for use in development, testing, and demonstration. Each license of Developer Edition entitles one developer to use the software on as many systems as necessary; additional developers can use the software by purchasing additional licenses. For rapid deployment into production, the database system of Developer Edition can easily be upgraded to Enterprise Edition.

▶ **Compact Edition**   A slim version of SQL Server that you can use on Pocket PCs, smart phones, tablet PCs, and desktop PCs. Compact Edition databases are generally used as embedded databases for desktop-based applications.

Installation Recommendations

During the installation process, you have to make many choices. As a general guideline, it is better to familiarize yourself with their effects before running the Setup program. You should answer the following questions before you start the installation process:

▶ Where will the root directory be stored?

▶ Should multiple instances of Database Engine be used?

▶ Which authentication mode for Database Engine should be used?

NOTE

Before you start the installation process, you should exactly know which SQL Server 2008 components you want to install (see also Figure 2-4). If not, please learn more about the existing components and make your decision now. (Most of these components are described in detail in this book. The description of other components can be found in Books Online.)

Where to Store the Root Directory

The root directory is where the Setup program stores all program files and those files that do not change as you use the SQL Server system. By default, the installation process stores all program files in the subdirectory **Microsoft SQL Server**, although you can change this setting during the installation process. Using the default name is recommended because it uniquely determines the version of the system.

How Many Instances of Database Engine to Run

With Database Engine, you can install and use several different instances. An *instance* is a database server that does not share its system and user databases with other instances (servers) running on the same computer.

There are two instance types:

▶ Default

▶ Named

The *default instance* of the database server operates the same way as the database servers in earlier versions of SQL Server, where only one database server without instance support existed. The computer name on which the instance is running specifies solely the name of the default instance. Any instance of the database server other than the default instance is called a *named instance*. To identify a named instance, you have to specify its name as well as the name of the computer on which the instance is running: for example, NTB11901\INSTANCE1. On one computer, there can be any number of named instances (in addition to the default instance). Additionally, you can configure named instances on a computer that does not have the default instance.

Although all instances running on a computer do not share most system resources (SQL Server and SQL Server Agent services, system and user databases, as well as registry keys), there are some components that are shared among them:

▶ SQL Server program group

▶ Analysis Services server

▶ Development libraries

The existence of only one SQL Server program group on a computer also means that only one copy of each utility exists, which is represented by an icon in the program group. (This includes SQL Server Books Online, too.) Therefore, each utility works with all instances configured on a computer.

You should consider using multiple instances if:

► You have different types of databases on your computer

► Your computer is powerful enough to manage multiple instances

The main purpose of multiple instances is to divide databases that exist in your organization into different groups. For instance, if the system manages databases that are used by different users (production databases, test databases, and sample databases), you should divide them to run under different instances. That way you can encapsulate your production databases from databases that are used by casual or inexperienced users. A single-processor machine will not be the right hardware platform to run multiple instances of Database Engine, because of limited resources. For this reason, you should consider the use of multiple instances only with multiprocessor computers.

Which Authentication Mode to Choose

In relation to Database Engine, there are two different authentication modes:

► **Windows mode**   Specifies security exclusively at the operating system level—that is, it specifies the way in which users connect to the Windows operating system using their user accounts and group memberships.

► **Mixed mode**   Allows users to connect to Database Engine using Windows authentication or SQL Server authentication. This means that some user accounts can be set up to use Windows security subsystem, while others can use the SQL Server security subsystem in addition to the Windows security subsystem.

Microsoft recommends the use of Windows mode. (For details, see Chapter 12.)

Installing SQL Server

If you have done an installation of a complex software product before, you probably recognize that feeling of uncertainty that accompanies starting the installation for the first time. This feeling comes from the complexity of the product to be installed and the diversity of questions to be answered during the installation process. Because you may not completely understand the product, you (or the person who installs the software) may be less than confident that you can give accurate answers for all the questions that the Setup program asks to complete its tasks. This section will help you to find your way through the installation by giving you answers to most of the questions beforehand.

To begin the installation, insert the SQL Server 2008 DVD into your DVD drive. The **Install Shield** wizard opens and prompts you to specify the location in which to save the extracted files. When you click Next, the **Install Shield** wizard extracts all necessary files from the DVD and completes its task.

Before Starting the Setup Program

There are several tasks that you should complete before starting the Setup program. The best place to start is to read the Release Notes. The benefit of Release Notes is that they contain the newest information, which is not necessarily provided in SQL Server Books Online (see Chapter 3 for more details about Books Online). Read this information carefully to get a picture of features that are modified shortly before the delivery of the final release. (Release Notes also contain the list of bugs; it might prove useful for you to know about some of them.)

Microsoft's web site is an additional source for further information. As with Release Notes, you can find many interesting documents on the Microsoft web site. Especially important are white papers that Microsoft provides during the implementation of each new SQL Server version. On the Microsoft site, you can search for and download documents that are of interest to you.

Starting the Setup Program and Installing Prerequisites

On the **Installation Prerequisites** page (see Figure 2-1), SQL Server 2008 Setup identifies which additional software components are necessary, before you start the installation of SQL Server 2008. To begin this process, click **Install**.

Installing SQL Server Components

After the successful installation of prerequisites, the installation process automatically shows the **SQL Server Installation Center** (see Figure 2-2) with the tasks that can be executed. To install SQL Server 2008, choose **New Installation**. This step launches a wizard that guides you during the installation process.

On the first page of the wizard, the **System Configuration Check** page (see Figure 2-3), the Setup program scans your computer for conditions that may block the installation process. If you click the **Show details** button, you can see all details concerning the

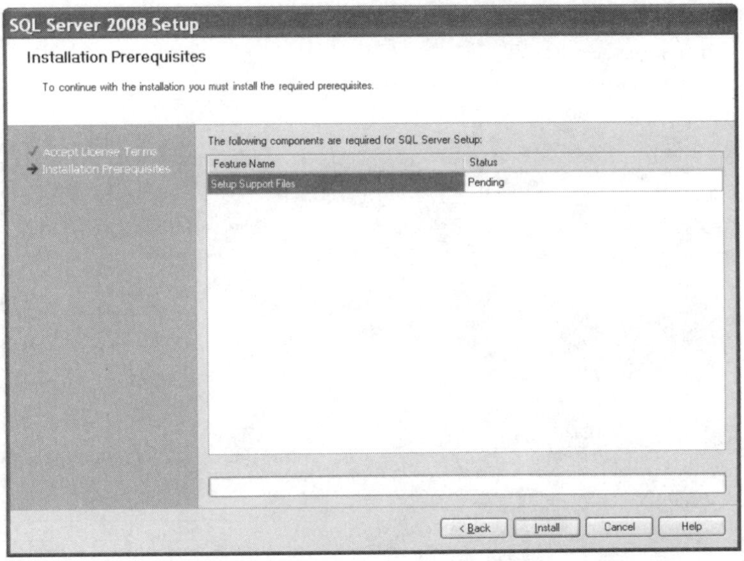

Figure 2-1   *Installation Prerequisites page*

check process. To proceed with the Setup process, click **Next**. On the **Registration Information** page, enter information in the corresponding text boxes and click **Next**.

On the **Feature Selection** page (see Figure 2-4), select the components to install by checking the corresponding check boxes. Also, toward the bottom of the page, you can specify the directory in which to store the shared components. After that, click **Next** to continue.

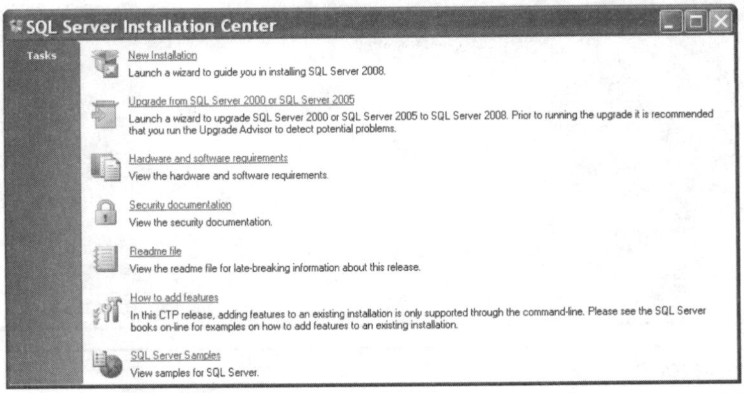

Figure 2-2   *SQL Server Installation Center*

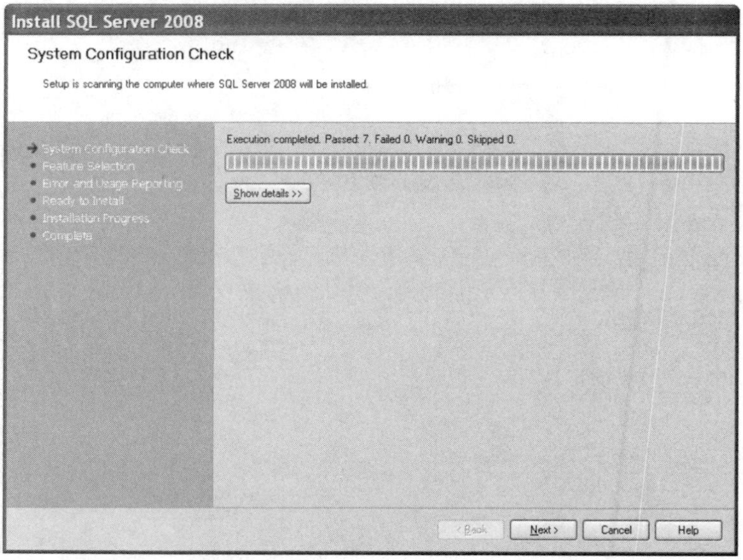

Figure 2-3 *System Configuration Check page*

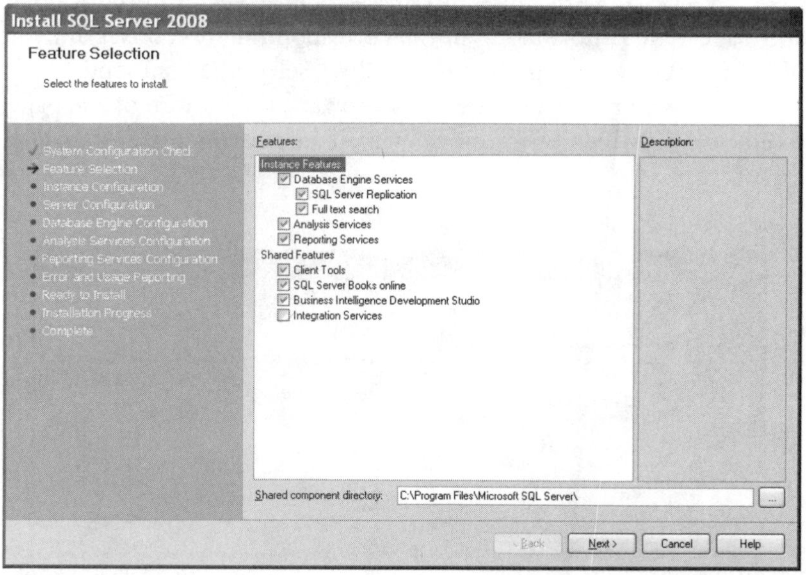

Figure 2-4 *Feature Selection page*

NOTE

Components of SQL Server that are selected will be installed one after the other in the order in which they are listed on the Feature Selection page. The installation process starts with the installation of Database Engine, followed by the installation of Analysis Services, and so on. Only the selected components will be installed.

On the **Instance Configuration** page (see Figure 2-5), you can choose between the installation of a default or named instance. (A detailed discussion of instances can be found in the section "How Many Instances of Database Engine to Run" in this chapter.) To install the default instance, click **Default instance**. If a default instance is already installed and you select **Default instance**, the Setup program upgrades it and additionally allows you to install additional components. (Therefore, you have another opportunity to install components that you skipped in the previous installation processes.)

To install a new named instance, click **Named instance** and then type a new name in the given text box. In the lower part of the page, you can see the list of instances already installed on your system. As you can see from Figure 2-5, the computer on which I installed the instance called INSTANCE1 already contains the default instance. (MSSQLSERVER is the name of the default instance for Database Engine.) Click **Next** to continue.

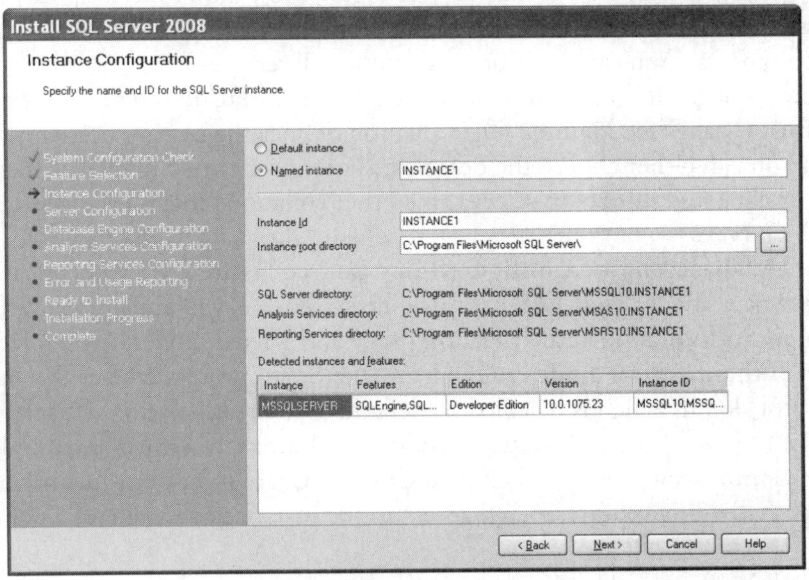

Figure 2-5   *Instance Configuration page*

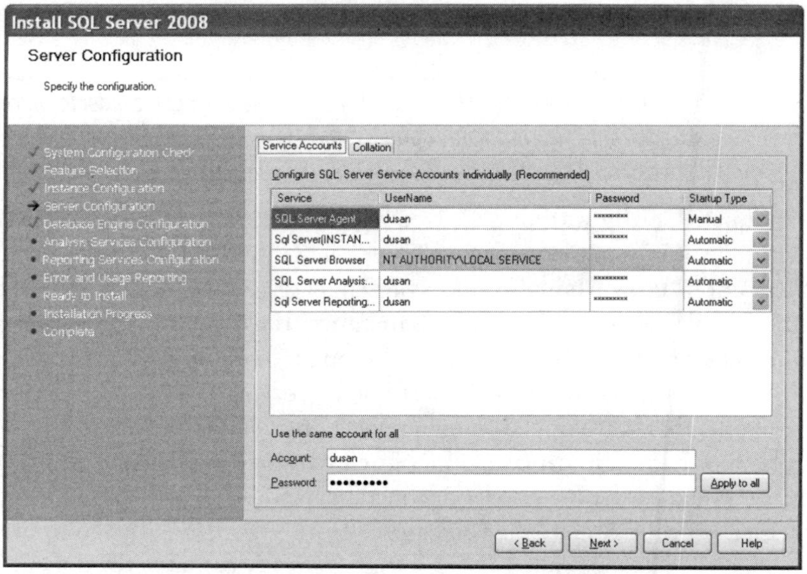

Figure 2-6   *Server Configuration (Service Accounts tab)*

The next page, **Server Configuration** (see Figure 2-6), allows you to specify usernames and corresponding passwords for services of all components that will be installed in the installation process. (You can apply one account for all services.)

To choose the collation of your instance, click the **Collation** tab of the **Server Configuration** page (see Figure 2-7). (Collation defines the sorting behavior for your instance.) You can either choose the default collations for the components that will be installed, or click **Customize** to select some other collations that are supported by the system. Click **Next** to continue.

On the **Database Engine Configuration** page (see Figure 2-8), you choose the authentication mode for your Database Engine system. As you already know, Database Engine supports Windows authentication mode and Mixed mode. If you select the **Windows authentication mode** radio button, the Setup process creates the **sa** (system administrator) login, which is disabled by default. (For the discussion of accounts, see Chapter 12.) If you choose the **Mixed Mode** radio button, you must enter and confirm the system administrator login. Click **Add Current User** if you want to add one or more users that will have unrestricted access to the instance of Database Engine.

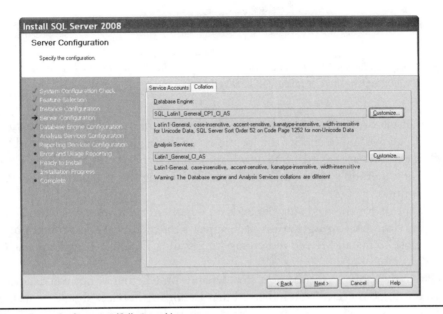

Figure 2-7   *Server Configuration (Collation tab)*

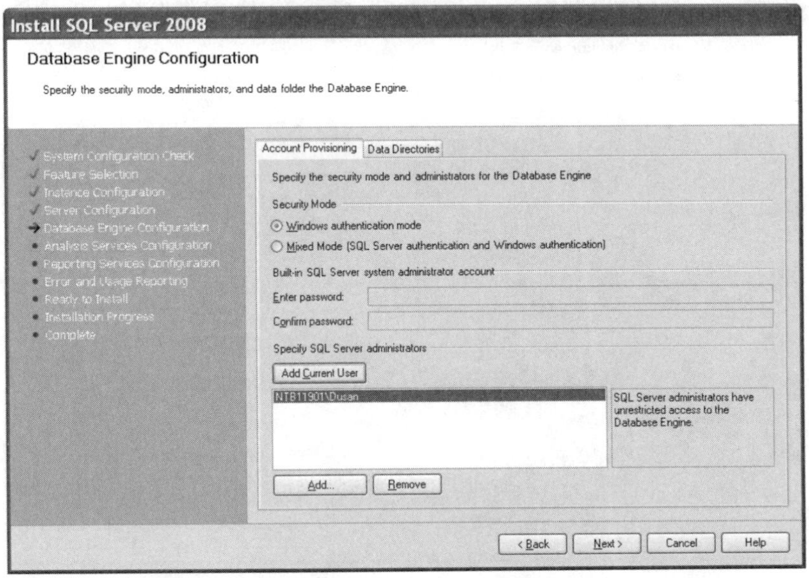

Figure 2-8   *Database Engine Configuration (Account Provisioning tab)*

NOTE

You can change the information concerning account provisioning after installation. In that case, you have to restart the Database Engine service called MSSQLSERVER.

The other tab of the **Database Engine Configuration** page, **Data Directories** (see Figure 2-9), allows you to specify the locations for all the directories in which Database Engine–related files are stored. (The new feature of SQL Server 2008 is that the storage location of the **tempdb** system database is specified during the installation process.) Click **Next** to continue.

What appears for the next step depends on whether or not you chose to install Analysis Services. (A **Configuration** page appears for each SQL Server component that you chose to install.) If you did choose to install it, Figure 2-10 will appear. Click **Next** to continue.

Similarly, what appears for the next step depends on whether or not you decided to install Reporting Services. If you indicated that Reporting Services should be installed, the **Reporting Services Configuration** page appears. In this step, you can decide just to

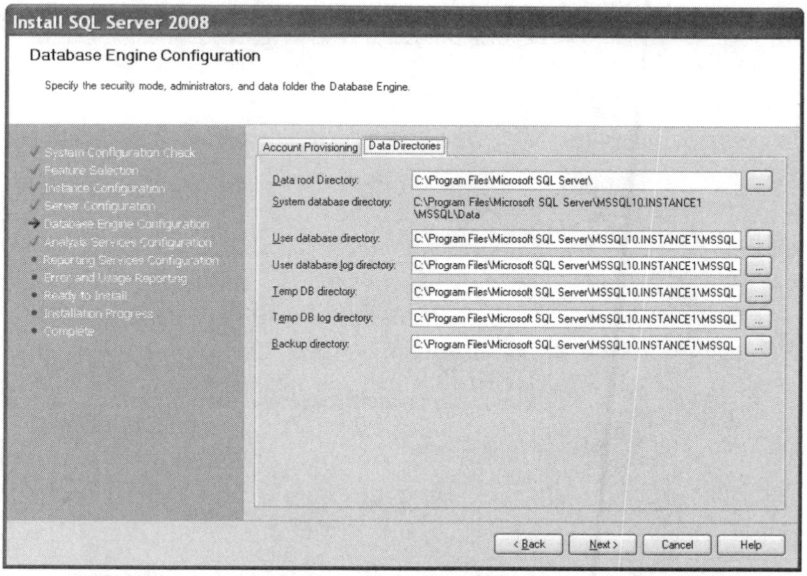

Figure 2-9 *Database Engine Configuration (Data Directories tab)*

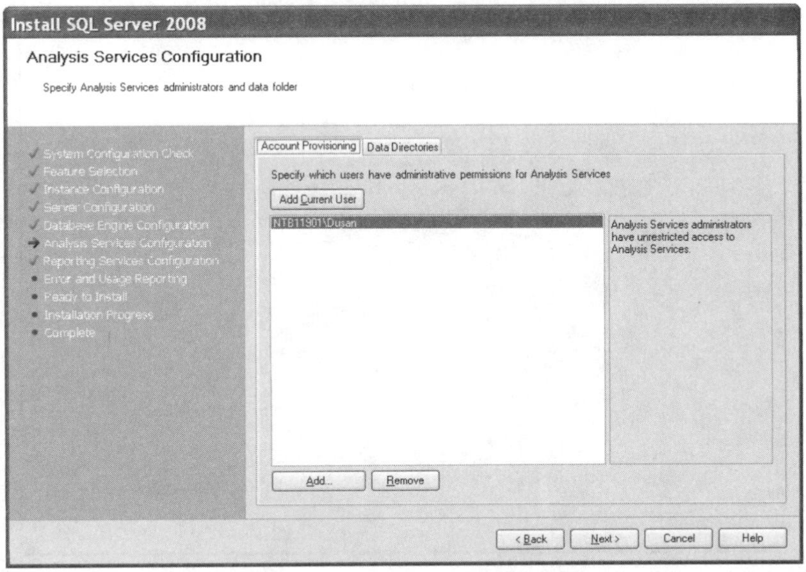

Figure 2-10   *Analysis Services Configuration page*

install the report server (without its configuration) or to install and configure it. The third alternative is to integrate the report server with Microsoft Office SharePoint Server (a server program that can be used to facilitate collaboration, provide content management features, and implement business processes). After that, click **Next** to continue.

On the **Error and Usage Reporting** page (see Figure 2-11), specify the information, if any, that you would like to send to Microsoft automatically. Clear both check boxes if you do not want to take part in this automatic reporting. Click **Next**.

The last page, before the installation process actually starts, is the **Ready to Install** page. This page allows you to review the summary of all SQL Server components that will be installed. To start the installation process, click **Install**. As you can see from Figure 2-12, Setup allows you to follow the progress of your installation process. If the installation process succeeds, click **Next**.

The **Complete** page appears, with the location of the file in which the summary log is stored. Click **Close** to complete the installation process. After that you can use all components, which you installed during the installation process.

The next section describes the use of an instance of Database Engine.

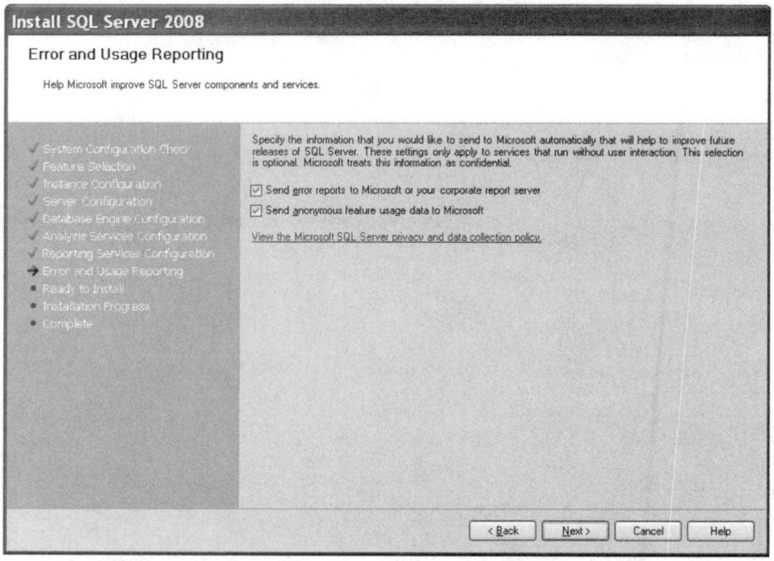

Figure 2-11 *Error and Usage Reporting page*

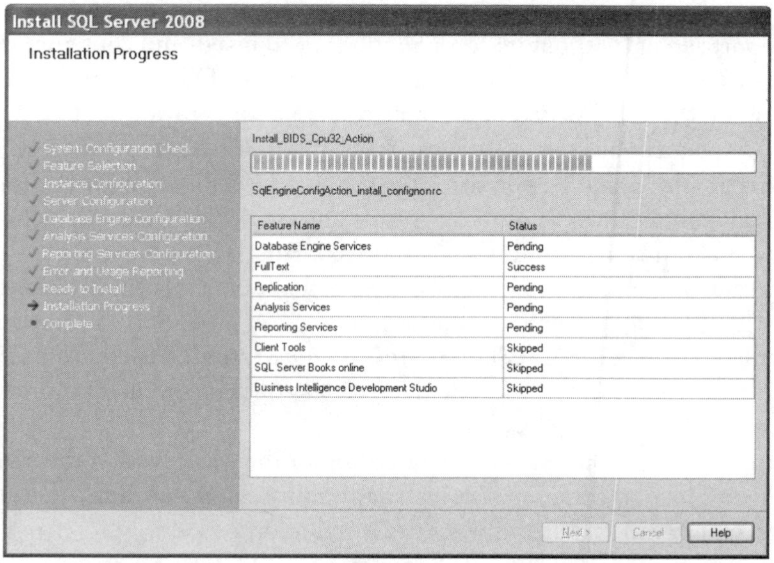

Figure 2-12 *Installation Progress page*

Starting and Stopping an Instance of Database Engine

The most convenient way to start an instance of Database Engine is automatically with the boot process of the computer. However, certain circumstances might require different handling of the system. Therefore, Database Engine offers several options for starting an instance:

▶ SQL Server Management Studio (see Chapter 3)

▶ The **sqlservr** application

▶ The **net** command

The **sqlservr** application can be used only to start an instance of Database Engine. This application is invoked using the following command:

sqlservr *option_list*

option_list contains all options that can be invoked using the application. Table 2-1 describes the most important options.

The **net start**, **net stop**, and **net pause** commands start, stop, and pause an instance of Database Engine, respectively. The **net** command in Example 2.1 starts the MSSQLSERVER service.

EXAMPLE 2.1

net start mssqlserver

Option	Description
–f	Indicates that the instance is started with the minimal configuration.
–m	Indicates that the instance is started in single-user mode. Use this option if you have problems with the system and want to perform maintenance on it (this option must be used to restore the **master** database).
–s instance_name	Specifies the instance of Database Engine. If no named instance is specified, **sqlservr** starts the default instance of Database Engine.

Table 2-1   *Most Important Options of the sqlservr Application*

Dedicated Connection to an Instance of Database Engine

After the successful start of an instance of Database Engine, the next step is to make a connection to it. Generally, you can make the connection by using SQL Server Management Studio (see Chapter 3). But, there are certain extraordinary situations in which "normal" users cannot connect to the instance. In that case, you can use the dedicated administrator connection (DAC).

The DAC is a special connection that can be used by DBAs in case of extreme server resource depletion. Even when there are not enough resources for other users to connect, Database Engine will attempt to free resources for the DAC.

NOTE

*DAC is available and supported through the **sqlcmd** utility using the **−A** option. (For the description of the **sqlcmd** utility, see Chapter 15.)*

Conclusion

The installation of SQL Server also requires some work in the preinstallation and postinstallation phases. In the preinstallation phase, the system administrator determines software and hardware requirements and prepares different specifications for the installation process.

The installation of SQL Server 2008 is streamlined compared to the previous version. Installation is divided in two phases. In the first phase, Setup gathers the necessary information from you, including which components you want to install, and after that starts the actual installation process.

The next chapter describes the most important component of SQL Server called SQL Server Management Studio.

Chapter 3

SQL Server Management Studio

In This Chapter

- ► **SQL Server Program Group and Books Online**
- ► **Introduction to SQL Server Management Studio**

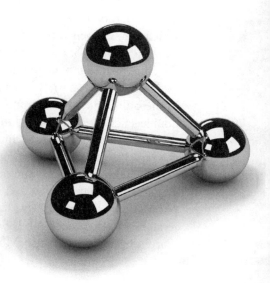

This chapter first discusses briefly the SQL Server program group and SQL Server Books Online, the online reference source with all necessary information concerning SQL Server. It then introduces SQL Server Management Studio, which is discussed in detail in relation to Database Engine and activities of end users. You will also learn all the functions of Management Studio, which are necessary for creating and executing any Transact-SQL statements.

SQL Server Program Group and Books Online

To see the SQL Server program group, click **Start, All Programs**, and finally **Microsoft SQL Server 2008**. The SQL Server program group comprises all applications you will use during your work with this system. This chapter looks only at two particular applications, SQL Server Books Online (BOL), which you can find in the **Documentation and Tutorials** directory, and SQL Server Management Studio, the primary focus of this chapter. Books Online is discussed briefly here.

Books Online is the online documentation that is delivered and installed with all other SQL Server software components. The toolbar of the **Books Online** window has, among others, buttons for four different features:

▶ Contents

▶ Index

▶ Search

▶ Help Favorites

If you click the **Contents** button, you see the contents of the whole online documentation divided into different books. Each specific topic is divided into subtopics, which can be opened by clicking the corresponding plus (+) symbol of the tree. You can view the content of each subfolder in the same way—that is, by clicking the + symbols of the corresponding book and all superfolders of that folder.

The **Index** pane shows an alphabetically sorted sequence of each keyword that appears in the online documentation. There are two ways to select one of the keywords: by double-clicking the keyword in the list or by typing the starting letters of it. In the latter case, the system selects (and highlights) the alphabetically first keyword in the list that has the typed letter(s) at its beginning.

The **Search** button is the most used button. It allows you to type a phrase (or a single word) that is then used in the search process to display all topics in which that phrase or word appears. (SQL Server 2008 uses its own Full Text Search component to support this process.) Besides the local search in Books Online, SQL Server 2008 searches the phrase also in MSDN Online and Codezone Community. (The Codezone

Community is a site for third-party tips, code samples, advices, and news from independent experts on the Microsoft .NET Framework and Microsoft Visual Studio.)

The results of the search process are displayed in the middle of the default pane. After clicking the **Search** button, the corresponding results appear in the pane. Each result includes the title of the document and a short description of the topic. The total number of search results appears also in the upper-right corner of the pane.

The **Help Favorites** tab allows you to store selected keywords (and phrases). Use this tab to display links to items, such as Help topics and web pages, that contain important information you might want to read again. This window also saves search queries so that you can save complex searches for future use. To bookmark a topic or web site, first open the topic or web site that you want to add to your list of favorites. Then, on the **Standard** toolbar, click the **Add to Help Favorites** icon. To select again one of the stored topics, double-click the entry in the list of your favorites.

Introduction to SQL Server Management Studio

SQL Server 2008 provides various tools that are used for different purposes, such as installation, configuration, auditing, and performance tuning. (All these tools will be discussed in different chapters of this book.)

NOTE

This chapter is dedicated to the activities of the end user. Therefore, only the functionality of SQL Server Management Studio with respect to the creation of database objects is described in detail. All administrative tasks and all tasks related to Analysis Services and other components that this tool supports are discussed beginning in Part III.

The administrator's primary tool for interacting with the system is SQL Server Management Studio. Both administrators and end users can use this tool to administer multiple servers, develop databases, and replicate data, among other things. To open this tool, click the Start menu, **All Programs**, **Microsoft SQL Server 2008**, and then **SQL Server Management Studio** in the SQL Server program group. Every user with access to the particular database server can also use SQL Server Management Studio.

SQL Server Management Studio comprises several different components that are used for the authoring, administration, and management of the overall system. The following are the main components used for these tasks:

- ▶   Registered Servers
- ▶   Object Explorer
- ▶   Query Editor
- ▶   Solution Explorer

The first two components are discussed in this introduction to SQL Server Management Studio. Query Editor and Solution Explorer are explained later in this chapter, in the section "Authoring Activities Using SQL Server Management Studio." To get to the main interface, you first must connect to a server, as described next.

Connecting to a Server

When you open SQL Server Management Studio, it displays the **Connect to Server** dialog box (see Figure 3-1), which allows you to specify the necessary parameters to connect to a server:

▶ **Server Type**   For purposes of this chapter, choose **Database Engine**.

NOTE

With SQL Server Management Studio, you can manage objects of Database Engine and Analysis Server, among others. This chapter demonstrates the use of Management Studio only with Database Engine.

▶ **Server Name**   Select or type the name of the server that you want to use. (Generally, you can connect SQL Server Management Studio to any of the installed products on a particular server.)

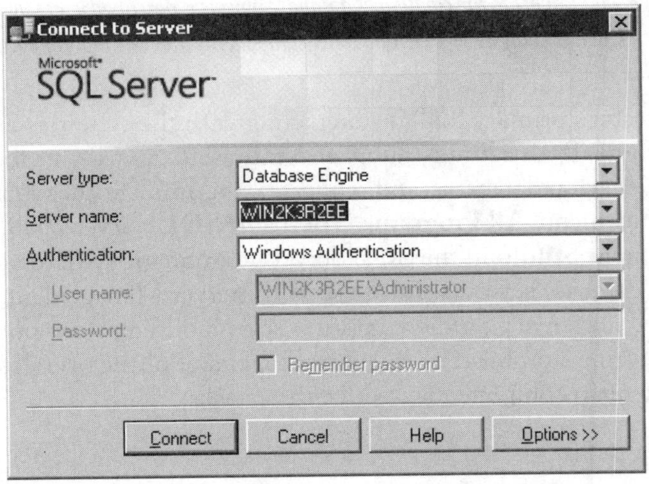

Figure 3-1   *The Connect to Server dialog box*

► **Authentication**   Choose between the two authentication types:

  ► **Windows Authentication**   Connect to SQL Server using your Windows account. This option is much simpler and is recommended for use by Microsoft.

  ► **SQL Server Authentication**   Database Engine uses its own authentication.

NOTE

For more information concerning SQL Server Authentication, see Chapter 12.

When you click **Connect**, Database Engine connects to the specified server. After connecting to the database server, the default SQL Server Management Studio window appears (see Figure 3-2). The default appearance is similar to Visual Studio, so users can leverage their experience of developing in Visual Studio to use SQL Server Management Studio more easily.

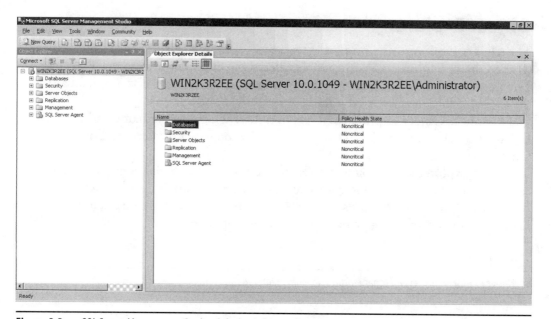

Figure 3-2   *SQL Server Management Studio: default window settings*

NOTE

SQL Server Management Studio gives you a unique interface to manage servers and create queries across all SQL Server components. This means that SQL Server Management Studio offers one interface for Database Engine, Analysis Services, Integration Services, and Reporting Services.

Registered Servers

Registered Servers is represented as a pane that allows you to maintain connections to already used servers. You can use these connections to check a server's status or to manage its objects. Each user has a separate list of registered servers, which is stored locally. (If the **Registered Servers** pane isn't visible, select its name from the **View** menu.)

You can add new servers to the list of all servers, or remove one or more existing servers from the list. You also can group existing servers into server groups. Each group should contain the servers that belong together logically. You can also group servers by server type, such as Database Engine, Analysis Services, Reporting Services, and Integration Services.

Object Explorer

The **Object Explorer** pane contains a tree view of all the database objects in a server. (If the **Object Explorer** pane isn't visible, select **Object Explorer** from the **View** menu.) The tree shows you a hierarchy of the objects on a server. Hence, if you expand a tree, the logical structure of a corresponding server will be shown.

To connect **Object Explorer** to a server, right-click the server name and choose **Connect**. To disconnect, click **Disconnect** in the toolbar and select the **Disconnect** function.

Object Explorer allows you to connect to multiple servers in the same pane. The server can be any of the existing servers for Database Engine, Analysis Services, Reporting Services, or Integration Services. This feature is user-friendly, because it allows you to manage all servers of the same or different types from one place.

NOTE

Object Explorer has several other features, explained later in this chapter.

Organizing and Navigating Management Studio's Panes

You can dock or hide each of the panes of Management Studio. By right-clicking the title bar at the top of the corresponding pane, you can choose between the following presentation possibilities:

▶ **Floating**   When a window's state is set to floating, it exists as a separate floating window on top of the rest of SQL Server Management Studio windows. Such a window can be moved anywhere around the screen.

▶ **Dockable**   Enables you to move panes of SQL Server Management Studio and dock them in different positions. To move a component, click and drag the title bar of the pane into the middle of the document window. The pane undocks and remains floating until you drop it.

▶ **Tabbed Document**   You can create a tabbed grouping using the Designer window. When this is done, the pane's state changes from dockable to tabbed document.

▶ **Hide**   Closes the window. (Alternatively, you can click the × in the upper-right corner of the window.) To display a closed window, select the component name from the **View** menu.

▶ **Auto Hide**   Minimizes the pane and stores it on the left side of the screen. To reopen (maximize) such a pane, move your mouse over the tabs on the left side of the screen and click the push pin to pin the pane in the open position.

NOTE

*The difference between the **Hide** and **Auto Hide** options is that the former option removes the pane from SQL Server Management Studio, while the latter collapses the pane to the side panel.*

To restore the default configuration, click the **Window** menu and select **Reset Window Layout**. The **Object Explorer** pane appears on the left, while the **Object Explorer Details** tab appears on the right side of SQL Server Management Studio. (The **Object Explorer Details** tab displays information about the currently selected node of **Object Explorer**.)

NOTE

You will find that often there are several ways of accomplishing the same task within SQL Server Management Studio. This chapter will indicate more than one way to do things, whereas only a single method will be given in subsequent chapters. Different people prefer different methods (some like to double-click, some like to click the +/– signs, some like to right-click, others like to use the pull-down menus, and others like to use the keyboard shortcuts as much as possible). Experiment with the different ways to navigate, and use the methods that feel most natural to you.

Within the **Object Explorer** and **Registered Servers** panes, a subobject appears only if you click the plus (+) sign of its direct predecessor in the tree hierarchy. To see the properties of an object, right-click the object and choose **Properties**. A minus (–) sign to the left of an object's name indicates that the object is currently expanded. To compress all subobjects of an object, click its minus sign. (Another possibility would be to double-click the folder, or press the LEFT ARROW key while the folder is selected.)

Using Management Studio with Database Engine

SQL Server Management Studio has two main purposes:

▶   Administration of the database servers

▶   Management of database objects

The following sections describe these features of SQL Server Management Studio.

Administering Database Servers

The administration tasks that you can perform by using SQL Server Management Studio are, among others, the following:

▶   Register servers

▶   Connecting to a server

▶   Create new server groups

▶   Start and stop SQL Server

The following subsections describe these administration tasks.

Registering Servers

SQL Server Management Studio separates the activities of registering servers and exploring databases and their objects. (Both of these activities can be done using Object Explorer.) Every server (local or remote) must be registered before use. A server can be registered during the first execution of SQL Server Management Studio or later. To register a database server, right-click the folder of your database server in **Object Explorer** and choose **Register**. (If the **Object Explorer** pane doesn't appear on your screen, select **View** and click **Object Explorer**.) The **New Server Registration** dialog box appears, as shown in Figure 3-3. Choose the name of the server that you want to register and the authentication mode (Windows Authentication or SQL Server Authentication).

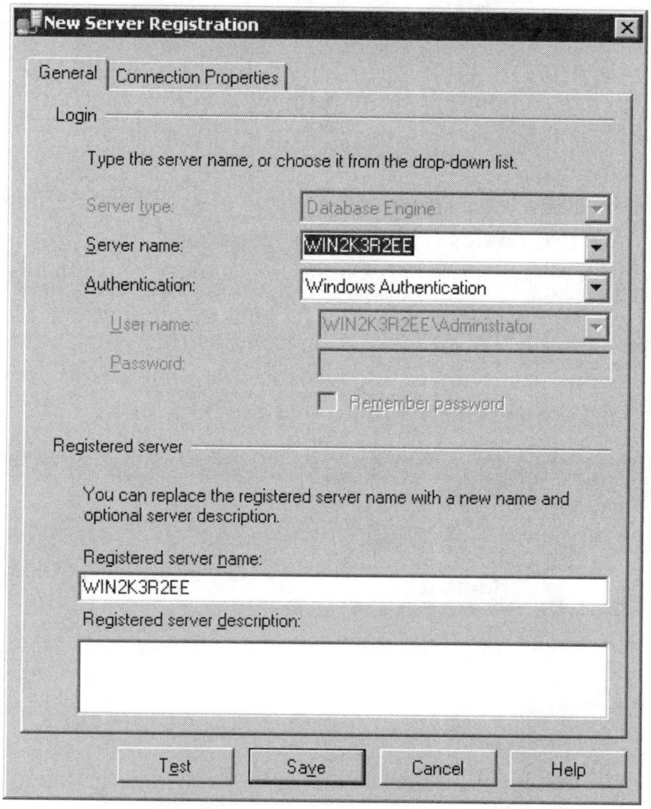

Figure 3-3   *The New Server Registration dialog box*

Connecting to a Server

SQL Server Management Studio also separates the tasks of registering a server and connecting to a server. This means that registering a server does not automatically connect you to the server. To connect to a server from the **Object Explorer** window, right-click the server name and choose **Connect**.

Creating a New Server Group

To create a new server group in the **Registered Servers** pane, right-click **Local Server Groups** and choose **New Server Group**. In the **New Server Group** properties dialog box, enter a (unique) group name and optionally describe the new group.

Managing Multiple Servers

SQL Server Management Studio allows you to administer multiple database servers (called instances) on one computer by using **Object Explorer**. Each instance of Database Engine has its own set of database objects (system and user databases) that are not shared between different instances.

To manage a server and its configuration, right-click the server name in **Object Explorer** and choose **Properties**. The **Server Properties** dialog box (see Figure 3-4) contains several different pages, such as **General**, **Security**, and **Permissions**.

The **General** page shows general properties of the server. The **Security** page contains the information concerning the authentication mode of the server and the login auditing mode. The **Permissions** page shows all logins and roles that can access the server. The lower part of the page shows all permissions that can be granted to the logins and roles.

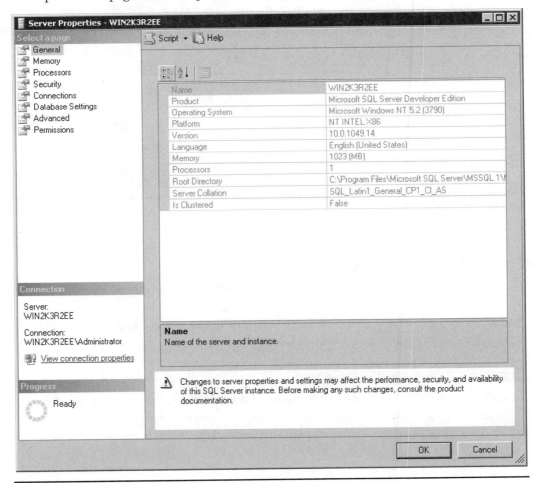

Figure 3-4   *The Server Properties dialog box*

You can replace the existing server name with a new name. Right-click the server in the **Object Explorer** window and choose **Register**. Now you can rename the server and modify the existing server description in the **Registered Server** frame.

NOTE

Do not rename servers, because changing names can affect other servers that reference them.

Starting and Stopping Servers

A Database Engine server can be started automatically each time the Windows operating system starts or by using SQL Server Management Studio. To start the server using Management Studio, right-click the selected server in the **Object Explorer** pane and click **Start** in the context menu. The menu also contains **Stop** and **Pause** functions that you can use to stop or pause the activated server, respectively.

Managing Databases Using Object Explorer

The following are the management tasks that you can perform by using SQL Server Management Studio:

- ▶ Create databases without using Transact-SQL
- ▶ Modify databases without using Transact-SQL
- ▶ Manage database objects and their usage
- ▶ Generate and execute SQL statements

Creating Databases Without Using Transact-SQL

You can create a new database by using **Object Explorer** or the Transact-SQL language. (Database creation using Transact-SQL is discussed in Chapter 5.) As the name suggests, you also use **Object Explorer** to explore the objects within a server. From the **Object Explorer** pane, you can inspect all the objects within a server and manage your server and databases. The existing tree contains, among other folders, the **Databases** folder. This folder has several subfolders, including one for the system databases and one for each new database that is created by a user. (System and user databases are discussed in detail in Chapter 15.)

To create a database using **Object Explorer**, right-click **Databases** and select **New Database**. In the **New Database** dialog box (see Figure 3-5), type the name of the new database in the **Database Name** field and then click **OK**. Each database has several

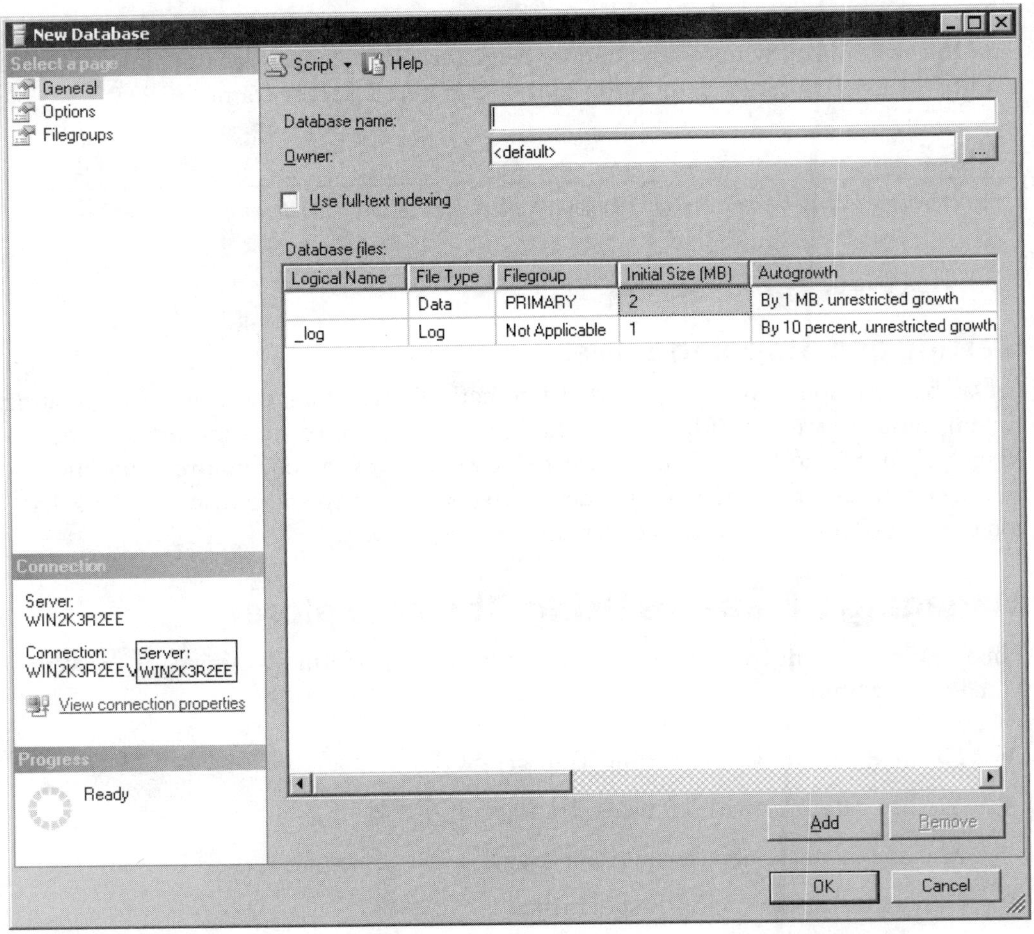

Figure 3-5   *The New Database dialog box*

different properties, such as file type, initial size, and so on. Database properties can be selected from the left pane of the **New Database** dialog box. There are several different pages (property groups):

► General

► Files (appears only for an existing database)

► Filegroups

► Options

► Permissions (appears only for an existing database)

▶ Extended Properties (appears only for an existing database)

▶ Mirroring (appears only for an existing database)

▶ Transaction Log Shipping (appears only for an existing database)

NOTE

*The system displays all property groups listed for an existing database. For a new database, as shown in Figure 3-5, there are only three different groups: **General**, **Options**, and **Filegroups**.*

The **General** page of the **Database Properties** dialog box (see Figure 3-6) displays, among other things, the database name, the owner of the database, its collation, and recovery model. The properties of the data files that belong to a particular database

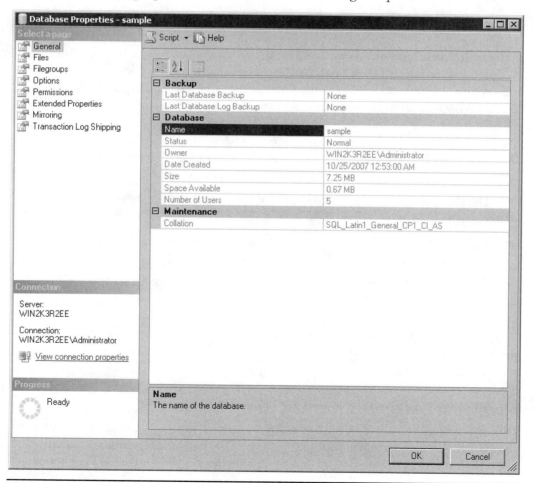

Figure 3-6   *Database Properties dialog box: General page*

comprise the name and initial size of the file, where the database will be stored, and the type of the file (PRIMARY, for instance). A database can be stored in multiple files.

NOTE

*SQL Server has dynamic disk space management. This means that databases can be set up to automatically expand and shrink as needed. If you want to change the **Autogrowth** property of the **Files** option, click ... in the **Autogrowth** column and make your changes in the **Change Autogrowth** dialog box. The **Enable Autogrowth** check box should be checked to allow the database to autogrow. Each time there is insufficient space within the file when data is added to the database, the server will request the additional space from the operating system. The amount (in megabytes) of the additional space is set by the number in the **File Growth** frame of the same dialog box. You can also decide whether the file can grow without any restrictions (the default value) or not. If you restrict the file growth, you have to specify the maximum file size.*

The **Filegroups** page of the **Database Properties** dialog box displays the name(s) of the filegroup(s) to which the database file belongs, the art of the filegroup (default or nondefault), and the allowed operation on the filegroup (read/write or read-only).

The **Options** page of the **Database Properties** dialog box enables you to display and modify all database-level options. There are several groups of options: **Automatic**, **Cursor**, **Miscellaneous**, **Recovery**, and **State**. For instance, the following four options exist for **State**:

- ▶ **Database Read-Only**   Allows read-only access to the database. This prohibits users from modifying any data. (The default value is False.)

- ▶ **Database State**   Describes the state of the database. (The default value is NORMAL.)

- ▶ **Restrict Access**   Restricts the use of the database to one user at a time. (The default value is MULTI_USER.)

- ▶ **Encryption Enabled**   Controls the database encryption state. (The default value is False.)

If you choose the **Permissions** page, the system opens the corresponding dialog box and displays all users and roles along with their permissions. (For the discussion of permissions, see Chapter 12.)

Modifying Databases Without Using Transact-SQL

Object Explorer can also be used to modify an existing database. Using this component, you can modify files and filegroups that belong to the database. To add new data files, right-click the database name and choose **Properties**. In the **Database Properties**

dialog box, select **Files**, click **Add**, and type the name of the new file. (In the **Add File** dialog box, you can also change the autogrowth properties and the location of each existing file.) You can also add a (secondary) filegroup for the database by selecting **Filegroups** and clicking **Add**.

NOTE

Only the system administrator or the database owner can modify the database properties just mentioned.

To delete a database using **Object Explorer**, right-click the database name and choose **Delete**.

Managing Tables Without Using Transact-SQL

After you create a database, your next task is to create all tables belonging to it. Again, you can create tables by using either **Object Explorer** or Transact-SQL. Again, only **Object Explorer** is discussed here.

To create a table using **Object Explorer**, expand the **Databases** folder, expand the database, right-click the **Tables** subfolder, and then click **New Table**. The creation of a table and all other database objects using the Transact-SQL language will be discussed in detail in Chapter 5.

To demonstrate the creation of a table using **Object Explorer**, the **department** table of the **sample** database will be used as an example. Enter the names of all columns with their properties. Column names, their data types, as well as the NULL property of the column must be entered in the two-dimensional matrix, as shown in the top-right pane of Figure 3-7.

All data types supported by the system can be displayed (and one of them selected) by clicking the arrow sign in the **Data Type** column (the arrow appears after the cell has been selected). Subsequently, you can type entries in the **Length**, **Precision**, and **Scale** rows for the chosen data type on the **Column Properties** tab (see the bottom-right pane of Figure 3-7). Some data types, such as CHAR, require a value for the **Length** row, and some, such as DECIMAL, require a value in the **Precision** and **Scale** rows. On the other hand, data types such as INTEGER do not need any of these entries to be specified. (The valid entries for a specified data type are highlighted in the list of all possible column properties.)

The check box in the **Allow Nulls** column must be checked if you want a table column to permit NULL values to be inserted into that column. Similarly, if there is a default value, it should be entered in the **Default Value or Binding** row of the **Column Properties** tab. (A default value is a value that will be inserted in a table column when there is no explicit value entered for it.)

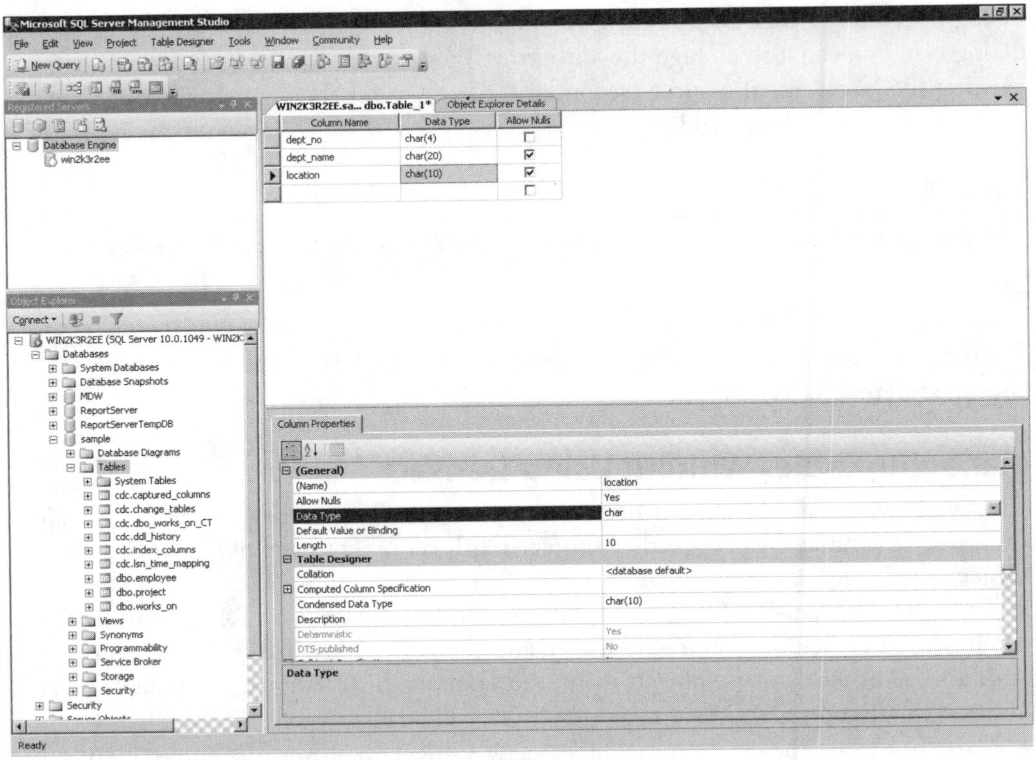

Figure 3-7 *Creating the department table using SQL Server Management Studio*

The column **dept_no** is the primary key of the **department** table. (For the discussion of primary keys of the **sample** database, see Chapter 1.) To specify a column as the primary key of a table, you must right-click the column and choose **Set Primary Key**. Finally, close the right pane with the information concerning the new table. After that, the system will display the **Choose Name** dialog box, where you can type the table name.

To view the properties of an existing table, double-click the folder of the database to which the table belongs, double-click **Tables**, and then right-click the name of the table and choose **Properties**. Figure 3-8 shows the **Table Properties** dialog box for the **employee** table.

To rename a table, right-click the name of the table in the **Tables** folder and choose **Rename**. To remove a table, right-click the name of the table in the **Tables** folder in the database to which the table belongs and select **Delete**.

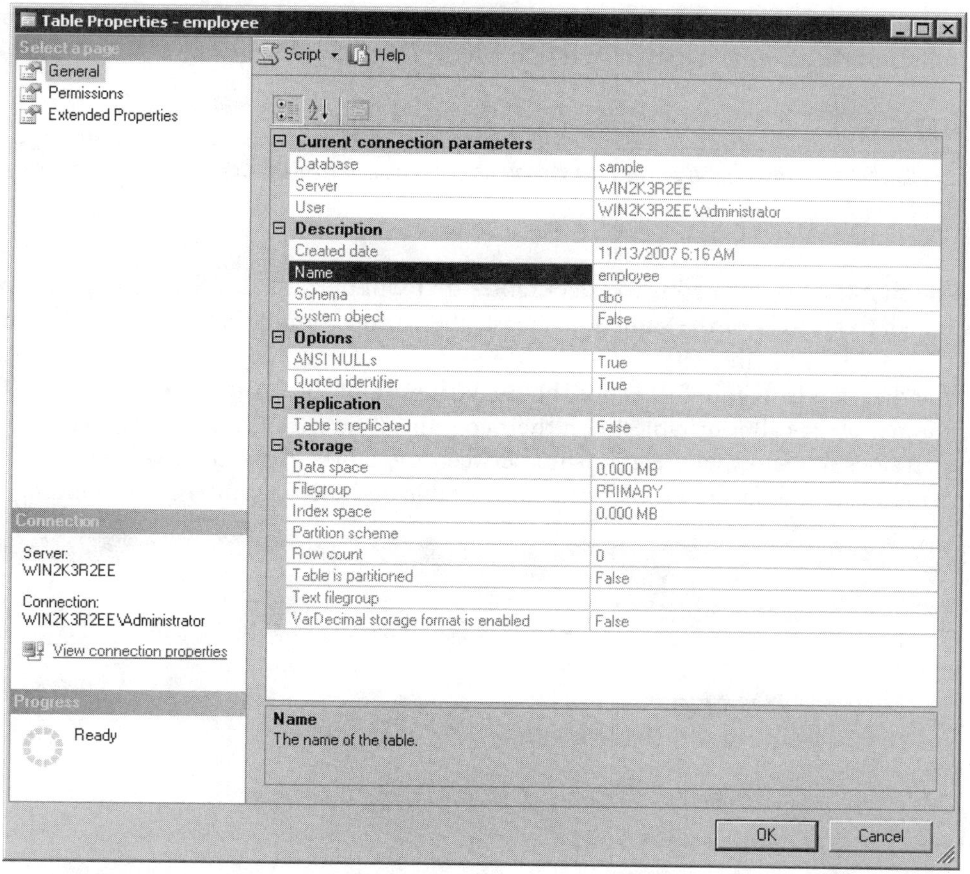

Figure 3-8   *Table Properties dialog box for the employee table*

NOTE

*You should now create the other three tables of the **sample** database.*

After you have created all four tables of the **sample** database (**employee, department, project,** and **works_on**), you can use another feature of SQL Server Management Studio to display the corresponding entity-relationship (ER) diagram of the **sample** database. (The process of converting the existing tables of a database into the corresponding ER diagram is called *reverse engineering*.)

To see the ER diagram of the **sample** database, right-click the **Database Diagrams** subfolder of the **sample** database and select **New Database Diagram**.

NOTE

If a dialog box opens asking you whether the support objects should be created, click Yes.

The first (and only) step is to select tables that will be added to the diagram. After adding all four tables of the **sample** database, the wizard completes the work and creates the diagram (see Figure 3-9).

The diagram in Figure 3-9 is not the final diagram of the **sample** database, because although it shows all four tables with their columns (and the corresponding primary keys), it does not show any relationship between the tables. A relationship between two tables is based on the primary key of one table and the (possible) corresponding

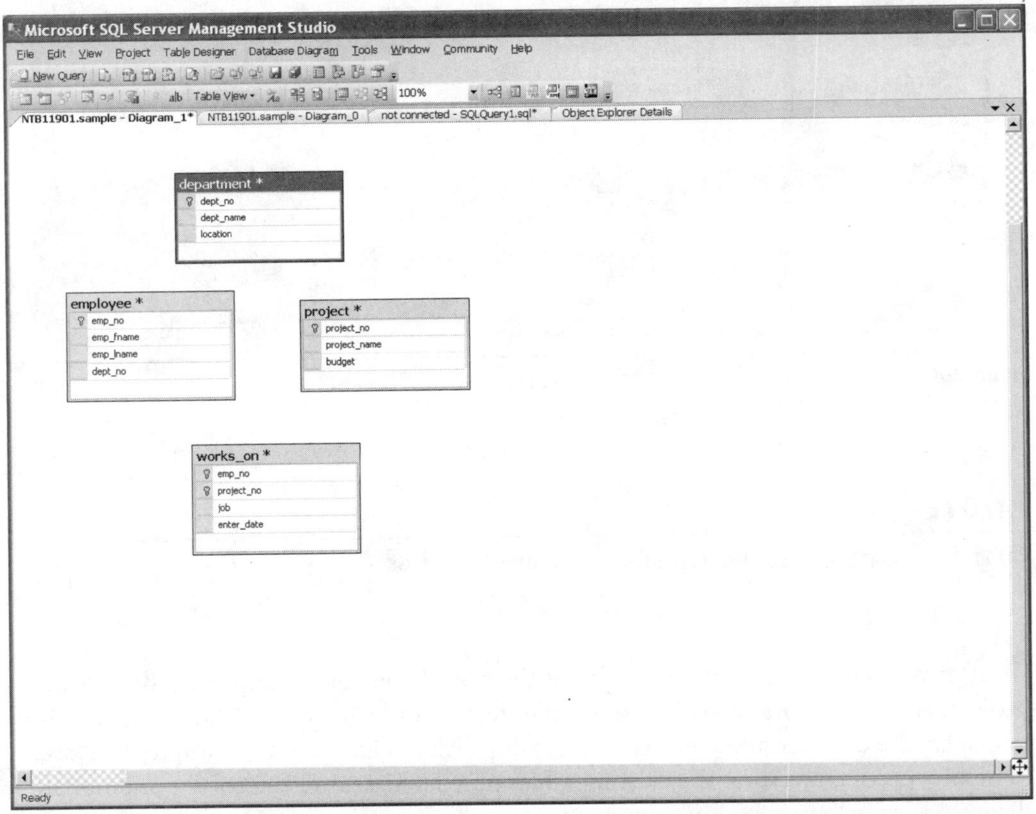

Figure 3-9   *First diagram of the sample database*

column(s) of the other table. (For a detailed discussion of these relationships and referential integrity, see Chapter 5.)

There are exactly three relationships between the existing tables of the **sample** database: first, the tables **department** and **employee** have a 1:N relationship, because for each value in the primary key column of the **department** table (**dept_no**), there is one or more corresponding values in the column **dept_no** of the **employee** table. Analogously, there is a relationship between the tables **employee** and **works_on**, because only those values that exist in the primary key of the **employee** table (**emp_no**) appear also in the column **emp_no** of the **works_on** table. (The third relationship is between the tables **project** and **works_on**, because only values that exist in the primary key of the **project** table (**pr_no**) appear also in the **pr_no** column of the **works_on** table.

To create each of the three relationships described, you have to redesign the diagram with the column that corresponds to the primary key column of the other table. (Such a column is called a *foreign key*.) To see how to do this, use the **employee** table and define its column **dept_no** as the foreign key of the **department** table:

1. Click the created diagram, right-click the graphical form of the **employee** table in the detail pane, and select **Relationships**. In the **Foreign Key Relationships** dialog box, click **Add**.

2. In the dialog box, expand **Tables and Columns Specification** column and click the ... button.

3. Select the table with the corresponding primary key (the **department** table).

4. Choose the **dept_no** column of this table as the primary key and the column with the same name in the **employee** table as the foreign key and click **OK**. Click Close.

Figure 3-10 shows the modified diagram after all three relationships in the **sample** database have been created.

Authoring Activities Using SQL Server Management Studio

SQL Server Management Studio gives you a complete authoring environment for all types of queries. You can create, save, load, and edit queries. SQL Server Management Studio allows you to work on queries without being connected to a particular server. This tool also gives you the option of developing your queries with different projects.

The authoring capabilities are associated with **Query Editor** as well as Solution Explorer. The former component will be discussed next.

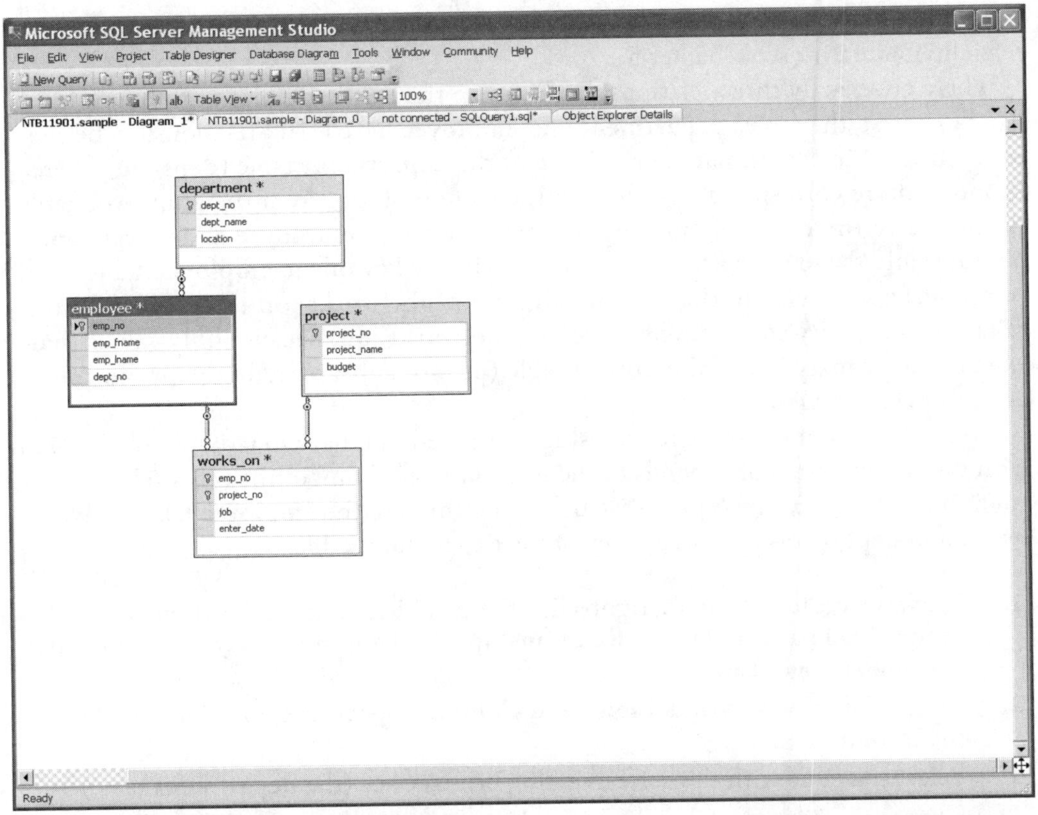

Figure 3-10   *The final diagram of the sample database*

Query Editor

To launch the **Query Editor** pane, click the **New Query** button in the toolbar of SQL Server Management Studio. If you expand it to show all the possible queries, it shows more than just a Database Engine query. By default, you get a new Database Engine query, but other queries are possible, such as MDX queries, XMLA queries, and other queries.

Once you open **Query Editor**, the status bar at the bottom of the pane tells you whether your query is in a connected or disconnected state. If you are not connected automatically to the server, the **Connect to SQL Server** dialog box appears, where you can type the name of the database server to which you want to connect and select the authentication mode.

NOTE

*Disconnected editing has more flexibility than connected editing. You can edit queries without having to choose a server, and you can disconnect a given **Query Editor** window from one server and connect it to another without having to open another window. (You can use disconnected editing if you click the **Cancel** button in the **Connect to SQL Server** dialog box.)*

Query Editor can be used by end users for the following tasks:

▶ Generating and executing Transact-SQL statements

▶ Storing the generated Transact-SQL statements in a file

▶ Generating and analyzing execution plans for generated queries

▶ Graphically illustrating the execution plan for a selected query

Query Editor contains an internal text editor and a selection of buttons in its toolbar. The main window is divided into a query pane (upper) and a results pane (lower). Users enter the Transact-SQL statements (queries) that they want to execute into the query pane, and after the system has processed the queries, the output is displayed in the results pane.

The example shown in Figure 3-11 demonstrates a query entered into Query Editor and the output returned. The first statement in the query pane, USE, specifies the **sample** database as the current database. The second statement, SELECT, retrieves all the rows of the **works_on** table. Clicking the **Query** button in the **Query Editor**'s toolbar and then selecting **Execute** or pressing F5 returns the results of these statements in the results pane of **Query Editor**.

NOTE

*You can open several different windows—that is, several different connections to one or more Database Engine instances. You create new connections by clicking the **New Query** button in the toolbar.*

The following additional information concerning the execution of the statement(s) is displayed in the status bar at the bottom of the **Query Editor** window:

▶ The status of the current operation (for example, "Query executed successfully")

▶ Database server name

▶ Current username and server process ID

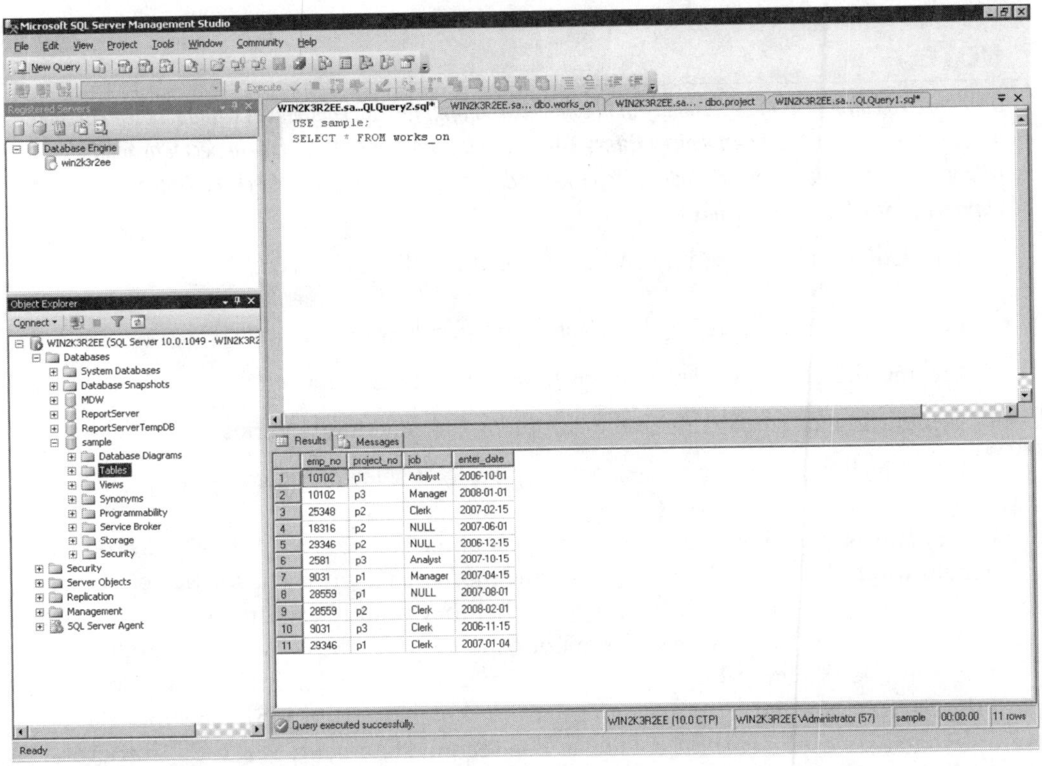

Figure 3-11   *Query Editor with a query and its results*

- ► Current database name
- ► Elapsed time for the execution of the last query
- ► The number of retrieved rows

One of the main features of SQL Server Management Studio is that it's easy to use, and that also applies to the **Query Editor** component. **Query Editor** supports a lot of features that make coding of Transact-SQL statements easier. First, **Query Editor** uses syntax highlighting to improve the readability of Transact-SQL statements. It displays all reserved words in blue, all variables in black, strings in red, and comments in green. (For a discussion of reserved words, see the next chapter.)

There is also the context-sensitive help function called **Dynamic Help** that enables you to get help on a particular statement. If you do not know the syntax of a statement, just highlight that statement in the editor and select the **Dynamic Help** option on the **Help** menu. You can also highlight options of different Transact-SQL statements to get the corresponding text from Books Online.

NOTE

SQL Server 2008 supports the SQL Intellisense tool. Intellisense is a form of automated autocompletion. In other words, this add-in allows you to access descriptions of frequently used elements of Transact-SQL statements without using the keyboard. (In future versions of SQL Server, this feature will be extended to support additional Transact-SQL elements.)

Object Explorer can also help you edit queries. For instance, if you want to see the corresponding CREATE TABLE statement for the **employee** table, drill down to this database object, right-click the table name, select **Script Table as**, and choose **CREATE to New Query Editor Window**. Figure 3-12 shows the **Query Editor** window with the CREATE TABLE statement. (This capability extends also to other objects, such as stored procedures and functions.)

Object Explorer is very useful if you want to display the graphical execution plan for a particular query. (The execution plan is the plan selected by the optimizer to execute a given query. This topic is discussed in detail in Chapter 20.) If you select the **Query**

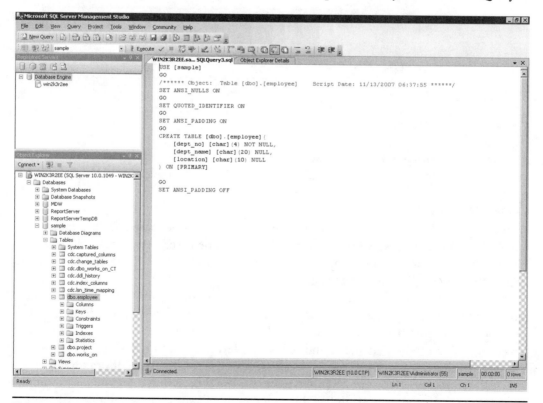

Figure 3-12   *The Query Editor windows with the CREATE TABLE statement*

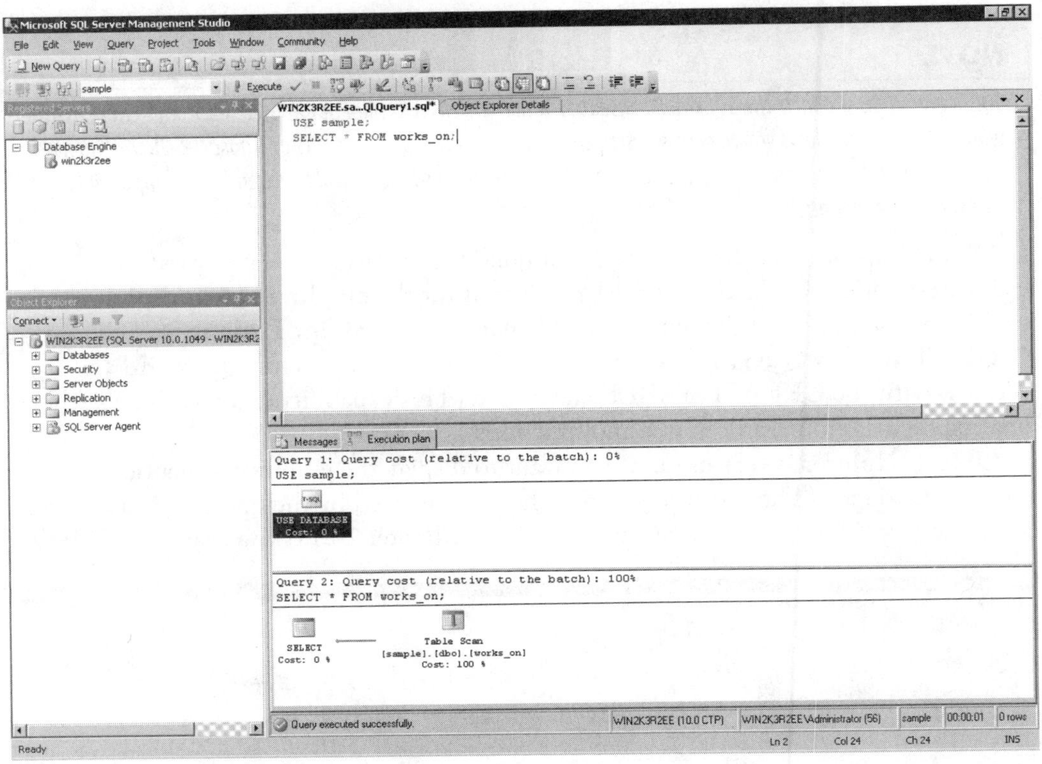

Figure 3-13 *The execution plan for the query from Figure 3-11*

function and **Display Estimated Execution Plan**, the system will display the graphical plan instead of the result set for the given query (see Figure 3-13).

Solution Explorer

Query editing in SQL Server Management Studio is solution-based. If you start a blank query using the **New Query** button, it will still be based on a blank solution. You can see this by choosing the component called **Solution Explorer** from the **View** menu, right after opening your blank query.

A solution can have zero, one, or more projects associated with it. A blank solution does not contain any project. If you want to associate a project with the solution, close your blank solution, **Solution Explorer**, and the **Query Editor** window, and start a new project by clicking the **File** menu and selecting **New** and then **Project**. In the **New Project** window, choose **SQL Server Scripts**. A project is a method of organizing files in a selected location. You can choose a name for the project and select its location on disk. When you create a new project, by default you will start a new solution. You can add a project to an existing solution using **Solution Explorer**.

Once the new project and solution are created, **Solution Explorer** shows nodes in each project for **Connections, Queries,** and **Miscellaneous.** To open a new **Query Editor** window, right-click the **Query** node and choose **New Query.**

SQL Server Management Studio supports version control using the integration with Microsoft Visual Source Safe. As already stated, **Solution Explorer** allows you to organize and store related scripts as parts of a project. These script files can be checked in and out of the version control system directly from **Solution Explorer.**

Conclusion

This chapter covered the most important SQL Server tool: SQL Server Management Studio. SQL Server Management Studio is very useful for end users and administrators alike. First, it allows many administrative functions to be performed. These are touched on here but are covered in more detail later in the book. This chapter discussed most important functions of SQL Server Management Studio concerning end users, such as database and table creation.

SQL Server Management Studio contains several components:

- ▶ **Registered Servers**   Allows you to register SQL Server instances and connect to them.

- ▶ **Object Explorer**   Contains a tree view of all the database objects in a server.

- ▶ **Query Editor**   Allows end users to generate, execute, and store Transact-SQL statements. Additionally, it provides the ability to analyze queries by displaying the execution plan.

- ▶ **Solution Explorer**   Allows you to create solutions. A solution can have zero or more projects associated with it.

The next chapter introduces the Transact-SQL language and describes its main components. After introducing the basic concepts and existing data types, the chapter also describes system functions that Transact-SQL supports.

Exercises

E.3.1

Using SQL Server Management Studio, create a database called **test**. Store the database in a file named **testdate_a** in the directory C:\tmp and allocate 10MB of space to it. Configure the file in which the database is located to grow in increments of 2MB, not to exceed a total of 20MB.

E.3.2

Using SQL Server Management Studio, change the transaction log for the **test** database. Give the file an initial size of 3MB, with growth of 20 percent. Allow the file for the transaction log to autogrow.

E.3.3

Using SQL Server Management Studio, allow only the database owner and system administrator to use the **test** database. Is it possible that both users could use the database at the same time?

E.3.4

Using SQL Server Management Studio, create all four tables of the **sample** database (see Chapter 1) with all their columns.

E.3.5

Using SQL Server Management Studio, view which tables the **AdventureWorks** database contains. After that, choose the **person.address** table and view its properties.

E.3.6

Using Query Editor, type the following Transact-SQL statement:

CREATE DATABASE test

Explain the error message shown in the result pane.

E.3.7

Store the Transact-SQL statement in E.3.6 in the file C:\tmp\createdb.sql.

E.3.8

Using Query Editor, how can you make the **test** database the current database?

E.3.9

Using Query Editor, make the **AdventureWorks** database the current database and execute the following Transact-SQL statement:

SELECT * FROM Sales.Customer

How can you stop the execution of the statement?

E.3.10

Using Query Editor, change the output of the SELECT statement (E.3.9) so that the results appear as the text (and not as the grid).

Part II

Transact-SQL Language

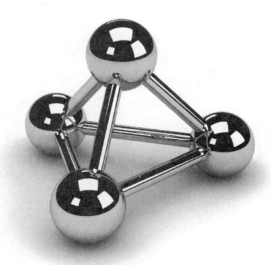

Chapter 4

SQL Components

In This Chapter

- ► **SQL's Basic Objects**
- ► **Data Types**
- ► **Transact-SQL Functions**
- ► **Scalar Operators**
- ► **NULL Values**

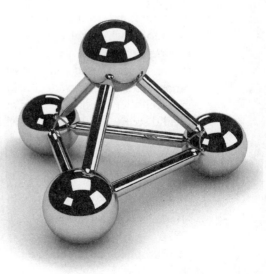

T his chapter introduces the elementary objects and basic operators supported by the Transact-SQL language. First, the basic language elements, including constants, identifiers, and delimiters, are described. Then, because every elementary object has a corresponding data type, data types are discussed in detail. Additionally, all existing operators and functions are explained. At the end of the chapter, NULL values are introduced.

SQL's Basic Objects

The language of Database Engine, Transact-SQL, has the same basic features as other common programming languages:

- ▶ Literal values (also called constants)
- ▶ Delimiters
- ▶ Comments
- ▶ Identifiers
- ▶ Reserved keywords

The following sections describe these features.

Literal Values

A *literal* value is an alphanumerical, hexadecimal, or numeric constant. A string constant contains one or more characters of the character set enclosed in two single straight quotation marks (' ') or double straight quotation marks (" ") (single quotation marks are preferred due to the multiple uses of double quotation marks, as discussed in a moment). If you want to include a single quotation mark within a string delimited by single quotation marks, use two consecutive single quotation marks within the string. Hexadecimal constants are used to represent nonprintable characters and other binary data. Each hexadecimal constant begins with the characters '0x' followed by an even number of characters or numbers. Examples 4.1 and 4.2 illustrate some valid and invalid string constants and hexadecimal constants.

EXAMPLE 4.1

Some valid string constants and hexadecimal constants follow:

'Philadelphia'
"Berkeley, CA 94710"
'9876'
'Apostrophe is displayed like this: can''t' (note the two consecutive single quotation marks)
0x53514C0D

EXAMPLE 4.2

The following are *not* string constants:

'AB'C' (odd number of single quotation marks)
'New York" (same type of quotation mark—single or double—must be used at each end of the string)

The numeric constants include all integer, fixed-point, and floating-point values with and without signs (see Example 4.3).

EXAMPLE 4.3

The following are numeric constants:

130
−130.00
−0.357E5 (scientific notation—nEm means n multiplied by 10^m)
22.3E-3

A constant always has a data type and a length, and both depend on the format of the constant. Additionally, every numeric constant has a precision and a scale factor. (The data types of the different kinds of literal values are explained later in this chapter.)

Delimiters

In Transact-SQL, double quotation marks have two meanings. In addition to enclosing strings, double quotation marks can also be used as delimiters for so-called *delimited identifiers*. Delimited identifiers are a special kind of identifier usually used to allow the use of reserved keywords as identifiers and also to allow spaces in the names of database objects.

NOTE

Differentiation between single and double quotation marks was first introduced in the SQL92 standard. In the case of identifiers, this standard differentiates between regular and delimited identifiers. Two key differences are that delimited identifiers are enclosed in double quotation marks and are case sensitive. (Transact-SQL also supports the use of square brackets instead of double quotation marks.) Double quotation marks are only used for delimiting strings. Generally, delimited identifiers were introduced to allow the specification of identifiers, which are otherwise identical to reserved keywords. Specifically, delimited identifiers protect you from using names (identifiers, variable names) that could be introduced as reserved keywords in one of the future SQL standards. Also, delimited identifiers may contain characters that are normally illegal within identifier names, such as blanks.

In Transact-SQL, the use of double quotation marks is defined using the QUOTED_ IDENTIFIER option of the SET statement. If this option is set to ON, which is the default value, an identifier in double quotation marks will be defined as a delimited identifier. In this case, double quotation marks cannot be used for delimiting strings.

Comments

There are two different ways to specify a comment in a Transact-SQL statement. Using the pair of characters /* and */ marks the enclosed text as a comment. In this case, the comment may extend over several lines. Furthermore, the characters -- (two hyphens) indicate that the remainder of the current line is a comment. (The two hyphens -- comply with the ANSI SQL standard, while /* and */ are the extensions of Transact-SQL.)

Identifiers

In Transact-SQL, identifiers are used to identify database objects such as databases, tables, and indices. They are represented by character strings that may include up to 128 characters and can contain letters, numerals, or the following characters: _, @, #, and $. Each name must begin with a letter or one of the following characters: _, @, or #. The character # at the beginning of a table or stored procedure name denotes a temporary object, while @ at the beginning of a name denotes a variable. As indicated earlier, these rules don't apply to delimited identifiers (also known as quoted identifiers), which can contain, or begin with, any character (other than the delimiters themselves).

Reserved Keywords

Each programming language has a set of names with reserved meanings, which must be written and used in the defined format. Names of this kind are called *reserved keywords*. Transact-SQL uses a variety of such names, which, as in many other programming languages, cannot be used as object names, unless the objects are specified as delimited or quoted identifiers.

NOTE

In Transact-SQL, the names of all data types and system functions, such as CHARACTER and INTEGER, are not reserved keywords. They can therefore be used for denoting objects. (Do not use data types and system functions as object names! Such a use makes Transact-SQL statements difficult to read and understand.)

Data Types

All the data values of a column must be of the same data type. (The only exception specifies the values of the SQL_VARIANT data type.) Transact-SQL uses different data types, which can be categorized as follows:

▶ Numeric data types

▶ Character data types

▶ Temporal (date and/or time) data types

▶ Miscellaneous data types

▶ DECIMAL with VARDECIMAL storage type

The following sections describe all these categories.

Numeric Data Types

Numeric data types are used to represent numbers. The following table shows the list of all numeric data types:

Data Type	Explanation
INTEGER	Represents integer values that can be stored in 4 bytes. The range of values is −2,147,483,648 to 2,147,483,647. INT is the short form for INTEGER.
SMALLINT	Represents integer values that can be stored in 2 bytes. The range of values is −32768 to 32767.
TINYINT	Represents nonnegative integer values that can be stored in 1 byte. The range of values is 0 to 255.
BIGINT	Represents integer values that can be stored in 8 bytes. The range of values is -2^{63} to $2^{63} - 1$.
DECIMAL(p,[s])	Describes fixed-point values. The argument **p** (precision) specifies the total number of digits with assumed decimal point **s** (scale) digits from the right. DECIMAL values are stored, depending on the value of **p**, in 5 to 17 bytes. DEC is the short form for DECIMAL.
NUMERIC(p,[s])	Synonym for DECIMAL.
REAL	Used for floating-point values. The range of positive values is approximately 2.23E − 308 to 1.79E + 308, and the range of negative values is approximately −1.18E − 38 to −1.18E + 38 (the value zero can also be stored).
FLOAT[(p)]	Represents floating-point values, like REAL. **p** defines the precision with **p** < 25 as single precision (4 byte) and **p** >= 25 as double precision (8 byte).
MONEY	Used for representing monetary values. MONEY values correspond to 8-byte DECIMAL values and are rounded to four digits after the decimal point.
SMALLMONEY	Corresponds to the data type MONEY but is stored in 4 bytes.

Character Data Types

There are two general forms of character data types. They can be strings of single-byte characters or strings of Unicode characters. (Unicode uses several bytes to specify one character.) Further, strings can have fixed or variable length. The following character data types are used:

Data Type	Explanation
CHAR[(n)]	Represents a fixed-length string of single-byte characters, where **n** is the number of characters inside the string. The maximum value of **n** is 8000. CHARACTER(n) is an additional equivalent form for CHAR(n). If **n** is omitted, the length of the string is assumed to be 1.
VARCHAR[(n)]	Describes a variable-length string of single-byte characters (0 < **n** ≤ 8000). In contrast to the CHAR data type, the values for the VARCHAR data type are stored in their actual length. This data type has two synonyms: CHAR VARYING and CHARACTER VARYING.
NCHAR[(n)]	Stores fixed-length strings of Unicode characters. The main difference between the CHAR and NCHAR data types is that each character of the NCHAR data type is stored in 2 bytes, while each character of the CHAR data type uses 1 byte of storage space. Therefore, the maximum number of characters in a column of the NCHAR data type is 4000.
NVARCHAR[(n)]	Stores variable-length strings of Unicode characters. The main difference between the VARCHAR and the NVARCHAR data types is that each NVARCHAR character is stored in 2 bytes, while each VARCHAR character uses 1 byte of storage space. The maximum number of characters in a column of the NVARCHAR data type is 4000.

NOTE

*The VARCHAR data type is identical to the CHAR data type except for one difference: if the content of a CHAR(n) string is shorter than **n** characters, the rest of the string is padded with blanks. (A value of the VARCHAR data type is always stored in its actual length.)*

Temporal Data Types

Transact-SQL supports the following temporal data types:

- ► DATETIME
- ► SMALLDATETIME
- ► DATE
- ► TIME
- ► DATETIME2
- ► DATETIMEOFFSET

The DATETIME and SMALLDATETIME data types specify a date and time, with each value being stored as an integer value in 4 bytes or 2 bytes, respectively. Values of DATETIME and SMALLDATETIME are stored internally as two separate numeric values. The date value of DATETIME is stored in the range 01/01/1753 to 12/31/9999. The analog value of SMALLDATETIME is stored in the range 01/01/1900 to 06/06/2079. The time component is stored in the second 4-byte (or 2-byte for SMALLDATETIME) field as the number of three-hundredths of a second (DATETIME) or minutes (SMALLDATETIME) that have passed since midnight.

The use of DATETIME and SMALLDATETIME is rather inconvenient if you want to store only the date part or time part. For this reason, SQL Server 2008 introduces the new data types DATE and TIME, which store just the DATE or TIME component of a DATETIME, respectively. The DATE data type is stored in 3 bytes and has the range 01/01/0001 to 12/31/9999. The TIME data type is stored in 3–5 bytes and has an accuracy of 100 nanoseconds (ns).

The DATETIME2 data type is also a new data type that stores high-precision date and time data. The data type can be defined for variable lengths depending on the requirement. (The storage size is 6–8 bytes). The accuracy of the time part is 100 ns. This data type isn't aware of Daylight Saving Time.

All the temporal data types described thus far don't have support for the time zone. The new data type called DATETIMEOFFSET has the time zone offset portion. For this reason, it is stored in 6–8 bytes. (All other properties of this data type are analogous to the corresponding properties of DATETIME2.)

The date value in Transact-SQL is by default specified as a string in a format like 'mmm dd yyyy' (e.g., 'Jan 10 1993') inside two single quotation marks or double quotation marks. (Note that the relative order of month, day, and year can be controlled by the SET DATEFORMAT statement. Additionally, the system recognizes numeric month values with delimiters of / or –.) Similarly, the time value is specified in the format 'hh:mm' and Database Engine uses 24-hour time (23:24, for instance).

NOTE

Transact-SQL supports a variety of input formats for DATETIME values. As you already know, both objects are identified separately; thus, date and time values can be specified in any order or alone. If one of the values is omitted, the system uses the default values. (The default value for time is 12:00 AM.)

Examples 4.4 and 4.5 show the different ways, how date or time values can be written using the different formats.

EXAMPLE 4.4

The following date descriptions can be used:

'28/5/1959' (with SET DATEFORMAT dmy)
'May 28, 1959'
'1959 MAY 28'

EXAMPLE 4.5

The following time expressions can be used:

'8:45 AM'
'4 pm'

Miscellaneous Data Types

Transact-SQL supports several data types that do not belong to any of the data type groups described previously:

- ▶ Binary data types
- ▶ BIT
- ▶ Large object data types
- ▶ CURSOR (discussed in Chapter 8)
- ▶ UNIQUEIDENTIFIER
- ▶ SQL_VARIANT
- ▶ TABLE (discussed in Chapter 8)
- ▶ XML (discussed in Chapter 28)
- ▶ Spatial (e.g., GEOGRAPHY and GEOMETRY) data types (discussed in Chapter 29)
- ▶ HIERARCHYID
- ▶ TIMESTAMP data type
- ▶ User-defined data types (discussed in Chapter 5)

The following sections describe each of these data types (other than those designated as being discussed in another chapter).

Binary and BIT Data Types

BINARY and VARBINARY are the two binary data types. They describe data objects being represented in the internal format of the system. They are used to store bit strings. For this reason, the values are entered using hexadecimal numbers.

The values of the BIT data type are stored in a single bit. Therefore, up to 8 bit columns are stored in 1 byte. The following table summarizes the properties of these data types:

Data Type	Explanation
BINARY[(n)]	Specifies a bit string of fixed length with exactly **n** bytes (0 < **n** ≤ 8000).
VARBINARY[(n)]	Specifies a bit string of variable length with up to **n** bytes (0 < **n** ≤ 8000).
BIT	Used for specifying the Boolean data type with three possible values: FALSE, TRUE, and NULL.

Large Object Data Types

Large objects (LOBs) are data objects with the maximum length of 2GB. These objects are generally used to store large text data and to load modules and audio/video files. Transact-SQL supports two different ways to specify and access LOBs:

▶ Use the data types VARCHAR(MAX), NVARCHAR(MAX), and VARBINARY(MAX)

▶ Use the so-called text/image data type

The following subsections describe the two forms of LOBs.

The MAX Specifier   Starting with SQL Server 2005, you can use the same programming model to access values of standard data types and LOBs. In other words, you can use convenient system functions and string operators to work with LOBs.

Database Engine uses the MAX specifier with the data types VARCHAR, NVARCHAR, and VARBINARY to define variable-length columns. When you use MAX by default (instead of an explicit value), the system analyzes the length of the particular string and decides whether to store the string as a convenient value or as a LOB. The MAX specifier indicates that the size of column values can reach the maximum LOB size of the current system. (In a future version of SQL Server, it is possible that MAX will have a higher maximum value for strings.)

Although the database system decides how a LOB will be stored, you can override this default specification using the **sp_tableoption** system procedure with the LARGE_VALUE_TYPES_OUT_OF_ROW option. If the option's value is set to 1, the data in columns declared using the MAX specifier will be stored separately from all other data. If this option is set to 0, Database Engine stores all values for the row size < 8060 bytes as regular row data.

In SQL Server 2008, you can apply the new FILESTREAM attribute to a VARBINARY(MAX) column to store large binary data directly in an NTFS file system. The main advantage of this attribute is that the size of the corresponding LOB is limited only by the file system volume size.

TEXT, NTEXT, and IMAGE Data Types The data types TEXT, NTEXT, and IMAGE constitute the so-called text/image data types. Data objects of the type IMAGE can contain any kind of data (load modules, audio/video), while data objects of the data types TEXT and NTEXT can contain any text data (that is, printable data).

The text/image data types are stored by default separately from all other values of a database using a B-tree structure that points to the fragments of that data. (A *B-tree structure* is a treelike data structure in which all of the bottom nodes are the same number of levels away from the root of the tree.) For columns of a text/image data type, Database Engine stores a 16-byte pointer in the data row that specifies where the data can be found.

If the amount of text/image data is less than 32KB, the pointer points to the root node of the B-tree structure, which is 84 bytes long. The root node points to the physical blocks of the data. If the amount of the data is greater than 32KB, Database Engine builds intermediate nodes between the data blocks and the root node.

For each table that contains more than one column with such data, all values of the columns are stored together. However, one physical page can hold only text/image data from a single table.

Although text/image data is stored separately from all other data, you can modify this using the **sp_tableoption** system procedure with the TEXT_IN_ROW option. Using this option, you can specify the maximum number of bytes, which are stored together with the regular data.

The text/image data types discussed this far have several limitations. You can't use them as local variables (in stored procedures or in groups of Transact-SQL statements). Also, they can't be a part of an index or can't be used in the following clauses of the SELECT statement: WHERE, ORDER BY, and GROUP BY. The biggest problem concerning all text/image data types is that you have to use special operators (READTEXT, WRITETEXT, and UPDATETEXT) to work with such data.

NOTE

The text/image data types are marked as a deprecated feature and will be removed in a future version of Database Engine. Use VARCHAR(MAX), NVARCHAR(MAX), and VARBINARY(MAX) instead.

UNIQUEIDENTIFIER Data Type

As its name implies, a value of the UNIQUEIDENTIFIER data type is a unique identification number stored as a 16-byte binary string. This data type is closely related to the globally unique identifier (GUID), which guarantees uniqueness worldwide. Hence, using this data type, you can uniquely identify data and objects in distributed systems.

The initialization of a column or a variable of the UNIQUEIDENTIFIER type can be provided using the functions NEWID and NEWSEQUENTIALID, as well as with a string constant written in a special form using hexadecimal digits and hyphens. (The functions NEWID and NEWSEQUENTIALID are described in the section "System Functions" later in this chapter.)

A column of the UNIQUEIDENTIFIER data type can be referenced using the keyword ROWGUIDCOL in a query to specify that the column contains ID values. (This keyword does not generate any values.) A table can have several columns of the UNIQUEIDENTIFIER type, but only one of them can have the ROWGUIDCOL keyword.

SQL_VARIANT Data Type

The SQL_VARIANT data type can be used to store values of various data types at the same time, such as numeric values, strings, and date values. (The only types of values that cannot be stored are TIMESTAMP values.) Each value of an SQL_VARIANT column has two parts: the data value and the information that describes the value. (This information contains all properties of the actual data type of the value, such as length, scale, and precision.)

Transact-SQL supports the SQL_VARIANT_PROPERTY function, which displays the attached information for each value of an SQL_VARIANT column. For the use of the SQL_VARIANT data type, see Example 5.5 in Chapter 5.

NOTE
Declare a column of a table using the SQL_VARIANT data type only if it is really necessary. A column should have this data type if its values may be of different types or if it is not possible to determine the type of a column during the database design process.

HIERARCHYID Data Type

The HIERARCHYID data type is used to store an entire hierarchy. It is implemented as a Common Language Runtime (CLR) user-defined type that comprises several system functions for creating and operating on hierarchy nodes. The following functions, among others, belong to the methods of this data type: **GetAncestor()**, **GetDescendant()**, **Read()**, and **Write()**. (The detailed description of this data type is outside the scope of this book.)

TIMESTAMP Data Type

The TIMESTAMP data type specifies a column being defined as VARBINARY(8) or BINARY(8), depending on nullability of the column. The system maintains a current value (not a date or time) for each database, which it increments whenever any row with a TIMESTAMP column is inserted or updated and sets the TIMESTAMP column to that value. Thus, TIMESTAMP columns can be used to determine the relative time when rows were last changed. (ROWVERSION is a synonym for TIMESTAMP.)

NOTE

The value stored in a TIMESTAMP column isn't important by itself. This column is usually used to detect whether a specific row has been changed since the last time it was accessed.

DECIMAL with VARDECIMAL Storage Format

The DECIMAL data type is typically stored on the disk as fixed-length data. Since SQL Server 2005 SP2, this data type can be stored as a variable-length column by using the new storage format called VARDECIMAL. Using VARDECIMAL, you can significantly reduce the storage space for a DECIMAL column in which values have significant difference in their lengths.

NOTE

VARDECIMAL is a storage format and not a data type.

The VARDECIMAL storage format is helpful when you have to specify the largest possible value for a field in which the stored values usually are much smaller. Table 4-1 shows this.

NOTE

The VARDECIMAL storage format works the same way for the DECIMAL data type as the VARCHAR data type works for alphanumerical data.

Precision	No. of Bytes: VARDECIMAL	No. of Bytes: Fixed Length
0 or NULL	2	5
1	4	5
20	12	13
30	16	17
38	20	17

Table 4-1   *Number of Bytes for Storing VARDECIMAL and Fixed Length*

To enable the VARDECIMAL storage format, you first have to enable it for the database and then enable it for the particular table of that database. The **sp_db_vardecimal_storage_format** system procedure is used for the first step, as Example 4.6 shows.

EXAMPLE 4.6

EXEC sp_db_vardecimal_storage_format 'sample', 'ON';

The VARDECIMAL STORAGE FORMAT option of the **sp_table option** system procedure is used to turn on this storage for the table. Example 4.7 turns on the VARDECIMAL storage format for the **project** table.

EXAMPLE 4.7

EXEC sp_tableoption 'project', 'vardecimal storage format', 1

As you already know, the main reason to use the VARDECIMAL storage format is to reduce the storage size of the data. If you want to test how much storage space could be gained by using this storage format, use the dynamic management view called **sys.sp_estimated_rowsize_reduction_for_vardecimal**. This dynamic management view gives you a detailed estimate for the particular table.

Transact-SQL Functions

Transact-SQL functions can be either aggregate functions or scalar functions. The following sections describe these function types.

Aggregate Functions

Aggregate functions are applied to a group of data values from a column. Aggregate functions always return a single value. Transact-SQL supports several groups of aggregate functions:

- ▶ Convenient aggregate functions
- ▶ Statistical aggregate functions
- ▶ User-defined aggregate functions
- ▶ Analytic aggregate functions

Statistical and analytic aggregates are discussed in Chapter 24. User-defined aggregates are beyond the scope of this book. That leaves the convenient aggregate functions, described next:

▶ **AVG**   Calculates the arithmetic mean (average) of the data values contained within a column. The column must contain numeric values.

▶ **MAX and MIN**   Calculate the maximum and minimum data value of the column, respectively. The column can contain numeric, string, and date/time values.

▶ **SUM**   Calculates the total of all data values in a column. The column must contain numeric values.

▶ **COUNT**   Calculates the number of (non-null) data values in a column. The only aggregate function not being applied to columns is COUNT(*). This function returns the number of rows (whether or not particular columns have NULL values).

▶ **COUNT_BIG**   Analogous to COUNT, the only difference being that COUNT_BIG returns a value of the BIGINT data type.

The use of convenient aggregate functions with the SELECT statement are described in detail in Chapter 6.

Scalar Functions

In addition to aggregate functions, Transact-SQL provides several scalar functions that are used in the construction of scalar expressions. (A scalar function operates on a single value or list of values, as opposed to aggregate functions, which operate on the data from multiple rows.) Scalar functions can be categorized as follows:

▶ Numeric functions

▶ Date functions

▶ String functions

▶ System functions

▶ Metadata functions

The following sections describe these function types.

Numeric Functions

Numeric functions within Transact-SQL are mathematical functions for modifying numeric values. The following numeric functions are available:

Function	Explanation
ABS(n)	Returns the absolute value (i.e., negative values are returned as positive) of the numeric expression **n**. Example: SELECT ABS(−5.767) = 5.767, SELECT ABS(6.384) = 6.384
ACOS(n)	Calculates arc cosine of **n**. **n** and the resulting value belong to the FLOAT data type.
ASIN(n)	Calculates the arc sine of **n**. **n** and the resulting value belong to the FLOAT data type.
ATAN(n)	Calculates the arc tangent of **n**. **n** and the resulting value belong to the FLOAT data type.
ATN2(n,m)	Calculates the arc tangent of **n/m**. **n**, **m**, and the resulting value belong to the FLOAT data type.
CEILING(n)	Returns the smallest integer value greater or equal to the specified parameter. Examples: SELECT CEILING(4.88) = 5 SELECT CEILING(−4.88) = −4
COS(n)	Calculates the cosine of **n**. **n** and the resulting value belong to the FLOAT data type.
COT(n)	Calculates the cotangent of **n**. **n** and the resulting value belong to the FLOAT data type.
DEGREES(n)	Converts radians to degrees. Examples: SELECT DEGREES(PI()/2) = 90.0 SELECT DEGREES(0.75) = 42.97
EXP(n)	Calculates the value e^n. Example: SELECT EXP(1) = 2.7183
FLOOR(n)	Calculates the largest integer value less than or equal to the specified value **n**. Example: SELECT FLOOR(4.88) = 4
LOG(n)	Calculates the natural (i.e., base e) logarithm of **n**. Examples: SELECT LOG(4.67) = 1.54 SELECT LOG(0.12) = −2.12
LOG10(n)	Calculates the logarithm (base 10) for **n**. Examples: SELECT LOG10(4.67) = 0.67 SELECT LOG10(0.12) = −0.92
PI()	Returns the value of the number pi (3.14).
POWER(x,y)	Calculates the value x^y. Examples: SELECT POWER(3.12,5) = 295.65 SELECT POWER(81,0.5) = 9
RADIANS(n)	Converts degrees to radians. Examples: SELECT RADIANS(90.0) = 1.57 SELECT RADIANS(42.97) = 0.75
RAND	Returns a random number between 0 and 1 with a FLOAT data type.

Function	Explanation
ROUND(n, p,[t])	Rounds the value of the number **n** by using the precision **p**. Use positive values of **p** to round on the right side of the decimal point and use negative values to round on the left side. An optional parameter **t** causes **n** to be truncated. Examples: SELECT ROUND(5.4567,3) = 5.4570 SELECT ROUND(345.4567,−1) = 350.0000 SELECT ROUND(345.4567,−1,1) = 340.0000
ROWCOUNT_BIG	Returns the number of rows that have been affected by the last Transact-SQL statement executed by the system. The return value of this function has the BIGINT data type.
SIGN(n)	Returns the sign of the value **n** as a number (+1 for positive, −1 for negative, and 0 for zero). Example: SELECT SIGN(0.88) = 1
SIN(n)	Calculates the sine of **n**. **n** and the resulting value belong to the FLOAT data type.
SQRT(n)	Calculates the square root of **n**. Example: SELECT SQRT(9) = 3
SQUARE(n)	Returns the square of the given expression. Example: SELECT SQUARE(9) = 81
TAN(n)	Calculates the tangent of **n**. **n** and the resulting value belong to the FLOAT data type.

Date Functions

Date functions calculate the respective date or time portion of an expression or return the value from a time interval. Transact-SQL supports the following date functions:

Function	Explanation
GETDATE()	Returns the current system date and time. Example: SELECT GETDATE() = 2008-01-01 13:03:31.390
DATEPART(item,date)	Returns the specified part **item** of a date **date** as an integer. Examples: SELECT DATEPART(month, '01.01.2005') = 1 (1 = January) SELECT DATEPART(weekday, '01.01.2005') = 7 (7 = Sunday)
DATENAME(item,date)	Returns the specified part **item** of the date **date** as a character string. Example: SELECT DATENAME(weekday, '01.01.2005') = Saturday
DATEDIFF(item,dat1,dat2)	Calculates the difference between the two date parts **dat1** and **dat2** and returns the result as an integer in units specified by the value **item**. Example: SELECT DATEDIFF(year, BirthDate, GETDATE()) AS age FROM employee; -> returns the age of each employee.
DATEADD(i,n,d)	Adds the number **n** of units specified by the value **i** to the given date **d**. Example: SELECT DATEADD(DAY,3,HireDate) AS age FROM employee; -> adds three days to the starting date of employment of every employee (see the **sample** database).

String Functions

String functions are used to manipulate data values in a column, usually of a character data type. Transact-SQL supports the following string functions:

Function	Explanation
ASCII(character)	Converts the specified character to the equivalent integer (ASCII) code. Returns an integer. Example: SELECT ASCII('A') = 65
CHAR(integer)	Converts the ASCII code to the equivalent character. Example: SELECT CHAR(65) = 'A'.
CHARINDEX(z1,z2)	Returns the starting position where the partial string **z1** first occurs in the string **z2**. Returns 0 if **z1** does not occur in **z2**. Example: SELECT CHARINDEX('bl', 'table') = 3.
DIFFERENCE(z1,z2)	Returns an integer, 0 through 4, that is the difference of SOUNDEX values of two strings **z1** and **z2**. (SOUNDEX returns a number that specifies the sound of a string. With this method, strings with similar sounds can be determined.) Example: SELECT DIFFERENCE('spelling', 'telling') = 2 (sounds a little bit similar, 0 = doesn't sound similar)
LEFT(z, length)	Returns the first **length** characters from the string **z**.
LEN(z)	Returns the number of characters, instead of the number of bytes, of the specified string expression, excluding trailing blanks.
LOWER(z1)	Converts all uppercase letters of the string **z1** to lowercase letters. Lowercase letters and numbers, and other characters, do not change. Example: SELECT LOWER('BiG') = 'big'
LTRIM(z)	Removes leading blanks in the string **z**. Example: SELECT LTRIM(' String') = 'String'
NCHAR(i)	Returns the Unicode character with the specified integer code, as defined by the Unicode standard.
QUOTENAME(char_string)	Returns a Unicode string with the delimiters added to make the input string a valid delimited identifier.
PATINDEX(%p%,expr)	Returns the starting position of the first occurrence of a pattern **p** in a specified expression **expr**, or zeros if the pattern is not found. Examples: 1) SELECT PATINDEX('%gs%', 'longstring') = 4; 2) SELECT RIGHT(ContactName, LEN(ContactName)-PATINDEX('% %',ContactName)) AS First_name FROM Customers; (The second query returns all first names from the **customers** column.)
REPLACE(str1,str2,str3)	Replaces all occurrences of the **str2** in the **str1** with the **str3**. Example: SELECT REPLACE('shave' , 's' , 'be') = behave

Function	Explanation
REPLICATE(z,i)	Repeats string **z i** times. Example: SELECT REPLICATE('a',10) = 'aaaaaaaaaa'
REVERSE(z)	Displays the string **z** in the reverse order. Example: SELECT REVERSE('calculate') = 'etaluclac'
RIGHT(z,length)	Returns the last **length** characters from the string **z**. Example: SELECT RIGHT('Notebook',4) = 'book'
RTRIM(z)	Removes trailing blanks of the string **z**. Example: SELECT RTRIM('Notebook ') = 'Notebook'
SOUNDEX(a)	Returns a four-character SOUNDEX code to determine the similarity between two strings. Example: SELECT SOUNDEX('spelling') = S145
SPACE(length)	Returns a string with spaces of length specified by **length**. Example: SELECT SPACE = ' '
STR(f,[len [,d]])	Converts the specified float expression **f** into a string. **len** is the length of the string including decimal point, sign, digits, and spaces (10 by default), and **d** is the number of digits to the right of the decimal point to be returned. Example: SELECT STR(3.45678,4,2) = '3.46'
STUFF(z1,a,length,z2)	Replaces the partial string **z1** with the partial string **z2** starting at position a, replacing **length** characters of **z1**. Examples: SELECT STUFF('Notebook',5,0, ' in a ') = 'Note in a book' SELECT STUFF('Notebook',1,4, 'Hand') = 'Handbook'
SUBSTRING(z,a,length)	Creates a partial string from string **z** starting at the position a with a length of **length**. Example: SELECT SUBSTRING('wardrobe',1,4) = 'ward'
UNICODE	Returns the integer value, as defined by the Unicode standard, for the first character of the input expression.
UPPER(z)	Converts all lowercase letters of string **z** to uppercase letters. Uppercase letters and numbers do not change. Example: SELECT UPPER('loWer') = 'LOWER'

System Functions

System functions of Transact-SQL provide extensive information about database objects. Most system functions use an internal numeric identifier (ID), which is assigned to each database object by the system at its creation. Using this identifier, the system can uniquely identify each database object. System functions provide information about the database system. The following table describes several system functions. (For the complete list of all system functions, please see Books Online.)

Function	Explanation
CAST(a AS type [(length)]	Converts an expression **a** into the specified data type **type** (if possible). **a** could be any valid expression. Example: SELECT CAST(3000000000 AS BIGINT) = 3000000000
COALESCE($a_1, a_2, \ldots$)	Returns for a given list of expressions a_1, a_2,... the value of the first expression that is not NULL.
COL_LENGTH(obj,col)	Returns the length of the column **col** belonging to the database object (table or view) **obj**. Example: SELECT COL_LENGTH('customers', 'cust_ID') = 10
CONVERT(type[(length)],a)	Equivalent to CAST, but the arguments are specified differently. CONVERT can be used with any data type.
CURRENT_TIMESTAMP	Returns the current date and time. Example: SELECT CURRENT_TIMESTAMP = '2008-01-01 17:22:55.670'
CURRENT_USER	Returns the name of the current user.
DATALENGTH(z)	Calculates the length (in bytes) of the result of the expression **z**. Example: SELECT DATALENGTH(ProductName) FROM products. (This query returns the length of each field.)
GETANSINULL('dbname')	Returns 1 if the use of NULL values in the database **dbname** complies with the ANSI SQL standard. (See also the explanation of NULL values at the end of this chapter.) Example: SELECT GETANSINULL('AdventureWorks') = 1
ISNULL(expr, value)	Returns the value of **expr** if that value is not null; otherwise, it returns **value** (see Example 5.22).
ISNUMERIC(expression)	Determines whether an expression is a valid numeric type.
NEWID()	Creates a unique ID number that consists of a 16-byte binary string intended to store values of the UNIQUEIDENTIFIER data type.
NEWSEQUENTIALID()	Creates a GUID that is greater than any GUID previously generated by this function on a specified computer. (This function can only be used as a default value for a column.)
NULLIF($expr_1, expr_2$)	Returns the NULL value if the expressions **$expr_1$** and **$expr_2$** are equal. Example: SELECT NULLIF(project_no, 'p1') FROM projects. (The query returns NULL for the project with the project_no = 'p1').
SERVERPROPERTY(propertyname)	Returns the property information about the database server.
SYSTEM_USER	Returns the login ID of the current user. Example: SELECT SYSTEM_USER = LTB13942\dusan
USER_ID([user_name])	Returns the identifier of the user **user_name**. If no name is specified, the identifier of the current user is retrieved. Example: SELECT USER_ID('guest') = 2
USER_NAME([id])	Returns the name of the user with the identifier **id**. If no name is specified, the name of the current user is retrieved. Example: SELECT USER_NAME = 'guest'

All string functions can be nested in any order; for example, REVERSE (CURRENT_USER).

Metadata Functions

Generally, metadata functions return information concerning the specified database and database objects. The following table describes several metadata functions. (For the complete list of all metadata functions, please see Books Online.)

Function	Explanation
COL_NAME(tab_id, col_id)	Returns the name of a column belonging to the table with the ID **tab_id** and column ID **col_id**. Example: SELECT COL_NAME(OBJECT_ID('employee') , 3) = 'emp_lname'
COLUMNPROPERTY (id, col, property)	Returns the information about the specified column. Example: SELECT COLUMNPROPERTY(object_id('project'), 'project_no', 'PRECISION') = 4
DATABASEPROPERTY(database, property)	Returns the named database property value for the specified database and property. Example: SELECT DATABASEPROPERTY('sample', 'IsNullConcat') = 0. (The **IsNullConcat** property corresponds to the option CONCAT_NULL_YIELDS_NULL, which is described at the end of this chapter.)
DB_ID([db_name])	Returns the identifier of the database **db_name**. If no name is specified, the identifier of the current database is returned. Example: SELECT DB_ID('AdventureWorks') = 6
DB_NAME([db_id])	Returns the name of the database with the identifier **db_id**. If no identifier is specified, the name of the current database is displayed. Example: SELECT DB_NAME(6) = 'AdventureWorks'
INDEX_COL(table, i, no)	Returns the name of the indexed column in the table **table**, defined by the index identifier **i** and the position **no** of the column in the index.
INDEXPROPERTY(obj_id, index_name, property)	Returns the named index or statistics property value of a specified table identification number, index or statistics name, and property name.
OBJECT_NAME(obj_id)	Returns the name of the database object with the identifier **obj_id**. Example: SELECT OBJECT_NAME(453576654) = 'products'
OBJECT_ID(obj_name)	Returns the identifier of the database object **obj_name**. Example: SELECT OBJECT_ID('products') = 453576654
OBJECTPROPERTY(obj_id,property)	Returns the information about the objects from the current database.

Scalar Operators

Scalar operators are used for operations with scalar values. Transact-SQL supports numeric and Boolean operators as well as concatenation.

There are unary and binary arithmetic operators. Unary operators are + and − (as signs). Binary arithmetic operators are +, −, *, /, and **%**. (The first four binary operators have their respective mathematical meanings, whereas **%** is the modulo operator.)

Boolean operators have two different notations depending on whether they are applied to bit strings or to other data types. The operators NOT, AND, and OR are applied to all data types (except BIT). They are described in detail in Chapter 6.

The bitwise operators for manipulating bit strings are listed here, and Example 4.8 shows how they are used:

~   Complement (i.e., NOT)

&   Conjunction of bit strings (i.e., AND)

| Disjunction of bit strings (i.e., OR)

∧   Exclusive disjunction (i.e., XOR or Exclusive OR)

EXAMPLE 4.8

```
~(1001001) = (0110110)
(11001001) | (10101101) = (11101101)
(11001001) & (10101101) = (10001001)
(11001001) ∧ (10101101) = (01100100)
```

The concatenation operator + can be used to concatenate two character strings or bit strings.

Global Variables

Global variables are special system variables that can be used as if they were scalar constants. Transact-SQL supports many global variables, which have to be preceded by the prefix **@@**. The following table describes several global variables. (For the complete list of all global variables, see Books Online.)

Variable	Explanation
@@CONNECTIONS	Returns the number of login attempts since starting the system.
@@CPU_BUSY	Returns the total CPU time (in units of milliseconds) used since starting the system.
@@ERROR	Returns the information about the return value of the last executed Transact-SQL statement.

Variable	Explanation
@@IDENTITY	Returns the last inserted value for the column with the IDENTITY property (see Chapter 6).
@@LANGID	Returns the identifier of the language that is currently used by the database system.
@@LANGUAGE	Returns the name of the language that is currently used by the database system.
@@MAX_CONNECTIONS	Returns the maximum number of actual connections to the system.
@@PROCID	Returns the identifier for the stored procedure currently being executed.
@@ROWCOUNT	Returns the number of rows that have been affected by the last Transact-SQL statement executed by the system.
@@SERVERNAME	Retrieves the information concerning the local database server. This information contains, among other things, the name of the server and the name of the instance.
@@SPID	Returns the identifier of the server process.
@@VERSION	Returns the current version of the database system software.

NULL Values

A NULL value is a special value that may be assigned to a column. This value is normally used when information in a column is unknown or not applicable. For example, in the case of an unknown home telephone number for a company's employee, it is recommended that the NULL value be assigned to the **home_telephone** column.

Any arithmetic expression results in a NULL if any operand of that expression is itself a NULL value. Therefore, in unary arithmetic expressions (if A is an expression with a NULL value), both +A and –A return NULL. In binary expressions, if one (or both) of the operands A or B has the NULL value, A + B, A – B, A * B, A / B, and A % B also result in a NULL. (The operands A and B have to be numerical expressions.)

If an expression contains a relational operation and one (or both) of the operands has (have) the NULL value, the result of this operation will be NULL. Hence, each of the expressions A = B, A <> B, A < B, and A > B also returns NULL.

In the Boolean AND, OR, and NOT, the behavior of the NULL values is specified by the following truth tables, where T stands for true, U for unknown (NULL), and F for false. In these tables, follow the row and column represented by the values of the Boolean expressions that the operator works on, and the value where they intersect represents the resulting value.

AND	T	U	F
T	T	U	F
U	U	U	F
F	F	F	F

OR	T	U	F
T	T	T	T
U	T	U	U
F	T	U	F

NOT	
T	F
U	U
F	T

Any NULL value in the argument of aggregate functions AVG, SUM, MAX, MIN, and COUNT is eliminated before the respective function is calculated (except for the function COUNT(*)). If a column contains only NULL values, the function returns NULL. The aggregate function COUNT(*) handles all NULL values the same as non-NULL values. If the column contains only NULL values, the result of the function COUNT(DISTINCT column_name) is 0.

A NULL value has to be different from all other values. For numeric data types, there is a distinction between the value zero and NULL. The same is true for the empty string and NULL for character data types.

A column of a table allows NULL values if its definition explicitly contains NULL. On the other hand, NULL values are not permitted if the definition of a column explicitly contains NOT NULL. If the user does not specify NULL or NOT NULL for a column with a data type (except TIMESTAMP), the following values are assigned:

▶ **NULL** If the ANSI_NULL_DFLT_ON option of the SET statement is set to ON

▶ **NOT NULL** If the ANSI_NULL_DFLT_OFF option of the SET statement is set to ON

If the SET statement isn't activated, a column will contain the value NOT NULL by default. (The columns of TIMESTAMP data type can only be declared as NOT NULL columns.)

There is also another option of the SET statement: CONCAT_NULL_YIELDS_NULL. This option influences the concatenation operation with a NULL value so that anything you concatenate to a NULL value will yield NULL again. For instance:

'San Francisco' + NULL = NULL

Conclusion

The basic features of Transact-SQL consist of data types, predicates, and functions. Data types comply with data types of the ANSI SQL92 standard. Transact-SQL supports a variety of useful system functions.

The next chapter introduces you to Transact-SQL statements in relation to SQL's data definition language. This part of Transact-SQL comprises all the statements needed for creating, altering, and removing database objects.

Exercises

E.4.1

What is the difference between the numeric data types INT, SMALLINT, and TINYINT?

E.4.2

What is the difference between the data types CHAR and VARCHAR? When should you use the latter (instead of the former) and vice versa?

E.4.3

How can you set the format of a column with the DATE data type so that its values can be entered in the form 'yyyy/mm/dd'?

In the following two exercises, use the SELECT statement in the Query Editor component window of SQL Server Management Studio to display the result of all system functions and global variables. (For instance, SELECT host_id() displays the ID number of the current host.)

E.4.4

Using system functions, find the ID number of the **test** database (Exercise 2.1).

E.4.5

Using the system variables, display the current version of the database system software and the language that is used by this software.

E.4.6

Using the bitwise operators **&**, |, and ^, calculate the following operations with the bit strings:

(11100101) & (01010111)
(10011011) | (11001001)
(10110111) ^ (10110001)

E.4.7

What is the result of the following expressions? (A is a numerical and B a logical expression.)

A + NULL
NULL = NULL
B OR NULL
B AND NULL

E.4.8

When can you use both single and double quotation marks to define string and temporal constants?

E.4.9

What is a delimited identifier and when do you need it?

Chapter 5

Data Definition Language

In This Chapter

- ► **Creating Database Objects**
- ► **Modifying Database Objects**
- ► **Removing Database Objects**

This chapter describes all the Transact-SQL statements concerning data definition language (DDL). The DDL statements are divided into three groups which are discussed in turn. The first group includes statements that create objects, the second group includes statements that modify the structure of objects, and the third group includes statements that remove objects.

Creating Database Objects

The organization of a database involves many different objects. All objects of a database can be physical or logical. The physical objects are related to the organization of the data on the physical device (disk). Database Engine's physical objects are files and filegroups. Logical objects represent a user's view of a database. Databases, tables, columns, and views (virtual tables) are examples of logical objects.

The first database object that has to be created is a database itself. Database Engine manages both system and user databases. An authorized user can create user databases, while system databases are generated during the installation of the database system. System databases are

- ▶ **master**
- ▶ **tempdb**
- ▶ **model**
- ▶ **msdb**
- ▶ **resource**

This chapter describes the creation, alteration, and removal of user databases, while all system databases will be covered in detail in Chapter 15.

Creation of a Database

Two basic methods are used to create a database. The first method involves using Object Explorer in SQL Server Management Studio (see Chapter 3). The second method involves using the Transact-SQL statement CREATE DATABASE. This statement has the following general form, the details of which are discussed next:

```
CREATE DATABASE db_name
    [ON [PRIMARY] { file_spec1 } ,...]
    [LOG ON {file_spec2} ,...]
      [COLLATE collation_name]
  [FOR {ATTACH | ATTACH_REBUILD_LOG } ]
```

NOTE

For the syntax of the Transact-SQL statements, the conventions used are those described in the section "Syntax Conventions" in Chapter 1. According to the conventions, optional items appear in brackets, [ ]. Items written in braces, { }, and followed by "..." are items that can be repeated any number of times.

db_name is the name of the database. The maximum size of a database name is 128 characters. (The rules for identifiers described in Chapter 4 apply to database names.) The maximum number of databases managed by a single system is 32,767.

All databases are stored in files. These files can be explicitly specified by the system administrator or implicitly provided by the system. If the ON option exists in the CREATE DATABASE statement, all files containing the data of a database are explicitly specified.

NOTE

Database Engine uses disk files to store data. Each disk file contains data of a single database. Files themselves can be organized into filegroups. Filegroups provide the ability to distribute data over different disk drives and to back up and restore subsets of the database (useful for very large databases).

file_spec1 represents a file specification, which includes further options such as the logical name of the file, the physical name, and the size. The PRIMARY option specifies the first (and most important) file that contains system tables and other important internal information concerning the database. If the PRIMARY option is omitted, the first file listed in the specification is used as the primary file.

A login account of Database Engine that is used to create a database is called a database owner. A database can have one owner, who always corresponds to a login account name. The login account, which is the database owner, has the special name **dbo**. This name is always used in relation to a database it owns.

dbo uses the LOG ON option to define one or more files as the physical destination of the transaction log of the database. If the LOG ON option is not specified, the transaction log of the database will still be created because every database must have at least one transaction log file. (Database Engine keeps a record of each change it makes to the database. The system keeps all those records, in particular before and after values, in one or more files called the transaction log. Each database of the system has its own transaction log. Transaction logs are discussed in detail in Chapter 13.)

With the COLLATE option, you can specify the default collation for the database. If the COLLATE option is not specified, the database is assigned the default collation of the **model** database, which is the same as the default collation of the database system.

The FOR ATTACH option specifies that the database is created by attaching an existing set of operating system files. If this option is used, you have to explicitly specify the first primary file. The FOR ATTACH_REBUILD_LOG option specifies that the database is created by attaching an existing set of operating system files. (Attaching and detaching a database is described later in this chapter.)

During the creation of a new database, Database Engine uses the **model** database as a template. The properties of the **model** database can be changed to suit the personal conception of the system administrator.

NOTE

If you have a database object that should exist in each user database, you should create that object in the ***model*** *database first.*

Example 5.1 creates a simple database without any further specifications. To execute this statement, type it in the **Query Editor** window of SQL Server Management Studio and press F5.

EXAMPLE 5.1

```
USE master;
CREATE DATABASE sample;
```

Example 5.1 creates a database named **sample**. This concise form of the CREATE DATABASE statement is possible, because almost all options of that statement have default values. The system creates by default, two files. The logical name of the data file is **sample** and its original size is 2MB. Similarly, the logical name of the transaction log is **sample_log** and its original size is 1MB. (Both size values, as well as other properties of the new database, depend on corresponding specifications in the **model** database.)

Example 5.2 creates a database with explicit specifications for database and transaction log files.

EXAMPLE 5.2

```
USE master;
CREATE DATABASE projects
  ON (NAME=projects_dat,
      FILENAME = 'C:\projects.mdf',
      SIZE = 10,
      MAXSIZE = 100,
      FILEGROWTH = 5)
```

```
LOG ON
  (NAME=projects_log,
    FILENAME = 'C:\projects.ldf',
    SIZE = 40,
    MAXSIZE = 100,
    FILEGROWTH = 10);
```

Example 5.2 creates a database called **projects**. Because the PRIMARY option is omitted, the first file is assumed as the primary file. This file has the logical name **projects_dat** and is stored in the file **projects.mdf**. The original size of this file is 10MB. Additional portions of 5MB of disk storage are allocated by the system, if needed. If the MAXSIZE option is not specified or is set to UNLIMITED, the file will grow until the disk is full. (The KB, TB, and MB suffixes can be used to specify kilobytes, terabytes, or megabytes, respectively—the default is MB.)

There is also a single transaction log file with the logical name **projects_log** and the physical name **projects.ldf**. All options of the file specification for the transaction log have the same name and meaning as the corresponding options of the file specification for the data file.

Using the Transact-SQL language, you can apply the USE statement to change the database context to the specified database. (The alternative way is to select the database name in the **Database** pull-down menu in the toolbar of SQL Server Management Studio.)

The system administrator can assign a default database to a user by using the CREATE LOGIN statement or the ALTER LOGIN Statement (see also Chapter 12). In this case, the users do not need to execute the USE statement if they want to use their default database.

Creation of a Database Snapshot

The CREATE DATABASE statement can also be used to create a database snapshot of an existing database (source database). A database snapshot is transactionally consistent with the source database as it existed at the time of the snapshot's creation.

The syntax for the creation of a snapshot is

```
CREATE DATABASE database_snapshot_name
  ON  (NAME = logical_file_name,
        FILENAME = 'os_file_name') [ ,...n ]
        AS SNAPSHOT OF source_database_name
```

As you can see, if you want to create a database snapshot, you have to add the AS SNAPSHOT OF clause in the CREATE DATABASE statement. Example 5.3 creates a snapshot of the **AdventureWorks** database and stores it in the C:\temp data directory. (You must create this directory before you start the following example.)

EXAMPLE 5.3

```
USE master;
CREATE DATABASE AdventurWorks_snapshot
   ON (NAME = 'AdventureWorks_Data' ,
       FILENAME = 'C:\temp\snapshot_DB.mdf')
       AS SNAPSHOT OF AdventureWorks;
```

An existing database snapshot is a read-only copy of the corresponding database that reflects the point in time when the database is copied. (For this reason, you can have multiple snapshots for an existing database.) The snapshot file (in Example 5.3, 'C:\temp\snapshot_DB.mdf') contains only the modified data that has changed from the source database. Therefore, the process of creating a database snapshot must include the logical name of each data file from the source database as well as new corresponding physical names (see Example 5.3).

While the snapshot contains only modified data, the disk space needed for each snapshot is just a small part of the overall space required for the corresponding source database.

NOTE

To create snapshots of a database, you need NTFS disk volumes, because only such volumes support the sparse file technology that is used for storing snapshots.

Database snapshots are usually used as a mechanism to protect data against user errors.

Attaching and Detaching Databases

All data of a database can be detached and then attached to the same or another database server. Detaching and attaching a database should be done if you want to move the database.

You can detach a database from a database server by using the **sp_detach_db** system procedure. (The detached database must be in single-user mode.)

To attach a database, use either the CREATE DATABASE statement or the **sp_attach_db** system procedure. When you attach a database, all data files must be available. If any data file has a different path from when the database was first created, you must specify the file's current path.

CREATE TABLE: A Basic Form

The CREATE TABLE statement creates a new base table with all corresponding columns and their data types. The basic form of the CREATE TABLE statement is

CREATE TABLE table_name
    (col_name1 type1 [NOT NULL| <u>NULL</u>]
    [{, col_name2 type2 [NOT NULL| <u>NULL</u>]} ...])

NOTE
Besides base tables, there are also some special kinds of tables such as temporary tables and views (see Chapters 6 and 11, respectively).

table_name is the name of the created base table. The maximum number of tables per database is limited by the number of objects in the database (there can be more than 2 billion objects in a database, including tables, views, stored procedures, triggers, and constraints). **col_name1**, **col_name2**,... are the names of the table columns. **type1**, **type2**,... are data types of corresponding columns (see Chapter 4).

NOTE
The name of a database object can generally contain four parts in the form:
[server_name.[db_name.[schema_name.]]]object_name
***object_name** is the name of the database object. **schema_name** is the name of the schema to which the object belongs. **server_name** and **db_name** are the names of the server and database to which the database object belongs. Table names, combined with the schema name, must be unique within the database. Similarly, column names must be unique within the table.*

The first constraint that will be discussed in this book is the existence and nonexistence of NULL values within a column. If NOT NULL is specified, the assignment of NULL values for the column is not allowed. (In that case, the column may not contain nulls, and if there is a NULL value to be inserted, the system returns an error message.)

As already stated, a database object (in this case, a table) is always created within a schema of a database. A user can create a table only in a schema for which she has ALTER permissions. Any user in the **sysadmin, db_ddladmin**, or **db_owner** role can create a table in any schema. (The ALTER permissions, as well as database and server roles, are discussed in detail in Chapter 12.)

The creator of a table must not be its owner. This means that you can create a table that belongs to someone else. Similarly, a table created with the CREATE TABLE statement must not belong to the current database if some other (existing) database name, together with the schema name, is specified as the prefix of the table name.

The schema to which a table belongs has two possible default names. If a table is specified without the explicit schema name, the system checks for a table name in the corresponding default schema. If the object name cannot be found in the default schema, the system searches in the **dbo** schema.

NOTE

You should always specify the table name together with the corresponding schema name. That way you can eliminate possible ambiguities.

Temporary tables are a special kind of base table. They are stored in the **tempdb** database and are automatically dropped at the end of the session. The properties of temporary tables and examples concerning them are given in Chapter 6.

Example 5.4 shows the creation of all tables of the **sample** database. (The **sample** database should be the current database.)

EXAMPLE 5.4

```
USE sample;
CREATE TABLE employee  (emp_no INTEGER NOT NULL,
            emp_fname CHAR(20) NOT NULL,
            emp_lname CHAR(20) NOT NULL,
            dept_no CHAR(4) NULL);
CREATE TABLE department(dept_no CHAR(4) NOT NULL,
            dept_name CHAR(25) NOT NULL,
            location CHAR(30) NULL);
CREATE TABLE project   (project_no CHAR(4) NOT NULL,
            project_name CHAR(15) NOT NULL,
            budget FLOAT NULL);
CREATE TABLE works_on  (emp_no INTEGER NOT NULL,
            project_no CHAR(4) NOT NULL,
            job CHAR (15) NULL,
            enter_date DATE NULL);
```

Besides the data type and the nullability, the column specification can contain the following options:

- ▶ DEFAULT clause
- ▶ IDENTITY property

The DEFAULT clause in the column definition specifies the default value of the column—that is, whenever a new row is inserted into the table, the default value for the particular column will be used if there is no value specified for it. A constant value, such as the system functions USER, CURRENT_USER, SESSION_USER, SYSTEM_USER, CURRENT_TIMESTAMP, and NULL, among others, can be used as the default values.

A column with the IDENTITY property allows only integer values, which are usually implicitly assigned by the system. Each value, which should be inserted in the column, is calculated by incrementing the last inserted value of the column. Therefore, the definition of a column with the IDENTITY property contains (implicitly or explicitly) an initial value and an increment. This property will be discussed in detail in the next chapter (see Example 6.41).

NOTE

Because Database Engine generates the values with the IDENTITY property, these values are always different, even when multiple users are adding rows at the same time. This feature is very useful in a multiuser environment, where it is quite difficult for an ordinary program to generate unique numeric values.

To close this section, Example 5.5 shows the creation of a table with a column of the SQL_VARIANT type.

EXAMPLE 5.5

```
USE sample;
CREATE TABLE Item_Attributes  (
     item_id INT NOT NULL,
     attribute NVARCHAR(30) NOT NULL,
     value SQL_VARIANT NOT NULL,
     PRIMARY KEY (item_id, attribute) )
```

In Example 5.5, the table contains the **value** column, which is of type SQL_VARIANT. As you already know from Chapter 4, the SQL_VARIANT data type can be used to store values of various data types at the same time, such as numeric values, strings, and date values. Note that in Example 5.5 the SQL_VARIANT data type is used for the column values, because different attribute values may be of different data types. For example, the size attribute stores an integer attribute value, and a name attribute stores a character string attribute value.

CREATE TABLE and Declarative Integrity Constraints

One of the most important features that a DBMS must provide is a way of maintaining the integrity of data. The constraints, which are used to check the modification or insertion of data, are called *integrity constraints*. The task of maintaining integrity constraints can be handled by the user in application programs or by the DBMS. The most important benefits of handling integrity constraints by the DBMS are the following:

▶ Increased reliability of data

▶ Reduced programming time

▶ Simple maintenance

Using the DBMS to define integrity constraints increases the reliability of data because there is no possibility that the integrity constraints can be forgotten by a programmer. (If an integrity constraint is handled by application programs, *all* programs concerning the constraint must include the corresponding code. If the code is omitted in one application program, the consistency of data is compromised.)

An integrity constraint not handled by the DBMS must be defined in every application program that uses the data involved in the constraint. In contrast, the same integrity constraint must be defined only once if it is to be handled by the DBMS. Additionally, application-enforced constraints are usually more complex to code than are database-enforced constraints.

If an integrity constraint is handled by the DBMS, the modification of the structure of the constraint must be handled only once, in the DBMS. The modification of a structure in application programs requires the modification of every program that involves the corresponding code.

There are two groups of integrity constraints handled by a DBMS:

▶ Declarative integrity constraints

▶ Procedural integrity constraints that are handled by triggers (for the definition of triggers, see Chapter 13)

The declarative constraints are defined using the DDL statements CREATE TABLE and ALTER TABLE. They can be column-level constraints or table-level constraints. Column-level constraints, together with the data type and other column properties, are placed within the declaration of the column, while table-level constraints are always defined at the end of the CREATE TABLE or ALTER TABLE statement, after the definition of all columns.

NOTE

There is only one difference between column-level constraints and table-level constraints: a column-level constraint can be applied only upon one column, while a table-level constraint can cover one or more columns of a table.

Each declarative constraint has a name. The name of the constraint can be explicitly assigned using the CONSTRAINT option in the CREATE TABLE statement or the ALTER TABLE statement. If the CONSTRAINT option is omitted, Database Engine assigns an implicit name for the constraint.

NOTE

Using explicit constraint names is strongly recommended. The search for an integrity constraint can be greatly enhanced if an explicit name for a constraint is used.

All declarative constraints can be categorized into several groups:

▶ DEFAULT clause

▶ UNIQUE clause

▶ PRIMARY KEY clause

▶ CHECK clause

▶ FOREIGN KEY clause and referential integrity

The definition of the default value using the DEFAULT clause was shown earlier in this chapter (see also Example 5.6). All other constraints are described in detail in the following sections.

The UNIQUE Clause

Sometimes more than one column or group of columns of the table have unique values and therefore can be used as the primary key. All columns or groups of columns that qualify to be primary keys are called *candidate keys*. Each candidate key is defined using the UNIQUE clause in the CREATE TABLE or the ALTER TABLE statement.

The UNIQUE clause has the following form:

```
[CONSTRAINT c_name]
    UNIQUE [CLUSTERED | NONCLUSTERED] ({ col_name1} ,...)
```

The CONSTRAINT option in the UNIQUE clause assigns an explicit name to the candidate key. The option CLUSTERED or NONCLUSTERED relates to the fact that Database Engine always generates an index for each candidate key of a table. The index can be clustered—that is, the physical order of rows is specified using the indexed order of the column values. If the order is not specified, the index is nonclustered (see also Chapter 10). The default value is NONCLUSTERED. **col_name1** is a column name that builds the candidate key. (The maximum number of columns per candidate key is 16.)

Example 5.6 shows the use of the UNIQUE clause.

EXAMPLE 5.6

```
USE sample;
CREATE TABLE projects  (project_no CHAR(4)  DEFAULT 'p1',
            project_name CHAR(15) NOT NULL,
            budget FLOAT NULL
            CONSTRAINT unique_no UNIQUE (project_no));
```

Each value of the **project_no** column of the **projects** table is unique, including the NULL value. (Just as with any other value with a UNIQUE constraint, if NULL values are allowed on a corresponding column, there can be at most one row with the NULL value for that particular column.) If an existing value should be inserted into the column **project_no**, the system rejects it. The explicit name of the constraint that is defined in Example 5.6 is **unique_no**.

The PRIMARY KEY Clause

The *primary key* of a table is a column or group of columns whose values are different in every row. Each primary key is defined using the PRIMARY KEY clause in the CREATE TABLE or the ALTER TABLE statement.

The PRIMARY KEY clause has the following form:

```
[CONSTRAINT c_name]
PRIMARY KEY [CLUSTERED | NONCLUSTERED] ({col_name1} ,...)
```

All options of the PRIMARY KEY clause have the same meaning as the corresponding options with the same name in the UNIQUE clause. In contrast to UNIQUE, the PRIMARY KEY column must be NOT NULL, and its default value is CLUSTERED.

Example 5.7 shows the specification of the primary key for the **employee** table of the **sample** database.

NOTE

*You have to drop the **employee** table (DROP TABLE employee) before you execute the following example.*

EXAMPLE 5.7

USE sample;
CREATE TABLE employee (emp_no INTEGER NOT NULL,
        emp_fname CHAR(20) NOT NULL,
        emp_lname CHAR(20) NOT NULL,
        dept_no CHAR(4) NULL,
        CONSTRAINT prim_empl PRIMARY KEY (emp_no));

The **employee** table is re-created and its primary key is defined in Example 5.7. The primary key of the table is specified using the declarative integrity constraint named **prim_empl**. This integrity constraint is a table-level constraint, because it is specified after the definition of all columns of the **employee** table.

Example 5.8 is equivalent to Example 5.7, except for the specification of the primary key of the **employee** table as a column-level constraint.

NOTE

*Again, you have to drop the **employee** table (DROP TABLE employee) before you execute the following example.*

EXAMPLE 5.8

USE sample;
CREATE TABLE employee
   (emp_no INTEGER NOT NULL CONSTRAINT prim_empl PRIMARY KEY,
    emp_fname CHAR(20) NOT NULL,
    emp_lname CHAR(20) NOT NULL,
    dept_no CHAR(4) NULL);

In Example 5.8, the PRIMARY KEY clause belongs to the declaration of the corresponding column, together with its data type and nullability. For this reason, it is called a column-level constraint.

The CHECK Clause

The *check constraint* specifies conditions for the data inserted into a column. Each row inserted into a table or each value updating the value of the column must meet these conditions. The CHECK clause is used to specify check constraints. This clause can be defined in the CREATE TABLE or ALTER TABLE statement. The syntax of the CHECK clause is

[CONSTRAINT c_name]
    CHECK [NOT FOR REPLICATION] expression

expression must evaluate to a Boolean value (*true* or *false*) and can reference any columns in the current table (or just the current column if specified as a column-level constraint), but no other tables. The CHECK clause is not enforced during a replication of the data if the option NOT FOR REPLICATION exists. (A database, or a part of it, is said to be replicated if it is stored at more than one site. Replication can be used to enhance the availability of data. Chapter 20 describes data replication.)

Example 5.9 shows how the CHECK clause can be used.

EXAMPLE 5.9

```
USE sample;
CREATE TABLE customer
    (cust_no INTEGER NOT NULL,
    cust_group CHAR(3) NULL,
    CHECK (cust_group IN ('c1', 'c2', 'c10')));
```

The **customer** table that is created in Example 5.9 contains the **cust_group** column with the corresponding check constraint. The database system returns an error if the **cust_group** column, after a modification of its existing values or after the insertion of a new row, would contain a value different from the values in the set ('c1', 'c2', 'c10').

The FOREIGN KEY Clause

A *foreign key* is a column or group of columns in one table that contains values that match the primary key values in the same or another table. Each foreign key is defined using the FOREIGN KEY clause combined with the REFERENCES clause.

The FOREIGN KEY clause has the following form:

```
[CONSTRAINT c_name]
    [[FOREIGN KEY] ({col_name1} ,...)]
    REFERENCES table_name ({col_name2},...)
        [ON DELETE {NO ACTION| CASCADE | SET NULL | SET DEFAULT}]
        [ON UPDATE {NO ACTION | CASCADE | SET NULL | SET DEFAULT}]
```

The FOREIGN KEY clause defines all columns explicitly that belong to the foreign key. The REFERENCES clause specifies the table name with all columns that build the corresponding primary key. The number and the data types of the columns in the FOREIGN KEY clause must match the number and the corresponding data types of columns in the REFERENCES clause (and, of course, both of these must match the number and data types of the columns in the primary key of the referenced table).

The table that contains the foreign key is called the *referencing table*, and the table that contains the corresponding primary key is called the *parent table* or *referenced table*. Example 5.10 shows the specification of the foreign key in the **works_on** table of the **sample** database.

NOTE

*You have to drop the **works_on** table before you execute the following example.*

EXAMPLE 5.10

```
USE sample;
CREATE TABLE works_on  (emp_no INTEGER NOT NULL,
      project_no CHAR(4) NOT NULL,
        job CHAR (15) NULL,
        enter_date DATE NULL,
        CONSTRAINT prim_works PRIMARY KEY(emp_no, project_no),
        CONSTRAINT foreign_works FOREIGN KEY(emp_no)
          REFERENCES employee (emp_no));
```

The **works_on** table in Example 5.10 is specified with two declarative integrity constraints: **prim_works** and **foreign_works**. Both constraints are table-level constraints, where the former specifies the primary key and the latter the foreign key of the **works_on** table. Further, the constraint **foreign_works** specifies the **employee** table as the parent table and its **emp_no** column as the corresponding primary key of the column with the same name in the **works_on** table.

The FOREIGN KEY clause can be omitted if the foreign key is defined as a column-level constraint, because the column being constrained is the implicit column "list" of the foreign key, and the keyword REFERENCES is sufficient to indicate what kind of constraint this is. The maximum number of FOREIGN KEY constraints in a table is 63.

A definition of the foreign keys in tables of a database imposes the specification of another important integrity constraint: the referential integrity, described next.

Referential Integrity

A *referential integrity* enforces insert and update rules for the tables with the foreign key and the corresponding primary key constraint. Examples 5.7 and 5.10 specify two such constraints: **prim_empl** and **foreign_works**. The REFERENCES clause in Example 5.10 determines the **employee** table as the parent table.

Possible Problems in Relation to Referential Integrity

There are four cases in which the modification of the values in the foreign key or in the primary key can cause problems. All of these cases will be shown using the

sample database. The first two cases affect modifications of the referencing table, while the last two concern modifications of the parent table.

Case 1

Insert a new row into the **works_on** table with the employee number 11111.

The insertion of the new row in the referencing table **works_on** introduces a new employee number for which there is no matching employee in the parent table (**employee**). If the referential integrity for both tables is specified as is done in Examples 5.7 and 5.10, Database Engine rejects the insertion of a new row. For readers who are familiar with the SQL language, the corresponding Transact-SQL statement is

```
USE sample;
INSERT INTO works_on (emp_no, ...)
    VALUES (11111, ...);
```

Case 2

Modify the employee number 10102 in all rows of the **works_on** table. The new number is 11111.

In Case 2, the existing value of the foreign key in the **works_on** table should be replaced using the new value, for which there is no matching value in the parent table **employee**. If the referential integrity for both tables is specified as is done in Examples 5.7 and 5.10, the database system rejects the modification of the rows in the **works_on** table. The corresponding Transact-SQL statement is

```
USE sample;
UPDATE works_on
    SET emp_no = 11111 WHERE emp_no = 10102;
```

Case 3

Modify the employee number 10102 in the corresponding row of the **employee** table. The new number is 22222.

In Case 3, the existing value of the primary key in the parent table and the foreign key of the referencing table is modified only in the parent table. The values in the referencing table are unchanged. Therefore, the system rejects the modification of the row with the employee number 10102 in the **employee** table. Referential integrity requires that no rows in the referencing table (the one with the FOREIGN KEY clause) can exist unless a corresponding row in the parent table (the one with the PRIMARY KEY clause) also exists. Otherwise, the rows in the parent table would be "orphaned." If the modification described above were permitted, then rows in the

works_on table having the employee number 10102 would be orphaned, and the system would reject it. The corresponding Transact-SQL statement is

USE sample;
UPDATE employee
   SET emp_no = 22222 WHERE emp_no = 10102;

Case 4

Delete the row of the **employee** table with the employee number 10102.

   Case 4 is similar to Case 3. The deletion would remove the employee for which matching rows exist in the referencing table. Example 5.11 shows the definition of tables of the **sample** database with all existing primary key and foreign key constraints. (If the **employee**, **department**, **project**, and **works_on** tables already exist, drop them first using the DROP TABLE **table_name** statement.)

EXAMPLE 5.11

```
USE sample;
CREATE TABLE department(dept_no CHAR(4) NOT NULL,
          dept_name CHAR(25) NOT NULL,
          location CHAR(30) NULL,
          CONSTRAINT prim_dept PRIMARY KEY (dept_no));
CREATE TABLE employee  (emp_no INTEGER NOT NULL,
       emp_fname CHAR(20) NOT NULL,
       emp_lname CHAR(20) NOT NULL,
       dept_no CHAR(4) NULL,
       CONSTRAINT prim_emp PRIMARY KEY (emp_no),
       CONSTRAINT foreign_emp FOREIGN KEY(dept_no) REFERENCES
department(dept_no));
CREATE TABLE project   (project_no CHAR(4) NOT NULL,
       project_name CHAR(15) NOT NULL,
       budget FLOAT NULL,
       CONSTRAINT prim_proj PRIMARY KEY (project_no));
CREATE TABLE works_on  (emp_no INTEGER NOT NULL,
 project_no CHAR(4) NOT NULL,
 job CHAR (15) NULL,
 enter_date DATE NULL,
 CONSTRAINT prim_works PRIMARY KEY(emp_no, project_no),
 CONSTRAINT foreign1_works FOREIGN KEY(emp_no) REFERENCES
employee(emp_no),
 CONSTRAINT foreign2_works FOREIGN KEY(project_no) REFERENCES
project(project_no));
```

The ON DELETE and ON UPDATE Options

Database Engine can react differently if the values of the primary key of a table should be modified or deleted. If you try to update values of a foreign key, and those modifications result in inconsistencies in the corresponding primary key (see Case 1 and Case 2 in the previous sections), the database system will always reject the modification and will display a message similar to the following:

Server: Msg 547, Level 16, State 1, Line 1
UPDATE statement conflicted with COLUMN FOREIGN KEY constraint
'FKemployee'. The conflict occurred in database 'sample', table 'employee',
column 'dept_no'. The statement has been terminated.

But if you try to modify the values of a primary key, and these modifications result in inconsistencies in the corresponding foreign key (see Case 3 and Case 4 in the previous sections), a database system could react very flexibly. Generally, there are four options for how a database system can react:

► **NO ACTION**   Allows you to modify (update or delete) only those values of the parent table that do not have any corresponding values in the foreign key of the referencing table.

► **CASCADE**   Allows you to modify (UPDATE or DELETE) all values of the parent table. If this option is specified, a row is UPDATEd (i.e., DELETED) from the referencing table if the corresponding value in the primary key has been updated, or the whole row with that value has been deleted from the parent table.

► **SET NULL**   Allows you again to update or delete all values of the parent table. If you want to update a value of the parent table and this modification would lead to data inconsistencies in the referencing table, the database system sets all corresponding values in the foreign key of the referencing table to NULL. Similarly, if you want to delete the row in the parent table and the deletion of the value in the primary key would lead to data inconsistencies, the database system sets all corresponding values in the foreign key to NULL. That way, all data inconsistencies are omitted.

► **SET DEFAULT**   Analogous to the SET NULL option, with one exception: all corresponding values in the foreign key are set to a default value. (Obviously, the default value must still exist in the primary key of the parent table after modification.)

NOTE

The Transact-SQL language supports all four alternatives.

Example 5.12 shows the use of the ON DELETE and ON UPDATE options.

EXAMPLE 5.12

```
USE sample;
CREATE TABLE works_on1
(emp_no INTEGER NOT NULL,
 project_no CHAR(4) NOT NULL,
 job CHAR (15) NULL,
 enter_date DATE NULL,
 CONSTRAINT prim_works1 PRIMARY KEY(emp_no, project_no),
 CONSTRAINT foreign1_works1 FOREIGN KEY(emp_no)
    REFERENCES employee(emp_no) ON DELETE CASCADE,
 CONSTRAINT foreign2_works1 FOREIGN KEY(project_no)
    REFERENCES project(project_no) ON UPDATE CASCADE);
```

Example 5.12 creates the **works_on1** table that uses the ON DELETE CASCADE and ON UPDATE CASCADE options. If you load the **works_on1** table with the content shown in Table 1-4, each deletion of a row in the **employee** table will cause the additional deletion of all rows in the **works_on1** table that have the corresponding value in the **emp_no** column. Similarly, each update of a value in the **project_no** column of the project table will cause the same modification on all corresponding values in the **project_no** column of the **works_on1** table.

Creating Other Database Objects

A relational database contains not only base tables that exist in their own right but also *views*, which are virtual tables. The data of a base table exists physically—that is, it is stored on a disk—while a view is derived from one or more base tables. The CREATE VIEW statement creates a new view from one or more existing tables (or views) using a SELECT statement, which is an inseparable part of the CREATE VIEW statement. Since the creation of a view always contains a query, the CREATE VIEW statement belongs to the data manipulation language (DML) rather than to the data definition language (DDL). For this reason, the creation and removal of views is discussed in Chapter 11, after the presentation of all Transact-SQL statements for data modification.

The CREATE INDEX statement creates a new *index* on a specified table. The indices are primarily used to allow efficient access to the data stored on a disk. The existence of an index can greatly improve the access to data. Indices, together with the CREATE INDEX statement, are discussed in detail in Chapter 10.

A *stored procedure* is an additional database object that can be created using the corresponding CREATE PROCEDURE statement. (A stored procedure is a special kind of sequence of statements written in Transact-SQL, using the SQL language and procedural extensions. Chapter 8 describes stored procedures in detail.)

A *trigger* is a database object that specifies an action as a result of an operation. This means that when a particular data-modifying action (modification, insertion, or deletion) occurs on a particular table, Database Engine automatically invokes one or more additional actions. The CREATE TRIGGER statement creates a new trigger. Triggers are described in detail in Chapter 14.

A *synonym* is a local database object that provides a link between itself and another object managed by the same or a linked database server. Using the CREATE SYNONYM statement, you can create a new synonym for the given object. Example 5.13 shows the use of this statement.

EXAMPLE 5.13

```
USE sample;
CREATE SYNONYM  prod
          FOR AdventureWorks.Production.Product;
```

Example 5.13 creates a synonym for the **Product** table in the Production Schema of the **AdventureWorks** database. This synonym can be used in DML statements, such as SELECT, INSERT, UPDATE, and DELETE.

NOTE

The main reason to use synonyms is to omit the use of lengthy names in DML statements. As you already know, the name of a database object can generally contain four parts. Introducing a (single-part) synonym for an object that has three or four parts can save you time when typing its name.

A *schema* is a database object that includes statements for creation of tables, views, and user privileges. (You can think of a schema as a construct that collects together several tables, corresponding views, and user privileges.)

NOTE

Database Engine treats the notion of schema the same way it is treated in the ANSI SQL standard. In the SQL standard, a schema is defined as a collection of database objects that is owned by a single principal and forms a single namespace. A namespace is a set of objects that cannot have duplicate names. For example, two tables can have the same name only if they are in separate schemas. In the versions previous to SQL Server 2005, database users and schemas are implicitly connected; that is, every database user is the owner of a schema that has the same name as the user. Also, the CREATE SCHEMA statement existed, but it did not actually create a schema. (Schema is a very important concept in the security model of Database Engine. For this reason, you can find a detailed description of schema in Chapter 12.)

Integrity Constraints and Domains

A *domain* is the set of all possible legitimate values that columns of a table may contain. Almost all DBMSs use base data types such as INT, CHAR, and DATE to define the set of possible values for a column. This method of enforcing "domain integrity" is incomplete, as can be seen from the following example.

The **person** table has a column, **zip**, that specifies the ZIP code of the city in which the person lives. This column can be defined using the SMALLINT or CHAR(5) data type. The definition with the SMALLINT data type is inaccurate, because the SMALLINT data type contains all positive and negative values between $-2^{15}-1$ and 2^{15}. The definition using CHAR(5) is even more inaccurate, because all characters and special signs can also be used in such a case. Therefore, an accurate definition of ZIP codes requires defining an interval of positive integers between 00601 and 99950 and assigning it to the **zip** column.

CHECK constraints (defined in the CREATE TABLE or ALTER TABLE statement) can enforce more precise domain integrity because their expressions are flexible, and they are always enforced when the column is inserted or modified.

The Transact-SQL language provides support for domains by creating alias data types using the CREATE TYPE statement. The following two sections describe alias and CLR data types.

Alias Data Types

An alias data type is a special kind of data type that is defined by users using the existing base data types. Such a data type can be used with the CREATE TABLE statement to define one or more columns in a database.

The CREATE TYPE statement is generally used to create an alias data type. The syntax of this statement is as follows:

CREATE TYPE [type_schema_name.] type_name
{ [FROM base_type [(precision [, scale])] [NULL | NOT NULL]]
   | [EXTERNAL NAME assembly_name [.class_name]]}

Example 5.14 shows the creation of an alias data type using the CREATE TYPE statement.

EXAMPLE 5.14

USE sample;
CREATE TYPE zip
  FROM SMALLINT NOT NULL;

Example 5.14 creates an alias type **zip** based on the standard data type CHAR(5). This user-defined data type can now be used as a data type of a table column, as shown in Example 5.15.

NOTE

*Again, you have to drop the **customer** table (DROP TABLE customer) before you execute the following example.*

EXAMPLE 5.15

USE sample;
CREATE TABLE customer
  (cust_no INT NOT NULL,
  cust_name CHAR(20) NOT NULL,
  city CHAR(20),
  zip_code ZIP,
  CHECK (zip_code BETWEEN 601 AND 99950)),

Example 5.15 uses the new **zip** data type to specify a column of the **customer** table. The values of this column have to be constrained to the region between 601 and 99950. As can be seen from Example 5.15, this can be done using the CHECK clause.

NOTE

Generally, Database Engine implicitly converts between compatible columns of different data types. This is valid for the alias data types too.

SQL Server 2008 additionally supports the creation of user-defined table types. Example 5.16 shows how you can use the CREATE TYPE statement to create such a table type.

EXAMPLE 5.16

USE sample;
CREATE TYPE person_table_t AS TABLE
   (name VARCHAR(30), salary DECIMAL(8,2));

The user-defined table type called **person_table_t** has two columns: **name** and **salary**. Such table types are usually used in relation to table-valued parameters (see Chapter 8).

CLR Data Types

The CREATE TYPE statement can also be applied to create a user-defined data type using .NET. In this case, the implementation of a user-defined data type is defined in a class of an assembly in the Common Language Runtime (CLR). This means that you can use one of the .NET languages like C# or Visual Basic to implement the new data type. Further description of the user-defined data types is outside the scope of this book.

Modifying Database Objects

The Transact-SQL language supports changing the structure of the following database objects, among others:

▶ Database

▶ Table

▶ Stored procedure

▶ View

▶ Schema

▶ Trigger

The following two sections describe, in turn, how you can alter a database and a table. The modification of the structure of each of the last four database objects is described in Chapters 8, 11, 12, and 14, respectively.

Altering a Database

The ALTER DATABASE statement changes the physical structure of a database. The Transact-SQL language allows you to change the following properties of a database:

▶ Change the name of the database using the **sp_rename** stored procedure (see the section, "Altering a Table")

▶ Add or remove one or more database files

▶ Add or remove one or more log files

▶ Add or remove filegroups

▶ Modify file or filegroup properties

▶ Set database options

The following subsections describe these different types of database alterations.

Adding or Removing Database Files, Log Files, or Filegroups

The ALTER DATABASE statement allows the addition and removal of database files. The clauses ADD FILE and REMOVE FILE specify the addition of a new file and the deletion of an existing file, respectively. (Additionally, a new file can be assigned to an existing filegroup using the TO FILEGROUP option.)

Example 5.17 shows how a new database file can be added to the **projects** database.

EXAMPLE 5.17

```
USE master;
GO
ALTER DATABASE projects
ADD FILE (NAME=projects_dat1,
    FILENAME = 'C:\projects1.mdf',   SIZE = 10,
    MAXSIZE = 100,   FILEGROWTH = 5);
```

The ALTER DATABASE statement in Example 5.17 adds a new file with the logical name **projects_dat1**. Its initial size is 10MB, and this file will grow using units of 5MB until it reaches the upper limit of 100MB.

The REMOVE FILE clause removes one or more files that belong to an existing database. The file can be a data file or a log file. The file cannot be removed unless it is empty.

Log files are added in the same way as database files. The only difference is that you use the ADD LOG FILE clause instead of ADD FILE.

The CREATE FILEGROUP clause creates a new filegroup, while DELETE FILEGROUP removes an existing filegroup from the system. Again, you cannot remove a filegroup unless it is empty.

Modifying File or Filegroup Properties

You can use the MODIFY FILE clause to change the following file properties:

▶ Change the logical name of a file using the NEWNAME option of the MODIFY FILE clause

▶ Increase the value of the SIZE property

▶ Change the FILENAME, MAXSIZE, or FILEGROWTH property

▶ Mark the file as OFFLINE

Similarly, you can use the MODIFY FILEGROUP clause to change the following filegroup properties:

▶ Change the name of a filegroup using the NAME option of the MODIFY FILEGROUP clause

▶ Mark the filegroup as the default filegroup using the DEFAULT option

▶ Mark the filegroup as read-only or read-write using the READONLY or READWRITE options

Setting Database Options

The SET clause of the ALTER DATABASE statement is used to set different database options. Some options must be set to ON or OFF, but most of them have a list of possible values. Each database option has a default value, which is set in the **model** database. Therefore, you can alter the **model** database to change the default values of specific options.

All options that you can set are divided into several groups. The most important groups are

▶ State options

▶ Auto options

▶ SQL options

The state options control the following:

- ▶ User access to the database (options are SINGLE_USER, RESTRICTED_USER, and MULTI_USER)

- ▶ The status of the database (options are ONLINE, OFFLINE, and EMERGENCY)

- ▶ The read/write modus (options are READ_ONLY and READ_WRITE)

The auto options control, among other things, the art of the database shutdown (the option AUTO_CLOSE) and how index statistics are built (the options AUTO_CREATE_STATISTICS and AUTO_UPDATE_STATISTICS).

The SQL options control the ANSI compliance of the database and its objects. All SQL options can be edited using the databaseproperty function and modified using the **sp_dboption** system procedure. The recovery options FULL, BULK-LOGGED, and SIMPLE, influence the art of database recovery.

Altering a Table

The ALTER TABLE statement modifies the schema of a table. The Transact-SQL language allows the following types of alteration:

- ▶ Add or drop one or more new columns

- ▶ Modify column properties

- ▶ Add or remove integrity constraints

- ▶ Enable or disable constraints

- ▶ Rename tables and other database objects

The following sections describe these types of changes.

Adding or Dropping a New Column

You can use the ADD clause of the ALTER TABLE statement to add a new column to the existing table. Only one column can be added for each ALTER TABLE statement. Example 5.18 shows the use of the ADD clause.

EXAMPLE 5.18

```
USE sample;
ALTER TABLE employee
    ADD telephone_no CHAR(12) NULL;
```

The ALTER TABLE statement in Example 5.18 adds the column **telephone_no** to the **employee** table. Database Engine populates the new column either with NULL or IDENTITY values or with the specified default. For this reason, the new column must either be nullable or must have a default constraint.

NOTE

There is no way to insert a new column in a particular position in the table. The column, which is added using the ADD clause, is always inserted at the end of the table.

The DROP COLUMN clause provides the ability to drop an existing column of the table, as shown in Example 5.19.

EXAMPLE 5.19

```
USE sample;
ALTER TABLE employee
    DROP COLUMN telephone_no;
```

The ALTER TABLE statement in Example 5.19 removes the **telephone_no** column, which was added to the employee table with the ALTER TABLE statement in Example 5.18.

Modifying Column Properties

The Transact-SQL language supports the ALTER COLUMN clause of ALTER TABLE to modify properties of an existing column. The following column properties can be modified:

- ▶ Data type
- ▶ Nullability

Example 5.20 shows the use of the ALTER COLUMN clause.

EXAMPLE 5.20

```
USE sample;
ALTER TABLE department
    ALTER COLUMN location CHAR(25) NOT NULL;
```

The ALTER TABLE statement in Example 5.20 changes the previous properties (CHAR(30), nullable) of the **location** column of the **department** table to new properties (CHAR(25), not nullable).

Adding or Removing Integrity Constraints

A new integrity constraint can be added to a table using the ALTER TABLE statement and its option called ADD CONSTRAINT. Example 5.21 shows how you can use the ADD CONSTRAINT clause in relation to a check constraint.

EXAMPLE 5.21

```
USE sample;
CREATE TABLE sales
    (order_no INTEGER NOT NULL,
     order_date DATE NOT NULL,
     ship_date DATE NOT NULL);
ALTER TABLE sales
    ADD CONSTRAINT order_check CHECK(order_date <= ship_date);
```

The CREATE TABLE statement in Example 5.21 creates the **sales** table with two columns of the DATE data type: **order_date** and **ship_date**. The subsequent ALTER TABLE statement defines an integrity constraint named **order_check**, which compares both of the values and displays an error message if the shipping date is earlier than the order date.

Example 5.22 shows how you can use the ALTER TABLE statement to additionally define the primary key of a table.

EXAMPLE 5.22

```
USE sample;
ALTER TABLE sales
    ADD CONSTRAINT primaryk_sales PRIMARY KEY(order_no);
```

The ALTER TABLE statement in Example 5.22 declares the primary key for the **sales** table.

Each integrity constraint can be removed using the DROP CONSTRAINT clause of the ALTER TABLE statement, as shown in Example 5.23.

EXAMPLE 5.23

```
USE sample;
ALTER TABLE sales
DROP CONSTRAINT order_check;
```

The ALTER TABLE statement in Example 5.23 removes the CHECK constraint called **order_check**, specified in Example 5.21.

NOTE

You cannot use the ALTER TABLE statement to modify a definition of an integrity constraint. In this case, the constraint must be re-created—that is, dropped and then added with the new definition.

Enabling or Disabling Constraints

As previously stated, an integrity constraint always has a name that can be explicitly declared using the CONSTRAINT option or implicitly declared by the system. The name of all (implicitly or explicitly) declared constraints for a table can be viewed using the system procedure **sp_helpconstraint**.

A constraint is enforced by default during future insert and update operations. Additionally, the existing values in the column(s) are checked against the constraint. Otherwise, a constraint that is created with the WITH NOCHECK option is disabled in the second case. In other words, if you use the WITH NOCHECK option, the constraint will be applied only to future insert and update operations. (Both options, WITH CHECK and WITH NOCHECK, can be applied only with the CHECK and FOREIGN KEY constraints.)

Example 5.24 shows how you can disable all existing constraints for a table.

EXAMPLE 5.24

USE sample;
ALTER TABLE sales
    NOCHECK CONSTRAINT ALL;

In Example 5.24, the keyword ALL is used to disable all the constraints on the **sales** table.

NOTE

Use of the NOCHECK option is not recommended. Any constraint violations that are suppressed may cause future updates to fail.

Renaming Database Objects

The **sp_rename** system procedure modifies the name of an existing table (and any other existing database object, such as database, view, or stored procedure). Examples 5.25 and 5.26 show the use of this system procedure.

EXAMPLE 5.25

USE sample;
EXEC sp_rename @objname = department, @newname = subdivision

Example 5.25 renames the **department** table to **subdivision**.

EXAMPLE 5.26

USE sample;
EXEC sp_rename @objname = 'sales.order_no' , @newname = ordernumber

Example 5.26 renames the **order_no** column in the **sales** table. If the object to be renamed is a column in a table, the specification must be in the form **table_name.column_name**.

NOTE

*Do not use the **sp_rename** system procedure, because changing object names can influence other database objects that reference them. Drop the object and re-create it with the new name.*

Removing Database Objects

All Transact-SQL statements that are used to remove a database object have the following general form:

DROP object_type object_name

Each CREATE object statement has the corresponding DROP object statement. The statement

DROP DATABASE database1 {, ...}

removes one or more databases. This means that all traces of the database are removed from your database system.

One or more tables can be removed from a database with the following statement:

DROP TABLE table_name1 {, ...}

All data, indices, and triggers belonging to the removed table are also dropped. (In contrast, all views that are defined using the dropped table are not removed.) Only the user with the corresponding privileges can remove a table.

In addition to DATABASE and TABLE, **objects** in the DROP statement can be, among others, the following:

▶ TYPE

▶ SYNONYM

▶ PROCEDURE

▶ INDEX

▶ VIEW

▶ TRIGGER

▶ SCHEMA

The statements DROP TYPE and DROP SYNONYM drop a type and a synonym, respectively. The rest of the statements are described in different chapters: DROP PROCEDURE in Chapter 8, DROP INDEX in Chapter 10, DROP VIEW in Chapter 11, DROP SCHEMA in Chapter 12 and DROP TRIGGER in Chapter 14.

Conclusion

The Transact-SQL language supports many data definition statements that create, alter, and remove database objects. The following database objects, among others, can be created and removed using the CREATE object and the DROP object statement, respectively:

▶ Database

▶ Table

▶ Schema

▶ View

▶ Trigger

▶ Stored procedure

▶ Index

A structure of all database objects in the preceding list can be altered using the ALTER **object** statement. Note that the ALTER TABLE statement is the only standardized statement from this list. All other ALTER **object** statements are Transact-SQL extensions to the SQL standard.

The next chapter addresses the data manipulation statement called SELECT.

Exercises

E.5.1

Using the CREATE DATABASE statement, create a new database named **test_db** with explicit specifications for database and transaction log files. The database file with the logical name **test_db_dat** is stored in the file C:\tmp\test_db.mdf and the initial size is 5MB, the maximum size is unlimited, and the file growth is eight percent. The log file called **test_db_log** is stored in the file C:\tmp\test_db_log.ldf and the initial size is 2MB, the maximum size is 10MB, and the file growth is 500KB.

E.5.2

Using the ALTER DATABASE statement, add a new log file to the **test_db** database. The log file is stored in the file C:\tmp\emp_log.ldf and the initial size of the file is 2MB, with growth of 2MB and an unlimited maximum size.

E.5.3

Using the ALTER DATABASE statement, change the file size of the **test_db** database to 10MB.

E.5.4

In Example 5.4, there are some columns of the four created tables defined with the NOT NULL specification. For which column is this specification required and for which is it not required?

E.5.5

Why are the columns **dept_no** and **project_no** in Example 5.4 defined as CHAR values (and not as numerical values)?

E.5.6

Create the tables **customers** and **orders** with the following columns. (Do not declare the corresponding primary and foreign keys.)

customers	orders
customerid char(5) not null	orderid integer not null
companyname varchar(40) not null	customerid char(5) not null
contactname char(30) null	orderdate date null
address varchar(60) null	shippeddate date null
city char(15) null	freight money null
phone char(24) null	shipname varchar(40) null
fax char(24) null	shipaddress varchar(60) null
	quantity integer null

E.5.7

Using the ALTER TABLE statement, add a new column named **shipregion** to the **orders** table. The fields should be nullable and contain integers.

E.5.8

Using the ALTER TABLE statement, change the data type of the column **shipregion** from INTEGER to CHARACTER with length 8. The fields may contain NULL values.

E.5.9

Delete the formerly created column **shipregion**.

E.5.10

Describe exactly what happens if a table is deleted with the DROP TABLE statement.

E.5.11

Re-create the tables **customers** and **orders**, enhancing their definition with all primary and foreign keys constraints.

E.5.12

Using SQL Server Management Studio, try to insert a new row into the **orders** table with the following values:

(10, 'ord01', getdate(), getdate(), 100.0, 'Windstar', 'Ocean', 1).

Why isn't that working?

E.5.13

Using the ALTER TABLE statement, add the current system date and time as the default value to the **orderdate** column of the **orders** table.

E.5.14

Using the ALTER TABLE statement, create an integrity constraint that limits the possible values of the **quantity** column in the **orders** table to values between 1 and 30.

E.5.15

Display all integrity constraints for the **orders** table.

E.5.16

Delete the primary key of the **customers** table. Why isn't that working?

E.5.17

Delete the integrity constraint called **prim_empl** defined in Example 5.7.

E.5.18

Rename the **city** column of the **customers** table. The new name is **town**.

Chapter 6

Queries

In This Chapter

I n this chapter you will learn how to use the SELECT statement to perform retrievals. This chapter describes every clause in this statement and gives numerous examples using the **sample** database to demonstrate the practical use of each clause. After that, aggregate functions and the set operators, as well as computed columns and temporary tables will be introduced. The second part of the chapter tells you more about complex queries. This part introduces the join operator. In addition to looking at all forms of the join operator, which is the most important operator for relational database systems, the chapter discusses correlated subqueries and the EXISTS function. The end of the chapter describes common table expressions, together with the APPLY operator.

SELECT Statement: A Basic Form and the WHERE Clause

The Transact-SQL language has one basic statement for retrieving information from a database: the SELECT statement. With this statement, it is possible to query information from one or more tables of a database (or even from multiple databases). The result of a SELECT statement is another table, also known as a *result set*.

The simplest form of the SELECT statement contains a SELECT list with a FROM clause. (All other clauses are optional.) This form of the SELECT statement has the following syntax:

SELECT [ALL |DISTINCT] column_list
    FROM {table1 [tab_alias1] } ,...

table1 is a name of the table from which information is retrieved. **tab_alias1** provides an alias for the name of the corresponding table. An *alias* is another name for the corresponding table and can be used as a shorthand way of referring to the table or as a way to refer to two logical instances of the same physical table. Don't worry; this will become clearer as examples are presented.

column_list contains one or more of the following specifications:

▶ The asterisk symbol (*), which specifies all columns of the named tables in the FROM clause (or from a single table when qualified, as in **table2.***)

▶ The explicit specification of column names to be retrieved

▶ The specification **column_name** [AS] **column_heading**, which is a way to replace the name of a column or to assign a new name to an expression

▶ An expression

▶ A system or an aggregate function

NOTE

In addition to the preceding specifications, there are other options that will be presented later in this chapter.

A SELECT statement can retrieve either certain columns or rows from a table. The first operation is called *SELECT list* (or *projection*), and the second one is called *selection*. The combination of both operations is also possible in a SELECT statement.

NOTE

*Before you start to execute queries in this chapter, please re-create the entire **sample** database.*

Example 6.1 shows the simplest retrieval form with the SELECT statement.

EXAMPLE 6.1

Get full details of all departments:

USE sample;
SELECT dept_no, dept_name, location
 FROM department;

The result is

dept_no	dept_name	location
d1	Research	Dallas
d2	Accounting	Seattle
d3	Marketing	Dallas

The SELECT statement in Example 6.1 retrieves all rows and all columns from the **department** table. If you include all columns of a table in a SELECT list (as in Example 6.1), you can use * as shorthand, but this notation is not recommended. The column names serve as column headings of the resulting output.

WHERE Clause

The simplest form of the SELECT statement, described in the previous section, is not very useful for queries. In practice, there are always several more clauses in a SELECT statement than in the statement shown in Example 6.1. The following is the syntax of a SELECT statement that references a table, with (almost) all possible clauses:

```
SELECT select_list
    [INTO new_table_]
    FROM table
    [WHERE search_condition]
    [GROUP BY group_by_expression]
    [HAVING search_condition]
    [ORDER BY order_expression [ASC | DESC] ];
```

NOTE

The clauses in the SELECT statement must be written in the syntactical order given in the preceding syntax—for example, the GROUP BY clause must come after the WHERE clause and before the HAVING clause. (The INTO clause is not significant as the other clauses. For this reason it will be discussed later.)

This section starts with the definition of the WHERE clause. Often, it is necessary to define one or more conditions that limit the selected rows. The WHERE clause specifies a Boolean expression (an expression that returns a value of TRUE or FALSE) that is tested for each row to be returned (potentially). If the expression is true, then the row is returned; if it is false, it is discarded.

Example 6.2 shows the use of the WHERE clause.

EXAMPLE 6.2

Get the names and numbers of all departments located in Dallas:

```
USE sample;
SELECT dept_name, dept_no
    FROM department
    WHERE location = 'Dallas';
```

The result is

dept_name	dept_no
Research	d1
Marketing	d3

In addition to the equal sign, the WHERE clause can contain other comparison operators, including the following:

<> (or !=)	not equal
<	less than
>	greater than
>=	greater than or equal
<=	less than or equal
!>	not greater than
!<	not less than

Example 6.3 shows the use of a comparison operator in the WHERE clause.

EXAMPLE 6.3

Get the last and first names of all employees with employee numbers = 15000:

```
USE sample;
SELECT emp_lname, emp_fname
  FROM employee
  WHERE emp_no >= 15000;
```

The result is

emp_lname	emp_fname
Smith	Matthew
Barrimore	John
James	James
Moser	Sybill

An expression can also be a part of the condition in the WHERE clause, as Example 6.4 shows.

EXAMPLE 6.4

Get the project names for all projects with a budget > 60000 £. The current rate of exchange is 0.51 £ per $1.

```
USE sample;
SELECT project_name
  FROM project
  WHERE budget*0.51 > 60000;
```

The result is

project_name
Apollo
Mercury

Comparisons of strings (that is, values of data types CHAR, VARCHAR, NCHAR or NVARCHAR) are executed in accordance with the collating sequence (in effect the "sort order" specified when Database Engine was installed). If two strings are compared using ASCII code (or any other code), each of the corresponding (first, second, third, and so on) characters will be compared. One character is lower in priority than the other if it appears in the code table before the other one. Two strings of different lengths are compared after the shorter one is padded at the right with blanks, so that the length of both strings is equal. Numbers compare algebraically. Values of temporal data types (such as DATE, TIME, and DATETIME) compare in chronological order.

NOTE

Columns with TEXT or IMAGE data types cannot be used in the WHERE clause, except with the LIKE and IS NULL operators.

Boolean Operators

WHERE clause conditions can either be simple or contain multiple conditions. Multiple conditions can be built using the Boolean operators AND, OR, and NOT. The behavior of these operators has been described in Chapter 4 using truth tables.

If two conditions are connected by the AND operator, rows are retrieved for which both conditions are true. If two conditions are connected by the OR operator, all rows of a table are retrieved in which either the first or the second condition (or both) is true, as shown in Example 6.5.

EXAMPLE 6.5

Get the employee numbers for all employees that work for either project p1 or project p2 (or both):

```
USE sample;
SELECT project_no, emp_no
  FROM works_on
  WHERE project_no = 'p1'
  OR project_no = 'p2';
```

The result is

project_no	emp_no
p1	10102
p2	25348
p2	18316
p2	29346
p1	9031
p1	28559
p2	28559
p1	29346

The result of Example 6.5 contains some duplicate values of the **emp_no** column. If this redundant information is to be eliminated, the DISTINCT option should be used, as shown here:

```
USE sample;
SELECT DISTINCT emp_no
   FROM works_on
   WHERE project_no = 'p1'
   OR project_no = 'p2';
```

In this case, the result is

emp_no
9031
10102
18316
25348
28559
29346

NOTE

Columns with TEXT or IMAGE data types cannot be retrieved with the DISTINCT option.

Note that the DISTINCT option can be used only once in a SELECT list, and it must precede all column names in that list. Therefore, Example 6.6 is *wrong*.

EXAMPLE 6.6 (EXAMPLE OF AN ILLEGAL STATEMENT)

```
USE sample;
SELECT emp_fname, DISTINCT emp_no
    FROM employee
    WHERE emp_lname = 'Moser';
```

The result is

```
Server: Msg 156, Level 15, State 1, Line 1
Incorrect syntax near the keyword 'DISTINCT'.
```

NOTE

When there is more than one column in the SELECT list, the DISTINCT clause displays all rows where the combination of columns is distinct.

The WHERE clause may include any number of the same or different Boolean operations. You should be aware that the three Boolean operations have different priorities for evaluation: the NOT operation has the highest priority, AND is evaluated next, and the OR operation has the lowest priority. If you do not pay attention to these different priorities for Boolean operations, you will get unexpected results, as Example 6.7 shows.

EXAMPLE 6.7

```
USE sample;
SELECT emp_no, emp_fname, emp_lname
    FROM employee
    WHERE emp_no = 25348 AND emp_lname = 'Smith'
    OR emp_fname = 'Matthew' AND dept_no = 'd1';
SELECT emp_no, emp_fname, emp_lname
    FROM employee
    WHERE ((emp_no = 25348 AND emp_lname = 'Smith')
    OR emp_fname ='Matthew') AND dept_no = 'd1';
```

The result is

emp_no	emp_fname	emp_lname
25348	Matthew	Smith

emp_no	emp_fname	emp_lname

As the results of Example 6.7 show, the two SELECT statements display two different result sets. In the first SELECT statement, the system evaluates both AND operators first (from the left to the right); then the OR operator is evaluated. In the second SELECT statement, the use of parentheses changes the operation execution, with all expressions within parentheses being executed first, in sequence from left to right. As you can see, the first statement returned one row, while the second one returned zero rows.

The existence of several Boolean operations in a WHERE clause complicates the corresponding SELECT statement and makes it error prone. In such cases, the use of parentheses is highly recommended, even if they are not necessary. The readability of such SELECT statements will be greatly improved, and possible errors can be avoided. Here is the first SELECT statement from Example 6.7, modified using the recommended form:

```
USE sample;
SELECT emp_no, emp_fname, emp_lname
   FROM employee
   WHERE (emp_no = 25348 AND emp_lname = 'Smith')
   OR (emp_fname = 'Matthew' AND dept_no = 'd1');
```

The third Boolean operator, NOT, changes the logical value of the corresponding condition. The truth table for NOT in Chapter 4 shows that the negation of the true value is false and vice versa; the negation of the NULL value is also NULL.

Example 6.8 shows the use of the NOT operator.

EXAMPLE 6.8

Get the employee numbers and first names of all employees who do not belong to the department d2:

```
USE sample
SELECT emp_no, emp_lname
   FROM employee
   WHERE NOT dept_no = 'd2';
```

The result is

emp_no	emp_lname
25348	Smith
10102	Jones
18316	Barrimore
28559	Moser

In this case, the NOT operator can be replaced by the comparison operator <> (not equal).

NOTE

This book uses the operator <> (instead of !=) to remain consistent with the ANSI SQL standard.

IN and BETWEEN Operators

An IN operator allows the specification of two or more expressions to be used for a query search. The result of the condition returns true if the value of the corresponding column equals one of the expressions specified by the IN predicate.

EXAMPLE 6.9

Get all the columns for every employee whose employee number equals 29346, 28559, or 25348:

```
USE sample;
SELECT emp_no, emp_fname, emp_lname
   FROM employee
   WHERE emp_no IN (29346, 28559, 25348);
```

The result is

emp_no	emp_fname	emp_lname
25348	Matthew	Smith
29346	James	James
28559	Sybill	Moser

An IN operator is equivalent to a series of conditions, connected with one or more OR operators. (The number of OR operators is equal to the number of expressions following the IN operator minus one.)

The IN operator can be used together with the Boolean operator NOT, as shown in Example 6.10. In this case, the query retrieves rows that do not include any of the listed values in the corresponding columns.

EXAMPLE 6.10

Get all columns for every employee whose employee number is neither 10102 nor 9031:

USE sample;
SELECT emp_no, emp_fname, emp_lname, dept_no
  FROM employee
  WHERE emp_no NOT IN (10102, 9031);

The result is

emp_no	emp_fname	emp_lname	dept_no
25348	Matthew	Smith	d3
18316	John	Barrimore	d1
29346	James	James	d2
2581	Elke	Hansel	d2
28559	Sybill	Moser	d1

In contrast to the IN operator, which specifies each individual value, the BETWEEN operator specifies a range, which determines the lower and upper bounds of qualifying values. Example 6.11 provides an example.

EXAMPLE 6.11

Get the names and budgets for all projects with a budget between $95,000 and $120,000, inclusive:

USE sample;
SELECT project_name, budget
  FROM project
  WHERE budget BETWEEN 95000 AND 120000;

The result is

project_name	budget
Apollo	120000.0
Gemini	95000.0

The BETWEEN operator searches for all values in the range inclusively; that is, qualifying values can be between *or equal to* the lower and upper boundary values.

The BETWEEN operator is logically equal to two individual comparisons, which are connected with the Boolean operator AND. Example 6.11 is equivalent to Example 6.12.

EXAMPLE 6.12

```
USE sample;
SELECT project_name, budget
   FROM project
   WHERE budget >= 95000 AND budget <= 120000;
```

Like the BETWEEN operator, the NOT BETWEEN operator can be used to search for column values that do not fall within the specified range. The BETWEEN operator can also be applied to columns with character and date values.

The two SELECT statements in Example 6.13 show a query that can be written in two different, but equivalent ways.

EXAMPLE 6.13

Get the names of all projects with a budget less than $100,000 and greater than $150,000:

```
USE sample;
SELECT project_name
   FROM project
   WHERE budget NOT BETWEEN 100000 AND 150000;
```

The result is

project_name
Gemini
Mercury

Using comparison operators, the query looks different:

```
USE sample;
SELECT project_name
   FROM project
   WHERE budget < 100000 OR budget > 150000;
```

NOTE

Although the English phrasing of the requirements, "Get the names of all projects with budgets that are less than $100,000 and greater than $150,000," suggests the use of the AND operator in the second SELECT statement presented in Example 6.13, the logical meaning of the query demands the use of the OR operator, because if you use AND instead of OR, you will get no results at all. (The reason is that there cannot be a budget that is at the same time less than $100,000 and greater than $150,000.) Therefore, the second query in the example shows a possible problem that can appear between English phrasing of an exercise and its logical meaning.

Queries Involving NULL Values

A NULL in the CREATE TABLE statement specifies that a special value called NULL (which usually represents unknown or not applicable values) is allowed in the column. These values differ from all other values in a database. The WHERE clause of a SELECT statement generally returns rows for which the comparison evaluates to true. The concern then regarding queries is, how will comparisons involving NULL values be evaluated in the WHERE clause?

All comparisons with NULL values will return false (even when preceded by NOT). To retrieve the rows with NULL values in the column, Transact-SQL includes the operator feature IS NULL. This specification in a WHERE clause of a SELECT statement has the following general form:

column IS [NOT] NULL

Example 6.14 shows the use of the IS NULL operator.

EXAMPLE 6.14

Get employee numbers and corresponding project numbers for employees with unknown jobs who work on project p2:

```
USE sample;
SELECT emp_no, project_no
  FROM works_on
  WHERE project_no = 'p2'
  AND job IS NULL;
```

The result is

emp_no	project_no
18316	p2
29346	p2

Because all comparisons with NULL values return false, Example 6.15 shows syntactically correct, but logically incorrect, usage of NULL.

EXAMPLE 6.15

```
USE sample;
SELECT project_no, job
  FROM works_on
  WHERE  job <> NULL;
```

The result is

project_no	job

The condition

column IS NOT NULL

is equivalent to the condition

NOT (column IS NULL)

The system function ISNULL allows a display of the specified value as substitution for NULL (see Example 6.16).

EXAMPLE 6.16

```
USE sample;
SELECT emp_no, ISNULL(job, 'Job unknown') AS task
  FROM works_on
  WHERE project_no = 'p1';
```

The result is

emp_no	task
10102	Analyst
9031	Manager
28559	Job unknown
29346	Clerk

Example 6.16 uses a column heading called **task** for the **job** column.

LIKE Operator

LIKE is an operator that is used for pattern matching; that is, it compares column values with a specified pattern. The data type of the column can be any character or date. The general form of the LIKE operator is

column [NOT] LIKE 'pattern'

pattern may be a string or date constant or expression (including columns of tables) and must be compatible with the data type of the corresponding column. For the specified column, the comparison between the value in a row and the pattern evaluates to true if the column value matches the pattern expression.

Certain characters within the pattern—called wildcard characters—have a specific interpretation. Two of them are

% (percent sign)   Specifies any sequence of zero or more characters
_ (underscore)   Specifies any single character

Example 6.17 shows the use of the wildcard characters **%** and _.

EXAMPLE 6.17

Get the first and last names and numbers of all employees whose first name contains the letter *a* as the second character:

```
USE sample;
SELECT emp_fname, emp_lname, emp_no
   FROM employee
   WHERE emp_fname LIKE '_a%';
```

The result is

emp_fname	emp_lname	emp_no
Matthew	Smith	25348
James	James	29346

In addition to the percent sign and the underscore, Transact-SQL supports other characters that have a special meaning when used with the LIKE operator. These characters ([,], and ^) are demonstrated in Examples 6.18 and 6.19.

EXAMPLE 6.18

Get full details of all departments whose location begins with a character in the range *C* through *F*:

```
USE sample;
SELECT *
  FROM department
  WHERE location LIKE '[C-F]%';
```

The result is

dept_no	dept_name	location
d1	Research	Dallas
d3	Marketing	Dallas

As shown in Example 6.18, the square brackets, [ ], delimit a range or list of characters. The order in which characters appear in a range is defined by the collating sequence, which is determined during the system installation.

The character ^ specifies the negation of a range or a list of characters. This character has this meaning only within a pair of square brackets, as shown in Example 6.19.

EXAMPLE 6.19

Get the numbers and first and last names of all employees whose last name does not begin with the letter *J, K, L, M, N,* or *O* and whose first name does not begin with the letter *E* or *Z*:

```
USE sample;
SELECT emp_no, emp_fname, emp_lname
  FROM employee
  WHERE emp_lname LIKE '[^J-O]%'
  AND emp_fname LIKE '[^EZ]%';
```

The result is

emp_no	emp_fname	emp_lname
25348	Matthew	Smith
18316	John	Barrimore

The condition

column NOT LIKE 'pattern'

is equivalent to the condition

NOT (column LIKE 'pattern')

Example 6.20 shows the use of the LIKE operator (together with NOT).

EXAMPLE 6.20

Get full details of all employees whose first name does not end with the character *n*:

```
USE sample;
SELECT emp_no, emp_fname, emp_lname
   FROM employee
   WHERE emp_fname NOT LIKE '%n';
```

The result is

emp_no	emp_fname	emp_lname
25348	Matthew	Smith
29346	James	James
2581	Elke	Hansel
9031	Elsa	Bertoni
28559	Sybill	Moser

Any of the wildcard characters (%, _, [,], or ^) enclosed in square brackets stands for itself. An equivalent feature is available through the ESCAPE option. Therefore, both SELECT statements in Example 6.21 have the same meaning.

EXAMPLE 6.21

```
USE sample;
SELECT project_no, project_name
   FROM project
   WHERE project_name LIKE '%[_]%';
SELECT project_no, project_name
       FROM project
       WHERE project_name LIKE '%!_%' ESCAPE '!';
```

The result is

project_no	project_name

project_no	project_name

Both SELECT statements search for the underscore as an actual character in the column **project_name**. In the first SELECT statement, this search is established by enclosing the sign _ in square brackets. The second SELECT statement uses a character (in Example 6.21, the character !) as an escape character. The escape character overrides the meaning of the underscore as the wildcard character and leaves it to be interpreted as an ordinary character. (The result contains no rows because there are no project names that include the underscore character.)

NOTE

The SQL standard only supports the use of %, _, and the ESCAPE operator. For this reason, if any wildcard character must stand for itself, using the ESCAPE operator instead of a pair of square brackets is recommended.

Subqueries

All previous examples in this chapter contain comparisons of column values with an expression, constant, or set of constants. Additionally, the Transact-SQL language offers the ability to compare column values with the result of another SELECT statement. Such construct, where one or more SELECT statements are nested in the WHERE clause of another SELECT statement, is called a *subquery*. The first SELECT statement of a subquery is called the *outer query*—in contrast to the *inner query*, which denotes the SELECT statement(s) used in a comparison. The inner query will be evaluated first, and the outer query receives the values of the inner query.

NOTE

An inner query can also be nested in an INSERT, UPDATE, or DELETE statement, which will be discussed later in this book.

There are two types of subqueries:

▶ Self-contained

▶ Correlated

In a self-contained subquery, the inner query is logically evaluated exactly once. A correlated subquery differs from a self-contained one in that its value depends upon a variable from the outer query. Therefore, the inner query of a correlated subquery is logically evaluated each time the system retrieves a new row from the outer query. This section shows examples of self-contained subqueries. The correlated subquery will be discussed later in the chapter, together with the join operation.

A self-contained subquery can be used with the following operators:

- ► Comparison operators
- ► IN operator
- ► ANY or ALL operator

Subqueries and Comparison Operators

Example 6.22 shows the self-contained subquery that is used with the operator =.

EXAMPLE 6.22

Get the first and last names of employees who work in the Research department:

```
USE sample;
SELECT emp_fname, emp_lname
  FROM employee
  WHERE dept_no =
  (SELECT dept_no
    FROM department
    WHERE dept_name = 'Research');
```

The result is

emp_fname	emp_lname
John	Barrimore
Sybill	Moser

The inner query of Example 6.22 is logically evaluated first. That query returns the number of the research department (d1). Thus, after the evaluation of the inner query, the subquery in Example 6.22 can be represented with the following equivalent query:

```
USE sample
SELECT emp_fname, emp_lname
  FROM employee
  WHERE dept_no = 'd1';
```

A subquery can be used with other comparison operators, too. Any comparison operator can be used, provided that the inner query returns exactly one row. This is obvious because comparison between particular column values of the outer query and a set of values (as a result of the inner query) is not possible. The following section shows how you can handle the case in which the result of an inner query contains a set of values.

Subqueries and the IN Operator

The IN operator allows the specification of a set of expressions (or constants) that are subsequently used for the query search. This operator can be applied to a subquery for the same reason—that is, when the result of an inner query contains a set of values.

Example 6.23 shows the use of the IN operator in a subquery.

EXAMPLE 6.23

Get full details of all employees whose department is located in Dallas:

```
USE sample;
SELECT *
  FROM employee
  WHERE dept_no IN
  (SELECT dept_no
     FROM department
     WHERE location = 'Dallas');
```

The result is

emp_no	emp_fname	emp_lname	dept_no
25348	Matthew	Smith	d3
10102	Ann	Jones	d3
18316	John	Barrimore	d1
28559	Sybill	Moser	d1

Each inner query may contain further queries. This type of subquery is called a subquery with multiple levels of nesting. The maximum number of inner queries in a subquery depends on the amount of memory Database Engine has for each SELECT statement. In the case of subqueries with multiple levels of nesting, the system first evaluates the innermost query and returns the result to the query on the next nesting level, and so on. Finally, the outermost query evaluates the final outcome.

Example 6.24 shows the query with multiple levels of nesting.

EXAMPLE 6.24

Get the last names of all employees who work on the project Apollo:

```
USE sample;
SELECT emp_lname
  FROM employee
  WHERE emp_no IN
  (SELECT emp_no
    FROM works_on
    WHERE project_no IN
    (SELECT project_no
      FROM project
      WHERE project_name = 'Apollo'));
```

The result is

emp_lname
Jones
James
Bertoni
Moser

The innermost query in Example 6.24 evaluates to the **project_no** value p1. The middle inner query compares this value with all values of the **project_no** column in the **works_on** table. The result of this query is the set of employee numbers: (10102, 29346, 9031, 28559). Finally, the outermost query displays the corresponding last names for the selected employee numbers.

Subqueries and ANY and ALL Operators

The operators ANY and ALL are always used in combination with one of the comparison operators. The general syntax of both operators is

column_name operator [ANY | ALL] query

where **operator** stands for a comparison operator and **query** is an inner query.

The ANY operator evaluates to true if the result of the corresponding inner query contains at least one row that satisfies the comparison. The keyword SOME is the synonym for ANY. Example 6.25 shows the use of the ANY operator.

EXAMPLE 6.25

Get the employee numbers, project numbers, and job names for employees who have not spent the most time on one of the projects:

```
USE sample
SELECT DISTINCT emp_no, project_no, job
  FROM works_on
  WHERE enter_date > ANY
  (SELECT  enter_date
    FROM works_on)
```

The result is

emp_no	project_no	job
2581	p3	Analyst
9031	p1	Manager
9031	p3	Clerk
10102	p3	Manager
18316	p2	NULL
25348	p2	Clerk
28559	p1	NULL
28559	p2	Clerk
29346	p1	Clerk
29346	p2	NULL

Each value of the **enter_date** column in Example 6.25 is compared with all values of this column. For all dates of the column, except the oldest one, the comparison is evaluated to true at least once. The row with the oldest date does not belong to the result because the comparison does not evaluate to true in any case. In other words, the expression "enter_date > ANY (SELECT enter_date FROM works_on)" is true if there are *any* (one or more) rows in the **works_on** table with a value of the **enter_date** column less than the value of **enter_date** for the current row. This will be true for all but the earliest value of the **enter_date** column.

The ALL operator evaluates to true if the evaluation of the table column in the inner query returns all values of that column.

NOTE

Do not use ANY and ALL operators! Every query using ANY or ALL can be better formulated with the EXISTS function, which is explained later in this chapter (see the section "Subqueries and the EXISTS Function"). Additionally, the semantic meaning of the ANY operator can be easily confused with the semantic meaning of the ALL operator, and vice versa.

SELECT Statement: Other Clauses and Functions

The following subsections describe the rest of the clauses that can be used in a query as well as aggregate functions and set operators. First, we discuss the GROUP BY clause and show several examples with the clause and the aggregate functions, which are supported by Transact-SQL. After that, the HAVING and ORDER BY clauses are introduced. This section also discusses the IDENTITY property and the existing set operators (UNION, INTERSECT and EXCEPT).

GROUP BY Clause

The GROUP BY clause defines one or more columns as a group such that all rows within any group have the same values for those columns. Example 6.26 shows the simple use of the GROUP BY clause.

EXAMPLE 6.26

Get all jobs of the employees:

```
USE sample;
SELECT job
  FROM works_on
  GROUP BY job;
```

The result is

job
NULL
Analyst
Clerk
Manager

In Example 6.26, the GROUP BY clause builds different groups for all possible values (NULL, too) appearing in the **job** column.

NOTE

There is a restriction regarding the use of columns in the GROUP BY clause. Each column appearing in the SELECT list of the query must also appear in the GROUP BY clause. This restriction does not apply to constants and to columns that are part of an aggregate function. (Aggregate functions are explained in the next subsection.) This makes sense, because only columns in the GROUP BY clause are guaranteed to have a single value for each group.

A table can be grouped by any combination of its columns. Example 6.27 shows the grouping of rows of the **works_on** table using two columns.

EXAMPLE 6.27

Group all employees using their project numbers and jobs:

```
USE sample;
SELECT project_no, job
   FROM works_on
   GROUP BY project_no, job;
```

The result is

project_no	job
p1	Analyst
p1	Clerk
p1	Manager
p1	NULL
p2	NULL
p2	Clerk
p3	Analyst
p3	Clerk
p3	Manager

The result of Example 6.27 shows that there are nine groups with different combinations of project numbers and jobs. The only two groups that contain more than one row are

p2	Clerk	25348, 28559
p2	NULL	18316, 29346

The sequence of the column names in the GROUP BY clause need not correspond to the sequence of the names in the SELECT list.

NOTE

Columns with the TEXT (or IMAGE) data type cannot be used in the GROUP BY clause.

Aggregate Functions

Aggregate functions are functions that are used to get summary values. All aggregate functions can be divided into several groups:

► Convenient aggregate functions

► Statistical aggregate functions

► User-defined aggregate functions

► Analytic aggregate functions

The first three types are described in the following sections, while analytic aggregate functions are explained in detail in Chapter 24.

Convenient Aggregate Functions

The Transact-SQL language supports six aggregate functions:

► MIN

► MAX

► SUM

► AVG

► COUNT

► COUNT_BIG

All aggregate functions operate on a single argument, which can be either a column or an expression. (The only exception is the second form of the COUNT and COUNT_BIG functions: COUNT(*) and COUNT_BIG(*).) The result of each aggregate function is a constant value, which is displayed in a separate column of the result.

The aggregate functions appear in the SELECT list, which can include a GROUP BY clause. If there is no GROUP BY clause in the SELECT statement, and the SELECT list includes at least one aggregate function, then no simple columns can be included in the SELECT list (other than as arguments of an aggregate function). Therefore, Example 6.28 is *wrong*.

EXAMPLE 6.28 (EXAMPLE OF AN ILLEGAL STATEMENT)

```
USE sample;
SELECT emp_lname, MIN(emp_no)
   FROM employee;
```

The **emp_lname** column of the **employee** table must not appear in the SELECT list of Example 6.28, because it is not the argument of an aggregate function. On the other hand, all column names that are not arguments of an aggregate function may appear in the SELECT list if they are used for grouping.

The argument of an aggregate function can be preceded by one of two keywords:

▶ **ALL**   Indicates that all values of a column are to be considered (ALL is default value)

▶ **DISTINCT**   Eliminates duplicate values of a column before the aggregate function is applied

MIN and MAX Aggregate Functions   The aggregate functions MIN and MAX compute the lowest and highest values in the column, respectively. If there is a WHERE clause, the MIN and MAX functions return the lowest or highest of values from selected rows. Example 6.29 shows the use of the aggregate function MIN.

EXAMPLE 6.29

Get the lowest employee number:

```
USE sample;
SELECT MIN(emp_no)  AS min_employee_no
   FROM employee;
```

The result is

min_employee_no
2581

The result of Example 6.29 is not user friendly. For instance, the name of the employee with the lowest number is not known. As already shown, the explicit specification of the **emp_name** column in the SELECT list is not allowed. To retrieve the name of the employee with the lowest employee number, use a subquery, as shown in Example 6.30, where the inner query contains the SELECT statement of the previous example.

EXAMPLE 6.30

Get the number and the last name of the employee with the lowest employee number:

```
USE sample;
SELECT emp_no, emp_lname
  FROM employee
  WHERE emp_no =
  (SELECT MIN(emp_no)
    FROM employee);
```

The result is

emp_no	emp_lname
2581	Hansel

Example 6.31 shows the use of the aggregate function MAX.

EXAMPLE 6.31

Get the employee number of the manager who was entered last in the **works_on** table:

```
USE sample;
SELECT emp_no
  FROM works_on
  WHERE enter_date =
  (SELECT MAX(enter_date)
    FROM works_on
    WHERE job = 'Manager');
```

The result is

emp_no
10102

The argument of the functions MIN and MAX can also be a string value or a date. If the argument has a string value, the comparison between all values will be provided using the actual collating sequence. For all arguments of temporal data types, the earliest date specifies the lowest value and the latest date the highest value in the column.

The DISTINCT option cannot be used with the aggregate functions MIN and MAX. All NULL values in the column that are the argument of the aggregate function MIN or MAX are always eliminated before MIN or MAX is applied.

SUM Aggregate Function   The aggregate function SUM calculates the sum of the values in the column. The argument of the function SUM must be numeric. Example 6.32 shows the use of the SUM function.

EXAMPLE 6.32

Calculate the sum of all budgets of all projects:

```
USE sample;
SELECT SUM (budget) sum_of_budgets
   FROM project;
```

The result is

sum_of_budgets
401500

The aggregate function in Example 6.32 groups all values of the projects' budgets and determines their total sum. For this reason, the query in Example 6.32 (as does each analog query) implicitly contains the grouping function. Starting with SQL Server 2008, you can write the grouping function explicitly in the query shown in Example 6.32 with the GROUP BY clause, as shown in Example 6.33.

EXAMPLE 6.33

```
SELECT SUM (budget) sum_of_budgets
   FROM project
   GROUP BY();
```

The use of the new syntax for the GROUP BY clause is recommended, because it defines a grouping explicitly. (Chapter 25 describes several other GROUP BY features that are new in SQL Server 2008.)

The use of the DISTINCT option eliminates all duplicate values in the column before the function SUM is applied. Similarly, all NULL values are always eliminated before SUM is applied.

AVG Aggregate Function   The aggregate function AVG calculates the average of the values in the column. The argument of the function AVG must be numeric. All NULL values are eliminated before the function AVG is applied. Example 6.34 shows the use of the AVG aggregate function.

EXAMPLE 6.34

Calculate the average of all budgets with an amount greater than $100,000:

```
USE sample;
SELECT AVG(budget) avg_budget
   FROM project
   WHERE budget > 100000;
```

The result is

avg_budget
153250

COUNT and COUNT_BIG Aggregate Functions   The aggregate function COUNT has two different forms:

```
COUNT ([DISTINCT] col_name)
COUNT (*)
```

The first form calculates the number of values in the **col_name** column. When the DISTINCT keyword is used, all duplicate values are eliminated before COUNT is applied. This form of COUNT does not count NULL values for the column.

Example 6.35 shows the use of the first form of the aggregate function COUNT.

EXAMPLE 6.35

Count all different jobs in each project:

```
USE sample;
SELECT project_no, COUNT(DISTINCT job) job_count
   FROM works_on
   GROUP BY project_no;
```

The result is

project_no	job_count
p1	4
p2	1
p3	3

As can be seen from the result of Example 6.35, all NULL values are eliminated before the function COUNT(DISTINCT job) is applied. (The sum of all values in the column is 8 instead of 11.)

The second form of the function COUNT, COUNT(*), counts the number of rows in the table. Or if there is a WHERE clause in the SELECT statement, it returns the number of rows for which the WHERE condition is true. In contrast to the first form of the function COUNT, the second form does not eliminate NULL values, because this function operates on rows and not on columns. Example 6.36 shows the use of COUNT(*).

EXAMPLE 6.36

Get the number of each job in all projects:

```
USE sample;
SELECT job, COUNT(*) job_count
    FROM works_on
    GROUP BY job;
```

The result is

job	job_count
NULL	3
Analyst	2
Clerk	4
Manager	2

The COUNT_BIG function is analogous to the COUNT function. The only difference between them is in relation to their return values: COUNT_BIG always returns a value of the BIGINT data type, while the COUNT function always returns a value of the INTEGER data type.

Statistical Aggregate Functions

The following aggregate functions belong to the group of statistical aggregate functions:

▶ **VAR**   Computes the variance of all the values listed in a column or expression.

▶ **VARP**   Computes the variance for the population of all the values listed in a column or expression.

▶ **STDEV**   Computes the standard deviation of all the values listed in a column or expression. (The standard deviation is computed as the square root of the corresponding variance.)

▶ **STDEVP**   Computes the standard deviation for the population of all the values listed in a column or expression.

Examples concerning statistical aggregate functions will be shown in Chapter 24.

User-Defined Aggregate Functions

Database Engine also supports the implementation of user-defined aggregate functions. Using these functions, you can implement and deploy aggregate functions that do not belong to aggregate functions supported by the system. These functions are a special case of user-defined functions, which will be described in detail in Chapter 8.

HAVING Clause

The HAVING clause defines the condition that is then applied to groups of rows. Hence, this clause has the same meaning to groups of rows that the WHERE clause has to the content of the corresponding table. The syntax of the HAVING clause is

HAVING condition

where **condition** contains aggregate functions or constants.
   Example 6.37 shows the use of the HAVING clause with the aggregate function COUNT(*).

EXAMPLE 6.37

Get project numbers for all projects employing fewer than four persons:

```
USE sample;
SELECT project_no
  FROM works_on
  GROUP BY project_no
  HAVING COUNT(*) < 4;
```

The result is

project_no
p3

In Example 6.37, the system uses the GROUP BY clause to group all rows according to existing values in the **project_no** column. After that, it counts the number of rows in each group and selects those groups with three or fewer rows.

The HAVING clause can also be used without aggregate functions, as shown in Example 6.38.

EXAMPLE 6.38

Group rows of the **works_on** table by job and eliminate those jobs that do not begin with the letter *M*:

```
USE sample;
SELECT job
  FROM works_on
  GROUP BY job
    HAVING job LIKE 'M%';
```

The result is

job
Manager

The HAVING clause can also be used without the GROUP BY clause, although doing so is uncommon in practice. In such a case, all rows of the entire table belong to a single group.

NOTE

Columns with the TEXT (or IMAGE) data type cannot be used with the HAVING clause.

ORDER BY Clause

The ORDER BY clause defines the particular order of the rows in the result of a query. This clause has the following syntax:

ORDER BY {[col_name | col_number [ASC | DESC]]} , ...

The **col_name** column defines the order. **col_number** is an alternative specification, which identifies the column by its ordinal position in the sequence of all columns in the SELECT list (1 for the first column, 2 for the second one, and so on). ASC indicates ascending order and DESC indicates descending order, with ASC as the default value.

> ### NOTE
>
> The columns in the ORDER BY clause need not appear in the SELECT list. However, the ORDER BY columns must appear in the SELECT list if SELECT DISTINCT is specified. Also, this clause may not reference columns from tables that are not listed in the FROM clause.

As the syntax of the ORDER BY clause shows, the order criterion may contain more than one column, as shown in Example 6.39.

EXAMPLE 6.39

Get department numbers and employee names for employees with employee numbers < 20000, in ascending order of last and first names:

```
USE sample;
SELECT emp_fname, emp_lname, dept_no
   FROM employee
   WHERE emp_no < 20000
   ORDER BY emp_lname, emp_fname;
```

The result is

emp_fname	emp_lname	dept_no
John	Barrimore	d1
Elsa	Bretoni	d2
Elke	Hansel	d2
Ann	Jones	d3

It is also possible to identify the columns in the ORDER BY clause by the ordinal position of the column in the SELECT list. The ORDER BY clause in Example 6.39 could be written in the following form:

ORDER BY 2,1

The use of column numbers instead of column names is an alternative solution, if the order criterion contains any aggregate function. (The other way is to use column headings, which then appear in the ORDER BY clause.) However, using column names rather than numbers in the ORDER BY clause is recommended to reduce the difficulty of maintaining the query if any columns need to be added or deleted from the SELECT list. Example 6.40 shows the use of column numbers.

EXAMPLE 6.40

For each project number, get the project number and the number of all employees, in descending order of the employee number:

```
USE sample;
SELECT project_no, COUNT(*) emp_quantity
   FROM works_on
   GROUP BY project_no
   ORDER BY 2 DESC
```

The result is

project_no	emp_quantity
p1	4
p2	4
p3	3

The Transact-SQL language orders NULL values at the beginning of all values if the order is ascending, and at the end of all values if the order is descending.

NOTE

Columns with the TEXT (or IMAGE) data type cannot be used in the ORDER BY clause.

SELECT Statement and IDENTITY Property

Columns with numeric data types, such as TINYINT, SMALLINT, INT, and BIGINT, can have the IDENTITY property. Database Engine generates values for such columns sequentially, starting with an initial value. Therefore, you can use the IDENTITY property to let the system generate unique numeric values for the table column of your choice.

Each table can have only one column with the IDENTITY property. The table owner can specify the starting number and the increment value, as shown in Example 6.41.

EXAMPLE 6.41

USE sample;
CREATE TABLE product
  (product_no INTEGER IDENTITY(10000,1) NOT NULL,
    product_name CHAR(30) NOT NULL,
    price MONEY);
SELECT IDENTITYCOL
    FROM product
    WHERE product_name = 'Soap';

The result could be

product_no
10005

The **product** table is created first in Example 6.41. This table has the column **product_no** with the IDENTITY property. The values of the **product_no** column are automatically generated by the system, beginning with 10000 and incrementing by 1 for every subsequent value: 10000, 10001, 10002, and so on.

Some system functions and variables are related to the IDENTITY property. Example 6.41 used the IDENTITYCOL variable. As can be seen from the result set of Example 6.41, this variable automatically refers to the column with the IDENTITY property.

To find out the starting value and the increment of the column with the IDENTITY property, you can use the IDENT_SEED and IDENT_INCR functions, respectively:

SELECT IDENT_SEED('product'), IDENT_INCR('product)'

As you already know, the system automatically sets identity values. If you want to supply your own values for particular rows, you must set the IDENTITY_INSERT option to ON before the explicit value will be inserted:

SET IDENTITY_INSERT table_name ON

NOTE

Because the IDENTITY_INSERT option can be used to specify any values for a column with the IDENTITY property, IDENTITY does not generally enforce uniqueness. Use the UNIQUE or PRIMARY KEY constraint for this task.

If you insert values after the IDENTITY_INSERT option is set to ON, the system presumes that the next value is the incremented value of the highest value that exists in the table at that moment.

Set Operators

In addition to the operators described in the previous sections, there are three set operators supported in the Transact-SQL language:

- ▶ UNION
- ▶ INTERSECT
- ▶ EXCEPT

UNION Set Operator

The result of the union of two sets is the set of all elements appearing in either or both of the sets. Accordingly, the union of two tables is a new table consisting of all rows appearing in either or both of the tables.

The general form of the UNION operator is

select_1 UNION [ALL] select_2 {[UNION [ALL] select_3]}...

select_1, **select_2**,... are SELECT statements that build the union. If the ALL option is used, all resulting rows, including duplicates, are to be displayed. The ALL option has the same meaning with the UNION operator as it has in the SELECT list. There is only one difference: the ALL option is the default in the SELECT list, but it must be specified with the UNION operator to display all resulting rows, including duplicates.

The **sample** database in its original form is not suitable for a demonstration of the UNION operator. For this reason, this section introduces a new table, **employee_enh**, which is identical to the existing **employee** table, up to the additional **domicile** column. The **domicile** column contains the place of residence of every employee.

The new **employee_enh** table has the following form:

emp_no	emp_fname	emp_lname	dept_no	domicile
25348	Matthew	Smith	d3	San Antonio
10102	Ann	Jones	d3	Houston
18316	John	Barrimore	d1	San Antonio
29346	James	James	d2	Seattle
9031	Elke	Bertoli	d2	Portland
2581	Elisa	Kim	d2	Tacoma
28559	Sybill	Moser	d1	Houston

Creation of the **employee_enh** table provides an opportunity to show the use of the INTO clause of the SELECT statement. SELECT INTO has two different parts: First, it creates the new table with the columns corresponding to the columns listed in the SELECT list. Second, it inserts the existing rows of the original table into the new table. (The name of the new table appears with the INTO clause, and the name of the source table appears in the FROM clause of the SELECT statement.)

Example 6.42 shows the creation of the **employee_enh** table.

EXAMPLE 6.42

```
USE sample;
SELECT  emp_no, emp_fname, emp_lname, dept_no
  INTO employee_enh
  FROM employee;
ALTER TABLE employee_enh
     ADD domicile CHAR(25) NULL;
```

In Example 6.42, SELECT INTO generates the **employee_enh** table and inserts all rows from the initial table (**employee**) into the new one. Finally, the ALTER TABLE statement appends the **domicile** column to the **employee_enh** table.

After the execution of Example 6.42, the **domicile** column contains no values. The values can be added using SQL Server Management Studio (see Chapter 3) or the following UPDATE statements:

```
USE sample;
UPDATE employee_enh SET domicile = 'San Antonio'
   WHERE emp_no = 25348;
UPDATE employee_enh SET domicile = 'Houston'
    WHERE emp_no = 10102;
UPDATE employee_enh SET domicile = 'San Antonio'
   WHERE emp_no = 18316;
UPDATE employee_enh SET domicile = 'Seattle'
   WHERE emp_no = 29346;
UPDATE employee_enh SET domicile = 'Portland'
   WHERE emp_no = 9031;
UPDATE employee_enh SET domicile = 'Tacoma'
   WHERE emp_no = 2581;
UPDATE employee_enh SET domicile = 'Houston'
    WHERE emp_no = 28559;
```

Example 6.43 shows the union of the tables **employee_enh** and **department**.

EXAMPLE 6.43

```
USE sample;
SELECT domicile
  FROM employee_enh
UNION
SELECT location
  FROM department;
```

The result is

domicile
San Antonio
Houston
Portland
Tacoma
Seattle
Dallas

Two tables can be connected with the UNION operator if they are compatible with each other. This means that both the SELECT lists must have the same number of columns, and the corresponding columns must have compatible data types. (For example, INT and SMALLINT are compatible data types.)

The ordering of the result of the union can be done only if the ORDER BY clause is used with the last SELECT statement, as shown in Example 6.44. The GROUP BY and HAVING clauses can be used with the particular SELECT statements, but not with the union itself.

EXAMPLE 6.44

Get the employee number for employees who either belong to department d1 or entered their project before 1/1/2007, in ascending order of employee number:

```
USE sample;
SELECT emp_no
  FROM employee
  WHERE dept_no = 'd1'
UNION
SELECT emp_no
```

```
FROM works_on
WHERE enter_date < '01.01.2007'
ORDER BY 1;
```

The result is

emp_no
9031
10102
18316
28559
29346

> **NOTE**
> *The UNION operator supports the ALL option. UNION with ALL means that duplicates are not removed from the result set.*

The OR operator can be used instead of the UNION operator if all SELECT statements connected by one or more UNION operators reference the same table. In this case, the set of the SELECT statements is replaced through one SELECT statement with the set of OR operators.

INTERSECT and EXCEPT Set Operators

The two other set operators are INTERSECT, which specifies the intersection, and EXCEPT, which defines the difference operator. The intersection of two tables is the set of rows belonging to both tables. The difference of two tables is the set of all rows, where the resulting rows belong to the first table but not to the second one. Example 6.45 shows the use of the INTERSECT operator.

EXAMPLE 6.45

```
USE sample;
SELECT emp_no
  FROM employee
  WHERE dept_no = 'd1'
INTERSECT
SELECT emp_no
  FROM works_on
  WHERE enter_date < '01.01.2008';
```

The result is

emp_no
18316
28559

> **NOTE**
>
> *Transact-SQL does not support the INTERSECT operator with the ALL option. (The same is true for the EXCEPT operator.)*

Example 6.46 shows the use of the EXCEPT set operator.

EXAMPLE 6.46

```
USE sample;
SELECT emp_no
  FROM employee
  WHERE dept_no = 'd3'
EXCEPT
SELECT emp_no
  FROM works_on
  WHERE enter_date > '01.01.2008';
```

The result is

emp_no
10102
25348

> **NOTE**
>
> *You should be aware that the three set operators have different priorities for evaluation: the INTERSECT operator has the highest priority, EXCEPT is evaluated next, and the UNION operator has the lowest priority. If you do not pay attention to these different priorities, you will get unexpected results when you use several set operators together.*

CASE Expressions

In database application programming, it is sometimes necessary to modify the representation of data. For instance, a person's gender can be coded using the values 1, 2, and 3 (for female, male, and child, respectively). Such a programming technique can reduce the time for the implementation of a program. The CASE expression in the Transact-SQL language makes this type of encoding easy to implement.

NOTE

CASE does not represent a statement (as in most programming languages) but an expression. Therefore, the CASE expression can be used (almost) everywhere where the Transact-SQL language allows the use of an expression.

The CASE expression has two different forms:

► Simple CASE expression
► Searched CASE expression

The syntax of the simple CASE expression is

```
CASE expression_1
  {WHEN expression_2 THEN result_1} ...
  [ELSE result_n]
END
```

A Transact-SQL statement with the simple CASE expression looks for the first expression in the list of all WHEN clauses that match **expression_1** and evaluates the corresponding THEN clause. If there is no match, the ELSE clause is evaluated.

The syntax of the searched CASE expression is

```
CASE
  {WHEN condition_1 THEN result_1} ...
    [ELSE result_n]
END
```

A Transact-SQL statement with the searched CASE expression looks for the first expression that evaluates to true. If none of the WHEN conditions evaluates to true, the value of the ELSE expression is returned. Example 6.47 shows the use of the searched CASE expression.

EXAMPLE 6.47

```
USE sample;
SELECT project_name,
   CASE
    WHEN budget > 0 AND budget < 100000  THEN 1
```

```
      WHEN budget >= 100000 AND budget < 200000  THEN 2
      WHEN budget >= 200000 AND budget < 300000  THEN 3
      ELSE 4
   END budget_weight
FROM project;
```

The result is

project_name	budget_weight
Apollo	2
Gemini	1
Mercury	2

In Example 6.47, budgets of all projects are weighted, and the calculated weights (together with the name of the corresponding project) are displayed.

Example 6.48 shows another example with the CASE expression, where the WHEN clause contains inner queries as part of the expression.

EXAMPLE 6.48

```
SELECT project_name,
        CASE
                WHEN p1.budget < (SELECT AVG(p2.budget) FROM project p2)
                        THEN 'below average'
                WHEN p1.budget = (SELECT AVG(p2.budget) FROM project p2)
                        THEN 'on average'
                WHEN p1.budget > (SELECT AVG(p2.budget) FROM project p2)
                        THEN 'above average'
        END budget_category
     FROM project p1;
```

The result is

project_name	budget_category
Apollo	below average
Gemini	below average
Mercury	above average

COMPUTE Clause

The COMPUTE clause uses aggregate functions (MIN, MAX, SUM, AVG, and COUNT) to calculate summary values that appear as additional rows in the result of a query. The aggregate functions used with the COMPUTE clause are referred to as row aggregate functions.

The aggregate functions are usually applied to rows of a table to calculate a scalar value, which then appears in the result query as an additional row (see Example 6.49). The query using this form of aggregate functions has, again, a row as a result.

NOTE

The result of a COMPUTE clause is not a table: it is a report. Hence, the COMPUTE clause, in contrast to all other described operators and clauses, does not belong to the relational model.

The COMPUTE clause has an optional BY option. BY defines the grouping form of the result. If BY is omitted, the row aggregate function is applied to all rows of a result query. The option BY **column_name** specifies that the values of the **column_ name** column are used to build groups. The ORDER BY clause is required if the COMPUTE clause with BY is used.

NOTE

Do not use the COMPUTE and COMPUTE BY clauses any more, because they are marked for deprecation in the next version of Database Engine. Use the GROUP BY ROLLUP statement instead (see Chapter 24).

Example 6.49 shows the use of the COMPUTE clause with the BY option.

EXAMPLE 6.49

```
USE sample;
SELECT emp_no, project_no, enter_date
  FROM works_on
  WHERE project_no = 'p1' OR project_no = 'p2'
  ORDER BY project_no
COMPUTE MIN(enter_date) BY project_no;
```

The result is

emp_no	project_no	enter_date
10102	p1	2006-10-01
9031	p1	2007-04-15
28559	p1	2007-08-01
29346	p1	2007-01-04

min
2006-10-01

emp_no	project_no	enter_date
25348	p2	2007-02-15
18316	p2	2007-06-01
29346	p2	2006-12-15
28559	p2	2008-02-01

min
2006-12-15

A COMPUTE clause can have multiple uses in a SELECT statement. Hence, Example 6.49 can be written using one SELECT statement and the following COMPUTE statements:

COMPUTE MIN(enter_date) BY project_no
COMPUTE MIN(enter_date)

There are several restrictions concerning the COMPUTE clause:

▶ SELECT INTO is not allowed (because the result of the COMPUTE clause is *not* a table).

▶ All columns in the COMPUTE clause must appear in a SELECT list.

▶ The name of each column in the COMPUTE BY clause must appear in the ORDER BY clause.

▶ The order of the columns in the COMPUTE BY and ORDER BY clauses must be identical.

Temporary Tables

A temporary table is a database object that is temporarily stored and managed by the database system. Temporary tables can be local or global. Local temporary tables have physical representation—that is, they are stored in the **tempdb** system database. They are specified with the prefix **#** (for example, **#table_name**).

A local temporary table is owned by the session that created it and is visible only to that session. Such a table is thus automatically dropped when the creating session terminates. (If you define a local temporary table inside a stored procedure, it will be destroyed when the corresponding procedure terminates.)

Global temporary tables are visible to any user and any connection after they are created, and are deleted when all users that are referencing the table disconnect from the database server. In contrast to local temporary tables, global ones are specified with the prefix **##**.

Examples 6.50 and 6.51 show how the temporary table **project_temp** can be created using two different Transact-SQL statements.

EXAMPLE 6.50

```
USE sample;
CREATE TABLE #project_temp
  (project_no CHAR(4) NOT NULL,
   project_name CHAR(25) NOT NULL);
```

EXAMPLE 6.51

```
USE sample;
SELECT project_no, project_name
  INTO #project_temp
  FROM project;
```

Examples 6.50 and 6.51 are similar. They use two different Transact-SQL statements to create the local temporary table **#project_temp**. However, Example 6.50 actually populates the temporary table with the data from the **project** table, while Example 6.51 leaves it empty.

Join Operator

The previous sections of this chapter demonstrated the use of the SELECT statement to query rows from one table of a database. If the Transact-SQL language supported only such simple SELECT statements, the attachment of two or more tables to retrieve data would not be possible. Consequently, all data of a database would have to be stored in one table. Although the storage of all the data of a database inside one table is possible, it has one main disadvantage—the stored data are highly redundant.

Transact-SQL provides the join operator, which retrieves data from more than one table. This operator is probably the most important operator for relational database systems, because it allows data to be spread over many tables and thus achieves a vital property of database systems—nonredundant data.

NOTE

The UNION operator also attaches two or more tables. However, the UNION operator always attaches two or more SELECT statements, while the join operator "joins" two or more tables using just one SELECT. Further, the UNION operator attaches rows of tables, while, as you will see later in this section, the join operator "joins" columns of tables.

The join operator is applied to base tables and views. In this chapter, joins between base tables are discussed, while joins concerning views will be discussed in Chapter 11.

There are several different forms of the join operator. This section discusses the following fundamental types:

▶ Natural join

▶ Cartesian product (cross join)

▶ Outer join

▶ Theta-join, self-join and semi-join

Before explaining different join forms, this section describes the different syntax forms of the join operator.

Two Syntax Forms to Implement Joins

To join tables, you can use two different forms:

▶ Explicit join syntax (ANSI SQL :1992 join syntax)

▶ Implicit join syntax (old style join syntax)

The ANSI SQL:1992 join syntax is introduced in the SQL92 standard and defines join operations explicitly—that is, using the corresponding name for each type of the join operation. The keywords concerning the explicit definition of join are

▶ CROSS JOIN

▶ [INNER] JOIN

▶ LEFT [OUTER] JOIN

▶ RIGHT [OUTER] JOIN

▶ FULL [OUTER] JOIN

CROSS JOIN specifies the Cartesian product of two tables. INNER JOIN defines the natural join of two tables, while LEFT OUTER JOIN and RIGHT OUTER JOIN characterize the join operations of the same names, respectively. Finally, FULL OUTER JOIN specifies the union of the right and left outer joins. (All these different join operations are explained in the following sections.)

The implicit join syntax is "old-style" syntax, where each join operation is defined implicitly via the WHERE clause, using the so-called join columns (see Example 6.52).

NOTE

Use of the explicit join syntax is recommended. This syntax enhances the readability of queries. For this reason, all examples in this chapter concerning the join operation are solved using the explicit syntax forms. In a few introductory examples, you will see the "old-style" syntax, too.

Natural Join

Natural join is best explained through the use of an example, so check out Example 6.52.

NOTE

The phrases "natural join" and "equi-join" are often used as synonyms, but there is a slight difference between them. In the equi-join operation, there is always one or more pairs of columns that have identical values in every row. The operation that eliminates such columns from the equi-join is called a natural join.

EXAMPLE 6.52

Get full details of each employee; that is, besides the employee's number, first and last names, and corresponding department number, also get the name of his or her department and its location, with duplicate columns displayed.

Explicit join syntax:

```
USE sample;
SELECT employee.*, department.*
    FROM employee INNER JOIN department
    ON employee.dept_no = department.dept_no;
```

The SELECT list in Example 6.52 includes all columns of the **employee** and **department** tables. The FROM clause in the SELECT statement specifies the tables that are joined as well as the explicit name of the join form (INNER JOIN). The ON clause is also part of the FROM clause; it specifies the join columns from both tables. The condition employee.dept_no = department.dept_no in Example 6.52 specifies a *join condition*, and both columns are said to be *join columns*.

The equivalent solution is as follows:

"Old-style" join syntax:

```
USE sample;
SELECT employee.*, department.*
   FROM employee, department
   WHERE employee.dept_no = department.dept_no;
```

The "old-style" join syntax contains two significant differences: the FROM clause of the query contains the list of tables that are joined, and the corresponding join condition is specified in the WHERE clause using join columns.

The result is

emp_no	emp_fname	emp_lname	dept_no	dept_no	dept_name	location
25348	Matthew	Smith	d3	d3	Marketing	Dallas
10102	Ann	Jones	d3	d3	Marketing	Dallas
18316	John	Barrimore	d1	d1	Research	Dallas
29346	James	James	d2	d2	Accounting	Seattle
9031	Elsa	Bertoni	d2	d2	Accounting	Seattle
2581	Elke	Hansel	d2	d2	Accounting	Seattle
28559	Sybill	Moser	d1	d1	Research	Dallas

NOTE

*It is strongly recommend that you use * in a SELECT list only when you are using interactive SQL, and avoid its use in an application program.*

Example 6.52 can be used to show how a join operation works. Note that this is just an illustration of how you can think about the join process; Database Engine actually has several strategies from which it chooses to implement the join operator. Imagine each row of the **employee** table combined with each row of the **department** table. The result of this combination is a table with 7 columns (4 from the table **employee** and 3 from the table **department**) and 21 rows (see Table 6-1).

In the second step, all rows from Table 6-1 that do not satisfy the join condition employee.dept_no = department.dept_no are removed. These rows are prefixed in Table 6-1 with the * sign. The rest of the rows represent the result of Example 6.52.

The semantics of the corresponding join columns must be identical. This means both columns must have the same logical meaning. It is not required that the corresponding join columns have the same name (or even an identical type), although this will often be the case.

NOTE

It is not possible for a database system to check the logical meaning of a column. (For instance, project number and employee number have nothing in common, although both columns are defined as integers.) Therefore, database systems can only check the data type and the length of string data types. Database Engine requires that the corresponding join columns have compatible data types, such as INT and SMALLINT.

emp_no	emp_fname	emp_lname	dept_no	dept_no	dept_name	location
*25348	Matthew	Smith	d3	d1	Research	Dallas
*10102	Ann	Jones	d3	d1	Research	Dallas
18316	John	Barrimore	d1	d1	Research	Dallas
*29346	James	James	d2	d1	Research	Dallas
*9031	Elsa	Bertoni	d2	d1	Research	Dallas
*2581	Elke	Hansel	d2	d1	Research	Dallas
28559	Sybill	Moser	d1	d1	Research	Dallas
*25348	Matthew	Smith	d3	d2	Accounting	Seattle
*10102	Ann	Jones	d3	d2	Accounting	Seattle
*18316	John	Barrimore	d1	d2	Accounting	Seattle
29346	James	James	d2	d2	Accounting	Seattle
9031	Elsa	Bertoni	d2	d2	Accounting	Seattle
2581	Elke	Hansel	d2	d2	Accounting	Seattle
*28559	Sybill	Moser	d1	d2	Accounting	Seattle
25348	Matthew	Smith	d3	d3	Marketing	Dallas
10102	Ann	Jones	d3	d3	Marketing	Dallas
*18316	John	Barrimore	d1	d3	Marketing	Dallas
*29346	James	James	d2	d3	Marketing	Dallas
*9031	Elsa	Bertoni	d2	d3	Marketing	Dallas
*2581	Elke	Hansel	d2	d3	Marketing	Dallas
*28559	Sybill	Moser	d1	d3	Marketing	Dallas

Table 6-1   *Result of the Cartesian Product Between the Tables employee and department*

The **sample** database contains three pairs of columns in which each column of the pair has the same logical meaning (and they have the same names as well). The **employee** and **department** tables can be joined using the columns **employee.dept_no** and **department.dept_no**. The join columns of the **employee** and **works_on** tables are the columns **employee.emp_no** and **works_on.emp_no**. Finally, the **project** and **works_on** tables can be joined using the join columns **project.project_no** and **works_on.project_no**.

The names of columns in a SELECT statement can be qualified. "Qualifying" a column name means that, to avoid any possible ambiguity about which table the column belongs to, the column name is preceded by its table name (or the alias of the table), separated by a period: **table_name.column_name**.

In most SELECT statements a column name does not need any qualification, although the use of qualified names is generally recommended for readability. If column names within a SELECT statement are ambiguous (like the columns **employee.dept_no** and **department.dept_no** in Example 6.52), the qualified names for the columns *must* be used.

In a SELECT statement with a join, the WHERE clause can include other conditions in addition to the join condition, as shown in Example 6.53.

EXAMPLE 6.53

Get full details of all employees who work on the project Gemini.

Explicit join syntax:

```
USE sample;
SELECT  emp_no, project.project_no, job, enter_date, project_name, budget
    FROM works_on JOIN project
    ON project.project_no = works_on.project_no
    WHERE project_name = 'Gemini';
```

"Old-style" join syntax:

```
USE sample;
SELECT  emp_no, project.project_no, job, enter_date, project_name, budget
  FROM works_on, project
  WHERE project.project_no = works_on.project_no
  AND project_name = 'Gemini';
```

NOTE

*The qualification of the columns **emp_no**, **project_name**, **job**, and **budget** in Example 6.53 is not necessary, because there is no ambiguity regarding these names.*

The result is

emp_no	project_no	job	enter_date	project_name	budget
25348	p2	Clerk	2007-02-15	Gemini	95000.0
18316	p2	NULL	2007-06-01	Gemini	95000.0
29346	p2	NULL	2006-12-15	Gemini	95000.0
28559	p2	Clerk	2008-02-01	Gemini	95000.0

From this point forward, all examples will be implemented using the explicit join syntax only.

Example 6.54 shows another use of the inner join.

EXAMPLE 6.54

Get the department number for all employees who entered their projects on October 15, 2007:

```
USE sample;
SELECT dept_no
    FROM employee JOIN works_on
    ON employee.emp_no = works_on.emp_no
    WHERE enter_date = '10.15.2007';
```

The result is

dept_no
d2

Joining More Than Two Tables

Theoretically, there is no upper limit on the number of tables that can be joined using a SELECT statement. (One join condition always combines two tables!) However, Database Engine has an implementation restriction: the maximum number of tables that can be joined in a SELECT statement is 64.

NOTE

Usually, a maximum of eight to ten tables are joined in a SELECT statement. If you need to join more than ten tables in a SELECT statement, your database design is probably not optimal.

Example 6.55 joins three tables of the **sample** database.

EXAMPLE 6.55

Get the first and last names of all analysts whose department is located in Seattle:

```
USE sample;
SELECT emp_fname, emp_lname
    FROM works_on JOIN employee ON works_on.emp_no=employee.emp_no
                  JOIN department ON employee.dept_no=department.dept_no
    AND location = 'Seattle'
    AND job = 'analyst';
```

The result is

emp_fname	emp_lname
Elke	Hansel

The result in Example 6.55 can be obtained only if you join at least three tables: **works_on**, **employee**, and **department**. These tables can be joined using two pairs of join columns:

(works_on.emp_no, employee.emp_no)
(employee.dept_no, department.dept_no)

Example 6.56 uses all four tables from the **sample** database to obtain the result set.

EXAMPLE 6.56

Get the names of projects (with redundant duplicates eliminated) being worked on by employees in the Accounting department:

```
USE sample;
SELECT DISTINCT project_name
    FROM project JOIN works_on
    ON project.project_no = works_on.project_no
        JOIN employee ON works_on.emp_no = employee.emp_no
        JOIN department ON employee.dept_no = department.dept_no
    WHERE dept_name = 'Accounting';
```

The result is

project_name
Apollo
Gemini
Mercury

Notice that when joining three tables, you use two join conditions (linking two tables each) to achieve a natural join. When you join four tables, you use three such join conditions. In general, if you join n tables, you need $n - 1$ join conditions to avoid a Cartesian product. Of course, more than $n - 1$ join conditions, as well as other conditions, are certainly permissible to further reduce the result set.

Cartesian Product

The previous section illustrated a possible method of producing a natural join. In the first step of this process, each row of the **employee** table is combined with each row of the **department** table. This intermediate result was made by the operation called Cartesian product. Example 6.57 shows the Cartesian product of the tables **employee** and **department**.

EXAMPLE 6.57

USE sample;
SELECT employee.*, department.*
   FROM employee CROSS JOIN department;

   The result of Example 6.57 is shown in Table 6-1. A Cartesian product combines each row of the first table with each row of the second one. In general, the Cartesian product of two tables such that the first table has *n* rows and the second table has *m* rows will produce a result with *n* times *m* rows (or *n*m*). Thus, the result set in Example 6.57 contains 7*3 = 21 rows.

   In practice, the use of a Cartesian product is highly unusual. Sometimes users generate the Cartesian product of two tables when they forget to include the join condition in the WHERE clause of the "old-style" join syntax. In this case, the output does not correspond to the expected result because it contains too many rows. (The existence of many and unexpected rows in the result is a hint that a Cartesian product of two tables, rather than the intended natural join, has been produced.)

Outer Join

In the previous examples of natural join, the result set included only rows from one table that have corresponding rows in the other table. Sometimes it is necessary to retrieve, in addition to the matching rows, the unmatched rows from one or both of the tables. Such an operation is called an *outer join*.

   Examples 6.58 and 6.59 show the difference between a natural join and the corresponding outer join. (All examples in this section use the **employee_enh** table.)

EXAMPLE 6.58

Get full details of all employees, including the location of their department, who live and work in the same city.

USE sample;
SELECT employee_enh.*, department.location
   FROM employee_enh JOIN department
      ON domicile = location;

The result is

emp_no	emp_fname	emp_lname	dept_no	domicile	location
29346	James	James	d2	Seattle	Seattle

Example 6.58 uses a natural join to display the result set of rows. If you would like to know all other existing living places of employees, you have to use the (left) outer join. This is called a *left* outer join because all rows from the table on the *left* side of the operator are returned, whether or not they have a matching row in the table on the right. In other words, if there are no matching rows in the table on the right side, the outer join will still return a row from the table on the left side, with NULL in each column of the other table (see Example 6.59). Database Engine uses the operator LEFT OUTER JOIN to specify the left outer join.

A *right* outer join is similar, but it returns all rows of the table on the *right* of the symbol. Database Engine uses the operator RIGHT OUTER JOIN to specify the right outer join.

EXAMPLE 6.59

Get full details for all employees plus locations of their departments, for all cities that are either the living places, or both living and working places, of employees:

```
USE sample;
SELECT employee_enh.*, department.location
    FROM employee_enh LEFT OUTER JOIN department
        ON domicile = location;
```

The result is

emp_no	emp_fname	emp_lname	dept_no	domicile	location
25348	Matthew	Smith	d3	San Antonio	NULL
10102	Ann	Jones	d3	Houston	NULL
18316	John	Barrimore	d1	San Antonio	NULL
29346	James	James	d2	Seattle	Seattle
9031	Elsa	Bertoni	d2	Portland	NULL
2581	Elke	Hansel	d2	Tacoma	NULL
28559	Sybill	Moser	d1	Houston	NULL

As you can see, when there is no matching row in the table on the right side (**department**, in this case), the left outer join still returns the rows from the table on the left side (**employee_enh**), and the columns of the other table are populated by NULL values. Example 6.60 shows the use of the right outer join operation.

EXAMPLE 6.60

Get full details of all departments, as well as all living places of their employees, for all cities that are either the locations of departments or the living and working places of an employee.

```
USE sample;
SELECT employee_enh.domicile, department.*
    FROM employee_enh RIGHT OUTER JOIN department
        ON domicile =location;
```

The result is

domicile	dept_no	dept_name	location
Seattle	d2	Accounting	Seattle
NULL	d1	Research	Dallas
NULL	d3	Marketing	Dallas

In addition to the left and right outer joins, there is also the full outer join, which is defined as the union of the left and right outer joins. In other words, all rows from both tables are represented in the result set. If there is no corresponding row in one of the tables, its columns are returned with NULL values. This operation is specified using the FULL OUTER JOIN operator.

Database Engine supports the proprietary syntax for left and right outer joins, *= and =*, only under a backward-compatibility flag. To enable this nonstandard syntax, you have to change the database's compatibility mode to that of SQL Server 2000, which is 80.

NOTE

Changing the compatibility mode is not recommended because you cannot use any new features from the following versions. For this reason, if you want to implement any kind of outer join, use the standardized join syntax.

Every outer join operation can be simulated using the UNION operator plus the NOT EXISTS function. Example 6.61 is equivalent to the example with the left outer join (Example 6.59).

EXAMPLE 6.61

Get full details for all employees, plus locations of their departments, for all cities that are either the living places, or both living and working places, of employees:

```
USE sample;
SELECT employee_enh.*, department.location
   FROM employee_enh JOIN department
   ON domicile = location
UNION
SELECT employee_enh.*, 'NULL'
   FROM employee_enh
   WHERE NOT EXISTS
   (SELECT *
     FROM department
     WHERE location = domicile);
```

The first SELECT statement in the union specifies the natural join of the tables **employee_enh** and **department** with the join columns **domicile** and **location**. This SELECT statement retrieves all cities that are at the same time the living places and working places of each employee. The second SELECT statement in the union retrieves, additionally, all rows from the **employee_enh** table that do not match the condition in the natural join.

Further Forms of Join Operations

The preceding sections discussed the most important join forms. This section shows you three other forms:

- ▶ Theta join
- ▶ Self-join
- ▶ Semi-join

The following subsections describe these forms.

Theta Join

Join columns need not be compared using the equality sign. A join operation using a general join condition—that is, using a comparison operator other than equality—is called a theta join. Example 6.62, which uses the **employee_enh** table, shows the theta join operation.

EXAMPLE 6.62

Get all the combinations of employee information and department information where the domicile of an employee alphabetically precedes the location of the department, in which that employee works.

USE sample;
SELECT emp_fname, emp_lname, domicile, location
   FROM employee_enh JOIN department
   ON domicile < location;

The result is

emp_fname	emp_lname	domicile	location
Matthew	Smith	San Antonio	Seattle
Ann	Jones	Houston	Seattle
John	Barrimore	San Antonio	Seattle
Elsa	Bertoni	Portland	Seattle
Sybill	Moser	Houston	Seattle

In Example 6.62, the corresponding values of columns **domicile** and **location** are compared. In every resulting row, the value of the **domicile** column is ordered alphabetically before the corresponding value of the **location** column.

Self-Join, or Joining a Table with Itself

In addition to joining two or more different tables, a natural join operation can also be applied to a single table. In this case, the table is joined with itself, whereby a single column of the table is compared with itself. The comparison of a column with itself means that the table name appears twice in the FROM clause of a SELECT statement. Therefore, you need to be able to reference the name of the same table twice. This can be accomplished using at least one alias name. The same is true for the column names in the join condition of a SELECT statement. In order to distinguish both column names, you use the qualified names. Example 6.63 joins the **department** table with itself.

EXAMPLE 6.63

Get full details of all departments located at the same location as at least one other department:

USE sample;
SELECT t1.dept_no, t1.dept_name, t1.location

```
FROM department t1 JOIN department t2
    ON  t1.location = t2.location
WHERE t1.dept_no <> t2.dept_no;
```

The result is

dept_no	dept_name	location
d3	Marketing	Dallas
d1	Research	Dallas

The FROM clause in Example 6.63 contains two aliases for the **department** table: **t1** and **t2**. The first condition in the WHERE clause specifies the join columns, while the second condition eliminates unnecessary duplicates by making certain that each department is compared with *different* departments.

Semi-Join

The semi-join is similar to the natural join, but the result of the semi-join is only the set of all rows from one table where one or more matches are found in the second table. Example 6.64 shows the semi-join operation.

EXAMPLE 6.64

```
USE sample;
SELECT emp_no, emp_lname, e.dept_no
 FROM employee e JOIN department d
 ON e.dept_no = d.dept_no
 WHERE location = 'Dallas';
```

The result is

emp_no	emp_lname	dept_no
25348	Smith	d3
10102	Jones	d3
18316	Barrimore	d1
28559	Moser	d1

As can be seen from Example 6.64, the SELECT list of the semi-join contains only columns from the **employee** table. This is exactly what characterize the semi-join operation. This operation is usually used in distributed query processing to minimize data transfer. Database Engine uses the semi-join operation to implement the feature called star join (see Chapter 26).

Correlated Subqueries

A subquery is said to be a *correlated subquery* if the inner query depends on the outer query for any of its values. Example 6.65 shows a correlated subquery.

EXAMPLE 6.65

Get the last names of all employees who work on project p3:

```
USE sample;
SELECT emp_lname
  FROM employee
  WHERE 'p3' IN
  (SELECT project_no
    FROM works_on
    WHERE works_on.emp_no = employee.emp_no);
```

The result is

emp_lname
Jones
Bertoni
Hansel

The inner query in Example 6.65 must be logically evaluated many times because it contains the **emp_no** column, which belongs to the **employee** table in the outer query, and the value of the **emp_no** column changes every time Database Engine examines a different row of the **employee** table in the outer query.

Let's walk through how the system might process the query in Example 6.65. First, the system retrieves the first row of the **employee** table (for the outer query) and compares the employee number of that column (25348) with values of the **works_on.emp_no** column in the inner query. Since the only **project_no** for this employee is p2, the inner query returns the value p2. The single value in the set is not equal to the constant value p3 in the outer query, so the outer query's condition (WHERE 'p3' IN …) is not met and no rows are returned by the outer query for this employee. Then, the system retrieves the next row of the **employee** table and repeats the comparison of employee numbers in both tables. The second employee has two rows in the **works_on** table with **project_no** values of p1 and p3, so the result set of the inner query is (p1,p3). One of the elements in the result set is equal to the constant value p3, so the condition is evaluated to true and the corresponding value of the **emp_lname** column in the second row (Jones) is displayed. The same process is applied to all rows of the **employee** table, and the final result set with three rows is retrieved.

More examples of correlated subqueries are shown in the next section.

Subqueries and the EXISTS Function

The EXISTS function takes an inner query as an argument and returns true if the inner query returns one or more rows, and returns false if it returns zero rows. This function will be explained using examples.

EXAMPLE 6.66

Get the last names of all employees who work on project p1:

```
USE sample;
SELECT emp_lname
  FROM employee
  WHERE EXISTS
  (SELECT *
    FROM works_on
    WHERE employee.emp_no = works_on.emp_no
    AND project_no = 'p1');
```

The result is

emp_lname
Jones
James
Bertoni
Moser

The inner query of the EXISTS function almost always depends on a variable from an outer query. Therefore, the EXISTS function usually specifies a correlated subquery.

Let's walk through how Database Engine might process the query in Example 6.66. First, the outer query considers the first row of the **employee** table (Smith). Next, the EXISTS function is evaluated to determine whether there are any rows in the **works_on** table whose employee number matches the one from the current row in the outer query, and whose **project_no** is p1. Because Mr. Smith does not work on the project p1, the result of the inner query is an empty set and the EXISTS function is evaluated to false. Therefore, the employee named Smith does not belong to the final result set. Using this process, all rows of the **employee** table are tested, and the result set is displayed.

Example 6.67 shows the use of the NOT EXISTS function.

EXAMPLE 6.67

Get the last names of all employees who work for departments not located in Seattle:

```
USE sample;
SELECT emp_lname
  FROM employee
  WHERE NOT EXISTS
  (SELECT *
    FROM department
    WHERE employee.dept_no = department.dept_no
    AND location = 'Seattle');
```

The result is

emp_lname
Smith
Jones
Barrimore
Moser

The SELECT list of an outer query involving the EXISTS function is not required to be of the form SELECT * as in the previous examples. The form SELECT column_list, where **column_list** is one or more columns of the table, is an alternate form. Both forms are equivalent, because the EXISTS function tests only the existence (i.e., nonexistence) of rows in the result set. For this reason, the use of SELECT * in this case is safe.

Should You Use Joins or Subqueries?

Almost all SELECT statements that join tables and use the join operator can be rewritten as subqueries and vice versa. Writing the SELECT statement using the join operator is often easier to read and understand and can also help Database Engine to find a more efficient strategy for retrieving the appropriate data. However, there are a few problems that can be easier solved using subqueries, and there are others that can be easier solved using joins.

Subquery Advantages

Subqueries are advantageous over joins when you have to calculate an aggregate value on the fly and use it in the outer query for comparison. Example 6.68 shows this.

EXAMPLE 6.68

Get the employee numbers and enter dates of all employees with enter dates equal to the earliest date:

```
USE sample
SELECT emp_no, enter_date
   FROM works_on
   WHERE enter_date = (SELECT min(enter_date)
                          FROM works_on)
```

This problem cannot be solved easily with a join, because you would have to write the aggregate function in the WHERE clause and it is not allowed. (You can solve the problem using two separate queries in relation to the **works_on** table.)

Join Advantages

Joins are advantageous over subqueries if the SELECT list in a query contains columns from more than one table. Example 6.69 shows this.

EXAMPLE 6.69

Get the employee numbers, last names, and jobs for all employees that entered their projects on October 15, 2007:

```
USE sample;
SELECT employee.emp_no, emp_lname, job
   FROM employee, works_on
   WHERE employee.emp_no = works_on.emp_no
   AND enter_date = '10.15.2007';
```

The SELECT list of the query in Example 6.69 contains columns **emp_no** and **emp_lname** from the **employee** table and the **job** column from the **works_on** table. For this reason, the equivalent solution with the subquery would display an error, because subqueries can display information only from the outer table.

Table Expressions

Table expressions are subqueries that are used where a table is expected. There are two types of table expressions:

▶ Derived tables

▶ Common table expressions

The following subsections describe these two forms of table expressions.

Derived Tables

A derived table is a table expression that appears in the FROM clause of a query. You can apply derived tables when the use of column aliases is not possible because another clause is processed by the SQL translator before the alias name is known. Example 6.70 shows an attempt to use a column alias where another clause is processed before the alias name is known.

EXAMPLE 6.70 (EXAMPLE OF AN ILLEGAL STATEMENT)

Get all existing groups of months from the **enter_date** column of the **works_on** table:

```
USE sample;
SELECT MONTH(enter_date) as enter_month
FROM works_on
      GROUP BY enter_month;
```

The result is

```
Message 207: Level 16, State 1, Line 4
      The invalid column 'enter_month'
```

The reason for the error message is that the GROUP BY clause is processed before the corresponding SELECT list, and the alias name **enter_month** is not known at the time the grouping is processed.

By using a derived table that contains the preceding query (without the GROUP BY clause), you can solve this problem, because the FROM clause is executed before the GROUP BY clause, as shown in Example 6.71.

EXAMPLE 6.71

```
USE sample;
SELECT enter_month
  FROM (SELECT MONTH(enter_date) as enter_month
      FROM works_on) AS m
GROUP BY enter_month;
```

The result is

enter_month
1
2
4
6
8
10
11
12

Generally, it is possible to write a table expression any place in a SELECT statement where a table can appear. (The result of a table expression is always a table or, in a special case, an expression.) Example 6.72 shows the use of a table expression in a SELECT list.

EXAMPLE 6.72

```
USE sample;
SELECT w.job, (SELECT e.emp_lname
                      FROM employee e WHERE e.emp_no = w.emp_no) AS name
    FROM works_on w
    WHERE w.job IN ('Manager', 'Analyst');
```

The result is

job	name
Analyst	Jones
Manager	Jones
Analyst	Hansel
Manager	Bertoni

Common Table Expressions

A common table expression (CTE) is a named table expression that is supported by Transact-SQL. There are two types of queries, which use CTE:

► Nonrecursive queries

► Recursive queries

The following sections describe both query types.

NOTE

This section also describes the APPLY operator, because it uses CTE in the same way as non-recursive and recursive queries do.

CTEs and Nonrecursive Queries

The nonrecursive form of a CTE can be used as an alternative to derived tables and views. Generally, a CTE is defined using the WITH statement and an additional query that refers to the name used in WITH (see Example 6.74).

NOTE

The WITH keyword is ambiguous in the Transact-SQL language. To avoid ambiguity, you have to use a semicolon (;) to terminate the statement preceding the WITH statement.

Examples 6.73 and 6.74 use the **AdventureWorks** database to show how CTEs can be used in nonrecursive queries. Example 6.73 uses the "convenient" features, while Example 6.74 solves the same problem using a nonrecursive query.

NOTE

*If you do not have the **AdventureWorks** database on your system, you can download it from www.codeplex .com/MSFTDBProdSamples.*

EXAMPLE 6.73

```
USE AdventureWorks;
SELECT SalesOrderID
 FROM Sales.SalesOrderHeader
  WHERE TotalDue > (SELECT AVG(TotalDue)
          FROM Sales.SalesOrderHeader
          WHERE YEAR(OrderDate) = '2002')
   AND Freight > (SELECT AVG(TotalDue)
          FROM Sales.SalesOrderHeader
          WHERE YEAR(OrderDate) = '2002')/2.5;
```

The query in Example 6.73 finds total dues whose values are greater than the average of all dues and whose freights are greater than 40 percent of the average of all dues.

The main property of this query is that it is space-consuming, because an inner query has to be written twice. One way to shorten the syntax of the query is to create a view containing the inner query, but that is rather complicated, because you would have to create the view and then drop it when you are done with the query. A better way is to write a CTE. Example 6.74 shows the use of the nonrecursive CTE, which shortens the definition of the query in Example 6.73.

EXAMPLE 6.74

```
USE AdventureWorks;
WITH price_calc(year_2002) AS
    (SELECT AVG(TotalDue)
        FROM Sales.SalesOrderHeader
        WHERE YEAR(OrderDate) = '2002')
SELECT SalesOrderID
    FROM Sales.SalesOrderHeader
    WHERE TotalDue > (SELECT year_2002  FROM price_calc)
AND Freight > (SELECT year_2002  FROM price_calc)/2.5;
```

The syntax for the WITH clause in nonrecursive queries is

```
WITH cte_name (column_list) AS
    ( inner_query)
outer_query
```

cte_name is the name of the CTE that specifies a resulting table. The list of columns that belong to the table expression is written in brackets. (The CTE in Example 6.74 is called **price_calc** and has one column, **year_2002**.) **inner_query** in the CTE syntax defines the SELECT statement, which specifies the result set of the corresponding table expression. After that, you can use the defined table expression in an outer query. (The outer query in Example 6.74 uses the CTE called **price_calc** and its column **year_2002** to simplify the inner query, which appears twice.)

CTEs and Recursive Queries

NOTE

The material in this subsection is complex. Therefore, skipping it on the first reading of the book is recommended.

You can use CTEs to implement recursion, because CTEs can contain references to themselves. The basic syntax for a CTE for recursive queries is

WITH cte_name (column_list) AS
  (anchor_member
  UNION ALL
  recursive_member)
outer_query

cte_name and **column_list** have the same meaning as in CTEs for nonrecursive queries. The body of the WITH clause comprises two queries that are connected with the UNION ALL operator. The first query will be invoked only once, and it starts to accumulate the result of the recursion. The first operand of UNION ALL does not reference the CTE (see Example 6.75). This query is called the *anchor query* or *seed*.

The second query contains a reference to the CTE and represents the recursive portion of it. For this reason it is called the *recursive member*. In the first invocation of the recursive part, the reference to the CTE represents the result of the anchor query. The recursive member uses the query result of the first invocation. After that, the system repeatedly invokes the recursive part. The invocation of the recursive member ends when the result of the previous invocation is an empty set.

The UNION ALL operator joins the rows accumulated so far, as well as the additional rows that are added in the current invocation. (Inclusion of UNION ALL means that no duplicate rows will be eliminated from the result.)

Finally, **outer query** defines a query specification that uses the CTE to retrieve all invocations of the union of both members.

The table definition in Example 6.75 will be used to demonstrate the recursive form of CTEs.

EXAMPLE 6.75

```
USE sample;
CREATE TABLE airplane
   (containing_assembly VARCHAR(10),
   contained_assembly VARCHAR(10),
   quantity_contained INT,
   unit_cost DECIMAL (6,2));
insert into airplane values ( 'Airplane', 'Fuselage',1, 10);
insert into airplane values ( 'Airplane', 'Wings', 1, 11);
insert into airplane values ( 'Airplane', 'Tail',1, 12);
insert into airplane values ( 'Fuselage', 'Cockpit', 1, 13);
insert into airplane values ( 'Fuselage', 'Cabin', 1, 14);
insert into airplane values ( 'Fuselage', 'Nose',1, 15);
```

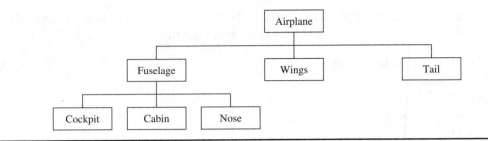

Figure 6-1 *Presentation of an Airplane and Its Parts*

insert into airplane values ('Cockpit', NULL, 1,13);
insert into airplane values ('Cabin', NULL, 1, 14);
insert into airplane values ('Nose', NULL, 1, 15);
insert into airplane values ('Wings', NULL,2, 11);
insert into airplane values ('Tail', NULL, 1, 12);

The **airplane** table contains four columns. The column **containing_assembly** specifies an assembly, while **contained_assembly** comprises the parts (one by one) that build the corresponding assembly. (Figure 6-1 shows graphically how an airplane with its parts could look.)

Suppose that the **airplane** table contains 11 rows, which are shown in Table 6-2. (The INSERT statements in Example 6.75 insert these rows in the **airplane** table.)

Example 6.76 shows the use of the WITH clause to define a query that calculates the total costs of each assembly.

Airplane	Fuselage	1	10
Airplane	Wings	1	11
Airplane	Tail	1	12
Fuselage	Cockpit	1	13
Fuselage	Cabin	1	14
Fuselage	Nose	1	15
Cockpit	NULL	1	13
Cabin	NULL	1	14
Nose	NULL	1	15
Wings	NULL	2	11
Tail	NULL	1	12

Table 6-2 *The Content of the Airplane Table*

EXAMPLE 6.76

USE sample;
WITH list_of_parts(assembly1, quantity, cost) AS
  (SELECT containing_assembly, quantity_contained, unit_cost
    FROM airplane
    WHERE contained_assembly IS NULL
  UNION ALL
  SELECT a.containing_assembly, a.quantity_contained,
      CAST(l.quantity*l.cost AS DECIMAL(6,2))
      FROM list_of_parts l,airplane a
      WHERE l.assembly1 = a.contained_assembly)
SELECT * FROM list_of_parts;

The WITH clause defines the CTE called **list_of_parts**, which contains three columns: **assembly**, **quantity**, and **cost**. The first SELECT statement in Example 6.76 will be invoked only once, to accumulate the results of the first step in the recursion process.

The SELECT statement in the last row of Example 6.76 displays the following result:

Assembly	Quantity	Costs
Cockpit	1	13.00
Cabin	1	14.00
Nose	1	16.500
Wings	2	11.00
Tail	1	12.00
Airplane	1	12.00
Airplane	1	22.00
Fuselage	1	16.500
Airplane	1	16.500
Fuselage	1	14.00
Airplane	1	14.00
Fuselage	1	13.00
Airplane	1	13.00

The first five rows in the preceding output show the result set of the first invocation of the anchor member of the query in Example 6.76. All other rows are the result of the recursive member (second part) of the query in the same example. The recursive member of the query will be invoked twice: the first time for the fuselage assembly and the second time for the airplane itself.

The query in Example 6.77 will be used to get the costs for each assembly with all its subparts.

EXAMPLE 6.77

```
USE sample;
WITH list_of_parts(assembly, quantity, cost) AS
  (SELECT containing_assembly, quantity_contained, unit_cost
    FROM airplane
    WHERE contained_assembly IS NULL
  UNION ALL
  SELECT a.containing_assembly, a.quantity_contained,
      CAST(l.quantity*l.cost AS DECIMAL(6,2))
       FROM list_of_parts l,airplane a
       WHERE l.assembly = a.contained_assembly )
SELECT assembly, SUM(quantity) parts, SUM(cost) sum_cost
  FROM  list_of_parts
  GROUP BY assembly;
```

The output of the query in Example 6.77 is as follows:

Assembly	Parts	Sum_cost
Airplane	5	76.00
Cabin	1	14.00
Cockpit	1	13.00
Fuselage	3	42.00
Nose	1	16.500
Tail	1	12.00
Wings	2	11.00

There are several restrictions for a CTE in a recursive query:

▶ The CTE definition must contain at least two SELECT statements (an anchor member and one recursive member) combined by the UNION ALL operator.

▶ The number of columns in the anchor and recursive members must be the same. (This is the direct consequence of using the UNION ALL operator.)

- ▶ The data type of a column in the recursive member must be the same as the data type of the corresponding column in the anchor member.
- ▶ The FROM clause of the recursive member must refer only once to the name of the CTE.
- ▶ The following options are not allowed in the definition part of a recursive member: SELECT DISTINCT, GROUP BY, HAVING, aggregation functions, TOP, and subqueries. (Also, the only join operation that is allowed in the query definition is an inner join.)

The APPLY Operator

The APPLY operator is similar to recursive queries, because it uses CTEs in the same way. This operator allows you to invoke a table-valued function for each row returned by an outer table expression of a query. The table-valued function acts as the right input, and the outer table expression acts as the left input. The right input is evaluated for each row from the left input, and the rows produced are combined for the final output. The list of columns produced by the APPLY operator is the set of columns in the left input followed by the list of columns returned by the right input. (See Chapter 8 for the detailed description of the APPLY operator.)

Conclusion

This chapter covered all the features of the SELECT statement regarding data retrieval from one or more tables. Every SELECT statement that retrieves data from a table must contain at least a SELECT list and the FROM clause. The FROM clause specifies the table(s) from which the data is retrieved. The most important optional clause is the WHERE clause, containing one or more conditions that can be combined using the Boolean operators AND, OR, and NOT. Hence, the conditions in the WHERE clause place the restriction on the selected row.

Exercises

E.6.1

Get all rows of the **works_on** table.

E.6.2

Get the employee numbers for all clerks.

E.6.3

Get the employee numbers for employees working on project p2 and having employee numbers lower than 10000. Solve this problem with two different but equivalent SELECT statements.

E.6.4

Get the employee numbers for employees who didn't enter their project in 2007.

E.6.5

Get the employee numbers for all employees who have a leading job (i.e., Analyst or Manager) in project p1.

E.6.6

Get the enter dates for all employees in project p2 whose jobs have not been determined yet.

E.6.7

Get the employee numbers and last names of all employees whose first names contain two letter *t*'s.

E.6.8

Get the employee numbers and first names of all employees whose last names have a letter *o* or *a* as the second character and end with the letters *es*.

E.6.9

Find the employee numbers of all employees whose departments are located in Seattle.

E.6.10

Find the last and first names of all employees who entered their projects on 04.01.2007.

E.6.11

Group all departments using their locations.

E.6.12

What is a difference between the DISTINCT and GROUP BY clauses?

E.6.13

How does the GROUP BY clause manage the NULL values? Does it correspond to the general treatment of these values?

E.6.14

What is the difference between COUNT(*) and COUNT(column)?

E.6.15

Find the highest employee number.

E.6.16

Get the jobs that are done by more than two employees.

E.6.17

Find the employee numbers of all employees who are clerks or work for department d3.

E.6.18

Why is the following statement wrong?

```
SELECT project_name
   FROM project
   WHERE project_no =
      (SELECT project_no FROM works_on WHERE Job = 'Clerk')
```

Write the correct syntax form for the statement.

E.6.19

What is a practical use of temporary tables?

E.6.20

What is a difference between global and local temporary tables?
   Write all solutions concerning the exercises that use a join operation using the explicit join syntax.

E.6.21

For the **project** and **works_on** tables, create the following:

   a.   Natural join

   b.   Cartesian product

E.6.22

If you intend to join several tables in a query (say **n** tables), how many join conditions are needed?

E.6.23

Get the employee numbers and job titles of all employees working on project Gemini.

E.6.24

Get the first and last names of all employees that work for departments Research or Accounting.

E.6.25

Get the enter dates of all clerks that belong to the department d1.

E.6.26

Get the names of projects on which two or more clerks are working.

E.6.27

Get the first and last names of the employees that are managers and that work on project Mercury.

E.6.28

Get the first and last names of all employees who entered the project at the same time as at least one other employee.

E.6.29

Get the employee numbers of the employees living in the same location and belonging to the same department as one another. (Hint: Use the extended **sample** database.)

E.6.30

Get the employee numbers of all employees belonging to the Marketing department. Find two equivalent solutions using

- ▶ The JOIN operator
- ▶ The correlated subquery

Chapter 7

Modification of a Table's Contents

In This Chapter

- ▶ **INSERT Statement**
- ▶ **UPDATE Statement**
- ▶ **DELETE Statement**
- ▶ **MERGE Statement**
- ▶ **OUTPUT Clause**

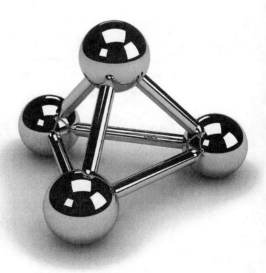

I n addition to the SELECT statement, which was introduced in Chapter 6, there are three other DML statements: INSERT, UPDATE, and DELETE. Like the SELECT statement, these three modification statements operate either on tables or on views. This chapter discusses these statements in relation to tables and gives examples of their use. Additionally, it explains two other statements: TRUNCATE TABLE and MERGE. Whereas the TRUNCATE TABLE statement is a Transact-SQL extension to the SQL standard, MERGE is a new and standardized feature in SQL Server 2008. At the end of the chapter the OUTPUT clause will be explained and several examples with the clause will be shown.

INSERT Statement

The INSERT statement inserts rows (or parts of them) into a table. It has two different forms:

- ▶ INSERT [INTO] tab_name [(col_list)]
  DEFAULT VALUES | VALUES ({ DEFAULT | NULL | *expression* } [,...*n*])
- ▶ INSERT INTO tab_name | view_name [(col_list)]
  {select_statement | execute_statement}

Using the first form, exactly one row (or part of it) is inserted into the **tab_name** table. The second form of the INSERT statement inserts the result set from the SELECT statement or from the stored procedure, which is executed using the EXECUTE statement. (The stored procedure must return data, which is then inserted into the table. The SELECT statement can select values from a different table or from the same table as the target of the INSERT statement, as long as the types of the columns are compatible.)

With both forms, every inserted value must have a data type that is compatible with the data type of the corresponding column of the table. To ensure compatibility, all character-based values and temporal data must be enclosed in apostrophes, while all numeric values need no such enclosing.

Inserting a Single Row

In both forms of the INSERT statement, the explicit specification of the column list is optional. This means that omitting the list of columns is equivalent to specifying a list of all columns in the table.

The option DEFAULT VALUES inserts default values for all the columns. If a column is of the data type TIMESTAMP or has the IDENTITY property, the value, which is automatically created by the system, will be inserted. For other data types, the column is set to the appropriate non-null default value if a default exists, or NULL, if it doesn't. If the column is not nullable, and has no DEFAULT value, then the INSERT statement fails and an error will be indicated.

Examples 7.1 through 7.4 insert rows into the four tables of the **sample** database. This action shows the use of the INSERT statement to load a small amount of data into a database.

EXAMPLE 7.1

Load data into the **employee** table:

```
USE sample;
INSERT INTO employee VALUES (25348, 'Matthew', 'Smith','d3');
INSERT INTO employee VALUES (10102, 'Ann', 'Jones','d3');
INSERT INTO employee VALUES (18316, 'John', 'Barrimore', 'd1');
INSERT INTO employee VALUES (29346, 'James', 'James', 'd2');
INSERT INTO employee VALUES (9031, 'Elsa', 'Bertoni', 'd2');
INSERT INTO employee VALUES (2581, 'Elke', 'Hansel', 'd2');
INSERT INTO employee VALUES (28559, 'Sybill', 'Moser', 'd1');
```

EXAMPLE 7.2

Load data into the **department** table:

```
USE sample;
INSERT INTO department VALUES ('d1', 'Research', 'Dallas');
INSERT INTO department VALUES ('d2', 'Accounting', 'Seattle');
INSERT INTO department VALUES ('d3', 'Marketing', 'Dallas');
```

EXAMPLE 7.3

Load data into the **project** table:

```
USE sample;
INSERT INTO project VALUES ('p1', 'Apollo', 120000.00);
INSERT INTO project VALUES ('p2', 'Gemini', 95000.00);
INSERT INTO project VALUES ('p3', 'Mercury', 186500.00);
```

EXAMPLE 7.4

Load data into the **works_on** table:

```
USE sample;
INSERT INTO works_on VALUES (10102,'p1', 'Analyst', '2006.10.1');
INSERT INTO works_on VALUES (10102, 'p3', 'Manager', '2008.1.1');
INSERT INTO works_on VALUES (25348, 'p2', 'Clerk', '2007.2.15');
INSERT INTO works_on VALUES (18316, 'p2', NULL, '2007.6.1');
INSERT INTO works_on VALUES (29346, 'p2', NULL, '2006.12.15');
INSERT INTO works_on VALUES (2581, 'p3', 'Analyst', '2007.10.15');
INSERT INTO works_on VALUES (9031, 'p1', 'Manager', '2007.4.15');
INSERT INTO works_on VALUES (28559, 'p1', 'NULL', '2007.8.1');
INSERT INTO works_on VALUES (28559, 'p2', 'Clerk', '2008.2.1');
INSERT INTO works_on VALUES (9031, 'p3', 'Clerk', '2006.11.15');
INSERT INTO works_on VALUES (29346, 'p1','Clerk', '2007.1.4');
```

There are a few different ways to insert values into a new row. Examples 7.5 through 7.7 show these possibilities.

EXAMPLE 7.5

```
USE sample;
INSERT INTO employee VALUES (15201, 'Dave', 'Davis', NULL);
```

The INSERT statement in Example 7.5 corresponds to the INSERT statements in Examples 7.1 through 7.4. The explicit use of the keyword NULL inserts the null value into the corresponding column.

The insertion of values into some (but not all) of a table's columns usually requires the explicit specification of the corresponding columns. The omitted columns must either be nullable or have a DEFAULT value.

EXAMPLE 7.6

```
USE sample;
INSERT INTO employee (emp_no, emp_fname, emp_lname)
       VALUES (15201, 'Dave', 'Davis');
```

Examples 7.5 and 7.6 are equivalent. The **dept_no** column is the only nullable column in the **employee** table because all other columns in the **employee** table were declared with the NOT NULL clause in the CREATE TABLE statement.

The order of column names in the VALUE clause of the INSERT statement can be different from the original order of those columns, which is determined in the CREATE TABLE statement. In this case, it is absolutely necessary to list the columns in the new order.

EXAMPLE 7.7

```
USE sample;
INSERT INTO employee (emp_lname, emp_fname, dept_no, emp_no)
      VALUES ('Davis', 'Dave', 'd1', 15201);
```

Inserting Multiple Rows

The second form of the INSERT statement inserts one or more rows selected with a subquery.

Example 7.8 shows how a set of rows can be inserted using the second form of the INSERT statement.

EXAMPLE 7.8

Get all the numbers and names for departments located in Dallas, and load the selected data into a new table:

```
USE sample;
CREATE TABLE dallas_dept
      (dept_no CHAR(4) NOT NULL,
       dept_name CHAR(20) NOT NULL);

INSERT INTO dallas_dept (dept_no, dept_name)
   SELECT dept_no, dept_name
      FROM department
      WHERE location = 'Dallas';
```

The new table created in Example 7.8, **dallas_dept,** has the same columns as the **department** table except for the **location** column. The subquery in the INSERT statement selects all rows with the value 'Dallas' in the **location** column. The selected rows will be subsequently inserted in the new table.

The content of the **dallas_dept** table can be selected with the following SELECT statement:

```
SELECT * FROM dallas_dept;
```

The result is

dept_no	dept_name
d1	Research
d3	Marketing

Example 7.9 is another example, which shows how multiple rows can be inserted using the second form of the INSERT statement.

EXAMPLE 7.9

Get all employee numbers, project numbers, and project enter dates for all clerks who work in project p2, and load the selected data into a new table:

```
USE sample;
CREATE TABLE clerk_t
   (emp_no INT NOT NULL,
    project_no CHAR(4),
    enter_date DATE);

INSERT INTO clerk_t (emp_no, project_no, enter_date)
   SELECT emp_no, project_no, enter_date
     FROM works_on
     WHERE job = 'Clerk'
     AND project_no = 'p2';
```

The new table, **clerk_t**, contains the following rows:

emp_no	project_no	enter_date
25348	p2	2007-02-15
28559	p2	2008-02-01

The tables **dallas_dept** and **clerk_t** (Examples 7.8 and 7.9) were empty before the INSERT statement inserted the rows. If, however, the table already exists and there are rows in it, the new rows will be appended.

NOTE

You can replace both statements (CREATE TABLE and INSERT) in Example 7.9 with the SELECT statement with the INTO clause (see Example 6.42 in Chapter 6).

Table Value Constructors and INSERT

SQL Server 2008 introduces a new feature called a *table* (or *row*) *value constructor*, which allows you to assign several tuples (rows) with a DML statement such as INSERT or UPDATE. Example 7.10 shows how you can assign several rows using such a constructor with an INSERT statement.

EXAMPLE 7.10

USE sample;
 INSERT INTO department VALUES ('d4', 'Human Resources', 'Chicago'),
                              ('d5', 'Distribution', 'New Orleans'),
                              ('d6', 'Sales', 'Chicago');

The INSERT statement in Example 7.10 inserts three rows at the same time in the **department** table using the table value constructor. As you can see from the example, the syntax of the constructor is rather simple. To use a table value constructor, list the values of each row inside the pair of brackets and separate each list from the others by using a comma.

UPDATE Statement

The UPDATE statement modifies values of table rows. This statement has the general form:

UPDATE tab_name
    { SET column_1 = {expression | DEFAULT | NULL} [,...*n*]
    [FROM tab_name1 [,...*n*]]
    [WHERE condition]

Rows in the **tab_name** table are modified in accordance with the WHERE clause. For each row to be modified, the UPDATE statement changes the values of the columns in the SET clause, assigning a constant (or generally an expression) to the associated column. If the WHERE clause is omitted, the UPDATE statement modifies all rows of the table. (The FROM clause will be discussed later in this section.)

NOTE

An UPDATE statement can only modify data of a single table.

EXAMPLE 7.11

Set the task of employee number 18316, who works on project p2, to be 'Manager':

```
USE sample;
UPDATE works_on
  SET job = 'Manager'
  WHERE emp_no = 18316
  AND project_no = 'p2';
```

The UPDATE statement in Example 7.11 modifies exactly one row of the **works_on** table, because the combination of the columns **emp_no** and **project_no** builds the primary key of that table and is therefore unique. This example modifies the task of the employee, which was previously unknown or set to NULL.

Example 7.12 modifies rows of a table with an expression.

EXAMPLE 7.12

Change the budgets of all projects to be represented in English pounds. The current rate of exchange is 0.51£ for $1.

```
USE sample;
UPDATE project
  SET budget = budget*0.51;
```

In the example, all rows of the **project** table will be modified because of the omitted WHERE clause. The modified rows of the **project** table can be displayed with the following Transact-SQL statement:

```
SELECT * FROM project;
```

The result is

project_no	project_name	budget
p1	Apollo	61200
p2	Gemini	48450
p3	Mercury	95115

EXAMPLE 7.13

Due to her illness, set all tasks on all projects for Mrs. Jones to NULL:

```
USE sample;
UPDATE works_on
```

```
   SET job = NULL
   WHERE emp_no IN
   (SELECT emp_no
      FROM employee
      WHERE emp_lname = 'Jones');
```

Example 7.13 uses an inner query in the WHERE clause of the UPDATE statement. Because of the use of the IN operator, more than one row can result from this query.

Example 7.13 can also be solved using the FROM clause of the UPDATE statement. The FROM clause contains the names of tables that are involved in the UPDATE statement. All these tables must be subsequently joined. Example 7.14 shows the use of the FROM clause. This example is identical to the previous one.

> **NOTE**
>
> *The FROM clause is a Transact-SQL extension to the ANSI SQL standard.*

EXAMPLE 7.14

```
USE sample;
UPDATE works_on
  SET job = NULL
  FROM works_on, employee
  WHERE emp_lname = 'Jones'
  AND works_on.emp_no = employee.emp_no;
```

Example 7.15 illustrates the use of the CASE expression in the UPDATE statement. (For a detailed discussion of this expression, refer to Chapter 6.)

EXAMPLE 7.15

The budget of each project should be increased by a percentage (20, 10, or 5) depending on its previous amount of money. Those projects with a lower budget will be increased by the higher percentages.

```
USE sample;
UPDATE project
  SET budget = CASE
      WHEN budget >0 and budget < 100000  THEN budget*1.2
      WHEN budget >= 100000 and budget < 200000  THEN budget*1.1
      ELSE budget*1.05
      END
```

DELETE Statement

The DELETE statement deletes rows from a table. This statement has two different forms:

```
DELETE FROM table_name
  [WHERE predicate];
```

```
DELETE table_name
    FROM table_name [,...]
    [WHERE condition];
```

All rows that satisfy the condition in the WHERE clause will be deleted. Explicitly naming columns within the DELETE statement is not necessary (or allowed), because the DELETE statement operates on rows and not on columns.

EXAMPLE 7.16

Delete all managers in the **works_on** table:

```
USE sample;
DELETE FROM works_on
  WHERE job = 'Manager';
```

The WHERE clause in the DELETE statement can contain an inner query.

EXAMPLE 7.17

Mrs. Moser is on leave. Delete all rows in the database concerning her:

```
USE sample;
DELETE FROM works_on
  WHERE emp_no IN
  (SELECT emp_no
    FROM employee
    WHERE emp_lname = 'Moser');
```

```
DELETE FROM employee
  WHERE emp_lname = 'Moser';
```

Example 7.17 can also be performed using the FROM clause, as Example 7.18 shows. This clause has the same semantics as the FROM clause in the UPDATE statement.

EXAMPLE 7.18

USE sample;
DELETE works_on
    FROM works_on, employee
    WHERE works_on.emp_no = employee.emp_no
    AND emp_lname = 'Moser';

DELETE FROM employee
    WHERE emp_lname = 'Moser';

The use of the WHERE clause in the DELETE statement is optional. If the WHERE clause is omitted, all rows of a table will be deleted, as shown in Example 7.19.

EXAMPLE 7.19

USE sample;
DELETE FROM works_on;

NOTE

There is a significant difference between the DELETE and the DROP TABLE statements. The DELETE statement deletes (partially or totally) the contents of a table, whereas the DROP TABLE statement deletes both the contents and the schema of a table. Thus, after a DELETE statement, the table still exists in the database (although possibly with zero rows), but after a DROP TABLE statement, the table no longer exists.

TRUNCATE TABLE Statement

The Transact-SQL language also supports the TRUNCATE TABLE statement. This statement normally provides a "faster executing" version of the DELETE statement without the WHERE clause. The TRUNCATE TABLE statement deletes all rows from a table more quickly than does the DELETE statement because it drops the contents of the table page by page, while DELETE drops the contents row by row.

NOTE

The TRUNCATE TABLE statement is a Transact-SQL extension to the SQL standard.

The TRUNCATE TABLE statement has the form:

TRUNCATE TABLE table_name

NOTE

If you want to delete all rows from a table, use the TRUNCATE TABLE statement. This statement is significantly faster than DELETE, because it is minimally logged and there are just a few entries in the log during its execution. (Logging is discussed in detail in Chapter 13.)

The OUTPUT Clause

The result of the execution of INSERT, UPDATE, or DELETE statements always contains only the text concerning the number of modified rows ("3 rows deleted," for instance). If the content of such a result doesn't fit your needs, you can use the OUTPUT clause, which displays explicitly the rows that are inserted or updated in the table or deleted from it.

The OUTPUT clause uses the **inserted** and **deleted** tables (explained in Chapter 14) to display the corresponding result. Also, the OUTPUT clause must be used with an INTO expression to fill a table. For this reason, you use a table variable to store the result.

Example 7.20 shows how the OUTPUT statement works with a DELETE statement.

EXAMPLE 7.20

```
USE sample;
DECLARE @del_table TABLE (emp_no INT, emp_lname CHAR(20));
DELETE employee
OUTPUT DELETED.emp_no, DELETED.emp_lname INTO @del_table
WHERE emp_no > 15000;
SELECT * FROM @del_table
```

The result is

emp_no	emp_lname
25348	Smith
18316	Barrimore
29346	James
28559	Moser

First, Example 7.20 declares the table variable **@del_table** with two columns: **emp_no** and **emp_lname**. This table will be used to store the deleted rows. The syntax of the DELETE statement is enhanced with the OUTPUT option:

```
OUTPUT DELETED.emp_no, DELETED.emp_lname INTO @del_table
```

Using this option, the system stores the deleted rows in the **deleted** table, which is then copied in the **@del** table variable.

Example 7.21 shows the use of the OUTPUT option in an UPDATE statement.

EXAMPLE 7.21

```
USE sample;
DECLARE @update_table TABLE
 (emp_no INT, project_no CHAR(20),old_job CHAR(20),new_job CHAR(20));
UPDATE works_on
SET job = NULL
OUTPUT DELETED.emp_no, DELETED.project_no,
    DELETED.job, INSERTED.job INTO @update_table
WHERE job = 'Clerk';
SELECT * FROM @update_table
```

The result is

emp_no	project_no	old_job	new_job
25348	p2	Clerk	NULL
28559	p2	Clerk	NULL
9031	p3	Clerk	NULL
29346	p1	Clerk	NULL

MERGE Statement

SQL Server 2008 introduces the SQL statement called MERGE. This statement combines the sequence of conditional INSERT and UPDATE commands in a single atomic statement, depending on the existence of a record.

The main application area for MERGE is a data warehouse environment (see Part IV of this book), where tables need to be refreshed periodically with new data arriving from online transaction processing (OLTP) systems. This new data may contain changes to existing rows in tables and/or new rows that need to be inserted. If a row in the new data corresponds to an item that already exists in the table, an UPDATE statement is performed. Otherwise, an INSERT statement is performed.

Prior to SQL Server 2008, these operations were expressed either as a sequence of INSERT and UPDATE statements or as batches (see Chapter 8), where, for each row, the decision is made whether to insert or update the data. Both these techniques have performance disadvantages: the former requires multiple data scans, and the latter operates on a record-by-record basis. By extending Transact-SQL with the new statement, SQL Server 2008 overcomes the deficiencies of the old approaches and simplifies the implementation of data warehousing applications.

Examples 7.22 and 7.23 show the use of the MERGE statement.

EXAMPLE 7.22

```
USE sample;
CREATE TABLE bonus
     (pr_no CHAR(4),
        bonus SMALLINT DEFAULT 100);
INSERT INTO bonus (pr_no) VALUES ('p1');
```

Example 7.22 creates the **bonus** table, which contains one row, (p1, 100). This table will be used for merging.

EXAMPLE 7.23

```
MERGE INTO bonus B
  USING (SELECT project_no, budget
          FROM project) E
     ON (B.pr_no = E.project_no)
     WHEN MATCHED THEN
          UPDATE SET B.bonus = E.budget * 0.1
     WHEN NOT MATCHED THEN
          INSERT (B.pr_no, B.bonus)
              VALUES (E.project_no, E.budget * 0.05);
```

The MERGE statement in Example 7.23 modifies the data in the **bonus** table depending on the existing values in the **pr_no** column. If a value from the **project_no** column of the **project** table appears in the **pr_no** column of the **bonus** table, the MATCHED branch will be executed and the existing value will be updated. Otherwise, the NON MATCHED branch will be executed and the corresponding INSERT statement inserts new rows in the **bonus** table.

The content of the bonus table after the execution of the MERGE statement is as follows:

pr_no	bonus
p1	12000
p2	4750
p3	9325

From the result set, you can see that a value of the **bonus** column represents 10 percent of the original value in the case of the UPDATE statement, and 5 percent in the case of the INSERT statement.

Conclusion

Generally, there are only three SQL statements that can be used to modify a table: INSERT, UPDATE, and DELETE. They are generic in that for all types of row insertion, you use only one statement: INSERT. The same is true for the modification of columns and deletion of rows with the UPDATE and DELETE statements, respectively.

The nonstandard statement TRUNCATE TABLE is just another form of the DELETE statement, but deleting of rows is executed faster with TRUNCATE TABLE than with DELETE. The MERGE statement is basically an "UPSERT" statement: it combines the UPDATE and the INSERT statements in one statement.

Chapters 5 through 7 have introduced all SQL statements that belong to DDL and DML. Most of these statements can be grouped together to build a sequence of Transact-SQL statements. Such a sequence is the basis for *stored procedures*, which will be covered in the next chapter.

Exercises

E.7.1

Insert the data of a new employee called Julia Long, whose employee number is 11111. Her department number is not known yet.

E.7.2

Create a new table called **emp_d1_d2** with all employees who work for department d1 or d2, and load the corresponding rows from the **employee** table. Find two different, but equivalent, solutions.

E.7.3

Create a new table of all employees who entered their projects in 2007 and load it with the corresponding rows from the **employee** table.

E.7.4

Modify the job of all employees in project p1 who are managers. They have to work as clerks from now on.

E.7.5

The budgets of all projects are no longer determined. Assign all budgets the NULL value.

E.7.6

Modify the jobs of the employee with the employee number 28559. From now on she will be the manager in all her projects.

E.7.7

Increase the budget of the project where the manager has the employee number 10102. The increase is 10 percent.

E.7.8

Change the name of the department for which the employee named James works. The new department name is Sales.

E.7.9

Change the enter date for the projects for those employees who work in project p1 and belong to department Sales. The new date is 12.12.2007.

E.7.10

Delete all departments that are located in Seattle.

E.7.11

The project p3 has been finished. Delete all information concerning this project in the sample database.

E.7.12

Delete the information in the **works_on** table for all employees who work for the departments located in Dallas.

Chapter 8

Stored Procedures and User-Defined Functions

In This Chapter

- ▶ Procedural Extensions
- ▶ Stored Procedures
- ▶ User-Defined Functions

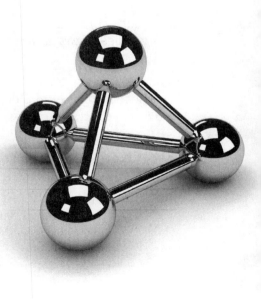

his chapter introduces batches and routines. A batch is a sequence of Transact-SQL statements and procedural extensions. A routine can be either a stored procedure or a user-defined function (UDF). The beginning of the chapter introduces all procedural extensions supported by Database Engine. After that, procedural extensions are used, together with Transact-SQL statements, to show how batches can be implemented. A batch can be stored as a database object, as either a stored procedure or a UDF. Some stored procedures are written by users, and others are provided by Microsoft and are referred to as *system stored procedures*. In contrast to user-defined stored procedures, UDFs return a value to a caller. All routines can be written either in Transact-SQL or in another programming language such as C# or Visual Basic. The end of the chapter introduces a new feature of SQL Server 2008—table-valued parameters.

Procedural Extensions

The preceding chapters introduced Transact-SQL statements that belong to the data definition language and the data manipulation language. Most of these statements can be grouped together to build a batch. As previously mentioned, a *batch* is a sequence of Transact-SQL statements and procedural extensions that are sent to the database system for execution together. The number of statements in a batch is limited by the size of the compiled batch object. The main advantage of a batch over a group of singleton statements is that executing all statements at once brings significant performance benefits.

There are a number of restrictions concerning the appearance of different Transact-SQL statements inside a batch. The most important is that the data definition statements CREATE VIEW, CREATE PROCEDURE, and CREATE TRIGGER must each be the only statement in a batch.

NOTE
To separate DDL statements from one another, use the GO statement.

The following sections describe each procedural extension of the Transact-SQL language separately.

Block of Statements

A block allows the building of units with one or more Transact-SQL statements. Every block begins with the BEGIN statement and terminates with the END statement, as shown in the following example:

```
BEGIN
statement_1
```

```
    statement_2
    ...
    END
```

A block can be used inside the IF statement to allow the execution of more than one statement, depending on a certain condition (see Example 8.1).

IF Statement

The Transact-SQL statement IF corresponds to the statement with the same name that is supported by almost all programming languages. IF executes one Transact-SQL statement (or more, enclosed in a block) *if* a Boolean expression, which follows the keyword IF, evaluates to true. If the IF statement contains an ELSE statement, a second group of statements can be executed if the Boolean expression evaluates to false.

NOTE

*Before you start to execute batches, stored procedures, and UDFs in this chapter, please re-create the entire **sample** database.*

EXAMPLE 8.1

```
USE sample;
IF (SELECT COUNT(*)
        FROM works_on
        WHERE project_no = 'p1'
        GROUP BY project_no ) > 3
    PRINT 'The number of employees in the project p1 is 4 or more'
    ELSE BEGIN
        PRINT 'The following employees work for the project p1'
        SELECT emp_fname, emp_lname
        FROM employee, works_on
        WHERE employee.emp_no = works_on.emp_no
        AND project_no = 'p1'
    END
```

Example 8.1 shows the use of a block inside the IF statement. The Boolean expression in the IF statement,

```
(SELECT COUNT(*)
        FROM works_on
        WHERE project_no = 'p1'
        GROUP BY project_no) > 3
```

is evaluated to true for the **sample** database. Therefore, the single PRINT statement in the IF part is executed. Notice that this example uses a subquery to return the number of rows (using the COUNT aggregate function) that satisfy the WHERE condition (project_no='p1'). The result of Example 8.1 is

The number of employees in the project p1 is four or more

NOTE

The ELSE part of the IF statement in Example 8.1 contains two statements: PRINT and SELECT. Therefore, the block with the BEGIN and END statements is required to enclose the two statements. (The PRINT statement is another statement that belongs to procedural extensions; it returns a user-defined message.)

WHILE Statement

The WHILE statement repeatedly executes one Transact-SQL statement (or more, enclosed in a block) *while* the Boolean expression evaluates to true. In other words, if the expression is true, the statement (or block) is executed, and then the expression is evaluated again to determine if the statement (or block) should be executed again. This process repeats until the expression evaluates to false.

A block within the WHILE statement can optionally contain one of two statements used to control the execution of the statements within the block: BREAK or CONTINUE. The BREAK statement stops the execution of the statements inside the block and starts the execution of the statement immediately following this block. The CONTINUE statement stops only the current execution of the statements in the block and starts the execution of the block from its beginning.

Example 8.2 shows the use of the WHILE statement.

EXAMPLE 8.2

```
USE sample;
WHILE (SELECT SUM(budget)
        FROM project) < 500000
    BEGIN
      UPDATE project SET budget = budget*1.1
      IF (SELECT MAX(budget)
          FROM project) > 240000
       BREAK
     ELSE CONTINUE
     END
```

In Example 8.2, the budget of all projects will be increased by 10 percent until the sum of budgets is greater than $500,000. However, the repeated execution will be stopped if the budget of one of the projects is greater than $240,000. The execution of Example 8.2 gives the following output:

(3 rows affected)
(3 rows affected)
(3 rows affected)

Local Variables

Local variables are an important procedural extension to the Transact-SQL language. They are used to store values (of any type) within a batch or a routine. They are "local" because they can only be referenced within the same batch in which they were declared. (Database Engine also supports global variables, which are described in Chapter 4.)

Every local variable must be defined using the DECLARE statement. (For the syntax of the DECLARE statement, see Example 8.3.) The definition of each variable contains its name and the corresponding data type. Variables are always referenced in a batch using the prefix @. The assignment of a value to a local variable is done using the following:

▶ The special form of the SELECT statement

▶ The SET statement

The usage of both statements for a value assignment is demonstrated in Example 8.3.

EXAMPLE 8.3

```
USE sample;
DECLARE @avg_budget MONEY, @extra_budget MONEY
     SET @extra_budget = 15000
     SELECT @avg_budget = AVG(budget) FROM project
     IF (SELECT budget
          FROM project
          WHERE project_no='p1') < @avg_budget
    BEGIN
     UPDATE project
          SET budget = budget + @extra_budget
          WHERE project_no ='p1'
     PRINT 'Budget for p1 increased by @extra_budget'
    END
    ELSE PRINT 'Budget for p1 unchanged'
```

The result is

Budget for p1 increased by @extra_budget

The batch in Example 8.3 calculates the average of all project budgets and compares this value with the budget of project p1. If the latter value is smaller than the calculated value, the budget of project p1 will be increased by the value of the local variable **@extra_budget**.

Miscellaneous Procedural Statements

The procedural extensions of the Transact-SQL language also contain the following statements:

▶ RETURN

▶ GOTO

▶ RAISEERROR

▶ WAITFOR

The RETURN statement has the same functionality inside a batch as the BREAK statement inside WHILE. This means that the RETURN statement causes the execution of the batch to terminate and the first statement following the end of the batch to begin executing.

The GOTO statement branches to a label, which stands in front of a Transact-SQL statement within a batch. The RAISEERROR statement generates a user-defined error message and sets a system error flag. A user-defined error number must be greater than 50000. (All error numbers <= 50000 are system defined and are reserved by Database Engine.) The error values are stored in the global variable @@ERROR.

The WAITFOR statement defines either the time interval (if the DELAY option is used) or a specified time (if the TIME option is used) that the system has to wait before executing the next statement in the batch. The syntax of this statement is

WAITFOR {DELAY 'time' | TIME 'time' | TIMEOUT 'timeout' }

The DELAY option tells the database system to wait until the specified amount of time has passed. TIME specifies a time in one of the acceptable formats for temporal data. (Example 13.5 in Chapter 13 shows the use of the WAITFOR statement.) TIMEOUT specifies the amount of time, in milliseconds, to wait for a message to arrive in the queue.

Handling Events with TRY and CATCH Statements

Versions of SQL Server previous to SQL Server 2005 require error handling code after every Transact-SQL statement that might produce an error. (You can handle errors using the @@ERROR global variable. Example 13.1 in Chapter 13 shows the use of this variable.) Starting with SQL Server 2005, you can capture and handle exceptions using two statements, TRY and CATCH. This section first explains what "exception" means and then discusses how these two statements work.

An exception is a problem (usually an error) that prevents the continuation of a program. With such a problem you cannot continue processing, because there is not enough information needed to handle the problem. For this reason, the existing problem will be relegated to another part of the program, which will handle the exception.

The role of the TRY statement is to capture the exception. (Because this process usually comprises several statements, the term "TRY block" typically is used instead of "TRY statement.") If an exception occurs within the TRY block, the part of the system called the exception handler delivers the exception to the other part of the program, which will handle the exception. This program part is denoted by the keyword CATCH and is therefore called the CATCH block.

NOTE

Exception handling using the TRY and CATCH statements is the common way that modern programming languages like C# and Java treat errors.

Exception handling with the TRY and CATCH blocks gives a programmer a lot of benefits, such as:

▶ Exceptions provide a clean way to check for errors without cluttering code.

▶ Exceptions provide a mechanism to signal errors directly rather than using some side effects.

▶ Exceptions can be seen by the programmer and checked during the compilations process.

Example 8.4 shows how exception handling with the TRY/CATCH works. It shows how you can use exception handling to insert all statements in a batch or to roll back the entire statement group if an error occurs. The example is based on the referential integrity between the **department** and **employee** tables. For this reason, you have to create both tables using the PRIMARY KEY and FOREIGN KEY constraints, as done in Example 5.11 in Chapter 5.

EXAMPLE 8.4

```
USE sample;
BEGIN TRY
  BEGIN TRANSACTION
    insert into employee values(11111, 'Ann', 'Smith','d2');
    insert into employee values(22222, 'Matthew', 'Jones','d4'); -- referential integrity error
    insert into employee values(33333, 'John', 'Barrimore', 'd2');
  COMMIT TRANSACTION
  PRINT 'Transaction committed'
END TRY
BEGIN CATCH
  ROLLBACK
  PRINT 'Transaction rolled back'
END CATCH
```

After the execution of the batch in Example 8.4, all three statements in the batch won't be executed at all, and the output of this example is

Transaction rolled back

The execution of Example 8.4 works as follows. The first INSERT statement is executed successfully. Then, the second statement causes the referential integrity error. Because all three statements are written inside the TRY block, the exception is "thrown" and the exception handler starts the CATCH block. CATCH rolls back all statements and prints the corresponding message. For this reason, the content of the **employee** table won't change.

NOTE

The statements BEGIN TRANSACTION, COMMIT TRANSACTION, and ROLLBACK are Transact-SQL statements concerning transactions. These statements start, commit, and roll back transactions, respectively. See Chapter 13 for the discussion of these statements and transactions generally.

Stored Procedures

A *stored procedure* is a special kind of batch written in Transact-SQL, using the SQL language and its procedural extensions. The main difference between a batch and a stored procedure is that the latter is stored as a database object. In other words, stored procedures are saved on the server side to improve the performance and consistency of repetitive tasks.

Database Engine supports stored procedures and system procedures. Stored procedures are created in the same way as all other database objects—that is, by using the DDL. System procedures are provided with Database Engine and can be used to access and modify the information in the system catalog. This section describes (user-defined) stored procedures, while system procedures are explained in different chapters of the book (see, for example, Chapters 14 and 21).

When a stored procedure is created, an optional list of parameters can be defined. The procedure accepts the corresponding arguments each time it is invoked. Stored procedures can optionally return a value, which displays the user-defined information or, in the case of an error, the corresponding error message.

A stored procedure is precompiled before it is stored as an object in the database. The precompiled form is stored in the database and used whenever the stored procedure is executed. This property of stored procedures offers an important benefit: the repeated compilation of a procedure is (almost always) eliminated, and the execution performance is therefore increased. This property of stored procedures offers another benefit concerning the volume of data that must be sent to and from the database system. It might take less than 50 bytes to call a stored procedure containing several thousand bytes of statements. The accumulated effect of this savings when multiple users are performing repetitive tasks can be quite significant.

Stored procedures can also be used for the following purposes:

▶ To control access authorization

▶ To create an audit trail of activities in database tables

The use of stored procedures provides security control above and beyond the use of the GRANT and REVOKE statements (see Chapter 12), which define different access privileges for a user. This is because the authorization to execute a stored procedure is independent of the authorization to modify the objects that the stored procedure contains, as described in the next section.

Stored procedures that audit write and/or read operations concerning a table are an additional security feature of the database. With the use of such procedures, the database administrator can track modifications made by users or application programs.

Creation and Execution of Stored Procedures

Stored procedures are created with the CREATE PROCEDURE statement, which has the following syntax:

```
CREATE PROC[EDURE] [schema_name.]proc_name
[({@param1} type1 [ VARYING] [= default1] [OUTPUT])] {, ...}
```

[WITH {RECOMPILE | ENCRYPTION | EXECUTE AS 'user_name'}]
[FOR REPLICATION]
AS batch | EXTERNAL NAME method_name

schema_name is the name of the schema to which the ownership of the created stored procedure is assigned. **proc_name** is the name of the new stored procedure.

@param1 is a parameter, while **type1** specifies its data type. The parameter in a stored procedure has the same logical meaning as the local variable for a batch. Parameters are values passed from the caller of the stored procedure and are used within the stored procedure. **default1** specifies the optional default value of the corresponding parameter. (Default can also be NULL.)

The OUTPUT option indicates that the parameter is a return parameter and can be returned to the calling procedure or to the system (see Example 8.8).

As you already know, the precompiled form of a procedure is stored in the database and used whenever the stored procedure is executed. If you want to generate the precompiled form each time the procedure is executed, use the WITH RECOMPILE option.

NOTE

The use of the WITH RECOMPILE option destroys one of the most important benefits of the stored procedures: the performance advantage gained by a single precompilation. For this reason, the WITH RECOMPILE option should be used only when database objects used by the stored procedure are modified frequently or when the parameters used by the stored procedure are volatile.

The EXECUTE AS clause specifies the security context under which to execute the stored procedure after it is accessed. By specifying the context in which the procedure is executed, you can control which user account the database engine uses to validate permissions on objects referenced by the procedure.

By default, only the members of the **sysadmin** fixed server role, and the **db_owner** and **db_ddladmin** fixed database roles, can use the CREATE PROCEDURE statement. However, the members of these roles may assign this privilege to other users by using the GRANT CREATE PROCEDURE statement. (For the discussion of user permissions, fixed server roles, and fixed database roles, see Chapter 12.)

Example 8.5 shows the creation of the simple stored procedure for the **project** table.

EXAMPLE 8.5

```
USE sample;
GO
CREATE PROCEDURE increase_budget (@percent INT=5)
     AS UPDATE project
          SET budget = budget + budget*@percent/100;
```

NOTE

The GO statement is used to separate two batches. (The CREATE PROCEDURE statement must be the first statement in the batch.)

The stored procedure **increase_budget** increases the budgets of all projects for a certain percentage value that is defined using the parameter **@percent**. The procedure also defines the default value (5), which is used if there is no argument at the execution time of the procedure.

NOTE

It is possible to create stored procedures that reference nonexistent tables. This feature allows you to debug procedure code without creating the underlying tables first, or even connecting to the target server.

In contrast to "base" stored procedures that are placed in the current database, it is possible to create temporary stored procedures that are always placed in the temporary system database called **tempdb**. You might create a temporary stored procedure to avoid executing a particular group of statements repeatedly within a connection. You can create *local* or *global* temporary procedures by preceding the procedure name with a single pound sign (**#proc_name**) for local temporary procedures and a double pound sign (**##proc_name**, for example) for global temporary procedures. A local temporary stored procedure can be executed only by the user who created it, and only during the same connection. A global temporary procedure can be executed by all users, but only until the last connection executing it (usually the creator's) ends.

The life cycle of a stored procedure has two phases: its creation and its execution. Each procedure is created once and executed many times. The EXECUTE statement executes an existing procedure. The execution of a stored procedure is allowed for each user who either is the owner of or has the EXECUTE privilege for the procedure (see Chapter 12). The EXECUTE statement has the following syntax:

```
[[EXEC[UTE]] [@return_status =] {proc_name
    | @proc_name_var}
    {[[@parameter1 =] value | [@parameter1=] @variable [OUTPUT]] | DEFAULT}..
    [WITH RECOMPILE]
```

All options in the EXECUTE statement, other than **return_status**, have the equivalent logical meaning as the options with the same names in the CREATE PROCEDURE statement. **return_status** is an optional integer variable that stores the return status of a procedure. The value of a parameter can be assigned using either a value (**value**) or a local variable (**@variable**). The order of parameter values is not relevant if they are named, but if they are not named, parameter values must be supplied in the order defined in the CREATE PROCEDURE statement.

The DEFAULT clause supplies the default value of the parameter as defined in the procedure. When the procedure expects a value for a parameter that does not have a defined default and either a parameter is missing or the DEFAULT keyword is specified, an error occurs.

NOTE

When the EXECUTE statement is the first statement in a batch, the word "EXECUTE" can be omitted from the statement. Despite this, it would be safer to include this word in every batch you write.

Example 8.6 shows the use of the EXECUTE statement.

EXAMPLE 8.6

```
USE sample;
EXECUTE increase_budget 10;
```

The EXECUTE statement in Example 8.6 executes the stored procedure **increase_budget** (Example 8.5) and increases the budgets of all projects by 10 percent each.

Example 8.7 shows the creation of a procedure that references the tables **employee** and **works_on**.

EXAMPLE 8.7

```
USE sample;
GO
CREATE PROCEDURE modify_empno (@old_no INTEGER, @new_no INTEGER)
    AS UPDATE employee
        SET emp_no = @new_no
        WHERE emp_no = @old_no
    UPDATE works_on
        SET emp_no = @new_no
        WHERE emp_no = @old_no
```

The procedure **modify_empno** in Example 8.7 demonstrates the use of stored procedures as part of the maintenance of the referential integrity (in this case, between the **employee** and **works_on** tables). Such a stored procedure can be used inside the definition of a trigger, which actually maintains the referential integrity (see Example 14.3).

Example 8.8 shows the use of the OUTPUT clause.

EXAMPLE 8.8

```
USE sample;
GO
CREATE PROCEDURE delete_emp @employee_no INT, @counter INT OUTPUT
    AS SELECT @counter = COUNT(*)
        FROM works_on
         WHERE emp_no = @employee_no
    DELETE FROM employee
        WHERE emp_no = @employee_no
     DELETE FROM works_on
        WHERE emp_no = @employee_no
```

This stored procedure can be executed using the following statements:

```
DECLARE @quantity INT
EXECUTE delete_emp @employee_no=28559, @counter=@quantity OUTPUT
```

The preceding example contains the creation of the **delete_emp** procedure as well as its execution. This procedure calculates the number of projects on which the employee (with the employee number **@employee_no**) works. The calculated value is then assigned to the **@counter** parameter. After the deletion of all rows with the assigned employee number from the **employee** and **works_on** tables, the calculated value will be assigned to the **@quantity** variable.

> **NOTE**
>
> *The value of the parameter will be returned to the calling procedure if the OUTPUT option is used. In Example 8.8, the **delete_emp** procedure passes the @**counter** parameter to the calling statement, so the procedure returns the value to the system. Therefore, the @**counter** parameter must be declared with the OUTPUT option in the procedure as well as in the EXECUTE statement.*

Changing the Structure of Stored Procedures

Database Engine also supports the ALTER PROCEDURE statement, which modifies the structure of a stored procedure. The ALTER PROCEDURE statement is usually used to modify Transact-SQL statements inside a procedure. All options of the ALTER PROCEDURE statement correspond to the options with the same name in the CREATE PROCEDURE statement. The main purpose of this statement is to avoid reassignment of existing privileges for the stored procedure.

NOTE

Database Engine supports the CURSOR data type. You use this data type to declare cursors inside a stored procedure. A cursor is a programming construct that is used to store the output of a query (usually a set of rows) and to allow end-user applications to display the rows record by record. A detailed discussion of cursors is out of the scope of this book.

A stored procedure (or a group of stored procedures with the same name) is removed using the DROP PROCEDURE statement. Only the owner of the stored procedure and the members of the **db_owner** and **sysadmin** fixed roles can remove the procedure.

Database Engine contains several catalog views in relation to stored procedures. The most important views are **sys.objects** and **sys.procedures**. All rows of **sys.objects** in which the value of the **type** column is equal to *P* are related to stored procedures. The **sys.procedures** view inherits several columns of **sys.objects** and contains additional information concerning their auto-execution.

Stored Procedures and CLR

In the versions previous to SQL Server 2005, you can use only Transact-SQL statements to create stored procedures. SQL Server 2005 introduced a new feature, Common Language Runtime (CLR), that allows you to develop different database objects (stored procedures, user-defined functions, triggers, user-defined aggregates, and user-defined types) using C# and Visual Basic. CLR also allows you to execute these database objects using the common run-time system.

NOTE

*You enable and disable the use of CLR through the **clr_enabled** option of the **sp_configure** system procedure. Execute the RECONFIGURE statement to update the running configuration value.*

Example 8.9 shows how you can enable the use of CLR.

EXAMPLE 8.9

```
USE sample;
EXEC sp_configure 'clr_enabled',1
RECONFIGURE
```

To implement, compile, and store procedures using CLR, you have to execute the following four steps in the given order:

1. Implement a stored procedure using C# (or Visual Basic) and compile the program, using the corresponding compiler.

2. Use the CREATE ASSEMBLY statement to create the corresponding executable file.
3. Store the procedure as a server object using the CREATE PROCEDURE statement.
4. Execute the procedure using the EXECUTE statement.

NOTE

Microsoft suggests using Transact-SQL as the default language for creating server-side objects.

Figure 8-1 shows how CLR works. You use a development environment such as Visual Studio to implement your program. After the implementation, start the C# or Visual Basic compiler to generate the object code. This code will be stored in a .dll file, which is the source for the CREATE ASSEMBLY statement. After the execution of this statement, you get the intermediate code. In the next step you use the CREATE PROCEDURE statement to store the executable as a database object. Finally, the stored procedure can be executed using the already-introduced EXECUTE statement.

Examples 8.10 through 8.14 demonstrate the whole process just described. Example 8.10 shows the C# program that will be used to demonstrate how you apply CLR to implement and deploy stored procedures.

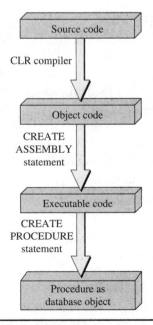

Figure 8-1   *The flow diagram for the execution of a CLR stored procedure*

EXAMPLE 8.10

```
using System;
using System.Data;
using System.Data.Sql;
using System.Data.SqlClient;
using Microsoft.SqlServer.Server;
using System.Data.SqlTypes;
public partial class StoredProcedures
{ [SqlProcedure]
    public static int GetEmployeeCount()
  {
    int iRows;
    SqlConnection conn = new SqlConnection("Context Connection=true");
    conn.Open();
    SqlCommand sqlCmd = conn.CreateCommand();
    sqlCmd.CommandText = "select count(*) as 'Employee Count' " + "from employee";
    iRows = (int)sqlCmd.ExecuteScalar();
    conn.Close();
    return iRows;
  }
};
```

This program uses a query to calculate the number of rows in the **employee** table. The **using** directives at the beginning of the program specify namespaces, such as **System.Data**. These directives allow you to specify class names in the source program without referencing the corresponding namespace. The **StoredProcedures** class is then defined, which is written with a [**SqlProcedure**] attribute. This attribute tells the compiler that the class is a stored procedure. Inside that class is defined a method called **GetEmployeeCount()**. The connection to the database system is established using the **conn** instance of the **SQLConnection** class. The **Open()** method is applied to that instance to open the connection. The **CreateCommand()** method, applied to **conn**, allows you to access the **SqlCommand** instance called **sqlCmd**.

The following lines of code

```
sqlCmd.CommandText =
"select count(*) as 'Employee Count' " + "from employee";
iRows = (int)sqlCmd.ExecuteScalar();
```

use the SELECT statement to find the number of rows in the **employee** table and to display the result. The command text is specified by setting the **CommandText** property of the **SqlCmd** instance returned by the call to the **CreateCommand()** method.

Next, the **ExecuteScalar()** method of the **SqlCommand** instance is called. This returns a scalar value, which is finally converted to the **int** data type and assigned to the **iRows** variable.

Example 8.11 shows the first step in deploying stored procedures using CLR.

EXAMPLE 8.11

```
csc /target:library GetEmployeeCount.cs
    /reference:"C:\Program Files\Microsoft SQL Server\MSSQL10.MSSQLSERVER\
MSSQL\Binn\sqlaccess.dll"
```

Example 8.11 demonstrates how to compile the C# method called **GetEmployeeCount** (Example 8.10). (Actually, this command can be used generally to compile any C# program, if you set the appropriate name for the source program.) **csc** is the command that is used to invoke the C# compiler. You invoke the **csc** command at the Windows command line. Before starting the command, you have to specify the location of the compiler using the PATH environment variable. At the time of writing this book, the C# compiler (the **csc .exe** file) can be found in the C:\WINDOWS\Microsoft.NET\Framework\v2.050727 directory. (You should select the appropriate version of the compiler.)

The **/target** option specifies the name of the C# program, while the **/reference** option defines the .dll file, which is necessary for the compilation process.

Example 8.12 shows the next step in creating the stored procedure. (Use SQL Server Management Studio to execute this statement.)

EXAMPLE 8.12

```
USE sample;
GO
CREATE ASSEMBLY GetEmployeeCount
    FROM 'C:\GetEmployeeCount.dll' WITH PERMISSION_SET = SAFE
```

The CREATE ASSEMBLY statement uses the managed code as the source to create the corresponding object, against which CLR stored procedures, UDFs, and triggers can be created. This statement has the following syntax:

```
CREATE ASSEMBLY assembly_name [ AUTHORIZATION owner_name ]
    FROM { dll_file}
    [WITH PERMISSION_SET = { SAFE | EXTERNAL_ACCESS | UNSAFE }]
```

assembly_name is the name of the assembly. The optional AUTHORIZATION clause specifies the name of a role as owner of the assembly. The FROM clause specifies the path where the assembly being uploaded is located. (Example 8.12 copied the .dll file generated from the source program from the **Framework** directory to the root of the C: drive.)

The WITH PERMISSION SET clause is a very important clause of the CREATE ASSEMBLY statement and should always be set. It specifies a set of code access permissions granted to the assembly. SAFE is the most restrictive permission set. Code executed by an assembly with this permission cannot access external system resources, such as files. EXTERNAL_ACCESS allows assemblies to access certain external system resources, while UNSAFE allows unrestricted access to resources, both within and outside the database system.

> **NOTE**
>
> *In order to store the information concerning assembly code, a user must have the ability to execute the CREATE ASSEMBLY statement. The user (or role) executing the statement is the owner of the assembly. It is possible to assign an assembly to another user by using the AUTHORIZATION clause of the CREATE SCHEMA statement.*

Database Engine also supports the ALTER ASSEMBLY and DROP ASSEMBLY statements. You can use the ALTER ASSEMBLY statement to refresh the system catalog to the latest copy of .NET modules holding its implementation. This statement also adds or removes files associated with the corresponding assembly. The DROP ASSEMBLY statement removes the specified assembly and all its associated files from the current database.

Example 8.13 creates the stored procedures based on the managed code implemented in Example 8.10.

EXAMPLE 8.13

```
USE sample;
GO
CREATE PROCEDURE GetEmployeeCount
AS EXTERNAL NAME GetEmployeeCount.StoredProcedures.GetEmployeeCount
```

The CREATE PROCEDURE statement in Example 8.13 is different from the same statement used in Examples 8.5 and 8.7, because it contains the EXTERNAL NAME option. This option specifies that the code is generated using CLR. The name in this clause is a three-part name:

assembly_name.class_name.method_name

- ▶ **assembly_name** is the name of the assembly (see Example 8.12).

- ▶ **class_name** is the name of the public class (see Example 8.10).

- ▶ **method_name**, which is optional, is the name of the method, which is specified inside the class.

Example 8.14 is used to execute the **GetEmployeeCount** procedure.

EXAMPLE 8.14

USE sample;
DECLARE @ret INT
EXECUTE @ret=GetEmployeeCount
PRINT @ret

The PRINT statement returns the current number of the rows in the **employee** table.

User-Defined Functions

In programming languages, there are generally two types of routines:

▶ Stored procedures

▶ User-defined functions (UDFs)

As discussed in the previous major section of this chapter, stored procedures are made up of several statements that have zero or more input parameters but usually do not return any output parameters. In contrast, functions always have one return value. This section describes the creation and use of UDFs.

Creation and Execution of User-Defined Functions

UDFs are created with the CREATE FUNCTION statement, which has the following syntax:

CREATE FUNCTION [schema_name.]function_name
    [({@param } type [= default]) {,...}
    RETURNS {scalar_type | [@variable] TABLE}
    [WITH {ENCRYPTION | SCHEMABINDING}
    [AS] {block | RETURN (select_statement)}

schema_name is the name of the schema to which the ownership of the created UDF is assigned. **function_name** is the name of the new function. **@param** is an input parameter, while **type** specifies its data type. Parameters are values passed from the caller of the UDF and are used within the function. **default** specifies the optional default value of the corresponding parameter. (Default can also be NULL.)

The RETURNS clause defines a data type of the value returned by the UDF. This data type can be any of the standard data types supported by the database system, including the TABLE data type. (The only standard data types that you cannot use is the TIMESTAMP data type.)

UDFs are either scalar-valued or table-valued. A scalar-valued function returns an atomic (scalar) value. This means that in the RETURNS clause of a scalar-valued function, you specify one of the standard data types. Functions are table-valued if the RETURNS clause returns a set of rows (see the next subsection).

The WITH ENCRYPTION option encrypts the information in the system catalog that contains the text of the CREATE FUNCTION statement. In that case, you cannot view the text used to create the function. (Use this option to enhance the security of your database system.)

The alternative clause, WITH SCHEMABINDING, binds the UDF to the database objects that it references. Any attempt to modify the structure of the database object that the function references fails. (The binding of the function to the database objects it references is removed only when the function is altered, so the SCHEMABINDING option is not specified anymore.)

Database objects that are referenced by a function must fulfill the following conditions if you want to use the SCHEMABINDING clause during the creation of that function:

▶ All views and UDFs referenced by the function must be schema-bound.

▶ All database objects (tables, views, or UDFs) must be in the same database as the function.

block is the BEGIN/END block that contains the implementation of the function. The final statement of the block must be a RETURN statement with an argument. (The value of the argument is the value returned by the function.) In the body of a BEGIN/END block, only the following statements are allowed:

▶ Assignment statements such as SET

▶ Control-of-flow statements such as WHILE and IF

▶ DECLARE statements defining local data variables

▶ SELECT statements containing SELECT lists with expressions that assign to variables that are local to the function

▶ INSERT, UPDATE, and DELETE statements modifying variables of the TABLE data type that are local to the function

By default, only the members of the **sysadmin** fixed server role and the **db_owner** and **db_ddladmin** fixed database roles can use the CREATE FUNCTION statement.

However, the members of these roles may assign this privilege to other users by using the GRANT CREATE FUNCTION statement (see Chapter 12).

Example 8.15 shows the creation of the function called **compute_costs**.

EXAMPLE 8.15

```
-- This function computes additional total costs that arise
-- if budgets of projects increase
USE sample;
GO
CREATE FUNCTION compute_costs (@percent INT =10)
   RETURNS DECIMAL(16,2)
 BEGIN
  DECLARE @additional_costs DEC (14,2), @sum_budget dec(16,2)
  SELECT @sum_budget = SUM (budget) FROM project
  SET @additional_costs = @sum_budget * @percent/100
  RETURN @additional_costs
 END
```

The function **compute_costs** computes additional costs that arise when all budgets of projects increase. The only input variable, **@percent**, specifies the percentage of increase of budgets. The BEGIN/END block first declares two local variables: **@additional_costs** and **@sum_budget**. The function then assigns to **@sum_budget** the sum of all budgets, using the special form of the SELECT statement. After that, the function computes total additional costs and returns this value using the RETURN statement.

Invoking User-Defined Functions

Each UDF can be invoked in Transact-SQL statements, such as SELECT, INSERT, UPDATE, or DELETE. To invoke a function, specify the name of it, followed by parentheses. Within the parentheses, you can specify one or more arguments. *Arguments* are values or expressions that are passed to the input parameters that are defined immediately after the function name. When you invoke a function, and all parameters have no default values, you must supply argument values for all of the parameters and you must specify the argument values in the same sequence in which the parameters are defined in the CREATE FUNCTION statement.

Example 8.16 shows the use of the **compute_costs** function (Example 8.15) in a SELECT statement.

EXAMPLE 8.16

```
USE sample;
SELECT project_no, project_name
   FROM project
   WHERE budget < dbo.compute_costs(25)
```

The result is

project_no	project_name
p2	Gemini

The SELECT statement in Example 8.16 displays names and numbers of all projects where the budget is lower than the total additional costs of all projects for a given percentage.

NOTE

Each function used in a Transact-SQL statement must be specified using its two-part name—that is, **schema_name.function_name**.

TABLE Data Type

As you already know, functions are table-valued if the RETURNS clause returns a set of rows. Depending on how the body of the function is defined, table-valued functions can be classified as inline or multistatement functions. If the RETURNS clause specifies TABLE with no accompanying list of columns, the function is an inline function. Inline functions return the result set of a SELECT statement as a variable of the TABLE data type (see Example 8.17). A multistatement table-valued function includes a name followed by TABLE. (The name defines an internal variable of the type TABLE.) You can use this variable to insert rows into it and then return the variable as the return value of the function.

Example 8.17 shows a function that returns a variable of the TABLE data type.

EXAMPLE 8.17

```
USE sample;
GO
CREATE FUNCTION employees_in_project (@pr_number CHAR(4))
   RETURNS TABLE
   AS RETURN (SELECT emp_fname, emp_lname
           FROM works_on, employee
             WHERE employee.emp_no = works_on.emp_no
           AND project_no = @pr_number)
```

The **employees_in_project** function is used to display names of all employees that belong to a particular project. The input parameter **@pr_number** specifies a project number. While the function generally returns a set of rows, the RETURNS clause contains the TABLE data type. (Note that the BEGIN/END block in Example 8.17 must be omitted, while the RETURN clause contains a SELECT statement.)

Example 8.18 shows the use of the **employees_in_project** function.

EXAMPLE 8.18

```
USE sample;
SELECT *
   FROM employees_in_project('p3')
```

The result is

emp_fname	emp_lname
Ann	Jones
Elsa	Bertoni
Elke	Hansel

Table-Valued Parameters

In all versions previous to SQL Server 2008, it was difficult to send many parameters to a routine. In that case you had to use a temporary table, insert the values into it, and then call the routine. Since SQL Server 2008, you can use table-valued parameters to simplify this task. These parameters are used to deliver a result set to the corresponding routine.

Example 8.19 shows the use of a table-valued parameter.

EXAMPLE 8.19

```
CREATE TYPE departmentType AS TABLE
 (dept_no CHAR(4),dept_name CHAR(25),location CHAR(30));
GO
CREATE TABLE #dallasTable
 (dept_no CHAR(4),dept_name CHAR(25),location CHAR(30));
GO
CREATE PROCEDURE insertProc
 @Dallas departmentType READONLY
 AS SET NOCOUNT ON
 INSERT INTO #dallasTable (dept_no, dept_name, location)
  SELECT * FROM @Dallas
```

```
GO
DECLARE @Dallas AS departmentType;
INSERT INTO @Dallas( dept_no, dept_name, location)
SELECT * FROM department
WHERE location = 'Dallas'
EXEC insertProc @Dallas;
```

Example 8.19 first defines the type called **departmentType** as a table. This means that its type is the TABLE data type, so rows can be inserted in it. In the **insertProc** procedure, the **@Dallas** variable, which is of the **departmentType** type, is specified. (The READONLY clause specifies that the content of the table variable cannot be modified.) In the subsequent batch, data is added to the table variable, and after that the procedure is executed. The procedure, when executed, inserts rows from the table variable into the temporary table **#dallasTable**. The content of the temporary table is as follows:

dept_no	dept_name	location
d1	Research	Dallas
d3	Marketing	Dallas

The use of table-valued parameters gives you the following benefits:

▶ It simplifies the programming model in relation to routines.

▶ It reduces the round trips to the server.

▶ The resulting table can have different numbers of rows.

The next section shows how table-valued function can be used with the APPLY operator.

Table-Valued Functions and APPLY

The APPLY operator can be combined with a table-valued function to produce the result, which is similar to the result set of a join operation between two tables. The following two examples shows how you can use APPLY.

EXAMPLE 8.20

```
-- generate function
CREATE FUNCTION dbo.fn_getjob(@empid AS INT)
    RETURNS TABLE AS
```

```
RETURN
    SELECT job
      FROM works_on
      WHERE emp_no = @empid
      AND job IS NOT NULL  AND project_no = 'p1';
```

The **fn_getjob**() function in Example 8.20 returns set of rows from the **works_on** table. This result set is "joined" in the following example with the content of the **employee** table.

EXAMPLE 8.21

```
-- use CROSS APPLY
SELECT E.emp_no, emp_fname, emp_lname, job
 FROM employee as E
   CROSS APPLY dbo.fn_getjob(E.emp_no) AS A
-- use OUTER APPLY
SELECT E.emp_no, emp_fname, emp_lname, job
 FROM employee as E
   OUTER APPLY dbo.fn_getjob(E.emp_no) AS A
```

The result is

emp_no	emp_fname	emp_lname	job
10102	Ann	Jones	Analyst
29346	James	James	Clerk
9031	Elsa	Bertoni	Manager
28559	Sybill	Moser	NULL

emp_no	emp_fname	emp_lname	job
25348	Matthew	Smith	NULL
10102	Ann	Jones	Analyst
18316	John	Barrimore	NULL
29346	James	James	Clerk
9031	Elsa	Bertoni	Manager
2581	Elke	Hansel	NULL
28559	Sybill	Moser	NULL

In the first query of Example 8.21 the result set of the table-valued function **fn_getjob**() is "joined" with the content of the **employee** table using the CROSS APPLY operator. **fn_getjob**() acts as the right input, and the **employee** table acts as the left input. The right input is evaluated for each row from the left input, and the rows produced are combined for the final output.

The second query is similar to the first one, but uses OUTER APPLY, which corresponds to the outer join operation of two tables.

Changing the Structure of UDFs

The Transact-SQL language also supports the ALTER FUNCTION statement, which modifies the structure of a UDF. This statement is usually used to remove the schema binding. All options of the ALTER FUNCTION statement correspond to the options with the same name in the CREATE FUNCTION statement.

A UDF is removed using the DROP FUNCTION statement. Only the owner of the function (or the members of the **db_owner** and **sysadmin** fixed database roles) can remove the function.

The **sys.objects** catalog view displays the information about existing UDFs. (See the values 'FN' [for scalar functions], 'FS' [for CLR functions], 'FT' [for table-valued functions], and 'IF' [for inline table-valued functions] in the **type** column.) The system procedure **sp_helptext** also provides relevant information about UDFs.

User-Defined Functions and CLR

The discussion in "Stored Procedures and CLR" earlier in the chapter is also valid for UDFs. The only difference is that you use the CREATE FUNCTION statement (instead of CREATE PROCEDURE) to store a UDF as a database object. Also, UDFs are used in different context from that of stored procedures, because UDFs always have a return value.

Example 8.22 shows the C# program used to demonstrate how UDFs are compiled and deployed.

EXAMPLE 8.22

```
using System;
using System.Data.Sql;
using System.Data.SqlTypes;
public class budgetPercent
{ private const float percent = 10;
    public static SqlDouble computeBudget(float budget)
    { float budgetNew;
      budgetNew = budget * percent;
      return budgetNew;
    }
};
```

The C# source program in Example 8.22 shows a UDF that calculates the new budget of a project using the old budget and the percental increase. (The description of the C# program is omitted, because this program is analog to the program in Example 8.10.) Example 8.23 shows the CREATE ASSEMBLY statement, which is necessary if you want to create a database object.

EXAMPLE 8.23

```
USE sample;
GO
CREATE ASSEMBLY computeBudget
FROM 'C:\computeBudget.dll'
WITH PERMISSION_SET = SAFE
```

The CREATE FUNCTION statement in Example 8.24 stores the **computeBudget** assembly as the database object, which can be used subsequently in data manipulation statements, such as SELECT, as shown in Example 8.25.

EXAMPLE 8.24

```
USE sample;
GO
CREATE FUNCTION ReturncomputeBudget (@budget Real)
RETURNS FLOAT
AS EXTERNAL NAME computeBudget.budgetPercent.computeBudget
```

EXAMPLE 8.25

```
USE sample;
SELECT dbo.ReturncomputeBudget (321.50)
```

The result is 3215.

NOTE

You can place an existing UDF at several places inside a SELECT statement. Example 8.16 shows its use with the WHERE clause, Example 8.18 in the FROM clause, and Example 8.25 in the SELECT list.

Conclusion

A stored procedure is a special kind of batch, written either in the Transact-SQL language or using Common Language Runtime (CLR). Stored procedures are used for the following purposes:

- ► To control access authorization
- ► To create an audit trail of activities in database tables
- ► To enforce consistency and business rules with respect to data modification
- ► To improve the performance of repetitive tasks

User-defined functions have a lot in common with stored procedures. The main difference is that UDFs do not support parameters but return a single data value, which can also be a table.

Microsoft suggests using Transact-SQL as the default language for creating server-side objects. (CLR is recommended as an alternative only when your program contains a lot of computation.)

The next chapter discusses system catalog of Database Engine.

Exercises

E.8.1

Create a batch that inserts 3000 rows in the **employee** table. The values of the **emp_no** column should be unique and between 1 and 3000. All values of the columns **emp_lname, emp_fname**, and **dept_no** should be set to 'Jane', ' Smith', and ' d1', respectively.

E.8.2

Modify the batch E.8.1 so that the values of the **emp_no** column should be generated randomly using the RAND function. (Hint: Use the temporal system functions DATEPART and GETDATE to generate the random values.)

Chapter 9

System Catalog

In This Chapter

▶ **Introduction to the System Catalog**

▶ **General Interfaces**

▶ **Proprietary Interfaces**

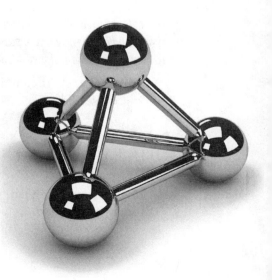

his chapter discusses the system catalog of Database Engine. The introduction is followed by a description of the structure of several catalog views, each of which allows you to retrieve metadata. The use of dynamic management views and dynamic management functions is also covered in the first part of the chapter. Four alternative ways for retrieving metadata information are discussed in the second part: system stored procedures, system functions, property functions, and the information schema.

Introduction to the System Catalog

The system catalog consists of tables describing the structure of objects such as databases, base tables, views, and indices. (These tables are called *system base tables*.) Database Engine frequently accesses the system catalog for information that is essential for the system to function properly.

Database Engine distinguishes the system base tables of the **master** database from those of a particular user-defined database. System tables of the **master** database belong to the system catalog, while system tables of a particular database form the database catalog. Therefore, system base tables occur only once in the entire system (if they belong exclusively to the **master** database), while others occur once in each database, including the **master** database.

In all relational database systems, system base tables have the same logical structure as base tables. As a result, the same Transact-SQL statements used to retrieve information in the base tables can also be used to retrieve information in system base tables.

NOTE

Since SQL Server 2005, the use of system base tables changed significantly. Generally, the system base tables cannot be accessed directly any more: you have to use existing interfaces to query the information from the system catalog. The only way to access system information from system base tables directly is to make a connection using the dedicated administrator connection (See Chapter 2).

There are several different interfaces that you can use to access the information in the system base tables:

▶ **Catalog views**   Present the primary interface to the metadata stored in system base tables. (Metadata is data that describes the attributes of objects in a database system.)

▶ **Dynamic management views (DMVs) and functions (DMFs)**   Generally used to observe active processes and the contents of the memory.

▶ **Information schema**   A standardized solution for the access of metadata that gives you a general interface not only for Database Engine, but for all existing relational database systems (assuming that the system supports the information schema).

▶ **System and property functions**   Allow you to retrieve system information. The difference between these two function types is mainly in their structure. Also, property functions can return more information than system functions.

▶ **System procedures**   Some system procedures can be used to access and modify the content of the system base tables.

Figure 9-1 shows a simplified form of Database Engine's system information and different interfaces that you can use to access it.

NOTE

This chapter shows you just an overview of the system catalog and the ways in which you can access metadata. Particular catalog views, as well as all other interfaces, that are specific for different topics (such as indices, security, etc.) are discussed in the corresponding chapters.

These interfaces can be grouped in two groups: *general* interfaces (catalog views, DMVs and DMFs, and the information schema), and *proprietary* interfaces in relation to Database Engine (system procedures and system and property functions).

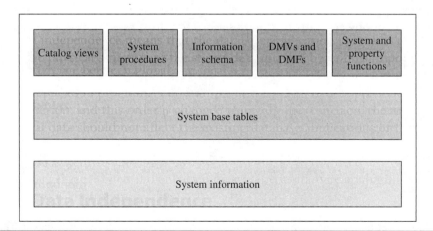

Figure 9-1   *Graphical presentation of different interfaces for the system catalog*

NOTE

"General" means that all relational database systems support such interfaces, but use different terminology. For instance, in Oracle's terminology, catalog views and DMVs are called "data dictionary views" and "V$ views," respectively.

The following section describes general interfaces. Proprietary interfaces are discussed later in the chapter.

General Interfaces

As already stated, the following interfaces are general interfaces:

- ▶ Catalog views
- ▶ DMVs and DMFs
- ▶ Information schema

Catalog Views

SQL Server 2005 introduced catalog views as a new interface to retrieve system information from the system catalog. Catalog views are the most general interface to the metadata and provide the most efficient way to obtain customized forms of this information (see Examples 9.1 through 9.3).

Catalog views belong to the **sys** schema, so you have to use the schema name when you access one of objects. This section describes the three most important catalog views:

- ▶ sys.objects
- ▶ sys.columns
- ▶ sys.database_principals

NOTE

You can find the description of other views either in different chapters of this book or in Books Online.

The **sys.objects** catalog view contains a row for each user-defined object in relation to the user's schema. There are two other catalog views that show similar information: **sys.system_objects** and **sys.all_objects**. The former contains a row for each system

Column Name	Description
name	Object name
object_id	Object identification number, unique within a database
schema_id	ID of the schema in which the object is contained
type	Object type

Table 9-1   *Selected Columns of the sys.objects Catalog View*

object, while the latter shows the union of all schema-scoped user-defined objects and system objects. (All three catalog views have the same structure.) Table 9-1 lists and describes the most important columns of the **sys.objects** catalog view.

The **sys.columns** catalog view contains a row for each column of an object that has columns, such as tables and views. Table 9-2 lists and describes the most important columns of the **sys.columns** catalog view.

The **sys.database_principals** catalog view contains a row for each security principal (that is, user, group, or role in a database). (For a detailed discussion of principals, see Chapter 12.) Table 9-3 lists and describes the most important columns of the **sys.objects** catalog view.

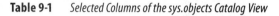

NOTE

SQL Server 2008 still supports so-called compatibility views for backward compatibility with SQL Server 2000. Each compatibility view has the same name (and the same structure) as the corresponding system base table of the SQL Server 2000 system. Compatibility views are a deprecated feature and will be removed in a future version of SQL Server.

Querying Catalog Views

As already stated in this chapter, all system tables have the same structure as base tables. Because system tables cannot be referenced directly, you have to query catalog views, which correspond to particular system tables. Examples 9.1 through 9.3 use existing catalog views to demonstrate how information concerning database objects can be queried.

Column Name	Description
object_id	ID of the object to which this column belongs
name	Column name
column_id	ID of the column (unique within the object)

Table 9-2   *Selected Columns of the sys.columns Catalog View*

Column Name	Description
name	Name of principal
principal_id	ID of principal (unique within the database)
type	Principal type

Table 9-3   *Selected Columns of the sys.database_principals Catalog View*

EXAMPLE 9.1

Get the table ID, user ID, and table type of the **employee** table:

```
USE sample;
SELECT object_id, principal_id, type
    FROM sys.objects
    WHERE name = 'employee';
```

The result is

object_id	principal_id	type
530100929	NULL	U

The **object_id** column of the **sys.objects** catalog view displays the unique ID number for the corresponding database object. The NULL value in the **principal_id** column tells that the object's owner is the same as the owner of the schema. *U* in the **type** column stands for the user (table).

EXAMPLE 9.2

Get the names of all tables of the **sample** database that contain the **project_no** column:

```
USE sample;
SELECT sys.objects.name
  FROM sys.objects INNER JOIN sys.columns
  ON sys.objects.object_id = sys.columns.object_id
  WHERE sys.objects.type = 'U'
  AND sys.columns.name = 'project_no';
```

The result is

name
project
works_on

EXAMPLE 9.3

Who is the owner of the **employee** table?

SELECT sys.database_principals.name
FROM sys.database_principals INNER JOIN sys.objects
ON sys.database_principals.principal_id = sys.objects.schema_id
WHERE sys.objects.name = 'employee'
AND sys.objects.type = 'U';

The result is

name
dbo

Dynamic Management Views and Functions

Dynamic management views (DMVs) and functions (DMFs) return server state information that can be used to observe active processes and therefore to tune system performance or to monitor the actual system state. In contrast to catalog views, the DMVs and DMFs are based on internal structures of the system.

NOTE

The main difference between catalog views and DMVs is in their application: catalog views display the static information about metada, while DMVs (and DMFs) are used to access dynamic properties of the system. In other words, you use DMVs to get insightful information about the database, individual queries, or an individual user.

DMVs and DMFs belong to the **sys** schema and their names start with the prefix **dm_**, followed by a text string that indicates the category to which the particular DMV or DMF belongs.

The following list identifies and describes some of these categories:

▶ **dm_db_***   Contains information about databases and their objects

▶ **dm_tran_***   Contains information in relation to transactions

▶ **dm_io_***   Contains information about I/O activities

▶ **dm_exec_***   Contains information related to the execution of user code

NOTE

Many DMVs and DMFs are discussed in subsequent chapters of the book. For instance, index-related DMVs and DMFs, which belong to the db_db_* category, are explained in the next chapter, while transaction-related DMVs and DMFs are discussed in Chapter 13.

Information Schema

The information schema consists of read-only views that provide information about all tables, views, and columns of Database Engine to which you have access. In contrast to the system catalog that manages the metadata applied to the system as a whole, the information schema primarily manages the environment of a database.

NOTE

The information schema was originally introduced in the SQL92 standard. Database Engine provides information schema views so that applications developed on other database systems can obtain its system catalog without having to use it directly. These standard views use different terminology, so when you interpret the column names, be aware that catalog = database and domain = user-defined data type.

The following sections provide a description of the most important information schema views.

Information_schema.tables

The **Information_schema.tables** view contains one row for each table in the current database to which the user has access. The view retrieves the information from the system catalog using the **sys.objects** catalog view. Table 9-4 lists and describes the four columns of this view.

Column	Description
TABLE_CATALOG	The name of the catalog (database) to which the view belongs
TABLE_SCHEMA	The name of the schema to which the view belongs
TABLE_NAME	The table name
TABLE_TYPE	The type of the table (can be BASE TABLE or VIEW)

Table 9-4   *The Information_schema.tables View*

Column	Description
TABLE_CATALOG	The name of the catalog (database) to which the column belongs
TABLE_SCHEMA	The name of the schema to which the column belongs
TABLE_NAME	The name of the table to which the column belongs
COLUMN_NAME	The column name
ORDINAL_POSITION	The column identification number
DATA_TYPE	The data type of the column

Table 9-5   *The Information_schema.columns View*

Information_schema.columns

The **Information_schema.columns** view contains one row for each column in the current database accessible by the user. The view retrieves the information from the **sys.columns** and **sys.objects** catalog views. Table 9-5 lists and describes the six most important columns of this view.

Information_schema.referential_constraints

The **information_schema.referentail_constraints** view contains one row for each referential constraint owned by the current user and defined in the current database. Table 9-6 lists and describes the most important columns of this view.

Column	Description
CONSTRAINT_CATALOG	The name of the catalog (database) to which the referential constraint belongs
CONSTRAINT_SCHEMA	The name of the schema to which the referential constraint belongs
CONSTRAINT_NAME	The constraint name
DELETE_RULE	The action that is taken if a DELETE statement violates referential integrity defined by this constraint (could be NO ACTION, CASCADE, SET NULL, or SET DEFAULT)
UPDATE_RULE	The action that is taken if an UPDATE statement violates referential integrity defined by this constraint (could be NO ACTION, CASCADE, SET NULL, or SET DEFAULT)

Table 9-6   *The Information_schema.referential_constraints View*

Proprietary Interfaces

The previous section describes the use of the general interfaces for accessing system base tables. You can also retrieve system information using one of the following proprietary mechanisms of Database Engine:

► System stored procedures

► System functions

► Property functions

The following sections describe these interfaces.

System Procedures

System procedures are used to provide many administrative and end-user tasks, such as renaming database objects, identifying users, and monitoring authorization and resources. Almost all existing system procedures access system base tables to retrieve and modify system information.

NOTE

The most important property of system procedures is that they can be used for easy and reliable modification of system base tables.

This section describes two system procedures: **sp_help** and **sp_depends**. Depending on the subject matter of the chapters, certain system procedures were discussed in previous chapters, and additional procedures will be discussed in later chapters of the book.

The **sp_help** system procedure displays information about one or more database objects. The name of any database object or data type can be used as a parameter of this procedure. If **sp_help** is executed without any parameter, information on all database objects of the current database will be displayed.

The **sp_depends** system procedure displays the dependency information among tables, views, triggers, and stored procedures.

Example 9.4 displays the dependency information for the modify_empno stored procedure. (This user-defined procedure is created in Chapter 8, Example 8.7.)

EXAMPLE 9.4

```
USE sample;
EXEC sp_depends @objname = 'modify_empno';
```

The result is

name	type	updated	selected	column
dbo.works_on	user table	yes	yes	emp_no
dbo.employee	user table	yes	yes	emp_no

The **sp_depends** system procedure in Example 9.4 displays the dependency information of the **modify_empno** procedure (created in Example 8.7 in Chapter 8). This information contains the names of the tables that are referenced in the procedure (**works_on** and **employee**).

System Functions

System functions are described in Chapter 5. Some of them can be used to access system base tables. Example 9.5 shows two SELECT statements that retrieve the same information using different interfaces.

```
USE sample;
SELECT object_id
  FROM sys.objects
  WHERE name = 'employee';
SELECT object_id('employee');
```

The second SELECT statement in Example 9.5 uses the system function **object_id** to retrieve the ID of the **employee** table. (This information can be stored in a variable and used when calling a command, or a system procedure, with the object's ID as a parameter.)

The following system functions, among others, access system base tables:

- ▶ OBJECT_ID(object_name)
- ▶ OBJECT_NAME(object_id)
- ▶ USER_ID([user_name])
- ▶ USER_NAME([user_id])
- ▶ DB_ID([db_name])
- ▶ DB_NAME([db_id])
- ▶ INDEX_COL(table, index_id, col_id)

As Example 9.6 demonstrates, using the INDEX_COL system function is much easier than retrieving the same information using the corresponding catalog views, for instance. (The INDEX_COL function displays the name of the column on which an index key is based.)

EXAMPLE 9.6

SELECT INDEX_COL('employee', 1,1) AS index_col_1

If there is a clustered index for the **emp_no** column of the **employee** table, the result is the following:

index_col_1
emp_no

Example 9.6 retrieves the clustered index (index_id = 1) of the first column (col_id = 1) of the **employee** table.

Property Functions

Property functions return properties of database objects, data types, or files. Generally, property functions can return more information than system functions can return, because property functions support dozens of properties (as parameters), which you can specify explicitly.

Almost all property functions return one of the following three values: 0, 1, or NULL. If the value is 0, the object does not have the specified property. If the value is 1, the object has the specified property. Similarly, the value NULL specifies that the existence of the specified property for the object is unknown to the system.

Database Engine supports, among others, the following property functions:

▶ OBJECTPROPERTY(id, property)

▶ COLUMNPROPERTY(id, column, property)

▶ FILEPROPERTY(filename, property)

▶ TYPEPROPERTY(type, property)

The OBJECTPROPERTY function returns information about objects in the current database (see Exercise E.9.2). The COLUMNPROPERTY function returns information about a column or procedure parameter. The FILEPROPERTY function returns the specified filename and property value for a given filename and property name.

The TYPEPROPERTY function returns information about a data type. (The description of existing properties for each property function can be found in Books Online.) The use of several property functions will be demonstrated in different chapters of this book.

Conclusion

The system catalog is a collection of system base tables belonging to the **master** database and existing user databases. Generally, system base tables cannot be queried directly by a user. Database Engine supports several different interfaces that you can use to access the information from the system catalog. Catalog views are the most general interface that you can apply to obtain system information. Dynamic management views (DMVs) and functions (DMFs) are similar to catalog views, but you use them to access dynamic properties of the system. System stored procedures provide easy and reliable access to system base tables. It is strongly recommended to exclusively use system procedures for modification of system information.

The information schema is a collection of views defined on system base tables that provide unified access to the system catalog for all database applications developed on other database systems. The use of the information schema is recommended if you intend to port your system from one database system to another.

The next chapter introduces you to database indices.

Exercises

E.9.1

Using catalog views, find the operating system path and filename of the **sample** database.

E.9.2

Using the OBJECTPROPERTY property function, find out whether the clustered index for the **employee** table of the **sample** database exists.

E.9.3

Using catalog views, find how many integrity constraints are defined for the **employee** table of the **sample** database.

E.9.4

Using catalog views, find out if there is any integrity constraint defined for the **dept_no** column of the **employee** table.

E.9.5

Using the information schema, display all user tables that belong to the **AdventureWorks** database.

E.9.6

Using the information schema, find all columns of the **employee** table with their ordinal positions and the corresponding data types.

Chapter 10

Indices

In This Chapter

- ▶ Introduction
- ▶ Transact-SQL and Indices
- ▶ Guidelines for Creating and Using Indices
- ▶ Indices on Computed Columns

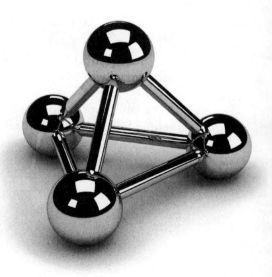

This chapter describes indices and their role in optimizing the response time of queries. The first part of the chapter discusses how indices are stored and the existing forms of them. The main part of the chapter explains three Transact-SQL statements pertaining to indices: CREATE INDEX, ALTER INDEX, and DROP INDEX. After that, index fragmentation and its impact on the performance of the system will be explained. The next part of the chapter gives you several general recommendations for how and when indices should be created. At the end of the chapter indices on computed columns will be described.

Introduction

Database systems generally use indices to provide fast access to relational data. An index is a separate physical data structure that enables queries to access one or more data rows fast. Proper tuning of indices is therefore a key for query performance.

An index is in many ways analogous to a book index. When you are looking for a topic in a book, you use its index to find the page(s) where that topic is described. Similarly, when you search for a row of a table, Database Engine uses an index to find its physical location. However, there are two main differences between a book index and a database index:

▶ As a book reader, you can decide whether or not to use the book's index. This possibility generally does not exist if you use a database system: the system component called query optimizer decides whether or not to use an existing index. (A user can manipulate the use of indices by using index hints, but their use is recommended only in a few special cases. The optimizer and index hints are described in Chapter 20.)

▶ A particular book's index is edited together with the book and does not change at all. This means that you can find a topic exactly on the page where it is determined in the index. By contrast, a database index can change each time the corresponding data is changed.

If a table does not have an appropriate index, the database system uses the table scan method to retrieve rows. *Table scan* means that each row is retrieved and examined in sequence (from first to last) and returned in the result set if the search condition in the WHERE clause evaluates to true. Therefore, all rows are fetched according to their physical memory location. This method is less efficient than an index access, as explained next.

Indices are stored in additional data structures called *index pages*. (The structure of index pages is very similar to the structure of data pages, as you will see in Chapter 15.) For each indexed row there is an *index entry*, which is stored in an index page.

Each index entry consists of the index key plus a pointer. For this reason, each index entry is significantly shorter than the corresponding row. Therefore, the number of index entries per (index) page is significantly higher than the number of rows per (data) page. This index property plays a very important role, because the number of I/O operations required to traverse the index structure is significantly lower than the number of I/O operations required to traverse the corresponding data pages. In other words, a table scan would probably result in many more I/O operations than a corresponding index access would.

Database Engine's indices are constructed using the B$^+$-tree data structure. As its name suggests, a B$^+$-tree has a treelike structure in which all of the bottommost nodes (leaf nodes) are the same number of levels away from the top (root node) of the tree. This property is maintained even when new data is added or deleted from the indexed column.

Figure 10-1 illustrates the structure of the B$^+$-tree and the direct access to the row of the **employee** table with the value 25348 in its **emp_no** column. (It is assumed that the **employee** table has an index on the **emp_no** column.) You can also see that each B$^+$-tree consists of a root node, leaf nodes, and zero or more intermediate nodes.

Searching for the data value 25348 can be executed as follows: Starting from the root of the B$^+$-tree, a search proceeds for a lowest key value greater than or equal to the value to be retrieved. Therefore, the value 29346 is retrieved from the root node; then

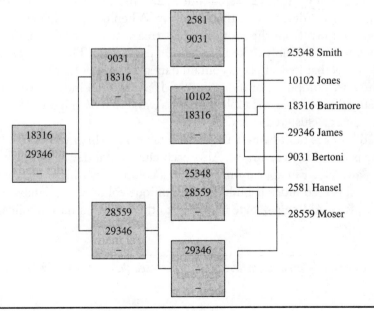

Figure 10-1   *B$^+$-tree for the emp_no column of the employee table*

the value 28559 is fetched from the intermediate level, and the searched value, 25348, is retrieved at the leaf level. With the help of the respective pointers, the appropriate row is retrieved. (An alternative, but equivalent, search method would be to search for smaller or equal values.)

Index access is generally the preferred and obviously advantageous method for accessing tables with many rows. With index access, it takes only a few I/O operations to find any row of a table in a very short time, whereas sequential access requires much more time to find a row physically stored at the end of the table.

NOTE

Besides convenient B+-tree indices and indices on computed columns, which will be described in this chapter, SQL Server supports other kinds of indices, such as partitioned, XML, and full-text indices. Partitioned indices are used with partitioned tables and are described in Chapter 26. Indices in relation to XML are explained in detail in Chapter 28. Full-text indices are out of the scope of this book.

The two existing index types, clustered and nonclustered indices, are described next, after which you will find out how to create an index.

Clustered Indices

A clustered index determines the physical order of the data in a table. Database Engine allows the creation of a single clustered index per table, because the rows of the table cannot be physically ordered more than one way. When using a clustered index, the system navigates down from the root of the B+-tree structure to the leaf nodes, which are linked together in a doubly linked list called a page chain. The important property of a clustered index is that its leaf pages contain data pages. (All other levels of a clustered index structure are composed of index pages.) If a clustered index is (implicitly or explicitly) defined for a table, the table is called a *clustered table*. Figure 10-2 shows the B+-tree structure of a clustered index.

A clustered index is built by default for each table, for which you define the primary key using the primary key constraint. Also, each clustered index is unique by default— that is, each data value can appear only once in a column for which the clustered index is defined. If a clustered index is built on a nonunique column, the database system will force uniqueness by adding a 4-byte identifier to the rows that have duplicate values.

NOTE

Clustered indices allow very fast access in the case that a query searches for a range of values (see Chapter 20).

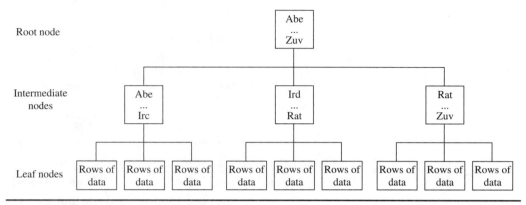

Root node

Intermediate
nodes

Leaf nodes

Figure 10-2   *Physical structure of a clustered index*

Nonclustered Indices

A nonclustered index has the same index structure as a clustered index, with two
important differences:

▶ A nonclustered index does not change the physical order of the rows in the table.

▶ The leaf pages of a nonclustered index consist of an index key plus a bookmark.

The physical order of rows in a table will not be changed if one or more nonclustered
indices are defined for that table. For each nonclustered index, Database Engine creates
an additional index structure that is stored in index pages.

A bookmark of a nonclustered index shows where to find the row corresponding
to the index key. The bookmark part of the index key can have two forms, depending
on the form of the table—that is, the table can be a clustered table or a heap. (In SQL
Server terminology, a *heap* is a table without a clustered index.) If a clustered index
exists, the bookmark of the nonclustered index shows the B+-tree structure of the table's
clustered index. If the table has no clustered index, the bookmark is identical to the
row identifier (RID), which contains three parts: the address of the file to which the
corresponding table belongs, the address of the physical block (page) in which the row
is stored, and the offset, which is the position of the row inside the page.

As the preceding discussion indicates, searching for data using a nonclustered index
could proceed in either of two different ways, depending on the form of the table:

▶ **Heap**   Traversal of the nonclustered index structure is followed by the retrieval of
the row using the RID.

▶ **Clustered table**   Traversal of the nonclustured index structure is followed by
traversal of the corresponding clustered index.

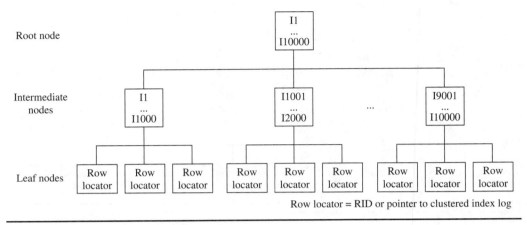

Root node

Intermediate nodes

Leaf nodes

Row locator = RID or pointer to clustered index log

Figure 10-3 *Structure of a nonclustered index*

In both cases, the number of I/O operations is quite high, so you should design a nonclustered index with care and only when you are sure that there will be significant performance gains by using it. Figure 10-3 shows the B⁺-tree structure of a nonclustered index.

Transact-SQL and Indices

Now that you are familiar with the physical structure of indices, this section describes how you can create, alter, and drop indices, obtain index fragmentation information, and edit index information, all of which will prepare you for the subsequent discussion of how you can use indices to improve performance of the system.

Creating Indices

The CREATE INDEX statement creates an index for the particular table. The general form of this statement is

```
CREATE [UNIQUE] [CLUSTERED |NONCLUSTERED] INDEX index_name
    ON table_name (column1 [ASC | DESC] ,...)
        [ INCLUDE ( column_name [ ,... ] ) ]
[WITH
        [FILLFACTOR=n]
        [[, ] PAD_INDEX = {ON | OFF}]
        [[, ] DROP_EXISTING = {ON | OFF}]
        [[, ] SORT_IN_TEMPDB = {ON | OFF}]
```

```
[[, ] IGNORE_DUP_KEY = {ON | OFF}]
[[, ] ALLOW_ROW_LOCKS = {ON | OFF}]
[[, ]ALLOW_PAGE_LOCKS = {ON | OFF}]
[[, ] STATISTICS_NORECOMPUTE = {ON | OFF}]
[[, ]ONLINE = {ON | OFF}]]
[ON file_group | "default"]
```

index_name identifies the name of the created index. An index can be established for one or more columns of a single table (**table_name**). **column1** is the name of the column for which the index is created. (As you can see from the syntax of the CREATE INDEX statement, you can specify an index for several columns of a table.) Database Engine supports indices on views too. Such views, called *indexed views*, are discussed in the next chapter.

NOTE

Each column of a table, except those with the text/image data types, can be indexed. This means that columns with VARBINARY(MAX), BIGINT, and SQL_VARIANT data types can be indexed, too.

An index can be either single or composite. A single index has one column, whereas a composite index is built on more than one column. Each composite index has certain restrictions concerning its length and number of columns. The maximum size of an index is 900 bytes, while the index can contain up to 16 columns.

The UNIQUE option specifies that each data value can appear only once in an indexed column. For a unique composite index, the combination of data values of all columns in each row must be unique. If UNIQUE is not specified, duplicate values in the indexed column(s) are allowed.

The CLUSTERED option specifies a clustered index. The NONCLUSTERED option (the default) specifies that the index does not change the order of the rows in the table. Database Engine allows a maximum of 249 nonclustered indices per table.

Database Engine has been enhanced to support indices with descending order on column values. The ASC option after the column name specifies that the index is created on the ascending order of the column's values, while DESC specifies the descending order. This gives you more flexibility for using an index. Descending indices should be used when you create a composite index on columns that have opposite sorting directions.

The INCLUDE option allow you to specify the nonkey columns, which are added to the leaf pages of the nonclustered index. Column names cannot be repeated in the INCLUDE list and cannot be used simultaneously as both key and nonkey columns. To understand the benefit of the INCLUDE option, you have to know what a *covering index* is. Significant performance gains can be achieved when *all* columns in a query are included in the index, because the query optimizer can locate all the column values within the index pages without having to access table data. This feature is called a covering index or covered query. So, if you include additional nonkey columns in the leaf pages of the nonclustered index, more queries will be covered and their performance will be significantly better. (Further discussion of this topic, as well as an example of how the query optimizer handles a covering index, can be found later in this chapter in the section "Covering Index.")

FILLFACTOR=n defines the storage percentage for each index page at the time the index is created. You can set the value of FILLFACTOR from 1 to 100. If the value of **n** is set to 100, each index page will be 100 percent filled—that is, the existing index leaf pages as well as nonleaf pages will have no space for the insertion of new rows. Therefore, this value is recommended only for static tables. (The default value, 0, also indicates that the leaf index pages are filled and the intermediate nonleaf pages contain one free entry each.)

If you set the FILLFACTOR option to a value between 1 and 99, the new index structure will be created with leaf pages that are not completely full. The bigger the value of FILLFACTOR, the smaller the space that is left free on an index page. For instance, setting FILLFACTOR to 60 means that 40 percent of each leaf index page is left free for future insertion of index rows. (Index rows will be inserted when you execute either the INSERT or the UPDATE statement.) For this reason, the value 60 could be a reasonable value for tables with rather frequent data modification. For all values of the FILLFACTOR option between 1 and 99, the intermediate nonleaf pages contain one free entry each.

NOTE

The FILLFACTOR value is not maintained—that is, it specifies only how much storage space is reserved with the existing data at the time the storage percentage is defined. If you want to reestablish the original value of the FILLFACTOR option, you need to use the ALTER INDEX statement, which is described later in this chapter.

The PAD_INDEX option is tightly connected to the FILLFACTOR option. The FILLFACTOR option mainly specifies the percentage of space that is left free on leaf index pages. On the other hand, the PAD_INDEX option specifies that the FILLFACTOR setting should be applied to the index pages as well as to the data pages in the index.

The DROP_EXISTING option allows you to enhance performance when re-creating a clustered index on a table that also has a nonclustered index. See the section 'Rebuilding an Index' later in the chapter for more details.

The SORT_IN_TEMPDB option is used to place into the **tempdb** system database the data from intermediate sort operations used while creating the index. This can result in a performance benefits if the **tempdb** database is placed on another disk drive from the data itself. (DROP_EXISTING is discussed in the section "Rebuilding an Index" later in the chapter.)

The IGNORE_DUP_KEY option causes the system to ignore the attempt to insert duplicate values in the indexed column(s). This option should be used only to avoid the termination of a long transaction in cases when the INSERT statement inserts duplicate data in the indexed column(s). If this option is activated and an INSERT statement attempts to insert rows that would violate the uniqueness of the index, the database system returns a warning rather than causing the entire statement to fail. Database Engine does *not* insert the rows that would add duplicate key values; it merely ignores those rows and adds the rest. (If this options is not set, the statement as a whole will be aborted.)

The ALLOW_ROW_LOCKS option specifies that the system uses row locks when this option is activated (set to ON). Similarly, the ALLOW_PAGE_LOCKS option specifies that the system uses page locks when this option is set to ON. (For the description of page and row locks, see Chapter 13.)

The STATISTICS_NORECOMPUTE option specifies that statistics of the specified index should not be automatically recomputed. The ON option creates either the specified index on the default file group ("default") or on the specified file group (**file_group**).

If you activate the ONLINE option, you can create, rebuild, or drop an index online. This option allows concurrent modifications to the underlying table or clustered index data and any associated indices during index execution. For example, while a clustered index is being rebuilt, you can continue to make updates to the underlying data and perform queries against the data. (This means that exclusive locks on the underlying data are not held during index rebuilding.)

NOTE

*Before you start to execute queries in this chapter, re-create the entire **sample** database.*

Example 10.1 shows the creation of a nonclustered index.

EXAMPLE 10.1

Create an index for the **emp_no** column of the **employee** table:

```
USE sample;
CREATE INDEX i_empno ON employee (emp_no);
```

Example 10.2 shows the creation of a unique composite index.

EXAMPLE 10.2

Create a composite index for the columns **emp_no** and **project_no** on the **works_on** table. The compound values in both columns must be unique. Eighty percent of each index leaf page should be filled.

```
USE sample;
CREATE UNIQUE INDEX i_empno_prno
      ON works_on (emp_no, project_no)
      WITH FILLFACTOR= 80;
```

The creation of a unique index for a column is not possible if the column already contains duplicate values. The creation of such an index is possible if each existing data value (including the NULL value) occurs only once. Also, any attempt to insert or modify an existing data value into a column with an existing unique index will be rejected by the system.

Obtaining Index Fragmentation Information

During the life cycle of an index, it can become *fragmented*, meaning the storage of data in its pages is done inefficiently. There are two forms of index fragmentation: internal and external. Internal fragmentation specifies the amount of data, which is stored within each page. External fragmentation occurs when the logical order of the pages is wrong.

To get information concerning internal index fragmentation, you use either the dynamic management view (DMV) called **sys.dm_db_index_physical_stats** or the DBCC SHOWCONTIG command. This section discusses only the DMV, because DBCC SHOWCONTIG is a deprecated feature.

sys.dm_db_index_physical_stats returns size and fragmentation information for the data and indices of the specified table. For each index, one row is returned for each level of the B$^+$-tree. Using this DMV, you can obtain information about the degree of fragmentation of rows on data pages. You can use this information to decide whether reorganization of the data is necessary.

Example 10.3 shows how you can use the **sys.dm_db_index_physical_stats** view. (You need to drop all existing indices on the **works_on** table before you start the batch.)

EXAMPLE 10.3

```
DECLARE @db_id INT;
DECLARE @tab_id INT;
DECLARE @ind_id INT;
```

```
SET @db_id = DB_ID('sample');
SET @tab_id = OBJECT_ID('employee');
SELECT avg_fragmentation_in_percent, avg_page_space_used_in_percent
 FROM sys.dm_db_index_physical_stats
(@db_id, @tab_id, NULL, NULL, NULL)
```

As you can see from Example 10.3, the **sys.dm_db_index_physical_stats** view has five parameters. The first three specify the IDs of the current database, table, and index, respectively. The forth specifies the partition ID (see Chapter 26), and the last one specifies the scan level that is used to obtain statistics. (You can always use NULL to specify the default value of the particular parameter.)

This view has several columns, of which **avg_fragmentation_in_percent** and **avg_page_space_used_in_percent** are the most important. The former specifies the average fragmentation in percent, while the latter defines the percentage of the used space.

Editing Index Information

After you have viewed the index fragmentation information, as discussed in the previous section, you can use the following system features to edit that information and to edit other index information:

- ▶ **sys.indexes** catalog view
- ▶ **sys.index_columns** catalog view
- ▶ **sp_helpindex** system procedure
- ▶ OBJECTPROPERTY property function
- ▶ SQL Server Management Studio
- ▶ **sys.dm_db_index_usage_stats** DMV
- ▶ **sys.dm_db_missing_index_details** DMV

The **sys.indexes** catalog view contains a row for each index and a row for each table without a clustered index. The most important columns of this view are **object_id**, **name**, and **index_id**. **object_id** is the name of the database object to which the index belongs, while **name** and **index_id** are the name and the ID of that index, respectively.

The **sys.index_columns** catalog view contains a row per column that is part of an index or a heap. This information can be used together with the information from the **sys.indexes** catalog view to obtain further properties of a specific index.

sp_helpindex displays all indices on a table as well as column statistics. The syntax of this procedure is

sp_helpindex [@db_object =] 'name',

where **db_object** is the name of a table.

The OBJECTPROPERTY property function has two properties in relation to indices: **IsIndexed** and **IsIndexable**. The former informs you whether a table or view has an index, while the latter specifies whether a table or view can be indexed.

To edit information about an existing index using SQL Server Management Studio, choose the database in the **Databases** folder and select **Tables**. Expand the **Indexes** folder. The list of all existing indices for that table is shown. After you double-click one of the indices, the system shows you the **Index Properties** dialog box with all properties of that index. (You can also use Management Studio to create a new index or drop an existing one.)

The **sys.dm_db_index_usage_stats** View returns counts of different types of index operations and the time each type of operation was last performed. Every individual seek, lookup, or update on the specified index by one query execution is counted as a use of that index and increments the corresponding counter in this DMV. That way you can get general information about how often an index is used i.e. indices which are used more heavily than the others.

The **sys.dm_db_missing_index_details** View returns detailed information about missing indices. The most important columns of this DMV are **index_handle** and **object_id**. The former identifies a particular missing index, while the latter specifies the table where the index is missing.

Altering Indices

Database Engine is one of a few database systems that support the ALTER INDEX statement. This statement can be used for index maintenance activities. The syntax of the ALTER INDEX statement is very similar to the syntax of the CREATE INDEX statement. In other words, this statement allows you to change the settings for the following options: ALLOW_ROW_LOCKS, ALLOW_PAGE_LOCKS, IGNORE_DUP_KEY, and STATISTICS_NORECOMPUTE.

In addition to the preceding options, the ALTER INDEX statement supports three other activities:

- ▶ Rebuilding an index using the REBUILD option
- ▶ Reorganizing leaf index pages using the REORGANIZE option
- ▶ Disabling an index using the DISABLE option

The following subsections discuss these options.

> **NOTE**
>
> The ALTER INDEX statement replaces a set of commands and system procedures that was used in versions previous to SQL Server 2005 for index maintenance.

Rebuilding an Index

There are three ways in which you can rebuild an index:

- ▶ Use the REBUILD option of the ALTER INDEX statement
- ▶ Use the DROP_EXISTING option of the CREATE INDEX statement
- ▶ Use the DBCC DBREINDEX command

With the REBUILD option, you can rebuild an index. If you specify ALL instead of an index name, all indices of the table will be rebuilt. (By allowing indices to be rebuilt dynamically, you don't have to drop and re-create them.)

The DROP_EXISTING option of the CREATE INDEX statement allows you to enhance performance when re-creating a clustered index on a table that also has a nonclustered index. It specifies that the existing clustered or nonclustered index should be dropped and the specified index rebuilt. As you already know, each nonclustered index in a clustered table contains in its leaf nodes the corresponding values of the table's clustered index. For this reason, all nonclustered indices must be rebuilt when a table's clustered index is dropped. Using the DROP_EXISTING option, you can prevent the nonclustered indices from being rebuilt twice.

> **NOTE**
>
> The DROP_EXISTING option is more powerful than REBUILD, because it is more flexible and offers several options, such as changing the columns that make up the index and changing a nonclustered index to a clustered one.

The DBCC DBREINDEX command rebuilds one or more indexes for a table in the specified database. (The DBREINDEX option is a deprecated feature and will be removed in one of the following versions of SQL Server.)

Reorganizing Leaf Index Pages

The REORGANIZE option of the ALTER INDEX statement specifies that the leaf pages of the corresponding index structure will be reorganized so that the physical order of the pages matches the left-to-right logical order of the leaf nodes. Therefore, this option removes some of the fragmentation from an index, thus improving performance. (REORGANIZE replaces the DBCC INDEXDEFRAG command.)

Disabling an Index

The DISABLE option disables an existing index. Each disabled index is unavailable for use until you enable it again. Note that a disabled index won't be maintained as changes to the corresponding data are made. For this reason, indices must be completely rebuilt if you want to use them again. To enable a disabled index, use the REBUILD option of the ALTER TABLE statement.

> **NOTE**
>
> *If you disable the clustered index of a table, the data won't be available, because all data pages are stored in the leaf level of the clustered index.*

Removing and Renaming Indices

The DROP INDEX statement removes one or more existing indices from the current database. Note that removing the clustered index of a table can be a very resource-intensive operation, because all nonclustered indices will have to be rebuilt. (All the nonclustered indices use the index key of the clustered index as a pointer in their leaf index pages.) Example 10.4 shows how the **i_empno** index can be dropped.

EXAMPLE 10.4

Remove the index created in Example 10.1:

```
USE sample;
DROP INDEX i_empno ON employee;
```

The DROP INDEX statement has an additional option, MOVE TO, which is analogous to the ON option of CREATE INDEX. In other words, you can use this option to specify a location to which to move the data rows that are currently in the leaf pages of the clustered index. The data is moved to the new location in the form of a heap. You can specify either a default or named file group as the new location.

> **NOTE**
>
> *The DROP INDEX statement cannot be used to remove indices that are implicitly generated by the system for integrity constraints, such as PRIMARY KEY or UNIQUE. To remove such indices, you must first drop the constraint.*

The **sp_rename** system procedure, which is discussed in Chapter 5, can be used to rename indices.

Guidelines for Creating and Using Indices

Although Database Engine does not have any practical limitations concerning the number of indices, it is advisable to limit them, for a couple of reasons. First, each index uses a certain amount of disk space, so it is possible that the total number of index pages could exceed the number of data pages within a database. Second, in contrast to the benefits of using an index for retrievals, inserts and updates have a direct impact on the maintenance of the index. The more indices on the tables, the more index reorganizations that are necessary. The rule of thumb is to choose indices wisely for frequent queries and evaluate index usage afterwards.

This section gives some recommendations for creating and using indices.

NOTE

The following recommendations are general rules of thumb. They ultimately depend on how your database will be used in production and which queries are used most frequently. An index on a column that is never used will be counterproductive.

Indices and Conditions in the WHERE Clause

If the WHERE clause in a SELECT statement contains a search condition with a single column, you should create an index on this column. The use of an index is especially recommended if the selectivity of the condition is high. The *selectivity* of a condition is defined as the ratio of the number of rows satisfying the condition to the total number of rows in the table. (High selectivity corresponds to a small ratio.) The most successful processing of a retrieval with the indexed column will be achieved if the selectivity of a condition is 5 percent or less.

The column should not be indexed if the selectivity of the condition is constantly 80 percent or more. In such a case, additional I/O operations will be needed for the existing index pages, which would eliminate any time savings gained by index access. In this particular case, a table scan would be faster, and the query optimizer would usually choose to use a table scan, rendering the index useless.

If a search condition in a frequently used query contains one or more AND operators, it is best to create a composite index that includes all the columns of the table specified in the WHERE clause of the SELECT statement. Example 10.5 shows the creation of a composite index that includes all the columns specified in the WHERE clause of the SELECT statement.

EXAMPLE 10.5

```
USE sample;
CREATE INDEX i_works ON works_on(emp_no, enter_date);
SELECT emp_no, project_no, enter_date
    FROM works_on
    WHERE emp_no = 29346 AND enter_date='1.4.2006';
```

The AND operator in this query contains two conditions. As such, both of the columns appearing in each condition should be indexed using a composite nonclustered index.

Indices and Join Operator

In the case of a join operation, it is recommended that you index each join column. Join columns often represent the primary key of one table and the corresponding foreign key of the other or the same table. If you specify the PRIMARY KEY and FOREIGN KEY integrity constraints for the corresponding join columns, only a non clustered index for the column with the foreign key should be created, because the system will implicitly create the clustered index for the PRIMARY KEY column.

Example 10.6 shows the creation of indices, which should be used if you have a query with a join operation and an additional filter.

EXAMPLE 10.6

```
USE sample;
SELECT emp_lname, emp_fname
    FROM employee, works_on
    WHERE employee.emp_no = works_on.emp_no
    AND enter_date = '10.15.2007';
```

For Example 10.6, the creation of two separate indices for the **emp_no** column in both the **employee** and **works_on** tables is recommended. Also, an additional index should be created for the **enter_date** column.

Covering Index

As you already know, significant performance gains can be achieved when *all* columns in the query are included in the index. Example 10.7 shows a covering index.

EXAMPLE 10.7

```
USE AdventureWorks;
GO
DROP INDEX Person.Address.IX_Address_StateProvinceID;
GO
CREATE INDEX i_address_zip
 ON Person.Address (PostalCode)
 INCLUDE (City, StateProvinceID);
GO
SELECT city, stateprovinceID
   FROM Person.Address
   WHERE PostalCode = 84407;
```

Example 10.7 first drops the **IX_Address_StateProvinceID** index of the **Address** table. In the second step, it creates the new index, which additionally includes two other columns, on the **PostalCode** column. Finally, the SELECT statement at the end of the example shows a query covered by the index. For this query, the system does not have to search for data in data pages, because the optimizer can find all the column values in the leaf pages of the nonclustered index.

NOTE

The use of covering indices is recommended, because index pages generally contain many more entries than the corresponding data pages contain. Also, to use this method, the filtered columns must be the first key columns in the index!

Indices on Computed Columns

Database Engine allows you to create the following special types of indices:

▶ Indices on computed columns

▶ Indices on views

This chapter discusses computed columns; indexed views are explained in the next chapter.

A *computed column* is a column of a table that is used to store the result of a computation of the table's data. Such a column can be either virtual or persistent. The following subsections describe these two forms of computed columns.

Virtual Computed Columns

A computed column without a corresponding clustered index is logical—that is, it is not physically stored on the hard disk. Hence, it is recomputed each time a row is accessed.

Example 10.8 demonstrates the use of virtual computed columns.

EXAMPLE 10.8

```
USE sample;
CREATE TABLE orders
    (orderid INT NOT NULL,
     price MONEY NOT NULL,
     quantity INT NOT NULL,
     orderdate DATETIME NOT NULL,
      total AS price * quantity,
     shippeddate AS DATEADD (DAY, 7, orderdate));
```

The **orders** table in Example 10.8 has two computed columns: **total** and **shippeddate**. The **total** column is computed using two other columns, **price** and **quantity,** while the **shippeddate** column is computed using the date function DATEADD and the column **orderdate**.

Persistent Computed Columns

Database Engine allows you to build indices on deterministic computed columns, where the underlying columns have precise data types. (A computed column is called deterministic if the same values will always be returned for the same table data.)

An indexed computed column can be created only if the following options of the SET statement are set to ON. (These options guarantee the determinism of the column.)

- ► QUOTED_IDENTIFIER
- ► CONCAT_NULL_YIELDS_NULL
- ► ANSI_NULLS
- ► ANSI_PADDING
- ► ANSI_WARNINGS

Also, the NUMERIC_ROUNDABORT option must be set to OFF.

NOTE

Columns used for indexed views must fulfill the same conditions as indexable computed columns. The section on indexed views in the next chapter shows how you can check whether the preceding options are appropriately set.

If you create a clustered index on a computed column, the values of the column will physically exist in the corresponding table rows, because leaf pages of the clustered index contain data rows (see the "Clustered Indices" section earlier in this chapter).

Example 10.9 shows the creation of a clustered index for the computed column **total** in Example 10.8.

EXAMPLE 10.9

CREATE CLUSTERED INDEX i1 ON orders (total);

After the execution of the CREATE INDEX statement in Example 10.9, the computed column **total** will physically exist. This means that all updates to the underlying columns that build the computed column will cause the modification of the computed column itself.

PERSISTED Option

Since SQL Server 2005, it is possible to mark a computed column explicitly as persistent, using the PERSISTED option. This option allows you to specify that the computed column will physically exist in the corresponding table rows, even if the corresponding clustered index isn't created. This feature is necessary for computed columns built upon approximate data types (FLOAT and REAL). (As you already know, you can create an index for a computed column only if the underlying columns have a precise data type.)

Conclusion

Indices are used to access data more efficiently. They can affect not only SELECT statements but also performance of INSERT, UPDATE, and DELETE statements. An index can be clustered or nonclustered, unique or nonunique, and single or composite. A clustered index physically sorts the rows of the table in the order of the specified column(s). A unique index specifies that each value can appear only once in that column of the table. A composite index is composed of more than one column.

A great feature in relation to indices is Database Engine Tuning Advisor (DTA), which will, among other things, analyze a sample of your actual workload (supplied via either a script file from you or a captured trace file from SQL Server Profiler) and recommend indices for you to add or delete based on that workload. Use of DTA is highly recommended. For more information on SQL Server Profiler and DTA, see Chapter 21.

The next chapter discusses the notion of a view.

Exercises

E.10.1

Create a nonclustered index for the **enter_date** column of the **works_on** table. Sixty percent of each index leaf page should be filled.

E.10.2

Create a unique composite index for the **l_name** and **f_name** columns of the **employee** table. Is there any difference if you change the order of the columns in the composite index?

E.10.3

How can you drop the index that is implicitly created for the primary key of a table?

E.10.4

Discuss the benefits and disadvantages of an index.

In the following four exercises, create indices that will improve performance of the queries. (Assume that all tables of the **sample** database that are used in the following exercises have a very large number of rows.)

E.10.5

```
SELECT emp_no, emp_fname, emp_lname
     FROM employee
     WHERE emp_lname = 'Smith'
```

E.10.6

```
SELECT emp_no, emp_fname, emp_lname
     FROM employee
     WHERE emp_lname = 'Hansel'
     AND emp_fname = 'Elke'
```

E.10.7

```
SELECT job
    FROM works_on, employee
    WHERE employee.emp_no = works_on.emp_no
```

E.10.8

```
SELECT emp_lname, emp_fname
    FROM employee, department
    WHERE employee.dept_no = department.dept_no
    AND dept_name = 'Research'
```

Chapter 11

Views

In This Chapter

- ▶ DDL Statements and Views
- ▶ DML Statements and Views
- ▶ Indexed Views

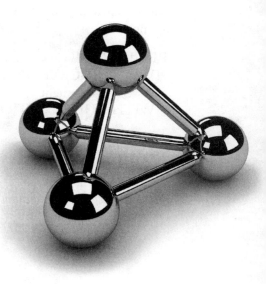

This chapter is dedicated exclusively to the database object called a *view*. The structure of this chapter corresponds to the structure of Chapters 5 to 7, in which the DDL and DML statements for base tables were described. The first section of this chapter covers the DDL statements concerning views: CREATE VIEW, ALTER VIEW, and DROP VIEW. The second part of the chapter describes the DML statements SELECT, INSERT, UPDATE, and DELETE with views. The SELECT statement will be looked at separately from the other three statements. In contrast to base tables, views cannot be used for modification operations without certain limitations. These limitations are described at the end of each corresponding section.

The alternative form of a view, called an indexed view, is described in the last major section of this chapter. This type of index materializes the corresponding query and allows you to achieve significant performance gains in relation to queries with aggregated data.

DDL Statements and Views

In the previous chapters, base tables were used to describe DDL and DML statements. A base table contains data stored on the disk. By contrast, views, by default, do not exist physically—that is, their content is not stored on the disk. (This is not true for so-called indexed views, which are discussed later in this chapter.) Views are database objects that are always derived from one or more base tables (or views) using metadata information. This information (including the name of the view and the way the rows from the base tables are to be retrieved) is the only information concerning views that is physically stored. Thus, views are also called *virtual tables*.

Creating a View

A view is created using the CREATE VIEW statement. The general form of this statement is

```
CREATE VIEW view_name [(column_list)]
    [WITH {ENCRYPTION | SCHEMABINDING | VIEW_METADATA}]
    AS select_statement
    [WITH CHECK OPTION]
```

NOTE

The CREATE VIEW statement must be the only statement in a batch. (This means that you have to use the GO statement to separate this statement from other statements in a statement group.)

view_name is the name of the defined view. **column_list** is the list of names to be used for columns in a view. If this optional specification is omitted, column names of the underlying tables are used. **select_statement** specifies the SELECT statement that retrieves rows and columns from one or more tables (or views). The WITH ENCRYPTION option encrypts the SELECT statement, thus enhancing the security of the database system.

The SCHEMABINDING clause binds the view to the schema of the underlying table. When SCHEMABINDING is specified, database objects referenced in the SELECT statement must include the two-part names in the form **owner.db_object**, where **db_object** may be a table, a view, or a user-defined function.

Any attempt to modify the structure of views or tables that are referenced in a view created with this clause fails. You have to drop the view or change it so that it no longer has the SCHEMABINDING clause if you want to apply the ALTER or DROP statement to the referenced objects. (The WITH CHECK OPTION clause is discussed in detail later in this chapter in the section "INSERT Statement and a View.")

When a view is created with the VIEW_METADATA option, all of its columns (except columns with the TIMESTAMP data type) can be updated if the view has INSERT or UPDATE INSTEAD OF triggers. (Triggers are described in Chapter 14.)

NOTE

The SELECT statement in a view cannot include the ORDER BY, INTO, or COMPUTE clauses. Additionally, a temporary table cannot be referenced in the query.

Views can be used for different purposes:

▶ To restrict the use of particular columns and/or rows of tables. Therefore, views can be used for controlling access to a particular part of one or more tables (see Chapter 12).

▶ To hide the details of complicated queries. If database applications need queries that involve complicated join operations, the creation of corresponding views can simplify the use of such queries.

▶ To restrict inserted and updated values to certain ranges.

Example 11.1 shows the creation of a view.

EXAMPLE 11.1

```
USE sample;
GO
CREATE VIEW v_clerk
  AS SELECT emp_no, project_no, enter_date
    FROM works_on
    WHERE job = 'Clerk';
```

The query in Example 11.1 retrieves the rows of the **works_on** table, for which the condition job = 'Clerk' evaluates to true. The **v_clerk** view is defined as the rows and columns returned by this query. Table 11-1 shows the **works_on** table with the rows that belong to the **v_clerk** view bolded.

Example 11.1 specifies the selection of rows—that is, it creates a horizontal subset from the base table **works_on**. It is also possible to create a view that limits the columns as well as the rows to be included in the view. Example 11.2 shows the creation of such a view.

EXAMPLE 11.2

```
USE sample;
GO
CREATE VIEW v_without_budget
  AS SELECT project_no, project_name
        FROM project;
```

emp_no	project_no	job	enter_date
10102	p1	Analyst	2006.10.1 00:00:00
10102	p3	Manager	2008.1.1 00:00:00
25348	**p2**	**Clerk**	**2007.2.15 00:00:00**
18316	p2	NULL	2007.6.1 00:00:00
29346	p2	NULL	2006.12.15 00:00:00
2581	p3	Analyst	2007.10.15 00:00:00
9031	p1	Manager	2007.4.15 00:00:00
28559	p1	NULL	2007.8.1. 00:00:00
28559	**p2**	**Clerk**	**2008.2.1 00:00:00**
9031	**p3**	**Clerk**	**2006.11.15 00:00:00**
29346	**p1**	**Clerk**	**2007.1.4 00:00:00**

Table 10-1   *The Base Table works_on*

The **v_without_budget** view in Example 11.2 contains all columns of the **project** table except the **budget** column.

As already stated, specifying column names with a view in the general format of the CREATE VIEW statement is optional. On the other hand, there are also two cases in which the explicit specification of column names is required:

▶   If a column of the view is derived from an expression or an aggregate function

▶   If two or more columns of the view have the same name in the underlying tables

Example 11.3 shows the explicit specification of column names in relation to a view.

EXAMPLE 11.3

```
USE sample;
GO
CREATE VIEW v_count(project_no, count_project)
   AS SELECT project_no, COUNT(*)
        FROM works_on
        GROUP BY project_no;
```

The column names of the **v_count** view in Example 11.3 must be explicitly specified because the SELECT statement contains the aggregate function COUNT(*), and all columns in a view must be named.

You can avoid the explicit specification of the column list in the CREATE VIEW statement if you use column headers, as in Example 11.4.

EXAMPLE 11.4

```
USE sample;
GO
CREATE VIEW v_count1
   AS SELECT project_no, COUNT(*) count_project
        FROM works_on
        GROUP BY project_no;
```

A view can be derived from another existing view, as shown in Example 11.5.

EXAMPLE 11.5

```
USE sample;
GO
CREATE VIEW v_project_p2
```

```
AS SELECT emp_no
    FROM v_clerk
    WHERE project_no ='p2';
```

The **v_project_p2** view in Example 11.5 is derived from the **v_clerk** view (see Example 11.1). Every query using the **v_project_p2** view is converted into the equivalent query on the underlying base table **works_on**.

You can also create a view using Object Explorer of SQL Server Management Studio. Select the database under which you want to create the view, right-click **Views**, and choose **New View**. The corresponding editor appears. Using the editor, you can do the following:

- ► Select underlying tables and columns from these tables for the view
- ► Name the view and define conditions in the WHERE clause of the corresponding query

Altering and Removing Views

The Transact-SQL language supports the nonstandard ALTER VIEW statement, which is used to modify the definition of the view query. The syntax of ALTER VIEW is analogous to that of the CREATE VIEW statement.

You can use the ALTER VIEW statement to avoid reassigning existing privileges for the view. Also, altering an existing view using this statement does not affect database objects (stored procedures, usually) that depend upon the view. Otherwise, if you use the DROP VIEW and CREATE VIEW statements to remove and re-create a view, any database object that uses the view will not work properly, at least in the time period between removing and re-creating the view.

Example 11.6 shows the use of the ALTER VIEW statement.

EXAMPLE 11.6

```
USE sample;
GO
ALTER VIEW v_without_budget
  AS SELECT project_no, project_name
      FROM project
      WHERE project_no >= 'p3';
```

The ALTER VIEW statement in Example 11.6 extends the SELECT statement of the **v_without_budget** view (see Example 11.2) with the new condition in the WHERE clause.

NOTE

The ALTER VIEW statement can also be applied to indexed views. This statement removes all indices that exist for such a view.

The DROP VIEW statement removes the definition of the specified view from the system tables. Example 11.7 shows the use of the DROP VIEW statement.

EXAMPLE 11.7

USE sample;
GO
DROP VIEW v_count;

If the DROP VIEW statement removes a view, all other views derived from it will be dropped, too, as demonstrated in Example 11.8.

EXAMPLE 11.8

USE sample;
GO
DROP VIEW v_clerk;

The DROP VIEW statement in Example 11.8 also implicitly removes the **v_project_p2** view (see Example 11.5). For instance, if you query the **v_project_p2** view, you will get the error: "Invalid object name: 'v_clerk'."

NOTE

A view is not automatically dropped if the underlying table is removed. This means that any view from the removed table must be exclusively removed using the DROP VIEW statement. On the other hand, if a table with the same logical structure as the removed one is subsequently created, the view can be used again.

Editing Information Concerning Views

sys.objects is the most important catalog view concerning views. As you already know, this catalog view contains information in relation to all objects of the current database. All rows of this view that have the value **V** for the **type** column are views.

Another catalog view called **sys.views** displays additional information about existing views. The most important column of this view is **with_check_option**, which instructs you whether or not WITH CHECK OPTION is specified.

Using the system procedure **sp_helptext**, you can display the query belonging to a particular view.

DML Statements and Views

Views are retrieved and modified with the same Transact-SQL statements that are used to retrieve and modify base tables. The following subsections discuss all four DML statements in relation to views.

View Retrieval

A view is used exactly like any base table of a database. You can think of selecting from a view as if the statement were transformed into an equivalent operation on the underlying base table(s). Example 11.9 shows this.

EXAMPLE 11.9

```
USE sample;
GO
CREATE VIEW v_d2
  AS SELECT emp_no, emp_lname
     FROM employee
     WHERE dept_no ='d2';
GO
SELECT emp_lname
   FROM v_d2
   WHERE emp_lname LIKE 'J%';
```

The result is

emp_lname
James

The SELECT statement in Example 11.9 is transformed into the following equivalent form, using the underlying table of the **v_d2** view:

```
SELECT emp_lname
   FROM employee
   WHERE emp_lname LIKE 'J%'
   AND dept_no ='d2';
```

The next three sections describe the use of views with the other three DML statements: INSERT, UPDATE, and DELETE. Data modification with these statements is treated in a manner similar to a retrieval. The only difference is that there are some restrictions on a view used for insertion, modification, and deletion of data from the table that it depends on.

INSERT Statement and a View

A view can be used with the INSERT statement as if it were a base table. When a view is used to insert rows, the rows are actually inserted into the underlying base table.

EXAMPLE 11.10

```
USE sample;
GO
CREATE VIEW v_dept
  AS SELECT dept_no, dept_name
      FROM department;
GO

INSERT INTO v_dept
   VALUES('d4', 'Development');
```

The **v_dept** view, which is created in Example 11.10, contains the first two columns of the **department** table. The subsequent INSERT statement inserts the row into the underlying table using the values 'd4' and 'Development'. The **location** column, which is not referenced by the **v_dept** view, is assigned a NULL value.

Using a view, it is generally possible to insert a row that does not satisfy the conditions of the view query's WHERE clause. The option WITH CHECK OPTION is used to restrict the insertion of only such rows that satisfy the conditions of the query. If this option is used, Database Engine tests every inserted row to ensure that the conditions in the WHERE clause are evaluated to true. If this option is omitted, there is no check of conditions in the WHERE clause, and therefore every row is inserted into the underlying table. This could lead to the confusing situation of a row being inserted using a view but subsequently not being returned by a SELECT statement against that view, because the WHERE clause is enforced for the SELECT. WITH CHECK OPTION is also applied to the UPDATE statement.

Examples 11.11 and 11.12 show the difference of applying and not applying WITH CHECK OPTION, respectively.

EXAMPLE 11.11

```
USE sample;
GO
CREATE VIEW v_2006_check
  AS SELECT emp_no, project_no, enter_date
      FROM works_on
      WHERE enter_date BETWEEN '01.01.2006' AND '12.31.2006'
      WITH CHECK OPTION;
GO

INSERT INTO v_2006_check
  VALUES (22334, 'p2', '1.15.2007');
```

In Example 11.11, the system tests whether the inserted value of the **enter_date** column evaluates to true for the condition in the WHERE clause of the SELECT statement. The attempted insert fails because the condition is not met.

EXAMPLE 11.12

```
USE sample;
GO
CREATE VIEW v_2006_nocheck
  AS SELECT emp_no, project_no, enter_date
      FROM works_on
      WHERE enter_date BETWEEN '01.01.2006' AND '12.31.2006';
GO

INSERT INTO v_2006_nocheck
  VALUES (22334, 'p2', '1.15.2007');
SELECT *
  FROM v_2006_nocheck;
```

The result is

emp_no	project_no	enter_date
10102	p1	2006-10-01
29346	p2	2006-12-15
9031	p3	2006-11-15

Because Example 11.12 does not use WITH CHECK OPTION, the INSERT statement is executed and the row is inserted into the underlying **works_on** table. Notice that the subsequent SELECT statement does not display the inserted row because it cannot be retrieved using the **v_2006_nocheck** view.

The insertion of rows into the underlying tables is *not* possible if the corresponding view contains any of the following features:

▶ The FROM clause in the view definition involves two or more tables and the column list includes columns from more than one table

▶ A column of the view is derived from an aggregate function

▶ The SELECT statement in the view contains the GROUP BY clause or the DISTINCT option

▶ A column of the view is derived from a constant or an expression

Example 11.13 shows a view that cannot be used to insert rows in the underlying base table.

EXAMPLE 11.13

```
USE sample;
GO
CREATE VIEW v_sum(sum_of_budget)
  AS SELECT SUM(budget)
       FROM project;
GO

SELECT *
  FROM v_sum;
```

Example 11.13 creates the **v_sum** view, which contains an aggregate function in its SELECT statement. Because the view in the example represents the result of an aggregation of many rows (and not a single row of the **project** table), it does not make sense to try to insert a row into the underlying table using this view.

UPDATE Statement and a View

A view can be used with the UPDATE statement as if it were a base table. When a view is used to modify rows, the content of the underlying base table is actually modified.

Example 11.14 creates a view that is then used to modify the **works_on** table.

EXAMPLE 11.14

```
USE sample;
GO
CREATE VIEW v_p1
  AS SELECT emp_no, job
      FROM works_on
      WHERE project_no = 'p1';
GO

UPDATE v_p1
   SET job = NULL
   WHERE job = 'Manager';
```

You can think of updating the view in Example 11.14 as if the UPDATE statement were transformed into the following equivalent statement:

```
UPDATE works_on
   SET job = NULL
   WHERE job = 'Manager'
   AND project_no = 'p1'
```

WITH CHECK OPTION has the same logical meaning for the UPDATE statement as it has for the INSERT statement. Example 11.15 shows the use of WITH CHECK OPTION with the UPDATE statement.

EXAMPLE 11.15

```
USE sample;
GO
CREATE VIEW v_100000
  AS SELECT project_no, budget
      FROM project
      WHERE budget > 100000
      WITH CHECK OPTION;
GO

UPDATE v_100000
   SET budget = 93000
   WHERE project_no = 'p3';
```

In Example 11.15, Database Engine tests whether the modified value of the **budget** column evaluates to true for the condition in the WHERE clause of the SELECT statement. The attempted modification fails because the condition is not met—that is, the value 93000 is not greater than the value 100000.

The modification of columns in the underlying tables is *not* possible if the corresponding view contains any of the following features:

► The FROM clause in the view definition involves two or more tables and the column list includes columns from more than one table

► A column of the view is derived from an aggregate function

► The SELECT statement in the view contains the GROUP BY clause or the DISTINCT option

► A column of the view is derived from a constant or an expression

Example 11.16 shows a view that cannot be used to modify row values in the underlying base table.

EXAMPLE 11.16

```
USE sample;
GO
CREATE VIEW v_uk_pound (project_number, budget_in_pounds)
   AS SELECT project_no, budget*0.65
        FROM project
        WHERE budget > 100000;
GO

SELECT *
   FROM v_uk_pound;
```

The result is

project_number	budget_in_pounds
p1	78000
p3	121225

The **v_uk_pound** view in Example 11.16 cannot be used with an UPDATE statement (nor with an INSERT statement) because the **budget_in_pounds** column is calculated using an arithmetic expression, and therefore does not represent an original column of the underlying table.

DELETE Statement and a View

A view can be used to delete rows of a table that it depends on, as shown in Example 11.17.

```
USE sample;
GO
CREATE VIEW v_project_p1
  AS SELECT emp_no, job
      FROM works_on
      WHERE project_no = 'p1';
GO

DELETE FROM v_project_p1
  WHERE job = 'Clerk';
```

Example 11.17 creates a view that is then used to delete rows from the **works_on** table. The deletion of rows in the underlying tables is *not* possible if the corresponding view contains any of the following features:

▶ The FROM clause in the view definition involves two or more tables and the column list includes columns from more than one table

▶ A column of the view is derived from an aggregate function

▶ The SELECT statement in the view contains the GROUP BY clause or the DISTINCT option

In contrast to the INSERT and the UPDATE statements, the DELETE statement allows the existence of a constant or an expression in a column of the view that is used to delete rows from the underlying table.

Example 11.18 shows a view that can be used to delete rows, but not to insert rows or modify column values.

```
USE sample;
GO
CREATE VIEW v_budget (budget_reduction)
  AS SELECT budget*0.9
      FROM project;
GO

DELETE FROM v_budget;
```

The DELETE statement in Example 11.18 deletes all rows of the **project** table, which is referenced by the **v_budget** view.

Indexed Views

As you already know from the previous chapter, there are two special index types: indices on computed columns and indices on views. This chapter discusses indices on views.

A view always contains a query that acts as a filter. Without indices created for a particular view, Database Engine builds dynamically the result set from each query that references a view. ("Dynamically" means that if you modify the content of a table, the corresponding view will always show the new information.) Also, if the view contains computations based on one or more columns of the table, the computations are performed each time you access the view.

Building dynamically the result set of a query can decrease performance, if the view with its SELECT statement processes many rows from one or more tables. If such a view is frequently used in queries, you could significantly increase performance by creating a clustered index on the view (see the next section). Creating a clustered index means that the system materializes the dynamic data into the leaf pages on an index structure.

Database Engine allows you to create indices on views. Such views are called indexed or materialized views. When a unique clustered index is created on a view, the view is executed and the result set is stored in the database in the same way a table with a clustered index is stored. This means that the leaf nodes of the clustered index's B$^+$-tree contain data pages (see also the description of the clustered table in Chapter 10).

NOTE

Indexed views are implemented through syntax extensions to the CREATE INDEX and CREATE VIEW statements. In the CREATE INDEX statement, you specify the name of a view instead of a table name. The syntax of the CREATE VIEW statement is extended with the SCHEMABINDING clause. For more information on extensions to this statement, see the description at the beginning of this chapter.

Creating an Indexed View

Creating an indexed view is a two-step process:

1.   Create the view using the CREATE VIEW statement with the WITH SCHEMABINDING clause.
2.   Create the corresponding clustered index.

Example 11.19 shows the first step, the creation of a typical view that can be indexed to gain performance. (This example assumes that **works_on** is a very large table.)

EXAMPLE 11.19

```
USE sample;
GO
CREATE VIEW v_enter_month
 WITH SCHEMABINDING
 AS SELECT emp_no, DATEPART(MONTH, enter_date)  AS enter_month
    FROM dbo.works_on;
```

The **works_on** table in the **sample** database contains the **enter_date** column, which represents the starting date of an employee in the corresponding project. If you want to retrieve all employees that entered their projects in a specified month, you can use the view in Example 11.19. To retrieve such a result set using index access, Database Engine cannot use a table index, because an index on the **enter_date** column would locate the values of that column by the date, and not by the month. In such a case, indexed views can help, as Example 11.20 shows.

EXAMPLE 11.20

```
USE sample;
GO
CREATE  UNIQUE CLUSTERED INDEX
    c_workson_deptno ON v_enter_month (enter_month, emp_no);
```

To make a view indexed, you have to create a unique clustered index on the column(s) of the view. (As previously already stated, a clustered index is the only index type that contains the data values in its leaf pages.) After you create that index, the database system allocates storage for the view, and then you can create any number of nonclustered indices because the view is treated as a (base) table.

An indexed view can be created only if the following options of the SET statement are set to ON (because the view must always display the same result set):

▶ QUOTED_IDENTIFIER

▶ CONCAT_NULL_YIELDS_NULL

▶ ANSI_NULLS

▶ ANSI_PADDING

▶ ANSI_WARNINGS

Also, the NUMERIC_ROUNDABORT option must be set to OFF.

There are several ways to check whether the options in the preceding list are appropriately set, as discussed in the upcoming section "Editing Information Concerning Indexed Views."

To create an indexed view, the view definition has to meet the following requirements:

▶ All referenced (system and user-defined) functions used by the view have to be deterministic—that is, they must always return the same result for the same arguments.

▶ The view must reference only base tables.

▶ The view and the referenced base table(s) must have the same owner and belong to the same database.

▶ The view must be created with the SCHEMABINDING option. SCHEMABINDING binds the view to the schema of the underlying base tables.

▶ The referenced user-defined functions must be created with the SCHEMABINDING option.

▶ The SELECT statement in the view cannot contain the following clauses and options: DISTINCT, UNION, COMPUTE, TOP, ORDER BY, MIN, MAX, COUNT, SUM (on a nullable expression), subqueries, derived tables, or OUTER.

The Transact-SQL language allows you to verify all of these requirements by using the **IsIndexable** parameter of the **objectproperty** property function, as shown in Example 11.21. If the value of the function is 1, all requirements are met and you can create the clustered index.

EXAMPLE 11.21

USE sample;
SELECT objectproperty(object_id('v_enter_month'), 'IsIndexable');

Modifying the Structure of an Indexed View

To drop the unique clustered index on an indexed view, you have to drop all nonclustered indices on the view, too. After you drop its clustered index, the view is treated by the system as a convenient view.

NOTE

If you drop an indexed view, all indices on that view are dropped.

If you want to change a standard view to an indexed one, you have to create a unique clustered index on it. To do so, you must first specify the SCHEMABINDING option for that view. You can drop the view and re-create it, specifying the SCHEMABINDING clause in the CREATE SCHEMA statement, or you can create another view that has the same text as the existing view but a different name.

> **NOTE**
>
> *If you create a new view with a different name, you must ensure that the new view meets all the requirements for an indexed view that are described in the preceding section.*

Editing Information Concerning Indexed Views

You can use the **sessionproperty** property function to test whether one of the options of the SET statement is activated (see the earlier section "Creating an Indexed View" for a list of the options). If the function returns 1, the setting is ON. Example 11.22 shows the use of the function to check how the QUOTED_IDENTIFIER option is set.

EXAMPLE 11.22

SELECT sessionproperty ('QUOTED_IDENTIFIER');

The easier way is to use the dynamic management view called **sys.dm_exec_sessions**, because you can retrieve all values using only one query. (Again, if the value of a column is 1, the corresponding option is set to ON.) Example 11.23 returns the value for the first four SET statement options from the list in "Creating an Indexed View." (The global variable **@@spid** is described in Chapter 4.)

EXAMPLE 11.23

```
USE sample;
SELECT quoted_identifier, concat_null_yields_null, ansi_nulls, ansi_padding
      FROM sys.dm_exec_sessions
      WHERE session_id = @@spid;
```

The **sp_spaceused** system procedure allows you to check whether the view is materialized—that is, whether or not it uses the storage space. The result of Example 11.24 shows that the **v_enter_month** view uses storage space for the data as well as for the defined index.

EXAMPLE 11.24

```
USE sample;
EXEC sp_spaceused 'v_enter_month';
```

The result is

name	rows	reserved	data	index_size	unused
v_enter_month	11	16KB	8KB	8KB	0KB

Benefits of Indexed Views

Besides possible performance gains for complex views that are frequently referenced in queries, the use of indexed views has two other advantages:

▶ The index of a view can be used even if the view is not explicitly referenced in the FROM clause.

▶ All modifications to data are reflected in the corresponding indexed view.

Probably the most important property of indexed views is that a query does not have to explicitly reference a view to use the index on that view. In other words, if the query contains references to columns in the base table(s) that also exist in the indexed views, and the optimizer estimates that using the indexed view is the best choice, it chooses the view indices in the same way it chooses table indices when they are not directly referenced in a query.

When you create an indexed view, the result set of the view (at the time the index is created) is stored on the disk. Therefore, all data that is modified in the base table(s) will also be modified in the corresponding result set of the indexed view.

Besides all the benefits that you can gain by using indexed views, there is also a (possible) disadvantage: indices on indexed views are usually more complex to maintain than indices on base tables, because the structure of a unique clustered index on an indexed view is more complex than a structure of the corresponding index on a base table.

The following types of queries can achieve significant performance benefits if a view that is referenced by the corresponding query is indexed:

▶ Queries that process many rows and contain join operations or aggregate functions

▶ Join operations and aggregate functions that are frequently performed by one or several queries

If a query references a standard view and the database system has to process many rows using the join operation, the optimizer will usually use a suboptimal join method. However, if you define a clustered index on that view, the performance of the query could be significantly enhanced, because the optimizer can use an appropriate method. (The same is true for aggregate functions.)

If a query that references a standard view does not process many rows, the use of an indexed view could still be beneficial if the query is used very frequently. (The same is true for groups of queries that join the same tables or use the same type of aggregates.)

If the restrictions on the types of views that can be indexed might prevent you from using an indexed view in a particular query, try to create partial solutions—each with the corresponding indexed view—and, after that, union all partial solutions to an entire one. For instance, you cannot design an indexed view to process the aggregation of data in tables from different databases and with the subsequent join of their results, because an indexed view cannot reference tables from several databases. You can, however, create an indexed view in each database that does the aggregation of data. If the optimizer can match the indexed view against all partial queries, at least the aggregation processing will speed up. While the join processing is not faster, the overall query is faster because it uses the aggregations stored in the indexed view.

Conclusion

Views can be used for different purposes:

- To restrict the use of particular columns and/or rows of tables—that is, to control access to a particular part of one or more tables

- To hide the details of complicated queries

- To restrict inserted and updated values to certain ranges

Views are created, retrieved, and modified with the same Transact-SQL statements that are used to create, retrieve, and modify base tables. The query on a view is always transformed into the equivalent query on an underlying base table. An update operation is treated in a manner similar to a retrieval. The only difference is that there are some restrictions on a view used for insertion, modification, and deletion of data from a table that it depends on. Even so, the way in which Database Engine handles the modification of rows and columns is more systematic than the way in which other relational database systems handle such modification.

Indexed views are used to increase performance of certain queries. When a unique clustered index is created on a view, the view becomes indexed–that is, its result set is physically stored in the same way a base table is stored.

The following chapter explains in detail the security issues of Database Engine.

Exercises

E.11.1

Create a view that comprises the data of all employees that work for the department d1.

E.11.2

For the project table, create a view that can be used by employees who are allowed to view all data of this table except the **budget** column.

E.11.3

Create a view that comprises the first and last names of all employees who entered their projects in the second half of the year 2007.

E.11.4

Solve Exercise E.11.3 so that the original columns **f_name** and **l_name** have new names in the view: **first** and **last**, respectively.

E.11.5

Use the view in E.11.1 to display full details of every employee whose last name begins with the letter *M*.

E.11.6

Create a view that comprises full details of all projects on which the employee named Smith works.

E.11.7

Using the ALTER VIEW statement, modify the condition in the view in E.11.1. The modified view should comprise the data of all employees that work either for the department d1 or d2, or both.

E.11.8

Delete the view created in E.11.3. What happens with the view created in E.11.4?

E.11.9

Using the view from E.11.2, insert the details of the new project with the project number p2 and the name Moon.

E.11.10

Create a view (with the WITH CHECK OPTION clause) that comprises the first and last names of all employees whose employee number is less than 10,000. After that, use the view to insert data for a new employee named Kohn with the employee number 22123, who works for the department d3.

E.11.11

Solve Exercise E.11.10 without the WITH CHECK OPTION clause and find the differences in relation to the insertion of the data.

E.11.12

Create a view (with the WITH CHECK OPTION clause) with full details from the **works_on** table for all employees that entered their projects during the years 2007 and 2008. After that, modify the entering date of the employee with the employee number 29346. The new date is 06/01/2006.

E.11.13

Solve Exercise E.11.12 without the WITH CHECK OPTION clause and find the differences in relation to the modification of the data.

Chapter 12

Security System of Database Engine

In This Chapter

- ► **Authentication**
- ► **Schemas**
- ► **Database Security**
- ► **Roles**
- ► **Authorization**
- ► **Tracking Changes**
- ► **Data Security and Views**

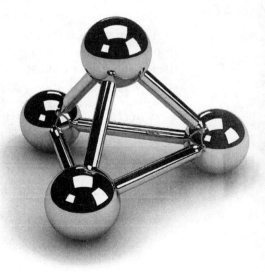

This chapter begins with a brief overview of the most important concepts of database security. It then discusses the specific features of the security system of Database Engine.

The following are the most important database security concepts:

▶ Authentication

▶ Encryption

▶ Authorization

▶ Tracking changes

Authentication requires evaluation of the following question: "Does this user have a legitimate right to access the system ?" Therefore, this security concept specifies the process of validating user credentials to prevent unauthorized users from using a system. Authentication can be checked by requesting the user to provide, for example:

▶ Something the user is acquainted with (usually a password)

▶ Something the user owns, such as a magnetic card or badge

▶ Physical characteristics of the user, such as a signature or fingerprints

Authentication is most commonly confirmed using a name and a password. This information is evaluated by the system to determine whether you are the user. This process can be strengthened using encryption.

Data encryption is the process of scrambling information so that it is incomprehensible until it is decrypted by the intended recipient. Several methods can be used to encrypt data, as discussed in the section "Encryption" a bit later in this chapter.

Authorization is the process that is applied after the identity of a user is verified through authentication. During this process, the system determines what resources the particular user can use. In other words, structural and system catalog information about a particular entity is now available only to principals—that is, subjects that have permission to access that entity.

Tracking changes means that actions of unauthorized users are followed and documented on your system. This process is useful to protect the system against users with elevated privileges.

The following sections describe in detail all of the security concepts defined here. Additionally, the end of the chapter describes how views can be used to secure data.

Authentication

Database Engine's security system includes two different security subsystems:

▶ Windows security

▶ SQL Server security

Windows security specifies security at the operating system level—that is, the method by which users connect to Windows using their Windows *user accounts*. (Authentication using this subsystem is also called Windows authentication.)

SQL Server security specifies the additional security necessary at the system level— that is, how users who have already logged on to the operating system can subsequently connect to the database server. SQL Server security defines a SQL Server login (also called "login") that is created within the system and is associated with a password. Some SQL Server logins are identical to the existing Windows user accounts. (Authentication using this subsystem is called SQL Server authentication.)

NOTE

In addition to Windows user accounts and logins, there are also Windows groups and SQL Server roles (also called "roles"). A Windows group is a collection of Windows user accounts. Assigning a user account membership to a group gives the user all the permissions granted to the group. Similarly, a role is a collection of logins. (Roles are discussed in detail later in this chapter.)

Based on these two security subsystems, Database Engine can operate in one of following authentication modes:

▶ Windows mode

▶ Mixed mode

Windows mode requires users to use Windows user accounts exclusively to log in to the system. The system accepts the user account, assuming it has already been validated at the operating system level. This kind of connection to a database system is called a *trusted connection*, because the system trusts that the operating system already validated the account and the corresponding password.

Mixed mode allows users to connect to Database Engine using Windows authentication or SQL Server authentication. This means that some user accounts can be set up to use the Windows security subsystem, while others can be set up to use both the SQL Server security subsystem and the Windows security subsystem.

NOTE

SQL Server authentication is provided for backward compatibility only. For this reason, use Windows authentication instead.

Implementing an Authentication Mode

You use SQL Server Management Studio to choose one of the existing authentication modes. (Chapter 3 discusses the SQL Server Management Studio interface in depth.) To set up Windows mode, right-click the server and click **Properties**. In the **Server Properties** dialog box, choose the **Security** page and click **Windows Authentication Mode**. To choose Mixed mode, the only difference is that you have to click **SQL Server and Windows Authentication Mode** in the **Server Properties** dialog box.

After a user successfully connects to Database Engine, the user's access to database objects is independent of whether Windows authentication or SQL Server authentication is used.

Before you learn how to set database server security, you need to understand encryption policies and mechanisms, discussed next.

Encrypting Data

Database Engine secures data with hierarchical encryption layers and a key management infrastructure. Each layer secures the layer beneath it, using a combination of certificates, asymmetric keys, and symmetric keys (see Figure 12-1).

The service master key in Figure 12-1 specifies the key that rules all other keys and certificates. The service master key is created automatically when you install Database Engine. (This key is encrypted using the Windows Data Protection API (DPAPI).

The important property of the service master key is that it is managed by the system. Although the system administrator can perform several maintenance tasks, the only one task, which should be done, is to back up the service master key, so you can restore the key, if it is corrupted.

As you can see in Figure 12-1, the database master key is the root encryption object for all keys, certificates, and data at the database level. Each database has a single database master key, which is created using the CREATE MASTER KEY statement. Because the database master key is protected by the service master key, it is possible for the system to automatically decrypt the database master key.

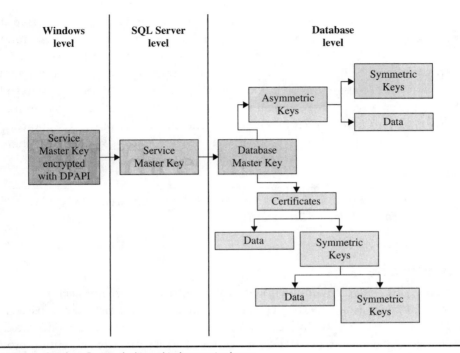

Figure 12-1   *Database Engine: the hierarchical encryption layers*

Once the database master key exists, users can use it to create user keys, which are created and manipulated by users. There are three forms of user keys: symmetric keys, asymmetric keys, and certificates. The following subsections describe the user keys.

Symmetric Keys

An encryption system that uses symmetric keys is one in which the sender and receiver of a message share a common key. Thus, this single key is used for both encryption and decryption.

Using symmetric keys has several benefits and one disadvantage. One advantage of using symmetric keys is that they can protect a significantly greater amount of data than can the other two types of user keys. Also, using this key type is significantly faster than using an asymmetric key.

On the other hand, in a distributed environment, using this type of key can make it almost impossible to keep encryption secure, because the same key is used to decrypt and encrypt data on both ends. So, the general recommendation is that symmetric keys should be used only with applications in which data is stored as encrypted text at one place.

The Transact-SQL language supports several statements and system functions related to symmetric keys. The CREATE SYMMETRIC KEY statement creates a new symmetric key, while the DROP SYMMETRIC KEY removes an existing symmetric key. Each symmetric key must be opened before you can use it to encrypt data or protect another new key. Therefore, you use the OPEN SYMMETRIC KEY statement to open a key.

After you open a symmetric key, you need to use the **EncryptByKey** system function for encryption. This function has two input parameters: the ID of the key and text, which has to be encrypted. For decryption, you use the **DecryptByKey** function.

NOTE

*See Books Online for detailed descriptions of all Transact-SQL statements related to symmetric keys as well as the system functions **EncryptByKey** and **DecryptByKey**.*

Asymmetric Keys

If you have a distributed environment or if a symmetric key does not keep your encryption secure, use asymmetric keys. An asymmetric key consists of two parts: a private key and the corresponding public key. Each key can decrypt data encrypted by the other key. Because of the existence of a private key, asymmetric encryption provides a higher level of security than does symmetric encryption.

The Transact-SQL language supports several statements and system functions related to asymmetric keys. The CREATE ASYMMETRIC KEY statement creates a new asymmetric key, while the ALTER ASYMMETRIC KEY statement changes the properties of an asymmetric key. The DROP ASYMMETRIC KEY statement drops an existing asymmetric key.

After you create an asymmetric key, use the **EncryptByAsymKey** system function to encrypt data. This function has two input parameters: the ID of the key and text, which has to be encrypted. For decryption, use the **DecryptByAsymKey** function.

NOTE

*See Books Online for detailed descriptions of all Transact-SQL statements related to asymmetric keys as well as the system functions **EncryptByAsymKey** and **DecryptByAsymKey**.*

Certificates

A public key certificate, usually simply called a certificate, is a digitally signed statement that binds the value of a public key to the identity of the person, device, or service that holds the corresponding private key. Certificates are issued and signed by a certification authority (CA). The entity that receives a certificate from a CA is the subject of that certificate. Certificates contain the following information.

- ▶ The subject's public key value
- ▶ The subject's identifier information
- ▶ Issuer identifier information
- ▶ The digital signature of the issuer

A primary benefit of certificates is that they relieve hosts of the need to maintain a set of passwords for individual subjects. When a host, such as a secure web server, designates an issuer as a trusted authority, the host implicitly trusts that the issuer has verified the identity of the certificate subject.

NOTE

Certificates provide the highest level of encryption in the Database Engine security model. The encryption algorithms for certificates are very processor-intensive. For this reason, use certificates sparingly.

The most important statement related to certificates is the CREATE CERTIFICATE statement. Examples 12.1 and 12.2 show the use of this statement.

EXAMPLE 12.1

```
USE sample;
CREATE MASTER KEY
ENCRYPTION BY PASSWORD = 'p1s4w9d16'
GO
CREATE CERTIFICATE cert01
    WITH SUBJECT = 'Certificate for dbo';
```

If you want to create a certificate without the ENCRYPTION BY option, you have first to create the database master key. (Each CREATE CERTIFICATE statement that does not include this option is protected by the database master key.) For this reason, the first statement in Example 12.1 is the CREATE MASTER KEY statement. After that, the CREATE CERTIFICATE statement is used to create a new certificate, **cert01**, which is owned by **dbo** in the **sample** database, if the current user is **dbo**.

EXAMPLE 12.2

```
USE sample;
        CREATE CERTIFICATE cert02
            ENCRYPTION BY PASSWORD = 'pGDFD4bb92DGvbd2439587y'
            WITH SUBJECT = 'SQL Server 2008';
```

Example 12.2 creates the new certificate called **cert02**. The ENCRYPTION BY PASSWORD option specifies the password that will be used to encrypt the private key.

Encryption Catalog Views

The most important encryption catalog views are the following:

- ▶ sys.symmetric_keys

- ▶ sys.asymmetric_keys

- ▶ sys.certificates

- ▶ sys.database_principals

The first three catalog views provide information about all symmetric keys, all asymmetric keys, and all the certificates installed in the current database, respectively. The **sys.database_principals** catalog view provides information about each of the principals in the current database. (You can join the last catalog view with any of the three others to see information about who owns a particular key.)

SQL Server 2008 Encryption Enhancements

SQL Server 2008 supports two new encryption features:

- ▶ Extensible Key Management (EKM)

- ▶ Transparent Data Encryption (TDE)

EKM allows third-party vendors to register their devices in Database Engine. Once the devices are registered, SQL Server logins can use the encryption keys stored on these modules as well as leverage advanced encryption features that these modules support. EKM also allows data protection from database administrators (except members of the **sysadmin** group). That way, you can protect the system against users with elevated privileges. Data can be encrypted and decrypted using Transact-SQL cryptographic statements, and SQL Server uses the external EKM device as the key store.

The following Transact-SQL statements support EKM:

- ▶ **CREATE CRYPTOGRAPHIC PROVIDER**   Creates a cryptographic provider within Database Engine from a third-party EKM vendor
- ▶ **DROP CRYPTOGRAPHIC PROVIDER**   Drops an existing provider

NOTE

Only the Enterprise and Developer editions of SQL Server 2008 support EKM.

Transparent Data Encryption introduces a new database option that encrypts the database files automatically, without needing to alter any applications. That way, you can prevent the database access of unauthorized persons, even if they obtain the database files or database backup files.

Encryption of the database file is performed at the page level. The pages in an encrypted database are encrypted before they are written to disk and decrypted when they are read into memory. Transparent data encryption does not increase the size of the encrypted database.

Setting Up System Security Using DDL

The security of Database Engine can be set up using either Transact-SQL statements or system procedures. This section discusses only Transact-SQL statements, because all corresponding system procedures (**sp_addlogin** and **sp_droplogin**) are deprecated features and will be removed in one of the following versions of SQL Server. The three Transact-SQL statements are CREATE LOGIN, ALTER LOGIN, and DROP LOGIN.

The CREATE LOGIN statement creates a new SQL Server login. The syntax is as follows:

```
CREATE LOGIN login_name
{ WITH option_list1   |
FROM {WINDOWS [ WITH option_list2 [,...] ]
| CERTIFICATE certname | ASYMMETRIC KEY key_name }}
```

login_name specifies the name of the login that is being created. As you can see from the syntax of the statement, you can use the WITH clause to specify one or more options for the login or use the FROM clause to define a certificate, asymmetric key, or Windows user account associated with the corresponding login.

option_list1 contains several options. The most important one is the PASSWORD option, which specifies the password of the login (see Example 12.3). (The other possible options are DEFAULT_DATABASE, DEFAULT_LANGUAGE, and CHECK_EXPIRATION.)

As you can see from the syntax of the CREATE LOGIN statement, the FROM clause contains one of the following options:

▶ **WINDOWS option** Specifies that the login will be mapped to an existing Windows user account (see Example 12.4). This clause can be specified with other suboptions, such as DEFAULT_DATABASE and DEFAULT_LANGUAGE.

▶ **CERTIFICATE option** Specifies the name of the certificate to be associated with this login.

▶ **ASYMMETRIC KEY option** Specifies the name of the asymmetric key to be associated with this login. (The certificate as well as the asymmetric key must already exist in the **master** database.)

The following examples show the creation of different login forms. Example 12.3 specifies the login called **mary**, with the password **you1know4it9**.

EXAMPLE 12.3

USE sample;
CREATE LOGIN mary WITH PASSWORD = 'you1know4it9';

Example 12.4 creates the login called **pete**, which will be mapped to a Windows user account with the same name.

EXAMPLE 12.4

USE sample;
CREATE LOGIN [NTB11901\pete] FROM WINDOWS;

NOTE

You have to alter the username and the computer name according to your environment.

The second security statement supported by Transact-SQL is ALTER LOGIN, which changes the properties of a particular login. Using the ALTER LOGIN statement, you can change the current password and its expiration properties, credentials, default database, and default language. You can also enable or disable the specified login.

Finally, the DROP LOGIN statement drops an existing login. A login cannot be dropped if it references (owns) other objects.

Managing Logins Using Management Studio

To create a new login using SQL Server Management Studio, expand the server, expand **Security**, right-click **Logins**, and click **New Login**. The **Login** dialog box (see Figure 12-2) appears. First, you have to decide between Windows authentication and SQL Server authentication. If you choose Windows authentication, the login name must be a valid Windows name, which is written in the form **domain\user_ name**. If you choose SQL Server authentication, you have to type the new login name and the corresponding password. Optionally, you may also specify the default database and language for the new login. (The default database is the database that the user is automatically connected to immediately after logging in to Database Engine.) After that, the user can log in to the system under the new account.

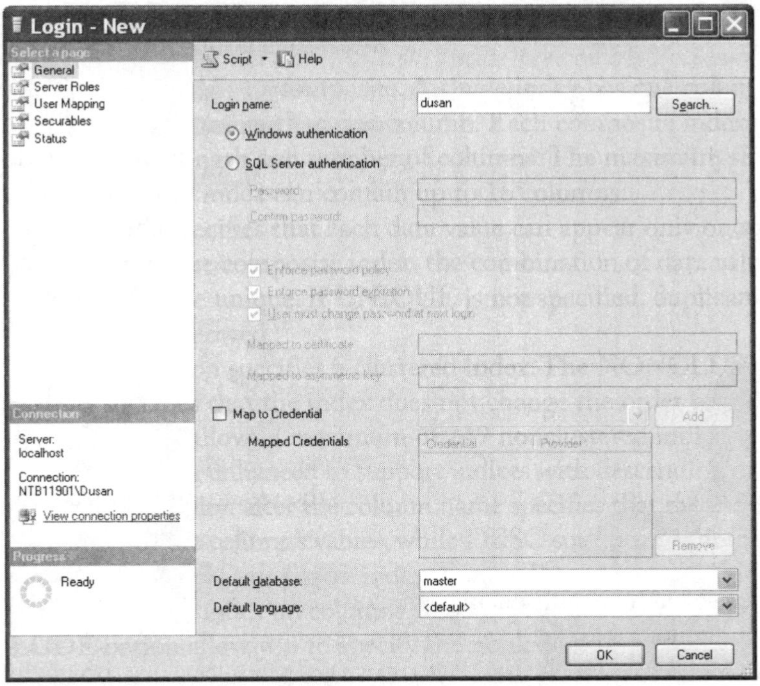

Figure 12-2   *Login dialog box*

Schemas

Database Engine uses schemas in its security model to simplify the relationship between users and objects, and thus schemas have a very big impact on how you interact with Database Engine.. This section describes the role of schemas in Database Engine security. The first subsection describes the relationship between schemas and users; the second subsection discusses all three Transact SQL statements related to schema creation and modification.

User-Schema Separation

A schema is a collection of database objects that is owned by a single person and forms a single namespace. (Two tables in the same schema cannot have the same name.) Since SQL Server 2005, the tight relationship between users and schemas has been broken. Now, Database Engine supports named schemas using the notion of a *principal*, an entity that can access objects. A principal can be either of the following:

▶ An indivisible principal

▶ A group principal

An indivisible principal represents a single user, such as a login or Windows user account. A group principal can be a group of users, such as a role or Windows group. Principals are ownerships of schemas, but the ownership of a schema can be transferred easily to another principal and without changing the schema name.

The separation of database users from schemas provides significant benefits, such as:

▶ One principal can own several schemas.

▶ Several indivisible principals can own a single schema via membership in roles or Windows groups.

▶ Dropping a database user does not require the renaming of objects contained by that user's schema.

Each database has a default schema, which is used to resolve the names of objects that are referred to without their fully qualified names. The default schema specifies the first schema that will be searched by the database server when it resolves the names of objects. The default schema can be set and changed using the DEFAULT_SCHEMA option of the CREATE USER or ALTER USER statement. If DEFAULT_SCHEMA is left undefined, the database user will have **dbo** as its default schema. (All default schemas are described in detail in the section "Default Database Schemas" later in this chapter.)

DDL Schema-Related Statements

There are three Transact-SQL schema-related statements:

▶ CREATE SCHEMA

▶ ALTER SCHEMA

▶ DROP SCHEMA

CREATE SCHEMA

Example 12.5 shows how schemas can be created and used to control database security.

> **NOTE**
> *Before you start Example 12.5, you have to create database users **peter** and **mary**. For this reason, first execute the Transact-SQL statements in Example 12.8.*

EXAMPLE 12.5

```
USE sample;
GO
CREATE SCHEMA my_schema AUTHORIZATION peter
GO
CREATE TABLE product
    (product_no CHAR(10) NOT NULL UNIQUE,
    product_name CHAR(20) NULL,
     price MONEY NULL);
GO
CREATE VIEW product_info
    AS SELECT product_no, product_name
        FROM product;
GO
GRANT SELECT TO mary;
DENY UPDATE TO mary;
```

Example 12.5 creates the **my_schema** schema, which comprises the **product** table and the **product_info** view. The database user called **peter** is the database-level principal that owns the schema. (You use the AUTHORIZATION option to define the principal of a schema. The principal may own other schemas and may not use the current schema as his or her default schema.)

> **NOTE**
>
> *The two other statements concerning permissions of database objects, GRANT and DENY, are discussed in detail at the end of this chapter. GRANT grants the SELECT permissions for all objects created in the schema, while DENY denies the UPDATE permissions for all objects of the schema.*

The CREATE SCHEMA statement can create a schema, create the tables and views it contains, and grant, revoke, or deny permissions on a securable in a single statement.

> **NOTE**
>
> *Securables are resources to which the SQL Server authorization system regulates access. There are three main securable scopes: server, database, and schema, which contain other securables, such us logins, database users, tables, and stored procedures.*

The CREATE SCHEMA statement is atomic. In other words, if any error occurs during the execution of a CREATE SCHEMA statement, none of the Transact-SQL statements specified in the schema will be executed.

Database objects that are created in a CREATE SCHEMA statement can be specified in any order, with one exception: a view that references another view must be specified after the referenced view.

A database-level principal could be a database user, role, or application role. (Roles and application roles are discussed in the "Roles" section later in the chapter.) The principal that is specified in the AUTHORIZATION clause of the CREATE SCHEMA statement is the owner of all objects created within the schema. Ownership of schema-contained objects can be transferred to any other database-level principal using the ALTER AUTHORIZATION statement (see Example 12.7).

The user needs the CREATE SCHEMA permission on the database to execute the CREATE SCHEMA statement. Also, to create the objects specified within the CREATE SCHEMA statement, the user needs the corresponding CREATE permissions.

ALTER SCHEMA

The ALTER SCHEMA statement transfers an object between different schemas of the same database. The syntax of the ALTER SCHEMA statement is as follows:

ALTER SCHEMA schema_name TRANSFER object_name

Example 12.6 shows the use of the ALTER SCHEMA statement.

EXAMPLE 12.6

```
USE AdventureWorks;
ALTER SCHEMA humanresources TRANSFER person.address;
```

Example 12.6 alters the schema called **humanresources** of the **AdventureWorks** database by transferring into it the **address** table from the **person** schema of the same database.

The ALTER SCHEMA statement can only be used to transfer objects between different schemas in the same database. (Single objects within a schema can be altered using the ALTER TABLE statement or the ALTER VIEW statement.)

DROP SCHEMA

The DROP SCHEMA statement removes a schema from the database. You can successfully execute the DROP SCHEMA statement for a schema only if the schema does not contain any objects. If the schema contains any objects, the DROP SCHEMA statement will be rejected by the system.

As previously stated, the system allows you to change the ownership of a schema by using the ALTER AUTHORIZATION statement. This statement modifies the ownership of an entity.

NOTE
The Transact-SQL language does not support the CREATE AUTHORIZATION and DROP AUTHORIZATION statements. You specify the ownership of an entity by using the CREATE SCHEMA statement.

Example 12.7 shows the use of the ALTER AUTHORIZATION statement to change the ownership of the **my_schema** schema.

EXAMPLE 12.7

```
USE sample;
ALTER AUTHORIZATION ON SCHEMA ::my_schema TO mary;
```

Database Security

A Windows user account or a login allows a user to log in to the system. A user who subsequently wants to access a particular database of the system also needs a database user account to work with the database. Therefore, users must have a database user account for each database they want to use. The database user account can be mapped from the existing Windows user accounts, Windows groups (of which the user is a member), logins, or roles.

Setting Up Database User Accounts

Database security permissions can be set up using Transact-SQL statements, Management Studio, or system procedures. This section does not explain how to set up user accounts with system procedures, because all corresponding system procedures (sp_grantdbaccess and sp_revokedbaccess) will be removed in a future version of SQL Server.

Adding Users Using Transact-SQL Statements

The CREATE USER statement adds a user to the current database. The syntax of this statement is

```
CREATE USER user_name
 [FOR {LOGIN login |CERTIFICATE cert_name |ASYMMETRIC KEY key_name}]
  [ WITH DEFAULT_SCHEMA = schema_name ]
```

user_name is the name that is used to identify the user inside the database. **login** specifies the login for which the user is being created. **cert_name** and **key_name** specify the corresponding certificate and asymmetric key, respectively. Finally, the WITH DEFAULT SCHEMA option specifies the first schema that will be searched by the server when it resolves the names of objects for this database user.

Example 12.8 demonstrates the use of the CREATE USER statement.

EXAMPLE 12.8

```
USE sample;
CREATE USER peter FOR LOGIN [NTB11901\pete];
CREATE USER mary FOR LOGIN mary WITH DEFAULT_SCHEMA =
my_schema;
```

NOTE

*To execute the first statement successfully, create the Windows account named **pete** and change the server name.*

The first CREATE USER statement creates the database user called **peter** for the Windows login called **pete**. **pete** will use **dbo** as its default schema, because the DEFAULT SCHEMA option is omitted. (Default schemas will be described in the section "Default Database Schemas" later in this chapter.)

The second CREATE USER statement creates a new database user with the name **mary**. This user has **my_schema** as her default schema. (The DEFAULT_SCHEMA option can be set to a schema that does not currently exist in the database.)

NOTE

Each database has its own specific users. Therefore, the CREATE USER statement must be executed once for each database where a user account should exist. Also, a SQL Server login can have only a single corresponding database user for a given database.

The ALTER USER statement modifies a database username, changes its default schema, or remaps a user to another login. Similar to the CREATE USER statement, it is possible to assign a default schema to a user before the creation of the schema.

The DROP USER statement removes a user from the current database. Users that own securables (that is, database objects) cannot be dropped from the database.

Adding Users Using SQL Server Management Studio

To add users to a database using SQL Server Management Studio, expand the server, expand the **Databases** folder, expand the database, and expand **Security**. Right-click **Users** and click **New User**. In the **Database User** dialog box (see Figure 12-3), enter a username and choose a corresponding login name. Optionally, you can choose database role memberships and schemas owned by this user.

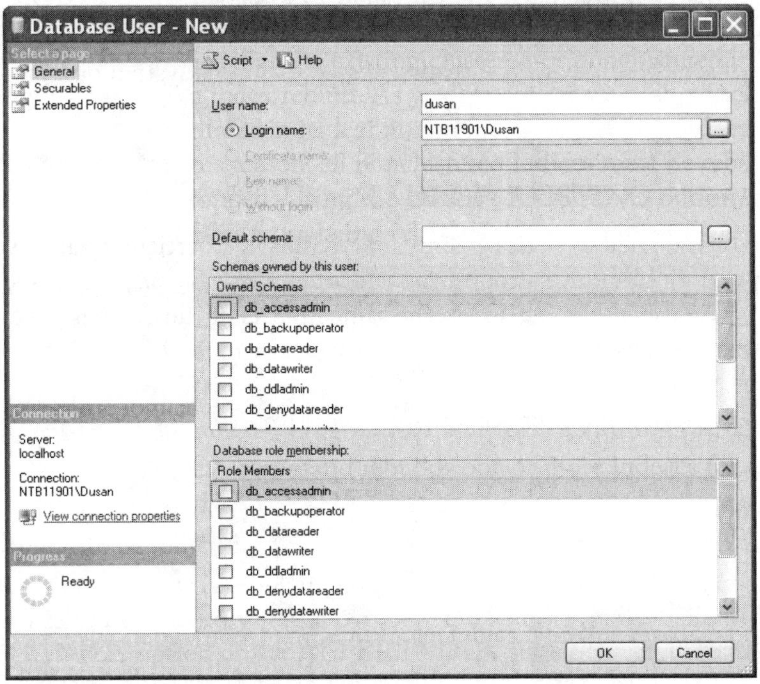

Figure 12-3   *Database User dialog box*

Default Database Schemas

Each database within the system has the following default database schemas:

- ▶ guest
- ▶ dbo
- ▶ INFORMATION_SCHEMA
- ▶ sys

Database Engine allows users without user accounts to access a database using the **guest** schema. (After creation, each database contains this schema.) You can apply permissions to the **guest** schema in the same way as you apply them to any other schema. Also, you can drop and add the guest schema from any database except the **master** and **tempdb** system databases.

Each database object belongs to one and only one schema, which is the default schema for that object. The default schema can be defined explicitly or implicitly. If the default schema isn't defined explicitly during the creation of an object, that object belongs to the **dbo** schema. Also, the login that is the owner of a database always has the special username **dbo** when using the database it owns.

The INFORMATION_SCHEMA schema contains all information schema views. The **sys** schema, as you may have already guessed, contains system objects, such as catalog views.

Roles

When several users need to perform similar activities in a particular database (and there is no corresponding Windows group), you can add a *database role*, which specifies a group of database users that can access the same objects of the database.

Members of a database role can be any of the following:

- ▶ Windows groups and user accounts
- ▶ SQL Server logins
- ▶ Other roles

The security architecture in Database Engine includes several "system" roles that have special implicit permissions. There are two types of predefined roles (in addition to user-defined roles):

▶ Fixed server roles

▶ Fixed database roles

Beside these two, the following sections also describe the following types of roles:

▶ Application roles

▶ User-defined roles

Fixed Server Roles

Fixed server roles are defined at the server level and therefore exist outside of databases belonging to the database server. Table 12-1 lists all existing fixed server roles.

The following two system procedures are used, respectively, to add members to and delete members from a fixed server role:

▶ sp_addsrvrolemember

▶ sp_dropsrvrolemember

NOTE
You cannot add or remove fixed server roles. Additionally, only the members of fixed server roles can execute the system procedures to add or remove logins to or from the role.

Each fixed server role has its implicit permissions within a database system. You can view the permissions for each fixed server role using the **sp_srvrolepermission** system procedure. Use Books Online to learn more about fixed server roles and their permissions.

Fixed Server Role	Description
sysadmin	Performs any activity in the database system
serveradmin	Configures server settings
setupadmin	Installs replication and manages extended procedures
securityadmin	Manages logins and CREATE DATABASE permissions and reads audits
processadmin	Manages system processes
dbcreator	Creates and modifies databases
diskadmin	Manages disk files

Table 12-1   *Fixed Server Roles*

The sa Login

The **sa** login is the login of the system administrator. In versions previous to SQL Server 2005, in which roles did not exist, the **sa** login was granted all possible permissions for system administration tasks. Now, the **sa** login is included just for backward compatibility. This login is always a member of the **sysadmin** fixed server role and cannot be removed from the role.

NOTE

*Use the **sa** login only when there is not another way to log in to the database system.*

Assigning a Login to a Fixed Server Role

To assign a login to a fixed server role using SQL Server Management Studio, expand the server, expand **Security**, and expand **Server Roles**. Right-click the role to which you want to add a login and then click **Properties**. On the **General** page of the **Server Role Properties** dialog box (see Figure 12-4), click **Add**. Search for the login you want to add. Such a login is then the member of the role and inherits all credentials, which are assigned to that role.

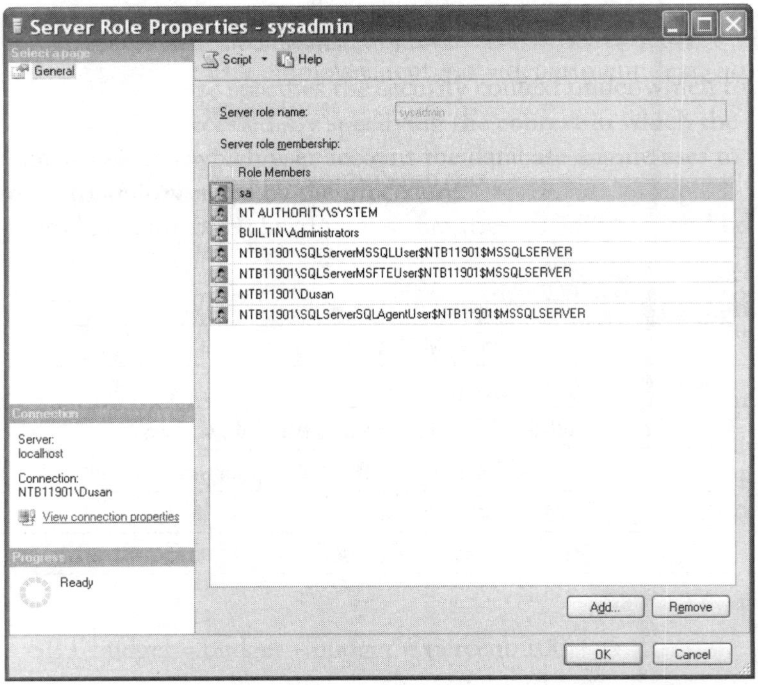

Figure 12-4   *Server Role Properties dialog box*

Fixed Database Roles

Fixed database roles are defined at the database level and therefore exist in each database belonging to the database server. Table 12-2 lists all of the fixed database roles. Members of the fixed database role can perform different activities. Use Books Online to learn which activities are allowed for each of the fixed database roles.

Besides the fixed database roles listed in Table 12-2, there is a special fixed database role called **public**, which is explained next.

public Role

The **public** role is a special fixed database role to which every legitimate user of a database belongs. It captures all default permissions for users in a database. This provides a mechanism for giving all users without appropriate permissions a set of (usually limited) permissions. The **public** role maintains all default permissions for users in a database and cannot be dropped. This role cannot have users, groups, or roles assigned to it because they belong to the role by default. (Example 12.19, later in the chapter, shows the use of the **public** role.)

By default, the **public** role allows users to do the following:

▶ View system tables and display information from the **master** system database using certain system procedures

▶ Execute statements that do not require permissions—for example, PRINT

Fixed Database Role	Description
db_owner	Users who can perform almost all activities in the database
db_accessadmin	Users who can add or remove users
db_datareader	Users who can see data from all user tables in the database
db_datawriter	Users who can add, modify, or delete data in all user tables in the database
db_ddladmin	Users who can perform all DDL operations in the database
db_securityadmin	Users who can manage all activities concerning security permissions in the database
db_backupoperator	Users who can back up the database
db_denydatareader	Users who cannot see any data in the database
db_denydatawriter	Users who cannot change any data in the database

Table 12-2   *Fixed Database Roles*

Assigning a User to a Fixed Database Role

To assign a user account to a fixed database role using SQL Server Management Studio, expand the server, expand **Databases**, expand the database, expand **Security**, expand **Roles**, and then expand **Database Roles**. Right-click the role to which you want to add a user and then click **Properties**. In the **Database Role** dialog box, click **Add** and browse for the user(s) you want to add. Such an account is then the member of the role and inherits all credentials, which are assigned to that role.

Application Roles

Application roles allow you to enforce security for a particular application. In other words, application roles allow the application itself to accept the responsibility of user authentication, instead of relying on the database system. For instance, if clerks in your company may change an employee's data only using the existing application (and not Transact-SQL statements or any other tool), you can create an application role for the application.

Application roles differ significantly from all other role types. First, application roles have no members, because they use the application only and therefore do not need to grant permissions directly to users. Second, you need a password to activate an application role.

When an application role is activated for a session by the application, the session loses all permissions applied to the logins, user accounts and groups, or roles in all databases for the duration of the session. Because these roles are applicable only to the database in which they exist, the session can gain access to another database only by virtue of permissions granted to the **guest** user account in the other database. For this reason, if there is no **guest** user account in a database, the session cannot gain access to that database.

Creating, Modifying, and Deleting Application Roles

You can create, modify, and delete application roles using either the Transact-SQL language or system procedures. Because all system procedures related to this topic (**sp_addapprole**, **sp_setapprole**, and **sp_dropapprole**) are deprecated features and will be removed in one of the following versions of SQL Server, this section discusses only the corresponding Transact-SQL statements.

The CREATE APPLICATION ROLE statement creates an application role for the current database. This statement has two options: one to specify the password and one to define the default schema—that is, the first schema that will be searched by the server when it resolves the names of objects for this role.

Example 12.9 adds a new application role called **weekly_reports** to the **sample** database.

EXAMPLE 12.9

USE sample;
CREATE APPLICATION ROLE weekly_reports
WITH PASSWORD ='x1y2z3w4',
          DEFAULT_SCHEMA =my_schema;

You can modify and remove application roles using the ALTER APPLICATION ROLE and DROP APPLICATION ROLE statements, respectively.

The ALTER APPLICATION ROLE statement changes the name, password, or default schema of an existing application role. The syntax of this statement is similar to the syntax of the CREATE APPLICATION ROLE statement. To execute the ALTER APPLICATION ROLE statement, you need the ALTER permission on the role.

The DROP APPLICATION ROLE statement removes the application role from the current database. If the application role owns any objects (securables), it cannot be dropped.

Activating Application Roles

After a connection is started, it must execute the **sp_setapprole** system procedure to activate the permissions that are associated with an application role. This procedure has the following syntax:

```
sp_setapprole [@rolename =] 'role' ,
          [@password =] 'password'
          [,[@encrypt =] 'encrypt_style']
```

role is the name of the application role defined in the current database, **password** specifies the corresponding password, and **encrypt_style** defines the encryption style specified for the password.

When you activate an application role using **sp_setapprole**, you need to know the following:

▶ After the activation of an application role, you cannot deactivate it in the current database until the session is disconnected from the system.

▶ An application role is always database bound—that is, its scope is the current database. If you change the current database within a session, you are allowed to perform other activities based on the permissions in that database.

NOTE

The design of application roles in SQL Server 2008 is suboptimal, because it is not uniform. To create and delete application roles, you use Transact-SQL. After that, the activation of application roles is done by a system procedure.

Managing Application Roles Using Management Studio

To create an application role using SQL Server Management Studio, expand the server, expand **Databases**, and then expand the database and its **Security** folder. Right-click **Roles**, click **New**, and then click **New Application Role**. In the **Application Role** dialog box, enter the name of the new role. Additionally, you must enter the password and may enter the default schema for the new role.

User-Defined Database Roles

Generally, user-defined database roles are applied when a group of database users needs to perform a common set of activities within a database and no applicable Windows group exists. These roles are created (deleted) using either Transact-SQL statements or system procedures. This section discusses only Transact-SQL statements, because system procedures concerning user-defined roles (**sp_addrole** and **sp_droprole**) are a deprecated feature.

Creating and Deleting User-Defined Roles

The CREATE ROLE statement creates a new user-defined database role in the current database. The syntax of this statement is

CREATE ROLE role_name [AUTHORIZATION owner_name]

   role_name is the name of the user-defined role to be created. **owner_name** specifies the database user or role that will own the new role. (If no user is specified, the role will be owned by the user that executes the CREATE ROLE statement.)

   The ALTER ROLE statement changes the name of a user-defined database role. Similarly, the DROP ROLE statement drops a role from the database. Roles that own database objects (securables) cannot be dropped from the database. To drop such a role, you must first transfer the ownership of those objects.

Roles and System Procedures

There are still several system procedures that you have to use if you need to add or remove members of a user-defined role:

- ▶ sp_addrolemember
- ▶ sp_droprolemember
- ▶ sp_helprole

After you add a role to the current database, you can use the system procedure **sp_addrolemember** to add members to the role. A role member can be any valid login, Windows user account or group, or another role. Only members of the **db_owner** database role can execute this system procedure. Additionally, role owners can execute **sp_addrolemember** to add a member to any role that they own.

The **sp_droprolemember** system procedure removes an existing member from the role. (It is not possible to use this system procedure to remove an existing Windows user account from a Windows group.) Only members of the **db_owner** or **db_securityadmin** database roles can execute this system procedure.

The **sp_helprole** system procedure displays information (role ID and name) about a particular role, or all roles in the current database if no role name is provided. Only the members of the **db_owner** or **db_securityadmin** roles can execute this system procedure.

NOTE

Again, the design of roles (in this case, user-defined database roles) in SQL Server 2008 is neither uniform nor optimal. To create and delete user-defined roles, you use Transact-SQL, whereas to add such roles to the current database, you use system procedures.

Example 12.10 shows how you can create and add members to a user-defined role.

EXAMPLE 12.10

```
USE sample;
CREATE ROLE marketing AUTHORIZATION peter;
GO
exec sp_addrolemember @rolename = 'marketing', @membername = 'peter';
exec sp_addrolemember @rolename = 'marketing', @membername = 'mary';
```

Example 12.10 first creates the user-defined role called **marketing**, and then, using the **sp_addrolemember** system procedure, adds two members, **peter** and **mary,** to the role.

Managing User-Defined Roles Using Management Studio

To create a user-defined role using SQL Server Management Studio, expand the server, expand **Databases,** and then expand the database and its **Security** folder. Right-click **Roles,** click **New,** and then click **New Database Role.** In the **Database Role** dialog box (see Figure 12-5), enter the name of the new role. Click **Add** to add members to the new role. Choose the members (users and/or other roles) of the new role and click **OK.**

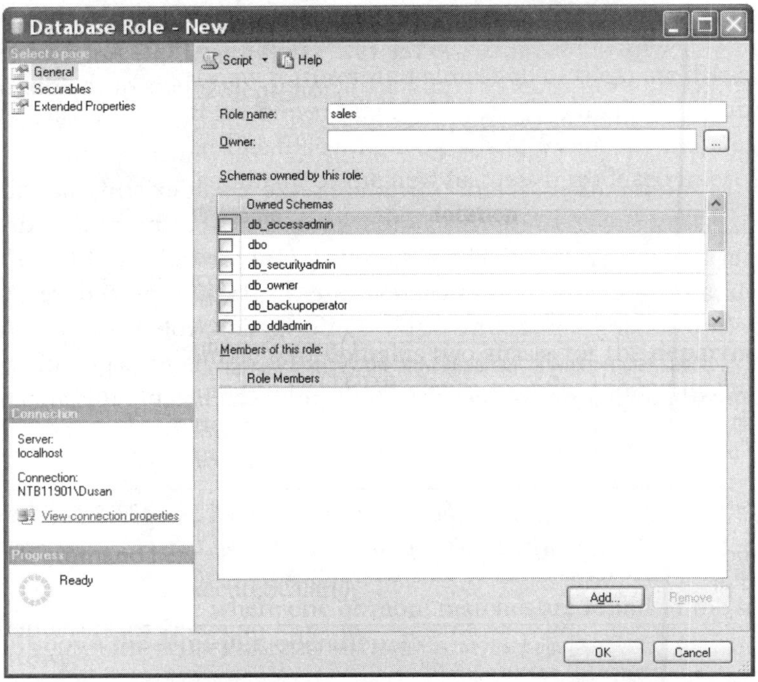

Figure 12-5 *Database Role dialog box*

Authorization

Only authorized users are able to execute statements or perform operations on an entity. If an unauthorized user attempts to do either task, the execution of the Transact-SQL statement or the operation on the database object will be rejected.

There are three Transact-SQL statements related to authorization:

▶ GRANT

▶ DENY

▶ REVOKE

Before you read about these three statements, you need to be aware of one of the most important security properties of Database Engine: it supports multiple scopes and permissions to help database administrators handle permissions. The authorization model separates the world into principals and securable. Every securable has associated permissions that can be granted to a principal. Principals, such as individuals, groups, or applications, can access entities. Entities are the resources to which the authorization subsystem regulates access. As previously stated, there are three securable scopes: server, database, and schema, which contain other securables, such as login, database users, tables, and stored procedures.

GRANT Statement

The GRANT statement grants permissions to securables. The syntax of the GRANT statement is

```
GRANT {ALL [PRIVILEGES]} | permission_list
    [ON [class::] securable]  TO principal_list [WITH GRANT OPTION]
    [AS principal ]
```

The ALL clause indicates that all permissions applicable to the specified securable will be granted to the specified principal. (For the list of specific securables, see Books Online.) **permission_list** specifies either statements or objects (separated by commas) for which the permissions are granted. **class** specifies either a securable class or a securable name for which permission will be granted. ON **securable** specifies the securable for which permissions are granted (see Example 12.15 later in this section). **principal_list** lists all accounts (separated by commas) to which permissions are granted. **principal** and the components of **principal_list** can be a Windows user account, a login or user account mapped to a certificate, a login mapped to an asymmetric key, a database user, a database role, or an application role.

Table 12-3 lists and describes all the permissions and lists the corresponding securables to which they apply.

NOTE

Table 12-3 shows only the most important permissions. The security model of Database Engine is hierarchical. Hence, there are many granular permissions that are not listed in the table. You can find the description of these permissions in Books Online.

The following examples demonstrate the use of the GRANT statement. To begin, Example 12.11 demonstrates the use of the CREATE permission.

EXAMPLE 12.11

```
USE sample;
GRANT CREATE TABLE, CREATE PROCEDURE
        TO peter, mary;
```

Permission	Applies To	Description
SELECT	Tables + columns, synonyms, views + columns, table-valued functions	Provides the ability to select (read) rows. You can restrict this permission to one or more columns by listing them. (If the list is omitted, all columns of the table can be selected.)
INSERT	Tables + columns, synonyms, views + columns	Provides the ability to insert rows.
UPDATE	Tables + columns, synonyms, views + columns	Provides the ability to modify column values. You can restrict this permission to one or more columns by listing them. (If the list is omitted, all columns of the table can be modified.)
DELETE	Tables + columns, synonyms, views + columns	Provides the ability to delete rows.
REFERENCES	User-defined functions (SQL and CLR), tables + columns, synonyms, views + columns	Provides the ability to reference columns of the foreign key in the referenced table when the user has no SELECT permission for the referenced table.
EXECUTE	Stored procedures (SQL and CLR), user-defined functions (SQL and CLR), synonyms	Provides the ability to execute the specified stored procedure or user-defined functions.
CONTROL	Stored procedures (SQL and CLR), user-defined functions (SQL and CLR), synonyms	Provides ownership-like capabilities; the grantee effectively has all defined permissions on the securable. A principal that has been granted CONTROL also has the ability to grant permissions on the securable. CONTROL at a particular scope implicitly includes CONTROL on all the securables under that scope (see Example 12.16).
ALTER	Stored procedures (SQL and CLR), user-defined functions (SQL and CLR), tables, views	Provides the ability to alter the properties (except ownership) of a particular securable. When granted on a scope, it also bestows the ability to ALTER, CREATE, or DROP any securable contained within that scope.
TAKE OWNERSHIP	Stored procedures (SQL and CLR), user-defined functions (SQL and CLR), tables, views, synonyms	Provides the ability to take ownership of the securable on which it is granted.
VIEW DEFINITION	Stored procedures (SQL and CLR), user-defined functions (SQL and CLR), tables, views, synonyms	Controls the ability of the grantee to see the metadata of the securable (see Example 12.15).
CREATE (Server securable)	n/a	Provides the ability to create the server securable.
CREATE (DB securable)	n/a	Provides the ability to create the database securable.

Table 12-3 *Permissions with Corresponding Securables*

In Example 12.11, the users **peter** and **mary** can execute the Transact-SQL statements CREATE TABLE and CREATE PROCEDURE. (As you can see from this example, the GRANT statement with the CREATE permission does not include the ON option.)

Example 12.12 allows the user **mary** to create user-defined functions in the **sample** database.

EXAMPLE 12.12

USE sample;
GRANT CREATE FUNCTION TO mary;

Example 12.13 shows the use of the SELECT permission within the GRANT statement.

EXAMPLE 12.13

USE sample;
GRANT SELECT ON employee
   TO peter, mary;

In Example 12.13, the users **peter** and **mary** can read rows from the **employee** table.

NOTE

When a permission is granted to a Windows user account or a login, this account (login) is the only one affected by the permission. On the other hand, if a permission is granted to a group or role, the permission affects all users belonging to the group (role).

Example 12.14 shows the use of the UPDATE permission within the GRANT statement.

EXAMPLE 12.14

USE sample;
GRANT UPDATE ON works_on (emp_no, enter_date) TO peter;

In Example 12.14, the user **peter** can modify two columns of the **works_on** table: **emp_no** and **enter_date**.

Example 12.15 shows the use of the VIEW DEFINITION permission.

EXAMPLE 12.15

USE sample;
GRANT VIEW DEFINITION ON OBJECT::employee TO peter;
GRANT VIEW DEFINITION ON SCHEMA::dbo TO peter;

Example 12.15 shows two GRANT statements for the VIEW DEFINITION permission. The first one allows the user **peter** to see metadata about the **employee** table of the **sample** database. (OBJECT is one of the base securables, and you can use this clause to give permissions for specific objects, such as tables, views, and stored procedures.) Because of the hierarchical structure of securables, you can use a "higher" securable to extend the VIEW DEFINITION (or any other base) permission. The second statement in Example 12.15 gives the user **peter** access to metadata of all the objects of the **dbo** schema of the **sample** database.

NOTE

In versions previous to SQL Server 2005, it is possible to query information on all database objects, even if these objects are owned by another user. The VIEW DEFINITION permission now allows you to grant or deny access to different pieces of your metadata and hence to decide which part of metadata is visible to other users.

Example 12.16 shows the use of the CONTROL permission.

EXAMPLE 12.16

```
USE sample;
GRANT CONTROL ON DATABASE::sample TO peter;
```

In Example 12.16, the user **peter** effectively has all defined permissions on the securable (in this case, the **sample** database). A principal that has been granted CONTROL also implicitly has the ability to grant permissions on the securable; in other words, the CONTROL permission includes the WITH GRANT OPTION clause (see Example 12.17). The CONTROL permission is the highest permission in relation to several base securables. For this reason, CONTROL at a particular scope implicitly includes CONTROL on all the securables under that scope. Therefore, the CONTROL permission of peter on the **sample** database implies all permissions on this database, all permissions on all assemblies in the database, all permissions on all schemas in the **sample** database, and all permissions on objects within the **sample** database.

By default, if user A grants a permission to user B, then user B can only use the permission to execute the Transact-SQL statement listed in the GRANT statement. The WITH GRANT OPTION gives user B the additional capability of granting the privilege to other users, as shown in Example 12.17.

EXAMPLE 12.17

```
USE sample;
GRANT SELECT ON works_on  TO mary
   WITH GRANT OPTION;
```

In Example 12.17, the user **mary** can use the SELECT statement to retrieve rows from the **works_on** table and also may grant this privilege to other users of the **sample** database.

DENY Statement

The DENY statement prevents users from performing actions. This means that the statement removes existing permissions from user accounts or prevents users from gaining permissions through their group/role membership that might be granted in the future. This statement has the following syntax:

DENY {ALL [PRIVILEGES] } | permission_list
 [ON [class::] securable] TO principal_list
[CASCADE] [AS principal]

All options of the DENY statement have the same logical meaning as the options with the same name in the GRANT statement. DENY has an additional option, CASCADE, which specifies that permissions will be denied to user A and any other users to whom user A passed this permission. (If the CASCADE option is not specified in the DENY statement, and the corresponding object permission was granted with the WITH GRANT OPTION, an error is returned.)

The DENY statement prevents the user, group, or role from gaining access to the permission granted through their group or role membership. This means that if a user belongs to a group (or role) and the granted permission for the group is denied to the user, this user will be the only one of the group who cannot use this permission. On the other hand, if a permission is denied for a whole group, all members of the group will be denied the permission.

NOTE

You can think of the GRANT statement as a "positive" and the DENY statement as a "negative" user authorization. Usually, the DENY statement is used to deny already existing permissions for groups (roles) to a few members of the group.

Examples 12.18 and 12.19 show the use of the DENY statement.

EXAMPLE 12.18

USE sample;
DENY CREATE TABLE, CREATE PROCEDURE
 TO peter;

The DENY statement in Example 12.18 denies two previously granted statement permissions to the user **peter**.

EXAMPLE 12.19

```
USE sample;
GRANT SELECT ON project
   TO PUBLIC;
DENY SELECT ON project
     TO peter, mary;
```

Example 12.19 shows the negative authorization of some users of the **sample** database. First, the retrieval of all rows of the **project** table is granted to all users of the **sample** database. After that, this permission is denied to two users: **peter** and **mary**.

REVOKE Statement

The REVOKE statement removes one or more previously granted or denied permissions. This statement has the following syntax:

```
REVOKE [GRANT OPTION FOR]
   { [ALL [PRIVILEGES] ] | permission_list ]}
[ON  [class:: ] securable ]
 FROM principal_list [CASCADE]  [ AS principal ]
```

The only new option in the REVOKE statement is GRANT OPTION FOR. (All other options have the same logical meaning as the options with the same names in the GRANT or DENY statement.) GRANT OPTION FOR is used to remove the effects of the WITH GRANT OPTION in the corresponding GRANT statement. This means that the user will still have the previously granted permissions but will no longer be able to grant the permission to other users.

NOTE

The REVOKE statement revokes "positive" permissions specified with the GRANT statement as well as "negative" permissions generated by the DENY statement. Therefore, its function is to neutralize the specified (positive or negative) permissions.

Example 12.20 shows the use of the REVOKE statement.

EXAMPLE 12.20

USE sample;
REVOKE SELECT ON project
  FROM PUBLIC;

The REVOKE statement in Example 12.20 revokes the granted permission for the
public role. At the same time, the existing "negative" permissions for the users **peter**
and **mary** are not revoked (as in Example 12.19), because the explicitly granted or
denied permissions are not affected by revoking roles or groups.

Managing Permissions Using Management Studio

Database users can perform activities that are granted to them. In this case, there is a
corresponding entry in the **sys.database_permissions** catalog view (that is, the value
of the **state** column is set to **G** for grant). A negative entry in the table prevents a
user from performing activities. The entry **D** (deny) in the **state** column overrides a
permission that was granted to a user explicitly or implicitly using a role to which the
user belongs. Therefore, the user cannot perform this activity in any case. In the last
case (value **R**), the user has no explicit privileges but can perform an activity if a role to
which the user belongs has the appropriate permission.

To manage permissions for a user or role using Management Studio, expand the
server and expand **Databases**. Right-click the database and click **Properties**. Choose
the **Permissions** page and click the **Add** button. In the Database Properties dialog
box, shown in Figure 12-6, you can select one or more object types (users and/or roles)
to which you want to grant or deny permissions. To grant a permission, check the
corresponding box in the **Grant** column and click **OK**. To deny a permission, check
the corresponding box in the **Deny** column. (The **With Grant** column specifies that
the user has the additional capability of granting the privilege to other users.) Blanks in
these columns mean no permission.

To manage permissions for a single database object using SQL Server Management
Studio, expand the server, expand **Databases**, expand the database, and then expand
Tables, **Views**, or **Synonyms**, depending on the database object for which you want
to manage permissions. Right-click the object, choose **Properties**, and select the
Permissions page. (Figure 12-7 shows the **Table Properties** dialog box for the **employee**
table.) Click the **Add** button to open the **Select Users or Roles** dialog box. Click **Object
Types** and select one or more object types (users, database roles, application roles). After
that, click **Browse** and check all objects to which permissions should be granted. To grant
a permission, check the corresponding box in the **Grant** column. To deny a permission,
check the corresponding box in the **Deny** column.

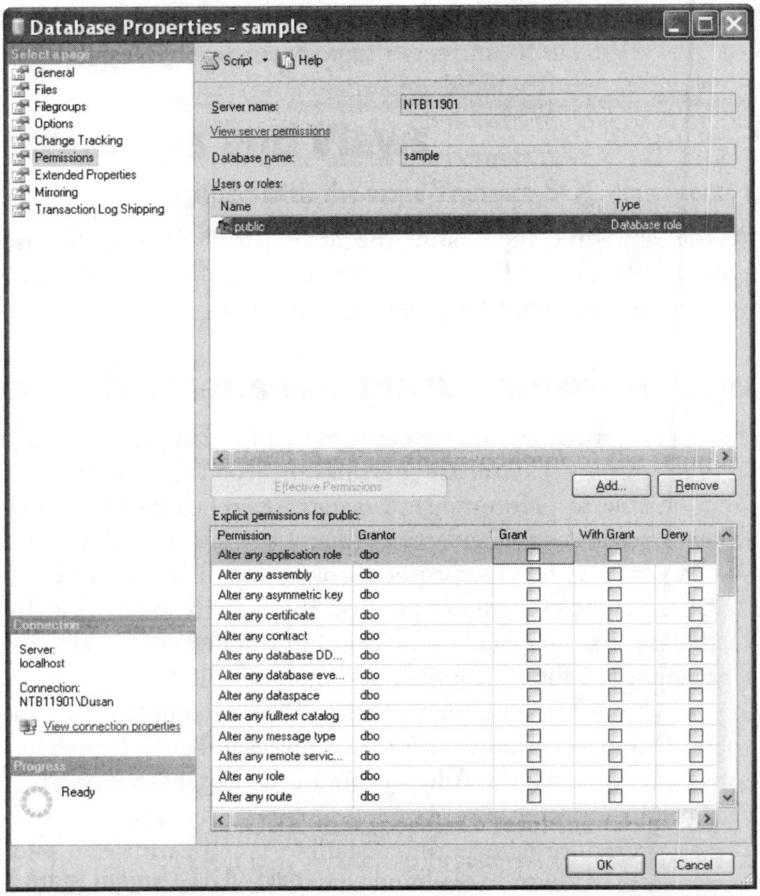

Figure 12-6   *Managing statement permissions using SQL Server Management Studio*

Tracking Changes

Tracking changes refers to documenting all insert, update, and delete activities that are applied to tables of the database. The tracked changes can then be viewed to find out who accessed the data and when they accessed it. There are two ways in which you can track changes:

▶   Using triggers
▶   Using change data capture (CDC)

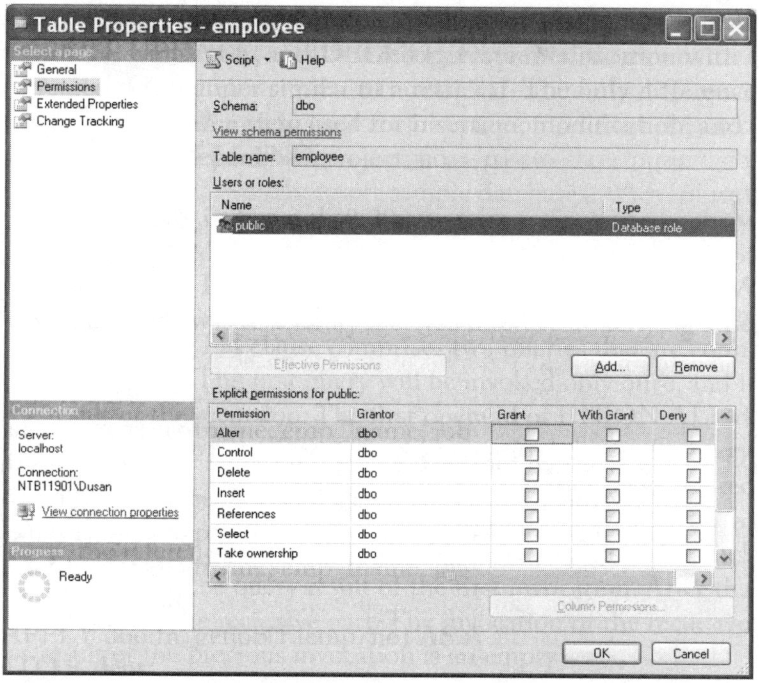

Figure 12-7   *Managing object permissions using SQL Server Management Studio*

You can use triggers to create an audit trail of activities in one or more tables of the database. The section "After Triggers" in Chapter 14 and Example 14.1 show how triggers can be used to track such changes. Therefore, the focus of this section is CDC.

CDC is a tracking mechanism that you can use to see changes as they happen. The primary goal of CDC is to audit who changed what data and when, but it can also be used to support concurrency updates. (If an application wants to modify a row, CDC can check the change tracking information to make sure that the row hasn't been changed since the last time the application modified the row. This check is called a "concurrency update".)

NOTE

CDC is available only in the SQL Server 2008 Enterprise and Developer editions.

Before a capture instance can be created for individual tables, the database that contains the tables must be enabled for CDC, which you do with the system stored procedure **sys.sp_cdc_enable_db** as shown in Example 12.21. (Only members of the **sysadmin** fixed server role can execute this procedure.)

EXAMPLE 12.21

```
USE sample;
EXECUTE sys.sp_cdc_enable_db
```

To determine whether the **sample** database is enabled for CDC, you can retrieve the value of the column **is_cdc_enabled** in the **sys.databases** catalog view. The value 1 indicates the activation of CDC for the particular database.

When a database is enabled for CDC, the **cdc** schema, **cdc** user, metadata tables, and other system objects are created for the database. The **cdc** schema contains the CDC metadata tables as well as the individual tracking tables that serve as a repository for CDC.

Once a database has been enabled for CDC, you can create a target table that will capture changes for a particular source table. You enable the table by using the stored procedure **sys.sp_cdc_enable_table**. (Only members of the **db_owner** fixed database role can execute this procedure.) Example 12.22 shows the use of this system stored procedure.

NOTE

The SQLServerAgent service must be running before you enable tables for CDC.

EXAMPLE 12.22

```
USE sample;
EXECUTE sys.sp_cdc_enable_table
    @source_schema = N'dbo', @source_name = N'works_on',
    @role_name = N'cdc_admin';
```

The **sys.sp_cdc_enable_table_change_data_capture** system procedure in Example 12.22 enables CDC for the specified source table in the current database. When a table is enabled for CDC, all DML statements are read from the transaction log and captured in the associated change table. The **@source_schema** parameter specifies the name of the schema in which the source table belongs. **@source_name** is the name of the source table on which you enable CDC. The **@role_name** parameter specifies the name of the database role used to allow access to data.

Creating a capture instance also creates a tracking table that corresponds to the source table. You can specify up to two capture instances for a source table. Example 12.23 changes the content of the source table (**works_on**).

EXAMPLE 12.23

```
USE sample;
INSERT INTO works_on VALUES (10102, 'p2', 'Analyst', NULL);
INSERT INTO works_on VALUES (9031, 'p2', 'Analyst', NULL);
INSERT INTO works_on VALUES (29346, 'p3', 'Clerk', NULL);
```

By default, at least one table-valued function is created to access the data in the associated change table. This function allows you to query all changes that occur within a defined interval. The function name is the concatenation of cdc.fn_cdc_get_all_ changes_ and the value assigned to the **@capture_instance** parameter. In this case, the parameter has the value dbo_works_on, as Example 12.24 shows.

EXAMPLE 12.24

```
USE sample;
SELECT *
FROM cdc.fn_cdc_get_all_changes_dbo_works_on
    (sys.fn_cdc_get_min_lsn('dbo_works_on'), sys.fn_cdc_get_max_lsn(), 'all');
```

The result is

__$start_lsn	__$update_mask	emp_no	project_no	job	enter_date
0x0000001C000001EF0003	0x0F	10102	p2	Analyst	NULL
0x0000001D000000100003	0x0F	9031	p2	Analyst	NULL
0x0000001D000000110003	0x0F	29346	p3	Clerk	NULL

Example 12.24 shows all changes that happened after the execution of the three INSERT statements. If you want to track all changes in a certain time interval, you can use a batch similar to the one shown in Example 12.25.

EXAMPLE 12.25

```
USE sample;
 DECLARE @from_lsn binary(10), @to_lsn binary(10);
  SELECT @from_lsn =
     sys.fn_cdc_map_time_to_lsn('smallest greater than', GETDATE() - 1);
```

```
SELECT @to_lsn =
    sys.fn_cdc_map_time_to_lsn('largest less than or equal', GETDATE());
SELECT * FROM
    cdc.fn_cdc_get_all_changes_dbo_works_on (@from_lsn, @to_lsn, 'all');
```

The only difference between Example 12.25 and Example 12.24 is that Example 12.25 uses two parameters (**@from_lsn** and **@to_lsn**) to define the beginning and end of the time interval. (The assignment of time boundaries is done using the **sys.fn_cdc_map_time_to_lsn()** function.)

Data Security and Views

As already stated in Chapter 11, views can be used for the following purposes:

▶ To restrict the use of particular columns and/or rows of tables

▶ To hide the details of complicated queries

▶ To restrict inserted and updated values to certain ranges

Restricting the use of particular columns and/or rows means that the view mechanism provides itself with the control of data access. For example, if the **employee** table also contains the salaries of each employee, then access to these salaries can be restricted using a view that accesses all columns of the table except the **salary** column. Subsequently, retrieval of data from the table can be granted to all users of the database using the view, while only a small number of (privileged) users will have the same permission for all data of the table.

The following three examples show the use of views to restrict the access to data.

EXAMPLE 12.26

```
USE sample;
GO
CREATE VIEW v_without_budget
  AS SELECT project_no, project_name
        FROM project;
```

Using the **v_without_budget** view, it is possible to divide users into two groups: the group of privileged users who can access the budget of all projects, and the group of common users who can access all rows from the **projects** table but not the data from the **budget** column.

EXAMPLE 12.27

```
USE sample;
GO
ALTER TABLE employee
  ADD user_name CHAR(60) DEFAULT SYSTEM_USER;
GO
CREATE VIEW v_my_rows
      AS SELECT emp_no, emp_fname, emp_lname, dept_no
          FROM employee
          WHERE user_name = SYSTEM_USER;
```

NOTE

The Transact-SQL statements in Example 12.27 must be separately executed, because the CREATE VIEW statement must be the first statement in the batch. That is why the GO statement is used (to mark the end of the first batch).

The schema of the **employee** table is modified in Example 12.27 by adding the new column **user_name**. Every time a new row is inserted into the **employee** table, the system login is inserted into the **user_name** column. After the creation of corresponding views, every user can retrieve only the rows that they inserted into the table. (The same is true for the UPDATE statement.)

EXAMPLE 12.28

```
USE sample;
GO
CREATE VIEW v_analyst
  AS SELECT employee.emp_no, emp_fname, emp_lname
      FROM employee, works_on
      WHERE employee.emp_no = works_on.emp_no
      AND job = 'Analyst';
```

The **v_analyst** view represents a horizontal and a vertical subset (in other words, it limits the rows and columns that can be accessed) of the **employee** table.

Conclusion

The following are the most important concepts of database system security:

▶ Authentication

▶ Encryption

- ▶ Authorization
- ▶ Tracking changes

Authentication is the process of validating user credentials to prevent unauthorized users from using a system. It is most commonly enforced by requiring a username and password. Data encryption is the process of scrambling information so that it is incomprehensible until it is decrypted by the intended recipient. Several different methods can be used to encrypt data.

During the authorization process, the system determines what resources the particular user can use. Database Engine supports authorization with the following Transact-SQL statements: GRANT, DENY, and REVOKE. Tracking changes means that actions of unauthorized users are followed and documented on your system. This process is useful to protect the system against users with elevated privileges.

The next chapter discusses the features concerning Database Engine as a multi-user software system and describes the notions of optimistic and pessimistic concurrency.

Exercises

E.12.1

What is a difference between Windows mode and Mixed mode?

E.12.2

What is a difference between a SQL Server login and a database user account?

E.12.3

Create three logins called **ann, burt,** and **chuck.** The corresponding passwords are **a1b2c3d4e5, d4e3f2g1h0,** and **f102gh285,** respectively. The default database is the **sample** database. After creating the logins, check their existence using the system catalog.

E.12.4

Create three new database usernames for the logins in E.12.3. The new names are **s_ann, s_burt,** and **s_charles.**

E.12.5

Create a new user-defined database role called **managers** and add three members (see E.12.4) to the role. After that, display the information for this role and its members.

E.12.6

Using the GRANT statement, allow the user **s_burt** to create tables and the user **s_ann** to create stored procedures in the **sample** database.

E.12.7

Using the GRANT statement, allow the user **s_charles** to update the columns **lname** and **fname** of the **employee** table.

E.12.8

Using the GRANT statement, allow the users **s_burt** and **s_ann** to read the values from the columns **emp_lname** and **emp_fname** of the **employee** table. (Hint: Create the corresponding view first.)

E.12.9

Using the GRANT statement, allow the user-defined role **managers** to insert new rows in the **project** table.

E.12.10

Revoke the SELECT rights from the user **s_burt**.

E.12.11

Using Transact-SQL, do not allow the user **s_ann** to insert the new rows in the **project** table either directly or indirectly (using roles).

E.12.12

Discuss the difference between the use of views and Transact-SQL statements GRANT, DENY, and REVOKE in relation to security.

E.12.13

Display the existing information about the user **s_ann** in relation to the **sample** database. (Hint: Use the system procedure **sp_helpuser**.)

Chapter 13

Concurrency Control

As you already know, data in a database is generally shared between many user application programs. The situation in which several user application programs read and write the same data at the same time is called *concurrency*. Thus, each DBMS must have some kind of control mechanism to solve concurrency problems.

A high level of concurrency is possible in a database system that can manage many active user applications without them interfering with each other. Conversely, a database system in which different active applications interfere with each other support a low level of concurrency.

This chapter begins by describing the two concurrency control models that Database Engine supports. The next section explains how concurrency problems can be solved using transactions. This discussion includes an introduction of the four properties of transactions, known as ACID properties, discussion of the Transact-SQL statements related to transactions, and an introduction of transaction logs. The third major section addresses locking and the three general lock properties: lock modes, lock resources, and lock duration. Deadlock, an important problem that can arise as a consequence of locking, is also introduced.

The behavior of transactions depends on the selected isolation level. Five forms of isolation levels are introduced, including whether each belongs to the pessimistic or the optimistic concurrency model. The differences between existing isolation levels and their practical meaning will be explained, too.

The end of the chapter introduces row versioning, which is how Database Engine implements the optimistic concurrency model. The two isolation levels related to this model—SNAPSHOT and READ COMMITTED SNAPSHOT—are discussed, as well as use of the **tempdb** system database as a version store.

Concurrency Models

Database Engine supports two different concurrency models:

► Pessimistic concurrency
► Optimistic concurrency

Pessimistic concurrency uses locks to block access to data that is used by another process at the same time. In other words, a database system that uses pessimistic concurrency assumes that a conflict between two or more processes can occur at any time and therefore locks resources (row, page, table), as they are required, for the duration of a transaction. As you will see in the section "Locking," pessimistic concurrency issues shared locks on data being read so that no other process can modify that data. Also, pessimistic concurrency issues exclusive locks for data being modified so that no other processes can read or modify that data.

Optimistic concurrency works on the assumption that a transaction is unlikely to modify data that another transaction is modifying at the same time. Database Engine supports optimistic concurrency so that older versions of data rows are saved, and any process that reads the same data uses the row version that was active when it started reading data. For that reason, a process that modifies the data can do so without any limitation, because all other processes that read the same data access the saved versions of the data. The only conflict scenario occurs when two or more write operations use the same data. In that case, the system displays an error so that the client application can handle it.

NOTE

The notion of optimistic concurrency is generally defined in a broader sense. Optimistic concurrency control works on the assumption that resource conflicts between multiple users are unlikely, and allows transactions to execute without using locks. Only when a user is attempting to change data are resources checked to determine if any conflicts have occurred. If a conflict occurs, the application must be (repeatedly) restarted.

Transactions

A transaction specifies a sequence of Transact-SQL statements that is used by database programmers to package together read and write operations, so that the database system can guarantee the consistency of data. There are two forms of transactions:

- ▶ **Implicit**   Specifies any single INSERT, UPDATE, or DELETE statement as a transaction unit.

- ▶ **Explicit**   Generally a group of Transact-SQL statements, where the beginning and the end of the group are marked using statements such as BEGIN TRANSACTION, COMMIT, and ROLLBACK.

The notion of a transaction is best explained through an example. In the **sample** database, the employee Ann Jones should be assigned a new employee number. The employee number must be modified in two different tables at the same time. The row in the **employee** table and all corresponding rows in the **works_on** table must be modified at the same time. (If only one of these tables is modified, data in the **sample** database would be inconsistent, because the values of the primary key in the **employee** table and the corresponding values of the foreign key in the **works_on** table for Mrs. Jones would not match.)

Example 13.1 shows how you can implement the problem discussed above using Transact-SQL statements.

EXAMPLE 13.1

```
USE sample;
BEGIN TRANSACTION /* The beginning of the transaction */
UPDATE employee
    SET emp_no = 39831
    WHERE emp_no = 10102
    IF (@@error <> 0)
        ROLLBACK /* Rollback of the transaction */
UPDATE works_on
    SET emp_no = 39831
    WHERE emp_no = 10102
    IF (@@error <> 0)
        ROLLBACK
COMMIT /*The end of the transaction */
```

The consistent state of data used in Example 13.1 can be obtained only if both UPDATE statements are executed or neither of them is executed. The global variable **@@error** is used to test the execution of each Transact-SQL statement. If an error occurs, **@@error** is set to a negative value and the execution of all statements is rolled back. (The Transact-SQL statements BEGIN TRANSACTION, COMMIT, and ROLLBACK are defined in the upcoming section "Transact-SQL Statements and Transactions.")

NOTE

*The Transact-SQL language supports exceptions. Instead of using the global variable @@**error**, used in Example 13.1, you can use TRY and CATCH statements to implement exception handling in a transaction. The use of these statements is discussed in Chapter 8.*

The next section explains the ACID properties of transactions. These properties guarantee that the data used by application programs will be consistent.

Properties of Transactions

Transactions have the following properties, which are known collectively by the acronym ACID:

- ▶ Atomicity
- ▶ Consistency
- ▶ Isolation
- ▶ Durability

The atomicity property guarantees the indivisibility of a set of statements that modifies data in a database and is part of a transaction. This means that either all data modifications in a transaction are executed or, in the case of any failure, all already executed changes are undone.

Consistency guarantees that a transaction will not allow the database to contain inconsistent data. In other words, the transactional transformations on data bring the database from one consistent state to another.

The isolation property separates concurrent transactions from each other. In other words, an active transaction can't see data modifications in a concurrent and incomplete transaction. This means that some transactions might be rolled back to guarantee isolation.

Durability guarantees one of the most important database concepts: persistence of data. This property ensures that the effects of the particular transaction persist even if a system error occurs. For this reason, if a system error occurs while a transaction is active, all statements of that transaction will be undone.

Transact-SQL Statements and Transactions

There are six Transact-SQL statements related to transactions:

- ▶ BEGIN TRANSACTION
- ▶ BEGIN DISTRIBUTED TRANSACTION
- ▶ COMMIT [WORK]
- ▶ ROLLBACK [WORK]
- ▶ SAVE TRANSACTION
- ▶ SET IMPLICIT_TRANSACTIONS

The BEGIN TRANSACTION statement starts the transaction. It has the following syntax:

```
BEGIN TRANSACTION [ {transaction_name | @trans_var }
  [WITH MARK ['description']]]
```

transaction_name is the name assigned to the transaction, which can be used only on the outermost pair of nested BEGIN TRANSACTION/COMMIT or BEGIN TRANSACTION/ROLLBACK statements. **@trans_var** is the name of a user-defined variable containing a valid transaction name. The WITH MARK option specifies that the transaction is to be marked in the log. **description** is a string that describes the mark. If WITH MARK is used, a transaction name must be specified. (For more information on transaction log marking for recovery, see Chapter 17.)

The BEGIN DISTRIBUTED TRANSACTION statement specifies the start of a distributed transaction managed by the Microsoft Distributed Transaction Coordinator (MS DTC). A *distributed* transaction is one that involves databases on more than one server. For this reason, where is a need for a coordinator, which will coordinate execution of statements on all involved servers. The server executing the BEGIN DISTRIBUTED TRANSACTION statement is the transaction coordinator and therefore controls the completion of the distributed transaction. (See Chapter 19 for a discussion of distributed transactions.)

The COMMIT WORK statement successfully ends the transaction started with the BEGIN TRANSACTION statement. This means that all modifications made by the transaction are stored on the disk. The COMMIT WORK statement is a standardized SQL statement. (The WORK clause is optional.)

NOTE

The Transact-SQL language also supports the COMMIT TRANSACTION statement, which is functionally equivalent to COMMIT WORK, with the exception that the former accepts a user-defined transaction name. COMMIT TRANSACTION is an extension of Transact-SQL in relation to the SQL standard.

In contrast to the COMMIT statement, the ROLLBACK WORK statement reports an unsuccessful end of the transaction. Programmers use this statement if they assume that the database might be in an inconsistent state. In this case, all executed modification operations within the transaction are rolled back. The ROLLBACK WORK statement is a standardized SQL statement. (The WORK clause is optional.)

NOTE

Transact-SQL also supports the ROLLBACK TRANSACTION statement, which is functionally equivalent to ROLLBACK WORK, with the exception that ROLLBACK TRANSACTION accepts a user-defined transaction name.

The SAVE TRANSACTION statement sets a savepoint within a transaction. A *savepoint* marks a specified point within the transaction so that all updates that follow can be canceled without canceling the entire transaction. (To cancel an entire transaction, use the ROLLBACK statement.)

NOTE

The SAVE TRANSACTION statement actually does not commit any modification operation; it only creates a target for the subsequent ROLLBACK statement with the label with the same name as the SAVE TRANSACTION statement.

Example 13.2 shows the use of the SAVE TRANSACTION statement.

EXAMPLE 13.2

```
BEGIN TRANSACTION;
INSERT INTO department (dept_no, dept_name)
    VALUES ('d4', 'Sales');
SAVE TRANSACTION a;
INSERT INTO department (dept_no, dept_name)
    VALUES ('d5', 'Research');
SAVE TRANSACTION b;
INSERT INTO department (dept_no, dept_name)
    VALUES ('d6', 'Management');
ROLLBACK TRANSACTION b;
INSERT INTO department (dept_no, dept_name)
    VALUES ('d7', 'Support');
ROLLBACK TRANSACTION a;
COMMIT TRANSACTION;
```

The only statement in Example 13.2 that is executed is the first INSERT statement. The third INSERT statement is rolled back by the ROLLBACK **b** statement, while the other two INSERT statements are rolled back by the ROLLBACK **a** statement.

NOTE

The SAVE TRANSACTION statement, in combination with the IF or WHILE statement, is a useful transaction feature for the execution of parts of an entire transaction. On the other hand, the use of this statement is contrary to the principle of operational databases that a transaction should be as short as possible, because long transactions generally reduce data availability.

As you already know, each Transact-SQL statement always belongs either implicitly or explicitly to a transaction. Database Engine provides implicit transactions for compliance with the SQL standard. When a session operates in the implicit transaction mode, selected statements implicitly issue the BEGIN TRANSACTION statement. This means that you do nothing to start an implicit transaction. However, the end of each implicit transaction must be explicitly committed or rolled back using the COMMIT or ROLLBACK statement. (If you do not explicitly commit the transaction, the transaction and all the data changes it contains are rolled back when the user disconnects.)

To enable an implicit transaction, you have to enable the IMPLICIT_ TRANSACTIONS clause of the SET statement. This statement sets the implicit transaction mode for the current session. When a connection is in the implicit transaction mode and the connection is not currently in a transaction, executing any of the following statements starts a transaction:

ALTER TABLE	FETCH	REVOKE
CREATE TABLE	GRANT	SELECT
DELETE	INSERT	TRUNCATE TABLE
DROP TABLE	OPEN	UPDATE

In other words, if you have a sequence of statements from the preceding list, each statement will represent a single transaction.

The beginning of an explicit transaction is marked with the BEGIN TRANSACTION statement. The end of an explicit transaction is marked with the COMMIT or ROLLBACK statement. Explicit transactions can be nested. In this case, each pair of statements BEGIN TRANSACTION/COMMIT or BEGIN TRANSACTION/ ROLLBACK is used inside one or more such pairs. (The nested transactions are usually used in stored procedures, which themselves contain transactions and are invoked inside another transaction.) The global variable **@@trancount** contains the number of active transactions for the current user.

BEGIN TRANSACTION, COMMIT, and ROLLBACK can be specified using a name assigned to the transaction. (The named ROLLBACK statement corresponds either to a named transaction or to the SAVE TRANSACTION statement with the same name.) You can use a named transaction only in the outermost statement pair of nested BEGIN TRANSACTION/COMMIT or BEGIN TRANSACTION/ ROLLBACK statements.

Transaction Log

Relational database systems keep a record of each change they make to the database during a transaction. This is necessary in case an error occurs during the execution of the transaction. In this situation, all previously executed statements within the transaction have to be rolled back. As soon as the system detects the error, it uses the stored records to return the database to the consistent state that existed before the transaction was started.

Database Engine keeps all stored records, in particular the before and after values, in one or more files called the *transaction log*. Each database has its own transaction log. Thus, if it is necessary to roll back one or more modification operations executed on the tables of the current database, Database Engine uses the entries in the transaction log to restore the values of columns that the database had before the transaction was started.

The transaction log is used to roll back or restore a transaction. If an error occurs and the transaction does not completely execute, the system uses all existing before values from the transaction log (called *before images*) to roll back all modifications since the start of the transaction. The process in which before images from the transaction log are used to roll back all modifications is called the *undo* activity.

Transaction logs also store so called after images. *After images* are all after values, which are used to roll forward all modifications since the start of the transaction. This process is called the *redo* activity and is applied during recovery of a database. (For further details concerning transaction logs and recovery, see Chapter 17.)

Every entry written into the log is uniquely identified using the log sequence number (LSN). All log entries that are part of the particular transaction are linked together, so that all parts of a transaction can be located for undo and redo activities.

Locking

Concurrency can lead to several negative effects, such as the reading of nonexistent data or loss of modified data. Consider this real-world example illustrating one of these negative effects, called *dirty read*: User U_1 in the personnel department gets notice of an address change for the employee Jim Smith. U_1 makes the address change, but when viewing the bank account information of Mr. Smith in the consecutive dialog step, he realizes that he modified the address of the wrong person. (The enterprise employs two persons with the name Jim Smith.) Fortunately, the application allows the user to cancel this change by clicking a button. U_1 clicks the button, knowing that he has committed no error.

At the same time, user U_2 in the technical department retrieves the data of the latter Mr. Smith to send the newest technical document to his home, because the employee seldom comes to the office. As the employee's address was wrongly changed just before U_2 retrieved the address, U_2 prints out the wrong address label and sends the document to the wrong person.

To prevent problems like these in the pessimistic concurrency model, every DBMS must have mechanisms that control the access of data by all users at the same time. Database Engine, like all relational DBMSs, uses locks to guarantee the consistency of the database in case of multiuser access. Each application program locks the data it needs, guaranteeing that no other program can modify the same data. When another application program requests the modification of the locked data, the system either stops the program with an error or makes a program wait.

Locking has several different aspects:

▶ Lock duration

▶ Lock modes

▶ Lock granularity

Lock duration specifies a time period during which a resource holds the particular lock. Duration of a lock depends on, among other things, the mode of the lock and the choice of the isolation level.

The next two sections describe lock modes and lock granularity.

NOTE

The following discussion concerns the pessimistic concurrency model. The optimistic concurrency model is handled using row versioning, and will be explained at the end of this chapter.

Lock Modes

Lock modes specify different kinds of locks. The choice of which lock mode to apply depends on the resource that needs to be locked. The following three lock types are used for row- and page-level locking:

▶ Shared (S)

▶ Exclusive (X)

▶ Update (U)

A *shared lock* reserves a resource (page or row) for reading only. Other processes cannot modify the locked resource while the lock remains. On the other hand, several processes can hold a shared lock for a resource at the same time—that is, several processes can read the resource locked with the shared lock.

An *exclusive lock* reserves a page or row for the exclusive use of a single transaction. It is used for DML statements (INSERT, UPDATE, and DELETE) that modify the resource. An exclusive lock cannot be set if some other process holds a shared or exclusive lock on the resource—that is, there can be only one exclusive lock for a resource. Once an exclusive lock is set for the page (or row), no other lock can be placed on the same resource.

NOTE

Page-level locking also allows an intent lock, described later in this section.

An *update lock* can be placed only if no other update or exclusive lock exists. On the other hand, it can be placed on objects that already have shared locks. (In this case, the update lock acquires another shared lock on the same object.) If a transaction that modifies the object is committed, the update lock is changed to an exclusive lock if there are no other locks on the object. There can be only one update lock for an object.

NOTE

Update locks prevent certain common types of deadlocks. (Deadlocks are described at the end of this section.)

Table 13-1 shows the compatibility matrix for shared, exclusive, and update locks. The matrix is interpreted as follows: suppose transaction T_1 holds a lock as specified in the first column of the matrix, and suppose some other transaction, T_2, requests a lock as specified in the corresponding column heading. In this case, "yes" indicates that a lock of T_2 is possible, whereas "no" indicates a conflict with the existing lock.

NOTE

Database Engine also supports other lock forms, such as latches and spinlocks. The description of these lock forms can be found in Books Online.

At the table level, there are five different types of locks:

▶ Shared (S)
▶ Exclusive (X)
▶ Intent shared (IS)
▶ Intent exclusive (IX)
▶ Shared with intent exclusive (SIX)

Shared and exclusive locks correspond to the row-level (or page-level) locks with the same names. Generally, an *intent* lock shows an intention to lock the next-lower resource in the hierarchy of the database objects. Therefore, intent locks are placed at

	Shared	Update	Exclusive
Shared	Yes	Yes	No
Update	Yes	No	No
Exclusive	No	No	No

Table 13-1   *Compatibility Matrix for Shared, Exclusive, and Update Locks*

	S	X	IS	SIX	IX
S	Yes	No	Yes	No	No
X	No	No	No	No	No
IS	Yes	No	Yes	Yes	Yes
SIX	No	No	Yes	No	No
IX	No	No	Yes	No	Yes

Table 13-2   *Compatibility Matrix for All Kinds of Table Locks*

a level in the object hierarchy above that which the process intends to lock. This is an efficient way to tell whether such locks will be possible, and it prevents other processes from locking the higher level before the desired locks can be attained.

Table 13-2 shows the compatibility matrix for all kinds of table locks. The matrix is interpreted exactly as the matrix in Table 13-1.

Lock Granularity

Lock granularity specifies which resource is locked by a single lock attempt. Database Engine can lock the following resources:

▶ Row

▶ Page

▶ Index key or range of index keys

▶ Table

▶ Extent

▶ Database itself

NOTE

The system automatically chooses the appropriate lock granularity.

A row is the smallest resource that can be locked. The support of row-level locking includes both data rows and index entries. Row-level locking means that only the row that is accessed by an application will be locked. Hence, all other rows that belong to the same page are free and can be used by other applications. Database Engine can also lock the page on which the row that has to be locked is stored.

NOTE

If a table is clustered, the data pages are stored at the leaf level of the (clustered) index structure and are therefore locked with index key locks instead of row locks.

Locking is also done on disk units, called *extents*, that are 64K in size (see Chapter 15). Extent locks are set automatically when a table (or index) grows and the additional disk space is needed.

Lock granularity affects concurrency. In general, the larger the lock granularity used, the more concurrency is reduced. This means that row-level locking maximizes concurrency because it leaves all but one row on the page unlocked. On the other hand, system overhead is increased because each locked row requires one lock. Page-level locking (and table-level locking) restricts the availability of data but decreases the system overhead.

Lock Escalation

If many locks of the same lock granularity are held during a transaction, Database Engine automatically upgrades these locks into a table lock. This process of converting many page-, row-, or index-level locks into one table lock is called *lock escalation*. The escalation threshold is the boundary at which the database system applies the lock escalation. Escalation thresholds are determined dynamically by the system and require no configuration. (Currently, the amount of threshold boundary is 5000 locks.)

The general problem with lock escalation is that the database server decides when to escalate a particular lock, and this decision might be suboptimal for applications with different requirements. For this reason, SQL Server 2008 enhances the syntax of the ALTER TABLE statement to allow you to change the lock escalation mechanism. This statement now supports the TABLE option with the following syntax:

SET (LOCK_ESCALATION = { TABLE | AUTO | DISABLE })

The TABLE option is the default value and it specifies that lock escalation will be done at table-level granularity. (This behavior is the same as in SQL Server 2005.) The AUTO option allows Database Engine to select the lock escalation granularity that is appropriate for the table schema. Finally, the DISABLE option allows you to disable lock escalation in most cases. (There are same cases in which Database Engine must take a table lock to protect data integrity.)

Example 13.3 disables the lock escalation for the **employee** table.

EXAMPLE 13.3

USE sample;
ALTER TABLE employee SET (LOCK_ESCALATION = DISABLE);

Affecting Locks

You can use either locking hints or the LOCK_TIMEOUT option of the SET statement to affect locks. The following subsections describe these features.

Locking Hints

Locking hints specify the type of locking used by Database Engine to lock table data. Table-level locking hints can be used when finer control of the types of locks acquired on a resource is required. (Locking hints override the current transaction isolation level for the session.)

All locking hints are written as a part of the FROM clause in the SELECT statement. You can use the following locking hints:

▶ **UPDLOCK**   Places update locks for each row of the table during the read operation. All update locks are held until the end of the transaction.

▶ **TABLOCK (TABLOCKX)**   Places a shared (or exclusive) table lock on the table. All locks are held until the end of the transaction.

▶ **ROWLOCK**   Replaces the existing shared table lock with shared row locks for each qualifying row of the table.

▶ **PAGLOCK**   Replaces a shared table lock with shared page locks for each page containing qualifying rows.

▶ **NOLOCK**   Synonym for READUNCOMMITTED (see the description of isolation-level hints later in this chapter).

▶ **HOLDLOCK**   Synonym for REPEATABLEREAD (see the description of isolation-level hints later in this chapter).

▶ **XLOCK**   Specifies that exclusive locks are to be taken and held until the transaction completes. If XLOCK is specified with ROWLOCK, PAGLOCK, or TABLOCK, the exclusive locks apply to the appropriate level of granularity.

▶ **READPAST**   Specifies that Database Engine does not read rows that are locked by other transactions.

NOTE

All these options can be combined in any order if the combination makes sense. (For example, the combination between TABLOCK and PAGLOCK is senseless, because both options are applied to different resources.)

LOCK_TIMEOUT Option

The LOCK_TIMEOUT option of the SET statement can be used to specify the number of milliseconds a transaction will wait for a lock to be released. The value of −1 (the default value) indicates no time-out; in other words, the transaction won't wait at all. (The READPAST locking hint provides an alternative to this SET option.)

Displaying Lock Information

Lock information can be displayed using either the **sp_lock** system procedure or the dynamic management view called **sys.dm_tran_locks**. Because **sp_lock** is a deprecated feature and won't be supported in the next release of SQL Server, this section describes only the **sys.dm_tran_locks** view.

sys.dm_tran_locks. The view returns information about currently active lock manager resources. Each row represents a currently active request for a lock that has been granted or is waiting to be granted. The columns of this view relate to two groups: resource and request. The resource group describes the resource on which the lock request is being made, and the request group describes the lock request. The most important columns of this view are as follows:

- ▶ **resource_type**   Represents the resource type
- ▶ **resource_database_id**   Specifies the ID of the database under which this resource is scoped
- ▶ **request_mode**   Specifies the mode of the request
- ▶ **request_status**   Specifies the current status of the request

Example 13.4 displays all the locks that are in a wait state.

EXAMPLE 13.4

```
SELECT resource_type, DB_NAME(resource_database_id) as db_name,
   request_session_id, request_mode, request_status
   FROM sys.dm_tran_locks
   WHERE request_status = 'WAIT;'
```

Deadlock

A *deadlock* is a special concurrency problem in which two transactions block the progress of each other. The first transaction has a lock on some database object that the other transaction wants to access, and vice versa. (In general, several transactions can cause a deadlock by building a circle of dependencies.) Example 13.5 shows the deadlock situation between two transactions.

NOTE

*The parallelism of processes cannot be achieved naturally using the small **sample** database, because every transaction in it is executed very quickly. Therefore, Example 13.5 uses the WAITFOR statement to pause both transactions for ten seconds to simulate the deadlock.*

EXAMPLE 13.5

```
BEGIN TRANSACTION               BEGIN TRANSACTION
UPDATE works_on                 UPDATE employee
   SET job = 'Manager'             SET dept_no = 'd2'
   WHERE emp_no = 18316            WHERE emp_no = 9031
   AND project_no = 'p2'        WAITFOR DELAY '00:00:10'
WAITFOR DELAY '00:00:10'        DELETE FROM works_on
UPDATE employee                    WHERE emp_no = 18316
   SET emp_lname = 'Green'          AND project_no = 'p2'
   WHERE emp_no = 9031          COMMIT
COMMIT
```

If both transactions in Example 13.5 are executed at the same time, the deadlock appears and the system returns the following output:

Server: Msg 1205, Level 13, State 45
Transaction (Process id 56) was deadlocked with another process and has been chosen as deadlock victim. Rerun your command.

As the output of Example 13.5 shows, the database system handles a deadlock by choosing one of the transactions as a "victim" (actually, the one that closed the loop in lock requests) and rolling it back. (The other transaction is executed after that.) A programmer can handle a deadlock by implementing the conditional statement that tests for the returned error number (1205) and then executes the rolled-back transaction again.

You can affect which transaction the system chooses as the "victim" by using the DEADLOCK_PRIORITY option of the SET statement. There are 21 different priority levels, from −10 to 10. The value LOW corresponds to −5, NORMAL (the default value) corresponds to 0, and HIGH corresponds to 5. The "victim" session is chosen according to the session's deadlock priority.

Isolation Levels

In theory, each transaction should be fully isolated from other transactions. But, in such a case, data availability is significantly reduced, because read operations in a transaction block write operations in other transactions, and vice versa. If data availability is an important issue, this property can be loosened using isolation levels. *Isolation levels* specify the degree to which data being retrieved in a transaction is protected from changes to the same data by other transactions. Before you are introduced to the existing isolation levels, the following section takes a look at scenarios that can arise if locking isn't used and, hence, there is no isolation between transactions.

Concurrency Problems

If locking isn't used and thus no isolation exists between transaction, the following four problems may appear:

- ► Lost update
- ► Dirty reads (discussed earlier, in the "Locking" section)
- ► Nonrepeatable reads
- ► Phantoms

The *lost update* concurrency problem occurs when no isolation is provided to a transaction from other transactions. This means that several transactions can read the same data and modify it. The changes to the data by all transactions, except those by the last transaction, are lost.

The *nonrepeatable read* concurrency problem occurs when one process reads data several times, and another process changes the same data between two read operations of the first one. Therefore, the values read by both read operations are different.

The *phantom* concurrency problem is similar to the nonrepeatable read concurrency problem, because two subsequent read operations can display different values, but in this case, the reason for this behavior lies in the different number of rows being read the first time and the second time. (Additional rows, called *phantoms*, are inserted by other transactions.)

Database Engine and Isolation Levels

Using isolation levels, you can specify which of the concurrency problems may occur and which you want to avoid. Database Engine supports the following five isolation levels, which control how your read operations are executed:

- ▶ READ UNCOMMITTED
- ▶ READ COMMITTED
- ▶ REPEATABLE READ
- ▶ SERIALIZABLE
- ▶ SNAPSHOT

READ UNCOMMITTED, REPEATABLE READ, and SERIALIZABLE are available only in the pessimistic concurrency model, whereas SNAPSHOT is available only in the optimistic concurrency model. READ COMMITTED is available in both models. The four isolation levels available in the pessimistic concurrency model are described next. SNAPSHOT is described in the next section, "Row Versioning."

READ UNCOMMITTED

READ UNCOMMITTED provides the simplest form of isolation between transactions, because it does not isolate the read operations from other transactions at all. When a transaction retrieves a row at this isolation level, it acquires no locks and respects none of the existing locks. The data that is read by such a transaction may be inconsistent. In this case, a transaction reads data that is updated from some other active transaction. If the latter transaction rolls back later, the former transaction reads data that never really existed.

Of the four concurrency problems described in the preceding section, READ UNCOMMITTED allows dirty reads, nonrepeatable reads, and phantoms.

NOTE

The READ UNCOMMITTED isolation level is usually very undesirable and should be used only when the accuracy of the data read is not important or the data is seldom modified.

READ COMMITTED

As you already know, the READ COMMITTED isolation level has two forms. The first form applies to the pessimistic concurrency model, while the second form applies to the optimistic concurrency model. This section discusses the former. The second form, READ COMMITTED SNAPSHOT, is discussed in the following section, "Row Versioning."

A transaction that reads a row and uses the READ COMMITTED isolation level tests only whether an exclusive lock is placed on the row. If no such lock exists, the transaction fetches the row. (This is done using a shared lock.) This action prevents the transaction from reading data that is not committed and that can be subsequently rolled back. After reading the data values, the data can be changed by some other transaction.

Shared locks used by this isolation level are released immediately after the data is processed. (Generally, all locks are released at the end of the transaction.) For this reason, the access to the concurrent data is improved, but nonrepeatable reads and phantoms can still happen.

NOTE

The READ COMMITTED isolation level is the default isolation level of Database Engine.

REPEATABLE READ

In contrast to the READ COMMITTED isolation level, REPEATABLE READ places shared locks on all data that is read and holds these locks until the transaction is committed or rolled back. Therefore, in this case, the execution of a query several times inside a transaction will always display the same result. The disadvantage of this isolation level is that concurrency is further reduced, because the time interval during which other transactions cannot update the same data is significantly longer than in the case of READ COMMITTED.

This isolation level does not prevent another transaction from inserting new rows, which are included in subsequent reads, so phantoms can appear.

SERIALIZABLE

SERIALIZABLE is the strongest isolation level, because it prevents all four concurrency problems already discussed. It acquires a range lock on all data that is read by the corresponding transaction. Therefore, this isolation level also prevents the insertion of new rows by another transaction until the former transaction is committed or rolled back.

NOTE

The SERIALIZABLE isolation level is implemented using a key-range locking method. This method locks individual rows and the ranges between them. A key-range lock acquires locks for index entries rather than locks for the particular pages or the entire table. In this case, any modification operation of another transaction cannot be executed, because the necessary changes of index entries are not possible.

Each isolation level in the preceding description reduces the concurrency more than the previous one. Thus, the isolation level READ UNCOMMITTED reduces concurrency the least. On the other hand, it also has the smallest isolation from concurrent transactions. SERIALIZABLE reduces concurrency the most, but guarantees full isolation between concurrent transactions.

Setting and Editing Isolation Levels

You can set an isolation level by using the following:

▶ The TRANSACTION ISOLATION LEVEL clause of the SET statement

▶ Isolation-level hints

The TRANSACTION ISOLATION LEVEL option of the SET statement provides five constant values, which have the same names and meanings as the standard isolation levels just described. The FROM clause of the SELECT statement supports several hints for isolation levels:

▶ READUNCOMMITTED

▶ READCOMMITTED

▶ REPEATABLEREAD

▶ SERIALIZABLE

These hints correspond to the isolation levels with the same name (but with a space in the name). The specification of isolation levels in the FROM clause of the SELECT statement overrides the current value set by the SET TRANSACTION ISOLATION LEVEL statement.

The DBCC USEROPTIONS statement returns, among other things, information about the isolation level. Look at the value of the isolation level option of this statement to find out the isolation level of your process.

Row Versioning

Database Engine supports an optimistic concurrency control mechanism based on row versioning. When data is modified using row versioning, logical copies of the data are maintained for all data modifications performed in the database. Every time a row is modified, the database system stores a before image of the previously committed row in the **tempdb** system database. Each version is marked with the transaction sequence number (XSN) of the transaction that made the change. (The XSN is used to uniquely identify each transaction.) The newest version of a row is always stored in the database and chained in the linked list to the corresponding version stored in **tempdb**. An old row version in the **tempdb** database might contain pointers to other, even older versions. Each row version is kept in the **tempdb** database as long as there are operations that might require it.

Row versioning isolates transactions from the effects of modifications made by other transactions without the need for requesting shared locks on rows that have been read. This significant reduction in the total number of locks acquired by this isolation level significantly increases availability of data. However, exclusive locks are still needed: transactions using the optimistic isolation level called SNAPSHOT request locks when they modify rows.

Row versioning is used, among other things, to

▶ Support the READ COMMITTED SNAPSHOT isolation level

▶ Support the SNAPSHOT isolation level

▶ Build the **inserted** and **deleted** tables in triggers

The following subsections describe the SNAPSHOT and READ COMMITTED SNAPSHOT isolation levels, while Chapter 14 discusses in detail the **inserted** and **deleted** tables.

READ COMMITTED SNAPSHOT Isolation Level

READ COMMITTED SNAPSHOT is a slight variation of the READ COMMITTED isolation level discussed in the previous section. It is a statement-level isolation, which means that any other transaction will read the committed values as they exist at the beginning of the statement. In the case of updates, this isolation level reverts from row versions to actual data to select rows to update and uses update locks on the data rows selected. Actual data rows that have to be modified acquire exclusive locks.

The main advantage of READ COMMITTED SNAPSHOT is that read operations do not block updates and updates do not block read operations. On the other hand, updates block other updates, because exclusive locks are set before an update operation is executed.

You use the SET clause of the ALTER DATABASE statement to enable the READ COMMITTED SNAPSHOT isolation level. After activation, no further changes are necessary. Any transaction specified with the READ COMMITTED isolation level will now run under READ COMMITTED SNAPSHOT.

SNAPSHOT Isolation Level

The SNAPSHOT isolation level is a transaction-level isolation, which means that any other transaction will read the committed values as they exist just before the snapshot transaction starts. Also, the snapshot transaction will return the initial value until it completes, even if another transaction changed it in the meantime. Therefore, only after the snapshot transaction ends will the other transaction read a modified value.

Transactions running under the SNAPSHOT isolation level acquire exclusive locks on data before performing the modification only to enforce constraints. Otherwise, locks are not acquired on data until the data is to be modified. When a data row meets the update criteria, the snapshot transaction verifies that the data row has not been modified by a concurrent transaction that committed after the transaction began. If the data row has been modified in a concurrent transaction, an update conflict occurs and the snapshot transaction is terminated. The update conflict is handled by the database system and there is no way to disable the update conflict detection.

Enabling the SNAPSHOT isolation level is a two-step process. First, on the database level, enable the ALLOW_SNAPSHOT_ISOLATION database option. Second, for each session that will use this isolation level, set the SET TRANSACTION ISOLATION LEVEL statement to SNAPSHOT. When these options are set, versions are built for all rows that are modified in the database.

READ COMMITTED SNAPSHOT vs. SNAPSHOT

The most important difference between the two optimistic isolation levels is that SNAPSHOT can result in update conflicts when a process sees the same data for the duration of its transaction and is not blocked. By contrast, the READ COMMITTED SNAPSHOT isolation level does not use its own XSN when choosing row versions. Each time a statement is started, such a transaction reads the latest XSN issued for that instance of the database system and selects the row based on that number.

Another difference is that the READ COMMITTED SNAPSHOT isolation level allows other transactions to modify the data before the row versioning transaction completes. This can lead to a conflict if another transaction modified the data between the time the row versioning transaction performs a read and subsequently tries to execute the corresponding write operation. (For an application based on the SNAPSHOT isolation level, the system detects the possible conflicts and sends the corresponding error message.)

Conclusion

Concurrency in multiuser database systems can lead to several negative effects, such as the reading of nonexistent data or loss of modified data. Database Engine, like all other DBMSs, solves this problem by using transactions. A transaction is a sequence of Transact-SQL statements that logically belong together. All statements inside a transaction build an atomic unit. This means that either all statements are executed or, in the case of failure, all statements are canceled.

The locking mechanism is used to implement transactions. The effect of the lock is to prevent other transactions from changing the locked object. Locking has the following aspects: lock modes, lock granularity, and lock duration. Lock mode specifies different kinds of locks, the choice of which depends on the resource that needs to be locked. Lock duration specifies a time period during which a resource holds the particular lock.

Database Engine provides a mechanism called a trigger that enforces, among other things, general integrity constraints. This mechanism is discussed in detail in the next chapter.

Exercises

E.13.1

What is a purpose of transactions?

E.13.2

What is the difference between a local and a distributed transaction?

E.13.3

What is the difference between implicit and explicit transaction mode?

E.13.4

What kinds of locks are compatible with an exclusive lock?

E.13.5

How can you test the successful execution of each T-SQL statement?

E.13.6

When should you use the SAVE TRANSACTION statement?

E.13.7

Discuss the difference between row-level and page-level locking.

E.13.8

Can a user explicitly influence the locking behavior of the system?

E.13.9

What is a difference between basic lock types (shared and exclusive) and an intent lock?

E.13.10

What does lock escalation mean?

E.13.11

Discuss the difference between the READ UNCOMMITTED and SERIALIZABLE isolation levels.

E.13.12

What is deadlock?

E.13.13

Which process is used as a victim in a deadlock situation? Can a user influence the decision of the system?

Chapter 14

Triggers

In This Chapter

- ▶ Introduction
- ▶ Application Areas for DML Triggers
- ▶ DDL Triggers
- ▶ Triggers and CLR

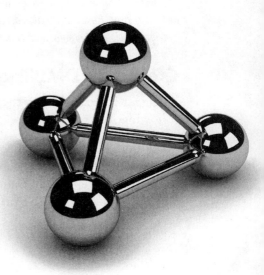

This chapter is dedicated to a mechanism called a *trigger*. The beginning of the chapter describes Transact-SQL statements for creating, deleting, and modifying triggers. After that, examples for different application areas for this database object are given. Each example is created using one of the following statements, INSERT, UPDATE, or DELETE. The second part of the chapter covers DDL triggers, which are based on DDL statements such as CREATE TABLE. Again, examples for different application areas related to DDL triggers are given. The end of the chapter discusses the implementation of triggers using CLR (Common Language Runtime).

Introduction

A trigger is a mechanism that is invoked when a particular action occurs on a particular table. Each trigger has three general parts:

- ▶ A name
- ▶ The action
- ▶ The execution

The maximum size of a trigger name is 128 characters. The action of a trigger can be either a DML statement (INSERT, UPDATE, or DELETE) or a DDL statement. Therefore, there are two trigger forms: DML triggers and DDL triggers. The execution part of a trigger usually contains a stored procedure or a batch.

NOTE

Database Engine allows you to create triggers using either Transact-SQL or CLR programming languages such as C# and Visual Basic. This section describes the use of Transact-SQL to implement triggers. The implementation of triggers using CLR programming languages is shown at the end of the chapter.

Creating a DML Trigger

A trigger is created using the CREATE TRIGGER statement, which has the following form:

```
CREATE TRIGGER [schema_name.]trigger_name
  ON {table_name | view_name}
    [WITH dml_trigger_option [,...]]
  {FOR | AFTER | INSTEAD OF} { [INSERT] [,] [UPDATE] [,] [DELETE]}
  [WITH APPEND]
  {AS  sql_statement  | EXTERNAL NAME method_name}
```

schema_name is the name of the schema to which the trigger belongs. **trigger_name** is the name of the trigger. **table_name** is the name of the table for which the trigger is specified. (Triggers on views are also supported, as indicated by the inclusion of **view_name**.)

The AFTER and INSTEAD OF options are two additional options that you can define for a trigger. (The FOR clause is a synonym for AFTER.) AFTER triggers fire after the triggering action occurs. INSTEAD OF triggers are executed instead of the corresponding triggering action. AFTER triggers can be created only on tables, while INSTEAD OF triggers can be created on both tables and views. Examples showing the use of these two trigger types are provided later in this chapter.

The INSERT, UPDATE, and DELETE options specify the trigger action. (The trigger action is the type of Transact-SQL statement that activates the trigger.) These three statements can be written in any possible combination. The DELETE statement is not allowed if the IF UPDATE option is used.

As you can see from the syntax of the CREATE TRIGGER statement, the AS sql_statement specification is used to determine the action(s) of the trigger. (You can also use the EXTERNAL NAME option, which is explained later in this chapter.)

NOTE

Database Engine allows you to create multiple triggers for each table and for each action (INSERT, UPDATE, and DELETE). By default, there is no defined order in which multiple triggers for a given modification action are executed. (You can define the order by using the first and last triggers, as described later in this chapter.)

Only the database owner, DDL administrators, and the owner of the table on which the trigger is defined have the authority to create a trigger for the current database. (In contrast to the permissions for other CREATE statements, this permission is not transferable.)

Modifying a Trigger's Structure

Transact-SQL also supports the ALTER TRIGGER statement, which modifies the structure of a trigger. The ALTER TRIGGER statement is generally used to modify the body of the trigger. All clauses and options of the ALTER TRIGGER statement correspond to the clauses and options with the same names in the CREATE TRIGGER statement.

The ALTER TRIGGER permissions default to members of the **db_owner** and **db_ddladmin** fixed database roles and to the table owner.

The DROP TRIGGER statement removes one or more existing triggers from the current database.

The following section describes deleted and inserted tables, which play a significant role in a triggered action.

Using Deleted and Inserted Tables

When creating a triggered action, you usually must indicate whether you are referring to the value of a column before or after the triggering action changes it. For this reason, two virtual tables with special names are used to test the effect of the triggering statement:

▶ **deleted**   Contains copies of rows that are deleted from the triggered table

▶ **inserted**   Contains copies of rows that are inserted into the triggered table

The structure of these tables is equivalent to the structure of the table for which the trigger is specified.

The **deleted** table is used if the DELETE or UPDATE clause is specified in the CREATE TRIGGER statement. The **inserted** table is used if the INSERT or UPDATE clause is specified in the CREATE TRIGGER statement. This means that for each DELETE statement executed in the triggered action, the **deleted** table is created. Similarly, for each INSERT statement executed in the triggered action, the **inserted** table is created.

An UPDATE statement is treated as a DELETE, followed by an INSERT. Therefore, for each UPDATE statement executed in the triggered action, the **deleted** and **inserted** tables are created (in this sequence).

The materialization of **inserted** and **deleted** tables is done using row versioning, which is discussed in detail in Chapter 13. When DML statements, such as INSERT, UPDATE, and DELETE executed on a table with corresponding triggers, all changes to the table are always versioned. When the trigger needs the information from the **deleted** table, it accesses the data from the version store. In the case of the **inserted** table, the trigger accesses the most recent versions of the rows.

NOTE

*Row versioning uses the **tempdb** database as the version store. For this reason, you must expect significant growth of this system database if your database contains many triggers that are often used.*

Application Areas for DML Triggers

The first part of the chapter introduced how you can create a DML trigger and modify its structure. This trigger form can be used to solve different problems. This section describes several application areas for DML triggers (AFTER triggers and INSTEAD OF triggers).

AFTER Triggers

As you already know, AFTER triggers fire after the triggering action has been processed. You can specify an AFTER trigger by using either the AFTER or FOR reserved keyword. AFTER triggers can be created only on base tables.

AFTER triggers can be used to perform the following actions, among others:

▶ Create an audit trail of activities in one or more tables of the database (see Example 14.1)

▶ Implement business rules (see Example 14.2)

▶ Enforce referential integrity (see Examples 14.3 and 14.4)

Creating an Audit Trail

Chapter 12 discussed how you can capture data changes using the mechanism called CDC (change data capture). DML triggers can also be used to solve the same problem. Example 14.1 shows how triggers can create an audit trail of activities in one or more tables of the database.

EXAMPLE 14.1

/* The audit_budget table is used as an audit trail of activities in the project table */

```
USE sample;
GO
CREATE TABLE audit_budget
  (project_no CHAR(4) NULL,
   user_name CHAR(16) NULL,
   date DATETIME NULL,
   budget_old FLOAT NULL,
   budget_new FLOAT NULL);
GO
```

```
CREATE TRIGGER modify_budget
   ON project AFTER UPDATE
   AS IF UPDATE(budget)
   BEGIN
   DECLARE @budget_old FLOAT
   DECLARE @budget_new FLOAT
   DECLARE @project_number CHAR(4)
   SELECT @budget_old = (SELECT budget FROM deleted)
   SELECT @budget_new = (SELECT budget FROM inserted)
   SELECT @project_number = (SELECT project_no FROM deleted)
   INSERT INTO audit_budget VALUES
   (@project_number,USER_NAME(),GETDATE(),@budget_old, @budget_new)
   END
```

Example 14.1 shows how triggers can be used to implement an audit trail of the activity within a table. This example creates the **audit_budget** table, which stores all modifications of the **budget** column of the **project** table. Recording all the modifications of this column will be executed using the **modify_budget** trigger.

Every modification of the **budget** column using the UPDATE statement activates the trigger. In doing so, the values of the rows of the **deleted** and **inserted** tables are assigned to the corresponding variables **@budget_old**, **@budget_new**, and **@project_number**. The assigned values, together with the username and the current date, will be subsequently inserted into the **audit_budget** table.

NOTE

Example 14.1 assumes that only one row will be updated at a time. Therefore, it is a simplification of a general case in which a trigger handles multirow updates. The implementation of such a general (and complicated) trigger is beyond the introductory level of this book.

If the following Transact-SQL statement is executed,

```
UPDATE project
   SET budget = 200000
   WHERE project_no = 'p2';
```

the content of the **audit_budget** table is as follows:

project_no	user_name	date	budget_old	budget_new
p2	Dbo	2008-01-31 14:00:05	95000	200000

Implementing Business Rules

Triggers can be used to create business rules for an application. Example 14.2 shows the creation of such a trigger.

EXAMPLE 14.2

-- The trigger total_budget is an example of using a trigger to implement a business rule

```
USE sample;
GO
CREATE TRIGGER total_budget
  ON project AFTER UPDATE
  AS IF UPDATE (budget)
  BEGIN
  DECLARE @sum_old1 FLOAT
  DECLARE @sum_old2 FLOAT
  DECLARE @sum_new FLOAT
  SELECT @sum_new = (SELECT SUM(budget) FROM inserted)
  SELECT @sum_old1 = (SELECT SUM(p.budget)
                        FROM project p WHERE p.project_no
      NOT IN (SELECT d.project_no FROM deleted d))
  SELECT @sum_old2 = (SELECT SUM(budget) FROM deleted)
  IF @sum_new > (@sum_old1 + @sum_old2) *1.5
  BEGIN
    PRINT 'No modification of budgets'
    ROLLBACK TRANSACTION
    END
  ELSE
      PRINT 'The modification of budgets executed'
  END
```

Example 14.2 creates the rule controlling the modification of the budget for the projects. The **total_budget** trigger tests every modification of the budgets and executes only such UPDATE statements where the modification does not increase the sum of all budgets by more than 50 percent. Otherwise, the UPDATE statement is rolled back using the ROLLBACK TRANSACTION statement.

Enforcing Integrity Constraints

As previously stated in Chapter 5, a DBMS handles two types of integrity constraints:

▶ Declarative integrity constraints, defined by using the CREATE TABLE and ALTER TABLE statements

▶ Procedural integrity constraints (handled by triggers)

The use of triggers to enforce integrity constraints has one significant advantage: triggers are more flexible than the declarative constraints, because *every* integrity constraint can be implemented using triggers. (The same is not true for declarative constraints.)

Example 14.3 shows how you can enforce the referential integrity for the **employee** and **works_on** tables using triggers.

EXAMPLE 14.3

```
USE sample;
GO
CREATE TRIGGER workson_integrity
  ON works_on AFTER INSERT, UPDATE
  AS IF UPDATE(emp_no)
    BEGIN
    IF (SELECT employee.emp_no
       FROM employee, inserted
       WHERE employee.emp_no = inserted.emp_no) IS NULL
    BEGIN
    ROLLBACK TRANSACTION
    PRINT 'No insertion/modification of the row'
    END
    ELSE PRINT 'The row inserted/modified'
    END
```

The **workson_integrity** trigger in Example 14.3 checks the referential integrity for the **employee** and **works_on** tables. This means that every modification of the **emp_no** column in the referenced **works_on** table is checked, and any violation of the constraint is rejected. (The same is true for the insertion of new values into the **emp_no** column.) The ROLLBACK TRANSACTION statement in the second BEGIN block rolls back the INSERT or UPDATE statement after a violation of the referential constraint.

The trigger in Example 14.3 checks case 1 and case 2 for referential integrity between the **employee** and **works_on** tables (see the definition of referential integrity in Chapter 5). Example 14.4 introduces the trigger that checks for the violation of integrity constraints between the same tables in case 3 and case 4.

EXAMPLE 14.4

```
USE sample;
GO
CREATE TRIGGER refint_workson2
  ON employee AFTER DELETE, UPDATE
  AS IF UPDATE (emp_no)
  BEGIN
   IF (SELECT COUNT(*)
     FROM WORKS_ON, deleted
     WHERE works_on.emp_no = deleted.emp_no) > 0
     BEGIN
     ROLLBACK TRANSACTION
     PRINT 'No modification/deletion of the row'
     END
   ELSE PRINT 'The row is deleted/modified'
  END
```

INSTEAD OF Triggers

A trigger with an INSTEAD OF clause replaces the corresponding triggering action. It is executed after the corresponding **inserted** and **deleted** tables are created, but before any integrity constraint or any other action is performed.

INSTEAD OF triggers can be created on tables as well as on views. When a Transact-SQL statement references a view that has an INSTEAD OF trigger, the database system executes the trigger instead of taking any action against any table. The trigger always uses the information in the **inserted** and **deleted** tables built for the view to create any statements needed to build the requested event.

There are certain requirements on column values that are supplied by an INSTEAD OF trigger:

▶ Values cannot be specified for computed columns.

▶ Values cannot be specified for columns with the TIMESTAMP data type.

▶ Values cannot be specified for columns with an IDENTITY property, unless the IDENTITY_INSERT option is set to ON.

These requirements are valid only for INSERT and UPDATE statements that reference a base table. An INSERT statement that references a view that has an INSTEAD OF trigger must supply values for all non-nullable columns of that view. (The same is true for an UPDATE statement: an UPDATE statement that references a view that has an INSTEAD OF trigger must supply values for each view column that does not allow nulls and that is referenced in the SET clause.)

Example 14.5 shows the different behavior during insertion of values for computed columns using a table and its corresponding view.

EXAMPLE 14.5

```
CREATE VIEW all_orders
   AS SELECT orderid, price, quantity, orderdate, total, shippeddate
   FROM orders;
GO
CREATE TRIGGER tr_orders
   ON all_orders INSTEAD OF INSERT
   AS BEGIN
     INSERT INTO orders
       SELECT orderid, price, quantity, orderdate
         FROM inserted
     END
```

Example 14.5 uses the **orders** table from Chapter 10 because the table contains two computed columns (see Example 10.8). The **all_orders** view retrieves all rows from this table. This view is used to specify a value for a view column that maps to a computed column in a base table. That way, an INSTEAD OF trigger can be used, which, in the case of an INSERT statement, is replaced by a batch that inserts the values into the base table via the **all_orders** view. (An INSERT statement that refers directly to the base table cannot supply a value for a computed column.)

First and Last Triggers

Database Engine allows multiple triggers to be created for each table or view and for each modification action (INSERT, UPDATE, and DELETE) on them. Additionally, you can specify the order of multiple triggers defined for a given action. Using the system stored procedure **sp_settriggerorder**, you can specify that one of the AFTER triggers associated with a table be either the first AFTER trigger or the last AFTER trigger executed for each triggering action. This system procedure has a parameter called **@order** that can contain three values:

▶ **first** Specifies that the trigger is the first AFTER trigger fired for a modification action.

▶ **last** Specifies that the trigger is the last AFTER trigger fired for a triggering action.

▶ **none** Specifies that there is no specific order in which the trigger should be fired. (This value is generally used to reset a trigger from being either first or last.)

NOTE

If you use the ALTER TRIGGER statement to modify the structure of a trigger, the order of that trigger (first or last) will be dropped.

Example 14.6 shows the use of the system stored procedure **sp_settriggerorder**.

EXAMPLE 14.6

```
EXEC sp_settriggerorder @triggername = 'modify_budget',
                        @order = 'first', @stmttype='update'
```

NOTE

There can be only one first and one last AFTER trigger on a table. The sequence in which all other AFTER triggers fire is undefined.

To display the order of a trigger, you can use the following:

▶ sp_helptrigger

▶ OBJECTPROPERTY function

The system procedure **sp_helptrigger** contains the **order** column, which displays the order of the specified trigger. Using the OBJECTPROPERTY function, you can specify either **ExecIsFirstTrigger** or **ExecIsLastTrigger** as the value of the second parameter of this function. The first parameter is always the identification number of the database object. The OBJECTPROPERTY function displays 1 if the particular property is true.

NOTE

Because an INSTEAD OF trigger is fired before data modifications are made to the underlying table, INSTEAD OF triggers cannot be specified as first or last triggers.

DDL Triggers

The first part of this chapter described DML triggers, which specify an action that is performed by the server when a modification of the table using an INSERT, UPDATE, or DELETE statement is executed. Database Engine allows you to define triggers for DDL statements, such as CREATE DATABASE, DROP TABLE, and ALTER TABLE. The syntax for DDL triggers is

```
CREATE TRIGGER [schema_name.]trigger_name
  ON {ALL SERVER | DATABASE }
[WITH {ENCRYPTION | EXECUTE AS clause_name]
  {FOR | AFTER } { event_group | event_type | LOGON}
  AS {batch  | EXTERNAL NAME method_name}
```

As you can see from the preceding syntax, DDL triggers are created the same way DML triggers are created. (The ALTER TRIGGER and DROP TRIGGER statements are used to modify and drop DDL triggers, too.) Therefore, this section describes only those options of CREATE TRIGGER that are new in the syntax for DDL triggers.

When you define a DDL trigger, you first must decide on the scope of your trigger. The DATABASE clause specifies that the scope of a DDL trigger is the current database. The ALL SERVER clause specifies that the scope of a DDL trigger is the current server.

After specifying the trigger's scope, you have to decide whether the trigger fires to a single DDL statement or a group of statements. **event_type** specifies a DDL statement that, after execution, causes a trigger to fire. **event_group** defines a name of a predefined group of Transact-SQL language events. The DDL trigger fires after execution of any Transact-SQL language event belonging to **event_group**. You can find the list of all event groups and types in Books Online. The LOGON keyword specifies a logon trigger (see Example 14.8, later in this section).

Besides the similarities that exist between DML and DDL triggers, there are several significant differences. The main difference between these two trigger forms is that a DDL trigger can be used to define as its scope an entire database or even an entire server, not just a single object. Also, DDL triggers do not support INSTEAD OF triggers. As you might have guessed, **inserted** and **deleted** tables are not necessary, because DDL triggers do not change a table's content.

The two different forms of DDL triggers, database-level and server-level, are described next.

Database-Level Triggers

Example 14.7 shows how you can implement a DDL trigger whose scope is the current database.

EXAMPLE 14.7

```
USE sample;
GO
CREATE TRIGGER prevent_drop_triggers
  ON DATABASE FOR DROP_TRIGGER
  AS PRINT 'You must disable "prevent_drop_triggers" to drop any trigger'
  ROLLBACK
```

The trigger in Example 14.7 prevents all users from deleting any trigger that belongs to the **sample** database. The DATABASE clause specifies that the **prevent_drop_triggers** trigger is a database-level trigger. The DROP_TRIGGER keyword is a predefined event type that prevents a deletion of any trigger.

Server-Level Triggers

Server-level triggers respond to changes on the server. You use the ALL SERVER clause to implement server-level triggers. Depending on the action, there are two different flavors of server-level triggers: conventional DDL triggers and logon triggers. The triggering action of conventional DDL triggers is based upon DDL statements, while the triggering action of logon triggers is a logon event.

Example 14.8 shows a server-level trigger that is at the same time a logon trigger.

EXAMPLE 14.8

```
USE master;
GO
CREATE LOGIN login_test WITH PASSWORD = 'login_test§$',
  CHECK_EXPIRATION = ON;
```

```
GO
GRANT VIEW SERVER STATE TO login_test;
GO
CREATE TRIGGER connection_limit_trigger
ON ALL SERVER WITH EXECUTE AS 'login_test'
FOR LOGON AS
BEGIN
IF ORIGINAL_LOGIN()= 'login_test' AND
   (SELECT COUNT(*) FROM sys.dm_exec_sessions
       WHERE is_user_process = 1 AND
          original_login_name = 'login_test') > 1
   ROLLBACK;
END;
```

Example 14.8 first creates the SQL Server login called **login_test**. This login is subsequently used in a server-level trigger. For this reason, it requires server permission VIEW SERVER STATE, which is given to it with the GRANT statement. After that, the **connection_limit_trigger** trigger is created. This trigger belongs to logon triggers, because of the LOGON keyword. The use of the **sys.dm_exec_sessions** view allows you to check if there is already a session established using the **login_test** login. In that case, the ROLLBACK statement is executed. That way, the **login_test** login can establish only one session at a time.

Triggers and CLR

Triggers, as well as stored procedures and user-defined functions, can be implemented using the Common Language Runtime (CLR). The following steps are necessary if you want to implement, compile, and store CLR triggers:

▶ Implement a trigger using C# or Visual Basic and compile the program using the corresponding compiler (see Examples 14.9 and 14.10).Use the CREATE ASSEMBLY statement to create the corresponding executable file (see Example 14.11).

▶ Create the trigger using the CREATE TRIGGER statement (see Example 14.12).

The following examples demonstrate these steps. Example 14.9 shows the C# source program that will be used to implement the trigger from Example 14.1.

NOTE

*Before you can create the CLR trigger in the following examples, you first have to drop the **prevent_drop_
triggers** trigger (see Example 14.7) and then drop the **modify_budget** trigger (see Example 14.1) by using the
DROP TRIGGER statement.*

EXAMPLE 14.9

```
using System;
using System.Data;
using System.Data.SqlClient;
using Microsoft.SqlServer.Server;
public class StoredProcedures
{
  public static void Modify_Budget()
  {
    SqlTriggerContext context = SqlContext.TriggerContext;
    if(context.IsUpdatedColumn(2)) //Budget
    {
      float budget_old;
      float budget_new;
      string project_number;
      SqlConnection conn = new SqlConnection("context connection=true");
      conn.Open();
      SqlCommand cmd = conn.CreateCommand();
      cmd.CommandText = "SELECT budget FROM DELETED";
      budget_old = (float)Convert.ToDouble(cmd.ExecuteScalar());
      cmd.CommandText = "SELECT budget FROM INSERTED";
      budget_new = (float)Convert.ToDouble(cmd.ExecuteScalar());
      cmd.CommandText = "SELECT project_no FROM DELETED";
      project_number = Convert.ToString(cmd.ExecuteScalar());
      cmd.CommandText = @"INSERT INTO audit_budget
                VALUES(@project_number, USER_NAME(), GETDATE(),
                  @budget_old, @budget_new)";
      cmd.Parameters.AddWithValue("@project_number",project_number);
      cmd.Parameters.AddWithValue("@budget_old",budget_old);
      cmd.Parameters.AddWithValue("@budget_new",budget_new);
      cmd.ExecuteNonQuery();
    }
  }
}
```

The **Microsoft.SQLServer.Server** namespace comprises all client classes that a C# program needs. **SqlTriggerContext** and **SqlFunction** are examples of the classes that belong to this namespace. Also, the **System.Data.SqlClient** namespace contains classes such as **SQLConnection** und **SQLCommand**, which are used to establish the connection and communication between the client and a database server. The connection is established using the connection string "context connection = true":

SqlConnection conn = new SqlConnection("context connection=true");

After that, the **StoredProcedure** class is defined, which is used to implement triggers. The **Modify_Budget()** method implements the trigger with the same name.

The instance of the **SQLTriggerContext** class called **context** allows the program to access the virtual table that is created during the execution of the trigger. The table stores the data that caused the trigger to fire. The **IsUpdatedColumn()** method of the **SQLTriggerContext** class allows you to find out whether the specified column of the table is modified.

The C# program contains two other important classes: **SQLConnection** and **SQLCommand**. An instance of **SQLConnection** is generally used to establish the connection to a database, while an instance of **SQLCommand** allows you to execute an SQL statement.

The following statements use the **Parameters** property of the **SQLCommand** class to display parameters and the **AddWithValue()** method to insert the value in the specified parameter:

cmd.Parameters.AddWithValue("@project_number",project_number);
cmd.Parameters.AddWithValue("@budget_old",budget_old);
cmd.Parameters.AddWithValue("@budget_new",budget_new);

Example 14.10 shows the execution of the **csc** command. Using this command, you can compile the C# program in Example 14.9.

EXAMPLE 14.10

csc /target:library Example14_9.cs
/reference:"c:\Program Files\Microsoft SQL Server\MSSQL.1\MSSQL\Binn\
sqlaccess.dll"

You can find the detailed description of the **csc** command in Chapter 8.

NOTE
*You enable and disable the use of CLR through the **clr_enabled** option of the **sp_configure** system procedure. Execute the RECONFIGURE statement to update the running configuration value (see Example 8.9).*

Example 14.11 shows the next two steps in creating the **modify_budget** trigger. (Use SQL Server Management Studio to execute these statements.)

EXAMPLE 14.11

```
CREATE ASSEMBLY Example14_9 FROM
      'C:\Programs\Microsoft SQL Server\assemblies\Example14_9.dll'
      WITH PERMISSION_SET=EXTERNAL_ACCESS
```

The CREATE ASSEMBLY statement uses the managed code as the source to create the corresponding object, against which the CLR trigger is created. The WITH PERMISSION SET clause in this example specifies that access permissions are set to the value EXTERNAL_ACCESS, which does not allow assemblies to access external system resources, except a few of them.

The following example creates the **modify_budget** trigger using the CREATE TRIGGER statement.

EXAMPLE 14.12

```
CREATE TRIGGER modify_budget ON project
   AFTER UPDATE AS
   EXTERNAL NAME Example14_9.StoredProcedures.Modify_Budget
```

The CREATE TRIGGER statement in Example 4.12 differs from the statement used in Examples 14.1 to 14.5, because it uses the EXTERNAL NAME option. This option specifies that the code is generated using CLR. The name in this clause is a three-part name. The first part is the name of the corresponding assembly, the second part (**StoredProcedures**) is the name of the public class defined in Example 14.9, and the third part (**Modify_Budget**) is the name of the method, which is specified inside the class.

Example 14.13 shows how the trigger in Example 14.3 can be implemented using the C# language.

NOTE

You have to drop the trigger called workson_integrity (see Example 14.3) using the DROP TRIGGER statement before you can create the CLR trigger in Example 14.13.

EXAMPLE 14.13

```
using System;
using System.Data;
using System.Data.SqlClient;
```

```
using Microsoft.SqlServer.Server;
public class StoredProcedures
{
    public static void WorksOn_Integrity()
    {
        SqlTriggerContext context = SqlContext.TriggerContext;
        if(context.IsUpdatedColumn(0)) //Emp_No
        {
            SqlConnection conn = new SqlConnection("context connection=true");
            conn.Open();
            SqlCommand cmd = conn.CreateCommand();
            cmd.CommandText = "SELECT employee.emp_no
                        FROM employee, inserted
                        WHERE employee.emp_no = inserted.emp_no";
            SqlPipe pipe = SqlContext.Pipe;
            if(cmd.ExecuteScalar() == null)
            {   System.Transactions.Transaction.Current.Rollback();
                pipe.Send("No insertion/modification of the row");
            }
            else
                pipe.Send("The row inserted/modified");
        }
    }
}
```

Only the two new features used in Example 14.13 require description. The **SqlPipe** class belongs to the **Microsoft.SQLServer.Server** namespace and allows you to send messages to the caller, such as:

pipe.Send("No insertion/modification of the row");

To set (or get) the current transaction inside a trigger, you use the **Current** property of the **Transaction** class. Example 14.13 uses the **Rollback()** method to roll back the whole transaction after violation of the integrity constraint.

Example 14.14 shows the creation of the assembly and the corresponding trigger based upon the C# program in Example 14.13. (Compilation of the C# program using the **csc** command as the intermediate step is necessary, but it is omitted here because it is analog to the same command in Example 14.10.)

EXAMPLE 14.14

```
CREATE ASSEMBLY Example14_13 FROM
    'C:\Programs\Microsoft SQL Server\assemblies\Example14_13.dll'
WITH PERMISSION_SET=EXTERNAL_ACCESS
GO
CREATE TRIGGER workson_integrity ON works_on
AFTER INSERT, UPDATE AS
EXTERNAL NAME Example14_13.StoredProcedures.WorksOn_Integrity
```

Conclusion

A trigger is a mechanism that resides in the database server and comes in two flavors: DML triggers and DDL triggers. DML triggers specify one or more actions that are automatically performed by the database server when a modification of the table using an INSERT, UPDATE, or DELETE statement is executed. (A DML trigger cannot be used with the SELECT statement.) On the other side, DDL triggers are based on DDL statements. They come in two flavors, depending on the scope of the trigger. The DATABASE clause specifies that the scope of a DDL trigger is the current database. The ALL SERVER clause specifies that the scope of a DDL trigger is the current server.

This chapter is the last chapter of the second part of the book. The next chapter starts the third part and discusses the system environment of Database Engine.

Exercises

E.14.1

Using triggers, define the referential integrity for the primary key of the **department** table, the **dept_no** column, which is the foreign key of the **works_on** table.

E.14.2

With the help of triggers, define the referential integrity for the primary key of the **project** table, the **project_no** column, which is the foreign key of the **works_on** table.

E.14.3

Using CLR, implement the trigger from Example 14.4.

Part III

SQL Server: System Administration

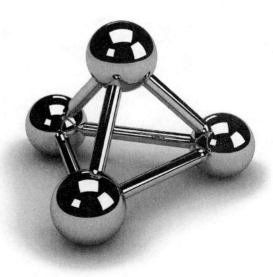

Chapter 15

System Environment of Database Engine

In This Chapter

- ▶ **System Databases**
- ▶ **Disk Storage**
- ▶ **Utilities and the DBCC Command**

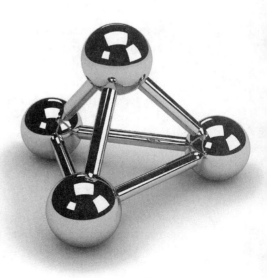

This chapter describes several features of Database Engine that belong to the system environment. First, the chapter provides a detailed description of system databases which are installed during the installation process. Another system-related topic is data storage. This chapter discusses several types of disk pages, as well as how different data types are stored on the disk. Finally, the **bcp**, the **sqlcmd** system utilities as well as the DBCC system command will be explained.

System Databases

During the installation of Database Engine, the following system databases are generated:

► master

► model

► tempdb

► msdb

NOTE

*There is another, "hidden" system database, called the **resource** database, which is used to store system objects, such as system stored procedures and functions. The content of this database is generally used for system upgrades.*

The following sections describe each of the system databases in turn.

master Database

The **master** database is the most important Database Engine database. It comprises all system tables that are necessary for your work. For example, the **master** database contains information about all other databases managed by Database Engine, system connections to clients, and user authorizations.

Because of the importance of this system database, you should always keep a current backup copy of it (see Chapter 17). Also, the **master** database is modified each time, when you perform several system operations. For this reason, you should back it up after the execution of such operations.

model Database

The **model** database is used as a template when user-defined databases are created. It contains the subset of all system tables of the **master** database, which every user-defined database needs. The system administrator can change the properties of the **model** database to adapt it to the specific needs of their system.

> **NOTE**
>
> *Because the **model** database is used as a model each time you create a new database, you can extend it with certain database objects and/or permissions. After that, all new databases will inherit the new properties. Use the ALTER DATABASE statement to extend or modify the **model** database.*

tempdb Database

The **tempdb** database provides the storage space for temporary tables and other temporary objects needed. For example, the system stores intermediate results of the calculation of each complex expression in the **tempdb** database. The **tempdb** database is used by all the databases belonging to the entire system. Its content is destroyed every time the system is restarted.

The system stores three different elements in the **tempdb** database:

▶ User objects

▶ Internal objects

▶ Version store

Private and global temporary tables, which are created by users, are stored in the **tempdb** database. The other objects stored in this system database are table variables and table-valued functions. All user objects stored in **tempdb** are treated by the system in the same way as any other database object. This means that entries concerning a temporary object are stored in the system catalog and you can retrieve information about it using the **sys.objects** catalog view.

Internal objects are similar to user objects, except that they are not visible using catalog views or other tools to retrieve metadata. There are three types of internal objects: work files, work tables, and sort units. Work files are created when the system retrieves information using particular operators. Work tables are created by the system when certain operations, such as spooling and recovering databases and tables by the DBCC command, are executed. Finally, sort units are created when a sort operation is executed.

Optimistic concurrency (see Chapter 13) uses the **tempdb** database as a place to store versions of rows. Hence, the **tempdb** database grows each time the system performs the following operations, among others:

▶ A trigger is executed

▶ An INSERT, UPDATE, or DELETE statement is executed in a database that allows snapshot isolation

NOTE

*Because of optimistic concurrency, the **tempdb** database is heavily used by the system. For this reason, make sure that **tempdb** is large enough and monitor its space regularly.*

msdb Database

The **msdb** database is used by the component called SQL Server Agent to schedule alerts and jobs (see Chapter 18). This system database contains task scheduling, exception handling, alert management, and system operator information; for example, the **msdb** database holds information for all the operators, such as e-mail addresses and pager numbers, and history information about all the backups and restore operations.

Disk Storage

The storage architecture of Database Engine contains two main units for storing database objects:

▶ Page
▶ Extent

NOTE

There are also other storage units, such as files and filegroups, which will be discussed in the next chapter.

The main unit of data storage is the page. The size of a page is always 8KB. Each page has a 96-byte header used to store the system information. Data rows are placed on the page immediately after the header.

Database Engine supports different page types. The most important are

▶ Data pages
▶ Index pages

NOTE

Data and index pages are actually physical parts of a database where the corresponding tables and indices are stored. The content of a database is stored in one or more files, and each file is divided in page units. Therefore, each table or index page (as a database physical unit) can be uniquely identified using a database ID, database file ID, and a page number.

When you create a table or index, the system allocates a fixed amount of space to contain the data belonging to the table or index. When the space fills, the space for additional storage must be allocated. The physical unit of storage in which space is allocated to a table (index) is called an *extent*. An extent comprises eight contiguous pages, or 64KB. There are two types of extents:

► Uniform extents

► Mixed extents

Uniform extents are owned by a single table or index, while mixed extents are shared by up to eight tables or indices. The system always allocates pages from mixed extents first. After that, if the size of the table (index) is greater than eight pages, it switches to uniform extents.

Properties of Data Pages

All types of data pages have a fixed size (8KB) and consist of the following three parts:

► Page header

► Space for data

► Row offset table

NOTE

This chapter does not include a separate discussion of the properties of index pages, because index pages are almost identical to data pages.

The following sections describe these parts.

Page Header

Each page has a 96-byte page header used to store the system information, such as page ID, the ID of the database object to which the page belongs, and the previous and next page in a page chain. As you may have already guessed, the page header is stored at the beginning of each page. Table 15-1 shows the information stored in the page header.

Space Reserved for Data

The part of the page reserved for data has a variable length that depends upon the number and length of rows stored on the page. For each row stored on the page, there is an entry in the space reserved for data and an entry in the row offset table at the end of the page. (A data row cannot span two or more pages, except for values of VARCHAR(MAX), and VARBINARY(MAX) data that are stored in their own specific pages.)

Page Header Information	Description
pageId	Database file number plus the page number
level	For index pages, the level of the page (leaf level is level 0, first intermediate level is level 1, and so on)
flagBits	Additional information concerning the page
nextPage	Database file number plus the page number of the next page in the chain (if a table has a clustered index)
prevPage	Database file number plus the page number of the previous page in the chain (if a table has a clustered index)
objId	ID of the database object to which the page belongs
lsn	Log sequence number (see Chapter 13)
slotCnt	Total number of slots used on this page
indexId	Index ID of the page (0, if the page is a data page)
freeData	Byte offset of the first available free space on the page
pminlen	Number of bytes in fixed-length part of rows
freeCnt	Number of free bytes on page
reservedCnt	Number of bytes reserved by all transactions
xactReserved	Number of bytes reserved by the most recently started transaction
xactId	ID of the most recently started transaction
tornBits	One bit per sector for detecting torn page write

Table 15-1   *Information Contained in the Page Header*

Each row is stored subsequently after already-stored rows, until the page is filled. If there is not enough space for a new row of the same table, it is stored on the next page in the chain of pages.

For all tables that have only fixed-length columns, the same number of rows is stored at each page. If a table has at least one variable-length column (a VARCHAR column, for instance), the number of rows per page may differ and the system then stores as many rows per page as will fit on it.

Row Offset Table

The last part of a page is tightly connected to a space reserved for data, because each row stored on a page has a corresponding entry in the row offset table (see Figure 15-1). The row offset table contains 2-byte entries consisting of the row number and the offset byte address of the row on the page. (The entries in the row offset table are in reverse order from the sequence of the rows on the page.) Suppose that each row of a table is fixed-length, 36 bytes in length. The first table row is stored at byte offset 96 of a page (because of the page header). The corresponding entry in the row offset table is written in the last 2 bytes of a page, indicating the row number (in the first byte) and the row offset (in the second byte). The next row is stored subsequently in the next 36 bytes of the page. Therefore, the corresponding entry in the row offset table is stored in the third- and fourth-to-last bytes of the page, indicating again the row number (1) and the row offset (132).

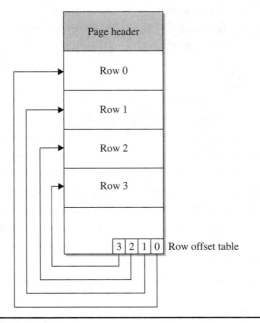

Figure 15-1   *The structure of a data page*

Types of Data Pages

Data pages are used to store data of a table. There are two types of data pages, each of which is used to store data in a different format:

► In-row data pages
► Row-overflow data pages

NOTE

The discussion in the previous section relates to all these types of data pages. The special properties of row-overflow data pages are explained in this section.

In-Row Data Pages

There is nothing special to say about in-row data pages: they are convenient pages in which to store data and index information. All non-LOB data is always stored in-row. Also, VARCHAR(MAX), NVARCHAR(MAX), VARBINARY(MAX), and XML values can be stored in-row, if the **large value types out of row** option of the **sp_ tableoption** system procedure is set to 0. In this case, all such values are stored directly in the data row, up to a limit of 8000 bytes and as long as the value can fit in the record. If the value does not fit in the record, a pointer is stored in-row and the rest is stored out of row in the LOB storage space.

Row-Overflow Data

Values of the VARCHAR(MAX), NVARCHAR(MAX), and VARBINARY(MAX) columns can be stored outside of the actual data page. As you already know, 8KB is the maximum size of a row on a data page, but you can exceed this size limit if you use columns of such large data types. In this case, the system stores the values of these columns in extra pages, which are called row-overflow pages.

The storage in row-overflow pages is done only under certain circumstances. The primary factor is the length of the row: if the row needs more than 8060 bytes, some of the column's values will be stored on overflow pages. (A value of a column cannot be split between the actual data page and a row-overflow page.)

As an example of how content of a table with large values is stored, Example 15.1 creates such a table and inserts a row into it.

EXAMPLE 15.1

```
USE sample;
CREATE TABLE mytable
    (col1 VARCHAR(1000),
     col2 VARCHAR(3000),
     col3 VARCHAR(3000),
     col4 VARCHAR(3000));
  INSERT INTO mytable
    SELECT REPLICATE('a', 1000), REPLICATE('b', 3000),
      REPLICATE('c', 3000), REPLICATE('d', 3000);
```

The query in Example 15.2 uses several catalog views to display information concerning page type description.

EXAMPLE 15.2

```
USE sample;
SELECT  rows, type_desc AS page_type, total_pages AS pages
    FROM sys.partitions p JOIN sys.allocation_units a ON
            p.partition_id = a.container_id
    WHERE object_id = object_id('mytable');
```

The result is

rows	page_type	pages
1	IN_ROW_DATA	2
1	ROW_OVERFLOW_DATA	2

In Example 15.2, the **sys.partition** and **sys.allocation_units** catalog views are joined together to display the information in relation to the **mytable** table and the storage of its row(s). The **sys.partition** view contains one row for each partition of each table or index. (Nonpartitioned tables, such as **mytable,** have only one partition unit.)

A set of pages of one particular data page type is called an *allocation unit.* Different allocation units can be displayed using the **type_desc** column of the **sys.allocation_units** catalog view. As you can see from the result of Example 15.2, for the single row of the **mytable** table, two convenient pages plus two row-overflow pages are allocated (or reserved) by the system.

NOTE

The performance of a system can significantly degrade if your queries access many row-overflow data pages.

Parallel Processing of Tasks

Database Engine can execute different database tasks in parallel. The following tasks can be parallelized:

▶ Bulk load

▶ Backup

▶ Query execution

▶ Indices

Database Engine allows data to be loaded in parallel using the **bcp** utility. (For the description of the **bcp** utility, see the next section of this chapter.) The table into which the data is loaded must not have any indices, and the load operation must not be logged. (Only applications using the ODBC or OLE DB-based APIs can perform parallel data loads into a single table.)

Database Engine can back up databases or transaction logs to multiple devices (tape or disk) using parallel striped backup. In this case, database pages are read by multiple threads one extent at a time.

Database Engine provides parallel queries to enhance the query execution. With this feature, the independent parts of a SELECT statement can be executed using several native threads on a computer. Each query that is planned for the parallel execution contains an exchange operator in its query execution plan. (An *exchange operator* is an operator in a query execution plan that provides process management, data redistribution, and flow control.) For such a query, the database system generates a parallel query execution plan. Parallel queries significantly improve the performance of the SELECT statements that process very large amounts of data.

On computers with multiple processor computers, Database Engine automatically uses more processors to perform index operations, such as creation and rebuilding of an index. The number of processors employed to execute a single index statement is determined by the configuration option **max degree of parallelism** as well as the current workload. If the database system detects that the system is busy, the degree of parallelism is automatically reduced before the statement is executed.

Utilities and the DBCC Command

Utilities are components that provide different features such as data reliability, data definition, and statistics maintenance functions. All utilities of Database Engine have two main properties:

▶ They are invoked using an operating system command

▶ Each utility has several optional parameters

This section describes the following utilities:

▶ bcp

▶ sqlcmd

Commands are Transact-SQL statements that affect the content of database systems. In contrast to utilities, commands are executed using SQL Server Management Studio. The only command discussed in this chapter is DBCC.

bcp Utility

bcp (Bulk Copy Program) is a useful utility that copies database data to/from a data file. Therefore, **bcp** is often used to transfer a large amount of data into a Database Engine database from another relational DBMS using a text file, or vice versa.

The syntax of the **bcp** utility is

bcp [[db_name.]schema_name]table_name {IN | OUT | QUERYOUT | FORMAT}
        file_name   [{–option parameter} ...]

db_name is the name of the database to which the table (**table_name**) belongs. IN or OUT specifies the direction of data transfer. The IN option copies data from the **file_name** file into the **table_name** table, and the OUT option copies rows from the **table_name** table into the **file_name** file. The FORMAT option creates a format file based on the options specified. If this option is used, the option **–f** must also be used.

NOTE

The IN option appends the content of the file to the content of the database table, whereas the OUT option overwrites the content of the file.

Data can be copied as either SQL Server–specific text or ASCII text. Copying data as SQL Server–specific text is referred to as working in native mode, whereas copying data as ASCII text is referred to as working in character mode. The parameter –n specifies native mode, and the parameter –c specifies character mode. Native mode is used to export and import data from one system managed by Database Engine to another system managed by Database Engine, and character mode is commonly used to transfer data between a Database Engine instance and other database systems.

Example 15.3 shows the use of the **bcp** utility. (You have to execute this statement from a command prompt.)

EXAMPLE 15.3

bcp AdventureWorks.Person.Address out "address.txt" –T –c

The **bcp** command in Example 15.3 exports the data from the **address** table of the **AdventureWorks** database in the output file **address.txt**. (Exactly 19,614 rows are transferred to the file.) The option **–T** specifies that the trusted connection is used. (*Trusted connection* means that the system uses integrated security instead of the user and password information.) The option –c specifies character mode; thus, the data is stored in the ASCII file.

NOTE

*Be aware that the BULK INSERT statement is an alternative to **bcp**. It supports all of the **bcp** options (although the syntax is a bit different) and offers much greater performance. BULK INSERT is described in Chapter 7.*

To import data from a file to a database table, you must have INSERT and SELECT permissions on the table. To export data from a table to a file, you must have SELECT permission on the table.

sqlcmd Utility

sqlcmd allows you to enter Transact-SQL statements, system procedures, and script files at the command prompt. The general form of this utility is

sqlcmd {option [parameter]} ...

where **option** is the specific option of the utility, and **parameter** specifies the value of the defined option. The **sqlcmd** utility has many options, the most important of which are described in Table 15-2.

Example 15.4 shows the use of **sqlcmd**.

Option	Description
–S server_name[\instance_name]	Specifies the name of the database server and the instance to which the connection is made. If this option is omitted, the connection is made to the database server set with the environment variable SQLSERVER. If this environment variable is not set, the connection is established to the local machine.
–U login_id	Specifies the SQL Server login. If this option is omitted, the value of the environment variable SQLCMDUSER is used.
–P password	Specifies a password corresponding to the login. If neither the **–U** option nor the **–P** option is specified, **sqlcmd** attempts to connect by using Windows authentication mode. Authentication is based on the account of the user who is running **sqlcmd**.
–c command_end	Specifies the batch terminator. (The default value is GO.) This option can be used to set the command terminator to a semicolon (;), which is the default terminator for almost all other database systems.
–i input_file	Specifies the name of the file that contains a batch or a stored procedure. The file must contain (at least one) command terminator. The sign < can be used instead of **–i**.
–o output_file	Specifies the name of the file that receives the result from the utility. The sign > can be used instead of **–o**.
–E	Uses a trusted connection (see Chapter 12) instead of requesting a password.
–e	Echoes each statement that runs as input.
–L	Shows a list of all database instances found on the network.
–t seconds	Specifies the number of seconds. The time interval defines how long the utility should wait before it considers the connection to the server to be a failure.
–?	Specifies standard request for all options of the **sqlcmd** utility.
–d dbname	Specifies which database should be a current database when **sqlcmd** is started.

Table 15-2   *Most Important Options of the sqlcmd Utility*

EXAMPLE 15.4

sqlcmd –S NTB11901 –i C:\ms0510.sql –o C:\ms0510.rpt

In Example 15.4, a user of the database system named NTB11900 executes the batch stored in the file ms0510.sql and stores the result in the output file ms0510.rpt. Depending on the authentication mode, the system prompts for the username and password (SQL Server authentication) or just executes the statement (Windows authentication).

Command	Description
:ED	Starts the text editor. This editor can be used to edit the current batch or the last executed batch. The editor is defined by the SQLCMDEDITOR environment variable. For instance, if you want to set the text editor to Microsoft WordPad, type SET SQLCMDEDITOR=wordpad.
:!!	Executes operating system commands. For example, **:!! dir** lists all files and directories in the current directory.
:r filename	Parses additional Transact-SQL statements and **sqlcmd** commands from the file specified by **filename** into the statement cache. It is possible to issue multiple **:r** commands. Hence, you can use this command to chain scripts with the **sqlcmd** utility.
:List	Prints the content of the statement cache.
:QUIT	Ends the session started by **sqlcmd**.
:EXIT [(statement)]	Allows you to use the result of a SELECT statement as the return value from **sqlcmd**.

Table 15-3   *Most Important Commands of the sqlcmd Utility*

The **sqlcmd** utility supports several specific commands that can be used within the utility, in addition to Transact-SQL statements. Table 15-3 describes the most important commands of the **sqlcmd** utility.

Example 15.5 shows the use of the **exit** command of the **sqlcmd** utility.

EXAMPLE 15.5

```
1>USE sample;
2>SELECT * FROM project
3>:EXIT(SELECT @@rowcount)
```

This example displays all rows from the **project** table and the number 3, if the **project** table contains three rows.

DBCC Command

The Transact-SQL language supports the DBCC (Database Console Commands) statement that act as a command for Database Engine. Depending on the options used with DBCC, the DBCC commands can be divided into the following groups:

▶ Maintenance

▶ Informational

▶ Validation

▶ Miscellaneous

NOTE

This section discusses only the validation commands. Other commands will be discussed in relation to their application. For example, if a command, such as DBCC SHOW_STATISTICS is related to query optimization, it is discussed in Chapter 20.

Validation Commands

The validation commands do consistency checking of the database. The following commands belong to this group:

- ► DBCC CHECKALLOC
- ► DBCC CHECKTABLE
- ► DBCC CHECKCATALOG
- ► DBCC CHECKDB

The DBCC CHECKALLOC command validates whether every extent indicated by the system has been allocated, as well as that there are no allocated extents that are not indicated by the system. Therefore, this command performs cross-referencing checks for extents.

The DBCC CHECKTABLE command checks the integrity of all the pages and structures that make up the table or indexed view. All performed checks are both physical and logical. The physical checks control the integrity of the physical structure of the page. The logical checks control, among other things, whether every row in the base table has a matching row in each nonclustered index, and vice-versa as well as indices are in their correct sort order. Using the PHYSICAL_ONLY option, you can validate only the physical structure of the page. This option causes a much shorter execution time of the command and is therefore recommended for frequent use on production systems.

The DBCC CHECKCATALOG command checks for catalog consistency within the specified database. It performs many cross-referencing checks between tables in the system catalog.

If you want to check the allocation and the structural and logical integrity of all the objects in the specified database, use DBCC CHECKDB. (As a matter of fact, this command performs all checks described above, in the given order.)

NOTE

All DBCC commands that validate the system use the snapshot technology (see Chapter 13) to provide the transactional consistency. In other words, the validation operations do not interfere with the other, ongoing database operations, because they use versions of current rows for validation.

Conclusion

This chapter described several features of the system environment of Database Engine:

▶ System databases

▶ Disk storage

▶ Utilities and commands

The system databases contain system information and high-level information about the whole database system. The most important of them is the **master** database.

The main unit of disk storage is the page. The size of pages is 8KB. The most important page type is the data page. (The form of an index page is almost identical to that of a data page.)

Database Engine supports a lot of utilities and commands. This chapter discussed two utilities (**sqlcmd** and **bcp**) and the DBCC validation commands.

The next chapter discusses how to manage databases instances and maintain databases.

Exercises

E.15.1

If you create a temporary database, where will its data be stored?

E.15.2

Change the properties of the **model** database so that its size is 4MB.

Chapter 16

Managing Instances and Maintaining Databases

In This Chapter

▶ **Declarative Management Framework**

▶ **Maintenance Plan Wizard**

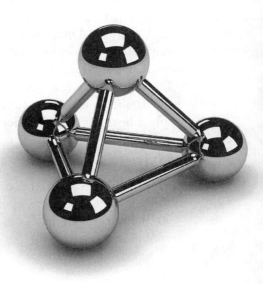

This chapter describes a framework for managing instances of Database Engine and a wizard for creating database maintenance plans. Declarative Management Framework (DMF) is a new feature of SQL Server 2008 that is used to manage whole instances or their databases. The Maintenance Plan Wizard supports several tasks that allow you to, among other things, check whether your database performs well and whether your tables and indices are free of inconsistencies.

Declarative Management Framework

The new Declarative Management Framework is a policy-based system for managing one or more server instances, databases, or other database objects. Before you learn how DMF works, though, you need to understand some key terms and concepts of DMF.

Key Terms

DMF manages entities called *managed targets*, which may be server instances, databases, tables, or indices. All managed targets that belong to an instance form a hierarchy. A *target set* is the set of managed targets that results from applying filters to the target hierarchy. For instance, if your managed target is a table, a target set could be all indices that belong to that table.

A *facet* is a set of logical properties that models the behavior or characteristics for certain types of managed targets. The number and characteristics of the properties are built into the facet and can be added or removed only by the maker of the facet. Some facets can be applied only to certain types of managed targets.

A *condition* is a Boolean expression that specifies a set of allowed states of a managed target with regard to a facet. Again, some conditions can be applied only to certain types of managed targets.

A *policy* is a DMF condition, together with the corresponding behavior. A policy can contain only one condition. Policies can be enabled or disabled. They are managed by users using categorization. A policy belongs to one and only one policy category. Database owners can subscribe a database to a set of policy categories. Only policies from the database's subscribed categories can govern that database. All databases implicitly subscribe to the default policy category.

Using DMF

This section presents an example to show how you can use DMF to create a policy. This example will create a policy whose condition is that the index fill factor will be 60 (percent) for all databases of the instance. (For a description of the FILLFACTOR option, see Chapter 10.)

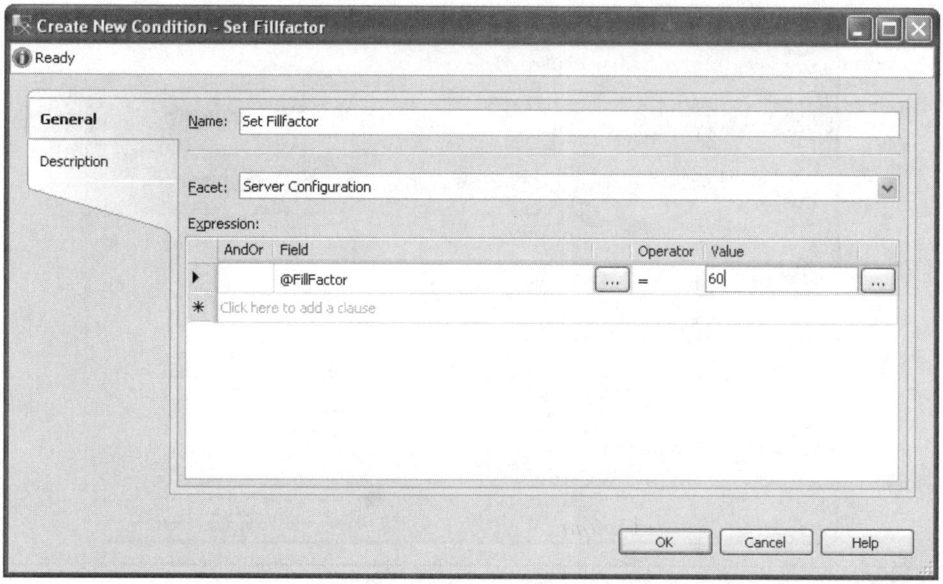

Figure 16-1   *The Create New Condition dialog box*

To create a policy, open SQL Server Management Studio, expand the server, expand **Management**, and expand **Policy Management**. The first step is to create a condition. Hence, right-click **Conditions** and select **New Condition**. In the **Create New Condition** dialog box (see Figure 16-1), type the condition name in the **Name** field (**Set Fillfactor**), and choose **Server Configuration** in the **Facet** drop-down list. (Setting fill factor for all databases of an instance is server-bound and belongs therefore to the server configuration.) In the **Field** column of the **Expression** frame, select **@FillFactor** from the drop-down menu and choose = as the operator. Finally, enter **60** in the **Value** field. Click **OK** and you have created a condition.

The next step is to create a policy based on the condition. In the **Policy Management** folder, right-click **Policies** and select **New Policy**. In the **Name** field of the **Create New Policy** dialog box (see Figure 16-2), type the name for the new policy (Policy Fillfactor 60). In the **Check Condition** drop-down list, select the condition that you have created (Fillfactor). (This condition can be found under the node called **Server Configurations**.) Select **On Demand** from the **Execution Mode** drop-down list and click **OK**.

NOTE

Policy administrators can run policies on demand, or enable automated policy execution by using one of the existing execution modes.

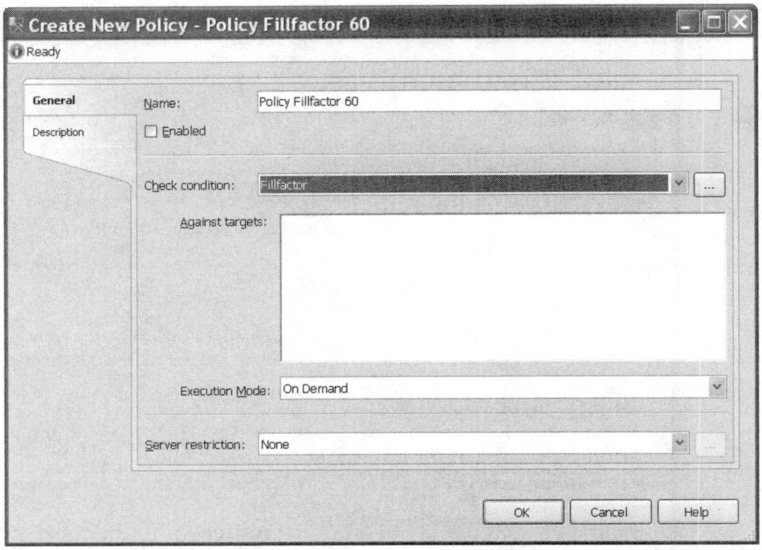

Figure 16-2 *The Create New Policy dialog box*

To test the policy, expand **Policies,** right-click the policy, and select **Test Policy.** The **Run Now** dialog box (see Figure 16-3) notifies you whether the policy fails for the existing databases.

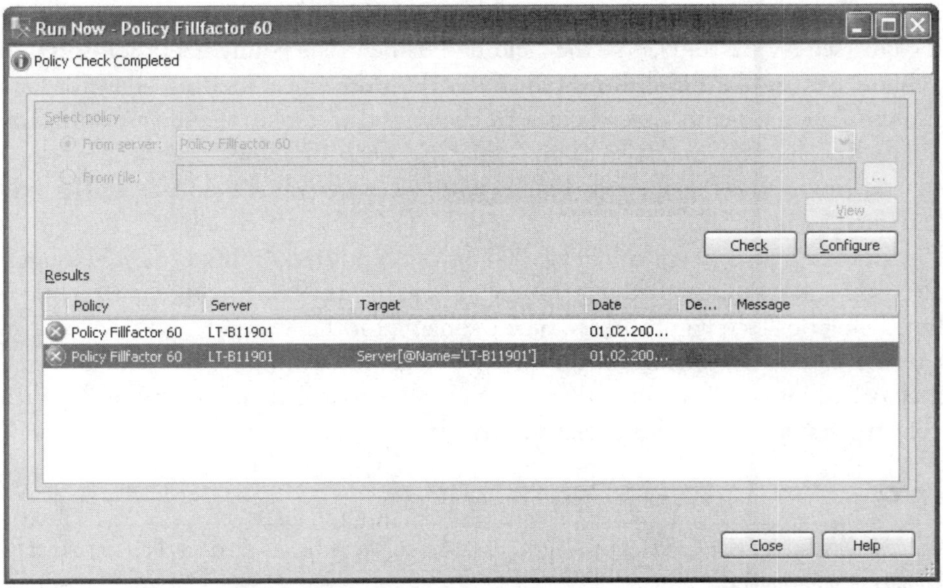

Figure 16-3 *The Run Now dialog box*

The process, described above, can be applied in the same way to dozens of different policies in relation to servers, databases and database objects.

Maintenance Plan Wizard

The Maintenance Plan Wizard provides you with the set of basic tasks needed to maintain a database. It ensures that that your database performs well, is regularly backed up, and is free of inconsistencies.

NOTE

To create or manage maintenance plans, you have to be a member of the sysadmin fixed server role.

To start the Maintenance Plan Wizard, expand the server, expand **Management**, right-click **Maintenance Plans**, and choose **Maintenance Plan Wizard**. As you can see from the starting page of the Maintenance Plan Wizard, you can perform the following administration tasks:

- ▶ Check database integrity
- ▶ Perform index maintenance
- ▶ Update database statistics
- ▶ Perform database backups

NOTE

The disadvantage of the wizard is that it doesn't support all the tasks that are available for use in a maintenance plan.

When you click **Next** on the starting page, the next wizard page, Select Plan Properties, enables you to select properties for your plan (see Figure 16-4), enter the plan's name and, optionally, describe it. Also, you can choose between separate schedules for each task or a single schedule for the entire plan. This example will check the integrity of the **sample** database, so name the plan **Integrity-Sample** and choose the **Single Schedule** radio button. The **Schedule** field allows you to create a schedule for the execution of the plan or to execute it on demand. Chapter 18 describes in detail how you can create such a schedule. (For purposes of this example, leave the **Schedule** field set to **No Schedule (On Demand)**.)

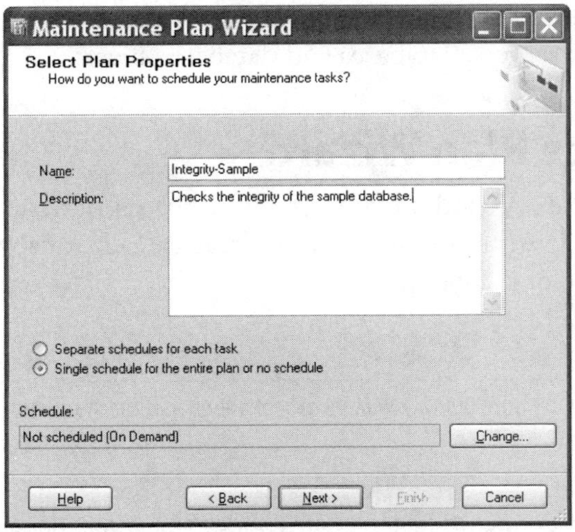

Figure 16-4   *The Select Plan Properties wizard page*

After you click **Next**, check the **Check Database Integrity** box on the **Select Plan Properties** wizard page. You can then specify the order in which the tasks should be performed. (In this case, there is no order, because there is only one task to be performed.)

The next two wizard pages enable you to specify the database(s) on which the task should be performed and to select report options (see Figure 16-5). The Select Report Options page allows you to write a report to a specific file and/or send an e-mail.

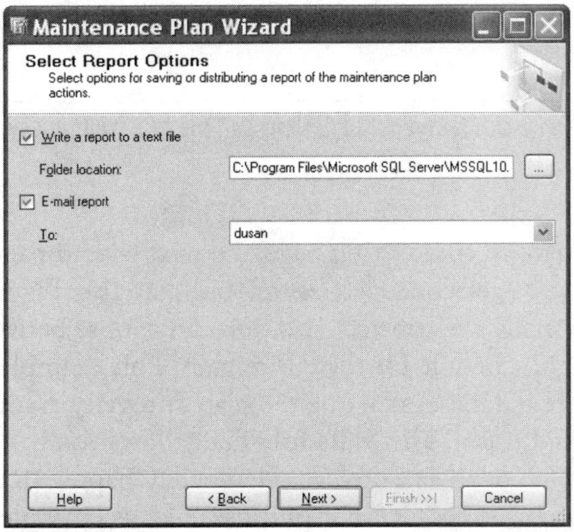

Figure 16-5   *The Select Report Options wizard page*

NOTE

An e-mail message can be sent only to an existing operator. Chapter 18 describes in detail how you can create an operator.

The second-to-last wizard page gives you a summary of all steps that will be executed. Click **Next**, and the wizard performs the task and creates a corresponding report.

To view the history of an existing maintenance plan, expand **Management**, expand **Maintenance Plans**, right-click the name of the plan, and choose **View History**. The Log File Viewer with the history of the selected plan is shown.

Conclusion

This short chapter described how you can use Declarative Management Framework and the Maintenance Plan Wizard. Declarative Management Framework is a policy-based system for managing one or more server instances, databases, or other database objects. It is very powerful tool, because it can manage everything: from the whole database system, till objects, such as tables or indices. On the other hand, the wizard can be used only for one task: to create plans for database maintenance.

The next chapter discusses how you can prevent the loss of data, using backup and recovery.

Exercises

E.16.1

Name all key DMF terms and discuss their roles and how they relate to one another.

E.16.2

Name all groups for which you can specify a condition.

E.16.3

Generate a policy that disables the use of the Common Language Runtime (CLR).

E.16.4

Name a database maintenance plan that can't be generated using the Maintenance Plan Wizard.

Chapter 17

Backup and Recovery

In This Chapter

This chapter covers two of the most important tasks concerning system administration: backup and recovery. Backup refers to the process of making copies of the database(s) and/or transaction logs to separate media that can later be used for recovery, if necessary. Recovery is the process of using the backup media to replace uncommitted, inconsistent, or lost data.

Performing backups is a precautionary measure that you have to take to prevent data loss. The reasons for data loss can be divided into the following groups:

▶ Program errors

▶ Administrator (human) errors

▶ Computer failures (system crash)

▶ Disk failures

▶ Catastrophes (fire, flood, earthquake) or theft

During execution of a program, conditions may arise that abnormally terminate the program. Such program errors concern only the database application and usually have no impact on the entire database system. Because these errors are based on faulty program logic, the database system cannot recover in such situations. The recovery should therefore be done by the programmer, who has to handle such exceptions using the COMMIT and ROLLBACK statements (see Chapter 13).

Another source of data loss is human error. Users with sufficient permissions (DBA, for instance) may accidentally lose or corrupt data (people have been known to drop the wrong table, update or delete data incorrectly, and so on). Of course, ideally, this would never happen, and you can establish practices that make it unlikely that production data is compromised in this way, but you have to recognize that people make mistakes, and data can be affected. The best that you can do is to try to avoid it, and be prepared to recover when it happens.

A computer failure may occur as a result of various different hardware or software errors. A hardware crash is an example of a system failure. In this case, the contents of the computer's main memory may be lost. A disk failure occurs either when a read/write head of the disk crashes or when the I/O system discovers corrupted disk blocks during I/O operations.

In the case of catastrophes or theft, the system must have enough information available to recover from the failure. This is normally done by means of media that offer the needed recovery information on a piece of hardware that is stored separately and thus has not been damaged or lost by the catastrophe or theft.

For most of the errors just described, backups, discussed next, can provide a recovery solution.

Backup Methods

Database backup is the process of dumping data (from a database, a transaction log, or a file) into backup devices that system creates and maintains. A backup device can be a disk file or a tape. Database Engine provides both static and dynamic backups. *Static backup* means that during the backup process, the only active session supported by the system is the one that creates the backup. In other words, user processes are not allowed during backup. *Dynamic backup* means that a database backup can be performed without stopping the database server, removing users, or even closing the files. (The users will not even know that the backup process is in progress.)

Database Engine provides four different backup methods:

- ► Full database backup
- ► Differential backup
- ► Transaction log backup
- ► File (or filegroup) backup

Full Database Backup

A full database backup captures the state of the database at the time the backup is started. During the full database backup, the system copies the data as well as the schema of all tables of the database and the corresponding file structures. If the full database backup is executed dynamically, the database system records any activity that takes place during the backup. Therefore, even all uncommitted transactions in the transaction log are written to the backup media.

Differential Backup

A differential backup creates a copy of only the parts of the database that have changed since the last full database backup. (As in a full database backup, any activity that takes place during a differential backup is backed up, too.) The advantage of a differential backup is speed. It minimizes the time required to back up a database, because the amount of data to be backed up is considerably smaller than in the case of a full database backup. (Remember that a full database backup includes a copy of all database pages.)

Transaction Log Backup

A transaction log backup considers only the changes recorded in the log. This form of backup is therefore not based on physical parts (pages) of the database, but rather on logical operations—that is, changes executed using the DML statements INSERT, UPDATE, and DELETE. Again, because the amount of data is smaller, this process can be performed significantly quicker than a full database backup and quicker than a differential backup.

> **NOTE**
>
> *It does not make sense to back up a transaction log unless a full database backup has been performed at least once.*

There are two main reasons to perform a transaction log backup: first, to store the data that has changed since the last transaction log backup or database backup on a secure medium; second (and more importantly), to properly close the transaction log up to the beginning of the active portion of it. (The active portion of the transaction log contains all uncommitted transactions.)

Using a full database backup and a valid chain of all closed transaction logs, it is possible to propagate a database copy on a different computer. This database copy can then be used to replace the original database in case of a failure. (The same scenario can be established using a full database backup and the last differential backup.)

Database Engine does not allow you to store the transaction log in the same file in which the database is stored. One reason for this is that if the file is damaged, the use of the transaction log to restore all changes since the last backup will not be possible.

Using a transaction log to record changes in the database is a common feature used by nearly all existing relational DBMSs. Nevertheless, situations may arise when it becomes helpful to switch this feature off. For example, the execution of a heavy load can last for hours. Such a program runs much faster when the logging is switched off. On the other hand, switching off the logging process is dangerous, as it destroys the valid chain of transaction logs. To ensure the database recovery, it is strongly recommended that you perform a full database backup after the successful end of the load.

One of the most common system failures occurs because the transaction log is filled up. Be aware that such a problem may cause a complete standstill of the system. If the storage used for the transaction log fills up to 100 percent, the system must stop all running transactions until the transaction log storage is freed again. This problem can only be avoided by making frequent backups of the transaction log: each time you close a portion of the actual transaction log and store it to a different storage media, that portion of the log becomes reusable, and the system thus regains disk space.

Some differences between log backups and differential backups are worth noting. The benefit of differential backups is that you save time in the restore process, because to recover a database completely, you need a full database backup and only the *latest* differential backup. If you use log backups for the same scenario, you have to apply a full database backup and *all* existing log backups to bring the database to a consistent state. A disadvantage of differential backups is that you cannot use them to recover data to a specific point in time, because they do not store intermediate changes to the database.

File or Filegroup Backup

File (or filegroup) backup allows you to back up specific database files (or filegroups) instead of the entire database. In this case, Database Engine backs up only files you specify. Individual files (or filegroups) can be restored from a database backup, allowing recovery from a failure that affects only a small subset of the database files. You can use either a database backup or a filegroup backup to restore individual files or filegroups. This means that you can use database and transaction log backups as your backup procedure and still be able to restore individual files (or filegroups) from the database backup.

Performing Backup

You can perform backup operations using the following:

▶ Transact-SQL statements
▶ SQL Server Management Studio

Each of these backup methods is described in the following sections.

Backing Up Using Transact-SQL Statements

All types of backup operations can be executed using two Transact-SQL statements:

▶ BACKUP DATABASE

▶ BACKUP LOG

Before I describe these two Transact-SQL statements, I will specify the existing types of backup devices.

Types of Backup Devices

Database Engine allows you to back up databases, transaction logs, and files to the following backup devices:

▶ Disk

▶ Tape

Disk files are the most common media used for storing backups. Disk backup devices can be located on a server's local hard disk or on a remote disk on a shared network resource. Database Engine allows you to append a new backup to a file that already contains backups from the same or different databases. By appending a new backup set to existing media, the previous contents of the media remain intact, and the new backup is written after the end of the last backup on the media. (Backup set includes all stored data of the object you chose to back up.) By default, Database Engine always appends new backups to disk files.

CAUTION

Do not back up to a file on the same physical disk where the database or its transaction log is stored! If the disk with the database crashes, the backup that is stored on the same disk will also be damaged.

Tape backup devices are generally used in the same way as disk devices. However, when you back up to a tape, the tape drive must be attached locally to the system. The advantage of tape devices in relation to disk devices is their simple administration and operation.

BACKUP DATABASE Statement

The BACKUP DATABASE statement is used to perform a full database backup or a differential database backup. This statement has the following syntax:

```
BACKUP DATABASE {db_name | @variable}
    TO device_list
    [MIRROR TO device_list2]
    [WITH | option_list]
```

db_name is the name of the database that should be backed up. (The name of the database can also be supplied using a variable, **@variable**.) **device_list** specifies one or more device names, where the database backup will be stored. **device_list** can be a list of names of disk files or tapes. The syntax for a device is as follows:

```
{ logical_device_name | @logical_device_name_var }
    | { DISK | TAPE } =  { 'physical_device_name' | @physical_device_name_var }
```

where the device name can be either a logical name (or a variable) or a physical name beginning with the DISK or TAPE keyword.

The MIRROR TO option indicates that the accompanying set of backup devices is a mirror within a mirrored media set. The backup devices must be identical in type and number to the devices specified in the TO clause. In a mirrored media set, all the backup devices must have the same properties. (See also the description of mirrored media in the section "Database Mirroring" later in this chapter.)

option_list comprises several options that can be specified for the different backup types. The most important options are the following:

- ▶ DIFFERENTIAL
- ▶ NOSKIP/SKIP
- ▶ NOINIT/INIT
- ▶ NOFORMAT/FORMAT
- ▶ UNLOAD/NOUNLOAD
- ▶ MEDIANAME, MEDIADESCRIPTION, and MEDIAPASSWORD
- ▶ BLOCKSIZE
- ▶ COMPRESSION

The first option, DIFFERENTIAL, specifies a differential database backup. All other clauses in the list concern full database backups.

The SKIP option disables the backup set expiration and name checking, which is usually performed by BACKUP DATABASE to prevent overwrites of backup sets. The NOSKIP option, which is the default, instructs the BACKUP statement to check the expiration date and name of all backup sets before allowing them to be overwritten.

The INIT option is used to overwrite any existing data on the backup media. This option does not overwrite the media header, if one exists. If there is a backup that has not yet expired, the backup operation fails. In this case, use the combination of SKIP and INIT options to overwrite the backup device. The NOINIT option, which is the default, appends a backup to existing backups on the media.

The FORMAT option is used to write a header on all of the files (or tape volumes) that are used for a backup. Therefore, use this option to initialize a backup medium. When you use the FORMAT option to back up to a tape device, the INIT option and the SKIP option are implied. Similarly, the INIT option is implied if the FORMAT option is specified for a file device. NOFORMAT, which is the default, specifies that the backup operation processes the existing media header and backup sets on the media volumes.

The UNLOAD and NOUNLOAD options are performed only if the backup medium is a tape device. The UNLOAD option, which is the default, specifies that the tape is automatically rewound and unloaded from the tape device after the backup is completed. Use the NOUNLOAD option if the database system should not rewind (and unload) the tape from the tape device automatically.

MEDIADESCRIPTION, MEDIANAME, and MEDIAPASSWORD specify the description, the name, and the password of the media set, respectively. The BLOCKSIZE option specifies the physical block size, in bytes. The supported sizes are 512, 1024, 2048, 4096, 8192, 16384, 32768, and 65536 (64KB) bytes. The default is 65536 bytes for tape devices and 512 bytes, otherwise.

SQL Server 2008 supports backup compression. To specify backup compression, use the COMPRESSION option of the BACKUP DATABASE statement. Example 17.1 backs up the **sample** database and compresses the backup file.

EXAMPLE 17.1

```
USE master;
BACKUP DATABASE sample
  TO DISK = 'C:\sample.bak'
  WITH INIT, COMPRESSION;
```

NOTE

If you get the "Access Denied" error for the C: directory, change the storage location of the sample.bak file to another directory (tmp, for instance).

If you want to know whether the particular backup file is compressed, use the output of the RESTORE HEADERONLY statement, which is described later in this chapter.

BACKUP LOG Statement

The BACKUP LOG statement is used to perform a backup of the transaction log. This statement has the following syntax:

```
BACKUP LOG {db_name | @variable}
  TO device_list
    [MIRROR TO device_list2]
  [WITH option_list]
```

db_name, **@variable**, **device_list**, and **device_list2** have the same meanings as the parameters with the same names in the BACKUP DATABASE statement. **option_list** has the same options as the BACKUP DATABASE statement and also supports the specific log options NO_TRUNCATE, NORECOVERY, and STANDBY.

You should use the NO_TRUNCATE option if you want to back up the transaction log without truncating it—that is, this option does not clear the committed transactions in the log. After the execution of this option, the system writes all recent database activities in the transaction log. Therefore, the NO_TRUNCATE option allows you to recover data right up to the point of the database failure.

The NORECOVERY option backs up the tail of the log and leaves the database in the restoring state. NORECOVERY is useful when failing over to a secondary database or when saving the tail of the log before a restore operation. The STANDBY option backs up the tail of the log and leaves the database in a read-only and standby state. (The restore operation and the standby state are explained later in this chapter.)

Backing Up Using Management Studio

Before you can perform a database or transaction log backup, you must specify (or create) backup devices. SQL Server Management Studio allows you to create disk devices and tape devices in a similar manner. In both cases, expand the server, expand **Server Objects**, right-click **Backup Devices**, and choose **New Backup Device**. In the **Backup Device** dialog box (see Figure 17-1), enter the name of either the disk device

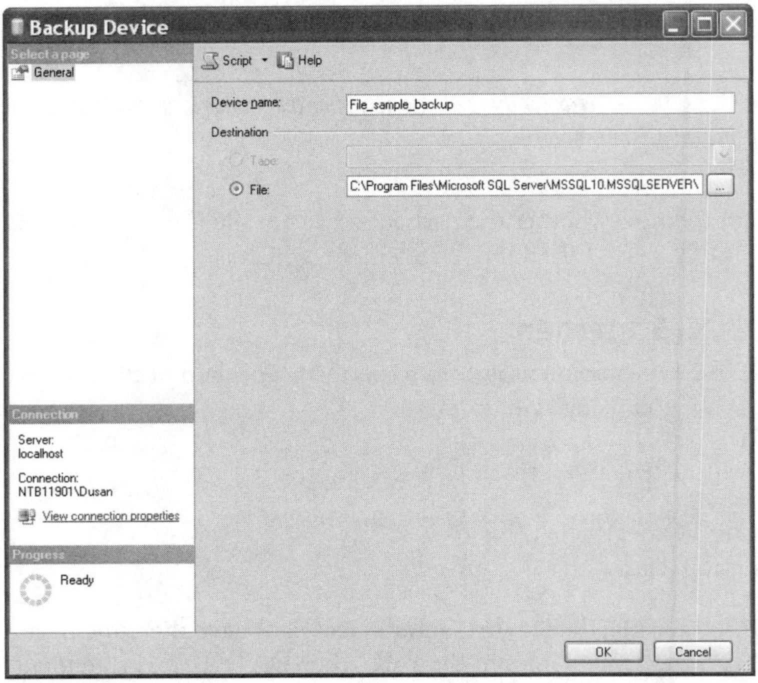

Figure 17-1   *The Backup Device dialog box*

(if you clicked **File**) or the tape device (if you clicked **Tape**). In the former case, you can click the ... button on the right side of the field to display existing backup device locations. In the latter case, if **Tape** cannot be activated, then no tape devices exist on the local computer.

After you specify backup devices, you can do a database backup. Expand the server, expand **Databases**, and right-click the database. After pointing to **Tasks**, choose **Back Up**. The **Back Up Database** dialog box appears (see Figure 17-2). On the **General** page of the dialog box, choose the backup type in the **Backup Type** drop-down list (Full, Differential, or Transaction Log), enter the backup set name in the **Name** field, and optionally enter a description of this set in the **Description** field. In the same dialog box, you can choose an expiration date for the backup.

In the **Destination** frame, select an existing device by clicking **Add**. (The **Remove** button allows you to remove one or more backup devices from the list of devices to be used.)

On the **Options** page (see Figure 17-3), to append to an existing backup on the selected device, click the **Append to the existing backup set** radio button. Choosing the **Overwrite all existing backup sets** radio button in the same frame overwrites any existing backups on the selected backup device.

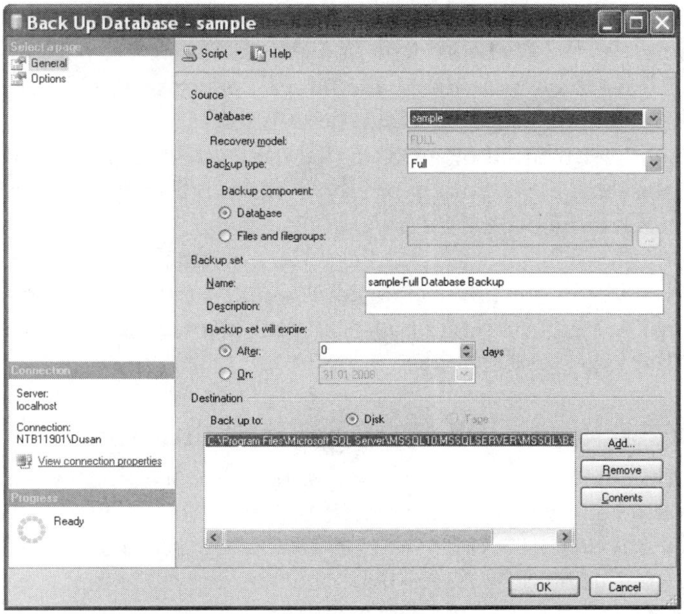

Figure 17-2   *The Back Up Database dialog box, General page*

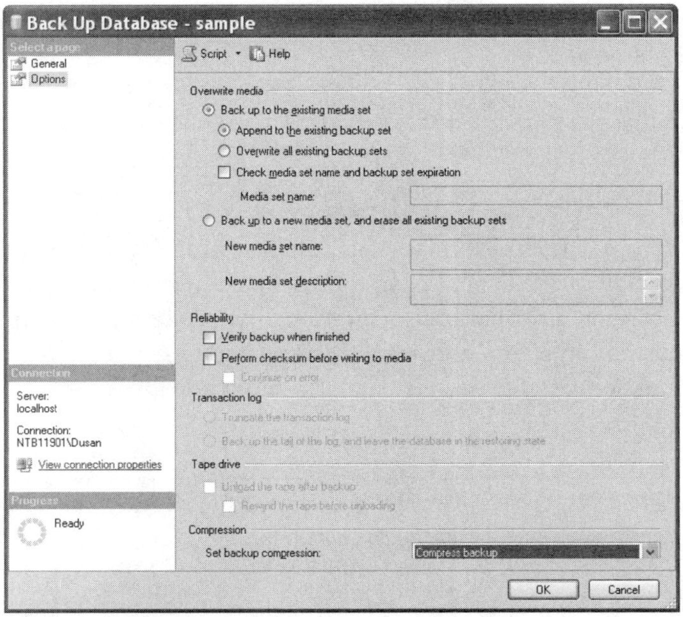

Figure 17-3   *The Back Up Database dialog box, Options page*

For verification of the database backup, click **Verify backup when finished** in the **Reliability** frame. On the **Options** page, you can also choose to back up to a new media set by clicking **Back up to a new media set, and erase all existing backup sets** and then entering the media set name and description.

For creation and verification of a differential database backup or transaction log backup, follow the same steps, but choose the corresponding backup type in the **Backup type** field on the **General** page.

After all options have been selected, click **OK**. The database or the transaction log is then backed up. The name, physical location, and the type of the backup devices can be shown by selecting the server, expanding the **Server Objects** folder, and finally expanding the **Backup Devices** folder.

Scheduling Backups with Management Studio

A well-planned timetable for the scheduling of backup operations will help you avoid system shortages when users are working. SQL Server Management Studio supports this planning by offering an easy-to-use graphical interface for scheduling backups. Scheduling backups using SQL Server Management Studio is explained in detail in the following chapter.

Determining Which Databases to Back Up

The following databases should be backed up regularly:

▶   The **master** database

▶   All production databases

Backing Up the master Database

The **master** database is the most important database of the system because it contains information about all of the databases in the system. Therefore, you should back up the **master** database on a regular basis. Additionally, you should back up the **master** database anytime certain statements and stored procedures are executed, because Database Engine modifies the **master** database automatically.

NOTE

*You can perform full database backups of the **master** database only. (The system does not support differential, transaction log, and file backups for the **master** database.)*

Many activities cause the modification of the **master** database. Some of them are listed here:

► The creation, alteration, and removal of a database

► The alteration of the transaction log

NOTE

*Without a backup of the **master** database, you must completely rebuild all system databases, because if the **master** database is damaged, all references to the existing user-defined databases are lost.*

Backing Up Production Databases

You should back up each production database on a regular basis. Additionally, you should back up any production database when the following activities are executed:

► After creating it

► After creating indices

► After clearing the transaction log

► After performing nonlogged operations

Always make a full database backup after it has been created, in case a failure occurs between the creation of the database and the first regular database backup. Remember that backups of the transaction log cannot be applied without a full database backup.

Backing up the database after creation of one or more indices saves time during the restore process, because the index structures are backed up together with the data. Backing up the transaction log after creation of indices does not save time during the restore process at all, because the transaction log only records the fact that an index was created (and does not record the modified index structure).

Backing up the database after clearing the transaction log is necessary because the transaction log no longer contains a record of database activity, which is used to recover the database. All operations that are not recorded to the transaction log are called nonlogged operations. Therefore, all changes made by these operations cannot be restored during the recovery process.

Performing Database Recovery

Whenever a transaction is submitted for execution, Database Engine is responsible either for executing the transaction completely and recording its changes permanently in the database or for guaranteeing that the transaction has no effect at all on the database. This approach ensures that the database is consistent in case of a failure, because failures do not damage the database itself, but instead affect transactions that are in progress at the time of the failure. Database Engine supports both automatic and manual recovery, which are discussed next in turn.

Automatic Recovery

Automatic recovery is a fault-tolerant feature that Database Engine executes every time it is restarted after a failure or shutdown. The automatic recovery process checks to see if the restoration of databases is necessary. If it is, each database is returned to its last consistent state using the transaction log.

During automatic recovery, Database Engine examines the transaction log from the last checkpoint to the point at which the system failed or was shut down. (A *checkpoint* is the most recent point at which all data changes are written permanently to the database from memory. Therefore, a checkpoint ensures the physical consistency of the data.) The transaction log contains committed transactions (transactions that are successfully executed, but their changes have not yet been written to the database) and uncommitted transactions (transactions that are not successfully executed before a shutdown or failure occurred). Database Engine rolls forward all committed transactions, thus making permanent changes to the database, and undoes the part of the uncommitted transactions that occurred before the checkpoint.

Database Engine first performs the automatic recovery of the **master** database, followed by the recovery of all other system databases. Then, all user-defined databases are recovered.

Manual Recovery

A manual recovery of a database specifies the application of the full backup of your database and subsequent application of all transaction logs in the sequence of their creation. (Alternatively, you can use the full database backup together with the last differential backup of the database.) After this, the database is in the same (consistent) state as it was at the point when the transaction log was backed up for the last time.

When you recover a database using a full database backup, Database Engine first re-creates all database files and places them in the corresponding physical locations. After that, the system re-creates all database objects.

Database Engine can process certain forms of recovery dynamically (in other words, while an instance of the database system is running). Dynamic recovery improves the availability of the system, because only the data being restored is unavailable. Dynamic recovery allows you to restore either an entire database file or a filegroup. (Microsoft calls dynamic recovery "online restore.")

Is My Backup Set Ready for Recovery?

After executing the BACKUP statement, the selected device (tape or disk) contains all data of the object you chose to back up. The stored data is called a *backup set*. Before you start a recovery process, you should be sure that

- ▶ The backup set contains the data you want to restore
- ▶ The backup set is usable

Database Engine supports a set of Transact-SQL statements that allows you to confirm that the backup set is usable and contains the proper data. The following four options, among others, belong to it:

- ▶ RESTORE LABELONLY
- ▶ RESTORE HEADERONLY
- ▶ RESTORE FILELISTONLY
- ▶ RESTORE VERIFYONLY

RESTORE LABELONLY   This statement is used to display the header information of the media (disk or tape) used for a backup process. The output of the RESTORE LABELONLY statement is a single row that contains the summary of the header information (name of the media, description of the backup process, and date of a backup process).

NOTE

RESTORE LABELONLY reads just the header file, so use this statement if you want to get a quick look at what your backup set contains.

RESTORE HEADERONLY   Whereas the RESTORE LABELONLY statement gives you concise information about the header file of your backup device, the RESTORE HEADERONLY statement gives you information about backups that are stored on a backup device. This statement displays a one-line summary for each backup on a backup device. In contrast to RESTORE LABELONLY, using RESTORE HEADERONLY can be time consuming if the device contains several backups.

The output of RESTORE HEADERONLY contains a **Compressed** column, which tells you whether the backup file is compressed (value 1) or not.

RESTORE FILELISTONLY   The RESTORE FILELISTONLY statement returns a result set with a list of the database and log files contained in the backup set. You can display information about only one backup set at a time. For this reason, if the specified backup device contains several backups, you have to specify the position of the backup set to be processed.

You should use RESTORE FILELISTONLY if you don't know exactly either which backup sets exist or where the files of a particular backup set are stored. In both cases, you can check all or part of the devices to make a global picture of existing backups.

RESTORE VERIFYONLY   After you have found your backup, you can do the next step: verify the backup without using it for the restore process. You can do the verification with the RESTORE VERIFYONLY statement, which checks the existence of all backup devices (tapes or files) and whether the existing information can be read.

In contrast to the previous three statements, RESTORE VERIFYONLY supports two specific options:

▶ **LOADHISTORY**   Causes the backup information to be added to the backup history tables

▶ **STATS**   Displays a message each time another percentage of the reading process completes and is used to gauge progress (the default value is 10)

Restoring Databases and Logs Using Transact-SQL Statements

All restore operations can be executed using two Transact-SQL statements:

▶ RESTORE DATABASE

▶ RESTORE LOG

The RESTORE DATABASE statement is used to perform the restore process for a database. The general syntax of this statement is

```
RESTORE DATABASE {db_name | @variable}
    [FROM device_list]
    [WITH option_list]
```

db_name is the name of the database that will be restored. (The name of the database can be supplied using a variable, **@variable**.) **device_list** specifies one or more names of devices on which the database backup is stored. (If you do not specify the FROM clause, only the process of automatic recovery takes place, not the restore of a backup, and you must specify either the RECOVERY, NORECOVERY, or STANDBY option. This action can take place if you want to switch over to a standby server.) **device_list** can be a list of names of disk files or tapes. **option_list** comprises several options that can be specified for the different backup forms. The most important options are

- ▶ RECOVERY/NORECOVERY/STANDBY
- ▶ CHECKSUM/NO_CHECKSUM
- ▶ REPLACE
- ▶ PARTIAL
- ▶ STOPAT
- ▶ STOPATMARK
- ▶ STOPBEFOREMARK

The RECOVERY option instructs Database Engine to roll forward any committed transaction and to roll back any uncommitted transaction. After the RECOVERY option is applied, the database is in a consistent state and is ready for use. This option is the default.

NOTE

Use the RECOVERY option either with the last transaction log to be restored or to restore with a full database backup without subsequent transaction log backups.

With the NORECOVERY option, Database Engine does not roll back uncommitted transactions because you will be applying further backups. After the NORECOVERY option is applied, the database is unavailable for use.

NOTE

Use the NORECOVERY option with all but the last transaction log to be restored.

The STANDBY option is an alternative to the RECOVERY and NORECOVERY options and is used with the standby server. (The standby server is discussed later, in the section "Using a Standby Server.") In order to access data stored on the standby server, you usually recover the database after a transaction log is restored. On the other hand, if you recover the database on the standby server, you cannot apply additional logs from the production server for the restore process. In that case, you use the STANDBY option to allow users read access to the standby server. Additionally, you allow the system the restoration of additional transaction logs. The STANDBY option implies the existence of the undo file that is used to roll back changes when additional logs are restored.

The CHECKSUM option initiates the verification of both the backup checksums and page checksums, if present. If checksums are absent, RESTORE proceeds without verification. The NO_CHECKSUM option explicitly disables the validation of checksums by the restore operation.

The REPLACE option replaces an existing database with data from a backup of a different database. In this case, the existing database is first destroyed, and the differences regarding the names of the files in the database and the database name are ignored. (If you do not use the REPLACE option, the database system performs a safety check that guarantees an existing database is not replaced if the names of files in the database, or the database name itself, differ from the corresponding names in the backup set.)

The PARTIAL option specifies a partial restore operation. With this option you can restore a portion of a database, consisting of its primary filegroup and one or more secondary filegroups, which are specified in an additional option called FILEGROUP. (The PARTIAL option is not allowed with the RESTORE LOG statement.)

The STOPAT option allows you to restore a database to the state it was in at the exact moment before a failure occurred by specifying a point in time. Database Engine restores all committed transactions that were recorded in the transaction log before the specified point in time. If you want to restore a database by specifying a point in time, execute the RESTORE DATABASE statement using the NORECOVERY clause. After that, execute the RESTORE LOG statement to apply each transaction log backup, specifying the name of the database, the backup device from which the transaction log backup will be restored, and the STOPAT clause. (If the backup of a log does not contain the requested time, the database will not be recovered.)

The STOPATMARK and STOPBEFOREMARK options specify to recover to a mark. This topic is described a bit later in the section "Recovering to a Mark."

The RESTORE DATABASE statement is also used to restore a database from a differential backup. The syntax and the options for restoring a differential backup are the same as for restoring from a full database backup. During a restoration from a differential backup, Database Engine restores only that part of the database that has changed since the last full database backup. Therefore, restore the full database backup *before* you restore a differential backup!

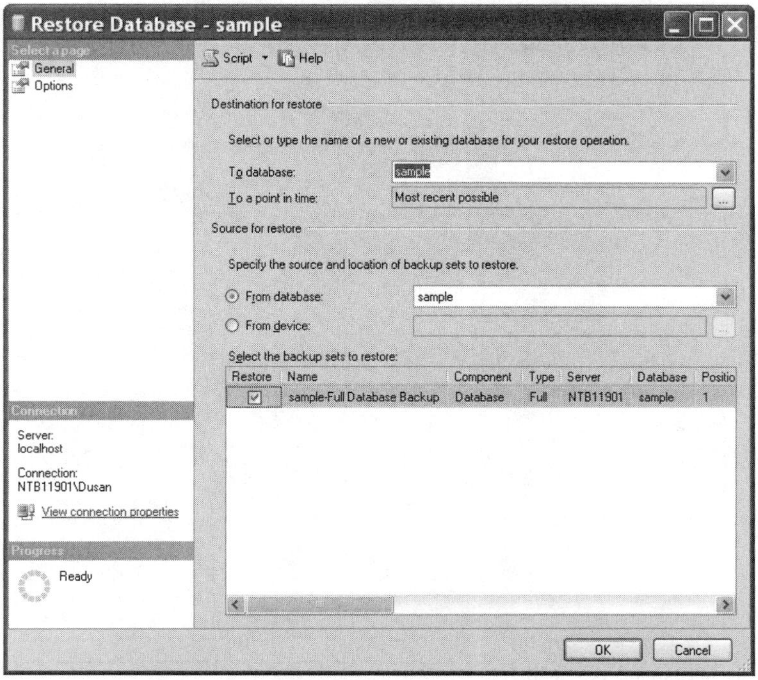

Figure 17-4   *The Restore Database dialog box, General page*

The RESTORE LOG statement is used to perform a restore process for a transaction log. This statement has the same syntax form and the same options as the RESTORE DATABASE statement.

Restoring Databases and Logs Using Management Studio

To restore a database from a full database backup, expand the server, choose **Databases**, and right-click the database. After pointing to **Tasks**, choose **Restore** and then **Database**. The **Restore Database** dialog box appears (see Figure 17-4). On the **General** page, select databases to which and from which you want to restore. Then check the type of a backup that you want to process (in this case, Full Database Backup).

NOTE

If you restore from the log backup, do not forget the sequence of restoring different types of backups. First restore the full database backup. Then restore all corresponding transaction logs in the sequence of their creation.

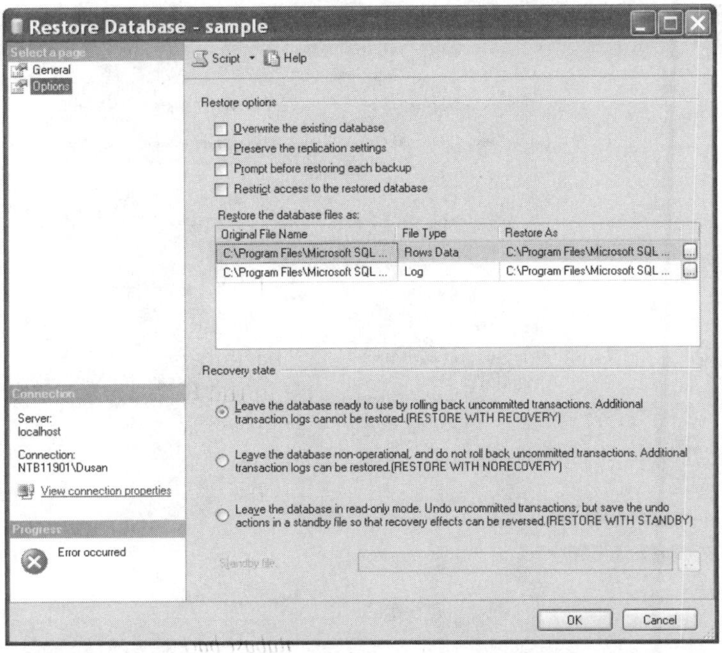

Figure 17-5   *The Restore Database dialog box, Options page*

To select the appropriate restore options, choose the **Options** page (see Figure 17-5) of the **Restore Database** dialog box. In the upper part of the window, choose one or more restore types. In the lower part of the window, you can choose one of the three existing options. Choosing the first option, **Leave the database ready to use by rolling back uncommitted transactions**, instructs Database Engine to roll forward any committed transaction and to roll back any uncommitted transaction. After applying this option, the database is in a consistent state and is ready for use. This option is equivalent to the RECOVERY option of the RESTORE DATABASE statement.

NOTE

Use this option only with the last transaction log to be restored or with a full database restore when no subsequent transaction logs need to be applied.

If you click the second option, **Leave the database non-operational, and do not roll back uncommitted transactions**, Database Engine does not roll back uncommitted transactions because you will be applying further backups. After you apply this option, the database is unavailable for use, and additional transaction logs should be restored. This option is equivalent to the NORECOVERY option of the RESTORE DATABASE statement.

NOTE

Use this option with all but the last transaction log to be restored or with a differential database restore.

Choosing the third option, **Leave the database in read-only mode**, specifies the file (in the **Standby file** dialog box) that is subsequently used to roll back the recovery effects. This option is equivalent to the STANDBY option in the RESTORE DATABASE statement.

The process of a database restoration from a differential database backup is equivalent to the process of a restoration from a full database backup. In this case, you have to check **Differential Database Backup** as the backup type in the **Restore Database** dialog box. The only difference to restoration with the full database backup is that only the first option in the lower half of the Options page (**Leave the database ready to use by rolling back uncommitted transactions**) can be applied to the restoration from a differential database backup.

NOTE

If you restore from a differential backup, first restore the full database backup before you restore the corresponding differential one. In contrast to transaction log backups, only the latest differential backup is applied, because it includes all changes since the full backup.

To restore a database with a new name, expand **Databases** and right-click the database. After pointing to **Tasks,** choose **Restore** and then **Database**. On the **General** page of the **Restore Database** dialog box, in the **To database** drop-down box enter the name of the database you want to create, and in the **From database** drop-down box enter the name of the database whose backup is used.

Recovering to a Mark

Database Engine allows you to use the transaction log to recover to a specific mark. Log marks correspond to a specific transaction and are inserted only if the transaction commits. This allows the marks to be tied to specific work and provides the ability to recover to a point that includes or excludes this work.

NOTE

If a marked transaction spans multiple databases on the same database server, the marks are recorded in the logs of all the affected databases.

The BEGIN TRANSACTION statement is enhanced to support transaction log marking. Use the WITH MARK clause to insert marks into the logs. Because the name of the mark is the same as its transaction, a transaction name is required. (The **description** option specifies a textual description of the mark.)

The transaction log records the mark name, description, database, user, date and time information, and the log sequence number (LSN). To allow their reuse, the transaction names are not required to be unique. The date and time information is used along with the name to uniquely identify the mark.

You can use the RESTORE LOG statement (with either the STOPATMARK clause or the STOPBEFOREMARK clause) to specify recovering to a mark. The STOPATMARK clause causes the recovery process to roll forward to the mark and include the transaction that contains the mark. If you specify the STOPBEFOREMARK clause, the recovery process excludes the transaction that contains the mark.

Both clauses just described support of an optional AFTER **datetime** clause. If this clause is omitted, recovery stops at the first mark with the specified name. If the clause is specified, recovery stops at the first mark with the specified name exactly at or after **datetime**.

Restoring the master Database

The corruption of the **master** system database can be devastating for the whole system, because it comprises all system tables that are necessary to work with the database system. The restore process for the **master** database is quite different from the same process for user-defined databases.

A damaged **master** database makes itself known through different failures. These failures include the following:

- Inability to start the MSSQLSERVER process
- An input/output error
- Execution of the DBCC command points to such a failure

Two different ways exist to recover the **master** database. The easier way is when you can start your database system. In that case, you just restore the **master** database from the full database backup. (The more difficult way is if you can't start your system. In that case, use the **sqlservr** command.)

To restore your **master** database, start your instance in single-user mode. As you already know, there are several ways to do it. My favorite way is to use the command window and execute the **sqlservr** application (from the command prompt) with the option **–m**. In the second step, you restore the **master** database together with all other databases using the last full database backup.

NOTE

*If there have been any changes to the **master** database since the last full database backup, you will need to re-create those changes manually.*

Restoring Other System Databases

The restore process for all system databases other than **master** is similar. Therefore, I will explain this process using the **msdb** database. The **msdb** database needs to be restored from a backup when either the **master** database has been rebuilt or the **msdb** database itself has been damaged. If the **msdb** database is damaged, restore it using the existing backups. If there have been any changes after the **msdb** database backup was created, re-create those changes manually.

NOTE

*You cannot restore a database that is being accessed by users. Therefore, when restoring the **msdb** database, the SQL Server Agent service should be stopped. (SQL Server Agent accesses the **msdb** database.)*

Recovery Models

A recovery model allows you to control to what extent you are ready to risk losing committed transactions if a database is damaged. It also determines the speed and size of your transaction log backups. Additionally, the choice of a recovery model has an impact on the size of the transaction log and therefore on the time period needed to back up the log. Database Engine supports three recovery models:

- ► Full
- ► Bulk-logged
- ► Simple

The following sections describe these recovery models.

Full Recovery Model

During full recovery, all operations are written to the transaction log. Therefore, this model provides complete protection against media failure. This means that you can restore your database up to the last committed transaction that is stored in the log file.

Additionally, you can recover data to any point in time (prior to the point of failure). To guarantee this, such operations as SELECT INTO and the execution of the **bcp** utility are fully logged too.

Besides point-in-time recovery, the full recovery model allows you also to recover to a log mark. Log marks correspond to a specific transaction and are inserted only if the transaction commits.

The full recovery model also logs all operations concerning the CREATE INDEX statement, implying that the process of data recovery now includes the restoration of index creations. That way, the re-creation of the indices is faster, because you do not have to rebuild them separately.

The disadvantage of this recovery model is that the corresponding transaction log may be very voluminous and the files on the disk containing the log will be filled up very quickly. Also, for such a voluminous log, you will need significantly more time for backup.

> **NOTE**
>
> *If you use the full recovery model, the transaction log must be protected from media failure. For this reason, using RAID 1 to protect transaction logs is strongly recommended. (RAID 1 is explained in the section "High Availability" later in this chapter.)*

Bulk-Logged Recovery Model

Bulk-logged recovery supports log backups by using minimal space in the transaction log for certain large-scale or bulk operations. The logging of the following operations is minimal and cannot be controlled on an operation-by-operation basis:

- ▶ SELECT INTO
- ▶ CREATE INDEX (including indexed views)
- ▶ **bcp** utility and BULK INSERT

Although bulk operations are not fully logged, you do not have to perform a full database backup after the completion of such an operation. During bulk-logged recovery, transaction log backups contain both the log and the results of a bulk operation. This simplifies the transition between full and bulk-logged recovery models.

The bulk-logged recovery model allows you to recover a database to the end of a transaction log backup (that is, up to the last committed transaction). Additionally, you can restore your database to any point in time if you haven't performed any bulk operations. The same is true for the restore operation to a named log mark.

The advantage of the bulk-logged recovery model is that bulk operations are performed much faster than under the full recovery model, because they are not fully logged. On the other side, Database Engine backs up all the modified extents, together with the log itself. Therefore, the log backup needs a lot more space than in the case of the full recovery. (The time to restore a log backup is significantly increased, too.)

Simple Recovery Model

In the simple recovery model, the transaction log is truncated whenever a checkpoint occurs. Therefore, you can recover a damaged database only by using the full database backup or the differential backup, because they do not require log backups. Backup strategy for this model is very simple: restore the database using existing database backups and, if differential backups exist, apply the most recent one.

> **NOTE**
>
> *The simple recovery model doesn't mean that there is no logging at all. The log content won't be used for backup purposes, but it is used at the checkpoint time, where all the transactions in the log are committed or rolled back.*

The advantages of the simple recovery model are that the performance of all bulk operations is very high and requirements for the log space are very small. On the other hand, this model requires the most manual work because all changes since the most recent database (or differential) backup must be redone. Point-in-time and page restore are not allowed with this recovery model. Also, file restore is available only for read-only secondary filegroups.

> **NOTE**
>
> *Do not use the simple recovery model for production databases.*

Changing and Editing a Recovery Model

You can change the recovery model by using the RECOVERY option of the ALTER DATABASE statement. The part of the syntax of the ALTER DATABASE statement concerning recovery models is

SET RECOVERY [FULL | BULK_LOGGED | SIMPLE]

There are two ways in which you can edit the current recovery model of your database:

▶ Using the **databasepropertyex** property function
▶ Using the **sys.databases** catalog view

If you want to display the current model of your database, use the RECOVERY clause of the **databaseproperty** function. Example 17.2 shows the query that displays the recovery model for the **sample** database. (The function displays one of the values FULL, BULK_LOGGED, or SIMPLE.)

EXAMPLE 17.2

SELECT databasepropertyex('sample', 'recovery')

The **recovery_model_desc** column of the **sys.databases** catalog view displays the same information as the **databasepropertyex** function, as Example 17.3 shows.

EXAMPLE 17.3

SELECT name, database_id, recovery_model_desc AS model
        FROM sys.databases
        WHERE name = 'sample'

The result is

name	database_id	model
sample	7	FULL

High Availability

Ensuring the availability of your database system and databases is one of the most important issues today. There are several techniques that you can use to ensure their availability, which can be divided in two groups: those that are components of Database Engine and those that are not implemented in the database server. The following two techniques are not part of Database Engine:

▶ Using a standby server
▶ Using RAID technology

The following techniques belong to the database system:

▶ Failover clustering

▶ Database mirroring

▶ Log shipping

▶ Replication

The following sections describe these components, other than replication, which is discussed in Chapter 19.

Using a Standby Server

A standby server is just what its name implies—another server that is standing by in case something happens to the production server (also called the primary server). The standby server contains files, databases (system and user-defined), and user accounts identical to those on the production server.

A standby server is implemented by initially restoring a full database backup of the database and applying transaction log backups to keep the database on the standby server synchronized with the production server. To set up a standby server, set the **read only** database option to true. This option prevents users from performing any write operations in the database.

The general steps to use a copy of a production database are as follows:

▶ Restore the production database using the RESTORE DATABASE statement with the STANDBY clause.

▶ Apply each transaction log to the standby server using the RESTORE LOG statement with the STANDBY clause.

▶ When applying the final transaction log backup, use the RESTORE LOG statement with the RECOVERY clause. (This final statement recovers the database without creating a file with before images, making the database available for write operations, too.)

After the database and transaction logs are restored, users can work with an exact copy of the production database. Only the noncommitted transactions at the time of failure will be permanently lost.

NOTE

If the production server fails, user processes are not automatically brought to the standby server. Additionally, all user processes need to restart any tasks with the uncommitted transactions due to the failure of the production server.

Using RAID Technology

RAID (redundant array of inexpensive disks) is a special disk configuration in which multiple disk drives build a single logical unit. This process allows files to span multiple disk devices. RAID technology provides improved reliability at the cost of performance decrease. Generally, there are six RAID levels, 0 through 5. Only three of these levels, levels 0, 1, and 5, are significant for database systems.

RAID can be hardware or software based. Hardware-based RAID is more costly (because you have to buy additional disk controllers), but it usually performs better. Software-based RAID can be supported either by the operating system or by the database system itself. Windows operating systems provide RAID levels 0, 1, and 5. RAID technology has impacts on the following features:

- ► Fault tolerance
- ► Performance

The benefits and disadvantages of each RAID level in relation to these two features are explained next.

RAID provides protection from hard disk failure and accompanying data loss with three methods: disk striping, mirroring, and parity. These three methods correspond to RAID levels 0, 1, and 5, respectively.

Disk Striping

RAID 0 specifies disk striping without parity. Using RAID 0, the data is written across several disk drives in order to allow data access more readily, and all read and write operations can be speeded up. For this reason, RAID 0 is the fastest RAID configuration. The disadvantage of disk striping is that it does not offer fault tolerance at all. This means that if one disk fails, all the data on that array become inaccessible.

Mirroring

Mirroring is the special form of disk striping that uses the space on a disk drive to maintain a duplicate copy of some files. Therefore, RAID 1, which specifies disk mirroring, protects data against media failure by maintaining a copy of the database (or a part of it) on another disk. If there is a drive loss with mirroring in place, the files for the lost drive can be rebuilt by replacing the failed drive and rebuilding the damaged files. The hardware configurations of mirroring are more expensive, but they provide additional speed. The advantage of the Windows solution for mirroring is that it can be configured to mirror disk partitions, while the hardware solutions are usually implemented on the entire disk.

In contrast to RAID 0, RAID 1 is much slower, but the reliability is higher. Also, RAID 1 costs much more than RAID 0, because each mirrored disk drive must be doubled. It can sustain at least one failed drive and may be able to survive failure of up to half the drives in the set of mirrored disks without forcing the system administrator to shut down the server and recover from file backup. (RAID 1 is the best-performing RAID option when fault tolerance is required.)

Mirroring also has performance impacts in relation to read and write operations. When mirroring is used, write operations decrease performance, because each such operation costs two disk I/O operations, one to the original and one to the mirrored disk drive. On the other hand, mirroring increases performance of read operations, because Database Engine will be able to read from either disk drive, depending on which one is least busy at the time.

Parity

Parity (RAID level 5) is implemented by calculating recovery information about data written to disk and writing this parity information on the other drives that form the RAID array. If a drive fails, a new drive is inserted into the RAID array and the data on that failed drive is recovered by taking the recovery information (parity) written on the other drives and using this information to regenerate the data from the failed drive.

The advantage of parity is that you need one additional disk drive to protect any number of existing disk drives. The disadvantages of parity concern performance and fault tolerance. Due to the additional costs associated with calculating and writing parity, additional disk I/O operations are required. (Read I/O operation costs are the same for mirroring and parity.) Also, using parity, you can sustain only one failed drive before the array must be taken offline and recovery from backup media must be performed. Because disk striping with parity requires additional costs associated with calculating and writing parity, RAID 5 requires four disk I/O operations, whereas RAID 0 requires only one operation and RAID 1 only two operations.

Failover Clustering

Failover clustering is probably the most important technology supported by Database Engine to achieve high availability. It is a process in which the operating system and database system work together to provide availability in the event of failures. A failover cluster consists of a group of redundant servers, called nodes, that share an external disk system. When a node within the cluster fails, the instance of Database Engine on that machine shuts down. Microsoft Cluster Service transfers resources from a failing machine to an equally configured target node automatically. The transfer of resources from one node to the other node in a cluster occurs very quickly.

The advantage of failover clustering is that it protects your system against hardware failures, because it provides a mechanism to automatically restart the database system on another node of the cluster. (It is the only high-availability technology with Database Engine that supports such server redundancy.) On the other hand, this technology has a single point of failure in the set of disks, which cluster nodes share and cannot protect from data errors. Another disadvantage of this technology is that it does not increase performance or scalability. In other words, an application cannot scale any further on a cluster than it can on one node.

Database Mirroring

As you already know from the previous section, failover clustering provides server redundancy, but it doesn't provide data file redundancy. A technology of Database Engine called database mirroring doesn't provide server redundancy, but provides both database redundancy and data file redundancy.

To set up database mirroring, use two servers with a database that will be mirrored from one server to the other. The former is called the principal server, while the latter is called the mirrored server. (The copy of the database on the mirrored server is called the mirrored database.)

Database mirroring allows continuous streaming of the transaction log from the principal server to the mirrored server. The copy of the transaction log activity is written to the log of the mirrored database, and the transactions are executed on it. If the principal server becomes unavailable, applications can reconnect to the database on the mirrored server without waiting for recovery to finish. Unlike failover clustering, the mirrored server is fully cached and ready to accept workloads because of its synchronized state. It is possible to implement up to four mirrored backup sets. (To implement mirroring, use the MIRROR TO option either of the BACKUP DATABASE, or BACKUP LOG statement.)

There is also the third server, called the witness server. It determines which server is the principal server and which is the mirrored server. This server is only needed when automatic failover is required. (To enable automatic failover, you must turn on the synchronous operating mode—that is, set the SAFETY option of the ALTER DATABASE statement to FULL.)

SQL Server 2008 Enhancements to Database Mirroring

SQL Server 2008 contains the following enhancements to database mirroring:

- ► Compression of stream data
- ► Improved use of log send buffers
- ► Read-ahead during the undo phase
- ► Write-ahead on the incoming stream on the mirrored server

Database Engine compresses the stream data if at least 12.5 percent compression ratio can be achieved. That way, the system reduces the consumption of log data that is sent from the principal server to mirrored server(s).

Previously, every log-flush operation on the principal server reserved a whole database mirroring log send buffer for its log records. In SQL Server 2008, if the most recently used log cache contains sufficient free space for the log records of the next log-flush operation, they are appended to that log cache.

After a failover, the new mirrored server must undo every change for which a page was written to disk locally but for which the log record might not have reached the new principal server. To undo such changed pages, the new mirrored server must first request and receive the corresponding pages from the new principal server. Performance of this part of the undo phase is enhanced in SQL Server 2008, because the new mirrored server sends read-ahead hints to the new principal server to indicate which pages will be requested later.

When receiving incoming log records, the mirrored server writes them to disk asynchronously. At the same time, the mirrored server processes log records that have already been written to disk.

Log Shipping

Log shipping allows the transaction logs from one database to be constantly sent and used by another database. This allows you to have a warm standby server and also provides a way to offload data from the source machine to read-only destination computers. The target database is an exact copy of the primary database, because the former receives all changes from the latter. You have the ability to make the target database a new primary database if the primary server, which hosts the original database, becomes unavailable. When the primary server becomes available again, you can reverse the server roles again.

Log shipping does not support automatic failover. Therefore, if the source database server fails, you must recover the target database yourself, either manually or through custom code.

> **NOTE**
>
> *Log shipping is similar to database mirroring in that it provides database redundancy. On the other hand, database mirroring significantly extends the capabilities of log shipping because it allows you to update the target database through a direct connection and in real time.*

Conclusion

The system administrator or database owner should periodically make a backup copy of the database and its transaction log to allow for recovery in the event of system errors, media failures, or other disasters (such as fire or theft). Database Engine enables you to make two kinds of backup copies of the database: full and differential. A full backup captures the state of the database at the time the statement is issued and copies it to the backup media (file or tape device). A differential backup copies the parts of the database that have changed since the last full database backup. The benefit of the differential backup is that it completes more rapidly than the full database backup for the same database. (There is also a transaction log backup, which copies transaction logs to a backup media.)

Database Engine performs automatic recovery each time a system failure occurs that does not cause any media failure. (Automatic recovery is also performed when the system is started after each shutdown of the system.) During automatic recovery, any committed transaction found in the transaction log is written to the database, and any uncommitted transaction is rolled back. After any media failure, it may be necessary to manually recover the database from the archived copy of it and its transaction logs. To recover a database, a full database backup and only the latest differential backup must be used. If you use transaction logs to restore a database, use the full database backup first and then apply all existing transaction logs in the sequence of their creation to bring the database to the consistent state that it was in before the last transaction log backup was created.

Database Engine supports several proprietary technologies that are used to enhance the availability of database systems and databases:

- ▶ Failover clustering
- ▶ Database mirroring
- ▶ Log shipping

Failover clustering is the most important technology of Database Engine in relation to high availability. It is the only technology that provides server redundancy. Database mirroring doesn't provide server redundancy, but guarantees database redundancy. Log shipping is similar to database mirroring, but supports only a subset of its capabilities.

The next chapter describes all system features that allow you to automate system administration tasks.

Exercises

E.17.1

Discuss the differences between the differential backup and transaction log backup.

E.17.2

When should you back up your production database?

E.17.3

How can you make a differential backup of the **master** database?

E.17.4

Discuss the use of different RAID technologies with regard to fault tolerance of a database and its transaction log.

E.17.5

What are the main differences between manual and automatic recovery?

E.17.6

Which statement should you use to verify your backup, without using it for the restore process?

E.17.7

Discuss the advantages and disadvantages of the three recovery models.

E.17.8

Discuss the similarities and differences between failover clustering, database mirroring, and log shipping.

Chapter 18

Automating System Administration Tasks

In This Chapter

- ▶ **Running and Configuring SQL Server Agent**
- ▶ **Creating Jobs and Operators**
- ▶ **Alerts**
- ▶ **Error Messages**

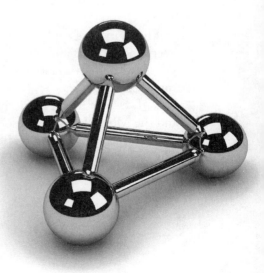

One of the most important advantages of Database Engine in relation to other relational DBMSs is its capability to automate administrative tasks and hence to reduce costs. The following are examples of some important tasks that are performed frequently and therefore could be automated:

▶ Backing up the database and transaction log

▶ Transferring data

▶ Dropping and re-creating indices

▶ Checking data integrity

You can automate all these tasks so that they occur on a regular schedule. For example, you can set the database backup task to occur every Friday at 8:00 P.M. and the transaction log backup task to occur daily at 12:00 P.M.

The components of Database Engine that are used in automation processes include the following:

▶ SQL Server service (MSSQLSERVER)

▶ Windows application log

▶ SQL Server Agent service

Why does Database Engine need these three components to automate processes? In relation to automation of administration tasks, the MSSQLSERVER service is needed to write events to the Windows application log. Some events are written automatically, and some must be raised by the system administrator (see the detailed explanation later in this chapter).

The Windows application log is where all operating system messages of Windows operating systems and messages of their components are written. The role of the Windows application log in the automation process is to notify SQL Server Agent about existing events.

SQL Server Agent is another service that connects to the Windows application log and the MSSQLSERVER service. The role of SQL Server Agent in the automation process is to take an action after a notification through the Windows application log. The action can be performed in connection with the MSSQLSERVER service or some other application. Figure 18-1 shows how these three components work together.

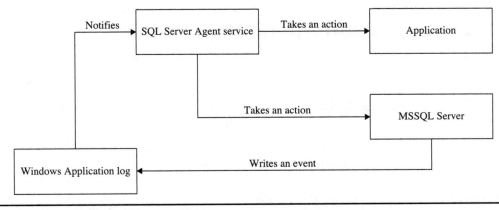

Figure 18-1   *SQL Server automation components*

Running and Configuring SQL Server Agent

SQL Server Agent executes jobs and fires alerts. As you will see in the upcoming sections, jobs and alerts are defined separately and can be executed independently. Nevertheless, jobs and alerts may also be complementary processes, because a job can invoke an alert and vice versa.

Consider an example: A job is executed to inform the system administrator about an unexpected filling of the transaction log that exceeds a tolerable limit. When this event occurs, the associated alert is invoked and, as a reaction, the system administrator may be notified by e-mail or pager.

Another critical event is a failure in backing up the transaction log. When this happens, the associated alert may invoke a job that truncates the transaction log. This reaction will be appropriate if the reason for the backup failure is an overflow (filling up) of the transaction log. In other cases (for example, the target device for the backup copy is full), such a truncation will have no effect. This example shows the close connection that may exist between events that have similar symptoms.

SQL Server Agent allows you to automate different administrative tasks. Before you can do this, the process has to be started. SQL Server Agent can be started in the same way as the MSSQLSERVER service. For more information, see Chapter 2.

As already stated, the invocation of an alert can also include the notification of one or more operators by e-mail using Database Mail. Database Mail is an enterprise solution for sending e-mail messages from Database Engine. Using Database Mail, your applications can send e-mail messages to users. The messages may contain query results, and may also include files from any resource on your network.

Creating Jobs and Operators

Generally, there are three steps to follow if you want to create a job:

1. Create a job and its steps
2. Create a schedule of the job execution if the job is not to be executed on demand
3. Notify operators about the status of the job

The following sections explain these steps using an example.

Creating a Job and Its Steps

A job may contain one or more steps. There are different ways in which a job step can be defined. The following list contains some of them.

▶ **Using Transact-SQL statements**   Many job steps contain Transact-SQL statements. For example, if you want to automate database or transaction log backups, you use the BACKUP DATABASE statement or BACKUP LOG statement, respectively.

▶ **Operating System (CmdExec)**   Some other jobs may require the execution of a SQL Server utility, which usually will be started with the corresponding command. For example, if you want to automate the data transfer from your database server to a data file, or vice versa, you could use the **bcp** utility.

▶ **Invoking a program**   As another alternative, it may be necessary to execute a program that has been developed using Visual Basic or some other programming language. In this case, you should always include the path drive letter in the **Command** text box when you start such a program. This is necessary because SQL Server Agent has to find the executable file.

If the job contains several steps, it is important to determine what actions should be taken in case of a failure. Generally, Database Engine starts the next job step if the previous one was successfully executed. However, if a job step fails, any job steps that follow will not be executed. Therefore, you should always specify how often each step should be retried in the case of failure. And, of course, it will be necessary to eliminate the reason for the abnormal termination of the job step (obviously, a repeated job execution will always lead to the same error if the cause is not repaired).

NOTE

The number of attempts depends on the type and content of the executed job step (batch, command, or application program).

You can create a job using the following:

▶ SQL Server Management Studio

▶ System stored procedures (sp_add_job and sp_add_jobstep)

SQL Server Management Studio is used in this example, which creates a job that backs up the **sample** database. To create this job, connect to an instance of Database Engine in **Object Explorer** and then expand that instance. Expand **SQL Server Agent**, right-click **Jobs**, and then click **New Job**. (SQL Server Agent must be running.) The **New Job** dialog box appears (see Figure 18-2). On the **General** page, enter a name for the job in the **Name** box. (As you can see in Figure 18-2, the name of the job for backing up the **sample** database is **backup_sample**.)

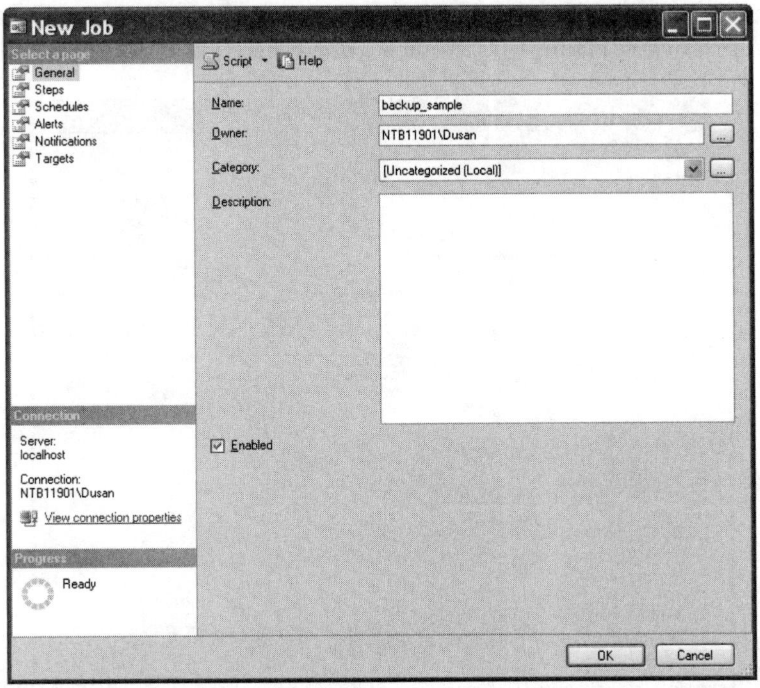

Figure 18-2 *New Job dialog box*

For the **Owner** field, click the ellipsis (…) button and choose the owner responsible for performing the job. In the **Category** drop-down list, choose the category to which the job belongs. In the example in Figure 18-2, the job **backup_sample** is not categorized, and the owner is the user who is creating the job. You can add a description of the job in the **Description** box, if you wish.

NOTE

If you have to manage several jobs, categorizing them is recommended. This is especially useful if your jobs are executed in a multiserver environment.

Check the **Enabled** check box to enable the job.

NOTE

All jobs are enabled by default. SQL Server Agent disables jobs if the job schedule is defined either at a specific time that has passed or on a recurring basis with an end date that has also passed. In both cases, you must re-enable the job manually.

Each job must have one or more steps. Therefore, in addition to defining job properties, you must create at least one step before you can save the job. To define one or more steps, click the **Steps** page in the **New Job** dialog box and click **New**. The **New Job Step** dialog box appears, as shown in Figure 18-3. Enter a name for the job step. (It is called **backup** in

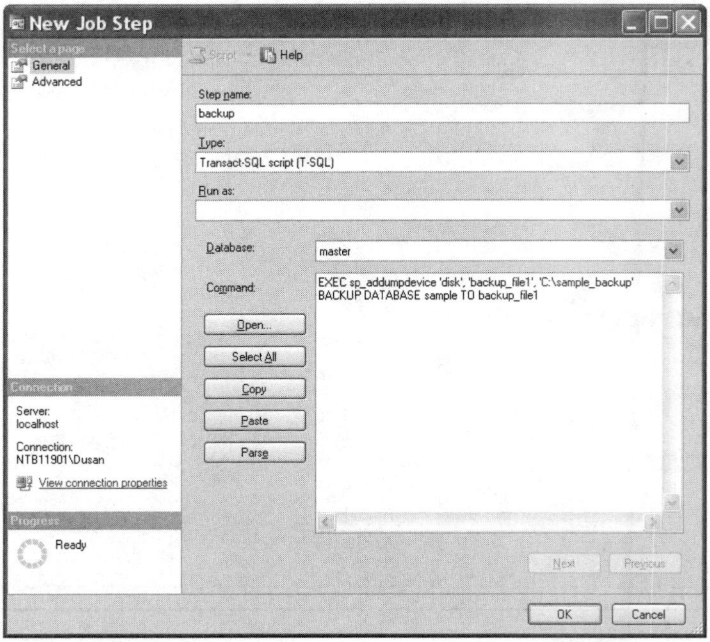

Figure 18-3   *New Job Step dialog box: General page*

the example.) In the **Type** drop-down list, choose **Transact-SQL script (T-SQL)**, because the backup of the sample database will be executed using the Transact-SQL statement BACKUP DATABASE.

In the **Database** drop-down list, choose the **master** database, because this system database must be the current database if you want to back up a database.

You can either enter the Transact-SQL statement directly in the **Command** box or invoke it from a file. In the former case, enter the following statements:

```
EXEC sp_addumpdevice 'disk', 'backup_file1', 'C:\sample_backup'
BACKUP DATABASE sample TO backup_file1
```

As you probably guessed, the **sp_addumpdevice** system procedure adds a backup device to an instance of Database Engine. To invoke the Transact-SQL statement from a file, click **Open** and select the file. The syntax of the statement(s) can be checked by clicking **Parse**.

Creating a Job Schedule

Each created job can be executed on demand (that is, manually by the user) or by using one or more schedules. A scheduled job can occur at a specific time or on a recurring schedule.

> **NOTE**
>
> *Each job can have multiple schedules. For example, the backup of the transaction log of a production database can be executed with two different schedules, depending on time of day. This means that during peak business hours, you can execute the backup more frequently than during nonpeak hours.*

To create a schedule for an existing job using SQL Server Management Studio, select the Schedules page in the **Job Properties** dialog box and click **New**. (The **Job Properties** dialog box is the same dialog box as in Figure 18-2). If the Job Properties dialog box is not active, expand SQL Server Agent, expand **Jobs**, and click the job you want to process.

> **NOTE**
>
> *If you get the warning, "The On Access action of the last step will be changed from Get Next Step to Quit with Success," click Yes.*

The **New Job Schedule** dialog box appears (see Figure 18-4).

For the **sample** database, set the schedule for the backup to be executed every Friday at 8:00 P.M. To do this, enter the name in the **Name** dialog box and choose **Recurring**

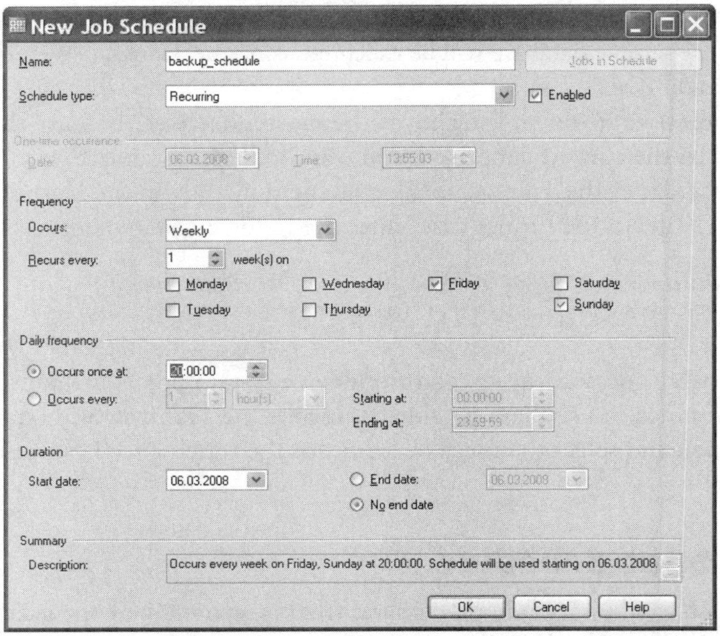

Figure 18-4   *New Job Schedule dialog box*

in the **Schedule type** drop-down list. In the **Frequency** section, select **Weekly** in the **Occur** drop-down list, and check **Friday**. In the **Daily frequency** section, click the **Occurs once at** radio button, and enter the time (**20:00:00**). In the **Duration** section, choose the start date in the **Start date** drop-down list, and then click the **End date** radio button and choose the end date in the corresponding drop-down list. (If the job should be scheduled without the end date, click **No end date**.)

Notifying Operators about the Job Status

When a job completes, several methods of notification are possible. For example, you can instruct the system to write a corresponding message to the Windows application log, hoping that the system administrator reads this log from time to time. A better choice is to explicitly notify one or more operators using e-mail, pager, and/or the **net send** command.

Before an operator can be assigned to a job, you have to create an entry for it. To create an operator using SQL Server Management Studio, expand **SQL Server Agent**, right-click **Operators**, and then click **New Operator**. The **New Operator** dialog box appears (see Figure 18-5). On the **General** page, enter the name of the operator in the **Name** box. Specify one or more methods of notifying the operator (via e-mail, pager, or the **net send** address). In the **Pager on duty schedule** section, enter the working hours of the operator.

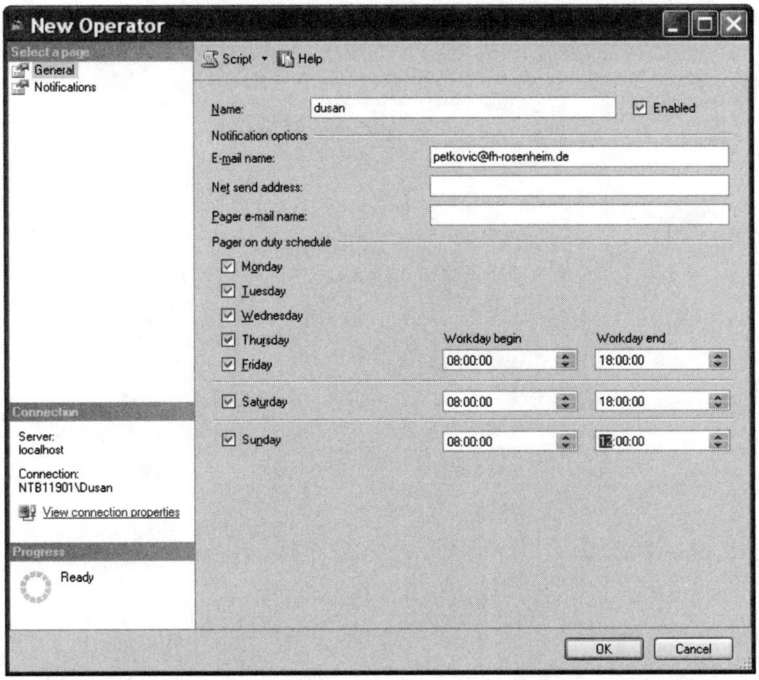

Figure 18-5   *New Operator Properties dialog box*

To notify one or more operators after the job finishes (successfully or unsuccessfully), return to the **Job Properties** dialog box of the job, select the **Notifications** page (see Figure 18-6), and check the corresponding boxes. (Besides e-mail, pager, or the **net send** command notification, in this dialog box you also have the option of writing the message to the Windows application log and/or deleting the job.)

Viewing the Job History Log

The database system stores the information concerning all job activities in the **sysjobhistory** system table of the **msdb** system database. Therefore, this table represents the job history log of your system. You can view the information in this table using SQL Server Management Studio. To do this, expand **SQL Server Agent**, expand **Jobs**, right-click the job, and click **View History**. The **Log File Viewer** dialog box shows the history log of the job.

Each row of the job history log is displayed in the details pane, which contains, among other information, the following:

▶   Date and time when the job step occurred

▶   Whether the job step completed successfully or unsuccessfully

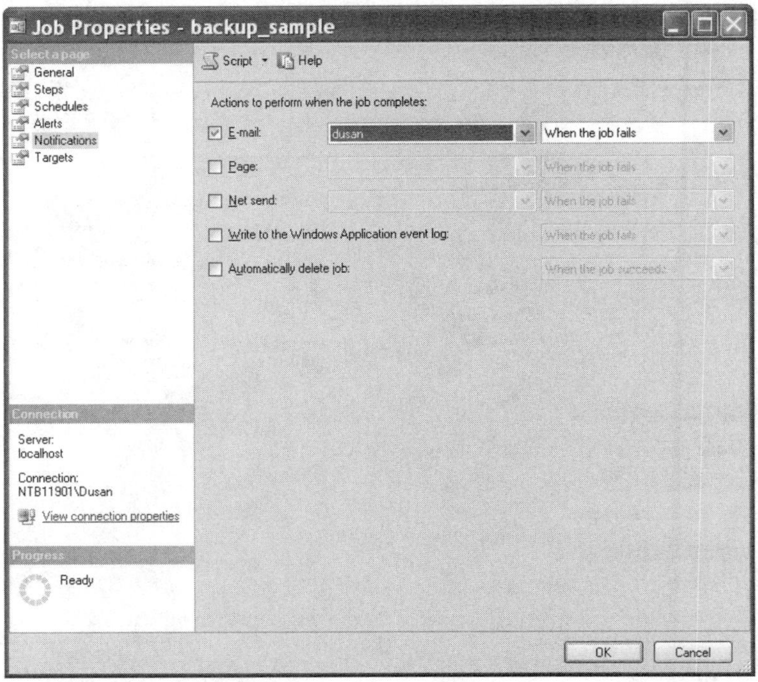

Figure 18-6   *Job Properties dialog box: Notifications page*

- ▶ Operators who were notified
- ▶ Duration of the job
- ▶ Errors or messages concerning the job step

By default, the maximum size of the job history log is 1000 rows, while the number of rows for a particular job is limited to 100. (The job history log is automatically cleared when the maximum size of rows is reached.) If you want to store the information about each job, and your system has several jobs, increase the size of the job history log and/or the number of rows per job. Using SQL Server Management Studio, right-click **SQL Server Agent** and click **Properties**. In the **SQL Server Agent Properties** dialog box, select the **History** page and enter the new values for the maximum job history log size and maximum job history rows per job. You can also check **Automatically remove agent history** and select a time interval when logs should be deleted.

Alerts

The information about execution of jobs and system error messages is stored in the Windows application log. SQL Server Agent reads this log and compares the stored messages with the alerts defined for the system. If there is a match, SQL Server Agent fires the alert. Therefore, alerts can be used to respond to potential problems (such as filling up the transaction log), different system errors, or user-defined errors. Before explaining how you create alerts, this section discusses system error messages and two logs, the SQL Server Agent error log and the Windows application log, which are used to capture all system messages (and thus most of the errors).

Error Messages

System errors are grouped in four different groups. Database Engine provides extensive information about each error. The information is structured and includes the following:

- ▶ A unique error message number
- ▶ An additional number between 0 and 25, which represents the error's severity level
- ▶ A line number, which identifies the line where the error occurred
- ▶ The error text

NOTE

The error text not only describes the detected error but also may recommend how to resolve the problem, which can be very helpful to the user.

Example 18.1 queries a nonexistent table in the **sample** database.

EXAMPLE 18.1

```
USE sample;
SELECT * FROM authors;
```

The result is

```
Msg 208, Level 16, State 1, Line 2
Invalid object name 'authors'.
```

All error messages are stored in the system table **sysmessages** of the **master** database. To view the information from this table, use the **sys.messages** catalog view. The three most important columns of this view are **message_id**, **severity**, and **text**.

Each unique error number has a corresponding error message. (The error message is stored in the **text** column, and the corresponding error number is stored in the **message_id** column of the **sys.messages** catalog view.) In Example 18.1, the message concerning the nonexistent or incorrectly spelled database object corresponds to error number –208.

The severity level of an error (the **severity** column of the **sys.messages** catalog view) is represented in the form of a number between 0 and 25. The levels between 0 and 10 are simply informational messages, where nothing needs to be fixed. All levels from 11 through 16 indicate different program errors and can be resolved by the user. The values 17 and 18 indicate software and hardware errors that generally do not terminate the running process. All errors with a severity level of 19 and greater are fatal system errors. The connection of the program generating such an error is closed, and its process will then be removed.

The messages relating to program errors (that is, the levels between 11 and 16) are shown on the screen only. All system errors (errors with a severity level of 19 or greater) will also be written to the log.

In order to resolve an error, you usually need to read the detailed description of the corresponding error. You can also find detailed error descriptions in Books Online.

System error messages are written to the SQL Server Agent error log and to the Windows application log. The following two sections describe these two components.

SQL Server Agent Error Log

SQL Server Agent creates an error log that records warnings and errors by default. The following warnings and errors are displayed in the log:

- ▶ Warning messages that provide information about potential problems
- ▶ Error messages that usually require intervention by a system administrator

The system maintains up to nine SQL Server Agent error logs. The current log is called **Current**, while all other logs have an extension that indicates the relative age of the log. For example, Archive #1 indicates the newest archived error log.

The SQL Server Agent error log is an important source of information for the system administrator. With it, he or she can trace the progress of the system and determine which corrective actions to take.

To view the SQL Server Agent error logs from SQL Server Management Studio, expand the instance in **Object Explorer**, expand **SQL Server Agent**, and expand **Error Logs**. Click one of the files to view the desired log. The log details appear in the details pane of the **Log File Viewer** dialog box.

Windows Application Log

Database Engine also writes system messages to the Windows application log. The Windows application log is the location of all operating system messages for the Windows operating systems, and it is where all application messages are stored. You can view the Windows application log using the Windows Event Viewer.

Viewing errors in the Windows application log has some advantages compared to viewing them in the SQL Server Agent error log. The most important is that the Windows application log provides an additional component for the search for desired strings.

To view information stored in the Windows application log, click **Start**, **Settings**, **Control Panel**, choose **Administrative Tools**, and select **Event Viewer**. In the **Event Viewer** window, you can choose between system, security, and application messages.

Defining Alerts to Handle Errors

An alert can be defined to raise a response to a particular error number or to the group of errors that belongs to a specific severity code. Furthermore, the definition of an alert for a particular error is different for system errors and user-defined errors. (The creation of alerts on user-defined errors is described later in this chapter.)

The rest of this section shows how you can create alerts using SQL Server Management Studio.

Creating Alerts on System Errors

Example 13.5, in which one transaction was deadlocked by another transaction, will be used to show how to create an alert about a system error number. If a transaction is deadlocked by another transaction, the victim must be executed again. This can be done, among other ways, by using an alert.

To create the deadlock (or any other) alert, expand **SQL Server Agent**, right-click **Alerts**, and click **New Alert**. In the **New Alert** dialog box (see Figure 18-7), enter the name of the alert in the **Name** box, select the alert type (**SQL Server event alert**), and choose <**all databases**> from the **Database name** drop-down list. Click **Error number**, and enter **1205**. (This error number indicates a deadlock problem, where the current process was selected as the "victim.")

The second step defines the response for the alert. In the same dialog box, click the **Response** page (see Figure 18-8). First check **Execute job**, and then select the job to execute when the alert occurs. (The example here defines a new job called **deadlock_all_db** that restarts the victim transaction.) Check **Notify operators**, and then in the **Operator list**, select operators and the methods of their notifications (e-mail, pager, and/or the **net send** command).

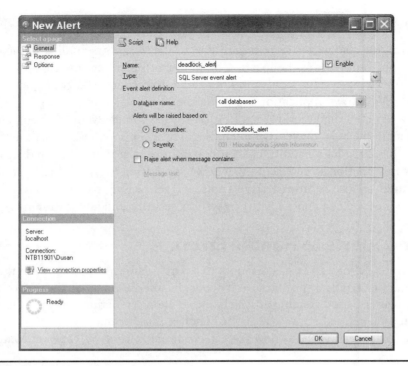

Figure 18-7 *New Alert dialog box: General page*

NOTE

In the preceding example, it is assumed that the victim process will be terminated. Actually, after receiving the deadlock error 1205, the program resubmits the failed transaction on its own.

Creating Alerts on a Group of Errors with the Same Severity Level

You can also define an alert that will raise a response on error severity levels. Each system error has a corresponding severity level that is a number between 0 and 25. The higher the severity level is, the more serious the error. Errors with severity levels 20 through 25 are fatal errors. Errors with severity levels 19 through 25 are written to the Windows application log.

NOTE

Always define an operator to be notified when a fatal error occurs.

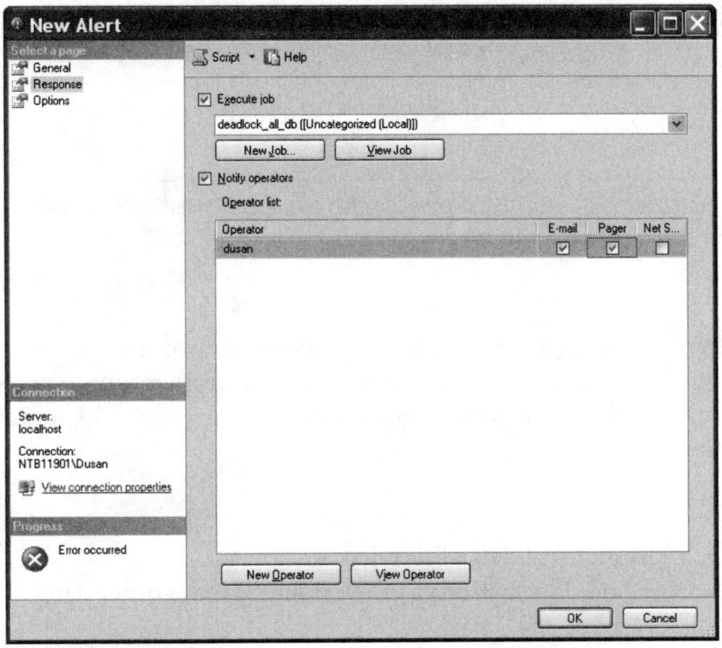

Figure 18-8   *New Alert dialog box: Response page*

As an example of how you can create alerts in relation to severity levels, here's how you use SQL Server Management Studio to create the particular alert for severity level 25. First, expand **SQL Server Agent**, right-click **Alerts**, and then click **New Alert**. In the **Name** box, enter a name for this alert (for example, **Severity 25 errors**). In the **Type** box, select **SQL Server event alert**. In the **Database name** drop-down list, select **sample** database. Click the **Severity** radio button and select **025 – Fatal Error**.

On the **Response** page, enter one or more operators to be notified via e-mail, pager and/or the **net send** command when an error of severity level 25 occurs.

Creating Alerts on User-Defined Errors

In addition to creating alerts on system errors, you can create alerts on customized error messages for individual database applications. Using such messages (and alerts), you can define solutions to problems that might occur in an application.

The following steps are necessary if you want to create an alert on a user-defined message:

1.   Create the error message
2.   Raise the error from a database application
3.   Define an alert on the error message

An example is the best way to illustrate the creation of such an alert: the alert is fired if the shipping date of a product is earlier than the order date. (For the definition of the **sales** table, see Chapter 5.)

NOTE

Only the first two steps are described here, because an alert on a user-defined message is defined similarly to an alert on a system error message.

Creating an Error Message   To create a user-defined error message, you can use either SQL Server Management Studio or the **sp_addmessage** stored procedure. Example 18.2 creates the error message for the example using the **sp_addmessage** stored procedure.

EXAMPLE 18.2

```
sp_addmessage @msgnum=50010, @severity=16,
@msgtext='The shipping date of a product is earlier than the order date',
@lang='us_english', @with_log='true'
```

The **sp_addmessage** stored procedure in Example 18.2 creates a user-defined error message with error number 50010 (the **@msgnum** parameter) and severity level 16 (the **@severity** parameter). All user-defined error messages are stored in the **sysmessages** system table of the **master** database and can be viewed by using the **sys.messages** catalog view. The error number Example 18.2 is 50010 because all user-defined errors must be greater than 50000. (All error message numbers less than 50000 are reserved for the system.)

For each user-defined error message, you can optionally specify the language using the **@lang** parameter in which the message is displayed. This specification may be necessary if multiple languages are installed on your computer. (When language is omitted, the session language is the default language.)

By default, user-defined messages are not written to the Windows application log. On the other hand, you must write the message to this log if you want to raise an alert on it. If you set the **@with_log** parameter of the **sp_addmessage** system procedure to true, the message will be written to the log.

Raising an Error Using Triggers   To raise an error from a database application, you invoke the RAISERROR statement. This statement returns a user-defined error message and sets a system flag in the **@@error** global variable. (You can also handle error messages using TRY/CATCH blocks.)

Example 18.3 creates the trigger **t_date_comp**, which returns a user-defined error of 50010 if the shipping date of a product is earlier than the order date.

> **NOTE**
> To execute Example 18.3, the table **sales** must exist (see Example 5.21).

EXAMPLE 18.3

```
USE sample;
GO
CREATE TRIGGER t_date_comp
  ON sales
  FOR INSERT AS
  DECLARE @order_date DATE
  DECLARE @shipped_date DATE
SELECT @order_date=order_date, @shipped_date=ship_date FROM INSERTED
  IF @order_date > @shipped_date
      RAISERROR (50010, 16, -1)
```

Now, if you insert the following row in the **sales** table, the shipping date of a product is earlier than the order date:

```
INSERT INTO sales VALUES (1, '01.01.2007', '01.01.2006')
```
the system will return the user-defined error message:
Msg 50010, Level 16, State 1, Procedure t_date_comp, Line 8

Conclusion

Database Engine allows you to automate and streamline many administrator tasks, such as database backups, data transfers, and index maintenance. For the execution of such tasks, SQL Server Agent must be running.

To automate a task, you have to execute several steps:

▶ Create a job

▶ Create operators

▶ Create alerts

Job and *task* are synonymous, so when you create a job, you create the particular task that you want to automate. The easiest way to create a job is to use SQL Server Management Studio, which allows you to define one or more job steps and create an execution schedule.

When a job (successfully or unsuccessfully) completes, you can notify one or more persons, using operators. Again, the general way to create an operator is to use SQL Server Management Studio.

Alerts are defined separately and can also be executed independently of jobs. An alert can handle individual system errors, user-defined errors, or groups of errors belonging to one of 25 severity levels.

The next chapter discusses data replication.

Exercises

E.18.1

Name several administrative tasks that could be automated.

E.18.2

You want to back up the transaction log of your database every hour during peak business hours and every four hours during nonpeak hours. What should you do?

E.18.3

You want to test performance of your production database in relation to locks and want to know whether the lock wait time is more than 30 seconds. How could you be notified automatically when this event occurs?

E.18.4

Specify all parts of a SQL Server error message.

E.18.5

Which are the most important columns of the **sys.messages** catalog view concerning errors?

Chapter 19

Data Replication

In This Chapter

- ▶ Distributed Data
- ▶ Replication—An Overview
- ▶ Managing Replication

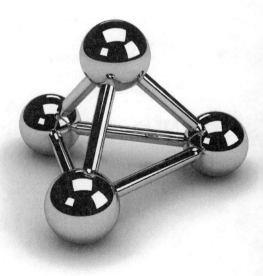

Besides distributed transactions, data replication is the way to achieve a distributed data environment. A general discussion of these two methods is given in the introductory part of this chapter. After that, replication elements are introduced, and the existing replication types are shown. The last part of the chapter covers various aspects of managing replications.

Distributed Data

Today, market forces require most companies to set up their computers (and the applications running on them) so that they focus on business and on customers. As a result, data used by these applications must be available ad hoc at different locations and at different times. Such a data environment is provided by several distributed databases that include multiple copies of the same information.

The traveling salesperson represents a good example of how a distributed data environment is used. During the day, the salesperson usually uses a laptop to query all necessary information from the database (prices and availability of products, for example) to inform customers on the spot. Afterwards, in the hotel room, the salesperson again uses the laptop—this time to transmit data (about the sold products) to headquarters.

From this scenario, you can see that a distributed data environment has several benefits compared to centralized computing:

► It is directly available to the people who need it, when they need it

► It allows local users to operate autonomously

► It reduces network traffic

► It makes nonstop processing cheaper

On the other hand, a distributed data environment is much more complex than the corresponding centralized model and therefore requires more planning and administration.

Methods for Distributing Data

There are two general methods for distributing data on multiple database servers:

► Distributed transactions
► Data replication

A distributed transaction is a transaction in which all updates to all locations (where the distributed data is stored) are gathered together and executed synchronously. Distributed database systems use a method called *two-phase commit* to implement distributed transactions.

Each database involved in a distributed transaction has its own recovery technique, which is used in case of error. (Remember that all statements inside a transaction are executed in their entirety or are cancelled.) A global recovery manager (called a coordinator) coordinates the two phases of distributed processing.

In the first phase of this process, the coordinator checks whether all participating sites are ready to execute their part of the distributed transaction. The second phase consists of the actual execution of the transaction at all participating sites. During this process, any error at any site causes the coordinator to stop the transaction. In this case, it sends a message to each local recovery manager to undo the part of the transaction that is already executed at that site.

NOTE

The Microsoft Distributed Transaction Coordinator (DTC) supports distributed transactions using two-phase commit.

During the data replication process, copies of the data are distributed from a source database to one or more target databases located on separate computers. Because of this, data replication differs from distributed transactions in two ways: timing and delay in time.

In contrast to the distributed transaction method, in which all data is the same on all participating sites at the same time, data replication allows sites to have different data at the same time. Additionally, data replication is an asynchronous process. This means there is a certain delay during which all copies of data are matched on all participating sites. (This delay can last from a couple of seconds to several days or weeks.)

Choosing a Data Distribution Method

Data replication is, in most cases, a better solution than distributed transactions because it is more reliable and cheaper. Experience with two-phase commit has shown that administration becomes very difficult if the number of participating sites increases. Also, the increased number of participating sites decreases the reliability, because the probability that a local part of a distributed transaction will fail increases with the increased number of nodes. (If one local part fails, the entire distributed transaction will fail, too.)

Another reason to use data replication instead of centralized data is performance: clients at the site where the data is replicated experience improved performance because they can access data locally rather than using a network to connect to a central database server.

Replication—An Overview

Generally, replication is based on two different concepts:

▶ Using transaction logs

▶ Using triggers

As already stated in Chapter 13, Database Engine keeps all values of modified rows ("before" as well as "after" values) in system files called transaction logs. If selected rows need to be replicated, the system starts a new process that reads the data from the transaction log and sends it to one or more target databases.

The other method is based upon triggers. The modification of a table that contains data to be replicated fires the corresponding trigger, which in turn creates a new table with the data and starts a replication process.

Both concepts have their benefits and disadvantages. The log-based replication is characterized by improved performance, because the process that reads data from the transaction log runs asynchronously and has little effect on the performance of the overall system. On the other hand, the implementation of log-based replication is very complex for database companies, because the database system not only has to manage additional processes and buffers but also has to solve the concurrency problems between system and replication processes that access the transaction log.

NOTE
Database Engine uses both concepts: the transaction log method for transactional replication processing, and triggers for merge replication processing. (Transactional and merge replication processing are described in detail later in this chapter.)

Publishers, Distributors, and Subscribers

Database Engine replication is based on the so-called publisher–subscriber metaphor. This metaphor describes the different roles servers can play in a replication process.

One or more servers publish data that other servers can subscribe to. In between there exists a distributor that stores the changes and forwards them further (to the subscribers). Hence, a node can have three roles in a replication scenario:

▶ **Publisher (or publishing server)**   Maintains its source databases, makes data available for replication, and sends the modified data to the distributor

▶ **Distributor (or distribution server)**   Receives all changes to the replicated data from the publisher and stores and forwards them to the appropriate subscribers

▶ **Subscriber (or subscription server)**   Receives and maintains published data

A database server can play many roles in a replication process. For example, a server can act as the publisher and the distributor at the same time. This scenario is appropriate for a process with few replications and few subscribers. If there are a lot of subscribers for the publishing information, the distributor can be located on its own server. Figure 19-1 shows a complex scenario in which there are multiple publishers and multiple subscribers. (See also the section "Replication Models" later in this chapter.)

NOTE

You can replicate only user-defined databases.

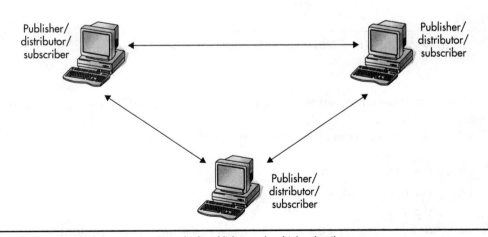

Figure 19-1   *Database Server can act as multiple publishers and multiple subscribers*

Publications and Articles

The unit of data to be published is called a *publication*. An *article* contains data from a table and/or one or more stored procedures. A table article can be a single table or a subset of data in a table. A stored procedure article can contain one or more stored procedures that exist at the publication time in the database.

A publication contains one or more articles. Each publication can contain data only from one database.

NOTE

A publication is the basis of a subscription. This means that you cannot subscribe directly to an article, because an article is always part of a publication.

A *filter* is the process that restricts information, producing a subset. Therefore, a publication contains one or more of the following items that specify types of table articles:

► Table

► Vertical filter

► Horizontal filter

► A combination of vertical and horizontal filters

NOTE

There are certain restrictions on filtering data regarding merge replication.

A vertical filter contains a subset of the columns in a table. A horizontal filter contains a subset of rows in a table.

A subscription can be initiated in two different ways:

► Using a push subscription

► Using a pull subscription

With a *push subscription*, all the administration of setting up subscriptions is performed on the publisher during the definition of a publication. Push subscriptions simplify and centralize administration, because the usual replication scenario contains one publisher and many subscribers. The benefit of a push subscription is higher security, because the initialization process is managed at one place. On the other hand, the performance of the distributor can suffer because the overall distribution of subscriptions runs at once.

With a *pull subscription*, the subscriber initiates the subscription. The pull subscription is more selective than the push subscription, because the subscriber can select publications to subscribe to. In contrast to the push subscription, the pull subscription should be used for publications with low security and a high number of subscribers.

NOTE

The downloading of data from the Internet is a typical form of pull subscription.

Replication Types

Database Engine provides the following replication types, which are discussed in the following subsections:

▶ Transactional

▶ Snapshot

▶ Merge

▶ Peer-to-peer

Transactional Replication

In transactional replication, the transaction log of the system is used to replicate data. All transactions that contain the data to be replicated are marked for replication. A component called Log Reader Agent searches for marked transactions and copies them from the transaction log on the publisher to the **distribution** database (see below). Another component—Distribution Agent—moves transactions to subscribers, where they are applied to the target tables in the subscription databases.

NOTE

All tables published using transactional replication must explicitly contain a primary key. The primary key is required to uniquely identify the rows of the published table, because a row is the transfer unit in transactional replication.

Transactional replication can replicate tables (or parts of tables) and one or more stored procedures. The use of stored procedures by transactional replication increases performance, because the amount of data to be sent over a network is usually significantly smaller. Instead of replicated data, only the stored procedure is sent to the subscribers, where it is executed. You can configure the delay of synchronization time between the publisher on one side and subscribers on the other during a transactional replication. (All these changes are propagated by Log Reader Agent and Distribution Agent.)

The **distribution** database is a system database that is installed on the distribution server when the replication process is initiated. This database holds all replicated transactions from publications and publishers that need to be forwarded to the subscribers. It is heavily used only by transactional replication.

NOTE

Before transactional replication can begin, a copy of the entire database must be transferred to each subscriber; this is performed by executing a snapshot.

Snapshot Replication

The simplest type of replication, snapshot replication, copies the data to be published from the publisher to all subscribers. (The difference between snapshot replication and transactional replication is that the former sends all the published data to the subscribers and the latter sends only the changes of data to the subscribers.)

Snapshot replication is tightly related to a component called Snapshot Agent. This component generates the schema and data of the published tables and stores them in files. The schema of a table and the corresponding data file builds the synchronization set that represents the snapshot of the table at a particular time. Whether the agent creates new snapshot files each time it runs depends on the type of replication and options chosen.

NOTE

Transactional and snapshot replications are one-way replications, meaning the only changes to the replicated data are made at the publishing server. Therefore, the data at all subscription servers is read-only, except for the changes made by replication processes.

In contrast to transactional replication, snapshot replication requires no primary key for tables. The reason is obvious: the unit of transfer in snapshot replication is a snapshot file and not a row of a table. Another difference between these two replication types concerns a delay in time: snapshot replication is replicated periodically, which means the delay is significant because all published data (changed and unchanged) is transferred from the publisher to the subscribers.

> **NOTE**
>
> *Snapshot replication does not use the **distribution** database directly. However, the **distribution** database contains status information and other details that are used by snapshot replication.*

Merge Replication

In transactional and snapshot replication, the publisher sends the data, and a subscriber receives it. (There is no possibility that a subscriber sends replicated data to the publisher.) Merge replication allows the publisher and subscribers to update data to be replicated. Because of that, conflicts can arise during a replication process.

After the creation of a publication at the publication server, Snapshot Agent prepares files containing table schema and data and stores them in the distribution working folder at the distributor site. (During merge replication, the **distribution** database contains only the status of the replication process.) The synchronization job is then used by another component—Merge Agent—that sends all changed data to the other sites. (Remember that Merge Agent can send replicated data to the subscribers as well as to the publisher.) Before the send process is started, Merge Agent also stores the appropriate information that is used to track updated conflicts.

When you use the merge replication scenario, the system makes three important changes to the schema of the publication database:

- ▶ It identifies a unique column for each replicated row
- ▶ It adds several system tables
- ▶ It creates triggers for tables in which data is replicated

Database Engine creates or identifies a unique column in the table with the replicated data. If the base table already contains a column with the UNIQUEIDENTIFIER data type and the ROWGUIDCOL property, the system uses that column to identify each replicated row. If there is no such column in the table, the system adds the column **rowguid** of the UNIQUEIDENTIFIER data type with the ROWGUIDCOL property.

> **NOTE**
>
> *UNIQUEIDENTIFIER columns may contain multiple occurrences of a value. The ROWGUIDCOL property additionally indicates that the values of the column of the UNIQUEIDENTIFIER data type uniquely identify rows in the table. Therefore, a column of the data type UNIQUEIDENTIFIER with the ROWGUIDCOL property contains unique values for each row across all networked computers in the world and thus guarantees the uniqueness of replicated rows across multiple copies of the table on the publisher and subscribers.*

The addition of new system tables provides the way to detect and resolve any update conflict. Database Engine stores all changes concerning the replicated data in the merge system tables **msmerge_contents** and **msmerge_tombstone** and joins them (using the **rowguid** property of the existing column with the UNIQUEIDENTIFIER data type) with the table that contains replicated data to resolve the conflict.

Database Engine creates triggers on tables that contain replicated data on all sites to track changes to the data in each replicated row. These triggers determine the changes made to the table, and they record them in the **msmerge_contents** and **msmerge_ tombstone** system tables.

Conflict detection is done by Merge Agent using the column lineage of the **msmerge_ contents** system table when a conflict is detected. The resolution of it can be either priority based or custom based.

Priority-based resolution means that any conflict between new and old values in the replicated row is resolved automatically based on assigned priorities. (The special case of the priority-based method specifies the "first wins" method, where the timely first change of the replicated row is the winner.) The priority-based method is the default. The *custom-based* method uses customized triggers based on business rules defined by the database administrator to resolve conflicts.

Peer-to-Peer Transactional Replication

Peer-to-peer is another form of transactional replication, in which each server is at the same time a publisher, distributor, and subscriber for the same data. In other words, all servers contain the same data, but each server is responsible for the modification of its own partition of data.

Peer-to-peer replication is best explained through an example. Suppose that a company has several branch offices in different cities and an office server has the same data set as all other servers. On the other hand, the entire data is partitioned in subsets, and each office server can update only its own subset of data. When data is modified on one of the office servers, the changes are replicated to all other servers (subscribers) in the peer-to-peer network. (Users in each office can read data without any restrictions.)

The benefits of this replication form are

▶ The entire system scales well

▶ The entire system provides high availability

A system that supports peer-to-peer replication scales well because each server serves only local users. (Users can update only the data partition that belongs to their local server. For read operations, all data is stored locally, too.)

The high availability is based upon the fact that if one or more servers go offline, all other servers can continue to operate, because all data they need for read and write operations is stored locally. When an offline server is online again, the replication process restarts and the server receives all data modifications that have happened at the other sites.

Conflict Detection in Peer-to-Peer Replication   In case of peer-to-peer replication you can change data at any node. Therefore, data changes at different nodes could conflict with each other. (If a row is modified at more than one node, it can cause a conflict.)

Peer-to-peer replication in SQL Server 2008 introduces the option to enable conflict detection across a peer-to-peer topology. With this option enabled, a conflicting change is treated as a critical error that causes the failure of Distribution Agent. In the event of a conflict, the scenario remains in an inconsistent state until the conflict is resolved and the data is made consistent on all participating servers.

NOTE

*You can enable conflict detection using the system procedures **sp_addpublication** or **sp_configure_peerconflictdetection**.*

Conflicts in peer-to-peer replication are detected by the stored procedures that apply changes to each node, based on a hidden column in each published table. This hidden column stores an identifier that combines together a unique ID that you specify for each node and the version of the row. The procedures are executed by Distribution Agent and they apply insert, update, and delete operations from other peers. If one of the procedures detects a conflict when it reads the hidden column value, it raises error 22815.

NOTE

The hidden column can be accessed only by a user that is logged in through the Dedicated Administrator Connection (see Chapter 2).

When a conflict occurs in peer-to-peer replication, the **Peer-to-peer conflict detection alert** is raised. You should configure this alert so that you are notified when a conflict occurs. (The previous chapter explains how alerts can be configured and discusses the ways to notify operators.) Books Online describes several approaches on how to handle the conflicts that occurred.

> **NOTE**
>
> *You should try to avoid conflicts in a peer-to-peer replication, even if the conflict detection is enabled.*

Replication Models

The previous section introduced different replication types that Database Engine uses to distribute data between different nodes. The replication types (transactional, snapshot, merge, and peer-to peer) provide the functionality for maintaining replicated data. *Replication models*, on the other hand, are used by a company to design its own data replication. (Each replication model can be implemented using one or more existing replication types.) Both replication type and replication model are usually determined at the same time.

Depending on requirements, several replication models can be used. Three of the basic ones are as follows:

- ▶ Central publisher with distributor
- ▶ Central subscriber with multiple publishers
- ▶ Multiple publishers with multiple subscribers

The following sections describe these models.

Central Publisher with Distributor

In the central publisher with distributor model, there is one publisher and usually one distributor. The publisher creates publications that are distributed by the distributor to several subscribers. (This model is the standard model.)

If the amount of publishing data is not very large, the publisher and distributor can reside on one server. Otherwise, using two separate servers is recommended because of performance issues. (If there is a heavy load of data to be published, the distributor is usually the bottleneck.) Figure 19-2 shows the replication model with the central publisher and the separate distributor.

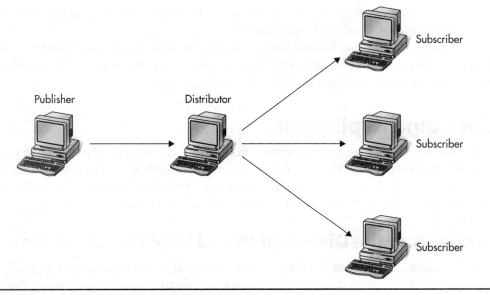

Figure 19-2   *Central publisher with separate distributor*

The publications designed by this model and received at a subscriber are usually read-only. Therefore, in most cases, transactional replication is the preferred replication type for this model, although snapshot replication can also be used.

Central Subscriber with Multiple Publishers

The scenario described at the beginning of this chapter of the traveling salesperson who transmits data to headquarters is a typical example of the central subscriber with multiple publishers. The data is gathered at a centralized subscriber, and several publishers send their data.

For this model, you can use either the transactional or merge replication type, depending on the use of replicated data. If publishers publish (and therefore update) the same data to the subscriber, merge replication should be used. If each publisher has its own data to publish, transactional replication or peer-to-peer replication should be used. (In this case, published tables will be filtered horizontally, and each publisher will be the exclusive owner of a particular table fragment.)

Multiple Publishers with Multiple Subscribers

The replication model in which some or all of the servers participating in data replication play the role of the publisher as well as the subscriber is known as multiple publishers with multiple subscribers. In most cases, this model includes several distributors that are usually placed at each publisher (see Figure 19-1).

This model can be implemented using merge replication only, because publications are modified at each publishing server. (The only other way to implement this model is to use the distributed transactions with two-phase commit.)

Managing Replication

All servers that participate in a replication must be registered. (Server registration is described in Chapter 3.) After registering servers, the distribution server, publishing server(s), and subscription server(s) must be set up. The following sections describe configuration of these processes using the corresponding wizards.

Configuring the Distribution and Publication Servers

Before you install publishing databases, you must install the distribution server and configure the distribution database. You can set up a distribution server by using the Configure Distribution Wizard. This wizard allows you to configure the distributor and the distribution database and to enable publisher(s). With the wizard you can

▶ Configure your server to be a distributor that can be used by other publishers

▶ Configure your server to be a publisher that acts as its own distributor

▶ Configure your server to be a publisher that uses another server as its distributor

This section shows a scenario for data replication of the **sample** database using two instances on the same computer: **NTB01112** and **NTB01112\INSTANCE1**. The former will be used as a publisher and distributor, while the latter will be the subscriber. The first step is to use the Configure Distribution Wizard to set up the **NTB01112** server to be a publisher that acts as its own distributor. (Additionally, the wizard will create the **distribution** database.)

NOTE
*You can also use the system procedures **sp_adddistributor** and **sp_adddistributiondb** to set up the distribution server and the **distribution** database. **sp_adddistributor** sets up the distribution server by creating a new row in the **sysservers** system table. **sp_adddistributiondb** creates a new distribution database and installs the distribution schema.*

To start the wizard, start SQL Server Management Studio, expand the instance, right-click **Replication**, and select **Configure Distribution**. The Configure Distribution

Wizard appears. On the first page, choose the distribution server and click **Next**. After that, select the folder in which snapshots from publisher(s) that use the distribution server will be stored and click **Next**. On the third page, select the name of the distribution database and log files. On the next page, enable the publisher(s) (the **NTB01112** server in this example), choose whether to finish the configuration process immediately or generate the script file to start the distribution configuration later and click **Next**. Figure 19-3 shows the summary of all steps that you have made to configure the **NTB01112** server as the distributor and publisher.

NOTE

*The existing publishing and distribution on a server can be disabled using the Disable Publishing and Distribution Wizard. To start the wizard, right-click **Replication** and select **Disable Publishing and Distribution**.*

After you configure the distribution and publishing servers, you must set up the publishing process. This is done with the New Publication Wizard, explained in the following section.

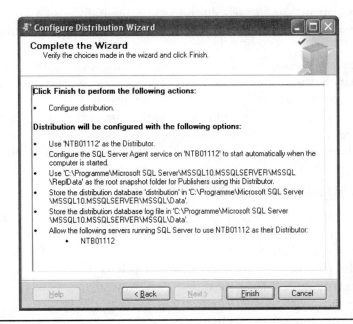

Figure 19-3   *Complete the Wizard page for the distributor and publisher(s)*

Setting Up Publications

You can use the New Publication Wizard to

▶ Select the data and database objects you want to replicate

▶ Filter the published data so the subscribers receive only the data they need

Assume that you want to publish the data of the **employee** table from the **NTB01112** server to the **NTB01112\INSTANCE1** instance using the snapshot replication type. In this case, the entire **employee** table is the publication unit.

To create a publication, expand the server node of the publishing server (**NTB01112**), expand the **Replication** folder, right-click the **Local Publications** folder, and select **New Publication**. The New Publication Wizard appears. On the first two pages, choose the database to publish (**sample**) and the publication type (in this case, the snapshot publication) and click **Next**. Then select at least one object for publication and click **Next** (in this example, select the entire **employee** table). The New Publication Wizard also allows you to filter (horizontally or vertically) the data that you want to publish. (This example will replicate the entire **employee** table.) The snapshot of the selected data can be initialized immediately and/or scheduled to run periodically. Also, you can finish the configuration process immediately or generate the script file to start the publication creation later.

On the next page, specify the security settings for Snapshot Agent. To do this, click the **Security Settings** button and type the Windows user account under which the Snapshot Agent process will run. (The user account must be entered in the form *domain_name\account_name*.) Figure 19-4 shows the summary of all steps made to set up the **employee** table as a publication unit.

The last step is to configure the subscription servers, discussed in the following section.

Configuring Subscription Servers

A task that concerns subscribers but has to be performed at the publisher is enabling the publisher to subscribe. Use SQL Server Management Studio to enable a subscriber at the publishing server. First expand the publishing server, expand **Replication**, right-click **Local Subscriptions**, and select **New Subscriptions**. The New Subscription Wizard appears. You can use the wizard to

▶ Create one or more subscriptions to a publication

▶ Specify where and when to run agents that synchronize the subscription

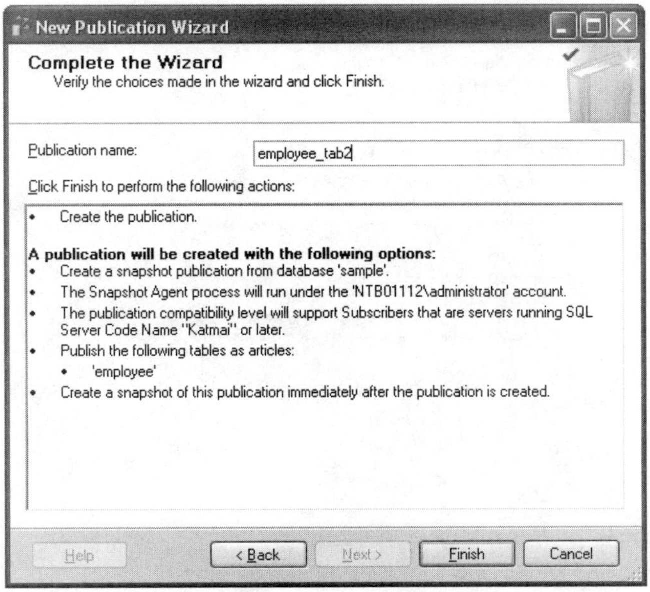

Figure 19-4   *Complete the Wizard page for the publication unit*

On the first page, choose the publication for which you want to create one or more subscriptions and click **Next**. (In this example, choose the **employee_tab2** publication, which was already generated with the New Publication Wizard.)

On the next page, Distribution Agent Location, you must choose between the push and pull subscriptions (see Figure 19-5). A push subscription means that the synchronization of subscriptions is administered centrally. For this replication, check **Run all agents at the Distributor**. To specify the pull distribution, check **Run each agent at its Subscriber**. Click **Next**.

On the next page, you must specify all subscription servers. If the subscription servers have not been added, click **Add SQL Server Subscriber** and select all servers to which data will be replicated and click **Next**. Before you finish the process, the wizard shows you the summary concerning the subscription configuration (see Figure 19-6).

NOTE

In Figure 19-6, the local administrator account is used. You should create a dedicated account for replication instead of using the administrator account.

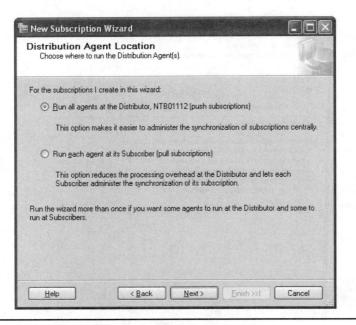

Figure 19-5 *Choice between the push and pull subscriptions*

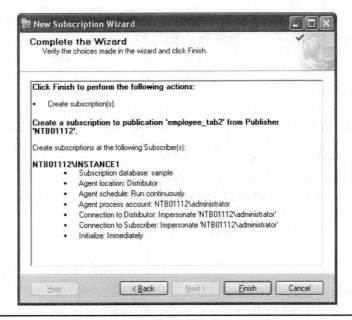

Figure 19-6 *Complete the Wizard page for the subscriber*

Conclusion

Data replication is the preferred method for data distribution, because it is cheaper than using distributed transactions. Database Engine allows you to choose one of four possible replication types (snapshot, transactional, merge, and peer-to-peer replication), depending on the physical model you use. Theoretically, any replication model can use any of the replication types, although each (basic) model has a corresponding type that is used in most cases.

A publication is the smallest unit of replication. A single database can have many publications with different replication types. (Otherwise, each publication corresponds to only one database.)

To configure the replication process, you must first set up the distribution server and the distribution system database and configure the publishing server(s). In the next step, you have to define one or more publications. Finally, you have to configure the subscription server(s). Database Engine supports these steps with three different wizards: the Configure Distribution Wizard, New Publication Wizard, and New Subscription Wizard.

The next two chapters discuss the overall performance of the system. Chapter 20 explains how the query optimizer of Database Engine works, while Chapter 21 discusses performance tuning. These chapters close the third part of the book.

Exercises

E.19.1

Why do you need a primary key for data replication? Which replication type requires a primary key?

E.19.2

How can you limit network traffic and/or database size?

E.19.3

Update conflicts are not recommended. How can you minimize them?

E.19.4

When does the system use Log Reader Agent, Merge Agent, and Snapshot Agent, respectively?

Chapter 20

Query Optimizer

In This Chapter

The question that generally arises when Database Engine (or any other relational database system) executes a query is how the data that is necessary for the query can be accessed and processed in the most efficient manner. The component of a database system that is responsible for the processing is called the query optimizer.

The task of the *query optimizer* (or just *optimizer*) is to consider a variety of possible execution strategies for querying the data in relation to a given query and to select the most efficient strategy. The selected strategy is called the *execution plan* of the query. The optimizer makes its decisions using considerations such as how big the tables are that are involved in the query, what indices exist, and what Boolean operator(s) (AND, OR, NOT) are used in the WHERE clause. Generally, these considerations are called *statistics*.

The beginning of the chapter introduces the phases of query processing and then explains in depth how the third phase, query optimization, works. This lays the foundation for the practical examples presented in the subsequent sections. Following that, you are introduced to the different tools that you can use to edit how the query optimizer does its work. The end of the chapter presents the optimization hints that you can give to the optimizer in special situations where it cannot find the optimal solution.

Phases of Query Processing

The task of the optimizer is to work out the most efficient execution plan for a given query. This task is done using the following four phases (see Figure 20-1):

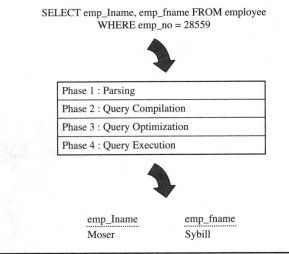

Figure 20-1 *Phases in processing a query*

NOTE

This chapter refers to using the query optimizer for queries in SELECT statements. The query optimizer is also used for INSERT, UPDATE, and DELETE statements. The INSERT statement can contain a subquery, while the UPDATE and DELETE statements often have a WHERE clause that has to be processed.

1. **Parsing**   The query's syntax is validated and the query is transformed in a tree. After that, the validation of all database objects, which are referenced by the query is checked. (For instance, the existence of all columns that are referenced in the query is checked and their IDs are determined.) After the validation process, the final query tree is formed.

2. **Query compilation**   The query tree is compiled by the query optimizer.

3. **Query optimization**   The query optimizer takes as input, the compiled query tree, generated in the previous step and investigates several access strategies before it decides how to process the given query. To find the most efficient execution plan, the query optimizer first makes the query analysis, during which it searches for search arguments and join operations. The optimizer then selects which indices to use. Finally, if join operations exist, the optimizer selects the join order and chooses one of the join processing techniques. (These optimization phases are discussed in detail in the following section.)

4. **Query execution**   After the execution plan is generated, it is permanently stored and executed.

NOTE

For some statements, parsing and optimization can be avoided if Database Engine knows that there is only one viable plan. (This process is called trivial plan optimization.) An example of a statement for which a trivial plan optimization can be used is the simple form of the INSERT statement.

How Query Optimization Works

As you already know from the previous section, the query optimization phase can be divided into the following phases:

▶ Query analysis

▶ Index selection

▶ Join order selection

▶ Choice of technique(s) for join processing

The following sections describe these phases.

Query Analysis

During the query analysis, the optimizer examines the query for search arguments, the use of the OR operator, and the existence of join criteria, in that order. Because the use of the OR operator and the existence of join criteria are self-explanatory, only search arguments are discussed.

A search argument is the part of a query that restricts the intermediate result set of the query. The main purpose of search arguments is to allow the use of existing indices in relation to the given expression. The following are examples of search arguments:

▶ emp_fname = 'Moser'

▶ salary >= 50000

▶ emp_fname = 'Moser' AND salary >= 50000

There are several expression forms that cannot be used by the optimizer as search arguments. To the first group belongs all expressions with the NOT (<>) operator. Also, if you use the expression on the left side of the operator, the existing expression cannot be used as a search argument.

The following are examples of expressions that are not search arguments:

▶ NOT IN ('d1', 'd2')

▶ emp_no <> 9031

▶ budget * 0.59 > 55000

The main disadvantage of expressions that cannot be used as search arguments is that the optimizer cannot use existing indices in relation to the expression to speed up the performance of the corresponding query. In other words, the only access that can be used in this case is the table scan.

Index Selection

The identification of search arguments allows the optimizer to decide whether one or more existing indices will be used. In this phase, the optimizer checks each search argument to see if there are indices in relation to the corresponding expression. If an index exists, the optimizer decides whether or not to use it. This decision depends on the selectivity of the corresponding expression. The *selectivity* of an expression is defined as the ratio of the number of rows satisfying the condition to the total number of rows in the table.

The optimizer checks the selectivity of an expression with the indexed column by using *statistics*, which are created in relation to the distribution of values in a column. The query optimizer uses this information to determine the optimal query plan by estimating the cost of using an index to execute the query.

The following sections discuss in detail selectivity of an expression with the indexed column and statistics. (Because statistics exist in relation to both indices and columns, they are discussed separately in two sections.)

NOTE

Database Engine automatically creates (index and column) statistics if the database option called AUTO_ CREATE_STATISTICS is activated. (This option is described later in this chapter.)

Selectivity of an Expression with the Indexed Column

As you already know, the optimizer uses indices to improve query execution time. When you query a table that doesn't have indices, or if the optimizer decides not to use an existing index, the system performs a table scan. During a table scan, Database Engine sequentially reads the table's data pages to find the rows that belong to the result set. Index access is an access method in which the database system reads and writes data pages using an existing index. Because index access significantly reduces the number of I/O read operations, it often outperforms table scans.

As you already know from Chapter 10, Database Engine uses a nonclustered index to search for data in one of two ways. If you have a heap (a table without a clustered index), the system first traverses the nonclustered index structure and then retrieves a row using the row identifier. If you have a clustered table, however, the traversal of the nonclustered index structure is followed by the traversal of the index structure of the table's clustered index. On the other hand, the use of a clustered index to search for data is always unique: Database Engine starts from the root of the corresponding B+-tree and usually after three or four read operations reaches the leaf nodes, where the data is stored. For this reason, the traversing of the index structure of a clustered index is almost always significantly faster than the traversing of the index structure of the corresponding nonclustered index.

From the discussion above, you can see that the answer to which access method (index scan or table scan) is faster isn't straightforward and depends on the selectivity and the index type.

Tests that I performed showed that a table scan often starts to perform better than a nonclustered index access when at least 10 percent of the rows are selected. In this case, the optimizer's decision of when to switch from nonclustered index access to table scan must not be correct. (If you think that the optimizer forces a table scan prematurely, you can use the INDEX query hint to change its decision, as discussed later in this chapter.)

For several reasons, the clustered index usually performs better than the nonclustered index. When the system scans a clustered index, it doesn't need to leave the b-tree structure to scan data pages, because the pages already exist at the leaf level of the tree. Also, a nonclustered index requires more I/O operations than a corresponding clustered index. Either the nonclustered index needs to read data pages after traversing the b-tree or, if a clustered index for another table's column(s) exists, the nonclustered index needs to read the clustered index's b-tree structure.

Therefore, you can expect a clustered index to perform significantly better than a table scan even when selectivity is poor (that is, the percentage of returned rows is high, because the query returns many rows). The tests that I performed showed that when the selectivity of an expression is 75 percent or less, the clustered index access is generally faster than the table scan.

Index Statistics

Index statistics are generally created when an index for the particular column(s) is created. The creation of index statistics for an index means that Database Engine creates a *histogram* based upon up to 200 values of the column. (Therefore, up to 199 intervals are built.) The histogram specifies, among other things, how many rows exactly match each interval, the average number of rows per distinct value inside the interval, and the density of values.

NOTE

Index statistics are always created for one column. If your index is a composite (multicolumn) index, the system generates statistics for the first column in the index.

If you want to create index statistics explicitly, you can use the following tools:

▶ **sp_createstats** system procedure
▶ SQL Server Management Studio

The **sp_createstats** system procedure creates single-column statistics for all columns of all user tables in the current database. The new statistic has the same name as the column where it is created.

To use SQL Server Management Studio for index statistics creation, expand the server, expand the **Databases** folder, expand the database, expand the **Tables** folder, expand the table, right-click **Statistics**, and click **New Statistics**. In the **New Statistics on Table** dialog box, specify the name for statistics and click **OK**.

As the data in a column changes, index statistics become out of date. The out-of-date statistics can significantly influence the performance of the query. Database Engine can automatically update index statistics if the database option AUTO_UPDATE_STATISTICS is activated (set to ON). In that case, any out-of-date statistics required by a query for optimization are automatically updated during query optimization.

There is also another database option, AUTO_CREATE_STATISTICS, that builds any missing statistics required by a query for optimization. Both options can be activated (or deactivated) using either the ALTER DATABASE statement or SQL Server Management Studio.

Column Statistics

As you already know from the previous section, Database Engine creates statistics for every existing index. The system can create statistics for nonindexed columns, too. These statistics are called *column statistics*. Together with index statistics, column statistics are used to optimize execution plans.

Database Engine creates statistics even for a nonindexed column that is a part of the condition in the WHERE clause.

There are several situations in which the existence of column statistics can help the optimizer to make the right decision. One of them is when you have a composite index on two or more columns. As you already know, for such an index, the system generates statistics only for the first column in the index. The existence of column statistics for the second column (and all other columns) of the composite index can help the optimizer to choose the optimal execution plan.

Database Engine supports two catalog views in relation to column statistics (these views can be used to edit the information concerning index statistics, too):

▶ sys.stats

▶ sys.stats_columns

The **sys.stats** view contains a row for each statistic of a table or a view. Besides the **name** column, which specifies the name of the statistics, this catalog view has, among others, two other columns:

▶ auto_created   Statistics created by the optimizer
▶ user_created   Statistics explicitly created by the user

The **sys.stats_columns** view contains additional information concerning columns that are part of the **sys.stats** view. (To ascertain this additional information, you have to join both views.)

Join Order Selection

Generally, the order in which two or more joined tables are written in the FROM clause of a SELECT statement doesn't influence the decision made by the optimizer in relation to their processing order.

As you will see in the next section, many different factors influence the decision of the optimizer regarding which table will be accessed first. On the other hand, you can influence the join order selection by using the FORCE ORDER hint (discussed in detail later in the chapter).

Join Processing Techniques

The join operation is the most time-consuming operation in query processing. Database Engine supports the following three different join processing techniques, so the optimizer can choose one of them depending on the statistics for both tables:

- ► Nested loops

- ► Merge join

- ► Hash join

The following subsections describe these techniques.

Nested Loops

Using nested loops is the processing technique that works by "brute force." In other words, for each row of the outer table, each row from the inner table is retrieved and compared. The pseudo-code in Algorithm 20.1 demonstrates the nested loops processing technique for two tables.

ALGORITHM 20.1

```
(A and B are two tables.)
for each row in the outer table A do:
    read the row
    for each row in the inner table B do:
        read the row
        if A.join_column = B.join_column then
            accept the row and add it to the resulting set
        end if
    end for
end for
```

In Algorithm 20.1, every row selected from the outer table (table A) causes the access of all rows of the inner table (table B). After that, the comparison of values is done and the row is added to the result set if the values in both columns are equal.

The nested loops method is very slow if there is no index for one of the join columns. Without indices, Database Engine would have to scan the outer table once and the inner table *n* times, where *n* is the number of rows of the outer table. Therefore, the query optimizer usually chooses this method if the join column of the *inner* table is indexed, so the inner table does not have to be scanned for each row in the outer table.

Merge Join

The merge join technique provides a cost-effective alternative to constructing an index for nested loops. The rows of the joined tables must be physically sorted using the values of the join column. Both tables are then scanned in order of the join columns, matching the rows with the same value for the join columns. The pseudo-code in Algorithm 20.2 demonstrates the merge join processing technique for two tables.

ALGORITHM 20.2

a. Sort the outer table A in ascending order using the join column
b. Sort the inner table B in ascending order using the join column
for each row in the outer table A do:
    read the row
    for each row from the inner table B with a value less than or equal to the join column
do:
        read the row
        if A.join_column = B.join_column then
            accept the row and add it to the resulting set
        end if
    end for
end for

The merge join processing technique has a high overhead if the rows from both tables are unsorted. However, this method is preferable when the values of both join columns are sorted in advance. (This is always the case when both join columns are primary keys of corresponding tables, because Database Engine creates by default the clustered index for the primary key of a table.)

Hash Join

The hash join technique is usually used when there are no indices for join columns. In the case of the hash join technique, both tables that have to be joined are considered as two inputs: the build input and the probe input. (The smaller table usually represents the build input.) The process works as follows:

1. The value of the join column of a row from the build input is stored in a hash bucket depending on the number returned by the hashing algorithm.

2. Once all rows from the build input are processed, the processing of the rows from the probe input starts.

3. Each value of the join column of a row from the probe input is processed using the same hashing algorithm.

4. The corresponding rows in each bucket are retrieved and used to build the result set.

NOTE

The hash join technique requires no index. Therefore, this method is highly applicable for ad hoc queries, where indices cannot be expected. Also, if the optimizer uses this processing technique, it could be a hint for you to create additional indices for one or both join columns.

Tools for Editing the Optimizer Strategy

Database Engine supports several tools that enable you to edit what the query optimizer is doing. You can use the following tools, among others:

▶ SET statement (to display textual or XML execution plans)

▶ Management Studio (to display graphical execution plans)

▶ Dynamic management views (DMVs) and functions

▶ SQL Server Profiler (discussed in detail in Chapter 21)

The following sections describe the first three tools.

NOTE

*All examples in this chapter use the **AdventureWorks** database. If your system doesn't contain this database, the introductory part of the book describes how you can download it.*

SET Statement

To understand the different options of the SET statement, you have to know that there are three different forms for how the execution plan of a query can be displayed:

▶ Textual form

▶ Using XML

▶ Graphical form

The first two forms use the SET statement, so these two forms are discussed in the following subsections. (The graphical form of execution plans is discussed a bit later, in the section "Management Studio and Graphical Execution Plans.")

Textual Execution Plans

The output of a textual execution plan is returned in the form of rows. Database Engine uses vertical bars to show the dependencies between the operations taking place. Textual execution plans can be displayed using the following options of the SET statement:

▶ SHOWPLAN_TEXT

▶ SHOWPLAN_ALL

Users running a query can display the textual execution plan for the query by activating (setting the option to ON) either SHOWPLAN_TEXT or SHOWPLAN_ALL, before they enter the corresponding SELECT statement. The SHOWPLAN_ALL option displays the same detailed information about the selected execution plan for the query as SHOWPLAN_TEXT with the addition of an estimate of the resource requirements for that statement.

Example 20.1 shows the use of the SET SHOWPLAN_TEXT option.

NOTE

Once you activate the SET SHOWPLAN_TEXT option, all consecutive Transact-SQL statements will not be executed until you deactivate this option with SET SHOWPLAN_TEXT OFF. (The SET SHOWPLAN_XML statement is another statement with the same property.)

EXAMPLE 20.1

```
SET SHOWPLAN_TEXT ON
GO
USE AdventureWorks;
```

```
SELECT * FROM HumanResources.Employee e JOIN
        HumanResources.EmployeeAddress a
            ON e.EmployeeID = a.EmployeeID
            AND e.EmployeeID = 10;
GO
SET SHOWPLAN_TEXT OFF
```

The following textual plan shows the output of Example 20.1:

```
StmtText
|--Nested Loops(Inner Join)
    |--Clustered Index Seek(OBJECT:([AdventureWorks].[HumanResources].
[Employee].
[PK_Employee_EmployeeID] AS [e]), SEEK:([e].[EmployeeID]=(10)) ORDERED
FORWARD)
    |--Clustered Index
Seek(OBJECT:([AdventureWorks].[HumanResources].[EmployeeAddress].
[PK_EmployeeAddress_EmployeeID_AddressID] AS [a]), SEEK:([a].
[EmployeeID]=(10)) ORDERED FORWARD)
```

If you take a look at the output of Example 20.1, you will see that there are three operators, **Nested Loops** and **Clustered Index Seek** (twice). (All operators are marked with a bar, |.) **Nested Loops** performs an inner join on the **employee** and **employeeaddress** tables. Each **Clustered Index Seek** operator seeks for the rows using the corresponding clustered indices of both tables. The indentation of operators determines the operator execution: the operator that is indented the furthest is executed first. If there are two or more operators with the same indentation, the processing of them is done from the top downwards. This means that in Example 20.1, the clustered index seek for the **employee** table is executed first. After that the same operator is applied to the **employeeaddress** table, and then both tables are joined using the nested loops processing techniques.

NOTE

Index access has two forms: index scan and index seek. Index scan processes the entire leaf level of an index tree, while index seek returns index values (or rows) from one or more ranges of an index.

XML Execution Plans

The phrase "XML execution plan" means that the execution plan of a query is displayed as an XML document. (For more information about XML, see Chapter 27.) The most important advantage of using XML execution plans is that such plans can be ported from one system to another, allowing you to use it in another environment (see the discussion below, how execution plans can be saved in a file).

The SET statement has two options in relation to XML:

► SHOWPLAN_XML

► STATISTICS XML

The SHOWPLAN_XML option returns information as a set of XML documents. In other words, if you activate this option, Database Engine returns detailed information about how the statements are going to be executed in the form of a well-formed XML document, without executing them. Each statement is reflected in the output by a single document. Each document contains the text of the statement, followed by the details of the execution steps.

Example 20.2 shows how the SHOWPLAN_XML option can be used.

EXAMPLE 20.2

```
SET SHOWPLAN_XML ON
GO
USE AdventureWorks;
SELECT * FROM HumanResources.Employee e JOIN
        HumanResources.EmployeeAddress a
            ON e.EmployeeID = a.EmployeeID
            AND e.EmployeeID = 10;
GO
SET SHOWPLAN_XML OFF
```

The main difference between the SHOWPLAN_XML and STATISTICS XML options is that the output of the latter is generated at run time. For this reason, STATISTICS XML includes the result of the SHOWPLAN_XML option as well as additional run-time information.

Each XML execution plan can be saved in a file. Using the default extension .sqlplan, the plan will be automatically displayed in graphical form when you use SQL Server Management Studio. That way, you can easily port execution plans from one computer to another, without storing images of corresponding execution plans.

NOTE

In SQL Server 2008 you can easily open the saved execution plan by double-clicking it. After that, the plan will be opened in SQL Server Management Studio and its graphical form will be displayed.

Other Options of the SET Statement

The SET statement has many other options, which are used in relation to locking, transaction, and date/time statements. Concerning statistics, Database Engine supports the following three options of the SET statement:

► STATISTICS IO

► STATISTICS TIME

► STATISTICS PROFILE

The STATISTICS IO option causes the system to display statistical information concerning the amount of disk activity generated by the query—for example, the number of read and write I/O operations processed with the query. The STATISTICS TIME option causes the system to display the processing, optimization, and execution time of the query.

When the STATISTICS PROFILE option is activated, each executed query returns its regular result set, followed by an additional result set that shows the profile of the query execution. (In other words, the result set contains the output of the SHOWPLAN_ALL option plus the additional result set.)

Example 20.3 shows the use of the STATISTICS PROFILE option of the SET statement.

EXAMPLE 20.3

```
SET STATISTICS PROFILE ON
GO
USE AdventureWorks;
SELECT * FROM HumanResources.Employee e JOIN
        HumanResources.EmployeeAddress a
            ON e.EmployeeID = a.EmployeeID
            AND e.EmployeeID = 10;
GO
SET STATISTICS PROFILE OFF
```

The result of Example 20.3, which is not shown because of its length, contains the output of the SET STATISTICS IO statement as well as the output of the SET SHOWPLAN_ALL statement.

Management Studio and Graphical Execution Plans

A graphical execution plan is the best way to display the execution plan of a query if you are a beginner or want to take a look at different plans in a short time. This form of display uses icons to represent operators in the query plan.

As an example of how graphical execution plans can be initiated and what they look like, Figure 20-2 shows the graphical execution plan for the query in Example 20.1. To display an execution plan in the graphical form, write the query in Query Editor of SQL Server Management Studio and click the **Display Estimated Execution Plan** button in the toolbar of Management Studio. (The alternative way is to click the **Query** menu and select **Display Estimated Execution Plan**.)

If you take a look at Figure 20-2, you will see that there is one icon for each operator of the execution plan. If you move the mouse to one of the icons, its detailed information appears, including the estimated I/O and CPU costs, estimated number of rows and

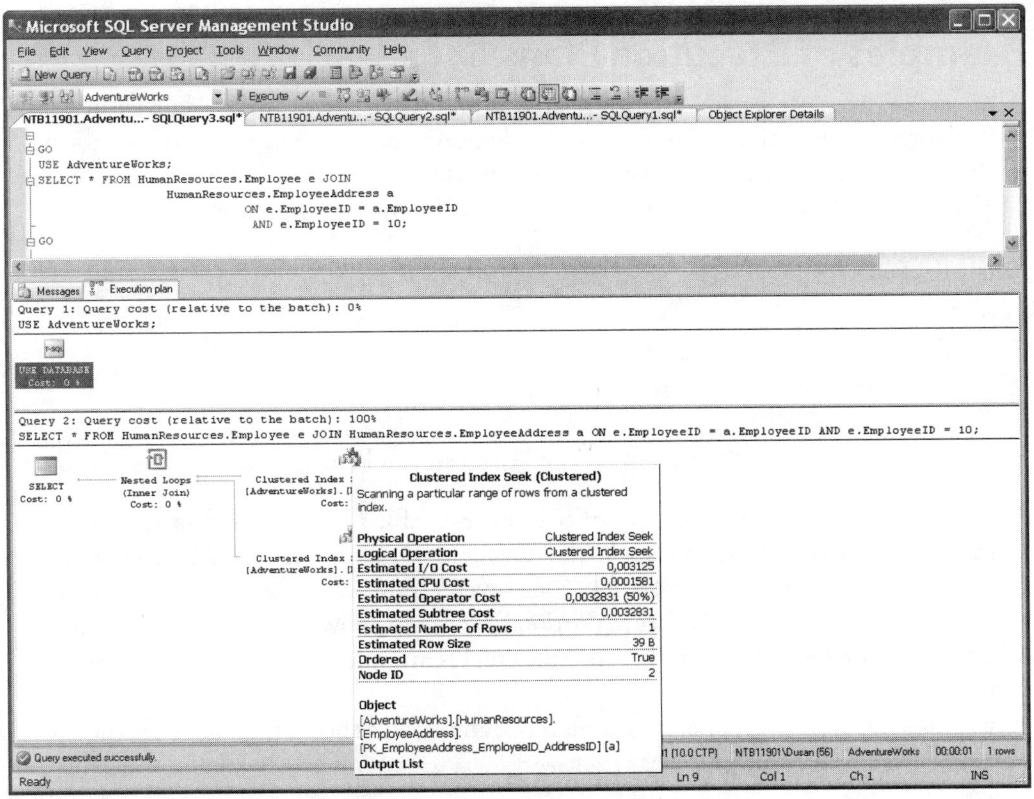

Figure 20-2   *Graphical execution plan for the query in Example 20.1*

their size, and the cost of the operator. The arrows between the icons represent the data flow. (You can also click an arrow, in which case the related information, such as estimated number of rows and estimated row size, will be displayed.)

NOTE

The thickness of arrows in the graphical execution plan is related to the number of rows returned by the corresponding operator. The thicker the arrow, the more rows will be returned.

As its name suggests, clicking the **Display Estimated Execution Plan** button displays the estimated plan of the query, without executing it. There is another button, **Include Actual Execution Plan**, that executes the query and additionally displays its execution plan. The actual execution plan contains additional information in relation to the estimated one, such as the actual number of processed rows and the actual number of executions for each operator.

Examples of Execution Plans

This section presents several queries related to the **AdventureWorks** database, together with their execution plans. These examples demonstrate the topics already discussed, enabling you to see how the query optimizer works in practice.

Example 20.4 introduces a new table (**new_addresses**) in the **sample** database.

EXAMPLE 20.4

```
USE sample;
SELECT * into new_addresses
 FROM AdventureWorks.Person.address;
GO
CREATE INDEX i_stateprov on new_addresses(StateProvinceID)
```

Example 20.4 copies the content of the **address** table from the **Person** schema of the **AdventureWorks** database in the new table of the **sample** database. This is necessary because the former table contains several indices, which hinders direct use of the **Address** table of the **AdventureWorks** database to show specific properties of the query optimizer. (Besides that, the example creates an index on the **StateProvinceID** column of that table.)

Example 20.5 shows a query with high selectivity and shows the plan that the optimizer chooses in such a case.

EXAMPLE 20.5

```
-- high selectivity
USE sample;
SELECT * FROM new_addresses a
    WHERE a.StateProvinceID = 32;
```

The textual output of Example 20.5 is

```
|--Nested Loops(Inner Join, OUTER REFERENCES:([Bmk1000]))
    |--Index Seek(OBJECT:([sample].[dbo].[new_addresses].[i_stateprov] AS [a]),
SEEK:([a].[StateProvinceID]=(32)) ORDERED FORWARD)
    |--RID Lookup(OBJECT:([sample].[dbo].[new_addresses] AS [a]),
SEEK:([Bmk1000]=[Bmk1000]) LOOKUP ORDERED FORWARD)
```

NOTE

The Nested Loops operator in the output is displayed even though the query in Example 20.5 accesses only one table. Since SQL Server 2005, this operator is shown always when there are two operators that are "joined" together (like the RID Lookup and Index Seek operators in Example 20.5).

The filter in Example 20.5 selects only one row from the **new_addresses** table. (The total count of rows in this table is 19614.) For this reason, the selectivity of the expression in the WHERE clause is very high (1/19614). In such a case, as you can see from the output of Example 20.5, the existing index on the **StateProvinceID** column is used by the optimizer.

Example 20.6 shows the same query as in Example 20.5, but with another filter.

EXAMPLE 20.6

```
-- low selectivity
USE sample;
SELECT * FROM new_addresses a
    WHERE a.StateProvinceID =9;
```

The textual plan of Example 20.6 is

```
|--Table Scan(OBJECT:([sample].[dbo].[new_addresses] AS [a]),
WHERE:([sample].[dbo].[new_addresses].[StateProvinceID] as [a].
[StateProvinceID]=(9)))
```

Although the query in Example 20.6 differs from the query in Example 20.5 only by a value on the right side of the condition in the WHERE clause, the execution plan that the optimizer chooses differs significantly. In this case, the existing index won't be used, because the selectivity of the filter is low. (The ratio of the number of rows satisfying the condition to the total number of rows in the table is 4564/19614 = 0.23, or 23 percent.)

Example 20.7 shows the use of the clustered index.

EXAMPLE 20.7

```
USE AdventureWorks;
SELECT * FROM HumanResources.Employee
   WHERE HumanResources.Employee.EmployeeID = 10;
```

The textual output of Example 20.7 is

```
|--Clustered Index Seek(OBJECT:([AdventureWorks].[HumanResources].
[Employee].
[PK_Employee_EmployeeID]), SEEK:([AdventureWorks].[HumanResources].
[Employee].[EmployeeID]=CONVERT_IMPLICIT(int,[@1],0)) ORDERED
FORWARD)
```

The query in Example 20.7 uses the **PK_Employee_EmployeeID** clustered index. This clustered index is created implicitly by the system because the **EmployeeID** column is the primary key of the **Employee** table.

Example 20.8 shows the use of the nested loops technique.

EXAMPLE 20.8

```
USE AdventureWorks;
SELECT  * FROM HumanResources.Employee e JOIN HumanResources.
EmployeeAddress a
  ON e.EmployeeID = a.EmployeeID
  AND e.EmployeeID = 10;
```

The textual output of Example 20.8 is

```
|--Nested Loops(Inner Join)
    |--Clustered Index
Seek(OBJECT:([AdventureWorks].[HumanResources].[Employee].
[PK_Employee_EmployeeID] AS [e]), SEEK:([e].[EmployeeID]=(10)) ORDERED
FORWARD)
    |--Clustered Index
Seek(OBJECT:([AdventureWorks].[HumanResources].[EmployeeAddress].
```

[PK_EmployeeAddress_EmployeeID_AddressID] AS [a]), SEEK:([a].
[EmployeeID]=(10))
ORDERED FORWARD)

The query in Example 20.8 uses the nested loops method even though the join columns of the tables are at the same time their primary keys. For this reason, one could expect that the merge join method would be used. The query optimizer decides to use nested loops because there is an additional filter (e.EmployeeID = 10) that reduces the result set of the query to a single row.

The slight modification of the query in Example 20.8 influences the optimizer to choose another join processing technique, as Example 20.9 shows.

EXAMPLE 20.9

```
USE AdventureWorks;
SELECT  * FROM HumanResources.Employee e JOIN
 HumanResources.EmployeeAddress a
  ON e.EmployeeID = a.EmployeeID;
```

The textual output of the query in Example 20.9 is

```
|--Merge Join(Inner Join, MERGE:([e].[EmployeeID])=([a].[EmployeeID]),
RESIDUAL:([AdventureWorks].[HumanResources].[EmployeeAddress].
[EmployeeID] as
 [a].[EmployeeID]=[AdventureWorks].[HumanResources].[Employee].[EmployeeID]
as
 [e].[EmployeeID]))
    |--Clustered Index
Scan(OBJECT:([AdventureWorks].[HumanResources].[Employee].
[PK_Employee_EmployeeID] AS [e]), ORDERED FORWARD)
    |--Clustered Index
Scan(OBJECT:([AdventureWorks].[HumanResources].[EmployeeAddress].
[PK_EmployeeAddress_EmployeeID_AddressID] AS [a]), ORDERED
FORWARD)
```

If you compare the queries in Examples 20.8 and 20.9, you will see that the latter doesn't have the condition e.EmployeeID = 10. (That is the only difference between the queries.) For this reason, the result set of Example 20.9 contains 290 rows. Because of this, the query optimizer decides that the use of the merge join method is advantageous in this case.

Example 20.10 shows the use of the hash join technique.

EXAMPLE 20.10

USE AdventureWorks;
SELECT * FROM Person.Address a JOIN Person.StateProvince s
  ON a.StateProvinceID = s.StateProvinceID;

The textual output of the query in Example 20.10 is

|--Hash Match(Inner Join, HASH:([s].[StateProvinceID])=([a].[StateProvinceID]))
    |--Clustered Index
Scan(OBJECT:([AdventureWorks].[Person].[StateProvince].
[PK_StateProvince_StateProvinceID] AS [s]))
    |--Clustered Index
 Scan(OBJECT:([AdventureWorks].[Person].[Address].[PK_Address_AddressID]
AS [a]))

Although both join columns in the ON clause are primary keys of the particular
tables (**Address** and **StateProvince**), the query optimizer doesn't choose the merge join
method. The reason is that *all* (19,614) rows of the **Address** table belong to the result
set. In such a case, the use of the hash join method is more beneficial than the other
two processing techniques.

Dynamic Management Views and Query Optimizer

There are many dynamic management views (and functions) that are directly related to
query optimization. In this section, the following DMVs are discussed:

▶ sys.dm_exec_query_optimizer_info

▶ sys.dm_exec_query_plan

▶ sys.dm_exec_query_stats

▶ sys.dm_exec_sql_text

▶ sys.dm_exec_text_query_plan

▶ sys.dm_exec_procedure_stats (new in SQL Server 2008)

sys.dm_exec_query_optimizer_info

The **sys.dm_exec_query_optimizer_info** view is probably the most important DMV
in relation to the work of the query optimizer because it returns detailed statistics
about its operation. You can use this view when tuning a workload to identify query
optimization problems or improvements.

The **sys.dm_exec_query_optimizer_info** view contains three columns: **counter**, **occurrence**, and **value**. The **counter** column specifies the name of the optimizer event, while the **occurrence** column displays the cumulative number of occurrences of these events. The value of the **value** column contains additional information concerning events. (Not all events deliver a **value** value.)

Using this view, you can, for example, display the total number of optimizations, the elapsed time value, and the final cost value to compare the query optimizations of the current workload and any changes observed during the tuning process.

Example 20.11 shows the use of the **sys.dm_exec_query_optimizer_info** view.

EXAMPLE 20.11

SELECT counter, occurrence, value
        FROM sys.dm_exec_query_optimizer_info
        WHERE value IS NOT NULL
        AND counter LIKE 'search 1%';

The result is

Counter	occurrence	value
search 1	117	1
search 1 time	95	0,0120736842105263
search 1 tasks	117	513,982905982906

Example 20.11 investigates how many times optimization Phase 1 is executed. (There are three optimization phases, Phase 0, Phase 1, and Phase 2, which are specified by the values **search 0**, **search 1**, and **search 2**, respectively.)

NOTE

Because of its complexity, the optimization process is broken into three phases. The first phase (Phase 0) considers only nonparallel execution plans. If the cost of Phase 0 isn't optimal, Phase 1 will be executed, in which both nonparallel plans and parallel plans are considered. Phase 2 takes into account only parallel plans.

sys.dm_exec_query_plan

As you already know, a stored procedure is created once and executed many times. For this reason, the execution plan for a stored procedure (or a batch) is placed in the procedure cache. That way, it can be used any time by the optimizer. You can examine the procedure cache using several DMVs. One of these is the **sys.dm_exec_query_plan** view, which returns all execution plans that are stored in the procedure cache of your system. (The execution plans are displayed in XML format.) Books Online contains several useful examples of this DMV.

Each query plan stored in the procedure cache is identified by a unique identifier called a *plan handle*. The **sys.dm_exec_query_plan** view requires a plan handle to retrieve the execution plan for a particular Transact-SQL query or batch. This handle can be displayed using the **sys.dm_exec_query_stats** DMV, which is discussed next.

sys.dm_exec_query_stats

The **sys.dm_exec_query_stats** view returns aggregate performance statistics for cached query plans. The view contains one row per query statement within the cached plan, and the lifetime of the rows is tied to the plan itself.

Example 20.12 "joins" the **sys.dm_exec_query_stats** and **sys.dm_exec_query_plan** views using the CROSS APPLY operator to return execution plans for all cached plans. Additionally, each SQL statement within a multistatement procedure or batch will be displayed separately. (CROSS APPLY is discussed in detail in Chapter 8.)

EXAMPLE 20.12

```
SELECT query_plan
    FROM sys.dm_exec_query_stats as qs
        CROSS APPLY sys.dm_exec_query_plan(qs.plan_handle);
```

sys.dm_exec_sql_text and sys.dm_exec_text_query_plan

The previous view, **sys.dm_exec_query_stats**, can be used with several other DMVs to display different properties of queries. In other words, each DMV that needs the plan handle to identify the query will be "joined" with the **sys.dm_exec_query_stats** view to display the required information. One such view is **sys.dm_exec_sql_text**. This view returns the text of the SQL batch that is identified by the specified handle. Books Online shows a very useful example that "joins" the **sys.dm_exec_sql_text** and **sys.dm_exec_query_stats** views to return the text of SQL queries that are being executed in batches, and then provides statistical information about them.

In contrast to the **sys.dm_exec_sql_text** view, **sys.dm_exec_text_query_plan** returns the execution plan of the batch in XML format. Similar to the previous views, this one is specified by the plan handle. (The plan specified by the plan handle can either be cached or currently executing.)

sys.dm_exec_procedure_stats

This DMV is similar to the **sys.dm_exec_query_stats** view. It returns aggregate performance statistics for cached stored procedures. The view contains one row per stored procedure, and the lifetime of the row is as long as the stored procedure remains cached. When a stored procedure is removed from the cache, the corresponding row is eliminated from this view.

NOTE

*The **sys.dm_exec_procedure_stats** view is one of several new views released with SQL Server 2008. Microsoft added about 50 new DMVs and functions to the new release.*

Optimization Hints

In most cases, the query optimizer chooses the fastest execution plan. However, there are some special situations in which the optimizer, for some particular reasons, cannot find the optimal solution. In such cases, you should use optimization hints to force it to use a particular execution plan that could perform better.

Optimization hints are optional parts in a SELECT statement that instruct the query optimizer to execute one specific behavior. In other words, by using optimization hints, you do not allow the query optimizer to search and find the way to execute a query because you tell it exactly what to do.

Why to Use Optimization Hints

You should use optimization hints only temporarily and for testing. In other words, avoid using them as a permanent part of a query. There are two reasons for this statement. First, if you force the optimizer to use a particular index and later define an index that results in better performance of the query, the query and the application to which it belongs cannot benefit from the new index. Second, Microsoft continuously strives to make the query optimizer better. If you bind a query to a specific execution plan, the query cannot benefit from new and improved features in the subsequent versions of SQL Server.

There are two reasons why the optimizer sometimes does not choose the fastest execution plan:

▶ The query optimizer is not perfect.

▶ The system does not provide the optimizer with the appropriate information.

NOTE

Optimization hints can help you only if the execution plan chosen by the optimizer is not optimal. If the system does not provide the optimizer with the appropriate information, use the AUTO_CREATE_STATISTICS and AUTO_UPDATE_STATISTICS database options to create or modify existing statistics.

Types of Optimization Hints

Database Engine supports the following types of optimization hints:

- ► Table hints
- ► Join hints
- ► Query hints
- ► Plan guides

The following sections describe these hints.

NOTE

The examples that follow demonstrate the use of optimization hints, but they don't give you any recommendations about using them in any particular queries. (In most cases shown in these examples, the use of hints would be counterproductive.)

Table Hints

You can apply table hints to a single table. The following table hints are supported:

- ► INDEX
- ► NOEXPAND
- ► FORCESEEK (new in SQL Server 2008)

The INDEX hint is used to specify one or more indices that are then used in a query. This hint is specified in the FROM clause of the query. You can use this hint to force index access if the optimizer for some reason chooses to perform a table scan for a given query. (Also, the INDEX hint can be used to prevent the optimizer from using a particular index.)

Examples 20.13 and 20.14 show the use of the INDEX hint.

EXAMPLE 20.13

```
USE sample;
SELECT * FROM new_addresses a WITH ( INDEX(i_stateprov))
    WHERE a.StateProvinceID = 9
```

The textual output of Example 20.13 is

```
|--Nested Loops(Inner Join, OUTER REFERENCES:([Bmk1000],
[Expr1004]) WITH UNORDERED PREFETCH)
     |--Index Seek(OBJECT:([sample].[dbo].[new_addresses].[i_stateprov] AS [a]),
SEEK:([a].[StateProvinceID]=(9)) ORDERED FORWARD)
     |--RID Lookup(OBJECT:([sample].[dbo].[new_addresses] AS [a]),
SEEK:([Bmk1000]=[Bmk1000]) LOOKUP ORDERED FORWARD)
```

Example 20.13 is identical to Example 20.6, but contains the additional INDEX hint. This hint forces the query optimizer to use the **i_stateprov** index. Without this hint, the optimizer chooses the table scan, as you can see from the output of Example 20.6.

The other form of the INDEX query hint, INDEX(0), forces the optimizer to not use any of the existing indices. Example 20.14 shows the use of this hint.

EXAMPLE 20.14

```
USE AdventureWorks;
SELECT * FROM Person.Address a
    WITH(INDEX(0))
    WHERE a.StateProvinceID = 32
```

The textual output of Example 20.14 is

```
|--Clustered Index
Scan(OBJECT:([AdventureWorks].[Person].[Address].[PK_Address_AddressID]
AS [a]),
    WHERE:([AdventureWorks].[Person].[Address].[StateProvinceID] as
[a].[StateProvinceID]=(32)))
```

NOTE

If a clustered index exists, INDEX(0) forces a clustered index scan and INDEX(1) forces a clustered index scan or seek. If no clustered index exists, INDEX(0) forces a table scan and INDEX(1) is interpreted as an error.

The execution plan of the query in Example 20.14 shows that the optimizer uses the clustered index scan, because of the INDEX(0) hint. Without this hint, the query optimizer itself would choose the nonclustered index scan. (You can check this by removing the hint in the query.)

The NOEXPAND hint specifies that any indexed view isn't expanded to access underlying tables when the query optimizer processes the query. The query optimizer treats the view like a table with the clustered index. (For a discussion of indexed views, see Chapter 11.)

The FORCESEEK table hint forces the optimizer to use only an index seek operation as the access path to the data in the table (or view) referenced in the query. You can use this table hint to override the default plan chosen by the query optimizer to avoid performance issues caused by an inefficient query plan. For example, if a plan contains table or index scan operators, and the corresponding tables cause a high number of reads during the execution of the query, forcing an index seek operation may yield better query performance. This is especially true when inaccurate cardinality or cost estimations cause the optimizer to favor scan operations at plan compilation time.

NOTE

The FORCESEEK hint can be applied to both clustered and nonclustered indices. This hint is a new feature in SQL Server 2008.

Join Hints

Join hints instruct the query optimizer how join operations in a query should be performed. They force the optimizer either to join tables in the order in which they are specified in the FROM clause of the SELECT statement or to use the join processing techniques explicitly specified in the statement. Database Engine supports several join hints:

- ► FORCE ORDER
- ► LOOP
- ► HASH
- ► MERGE

The FORCE ORDER hint forces the optimizer to join tables in the order in which they are specified in a query. Example 20.15 shows the use of this join hint.

EXAMPLE 20.15

```
USE AdventureWorks;
SELECT e.EmployeeID, e.LoginID, d.DepartmentID
  FROM HumanResources.Employee e, HumanResources.Department d,
    HumanResources.EmployeeDepartmentHistory h
  WHERE d.DepartmentID = h.DepartmentID
```

AND h.EmployeeID = e.EmployeeID
AND h.EndDate IS NOT NULL
OPTION(FORCE ORDER);

The textual output of Example 20.15 is

```
|--Merge Join(Inner Join, MERGE:([d].[DepartmentID],
[e].[EmployeeID])=([h].[DepartmentID], [h].[EmployeeID]),
RESIDUAL:([AdventureWorks].[HumanResources].[Department].[DepartmentID]
as
[d].[DepartmentID]=[AdventureWorks].[HumanResources].
[EmployeeDepartmentHistory].
[DepartmentID] as [h].[DepartmentID] AND
[AdventureWorks].[HumanResources].[EmployeeDepartmentHistory].
[EmployeeID] as
[h].[EmployeeID]=[AdventureWorks].[HumanResources].[Employee].[EmployeeID]
as
[e].[EmployeeID]))
     |--Sort(ORDER BY:([d].[DepartmentID] ASC, [e].[EmployeeID] ASC))
     |   |--Nested Loops(Inner Join)
     |       |--Index
Scan(OBJECT:([AdventureWorks].[HumanResources].[Employee].
[AK_Employee_LoginID] AS [e]))
     |       |--Clustered Index
Scan(OBJECT:([AdventureWorks].[HumanResources].[Department].
[PK_Department_DepartmentID] AS [d]))
     |--Sort(ORDER BY:([h].[DepartmentID] ASC, [h].[EmployeeID] ASC))
         |--Clustered Index
Scan(OBJECT:([AdventureWorks].[HumanResources].
[EmployeeDepartmentHistory].
[PK_EmployeeDepartmentHistory_EmployeeID_StartDate_DepartmentID] AS [h]),
WHERE:([AdventureWorks].[HumanResources].[EmployeeDepartmentHistory].
[EndDate] as
[h].[EndDate] IS NOT NULL))
```

As you can see from the textual output of Example 20.15, the optimizer performs
the join operation in the order in which the tables appear in the query. This means that
the **Employee** table will be processed first, then the **Department** table, and finally the
EmployeeDepartmentHistory table. (If you execute the query without the FORCE

ORDER hint, the query optimizer will process the tables in the opposite order: first **EmployeeDepartmentHistory**, then **Department**, and then **Employee**.)

> **NOTE**
>
> *Keep in mind that this does not necessarily mean that the new execution plan performs better than that chosen by the optimizer.*

The query hints LOOP, MERGE, and HASH force the optimizer to use the loop join method, merge join technique, and hash join technique, respectively. These three join hints can be used only when the join operation conforms to the SQL standard—that is, when the join is explicitly indicated with the JOIN keyword in the FROM clause of a SELECT statement.

Example 20.16 shows a query that uses the merge join method because the hint with the same name is explicitly defined in the SELECT statement. (You can apply the other two hints, HASH and LOOP, in the same way.)

EXAMPLE 20.16

```
USE AdventureWorks;
SELECT * FROM Person.Address a JOIN Person.StateProvince s
  ON a.StateProvinceID = s.StateProvinceID
  OPTION (MERGE JOIN);
```

The textual output of Example 20.16 is

```
|--Merge Join(Inner Join, MERGE:([s].[StateProvinceID])=([a].[StateProvinceID]),
RESIDUAL:([AdventureWorks].[Person].[StateProvince].[StateProvinceID] as
[s].[StateProvinceID]=[AdventureWorks].[Person].[Address].[StateProvinceID] as
[a].[StateProvinceID]))
     |--Clustered Index
Scan(OBJECT:([AdventureWorks].[Person].[StateProvince].
[PK_StateProvince_StateProvinceID] AS [s]), ORDERED FORWARD)
     |--Sort(ORDER BY:([a].[StateProvinceID] ASC))
         |--Clustered Index
Scan(OBJECT:([AdventureWorks].[Person].[Address].[PK_Address_AddressID]
AS [a]))
```

As you can see from the output of Example 20.16, the query optimizer is forced to use the merge join processing technique. (If the hint is removed, the query optimizer chooses the hash join technique.)

The specific join hint can be written either in the FROM clause of a query or using the OPTION clause at the end of it. The use of the OPTION clause is recommended if you want to write several *different* hints together. Example 20.17 is identical to Example 20.16, but specifies the join hint in the FROM clause of the query. (Note that in this case the INNER keyword is required.)

EXAMPLE 20.17

```
USE AdventureWorks;
SELECT * FROM Person.Address a INNER MERGE JOIN Person.StateProvince s
  ON a.StateProvinceID = s.StateProvinceID;
```

The output of Example 20.17 is the same as the output of Example 20.16.

Query Hints

There are several query hints, which are used for different purposes. This section discusses the following two query hints. (You can find the list of all other query hints in Books Online.)

► FAST n

► OPTIMIZE FOR

The FAST n hint specifies that the query is optimized for fast retrieval of the first n rows. After the first n rows are returned, the query continues execution and produces its full result set.

NOTE

This query can be very helpful if you have a very complex query with many result rows, requiring a lot of time for processing. Generally, a query is processed completely and then the system displays the result. This query hint forces the system to display the first n rows immediately after their processing.

The OPTIMIZE FOR hint forces the query optimizer to use a particular value for a local variable when the query is compiled and optimized. The value is used only during query optimization, and not during query execution. This query hint can be used when you create plan guides, which are discussed in the next section.

Example 20.18 shows the use of the OPTIMIZE FOR query hint.

EXAMPLE 20.18

```
DECLARE @city_name nvarchar(30)
SET @city_name = 'Newark'
```

```
SELECT * FROM Person.Address
    WHERE City = @city_name
        OPTION ( OPTIMIZE FOR (@city_name = 'Seattle') );
```

Although the value of the **@city_name** variable is set to Newark, the OPTIMIZE FOR hint forces the optimizer to use the value Seattle for the variable when optimizing the query.

Plan Guides

As you know from the previous section, hints are explicitly specified in the SELECT statement to influence the work of the query optimizer. Sometimes you cannot or do not want to change the text of the SELECT statement directly. In that case, it is still possible to influence the execution of queries by using plan guides. In other words, plan guides allow you to use a particular optimization hint every time the condition for it is met, without changing the syntax of the statement.

Plan guides are created using the **sp_create_plan_guide** system procedure. This procedure creates a plan guide for associating query hints or actual query plans with queries in a database. Another system procedure, **sp_control_plan_guide**, enables, disables, or drops an existing plan guide.

NOTE

There are no Transact-SQL DDL statements for creation and deletion of plan guides. A subsequent SQL Server version will hopefully support such statements.

Database Engine supports three types of plan guides:

▶ **SQL**   Matches queries that execute in the context of stand-alone Transact-SQL statements and batches that are not part of a database object

▶ **OBJECT**   Matches queries that execute in the context of routines and DML triggers

▶ **TEMPLATE**   Matches stand-alone queries that are parameterized to a specified form

To edit information related to plan guides, use the **sys.plan_guides** catalog view. This view contains a row for each plan guide in the current database. The most important columns are **plan_guide_id**, **name**, and **query_text**. The **plan_guide_id** column specifies the unique identifier of the plan guide, while **name** defines its name. The **query_text** column specifies the text of the query on which the plan guide is created.

Conclusion

The query optimizer is the part of Database Engine that decides how to best perform a query. It generates several query execution plans for the given query and selects the plan with the lowest cost.

The query optimization phase can be divided into the following phases: query analysis, index selection, and join order selection. During the query analysis phase, the optimizer examines the query for search arguments, the use of the OR operator, and the existence of join criteria, in that order. The identification of search arguments allows the optimizer to decide whether one or more existing indices will be used.

The order in which two or more joined tables are written in the FROM clause of a SELECT statement, doesn't influence the optimizer's decision regarding their processing order. Database Engine supports three different join processing techniques that can be used by the optimizer. Which technique the optimizer chooses, depends on existing statistics for joined tables.

Database Engine supports many tools that can be used to edit execution plans. The most important are textual and graphical display of the plan and dynamic management views.

You can influence the work of the optimizer by using optimization hints. Database Engine supports many optimization hints, which can be grouped in the following groups: table hints, join hints and query hints.

The next chapter discusses performance tuning.

Chapter 21

Performance Tuning

In This Chapter

- ▶ Factors that Affect Performance
- ▶ Monitoring Performance
- ▶ Choosing the Right Tool
- ▶ SQL Server 2008 Performance Tools

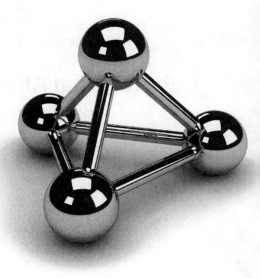

I mproving the performance of a database system requires many decisions, such as where to store data and how to access the data. This task is different from other administrative tasks because it comprises several different steps that concern all aspects of software and hardware. If the database system is not performing optimally, the system administrator must check many factors and possibly tune software (operating system, database system, database applications) as well as hardware.

The performance of Database Engine (and any other relational DBMS) is measured by two criteria:

▶ Response time

▶ Throughput

Response time measures the performance of an individual transaction or program. Response time is treated as the length of time from the moment a user enters a command or statement until the time the system indicates that the command (statement) has completed. To achieve optimum response time of an overall system, almost all existing commands and statements (80 to 90 percent of them) must not cross the specified response time limit.

Throughput measures the overall performance of the system by counting the number of transactions that can be handled by Database Engine during the given time period. (The throughput is typically measured in transactions per second.) Therefore, there is a direct relation between response time of the system and its throughput: when the response time of a system degrades (for example, because many users concurrently use the system), the throughput of the system degrades too.

This chapter discusses performance issues and the tools for tuning the database system that are relevant to daily administration of the system. In the first part of the chapter the factors that affect performance are described. After that, some tips on how to choose the right tool for the administration job are given. At the end of the chapter tools for monitoring the database system are presented.

Factors that Affect Performance

Factors affecting performance fall into three general categories:

▶ Database applications

▶ Database system

▶ System resources

These factors in turn can be affected by several other factors, as discussed in the following sections.

Database Applications and Performance

The following factors can affect the performance of database applications:

- ► Application-code efficiency
- ► Physical design

Application-Code Efficiency

Applications introduce their own load on the system software and on Database Engine. For this reason, they can contribute to performance problems if you make poor use of system resources. Most performance problems in application programs are caused by the improper choice of Transact-SQL statements and their sequence in an application program.

The following list gives some of the ways how you can improve overall performance by modifying code in an application:

- ► Use clustered indices.
- ► Do not use the NOT IN predicate.

Clustered indices generally improve performance. Performance of a range query is the best if you use a clustered index for the column in the filter. Even if you retrieve only a few rows, there are no differences between the use of a nonclustered index and a clustered index.

The NOT IN predicate is not optimizable; in other words, the query optimizer cannot use it as a search argument (SARG; for the definition, see Chapter 20). Therefore, the expression with the NOT IN predicate always results in a table scan.

> **NOTE**
>
> *More hints on how code modification can improve overall performance are given in Chapter 20.*

Physical Design

During physical database design, you choose the specific storage structures and access paths for the database files. In this design step, it is sometimes recommended that you denormalize some of the tables in the database to achieve good performance for various

emp_no	emp_fname	emp_lname	dept_no
25348	Matthew	Smith	d3
10102	Ann	Jones	d3
18316	John	Barrimore	d1
29346	James	James	d2
9031	Elke	Hansel	d2
28559	Sybill	Moser	d1

dept_no	dept_name	location
d1	Research	Dallas
d2	Accounting	Seattle
d3	Marketing	Dallas

Table 21-1   *The employee and department Tables*

database applications. Denormalizing tables means that two or more normalized tables are coupled together, resulting in some redundant data.

To demonstrate the process of denormalization, consider this example: Table 21-1 shows two tables from the **sample** database, **department** and **employee**, that are normalized. (For more information on data normalization, see Chapter 1.) Data in those two tables can be specified using just one table, **dept_emp** (see Table 21-2), which shows the denormalized form of data stored in the tables **department** and **employee**. In contrast to the tables **department** and **employee**, which do not contain any data redundancies, the **dept_emp** table contains a lot of redundancies, because two columns of this table (**dept_name** and **location**) are dependent on the **dept_no** column.

emp_no	emp_fname	emp_lname	dept_no	dept_name	location
25348	Matthew	Smith	d3	Marketing	Dallas
10102	Ann	Jones	d3	Marketing	Dallas
18316	John	Barrimore	d1	Research	Dallas
29346	James	James	d2	Accounting	Seattle
9031	Elke	Hansel	d2	Accounting	Seattle
28559	Sybill	Moser	d1	Research	Dallas

Table 21-2   *The dept_emp Table*

Data denormalization has two benefits and two disadvantage. First the benefits. If you have a column that is dependent on another column of the table (such as the **dept_name** column in the **dept_emp** table, which is dependent on the **dept_no** column) for data often required by queries, you can avoid the use of the join operation, which would affect the performance of applications. Second, denormalized data requires fewer tables than normalized data.

On the other hand, a denormalized table requires additional amounts of disk space, and data modification is difficult because of data redundancy.

Another option in the physical database design that contributes to good performance is the creation of indices. Chapter 10 gives several guidelines for the creation of indices, and examples are given later in this chapter.

Database Engine and Performance

Database Engine can substantially affect the performance of an entire system. The two most important components of Database Engine that affect performance are

- ▶ Optimizer
- ▶ Locks

Optimizer

The optimizer formulates several query execution plans for fetching the data rows that are required to process a query and then decides which plan should be used. The decision concerning the selection of the most appropriate execution plan includes which indices should be used, how to access tables, and the order of joining tables. All of these decisions can significantly affect the performance of database applications. The optimizer is discussed in detail in the previous chapter.

Locks

The database system uses locks as the mechanism for protecting one user's work from another's. Therefore, locks are used to control the access of data by all users at the same time and to prevent possible errors that can arise from the concurrent access of the same data.

Locking affects the performance of the system through its granularity—that is, the size of the object that is being locked and the isolation level. Row-level locking provides the best system performance, because it leaves all but one row on the page unlocked and hence allows more concurrency than page- or table-level locking.

Isolation levels affect the duration of the lock for SELECT statements. Using the lower isolation levels, such as READ UNCOMMITTED and READ COMMITTED, the data availability, and hence the concurrency, of the data can be improved. (Locking and isolation levels are explained in detail in Chapter 13.)

System Resources and Performance

Database Engine runs on the Windows operating systems, which in themselves use underlying system resources. These resources have a significant impact on the performance of the operating system as well as the database system. Performance of any database system depends on four main system resources:

► Central processing unit (CPU)

► Memory

► Disk I/O

► Network

The CPU, together with memory, is the key component for marking the speed of a computer. It is also the key to the performance of a system, because it manages other resources of the system and executes all applications. It executes user processes and interacts with other resources of your system. Performance problems in relation to the CPU can occur when the operating system and user programs are making too many requests on it. Generally, the more CPU power available for your computer, the better the overall system is likely to perform.

Database Engine dynamically acquires and frees memory as needed. Performance problems concerning memory can occur only if there is not enough of it to do the required work. When this occurs, many memory pages are written to a pagefile. (The notion of a *pagefile* is explained in detail later in this chapter.) If the process of writing to a pagefile happens very often, the performance of the system can degrade. Therefore, similarly to the CPU rule, the more memory available for your computer, the better the system is likely to perform.

There are two issues concerning disk I/O: disk speed and disk transfer rate. The disk speed determines how fast read and write operations to disk are executed. The disk transfer rate specifies how much data can be written to disk during a time unit (usually measured in seconds). Obviously, the faster the disk, the larger the amount of data being processed. Also, more disks are generally better than a single disk when many users are using the database system concurrently. (In this case, access to data is usually spread across many disks, thus improving the overall performance of the system.)

For a client/server configuration, a database system sometimes performs poorly if there are many client connections. In that case, the amount of data that needs to be transferred across the network possibly exceeds the network capacity. To avoid such a performance bottleneck, the following general recommendations should be taken into account:

▶ If a database server sends any rows to an application, only the rows needed by the application should be sent.

▶ If a long-lasting user application executes strictly on a client side, move it to a server side (by executing it as a stored procedure, for example).

All four of these system resources are dependent on each other. This means that performance problems in one resource can cause performance problems in the other resources. Similarly, an improvement concerning one resource can significantly increase performance of some other (or even all) resources. For example:

▶ If you increase the number of CPUs, each CPU can share the load evenly and therefore can remedy the disk I/O bottleneck. On the other hand, the inefficient use of the CPU is often the result of a preexisting heavy load on disk I/O and/or memory.

▶ If more memory is available, there is more chance of finding a page needed by the application (rather than reading the page from disk), which results in a performance gain. By contrast, reading from the disk drive instead of drawing from the immensely faster memory slows the system down considerably, especially if there are many concurrent processes.

The following sections describe in detail disk I/O and memory.

Disk I/O

One purpose of a database is to store, retrieve, and modify data. Therefore, Database Engine, like any other database system, must perform a lot of disk activity. In contrast to other system resources, a disk subsystem has two moving parts: the disk itself and the disk head. The rotation of the disk and the movement of the disk head need a great deal of time; therefore, disk reads and writes are two of the highest-cost operations that a database system performs. (For instance, access to a disk is usually slower than memory access by a factor of two or more.)

Database Engine stores the data in 8KB pages. The buffer cache of RAM is also divided into 8KB pages. The system reads data in units of pages. Reads occur not only for data retrieval, but also for any modification operations such as UPDATE and DELETE because the database system must read the data before it can be modified.

If the needed page is in the buffer cache, it will be read from memory. This I/O operation is called *logical I/O* or *logical read*. If it is not in memory, the page is read from disk and put in the buffer cache. This I/O operation is called *physical I/O* or *physical read*. The buffer cache is shared because Database Engine uses the architecture with only one memory address space. Therefore, many users can access the same page. A logical write occurs when data is modified in the buffer cache. Similarly, a physical write occurs when the page is written from the buffer cache to disk. Therefore, more logical write operations can be made on one page before it is written to disk.

Database Engine has a few components that have great impact on performance because they significantly consume the I/O resources:

- ► Read ahead
- ► Checkpoint

Read ahead is described in the following section, while checkpoint is explained in detail in Chapter 17.

Read Ahead   The optimal behavior of a database system would be to read data and never have to wait for a disk read request. The best way to perform this task is to know the next several pages that the user will need and to read them from the disk into the buffer pool *before* they are requested by the user process. This mechanism is called *read ahead*, and it allows the system to optimize performance by processing large amounts of data effectively.

The component of Database Engine called Read Ahead Manager manages the read-ahead processes completely internally, so a user has no way to influence this process. Instead of using the usual 8KB pages, Database Engine uses 64KB blocks of data as the unit for read-ahead reads. That way, the throughput for I/O requests is significantly increased. The read-ahead mechanism is used by the database system to perform large table scans and index range scans. Table scans are performed using the information that is stored in index allocation map (IAM) pages to build a serial list of the disk addresses that must be read. (IAM pages are allocation pages containing information about the extents that a table or index uses.) This allows the database system to optimize its I/O as large sequential reads in disk order. Read Ahead Manager reads up to 2MB of data at a time. Each extent is read with a single operation.

NOTE

Database Engine provides multiple serial read-ahead operations at once for each file involved in the table scan. This feature can take advantage of striped disk sets.

For index ranges, Database Engine uses the information in the intermediate level of index pages immediately above the leaf level to determine which pages to read. The system scans all these pages and builds a list of the leaf pages that must be read. During this operation, the contiguous pages are recognized and read in one operation. When there are many pages to be retrieved, Database Engine schedules a block of reads at a time.

The read-ahead mechanism can also have negative impacts on performance if too many pages for a process are read and the buffer cache is unnecessarily filled up. The only thing you can do in this case is create the indices you will actually need.

There are several performance counters and dynamic management views that are related to read-ahead activity. They are explained in detail later in this chapter.

Memory

Memory is a crucial resource component, not only for the running applications but also for the operating system. When an application is executed, it is loaded into memory and a certain amount of memory is allocated to the application. (In Microsoft terminology, the total amount of memory available for an application is called its *address space*.)

Windows operating systems support virtual memory. This means that the total amount of memory available to applications is the amount of physical memory (or RAM) in the computer plus the size of the specific file on the disk drive called pagefile. (The name of the pagefile on Windows operating systems is **pagefile.sys**.) Once data is moved out of its location in RAM, it resides in the pagefile. If the system is asked to retrieve data that is not in the proper RAM location, it will load the data from the location where it is stored and additionally produce a so-called page fault.

NOTE

pagefile.sys should be placed on a different drive from the drive on which files used by Database Engine are placed, because the paging process can have an impact on disk I/O activities.

For an entire application, only a portion of it resides in RAM. (Recently referenced pages can usually be found in RAM.) When the information the application needs is not in RAM, the operating system must page (that is, read the page from the pagefile into RAM). This process is called *demand paging*. The more the system has to page, the worse the performance is.

NOTE

When a page in RAM is required, the oldest page of the address space for an application is moved to the pagefile to make room for the new page. The replacement of pages is always limited to the address space of the current application. Therefore, there is no chance that pages in the address space of other running applications will be replaced.

As you already know, a page fault occurs if the application makes a request for information and the data page that contains that information is not in the proper RAM location of the computer. The information may either have been paged out to the pagefile or be located somewhere else in RAM. Therefore, there are two types of page fault:

- **Hard page fault** The page has been paged out (to the pagefile) and has to be brought into RAM from the disk drive.
- **Soft page fault** The page is found in another location in RAM.

Soft page faults consume only RAM resources. Therefore, they are better for performance than hard page faults, which cause disk reads and writes to occur.

NOTE

Page faults are normal in a Windows operating system environment because the operating system requires pages from the running applications to satisfy the need for memory of the starting applications. However, excessive paging (especially with hard page faults) is a serious performance problem because it can cause disk bottlenecks and start to consume the additional power of the processor.

Monitoring Performance

All the factors that affect performance can be monitored using different components. These components can be grouped in the following categories:

- Counters of Performance Monitor
- Dynamic management views and catalog views
- DBCC command
- System stored procedures

This section first gives an overview of Performance Monitor and then describes all components for monitoring performance in relation to the four factors: CPU, memory, disk access, and network.

Performance Monitor: An Overview

Performance Monitor is a Windows graphical tool that provides the ability to monitor Windows activities as well as database system activities. The benefit of this tool is that it is tightly integrated with Windows operating systems and therefore displays reliable values concerning different performance issues. Performance Monitor provides a lot of performance objects, and each performance object contains several counters. These counters can be monitored locally or over the network.

Performance Monitor supports three different presentation modes:

▶ **Graphic mode**   Displays the selected counters as colored lines, with the X axis representing time and the Y axis representing the value of the counter. (This is the default display mode.)

▶ **Histogram mode**   Displays the selected counters as colored horizontal bars that represent the data sampling values.

▶ **Report mode**   Displays the values of counters textually.

To start Performance Monitor, click **Start**, **Control Panel**, **Administrative Tools**, and finally **Performance**. The starting window of Performance Monitor, shown in Figure 21-1, contains three default counters: **Pages/sec** (Object: Memory), **Avg. Disk Queue Length** (Object: PhysicalDisk), and **% Processor Time** (Object: Processor). These three counters are important, but you will need to display the values of several other counters.

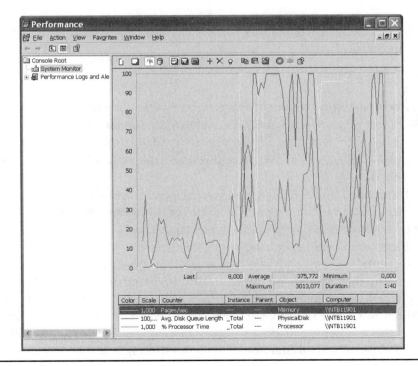

Figure 21-1   *Performance Monitor*

To add a counter for monitoring, click the plus sign in the tool bar of Performance Monitor, select the performance object to which the counter belongs, choose the counter, and click **Add**. To remove a counter, highlight the line in the bottom area and click **Delete**.

Monitoring the CPU

This section describes several Performance Monitor counters related to monitoring the CPU:

▶   % Processor Time (Object: Processor)

▶   % Interrupt Time (Object: Processor)

▶   Interrupts/sec (Object: Processor)

▶   Processor Queue Length (Object: System)

This section also describes one system procedure and two views related to monitoring the CPU:

▶   sp_monitor

▶   sys.sysprocesses

▶   sys.dm_exec_requests

The **% Processor Time** counter displays system-wide CPU usage and acts as the primary indicator of processor activity. The value of this counter should be between 80 and 90. You should try to reduce CPU usage if the value of the counter is constantly greater than 90. (CPU usage of 100 percent is acceptable only if it happens for short periods of time.)

The **% Interrupt Time** counter shows you the percentage of time that the CPU spends servicing hardware interrupts. The values of this counter are important if at least one piece of hardware is trying to get processor time. If only one piece of hardware causes problems, the solution could be to upgrade it.

The **Interrupts/sec** counter displays the number of times per second the processor receives hardware interrupts for service requests from peripheral devices. This number generally can be high in environments with high disk utilization or networking demands.

The **Processor Queue Length** counter indicates how many threads are waiting for execution. If this counter is consistently higher than 5 when the processor utilization approaches 100 percent, then there are more active threads available than the machine's processors are able to handle.

The **sp_monitor** system procedure displays statistics—for example, the number of seconds the CPU has been doing system activities, the number of seconds the system has been idle, the number of read/write operations, and the number of logins (or attempted logins) to the system.

The **sys.sysprocesses** catalog view can be useful if you want to identify processes that use the most processor time. The view contains information about processes that are running on an instance. These processes can be client processes or system processes. The view belongs to the **master** system database. For this reason, you must use the three-part name (**master.dbo.sysprocesses**) to access the view. The most important columns of the view are **spid** (session ID), **dbid** (ID of the current database), **uid** (ID of the user who executes the current command), and **cpu** (cumulative CPU time for the process).

The **sys.dm_exec_requests** view provides the same information as the **sys.sysprocesses** catalog view, but the names of the corresponding columns are different. Example 21.1 shows the use of this dynamic management view. (The column names are self-explanatory.)

EXAMPLE 21.1

```
SELECT session_id, database_id, user_id, cpu_time, sql_handle
    FROM sys.dm_exec_requests
    order by cpu_time DESC
```

The **sql_handle** column of the view points to the area in which the entire batch is stored. If you want to reduce the information to only one statement, you have to use the columns **statement_start_offset** and **statement_end_offset** to shorten the result.

NOTE
This dynamic management view is especially worthwhile if you want to identify long-running queries.

Monitoring Memory

This section describes several Performance Monitor counters related to monitoring memory:

- ▶ Buffer Cache Hit Ratio (Object: Memory)
- ▶ Pages/sec (Object: Memory)
- ▶ Page Faults/sec (Object: Memory)

This section also describes one command and two views related to monitoring memory:

- ► DBCC MEMORYSTATUS
- ► sys.dm_os_memory_clerks
- ► sys.dm_os_memory_objects

The **Buffer Cache Hit Ratio** counter displays the percentage of pages that did not require a read from disk. The higher this ratio, the less often the system has to go to the hard disk to fetch data, and performance overall is boosted. Note that there is no right value for this counter because it is application specific.

NOTE

This counter is different from most other counters, because it is not a real-time measurement, but rather an average value of all the days since the last restart of Database Engine.

The **Pages/sec** counter displays the amount of paging (that is, the number of pages read or written to disk per second). The counter is an important indicator of the types of faults that cause performance problems. If the value of this counter is too high, you should consider adding more physical memory.

The **Page Faults/sec** counter displays the average number of page faults per second. This counter includes both soft page and hard page faults. Page faults occur when a system process refers to a virtual memory page that is not currently within the working set in the physical memory. If the requested page is on the standby list or a page currently shared with another process, a *soft page fault* is generated and the memory reference is resolved without physical disk access. However, if the referenced page is currently in the paging file, a *hard page fault* is generated and the data must be fetched from the disk.

The DBCC MEMORYSTATUS command provides a snapshot of the current memory status of Database Engine. The command's output is useful in troubleshooting issues that relate to the memory consumption of Database Engine or to specific out-of-memory errors (many of which automatically print this output in the error log).

The **sys.dm_os_memory_clerks** view returns the set of all memory clerks that are active in the current instance. You can use this view to find memory allocations by different memory types.

NOTE

The Database Engine memory manager consists of a three-layer hierarchy. At the bottom of the hierarchy are memory nodes. The next level consists of memory clerks, memory caches, and memory pools. The last layer consists of memory objects. These objects are generally used to allocate memory.

The **sys.dm_os_memory_objects** view returns memory objects that are currently allocated by the database system. This dynamic management view is primarily used to analyze memory usage and to identify possible memory leaks, as shown in Example 21.2.

EXAMPLE 21.2

```
SELECT type , SUM(pages_allocated_count) AS total_memory
   FROM sys.dm_os_memory_objects
   GROUP BY type
   ORDER BY total_memory DESC
```

Example 21.2 groups all memory objects according to their type and then uses the values of the **pages_allocated_count** column to display the total memory of each group.

Monitoring the Disk System

This section describes several Performance Monitor counters related to monitoring the disk system:

- ► % Disk Time (Object: Physical Disk)
- ► Current Disk Queue Length (Object: Physical Disk)
- ► Disk Read Bytes/sec (Object: Physical Disk)
- ► Disk Write Bytes/sec (Object: Physical Disk)
- ► % Disk Time (Object: Logical Disk)
- ► Current Disk Queue Length (Object: Logical Disk)
- ► Disk Read Bytes/sec (Object: Logical Disk)
- ► Disk Write Bytes/sec (Object: Logical Disk)

As you can see from the preceding list, the names of the Performance Monitor counters for the Physical Disk object and the Logical Disk object are the same (The difference between physical and logical objects is explained in Chapter 5.) These counters have the same purpose for each of the objects as well, so the following descriptions explain the counters only for the Physical Disk object.

This section also describes one view related to monitoring the disk system:

▶ sys.dm_os_wait_stats

The **% Disk Time** counter displays the amount of time that the hard disk actually has to work. It provides a good relative measure of how busy your disk system is, and it should be used over a longer period of time to indicate a potential need for more I/O capacity.

The **Current Disk Queue Length** counter tells you how many I/O operations are waiting for the disk to become available. This number should be as low as possible.

The **Disk Read Bytes/sec** counter shows the rate at which bytes were transferred from the hard disk during read operations, while **Disk Write Bytes/sec** provides the rate at which bytes were transferred to the hard disk during write operations.

The **sys.dm_os_wait_stats** view returns information about the waits encountered by threads that are in execution. Use this view to diagnose performance issues with Database Engine and also with specific queries and batches. The most important columns of this view are **wait_type** and **waiting_tasks_count**. The former displays the names of the wait types, while the latter displays the number of waits on the corresponding wait type.

Monitoring the Network Interface

This section describes several Performance Monitor counters related to monitoring the network:

▶ Bytes Total/sec (Object: Network Interface)

▶ Bytes Received/sec (Object: Network Interface)

▶ Bytes Sent/sec (Object: Network Interface)

This section also describes a command and a view related to monitoring the network interface:

▶ DBCC PERFMON

▶ sys.dm_exec_connections

NOTE

*The **sp_monitor** system procedure, described earlier in the section "Monitoring the CPU," can be very useful to monitor data concerning the network interface because it displays the information in relation to packets sent and received as a running total.*

The **Bytes Total/sec** counter monitors the number of bytes that are sent over the network per second. (This includes both Database Engine and non-Database Engine network traffic.) Assuming your server is a dedicated database server, the vast majority of the traffic measured by this counter should be from Database Engine. A consistently low value for this counter indicates that network problems may be interfering with your application.

To find out how much data is being sent back and forth from your server to the network, use the **Bytes Received/sec** and **Bytes Sent/sec** counters. The former displays the rate at which network data (in bytes) are received, while the latter checks the outbound rate. These counters will help you to find out how busy your actual server is over the network.

The DBCC PERFMON command displays information about the I/O work that Database Engine has performed, as well as network statistics. Concerning the network, this command provides you with detailed information of actual bytes read and written (the **Network Bytes Read** and **Network Bytes Written** options, respectively).

NOTE

DBCC PERFMON might be deprecated in one of the following versions of SQL Server.

The **sys.dm_exec_connections** view returns information about the connections established to the instance of Database Engine and the details of each connection. Two important columns of this dynamic management view are **num_reads** and **num_writes**. The former displays the number of packet reads that have occurred over this connection, while the latter provides information about the number of packet writes that have occurred over this connection.

Choosing the Right Tool

The choice of an appropriate tool depends on the performance factors to be monitored and the type of monitoring. The type of monitoring can be

► Real time

► Delayed (by saving information in the file, for example)

Real-time monitoring means that performance issues are investigated as they are happening. If you want to display the actual values of one or a few performance factors, such as the number of users or number of attempted logins, use the existing dynamic management views because of their simplicity. In fact, DMVs can only be used for real-time monitoring. Therefore, if you want to trace performance activities during a specific time period, you have to use a tool such as SQL Server Profiler (see the next section).

Probably the best all-around tool for monitoring is Performance Monitor because of its many options. First, you can choose the performance activities you want to track and display them simultaneously. Second, Performance Monitor allows you to set thresholds on specific counters (performance factors) to generate alerts that notify operators. This way, you can react promptly to any performance bottlenecks. Third, you can report performance activities and investigate the resulting chart log files later.

Also, the use of DMVs is strongly recommended because of their simplicity. The first group of DMVs was released with SQL Server 2005, and each new version will support more and more DMVs, which can be used for variety of tasks.

The following sections describe SQL Server Profiler and Database Engine Tuning Advisor.

SQL Server Profiler

SQL Server Profiler is a graphical tool that lets system administrators monitor and record database and server activities, such as login, user, and application information. SQL Server Profiler can display information about several server activities in real time, or it can create filters to focus on particular events of a user, types of commands, or types of Transact-SQL statements. Among others, you can monitor the following events using SQL Server Profiler:

▶ Login connections, attempts, failures, and disconnections

▶ CPU use of a batch

▶ Deadlock problems

▶ All DML statements (SELECT, INSERT, UPDATE, and DELETE)

▶ The start or end of a stored procedure

The most useful feature of SQL Server Profiler is the ability to capture activities in relation to queries. These activities can be used as input for Database Engine Tuning Advisor, which allows you to select indices and indexed views for one or more queries. For this reason, the following section discusses the features of SQL Server Profiler together with Database Engine Tuning Advisor.

Database Engine Tuning Advisor

Database Engine Tuning Advisor is part of the overall system and allows you to automate the physical design of your databases. As mentioned, Database Engine Tuning Advisor is tightly connected to SQL Server Profiler, which can display information about several server activities in real time, or it can create filters to focus on particular events of a user, types of commands, or Transact-SQL statements.

The specific feature of SQL Server Profiler that is used by Database Engine Tuning Advisor is its ability to watch and record batches executed by users and to provide performance information, such as CPU use of a batch and corresponding I/O statistics.

Providing Information for Database Engine Tuning Advisor

Database Engine Tuning Advisor is usually used together with SQL Server Profiler to automate tuning processes. You use SQL Server Profiler to record into a trace file information about the workload being examined. (As an alternative to a workload file, you can use any file that contains a set of Transact-SQL statements. In this case, you do not need SQL Server Profiler.) Database Engine Tuning Advisor can then read the file and recommend several physical objects, such as indices, indexed views, and partitioning schema, that should be created for the given workload.

Example 21.3 shows how Database Engine Tuning Advisor evaluates the file created by SQL Server Profiler. The **orders** and **order_details** tables will be used to demonstrate the recommendation of physical objects by Database Engine Tuning Advisor.

EXAMPLE 21.3

```
USE sample;
CREATE TABLE orders
  (orderid INTEGER NOT NULL,
   orderdate DATE,
   shippeddate DATE,
   freight money);

CREATE TABLE order_details
  (productid INTEGER NOT NULL,
   orderid INTEGER NOT NULL,
   unitprice money,
   quantity INTEGER);
```

To demonstrate the use of Database Engine Tuning Advisor, many more rows are needed in both tables. Examples 21.4 and 21.5 insert 3000 rows in the **orders** table and 30,000 rows in the **order_details** table, respectively.

EXAMPLE 21.4

```
-- This procedure inserts 3000 rows in the table orders
USE sample;
declare @i int, @order_id integer
       declare @orderdate datetime
       declare @shipped_date datetime
       declare @freight money
       set @i = 1
       set @orderdate = getdate()
       set @shipped_date = getdate()
       set @freight = 100.00
     while @i < 3001
     begin
     insert into orders (orderid, orderdate, shippeddate, freight)
       values(@i, @orderdate, @shipped_date, @freight)
     set @i = @i+1
     end
```

EXAMPLE 21.5

```
-- This procedure inserts 30000 rows in order_details and modifies some of them
USE sample
declare @i int, @j int
       set @i = 3000
       set @j = 10
       while @j > 0
       begin
       if @i > 0
         begin
         insert into order_details (productid, orderid, quantity)
             values (@i, @j, 5)
       set @i = @i – 1
         end
       else begin
         set @j = @j – 1
         set @i = 3000
         end
       end

go
update order_details set quantity = 3
     where productid in (1511, 2678)
```

The query in Example 21.6 will be used as an input file for SQL Server Profiler. (Assume that no indices are created for the columns that appear in the SELECT statement.)

EXAMPLE 21.6

```
USE sample;
SELECT orders.orderid, orders.shippeddate
    FROM orders
    WHERE orders.orderid between 806 and 1600
    and not exists (SELECT order_details.orderid
                        FROM order_details
                        WHERE order_details.orderid = orders.orderid);
```

First, set up SQL Server Profiler by clicking **All Programs, Microsoft SQL Server 2008, Performance Tools, SQL Server Profiler**. On the **File** menu, select **New Trace**. After connecting to the server, the **Trace Properties** dialog box appears. Type a name for the trace and select an output .trc file for the Profiler information (in the **Save to file** field). Click **Run** to start the capture and use SQL Server Management Studio to execute the query in Example 21.6. Finally, stop SQL Server Profiler by choosing **Stop Trace** on the **File** menu and select the corresponding trace.

Working with Database Engine Tuning Advisor

Database Engine Tuning Advisor analyzes a workload and recommends the physical design of one or more databases. The analysis will include recommendations to add, remove, or modify the physical database structures, such as indices, indexed views, and partitions. Database Engine Tuning Advisor will recommend a set of physical database structures that will optimize the tasks included in the workload.

To use Database Engine Tuning Advisor, shown in Figure 21-2, click **Start, All Programs, Microsoft SQL Server 2008, Performance Tools, Database Engine Tuning Advisor**. (The alternative way is to start SQL Server Profiler, click **Tools**, and select **Database Engine Tuning Advisor**.)

In the **Session name** field, type the name of the session for which Database Engine Tuning Advisor will create tuning recommendations. In the **Workload** frame, select either **File** or **Table**. If you select **File**, enter the name of the trace file. If you choose **Table**, the name of the table that is created by SQL Server Profiler must be entered. (Using SQL Server Profiler, you can capture and save data about each workload to a file or to a SQL Server table.)

In the **Select databases and tables to tune** frame, choose one or more databases and/or one or more tables that you want to tune. (Database Engine Tuning Advisor

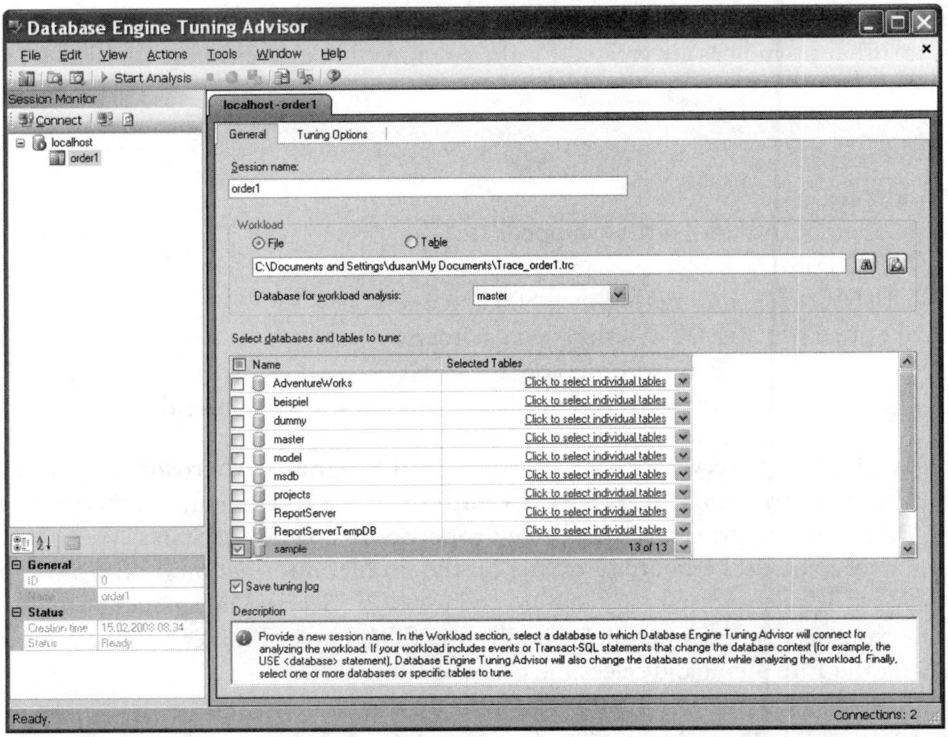

Figure 21-2   *Database Engine Tuning Advisor: General tab*

can tune a workload that involves multiple databases. This means that the tool can recommend indices, indexed views, and partitioning schema on any of the databases in the workload.)

To choose options for tuning, click the **Tuning Options** tab (see Figure 21-3). All options on this tab are divided into three groups:

▶ Physical Design Structures (PDS) to use in database

▶ Partitioning Strategy to employ

▶ Physical Design Structures (PDS) to keep in database

The first group of options allows you to choose which physical structures (indices and/or indexed views) should be recommended by Database Engine Tuning Advisor, after tuning the existing workload. (The **Evaluate utilization of existing PDS only** option causes Database Engine Tuning Advisor to analyze the existing physical structures and recommend which of them should be deleted.)

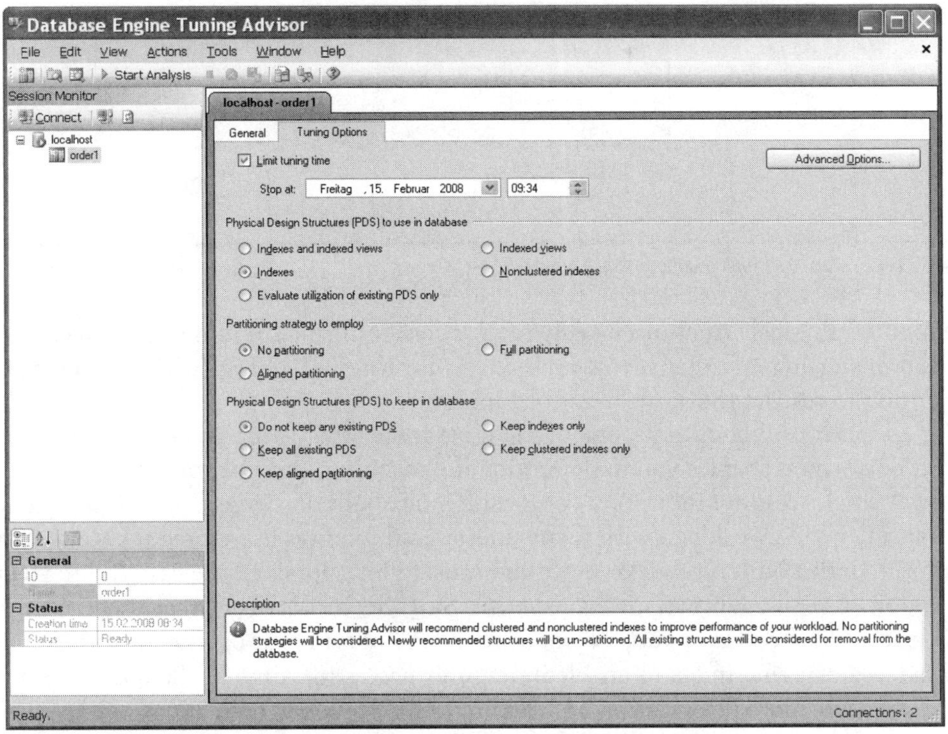

Figure 21-3 *Database Engine Tuning Advisor: Tuning Options tab*

The **Partitioning strategy to employ** group of options allows you to choose whether or not partitioning recommendations should be made. If you opt for partitioning recommendations, you can also choose the type of partitioning, full or aligned. (Partitioning is discussed in detail in Chapter 26.)

The last options group, **Physical Design Structures (PDS) to keep in database**, enables you to decide which, if any, existing structures should remain intact in the database after the tuning process.

For large databases, tuning physical structures usually requires a significant amount of time and resources. Instead of starting an exhaustive search for possible indexes, Database Engine Tuning Advisor offers (by default) the restrictive use of resources. This operation mode still gives very accurate results, although the number of resources tuned is significantly reduced.

During the specification of tuning options, you can define additional customization options by clicking **Advanced Options**, which opens the **Advanced Tuning Options** dialog box (see Figure 21-4). Checking the check box at the top of the dialog box enables you to define the maximum space for recommendations. (For large databases,

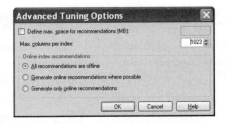

Figure 21-4   *Advanced Tuning Options dialog box*

selection of physical structures usually requires a significant amount of resources. Instead of starting an exhaustive search, Database Engine Tuning Advisor offers you the option to restrict the space used for tuning.)

Of all index tuning options, one of the most interesting is the second option in this dialog box, which enables you to determine the maximum number of columns per index. A single-column index or a composite index built on two columns can be used several times for a workload with many queries and requires less storage space than a composite index built on four or more columns. (This applies in the case where you use a workload file on your own instead of using SQL Server Profiler's trace for the specific workload.) On the other hand, a composite index built on four or more columns may be used as a covering index to enable index-only access for some of the queries in the workload. (For more information on covering indices, see Chapter 10.)

After you select options in the **Advanced Tuning Options** dialog box, click **OK** to close it. You can then start the analysis of the workload. To start the tuning process, choose **Actions** in the toolbar and select **Start Analysis**. After you start the tuning process for the trace file of the query in Example 21.6, Database Engine Tuning Advisor creates tuning recommendations, which you can view by clicking the **Recommendations** tab, as shown in Figure 21-5. As you can see, Database Engine Tuning Advisor recommends the creation of two indices.

Database Engine Tuning Advisor recommendations concerning physical structures can be viewed using a series of reports that provide information about very interesting options. These reports enable you to see how Database Engine Tuning Advisor evaluated the workload. To see these reports, click the **Reports** tab in the **Database Engine Tuning Advisor** dialog box after the tuning process is finished. You can see the following reports, among others:

▶ Index usage report (current and recommended)

▶ Index detail report (current and recommended)

▶ Table access report

▶ Workload analysis report

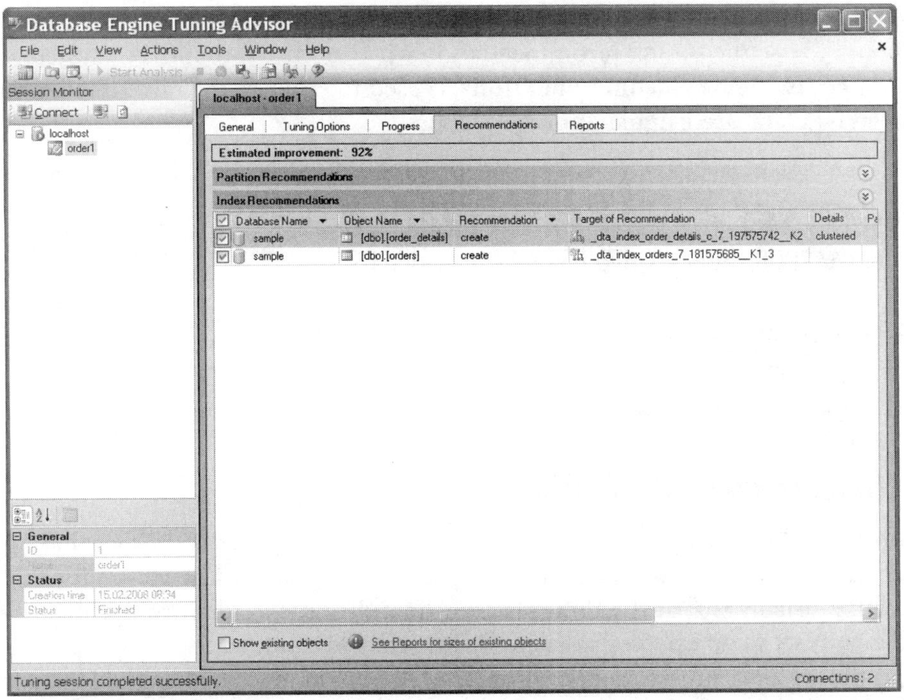

Figure 21-5   *Database Engine Tuning Advisor: Recommendations tab*

Index usage report (recommended) displays information about the expected usage of the recommended indexes and their estimated sizes. **Index usage report (current)** presents the same information for the existing configuration.

Index detail report (recommended) displays information about the names of all recommended indices and their types. **Index detail report (current)** presents the same information for the actual configuration, before the tuning process was started.

Table access report displays information about the costs of all queries in the workload (using tables in the database).

Workload analysis report provides information about the relative frequencies of all data modification statements. (Costs are calculated relative to the most expensive statement with the current index configuration.)

There are three ways how you can apply recommendations: immediately, scheduled, or after saving to the file. If you click the **Actions** menu and select **Apply Recommendations**, the recommendations will be applied immediately. Similarly, if you select **Save Recommendations** on the same menu, the recommendations will be saved to the file. (This alternative is useful if you generate the script with one (test) system and intend to use the tuning recommendation with another (production) system.) The third option, **Evaluate Recommendations**, is used to evaluate the recommendations produced by Database Engine Tuning Advisor.

SQL Server 2008 Performance Tools

SQL Server 2008 supports two new performance tools:

► Performance Data Collector
► Resource Governor

Performance Data Collector

One of the problems that database administrators generally face is the fact that performance problems sometimes are very hard to track down. The reason for this is that a DBA usually isn't at the right place at the right time to identify a problem and thus has to react to an existing problem by first tracking it down.

SQL Server 2005 introduced Performance Dashboard to solve this problem, but this was not a comprehensive solution. In SQL Server 2008, Microsoft has included an entire infrastructure to solve the problem. A key component of this new infrastructure is Performance Data Collector, a component that is installed in an SQL instance and can be configured to run either on a defined schedule or nonstop. The tool has two tasks:

► To collect different sets of data related to performance
► To store this data in a relational database

The data can then be used for comparison with already existing data that has been gathered in the past. The collected sets of data can be used to troubleshoot, tune, and monitor the state of one or more instance of Database Engine. This data can then be stored in Management Data Warehouse (MDW), which is another component of this tool. MDW is a database that is used as a repository for all gathered data.

To use Performance Data Collector, you have to configure MDW first. To do this, expand the server, expand **Management**, right-click **Data Collection**, and click **Configure Management Data Warehouse**. The Configure Management Data Warehouse Storage wizard appears. In the first step after the opening page, you have to select a server and

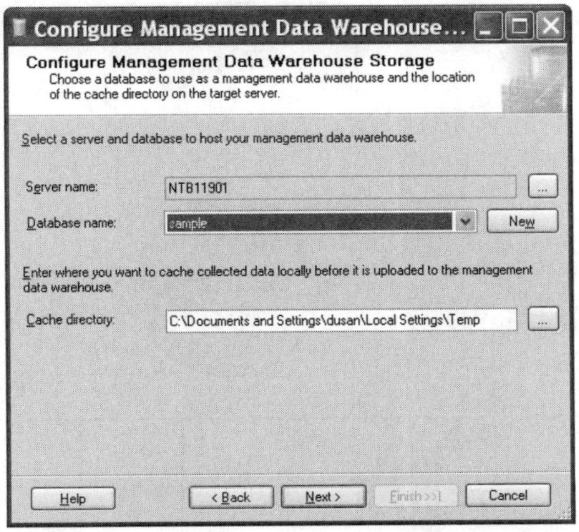

Figure 21-6   *Configuring MDW storage with the wizard*

database to host your management data warehouse (see Figure 21-6). In the next step of the wizard, map existing logins, users, roles, and groups to data warehouse roles. The last step finishes the wizard and starts data collection.

Once the Performance Data Collector is configured and active, the system will start collecting performance information and uploading the data to MDW.

Resource Governor

One of the biggest problems in the previous versions of SQL Server is trying to manage resources with the competing workloads on a shared database server. You can solve this problem using either server virtualization or several instances. In both cases, it is not possible for an instance to ascertain whether the other instances (or virtual machines) are using memory and the CPU. The new Resource Governor tool manages such a situation by enabling one instance to reserve a portion of the CPU (or another resource) for a particular process.

Generally, Resource Governor enables DBAs to define resource limits and priorities for different workloads. That way, consistent performance for processes can be achieved.

Resource Governor has two main components: resource groups and resource pools (see Figure 21-7). When a process connects to Database Engine, it is classified and then assigned to a resource group based on that classification. (The classification is done using either a built-in classifier or a user-defined function.) One or more resource groups are then assigned to specific resource pools.

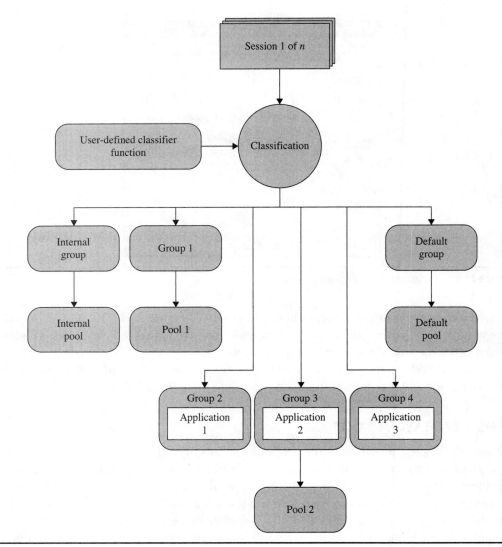

Figure 21-7   *Architecture of Resource Governor*

As you can see in Figure 21-7, there are two different resource groups:

▶ Internal group
▶ Default group

The internal group is used to execute certain system functions, while the default group is used when the process doesn't have a defined classification.

The following scenario describes the steps you might apply to create different workloads and decide which resources are applied to which workload group:

▶ Create workload groups by using the CREATE WORKLOAD statement.

▶ For each workload group, define the corresponding UDF. (Such UDFs can be used to create any association between a workload group and users.)

▶ Bind the functions with Resource Governor by using the ALTER RESOURCE GOVERNOR statement.

▶ Determine which workload group gets which resources by using the ALTER WORKLOAD GROUP statement.

▶ Execute the ALTER RESOURCE GOVERNOR statement with the RECONFIGURE option to apply changes to Resource Governor.

Conclusion

Performance issues can be divided into proactive and reactive response areas. Proactive issues concern all activities that affect performance of the overall system and that will affect future systems of an organization. Proper database design and proper choice of the form of Transact-SQL statements in application programs belong to the proactive response area. Reactive performance issues concern activities that are undertaken after the performance bottleneck occurs. SQL Server offers a variety of tools (graphical components, Transact-SQL statements, and stored procedures) that can be used to view and trace performance problems of an SQL Server system.

Of all components, Performance Monitor and dynamic management views are the best tools for monitoring because you can use them to track, display, report, and trace any performance bottlenecks.

The next chapter starts the Analysis Services part of the book. It introduces general terms and concepts that you need to know about this important topic.

Exercises

E.21.1

Discuss the differences between SQL Server Profiler and Database Engine Tuning Advisor.

E.21.2

Discuss the differences between Performance Data Collector and Resource Governor.

Part IV

SQL Server and Business Intelligence

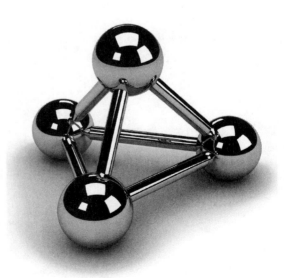

Chapter 22

Business Intelligence—
An Introduction

In This Chapter

- ▶ **Online Transaction Processing vs. Business Intelligence**
- ▶ **Data Warehouses and Data Marts**
- ▶ **Data Warehouse Design Using Dimensional Model**
- ▶ **Cubes and Their Architectures**
- ▶ **Data Access**

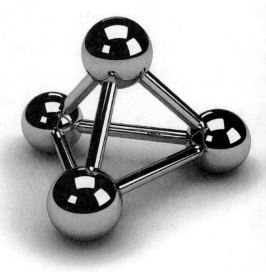

The goal of this chapter is to introduce you to an important area of database technology: business intelligence (BI). The first part of the chapter explains the difference between the online transaction processing world on one side and the BI world on the other side. A *data store* for a BI process can be either a data warehouse or a data mart. Both types of data store are discussed, and their differences are listed in the second part of the chapter. The design of data in BI and the need for creation of aggregate tables are explained at the end of the chapter.

Online Transaction Processing vs. Business Intelligence

From the beginning, relational database systems were used almost exclusively to capture primary business data such as orders and invoices using processing based on transactions. This focus on business data has its benefits and its disadvantages. One benefit is that the poor performance of early database systems improved dramatically, so today many database systems can execute thousands of transactions per second (using appropriate hardware). On the other hand, the focus on transaction processing prevented people in the database business from seeing another natural application of database systems: using them to filter and analyze needed information out of all the existing data in an enterprise or department.

Online Transaction Processing

As already stated, performance is one of the main issues for systems that are based upon transaction processing. These systems are called online transaction processing (OLTP) systems. A typical example of an operation performed by an OLTP system is withdrawing money from a bank account using a teller machine. OLTP systems have some important properties, such as:

▶ Short transactions—that is, high throughput of data

▶ Many (possibly hundreds or thousands of) users

▶ Continuous read and write operations based on a small number of rows

▶ Data of medium size that is stored in a database

The performance of a database system will increase if transactions in the database application programs are short. The reason is that transactions use locks (see Chapter 13) to prevent possible negative effects of concurrency issues. If transactions are long lasting, the number of locks and their duration increases, decreasing the data availability for other transactions and thus their performance.

Large OLTP systems usually have many users working on the system simultaneously. A typical example is a reservation system for an airline company, which must process thousands of requests for travel arrangements in a single country, or all over the world, almost immediately. In this type of system, most users expect that their response-time requirements will be fulfilled by the system and the system will be available at working hours (or 24 hours a day, seven days a week).

Users of an OLTP system execute their DML statements continuously—that is, they use both read and write operations at the same time and steadily. (Because data of an OLTP system is continuously modified, that data is highly dynamic.) All operations (or results of them) on a database usually include only a small amount of data, although it is possible that the database system must access many rows from one or more tables stored in the database.

In recent years, the amount of data stored in an *operational* database (that is, a database managed by an OLTP system) has increased steadily. Today, there are many databases that store several or even dozens of gigabytes of data. As you will see, this amount of data is still relatively small in relation to data warehouses.

Business Intelligence Systems

Business intelligence is the process of integrating enterprise-wide data into a single data store from which end users can run ad hoc queries and reports to analyze the existing data. In other words, the goal of BI is to keep data that can be accessed by users who make their business decisions on the basis of the analysis. These systems are often called *analytic* or *informative* systems, because by accessing data, users get the necessary information for making better business decisions.

The goals of BI systems are different from the goals of OLTP systems. The following is a query that is typical for a BI system: "What is the best-selling product category for each sales region in the third quarter of the year 2005?" Therefore, a BI system has very different properties from those listed for an OLTP system in the preceding section. The most important properties of a BI system are as follows:

▶ Periodic write operations (load) with queries based on a huge number of rows

▶ Small number of users

▶ Large size of data stored in a database

Besides data load that is executed at regular intervals (usually daily), BI systems are mostly read-only systems. (Therefore, the nature of the data in such a system is static.) As will be explained in detail later in this chapter, data is gathered from different sources, cleaned (made consistent), and loaded into a database called a data warehouse (or data mart). The cleaned data is usually not modified—that is, users query data using

SELECT statements to obtain the necessary information (and modification operations are very seldom).

Because BI systems are used to gain information, the number of users that simultaneously use such a system is relatively small in relation to the number of users that simultaneously use an OLTP system. Users of a BI system usually generate reports that display different factors concerning the finances of an enterprise (or department), or they execute complex queries to compare data.

NOTE

Another difference between OLTP and BI systems that actually affects the user's behavior is the daily schedule— that is, how those systems are used during a day. An OLTP system can be used nonstop (if it is designed for such a use), whereas a BI system can be used only as soon as data is made consistent and is loaded into the database.

In contrast to databases in OLTP systems that store only current data, BI systems must also track historical data. (Remember that BI systems make comparisons between data gathered in different time periods.) For this reason, the amount of data stored in a data warehouse is very large.

Data Warehouses and Data Marts

A *data warehouse* can be defined as a database that includes all corporate data and that can be uniformly accessed by users. That's the concise definition; explaining the notion of a data warehouse is much more involved. An enterprise usually has a large amount of data stored at different times and in different databases (or data files) that are managed by distinct DBMSs. These DBMSs need not be relational: some enterprises still have databases managed by hierarchical or network database systems. A special team of software specialists examines source databases (and data files) and converts them into a target store: the data warehouse. Additionally, the converted data in a data warehouse must be consolidated, because it holds the information that is the key to the corporation's operational processes. (*Consolidation* of data means that all equivalent queries executed upon a data warehouse at different times provide the same result.) The data consolidation in a data warehouse is provided in several steps:

▶ Data assembly from different sources (also called extraction)

▶ Data cleaning (in other words, transformation process)

▶ Quality assurance of data

Data must be carefully assembled from different sources. In this process, data is extracted from the sources, converted to an intermediate schema, and moved to a temporary work area. For data extraction, you need tools that extract exactly the data that must be stored in the data warehouse.

Data cleaning ensures the integrity of data that has to be stored in the target database. For example, data cleaning must be done on incorrect entries in data fields, such as addresses, or incompatible data types used to define the same date fields in different sources. For this process, the data cleaning team needs special software. An example will help explain the process of data cleaning more clearly. Suppose that there are two data sources that store personal data about employees and that both databases have the attribute **Gender**. In the first database, this attribute is defined as CHAR(6), and the data values are "female" and "male." The same attribute in the second database is declared as CHAR(1), with the values "f" and "m." The values of both data sources are correct, but for the target data source you must clean the data—that is, represent the values of the attribute in a uniform way.

The last part of data consolidation—quality assurance of data—involves a data validation process that specifies the data as the end user should view and access it. Because of this, end users should be closely involved in this process. When the process of data consolidation is finished, the data will be loaded in the data warehouse.

NOTE

The whole process of data consolidation is called ETL (extraction, transformation, loading). Microsoft provides a component called SQL Server Integration Services (SSIS) to support users during the ETL process.

By their nature (as a store for the overall data of an enterprise), data warehouses contain huge amounts of data. (Some data warehouses contain dozens of terabytes or even petabytes of data.) Also, because they must encompass the enterprise, implementation usually takes a lot of time, which depends on the size of the enterprise. Because of these disadvantages, many companies start with a smaller solution called a data mart.

Data marts are data stores that include all data at the department level and therefore allow users to access data concerning only a single part of their organization. For example, the marketing department stores all data relevant to marketing in its own data mart, the research department puts the experimental data in the research data mart, and so on. Because of this, a data mart has several advantages over a data warehouse:

▶ Narrower application area

▶ Shorter development time and lower cost

▶ Easier data maintenance

▶ Bottom-up development

As already stated, a data mart includes only the information needed by one part of an organization, usually a department. Therefore, the data that is intended for use by such a small organizational unit can be more easily prepared for the end user's needs.

The development time for a data warehouse averages two years and costs $5 million. On the other hand, costs for a data mart average $200,000, and such a project takes about three to five months. For these reasons, development of a data mart is preferred, especially if it is the first BI project in your organization.

The fact that a data mart contains significantly smaller amounts of data than a data warehouse helps you to reduce and simplify all tasks, such as data extraction, data cleaning, and quality assurance of data. It is also easier to design a solution for a department than for the entire organization. (For more information on BI design and a dimensional model, see the next section of this chapter.)

If you design and develop several data marts in your organization, it is possible to unite them all in one big data warehouse. This bottom-up process has several advantages over designing a data warehouse at once: first, each data mart may contain identical target tables that can be unified in a corresponding data warehouse. Second, some tasks are logically enterprise-wide, such as the gathering of financial information by the accounting department. If the existing data marts will be linked together to build a data warehouse for an enterprise, a global repository (that is, the data catalog that contains information about all data stored in sources as well as in the target database) is required.

NOTE

Be aware that building a data warehouse by linking data marts can be very troublesome because of possible significant differences in the structure and design of existing data marts. Different parts of an enterprise may use different data models and have different instructions for data representation. For this reason, at the beginning of this bottom-up process, it is strongly recommended that you make a single view of all data that will be valid at the enterprise level; do not allow departments to design data separately.

Data Warehouse Design Using Dimensional Model

Only a well-planned and well-designed database will allow you to achieve good performance. Relational databases and data warehouses have a lot of differences that require different design methods. Relational databases are designed using the well-known entity-relationship (ER) model, while the dimensional model is used for the design of data warehouses and data marts.

Using relational databases, data redundancy is removed using normal forms (see Chapter 1). The normalization process divides each table of a database that includes redundant data into two separate tables. The process of normalization should be finished when all tables of a database contain only nonredundant data.

The highly normalized tables are advantageous for OLTP, because in this case all transactions can be made as simple and short as possible. On the other hand, BI processes are based on queries that operate on a huge amount of data and are neither simple nor short. Therefore, the highly normalized tables do not suit the design of data warehouses, because the goal of BI systems is significantly different: there are few concurrent transactions, and each transaction accesses a very large number of records. (Imagine the huge amount of data belonging to a data warehouse that is stored in hundreds of tables. Most queries will join dozens of large tables to retrieve data. Such queries cannot be performed well, even if you use hardware with parallel processors and a database system with the best query optimizer.)

Data warehouses cannot use the ER model because this model is suited to design databases with nonredundant data. The logical model used to design data warehouses is called a *dimensional model*.

NOTE
There is another important reason why the ER model is not suited to the design of data warehouses: the use of data in a data warehouse is unstructured. This means the queries are partly executed ad hoc, allowing a user to analyze data in totally different ways. (On the other hand, OLTP systems usually have database applications that are hard-coded and therefore contain queries that are not modified often.)

In dimensional modeling, every model is composed of one table that stores measures and several other tables that describe dimensions. The former is called the *fact table*, and the latter are called *dimension tables*. Examples of data stored in a fact table include inventory sales and expenditures. Dimension tables usually include time, account, product, and employee data. Figure 22-1 shows an example of a dimensional model.

Each dimension table usually has a single-part primary key and several other attributes that describe this dimension closely. On the other hand, the primary key of the fact table is the combination of the primary keys of all dimension tables (see Figure 22-1). For this reason, the primary key of the fact table is made up of several foreign keys. (The number of dimensions also specifies the number of foreign keys in the fact table.) As you can see in Figure 22-1, the tables in a dimensional model build a star-like structure. Therefore, this model is often called a *star schema*.

Another difference in the nature of data in a fact table and the corresponding dimension tables is that most nonkey columns in a fact table are numeric and additive, because such data can be used to execute necessary calculations. (Remember that a typical query on a data warehouse fetches thousands or even millions of rows at a time, and the only useful operation upon such a huge amount of rows is to apply an aggregate function [sum, maximum, or average]). For example, columns like

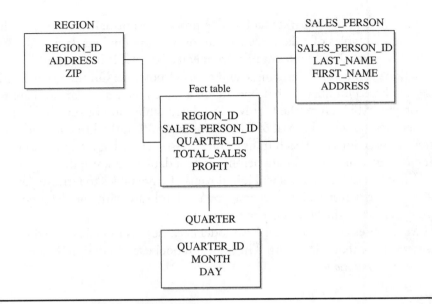

Figure 22-1   *Example of the dimensional model: star schema*

Units_of_product_sold, Total_sales, Profit, or **Dollars_cost** are typical columns in the fact table. (Numerical columns of the fact table that do not build the primary key of the table are called *measures*.)

On the other hand, columns of dimension tables are strings that contain textual descriptions of the dimension. For instance, columns such as **Address, Location,** and **Name** often appear in dimension tables. (These columns are usually used as headers in reports.) Another consequence of the textual nature of columns of dimension tables and their use in queries is that each dimension table contains many more indices than the corresponding fact table. (A fact table usually has only one unique index composed of all columns belonging to the primary key of that table.) Table 22-1 summarizes the differences between fact and dimension tables.

Fact Table	Dimension Table
Usually one in a dimensional model	Many (12–20)
Contains most rows of a data warehouse	Contains relatively small amount of data
Composite primary key (contains all primary keys of dimension tables)	Usually one column of a table builds the primary key of the table
Columns are numeric and additive	Columns are descriptive and therefore textual

Table 22-1   *The Differences Between Fact and Dimension Tables*

NOTE

Sometimes it is necessary to have multiple fact tables in a data warehouse because you may have different sets of measures, and each set has to be tied to a different fact table.

Columns of dimension tables are usually highly *denormalized*, which means that a lot of columns depend on each other. The denormalized structure of dimension tables has one important purpose: all columns of such a table are used as column headers in reports. If the denormalization of data in a dimension table is not desirable, a dimension table can be decomposed into several subtables. This is usually necessary when columns of a dimension table build hierarchies. (For example, the **product** dimension could have columns such as **Product_id**, **Category_id**, and **Subcategory_id** that build three hierarchies, with the primary key, **Product_id**, as the root.) This structure, in which each level of a base entity is represented by its own table, is called a *snowflake schema.* Figure 22-2 shows the snowflake schema of the **product** dimension.

The extension of a star schema into a corresponding snowflake schema has some benefits (reduction of used disk space, for example) and one main disadvantage: the snowflake schema requires more join operations to get information from lookup tables, which negatively impacts performance. For this reason, the performance of queries based on the snowflake schema is generally slow. Therefore, the design using the snowflake schema is recommended only in a few very specialized cases.

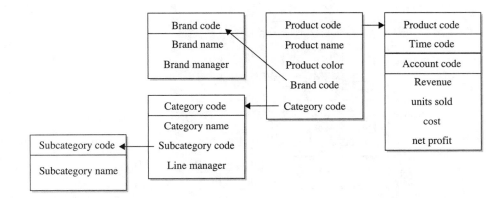

Figure 22-2   *The snowflake schema*

Cubes and Their Architectures

BI systems support different types of data storage. Some of these data storage types are based upon a multidimensional database that is also called a cube. A *cube* is a subset of data from the data warehouse that can be organized into multidimensional structures. To define a cube, you first select a fact table from the dimensional schema and identify numerical columns (measures) of interest within it. Then you select dimension tables that provide descriptions for the set of data to be analyzed. To demonstrate this, consider how the cube for car sales analysis might be defined. For example, the fact table may include the measures **Cars_sold**, **Total_sales**, and **Costs**, while the tables **Models**, **Quarters**, and **Region** specify dimension tables. The cube in Figure 22-3 shows all three dimensions: **Models**, **Regions**, and **Quarters**.

In each dimension there are discrete values called *members*. For instance, the **Regions** dimension may contain the following members: ALL, North America, South America, and Europe. (The ALL member specifies the total of all members in a dimension.)

Additionally, each cube dimension can have a hierarchy of levels that allows users to ask questions at a more detailed level. For example, the **Regions** dimension can include the following level hierarchies: **Country**, **Province**, and **City**. Similarly, the **Quarters** dimension can include **Month**, **Week**, and **Day** as level hierarchies.

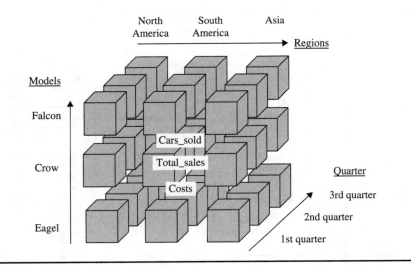

Figure 22-3 *Cube with dimensions Models, Quarters, and Regions*

NOTE

Cubes and multidimensional databases are managed by special systems called multidimensional database systems (MDBMS). SQL Server's MDBMS is called Analysis Services.

The physical storage of a cube is described after the following discussion of aggregates.

Aggregations

Data is stored in the fact table in its most detailed form so that corresponding reports can make use of it. On the other hand (as stated earlier), a typical query on a fact table fetches thousands or even millions of rows at a time, and the only useful operation upon such a huge amount of rows is to apply an aggregate function (sum, maximum, or average). This different use of data can reduce performance of ad hoc queries if they are executed on low-level (atomic) data, because time- and resource-intensive calculations will be necessary to perform each aggregate function.

For this reason, low-level data from the fact table should be summarized in advance and stored in intermediate tables. Because of their "aggregated" information, such tables are called *aggregate tables*, and the whole process is called *aggregation*.

NOTE

An aggregate row from the fact table is always associated with one or more aggregate dimension table rows. For example, the dimensional model in Figure 22-1 could contain the following aggregate rows: monthly sales aggregates by salespersons by region and region-level aggregates by salespersons by day.

An example will show why low-level data should be aggregated. An end user may want to start an ad hoc query that displays the total sales of the organization for the last month. This would cause the server to sum all sales for each day in the last month. If there are an average of 500 sales transactions per day in each of 500 stores of the organization, and data is stored at the transaction level, this query would have to read 7,500,000 ($500 \times 500 \times 30$ days) rows, and build the sum to return the result. Now consider what happens if the data is aggregated in a table that is created using monthly sales by store. In this case, the table will have only 500 rows (the monthly total for each of 500 stores), and the performance gain will be dramatic.

How Much to Aggregate?

Concerning aggregation, there are two extreme solutions: no aggregation at all, and exhaustive aggregation for every possible combination of queries that users will need. From the preceding discussion, it should be clear that no aggregation at all is out of the question, because of performance issues. (The data warehouse without any aggregation table probably cannot be used at all as a production data store.) The opposite solution is also not acceptable, for several reasons:

▶ Enormous amount of disk space needed to store additional data

▶ Overwhelming maintenance of aggregate tables

▶ Initial data load too long

Storing additional data that is aggregated at every possible level consumes an additional amount of disk space that increases the initial disk space by a factor of six or more (depending on the amount of the initial disk space and the number of queries that users will need). The creation of tables to hold the aggregates for all existing combinations is an overwhelming task for the system administrator. Finally, building aggregates at initial data load can have devastating results if this load already lasts for a long time and the additional time is not available.

From this discussion you can see that aggregate tables should be carefully planned and created. During the planning phase, keep these two main considerations in mind when determining what aggregates to create:

▶ Where is the data concentrated?

▶ Which aggregates would most improve performance?

The planning and creation of aggregate tables is dependent on the concentration of data in the columns of the base fact table. In a data warehouse, where there is no activity on a given day, the corresponding row is not stored at all. So if the system loads a large number of rows, as compared to the number of all rows that can be loaded, aggregating by that column of the base fact table improves performance enormously. In contrast, if the system loads few rows, as compared to the number of all rows that can be loaded, aggregating by that column is not efficient.

Here is another example to demonstrate the preceding discussion. For products in the grocery store, only a few of them (say, 15 percent) are actually sold on a given day. If we have a dimensional model with three dimensions, **Product**, **Store**, and **Time**, only 15 percent of the combination of the three corresponding primary keys for the particular day and for the particular store will be occupied. The daily product sales data will thus be *sparse*. In contrast, if all or many products in the grocery store are sold on a given day (because of a special promotion, for example), the daily product sales data will be *dense*.

To find out which dimensions are sparse and which are dense, you have to build rows from all possible combinations of tables and evaluate them. Usually the **Time** dimension is dense, because there are always entries for each day. Given the dimensions

Product, **Store**, and **Time**, the combination of the **Store** and **Time** dimensions is dense, because for each day there will certainly be data concerning selling in each store. On the other hand, the combination of the **Store** and **Product** dimensions is sparse (for the reasons previously discussed). In this case, the dimension **Product** is generally sparse, because its appearance in combination with other dimensions is sparse.

The choice of aggregates that would most improve performance depends on end users. Therefore, at the beginning of a BI project, you should interview end users to collect information on how data will be queried, how many rows will be retrieved by these queries, and other criteria.

Physical Storage of a Cube

Online analytical processing (OLAP) systems usually use one of the following three different architectures to store multidimensional data:

- ▶ Relational OLAP (ROLAP)
- ▶ Multidimensional OLAP (MOLAP)
- ▶ Hybrid OLAP (HOLAP)

Generally, these three architectures differ in the way in which they store leaf-level data and precomputed aggregates. (Leaf-level data is the finest grain of data that is defined in the cube's measure group. Therefore, the leaf-level data corresponds to the data of the cube's fact table.)

In ROLAP, the precomputed data isn't stored. Instead, queries access data from the relational database and its tables in order to bring back the data required to answer the question. MOLAP is a type of storage in which the leaf-level data and its aggregations are stored using a multidimensional cube.

Although the logical content of these two storage types is identical for the same data warehouse and both ROLAP and MOLAP analytic tools are designed to allow analysis of data through the use of data through the use of a dimensional data model, there are some significant differences between them. The advantages of ROLAP storage type are as follows:

- ▶ Data must not be duplicated
- ▶ Materialized (i.e., indexed) views can be used for summaries

If the data should also be stored in a multidimensional database, a certain amount of data must be duplicated. Therefore, the ROLAP storage type does not need additional storage to copy the leaf-level data. Also, the calculation of summaries (see the next section) can be executed very quickly with ROLAP if the corresponding summary tables are generated using materialized views.

On the other hand, MOLAP also has several advantages over ROLAP:

▶ Aggregates are stored in a multidimensional form

▶ Query response is generally faster

Using MOLAP, many aggregates are precomputed and stored in a multidimensional cube. That way the system does not have to calculate the result of such an aggregate each time it is needed. In the case of MOLAP, the database engine and the database itself are usually optimized to work together, so the query response may be faster than in ROLAP.

HOLAP storage is a combination of the MOLAP and ROLAP storage types. Precomputed data is stored as in the case of the MOLAP storage, while the leaf-level data is left in the relational database. (Therefore, for queries using summaries, HOLAP is identical to MOLAP.) The advantage of HOLAP storage is that the leaf-level data is not duplicated.

Data Access

Data in a data warehouse can be accessed using three general techniques:

▶ Reporting

▶ OLAP

▶ Data mining

Reporting is the simplest form of data access. A report is just a presentation of a query result in a tabular form. (Reporting is discussed in detail in Chapter 25.) With OLAP, you analyze data interactively; that is, it allows you to perform comparisons and calculations along any dimension in a data warehouse.

NOTE

Transact-SQL supports all standardized functions and constructs in relation to SQL/OLAP. This topic will be discussed in detail in Chapter 24.

Data mining is used to explore and analyze large quantities of data in order to discover significant patterns. This discovery is not the only task of data mining: using this technique, you must be able to turn the existing data into information and turn the information into action. In other words, it is not enough to analyze data; you have to apply the results of data mining meaningfully and take action upon the given results. (Data mining, as the most complex of the three techniques, will not be covered in this introductory book.)

Conclusion

At the beginning of a BI project, the main question is what to build: a data warehouse or a data mart. Probably the best answer is to start with one or more data marts that can later be united in a data warehouse. Most of the existing tools in the BI market support this alternative.

In contrast to operational databases that use ER models for their design, the design of data warehouses is best done using a dimensional model. These two models show significant differences. If you are already acquainted with the ER model, the best way to learn and use the dimensional model is to forget everything about the ER model and start modeling from scratch.

After this introductory discussion of general considerations about the BI process, the next chapter discusses the server part of Microsoft Analysis Services.

Exercises

E.22.1

Discuss the differences between operative and analytic systems.

E.22.2

Discuss the differences between the ER and dimensional models.

E.22.3

At the beginning of a project with a data warehouse, there is the so-called ETL (extracting, transforming, loading) process. Explain the three subprocesses.

E.22.4

Discuss the differences between a fact table and corresponding dimension tables.

E.22.5

Discuss the benefits of the three storage types (MOLAP, ROLAP, and HOLAP.)

E.22.6

Why it is necessary to aggregate data stored in a fact table?

Chapter 23

Microsoft Analysis Services

In This Chapter

- ► **BI Development Studio**
- ► **Analysis Services and Cubes**

Microsoft Analysis Services is a group of services that is used to manage data that is stored in a data warehouse or data mart. Analysis Services organizes data from a data warehouse into multidimensional cubes (see Chapter 22) with aggregates to allow the execution of sophisticated reports and complex queries. The key features of Analysis Services are

▶ Ease of use

▶ Flexible data model

▶ Several supported APIs

Analysis Services offer wizards for almost every task that is executed during the design and implementation of a data warehouse. For example, Data Source Wizard allows you to specify one or more data sources, while Cube Wizard is used to create a multidimensional cube where aggregate data is stored.

Ease of use is guaranteed by Business Intelligence (BI) Development Studio. You can use this tool to develop databases and other data warehousing objects. This means that BI Development Studio offers one interface for developing both Analysis Services projects and SQL Server Integration Services and Reporting Services projects.

In contrast to most other data warehousing systems, Analysis Services allows you to use the architecture that is most appropriate for a specific data warehousing system. You can choose between the three architectures (MOLAP, ROLAP, and HOLAP), which are discussed in detail in the previous chapter.

BI Development Studio

The main component of Analysis Services is Business Intelligence Development Studio, a management tool that provides one development platform for Integration Services, Reporting Services data mining, and Analysis Services. Built on Visual Studio, BI Development Studio supports an integrated development platform for system developers in the business intelligence area. Debugging, source control, and code development are available for all components of the BI application.

You can use BI Development Studio not only to create and manage cubes, but also to design capabilities for SQL Server Reporting Services and SQL Server Integration Services. (Reporting Services is discussed in Chapter 25, while Integration Services is beyond the scope of this book.)

NOTE

The user interface of BI Development Studio is very similar to the interface of SQL Server Management Studio. However, these two tools differ in their deployment: you should use BI Development Studio to develop BI projects, while you should use SQL Server Management Studio mainly to operate and maintain BI database objects.

In this chapter, BI Development Studio is used to create a cube based upon the **AdventureWorksDW** database and to process it. To start BI Development Studio, click **Start**, **All Programs**, **Microsoft SQL Server 2008**, and finally **SQL Server Business Intelligence Development Studio**.

Creating a New Project

The first step in building an analytic application is to create a new project. To build a project click **File**, select **New**, and choose **Project**. In the **New Project** dialog box (see Figure 23-1), click the **Business Intelligence Projects** folder in the **Project Types** pane. In the **Templates** pane, select **Analysis Services Project**. Type the name of the project and its location in the **Name** and **Location** text boxes, respectively. For purposes of this example, name the project **Project1**, as shown in Figure 23-1. The new project will be created after you click **OK**.

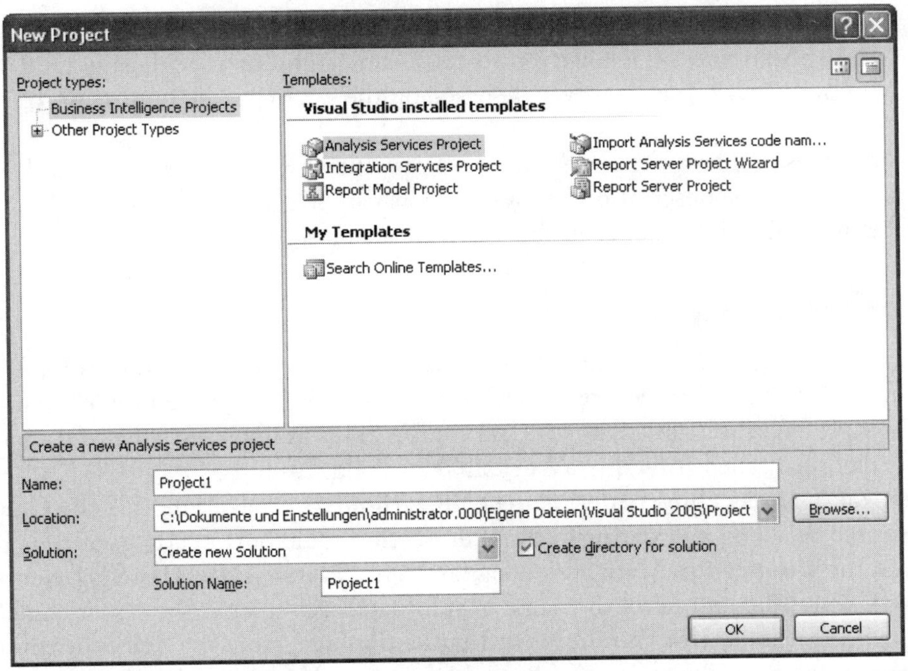

Figure 23-1   *The New Project dialog box*

The new project is always created in a new solution. Hence, the solution is the largest management unit in BI Development Studio, and always comprises one or more projects. (If the Solution Explorer pane, which allows you to view and manage objects in a solution or a project, is not visible, you can view it by clicking **View** in the menu bar and selecting **Solution Explorer.**)

Take a look at the **Solution Explorer** pane with the newly created project. Beneath the project node there are the following folders, among others:

- ▶ **Data Sources** Stores the information for connecting to the source database.

- ▶ **Data Source Views** Contains information concerning the subset of tables in a source database.

- ▶ **Cubes** Comprises all cubes that belong to the project.

- ▶ **Dimensions** Contains all dimensions. Analysis Services supports three types of dimensions. *Shared dimension*s (also called conformed dimensions) are dimensions that are shared among two or more cubes in the database. Typical shared dimensions are **Time**, **Product**, and **Customer**. *Private dimensions* are created for an individual cube. A *linked dimension* is based on a dimension that is stored in another Analysis Services database. The source database for a linked dimension can be on the same server or on a different server.

- ▶ **Mining Structures** Allows you to create a data mining model using the Data Mining Wizard. These models are based on the existing cube information.

Besides these folders, there are several other folders (Roles, Assemblies, and Miscellaneous). The description of these folders can be found in Books Online.

Once the project is created, you should create a data source.

Creating a Data Source

To create a data source, right-click the **Data Sources** folder in the **Solution Explorer** pane and select **New Data Source**. The **Data Source Wizard** appears, which guides you through the process of creating a data source. (This example uses the SQL Server sample database called **AdventureWorksDW** as the data source.)

First, on the **Select how to define the connection** page, make sure that the **Create a data source based on an existing or new connection** radio button is chosen and click **New**. In the **Connection Manager** dialog box, select **Native OLE DB/SQL Server Native Client 10.0** and select the name of your database server as the server name. In the same step, choose **Use Windows Authentication** and, from the **Select or enter a database name** drop-down list, choose the **AdventureWorksDW** database. Before you click **OK**, click the **Test Connection** button to test the connection to the database.

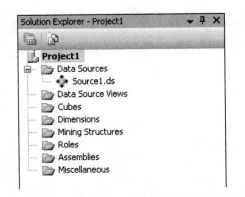

Figure 23-2   *The Solution Explorer pane with new data source*

Finally, on the **Completing the Wizard** page, give the new data source a name (for this example, call it **Source1**) and click **Finish**. The new data source appears in the **Solution Explorer** pane in the **Data Sources** folder (see Figure 23-2).

The next step is to create a view that corresponds to the selected data source.

Creating a Data Source View

A data source view is used to define the schema information you want to use in your solution. In other words, a data source view contains information concerning the subset of tables from the specified source database. (You should create a data source view when your database comprises hundreds of tables, of which only a few are useful in a BI application.)

To create such a view, right-click the **Data Source Views** folder in the **Solution Explorer** pane and select **New Data Source View**. The **Data Source View Wizard** guides you through the steps that are necessary to create a data source view. (This example creates a view called **View1**, which is based upon the **Customer** and **Project** tables as well as their related tables.)

First, on the **Select a Data Source** page, select an existing relational data source (for this example, select **Source1**) and click **Next**. On the next page—**Select Tables and Views**— you select tables that belong to your cube either as dimension tables or fact tables. (To select a table, mark its name and click the > button in the middle of the window. Again, click Finish. After that, the table appears in the **Included objects** pane.) For this example, select the **customer** and **product** tables from the **AdventureWorksDW** database. These tables are called **DimCustomer** and **DimProduct**, respectively, and will be used to build cube dimensions. Also, by clicking the **Add Related Tables** button, you instruct the system to find tables that are related to the two selected tables. (To find related tables, the system searches all primary key/foreign key relationships that exist in the database.)

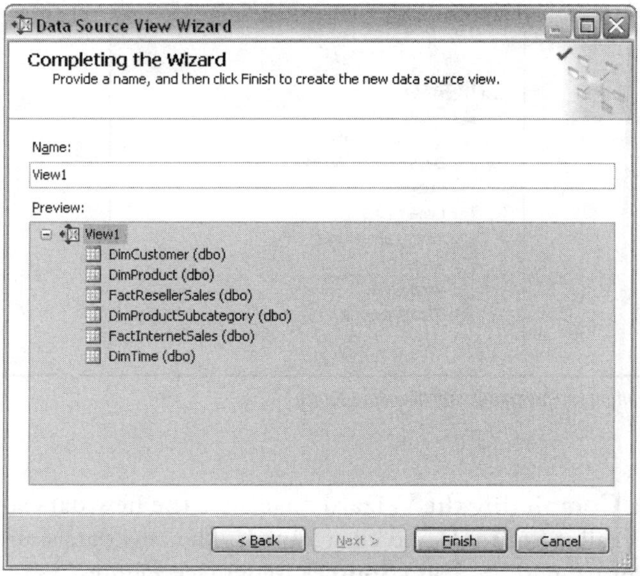

Figure 23-3   *The Completing the Wizard page*

Also add the **DimTime** table, because the time dimension is (almost) always a part of a cube. After that, click **Next**. On the **Completing the Wizard** page, the system shows the tables, which you can see in see Figure 23-3:

- ► DimCustomer
- ► DimProduct
- ► FactResellerSales
- ► DimProductSubcategory
- ► FactInternetSales
- ► DimTime

Click Finish. After the tables are selected, the wizard is completed and Data Source View Designer shows the selected tables (see Figure 23-4). (Data Source View Designer is a tool that is used to show a graphical representation of the data schema you have defined.)

Data Source View Designer offers several useful functions. To inspect the objects you have in your source view, move your mouse pointer to the cross-arrow icon in the bottom-right corner. When the pointer changes to a cross-arrow icon, click the icon. The **Navigation** window appears. Now you can navigate from one part of the diagram to another part. (If you want to find a specific table, use the **Data Source View** function

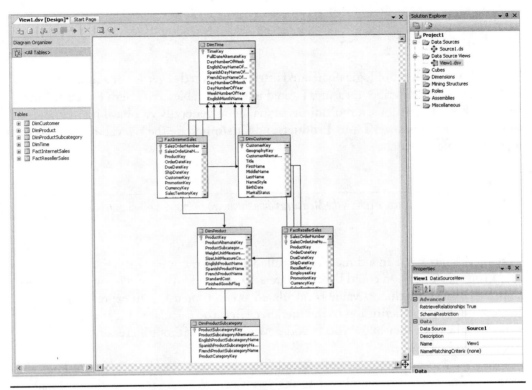

Figure 23-4   *Data Source View Designer with the selected tables*

in the menu bar and select **Find Table**.) To view the data in a table, right-click the table and then click **Explore Data**.

You can also create named queries, which are queries that are persistently stored and therefore can be accessed like any table. To create such a query, click the **Data Source View** function in the menu bar and then select the **New Named Query** icon. The **Create Named Query** dialog box allows you to create any query in relation to selected tables.

Analysis Services and Cubes

A *cube* is a multidimensional structure that contains all or a part of the data from a data warehouse. Each cube contains the following components:

- ▶   Dimensions
- ▶   Members
- ▶   Hierarchies
- ▶   Cells

- ► Levels
- ► Properties

A *dimension* is a set of logically related attributes (stored together in a dimensional table) that closely describes measures (stored in the fact table). Although the term "cube" implies three dimensions, a multidimensional cube generally can have many more dimensions. For instance, **Time**, **Product**, and **Customer** are the typical dimensions that are part of many models.

NOTE

*One important dimension of a cube is the **Measures** dimension, which includes all measures defined in the fact table.*

Each discrete value in a dimension is called a *member*. For instance, the members of a **Product** dimension could be Computers, Disks, and CPUs. Each member can be calculated, meaning that its value is calculated at run time using an expression that is specified during the definition of the member. (Because calculated members are not stored on the disk, they allow you to add new members without increasing the size of a corresponding cube.)

Hierarchies specify groupings of multiple members within each dimension. They are used to refine queries concerning data analysis. *Cells* are parts of a multidimensional cube that are identified by coordinates (x-, y-, and z-coordinate, if the cube is three-dimensional). This means that a cell is a set containing members from each dimension. For instance, consider the three-dimensional cube in Chapter 22 (see Figure 22-3) that represents car sales for a single region within a quarter. The cells with the following coordinates belong, among others, to the cube:

- ► First quarter, South America, Falcon
- ► Third quarter, Asia, Eagle

When you define hierarchies, you define them in terms of their levels. In other words, *levels* describe the hierarchy from the highest (most summarized) level to the lowest (most detailed) level of data. The following list displays the possible hierarchy levels for the time dimension:

- ► Quarter (Q1, Q2, Q3, Q4)
- ► Month (January, February, …)
- ► Day (Day1, Day2, …)

Creating a Cube

Before you create a cube, you must specify one or more data sources and create a data source view, as described earlier in the chapter. After that, you can use the Cube Wizard to create a cube.

To create a cube, right-click the **Cubes** folder of the particular project in the **Solution Explorer** pane and select **New Cube**. The Cube Wizard appears. Then, on the **Select Creation Method** page, choose **Use existing tables** and click **Next**. On the **Select Measure Group Tables** page, select the data source view, click the **Suggest** button, and then click **Next**.

On the **Select Measure** page, select the following measures: **SalesAmount** (in the **FactResellerSales** fact table) and **TotalProductCost** (in the **FactInternetSales** fact table). Click **Next**. On the **Select New Dimensions** page, select all three dimensions (**DimTime**, **DimProduct**, and **DimCustomer**) to be created, based on available tables. The final page, **Completing the Wizard**, shows the summary of all selected measures and dimensions (see Figure 23-5). Click **Finish** to finish the work.

Designing Storage Aggregation and Processing the Cube

As you already know, basic data from the fact table can be summarized in advance and stored in persistent tables. This process is called "aggregation," and it can significantly

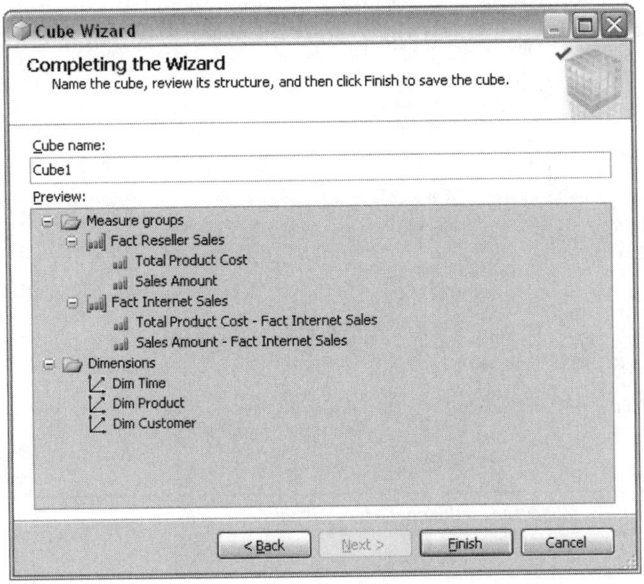

Figure 23-5   *Completing the Wizard page*

enhance the response time of queries, because scanning millions of rows to calculate the aggregation on the fly can take a very long time.

There is a tradeoff between storage requirements and the percentage of possible aggregations that are calculated and stored. Calculating all possible aggregations in a cube and their storage on the disk results in the fastest possible response time for all queries, because the response to each query is almost immediate. The disadvantage of this approach is that the storage and processing time required for the aggregations can be substantial.

On the other hand, if no aggregations are calculated and stored, you do not need any additional disk storage, but response time for queries concerning aggregate functions will be slow, because each aggregate has to be calculated on the fly.

Analysis Services provides the Aggregation Design Wizard to help you design aggregations optimally. To start the wizard, click the **Partitions** tab in the **Cube Designer**. (Figure 23-6 shows the Partitions tab for the **FactInternetSales** fact table.) In the table that appears in the Cube Designer (**FactInternetSales**), click the value under the **Aggregations** column. After that, click … in the same field. That starts the Aggregation Design Wizard.

In the first step of the wizard, you review aggregation usage settings in the window with the same name. In this step, you can include or exclude the attributes that appear on the page.

The next step after selecting the storage structure is to specify the number of members in each attribute. You do this on the **Specify Objects Counts** page. For each selected cube objects you must enter the estimated count value or partition count value, before you start the wizard, clicking **Count** button to start the wizard, which counts and displays the obtained count number.

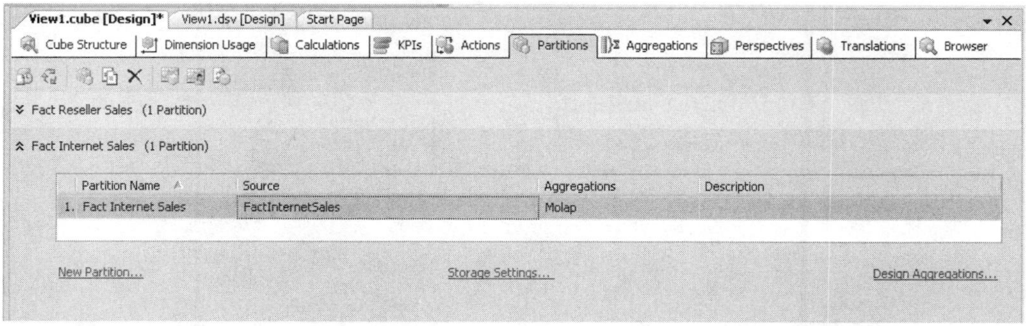

Figure 23-6   *The Partitions tab for the FactInternetSales fact table*

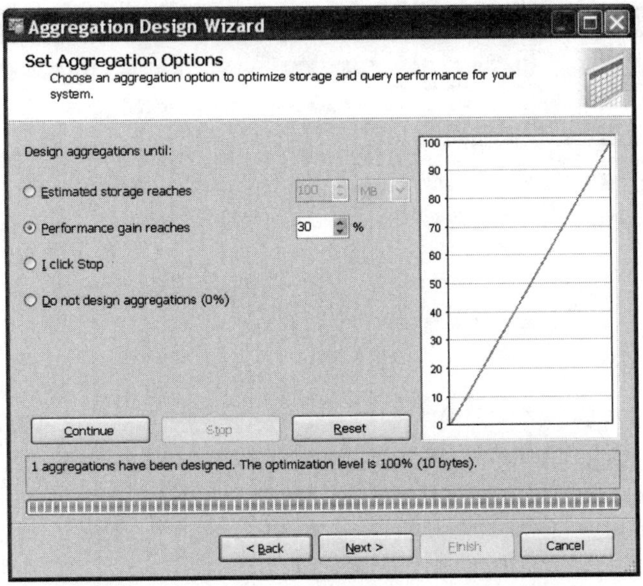

Figure 23-7   *The Set Aggregation Options page*

In the second-to-last step, the **Set Aggregation Options** page, shown in Figure 23-7, choose one of the four options to specify up to what point (or not at all) aggregations should be designed:

- **Estimated storage reaches__MB**   Specifies the maximum amount of disk storage that should be used for precomputed aggregations. The larger the amount, the more precalculated aggregations that will be created.

- **Performance gain reaches__%**   Specifies the performance gain that you want to achieve. The higher the percentage of precomputed aggregations, the better the performance.

- **I click Stop**   Enables you to decide when to stop the design process.

- **Do not design aggregation (0%)**   Specifies that no precomputed aggregations should be created.

After you click the **Start** button and the **Next** button, the **Completing the wizard** page appears. On this page, you can choose whether to process aggregations immediately (**Deploy and process now**) or later (**Save the aggregations but do not process them**).

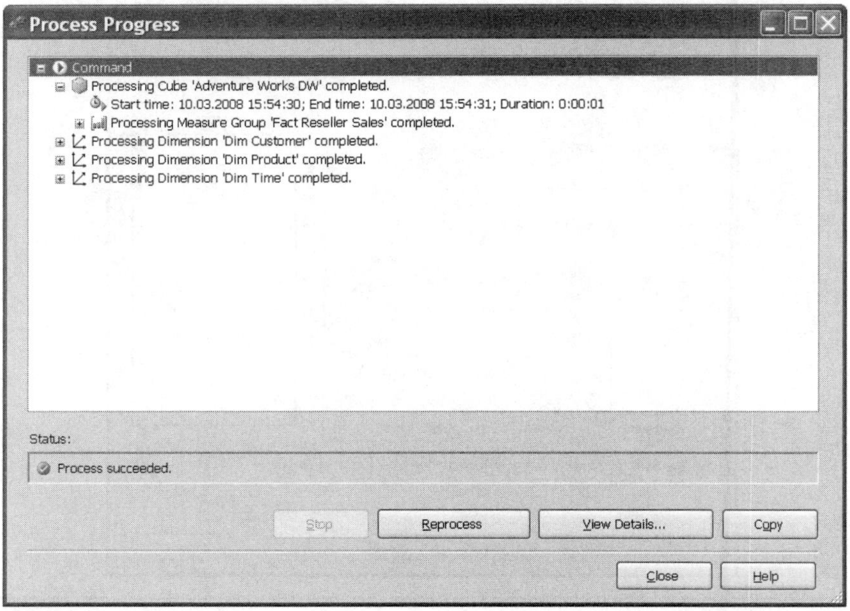

Figure 23-8   *The process progress window*

The **Process Progress** window shows the deployment progress of processing the cube (see Figure 23-8).

NOTE

A cube must be processed when you first create it and each time you modify it. If a cube has a lot of data and precomputed aggregations, processing the cube can be very time consuming.

Browsing a Cube

To browse a cube, right-click the cube name and select **Browse**. The **Browse** view appears. You can add any of the dimensions to the view by right-clicking the dimension name in the left pane and selecting **Add to Column Area** or **Add to Row Area**. You can also add a measure from the same pane if you right-click the measure and select **Add to Data Area**. Figure 23-9 shows the sales amounts for Internet sales for different customers and different products. To show these amounts, right-click the **DimProduct** table and select **Add to Column Area**. Also right-click the **DimCustomer** table and select **Add to Row Area**. The measure **SalesAmount** from the **FactInternetSales** fact table will be dropped analogously.

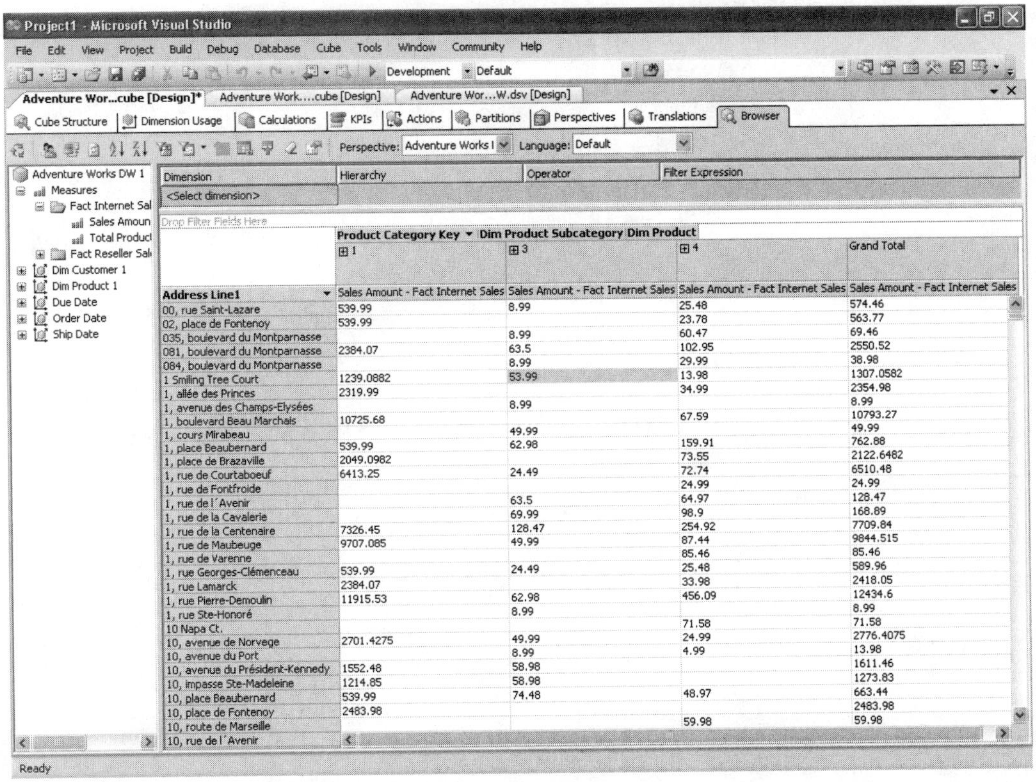

Figure 23-9   *Crosstab with sales amounts for Internet sales*

> **NOTE**
> *You can use ALT-SHIFT-ENTER to enlarge the **Browse** view of the Cube Designer. The same keystroke combination reverts back to normal view.*

Conclusion

With its Analysis Services, Microsoft offers a set of data warehousing services that can be used for entry- and intermediate-level data analysis. In particular, its ease of use through BI Development Studio, which is based upon Visual Studio, will give users an easy way to design and develop data warehouses and data marts.

The next chapter describes SQL/OLAP extensions in Transact-SQL.

Chapter 24

Business Intelligence and Transact-SQL

In This Chapter

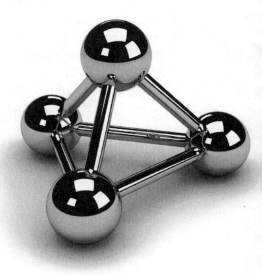

P art II of this book showed the power of the Transact-SQL language for managing traditional business data. Prior to SQL Server 2000, the Transact-SQL language did not handle complex data analysis particularly well. From its inception, Transact-SQL has provided several aggregate functions that can be used to compute simple summary data, and the GROUP BY clause, which offers elementary grouping of data.

SQL Server 2000 was the first version of SQL Server to provide complex data analysis facilities, such as the CUBE operator and the TOP clause. SQL Server 2005 extended significantly these facilities, introducing ranking functions and several relational operators. SQL Server 2008 introduces the standardized syntax for the ROLLUP and CUBE operators, as well as grouping sets, which allow you to compute groups on several different sets of grouping columns.

After a short introduction to SQL/OLAP, this chapter discusses the following topics concerning analytic functions:

- ▶ Window construct

- ▶ Extensions of the GROUP BY clause

- ▶ Analytic query functions

- ▶ Nonstandard analytic functions

Introduction to SQL/OLAP

Have you ever tried to write a Transact-SQL query that computes the percentage change in values between last two quarters? Or one that implements cumulative sums or sliding aggregations? If you have ever tried, you know how difficult these tasks are. Today, you don't have to implement them any more. The SQL:1999 standard has adopted a set of online analytical processing (OLAP) functions that enable you to easily perform these calculations as well as many others that used to be very complex for implementation. This part of the SQL standard is called SQL/OLAP. Therefore, SQL/OLAP comprises all functions and operators that are used for data analysis.

Using OLAP functions has several advantages for users:

- ▶ Users with standard knowledge of the SQL language can easily specify the calculations they need.

- ▶ Database systems, such as Database Engine, can perform these calculations much more efficiently.

▶ Because there is a standard specification of these functions, they're now much more economical for tool and application vendors to exploit.

▶ Almost all the analytic functions proposed by the SQL:1999 standard are implemented in enterprise database systems in the same way. For this reason, you can port queries in relation to SQL/OLAP from one system to another, without any code changes.

Database Engine offers many extensions to the SELECT statement that can be used primarily for analytic operations. Some of these extensions are defined according to the SQL:1999 standard and some are not. The following sections describe both standard and nonstandard SQL/OLAP functions and operators.

Window Construct

The most important extension of Transact-SQL concerning data analysis is the window construct. A window (in relation to SQL/OLAP) defines a partitioned set of rows to which a function is applied. The number of rows that belong to a window is dynamically determined in relation to the user's specifications. The window construct is specified using the OVER clause.

The standardized window construct has three main parts:

▶ Partitioning

▶ Ordering

▶ Aggregation grouping

NOTE

SQL Server 2008 doesn't support aggregation grouping, so this feature is not discussed here.

Before you delve into the window construct and its parts, take a look at the table that will be used for the examples. Example 24.1 creates the **project_dept** table, shown in Table 24-1, which is used in this chapter to demonstrate Transact-SQL extensions concerning SQL/OLAP.

dept_name	emp_cnt	budget	date_month
Research	5	50000	01.01.2007
Research	10	70000	02.01.2007
Research	5	65000	07.01.2007
Accounting	5	10000	07.01.2007
Accounting	10	40000	02.01.2007
Accounting	6	30000	01.01.2007
Accounting	6	40000	02.01.2008
Marketing	6	100000	01.01.2008
Marketing	10	180000	02.01.2008
Marketing	3	100000	07.01.2008
Marketing	NULL	120000	01.01.2008

Table 24-1 *Content of the project_dept table*

EXAMPLE 24.1

```
USE sample;
create table project_dept
    ( dept_name char( 20 ) not null,
    emp_cnt int null,
    budget float,
    date_month date );
```

The **project_dept** table contains several departments and their employee counts as well as budgets of projects that are controlled by each department. Example 24.2 shows the INSERT statements that are used to insert the rows shown in Table 24-1.

EXAMPLE 24.2

```
INSERT INTO project_dept VALUES
    ('Research', 5, 50000, '01.01.2007');
INSERT INTO project_dept VALUES
    ('Research', 10, 70000, '02.01.2007');
INSERT INTO project_dept VALUES
    ('Research', 5, 65000, '07.01.2007');
INSERT INTO project_dept VALUES
    ('Accounting', 5, 10000, '07.01.2007');
```

```
INSERT INTO project_dept VALUES
   ('Accounting', 10, 40000, '02.01.2007');
INSERT INTO project_dept VALUES
   ('Accounting', 6, 30000, '01.01.2007');
INSERT INTO project_dept VALUES
   ('Accounting', 6, 40000, '02.01.2008');
INSERT INTO project_dept VALUES
   ('Marketing', 6, 100000, '01.01.2008');
INSERT INTO project_dept VALUES
   ('Marketing', 10, 180000, '02.01.2008');
INSERT INTO project_dept VALUES
   ('Marketing', 3, 100000, '07.01.2008');
INSERT INTO project_dept VALUES
   ('Marketing', NULL, 120000, '01.01.2008');
```

Partitioning

Partitioning allows you to divide the result set of a query into groups, so that each row from a partition will be displayed separately. If no partitioning is specified, the entire set of rows comprises a single partition. Although the partitioning looks like a grouping using the GROUP BY clause, it is not the same thing. The GROUP BY clause collapses the rows in a partition into a single row, whereas the partitioning within the window construct simply organizes the rows into groups without collapsing them.

The following two examples show the difference between partitioning using the window construct and grouping using the GROUP BY clause. Suppose that you want to calculate several different aggregates concerning employees in each department. Example 24.3 shows how the OVER clause with the PARTITION BY clause can be used to build partitions.

EXAMPLE 24.3

Using the window construct, build the partition according to the values in the **dept_name** column and calculate the sum and the average for the Accounting and Research departments:

```
USE sample;
SELECT dept_name,  budget,
        SUM( emp_cnt ) OVER( PARTITION BY dept_name ) AS emp_cnt_sum,
        AVG( budget ) OVER( PARTITION BY dept_name )  AS budget_avg
         FROM project_dept
         WHERE dept_name IN ('Accounting', 'Research');
```

The result is

dept_name	budget	emp_cnt_sum	budget_avg
Accounting	10000	27	30000
Accounting	40000	27	30000
Accounting	30000	27	30000
Accounting	40000	27	30000
Research	50000	20	61666.6666666667
Research	70000	20	61666.6666666667
Research	65000	20	61666.6666666667

Example 24.3 uses the OVER clause to define the corresponding window. Inside it, the PARTITION BY option is used to specify partitions. (The partitions are grouped using the values in the **dept_name** column.) Finally, an aggregate (or some other) function is applied to the partitions. Again, as you can see from the result of the example, the partitioning organizes the rows into groups without collapsing them.

Example 24.4 shows a similar query that uses the GROUP BY clause.

EXAMPLE 24.4

Group the values in the **dept_name** column for the Accounting and Research departments and calculate the sum and the average for these two groups:

```
USE sample;
SELECT dept_name,
  SUM(emp_cnt) AS cnt, AVG( budget ) AS budget_avg
    FROM project_dept
    WHERE dept_name IN ('Accounting', 'Research')
    GROUP BY dept_name;
```

The result is

dept_name	cnt	budget_avg
Accounting	27	30000
Research	20	61666.6666666667

As already stated, when you use the GROUP BY clause, each group collapses in one row.

NOTE

There is another significant difference between the OVER and GROUP BY clauses. As can be seen from Example 24.2, when you use the OVER clause, the corresponding SELECT list can contain any column name from the table. This is obvious, because partitioning organizes the rows into groups without collapsing them.

Ordering

The ordering within the window construct is like the ordering in a query: first, you use the ORDER BY clause to specify the particular order of the rows in the result set. Second, it includes a list of sort keys and indicates whether they should be sorted in ascending or descending order. The most important difference is that ordering inside a window is applied only *within* each partition.

SQL Server 2008 doesn't support ordering inside a window construct *for aggregate functions*. In other words, the OVER clause for aggregate functions can contain only the PARTITION BY clause. (In spite of this limitation, ordering inside a window works for ranking functions.) Example 24.5, which is supported by the SQL standard, displays an error.

EXAMPLE 24.5(DISPLAYS AN ERROR)

Using the window construct, partition the rows of the **project_dept** table using the values in the **dept_name** column and sort the rows in each partition using the values in the **budget** column:

```
USE sample;
SELECT dept_name, budget, emp_cnt
    SUM(budget) OVER(PARTITION BY dept_name ORDER BY budget) AS
sum_dept
    FROM project_dept;
```

Example 24.6 uses the conventional Transact-SQL features to solve the problem in Example 24.5, which is called "cumulative aggregations," or in this case "cumulative sums." Cumulative aggregations accumulate data from the first value within the partition up to the current value.

EXAMPLE 24.6

Group the **project_dept** table using the values in the **dept_name** column and sort the rows in each partition using the values in the **budget** column:

```
USE sample;
SELECT p1.dept_name, p1.budget, p1.emp_cnt,
```

```
            SUM (p2.budget) AS cumulative_budget
     FROM project_dept p1 JOIN project_dept p2
           ON p1.dept_name =p2.dept_name
           AND p2.budget <= p1.budget
     GROUP BY p1.dept_name, p1.budget, p1.emp_cnt
     ORDER BY p1.dept_name, p1.budget, p1.emp_cnt;
```

NOTE

The SQL standard defines an additional part of the window construct called aggregation grouping. With aggregation grouping, you can define a set of rows on which the aggregate function operates for each row in the partition. Transact-SQL doesn't support aggregation grouping.

You can use several columns from a table to build different partitioning schemas in a query, as shown in Example 24.7.

EXAMPLE 24.7

Using the window construct, build two partitions for the Accounting and Research departments: one using the values of the **budget** column and the other using the values of the **dept_name** column. Calculate the sums for the former partition and the averages for the latter partition.

```
USE sample;
SELECT dept_name, CAST( budget AS INT ) AS budget,
 SUM( emp_cnt ) OVER( PARTITION BY budget ) AS emp_cnt_sum,
 AVG( budget ) OVER( PARTITION BY dept_name )  AS budget_avg
 FROM project_dept
WHERE dept_name IN ('Accounting', 'Research');
```

The result is

dept_name	budget	emp_cnt_sum	budget_avg
Accounting	10000	5	30000
Accounting	30000	6	30000
Accounting	40000	16	30000
Accounting	40000	16	30000
Research	50000	5	61666.6666666667
Research	65000	5	61666.6666666667
Research	70000	10	61666.6666666667

The query in Example 24.7 has two different partitioning schemas: one over the values of the **budget** column and one over the values of the **dept_name** column. The former is used to calculate the number of employees in relation to the departments with the same budget. The latter is used to calculate the average value of budgets of departments grouped by their names.

Extensions of GROUP BY

Transact-SQL extends the GROUP BY clause with the following operators:

► CUBE

► ROLLUP

► GROUPING SETS

The GROUP BY clause has also an additional GROUPING function, which will be discussed after the operators mentioned above.

CUBE Operator

This section looks at the differences between grouping using the GROUP BY clause alone and grouping using GROUP BY in combination with the CUBE operator. The main difference is that the GROUP BY clause defines one or more columns as a group such that all rows within any group have the same values for those columns. CUBE and ROLLUP provide additional summary rows for grouped data. These summary rows are also called multidimensional summaries.

The following two examples demonstrate these differences. Example 24.8 applies the GROUP BY clause to group the rows of the **project_dept** table using two criteria: **dept_name** and **emp_cnt**.

EXAMPLE 24.8

Using GROUP BY, group the rows of the **project_dept** table using the **dept_name** and **emp_cnt** columns:

```
USE sample;
SELECT dept_name, emp_cnt, SUM(budget) sum_of_budgets
    FROM project_dept
    WHERE dept_name IN ('Accounting', 'Research')
    GROUP BY dept_name, emp_cnt;
```

The result is

dept_name	emp_cnt	sum_of_budgets
Accounting	5	10000
Research	5	115000
Accounting	6	70000
Accounting	10	40000
Research	10	70000

Example 24.9 and its result set shows the difference when you additionally use the CUBE operator.

EXAMPLE 24.9

Group the rows of the **project_dept** table that belong to the Accounting and Research departments using the **dept_name** and **emp_cnt** columns and additionally display all possible summary rows:

```
USE sample;
SELECT dept_name, emp_cnt, SUM(budget) sum_of_budgets
    FROM project_dept
     WHERE dept_name IN ('Accounting', 'Research')
     GROUP BY CUBE (dept_name, emp_cnt);
```

The result is

dept_name	emp_cnt	sum_of_budgets
Accounting	5	10000
Accounting	6	70000
Accounting	10	40000
Accounting	NULL	120000
Research	5	115000
Research	10	70000
Research	NULL	185000
NULL	NULL	305000
NULL	5	125000
NULL	6	70000
NULL	10	110000

The main difference between the last two examples is that the result set of Example 24.8 displays only the values in relation to the grouping, while the result set of Example 24.9 contains, additionally, all possible summary rows. The placeholder for the values in the unneeded columns of summary rows is displayed as NULL. For example, the following row from the result set

NULL   NULL   305000

shows the sum of all budgets of all existing projects in the table, while the row

NULL   5   125000

shows the sum of all budgets for all projects that employ exactly five employees.

NOTE

Because the CUBE operator displays every possible combination of groups and summary rows, the number of rows is the same, regardless of the order of columns in the GROUP BY clause.

The syntax of CUBE in Example 24.9 corresponds to the standardized syntax of that operator. This syntax is introduced in SQL Server 2008. Example 24.10 is equivalent to Example 24.9 but uses the old-style syntax.

EXAMPLE 24.10

Group the rows of the **project_dept** table that belong to the Accounting and Research departments using the **dept_name** and **emp_cnt** columns and additionally display all possible summary rows:

```
USE sample;
SELECT dept_name, emp_cnt, SUM(budget) sum_of_budgets
    FROM project_dept
     WHERE dept_name IN ('Accounting', 'Research')
     GROUP BY dept_name, emp_cnt
     WITH CUBE;
```

ROLLUP Operator

In contrast to CUBE, which returns every possible combination of groups and summary rows, the group hierarchy using ROLLUP is determined by the order in which the grouping columns are specified. Example 24.11 shows the use of the ROLLUP operator.

EXAMPLE 24.11

Group the rows of the **project_dept** table that belong to the Accounting and Research departments using the **dept_name** and **emp_cnt** columns and additionally display summary rows for the **dept_name** column:

```
USE sample;
SELECT dept_name, emp_cnt, SUM(budget) sum_of_budgets
    FROM project_dept
     WHERE dept_name IN ('Accounting', 'Research')
     GROUP BY ROLLUP (dept_name, emp_cnt);
```

The result is

dept_name	emp_cnt	sum_of_budgets
Accounting	5	10000
Accounting	6	70000
Accounting	10	40000
Accounting	NULL	120000
Research	5	115000
Research	10	70000
Research	NULL	185000
NULL	NULL	305000

As you can see from the result of Example 24.11, the number of retrieved rows in this example is smaller than the number of displayed rows in the example with the CUBE operator. The reason is that the summary rows are displayed only for the first column in the GROUP BY clause.

NOTE

The syntax used in Example 24.11 is the standardized syntax that was introduced in SQL Server 2008. The old-style syntax for ROLLUP is similar to the syntax for CUBE, which is shown in Example 24.10.

GROUPING Function

As you already know, NULL is used in combination with CUBE and ROLLUP to specify the placeholder for the values in the unneeded columns. In such a case, it isn't possible to distinguish NULL in relation to CUBE and ROLLUP from the NULL value. Transact-SQL supports the standardized GROUPING function, which allows you to resolve the problem with the ambiguity of NULL. The GROUPING function returns 1 if the NULL in the result set is in relation to CUBE or ROLLUP, and 0 if it represents the group of NULL values.

Example 24.12 shows the use of the GROUPING function.

EXAMPLE 24.12

Using the GROUPING function, clarify which NULL values in the result of the following SELECT statement display summary rows:

```
USE sample;
SELECT dept_name, emp_cnt, SUM(budget) sum_b, GROUPING(emp_cnt) gr
       FROM project_dept
        WHERE dept_name IN ('Accounting', 'Marketing')
        GROUP BY ROLLUP (dept_name, emp_cnt);
```

The result is

dept_name	emp_cnt	sum_b	gr
Accounting	5	10000	0
Accounting	6	70000	0
Accounting	10	40000	0
Accounting	NULL	120000	1
Marketing	NULL	120000	0
Marketing	3	100000	0
Marketing	6	100000	0
Marketing	10	180000	0
Marketing	NULL	500000	1
NULL	NULL	620000	1

If you take a look at the grouping column (**gr**), you will see that some values are 0 and some are 1. The value 1 indicates that the corresponding NULL in the **emp_cnt** column specifies a summary value.

Grouping SETS Operator

Grouping sets are an extension to the GROUP BY clause that lets users define several groups in the same query. You use the GROUPING SETS operator to implement grouping sets. Example 24.13 shows the use of this operator.

EXAMPLE 24.13

Calculate the sum of budgets for the Accounting and Research departments using the combination of values of the **dept_name** and **emp_cnt** columns first, and after that using the values of the single column **dept_name**:

```
USE sample;
SELECT dept_name, emp_cnt, SUM(budget) sum_budgets
        FROM project_dept
        WHERE dept_name IN ('Accounting', 'Research')
        GROUP BY GROUPING SETS ((dept_name, emp_cnt),(dept_name));
```

The result is

dept_name	emp_cnt	sum_budgets
Accounting	5	10000
Accounting	6	70000
Accounting	10	40000
Accounting	NULL	120000
Research	5	115000
Research	10	70000
Research	NULL	185000

As you can see from the result set of Example 24.13, the query uses two different groupings to calculate the sum of budgets: first using the combination of values of the **dept_name** and **emp_cnt** columns, and second using the values of the single column **dept_name**.

You can use the series of grouping sets to replace the ROLLUP and CUBE operators. For instance, the following series of grouping sets

GROUP BY GROUPING SETS ((dept_name, emp_cnt), (dept_name), ())

is equivalent to the following ROLLUP clause:

GROUP BY ROLLUP (dept_name, emp_cnt)

Also,

GROUP BY GROUPING SETS ((dept_name, emp_cnt), (emp_cnt, dept_name), (dept_name), ())

is equivalent to the following CUBE clause:

GROUP BY CUBE (dept_name, emp_cnt)

OLAP Query Functions

Transact-SQL supports two groups of functions that are categorized as OLAP query functions:

▶ Ranking functions

▶ Statistical aggregate functions

The following subsections describe these functions.

> **NOTE**
>
> The GROUPING function, discussed previously, also belongs to the OLAP functions.

Ranking Functions

Ranking functions return a ranking value for each row in a partition group. Transact-SQL supports the following ranking functions:

▶ RANK

▶ DENSE_RANK

▶ ROW_COUNT

Example 24.14 shows the use of the RANK function.

EXAMPLE 24.14

Find all departments with a budget not greater than 30000, and display the result set in descending order:

```
USE sample;
SELECT RANK() OVER(ORDER BY budget DESC) AS rank_budget,
            dept_name, emp_cnt, budget
    FROM project_dept
    WHERE budget <= 30000;
```

The result is

rank_budget	dept_name	emp_cnt	budget
1	Accounting	6	30000
2	Accounting	5	10000

Example 24.14 uses the RANK function to return a number (in the first column of the result set) that specifies the rank of the row among all rows. The example uses the OVER clause to sort the result set by the **budget** column in the descending order. (In this example, the PARTITION BY clause is omitted. For this reason, the whole result set will belong to only one partition.)

NOTE

The RANK function uses logical aggregation. In other words, if two or more rows in a result set are tied (have a same value in the ordering column), they will have the same rank. The row with the subsequent ordering will have a rank that is one plus the number of ranks that precede the row. For this reason, the RANK function displays "gaps" if two or more rows have the same ranking.

Example 24.15 shows the use of the two other ranking functions, DENSE_RANK and ROW_NUMBER.

EXAMPLE 24.15

Find all departments with a budget not greater than 40000, and display the dense rank and the sequential number of each row in the result set:

```
USE sample;
SELECT DENSE_RANK() OVER( ORDER BY budget DESC ) AS rank_budget,
    ROW_NUMBER() OVER( ORDER BY budget DESC ) AS row_number,
    dept_name, emp_cnt, budget
  FROM project_dept
  WHERE budget <= 40000;
```

The result is

rank_budget	row_number	dept_name	emp_cnt	budget
1	1	Accounting	10	40000
1	2	Accounting	6	40000
2	3	Accounting	6	30000
3	4	Accounting	5	10000

The first two columns in the result set of Example 24.15 show the values for the DENSE_RANK and ROW_NUMBER functions, respectively. The output of the DENSE_RANK function is similar to the output of the RANK function (see Example 24.14). The only difference is that the DENSE_RANK function returns no "gaps" if two or more ranking values are equal and thus belong to the same ranking.

The use of the ROW_NUMBER function is obvious: it returns the sequential number of a row within a result set, starting at 1 for the first row.

In the last two examples, the OVER clause is used to determine the ordering of the result set. As you already know, this clause can be also used to divide the result set produced by the FROM clause into groups (partitions), and then to apply an aggregate or ranking function to each partition separately.

Example 24.16 shows how the RANK function can be applied to partitions.

EXAMPLE 24.16

Using the window construct, partition the rows of the **project_dept** table according to the values in the **date_month** column. Sort the rows in each partition and display them in ascending order.

```
USE sample;
SELECT date_month, dept_name, emp_cnt, budget,
    RANK() OVER( PARTITION BY date_month ORDER BY emp_cnt desc ) AS
rank
    FROM project_dept;
```

The result is

date_month	dept_name	emp_cnt	budget	rank
2007-01-01	Accounting	6	30000	1
2007-01-01	Research	5	50000	2
2007-02-01	Research	10	70000	1
2007-02-01	Accounting	10	40000	1
2007-07-01	Research	5	65000	1
2007-07-01	Accounting	5	10000	1
2008-01-01	Marketing	6	100000	1
2008-01-01	Marketing	NULL	120000	2
2008-02-01	Marketing	10	180000	1
2008-02-01	Accounting	6	40000	2
2008-07-01	Marketing	3	100000	1

The result set of Example 24.16 is divided (partitioned) into eight groups according to the values in the **date_month** column. After that the RANK function is applied to each partition. If you take a closer look and compare the previous example with Example 24.5, you will see that the last example works, while Example 24.5 displays an error, although both examples use the same window construct. As previously stated, Transact-SQL currently supports the OVER clause for aggregate functions only with the PARTITION BY clause, but in the case of ranking functions, the system supports general SQL standard syntax with the PARTITION BY and ORDER BY clauses.

Statistical Aggregate Functions

Chapter 6 introduced statistical aggregate functions. There are four of them:

▶ **VAR** Computes the variance of all the values listed in a column or expression.

▶ **VARP** Computes the variance for the population of all the values listed in a column or expression.

▶ **STDEV** Computes the standard deviation of all the values listed in a column or expression. (The standard deviation is computed as the square root of the corresponding variance.)

▶ **STDEVP** Computes the standard deviation for the population of all the values listed in a column or expression.

You can use statistical aggregate functions with or without or with the window construct. Example 24.17 shows how the functions VAR and STDEV can be used in relation to the window construct.

EXAMPLE 24.17

Using the window construct, calculate the variance and standard deviation of budgets in relation to partitions formed using the values of the **dept_name** column:

```
USE sample;
SELECT dept_name,  budget,
        VAR(budget) OVER(PARTITION BY dept_name) AS budget_var,
        STDEV(budget) OVER(PARTITION BY dept_name)  AS budget_stdev
         FROM project_dept
         WHERE dept_name in ('Accounting', 'Research');
```

The result is

dept_name	budget	budget_var	budget_stdev
Accounting	10000	200000000	14142.135623731
Accounting	40000	200000000	14142.135623731
Accounting	30000	200000000	14142.135623731
Accounting	40000	200000000	14142.135623731
Research	50000	108333333,333333	10408.3299973306
Research	70000	108333333,333333	10408.3299973306
Research	65000	108333333,333333	10408.3299973306

Example 24.17 uses the statistical aggregate functions VAR and STDEV to calculate the variance and standard deviation of budgets in relation to partitions formed using the values of the **dept_name** column.

Nonstandard Analytic Functions

SQL Server contains several OLAP functions that are not specified in the SQL standard. The following functions and operators belong to nonstandard SQL/OLAP:

▶ TOP

▶ NTILE

▶ PIVOT and UNPIVOT

The following sections describe these analytic functions and operators.

TOP Clause

The TOP clause specifies the first n rows of the query result that are to be retrieved. This clause should always be used with the ORDER BY clause, because the result of such a query is always well defined and can be used in table expressions. (A table expression specifies a sample of a grouped result table.) A query with TOP but without the ORDER BY clause is nondeterministic, meaning that multiple executions of the query with the same data must not always display the same result set.

Example 24.18 shows the use of this clause.

EXAMPLE 24.18

Retrieve the four projects with the highest budgets:

```
USE sample
SELECT TOP (4) dept_name, budget
  FROM project_dept
  ORDER BY budget DESC;
```

The result is

dept_name	budget
Marketing	180000
Marketing	120000
Marketing	100000
Marketing	100000

As you can see from Example 24.18, the TOP clause is part of the SELECT list and is written in front of all column names in the list.

NOTE

Beginning with SQL Server 2005, you should write the input value of TOP inside parentheses, because the system supports any self-contained expression as input.

The TOP clause is the nonstandard Transact-SQL implementation used to display the ranking of the top *n* rows from a table. The equivalent query to Example 24.18, which uses the window construct and the RANK function, is shown in Example 24.19.

EXAMPLE 24.19

Retrieve the four projects with the highest budgets:

```
USE sample;
SELECT dept_name, budget
    FROM (SELECT dept_name, budget,
            RANK() OVER (ORDER BY budget DESC) AS rank_budget
            FROM project_dept) part_dept
    WHERE rank_budget <= 4;
```

The TOP clause can also be used with the additional PERCENT option. In that case, the first *n* percent of rows are retrieved from the result set. The additional option

WITH TIES specifies that additional rows will be retrieved from the query result if they have the same value in the ORDER BY column(s) as the last row that belongs to the displayed set. Example 24.20 shows the use of the PERCENT and WITH TIES options.

EXAMPLE 24.20

Retrieve the top 25 percent of rows with the smallest number of employees:

```
USE sample;
SELECT TOP (25) PERCENT WITH TIES  emp_cnt, budget
  FROM project_dept
ORDER BY emp_cnt ASC;
```

The result is

emp_cnt	budget
NULL	120000
3	100000
5	50000
5	65000
5	10000

The result of Example 24.20 contains five rows, because there are three projects with five employees.

Beginning with SQL Server 2005, you can use the TOP clause with UPDATE, DELETE, and INSERT statements. Example 24.21 shows the use of this clause with the UPDATE statement.

EXAMPLE 24.21

Find the three projects with the highest budget amounts and reduce them by 10 percent:

```
USE sample
UPDATE TOP (3) project_dept
  SET budget = budget * 0.9
  WHERE budget in (SELECT TOP (3) budget
  FROM project_dept
  ORDER BY budget desc);
```

Example 24.22 shows the use of the TOP clause with the DELETE statement.

EXAMPLE 24.22

Delete the four projects with the smallest budget amounts:

```
USE sample
DELETE TOP (4)
  FROM project_dept
  WHERE budget IN
          (SELECT TOP (4) budget FROM project_dept
              ORDER BY budget ASC);
```

In Example 24.22, the TOP clause is used first in the subquery, to find the four projects with the smallest budget amounts, and then in the DELETE statement, to delete these projects.

NTILE Function

The NTILE function belongs to the ranking functions. It distributes the rows in a partition into a specified number of groups. For each row, the NTILE function returns the number of the group to which the row belongs. For this reason, this function is usually used to arrange rows into groups.

Example 24.23 shows the use of the NTILE function.

EXAMPLE 24.23

```
USE sample
SELECT dept_name, budget,
  CASE NTILE(3) OVER (ORDER BY budget ASC)
    WHEN 1 THEN 'Low'
    WHEN 2 THEN 'Medium'
    WHEN 3 THEN 'High'
  END AS groups
FROM project_dept;
```

The result is

dept_name	budget	groups
Accounting	10000	Low
Accounting	30000	Low
Accounting	40000	Low
Accounting	40000	Low
Research	50000	Medium

dept_name	budget	groups
Research	65000	Medium
Research	70000	Medium
Marketing	100000	Medium
Marketing	100000	High
Marketing	120000	High
Marketing	180000	High

PIVOT and UNPIVOT Operators

PIVOT and UNPIVOT are nonstandard relational operators that are supported by Transact-SQL. You can use them to manipulate a table-valued expression into another table. PIVOT transforms such an expression by turning the unique values from one column in the expression into multiple columns in the output, and it performs aggregations on any remaining column values that are desired in the final output.

Example 24.24 shows how PIVOT works.

EXAMPLE 24.24

```
USE sample;
SELECT *, month(date_month) as month, year(date_month) as year
 INTO project_dept_pivot
FROM project_dept;
GO
SELECT year, [1] as January, [2] as February, [7] July FROM
   (SELECT budget, year, month from project_dept_pivot) p2
   PIVOT (SUM(budget)  FOR month IN ([1],[2],[7])) AS P;
```

The result is

Year	January	February	July
2007	80000	11000	75000
2008	220000	200000	100000

The first part of Example 24.24 creates a new table, **project_dept_pivot**, which will be used to demonstrate how the PIVOT operator works. This table is identical to the table **project_dept** (introduced in Example 24.1), except for the two additional columns: **month** and **year**. The **year** column of the **project_dept_pivot** table contains the years 2007 and 2008, which appear in the **date_month** column of the **project_dept** table. Also, the **month** columns of the **project_dept_pivot** table (**january, february,** and **july**) contain the summaries of budgets corresponding to these months in the **project_dept** table.

The second SELECT statement contains an inner query, which is embedded in the FROM clause of the outer query. The PIVOT clause is part of the inner query. It starts with the specification of the aggregation function: SUM (of budgets). The second part specifies the pivot column (**month**) and the values from that column to be used as column headings (in Example 24.24, the first, second, and seventh months of the year). The value for a particular column in a row is calculated using the specified aggregate function over the rows that match the column heading.

NOTE

As you can see from Example 24.24, using all possible values of the pivot column is not required.

The UNPIVOT operator performs the reverse operation of PIVOT, by rotating columns into rows. Example 24.25 shows the use of this operator.

EXAMPLE 24.25

```
CREATE TABLE project_dept_pvt (year int, January float, February float, July float);
INSERT INTO project_dept_pvt VALUES (2007, 80000, 110000, 75000);
INSERT INTO project_dept_pvt VALUES (2008, 50000, 80000, 30000);
--UNPIVOT the table
SELECT year, month, budget
FROM
   (SELECT year, January, February, July
      FROM project_dept_pvt) p
         UNPIVOT (budget FOR month IN (January, February, July)
      )AS unpvt
```

The result is

year	month	budget
2007	January	80000
2007	February	110000
2007	July	75000
2008	January	50000
2008	February	80000
2008	July	30000

Example 24.25 uses the **project_dept_pvt** table to demonstrate the UNPIVOT relational operator. UNPIVOT's first input is the column name (**budget**), which holds the normalized values. After that, the FOR option is used to determine the target

column name (**month**). Finally, as part of the IN option, the selected values of the target column name are specified.

NOTE

UNPIVOT is not the exact reverse of PIVOT, because any NULL values in the table being transformed cannot be used as column values in the output.

Conclusion

SQL/OLAP extensions in Transact-SQL support data analysis facilities. There are four main parts of SQL/OLAP that are supported by SQL Server 2008:

▶ Window construct

▶ Extensions of the GROUP BY clause

▶ OLAP query functions

▶ Nonstandard analytic functions

The window construct is the most important extension. In combination with ranking and aggregate functions, it allows you to easily calculate analytic functions, such as cumulative and sliding aggregates, as well as rankings. There are three extensions to the GROUP BY clause that are described in the SQL standard and supported by SQL Server 2008: the CUBE, ROLLUP and GROUPING SETS operators.

The most important analytic query functions are ranking functions: RANK, DENSE_RANK, and ROW_NUMBER. Transact-SQL supports several nonstandard analytic functions and operators, such as TOP, NTILE, PIVOT, and UNPIVOT.

The next chapter describes Reporting Services, a business intelligence component of SQL Server.

Exercises

E.24.1

Find the average number of the employees in the Accounting department. Solve this problem:

    a. using the window construct

    b. using the GROUP BY clause

E.24.2

Using the window construct, find the department with the highest budget for the years 2007 and 2008.

E.24.3

Find the sum of employees according to the combination of values in the departments and budget amounts. All possible summary rows should be displayed, too.

E.24.4

Solve E.24.3 using the ROLLUP operator. What is the difference between this result set and the result set of E.24.3?

E.24.5

Using the RANK function, find the three departments with the highest number of employees.

E.24.6

Solve E.24.5 using the TOP clause.

E.24.7

Calculate the ranking of all departments for the year 2008 according to the number of employees. Display the values for the DENSE_RANK and ROW_NUMBER functions, too.

Chapter 25

Microsoft Reporting Services

This chapter describes the SQL Server enterprise reporting tool called Reporting Services. The first part of the chapter discusses the general structure of a report and explains the main components of Reporting Services. After that, you'll see how you can create reports by using the Report Server Project Wizard. The processing of a report is then explained. Finally, different ways to deliver a designed and deployed report are shown.

Introduction to Microsoft Reporting Services

Before you learn about the components of Reporting Services, you should understand the structure of reports. Each report has the following two instruction sets, which together specify the content of the report:

▶ **Data definition**   Specifies data sources and a dataset. A *dataset* is the information retrieved from data sources. The content of the dataset is defined using Query Designer, a tool that builds a query used in your report to select data.

▶ **Report layout**   Enables you to present selected data to the user. You can specify which column values correspond to which fields and the form and location of headings and page numbers.

When the information concerning data definition and report layout is gathered, Reporting Services stores it using the Report Definition Language (RDL). RDL is an XML-based language that is used exclusively for storing report definitions. RDL is an open schema language, meaning that developers can extend the language with additional attributes and elements.

Reporting Services includes three main components, which represent an application layer, a server layer, and a metadata layer, respectively:

▶ Report Manager
▶ Report Server
▶ Report Catalog

The following sections describe these components.

Report Manager

Report Manager is a web-based report access and management tool that runs using Internet Explorer. You can use this tool to create, secure, and maintain the hierarchy of items of a single report server instance. As a report server administrator, you use Report Manager to configure site properties and defaults and to create shared schedules and shared data sources, which makes schedules and data source connections more manageable. You can also use Report Manager to configure role-based security.

Report Server

Report Server is the main component of Reporting Services. It is implemented as a web service as well as a Windows service. The web service comprises a set of interfaces that client applications can use to access reports over a web server. The Windows service provides scheduling and delivery services. Both services work together and constitute a single report server instance.

As you can see from Figure 25-1, Report Server includes several components:

▶ Report processor

▶ Data providers

▶ Renderers

▶ Request handler

The report processor manages the execution of a report. It retrieves the definition of the report, which is done in RDL, and determines what is needed for the report. Also, the report processor manages the work of other components that are used to produce a report.

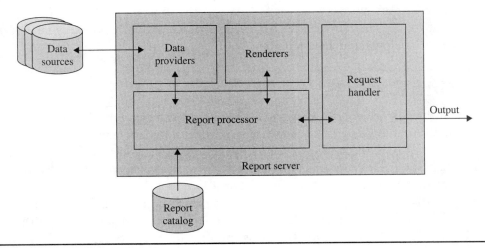

Figure 25-1   *Components of Report Server*

The report processor also retrieves the data that is used to load the dataset. After that, it selects a data provider that knows how to get information out of the data source. The task of the data provider is to connect to the data source, get the information for the report, and return it to the processor.

When data providers deliver the data for the report, the report processor can begin to process the report's layout. To generate the layout, the processor has to know the format of the report (HTML or PDF, for instance). The renderers are used to build the corresponding format.

The request handler receives requests for reports and sends them to the report processor. It also delivers the completed report. (The different forms of report delivery will be discussed later in the chapter.)

Report Catalog

Report Catalog contains two databases which are used to store the definitions of all existing reports that belong to a particular Report Server. The stored information includes report names, descriptions, data source connection information, credential information, parameters, and execution properties. Report Catalog also stores security settings and information concerning scheduling and delivering data.

Reporting Services uses two databases, the Report Server database and the Report Server temporary database, to separate persistent data storage from temporary storage requirements. The databases are created together and bound by name. By default, the database names are **reportserver** and **reportservertempdb**. The former is used to store Report Catalog, while the latter is used as temporary storage. (The Report Server temporary database is used to store session data, cached reports, and work tables that are generated by the report.)

Now that you are familiar with the components of Reporting Services, you will learn how to create, deploy, and deliver reports.

Creating Reports

You use Business Intelligence Development Studio to create a report. BI Development Studio, introduced in Chapter 23, is the integrated development environment built on Visual Studio and designed for the BI system developer. To start BI Development Studio, click **Start, All Programs, Microsoft SQL Server 2008**, and choose **SQL Server Business Intelligence Development Studio**.

The first step in building a report is to create a new project to which the report should belong. To build a project, click **File**, select **New**, and choose **Project**. In the **New Project** dialog box, select the **Business Intelligence Projects** folder in the **Project**

types pane. Type the name of the project and its location in the **Name** and **Location** text boxes, respectively. The project in this example is called **Report1**, as you can see in Figure 25-2.

In the **Templates** pane of the **New Project** dialog box (see Figure 25-2), you will see three project templates related to reports. The Report Server Project template creates an empty report and leaves you alone to do the rest of the work. The Report Server Project Wizard guides you during the creation phase of a new report. The Report Model Project template creates a data model for use with Report Builder.

NOTE

Generally, Reporting Services reports are built using either Report Builder or Report Designer. Report Builder allows you to do ad hoc reporting, without knowing anything about database structure and a creation of queries using query languages, such as SQL. Report Designer lets you build a report from scratch. It offers many more features for creating reports than Report Builder offers.

In this section, you will use the Report Server Project Wizard template to see how to create a report. Therefore, select the **Report Server Project Wizard** icon and click **OK**.

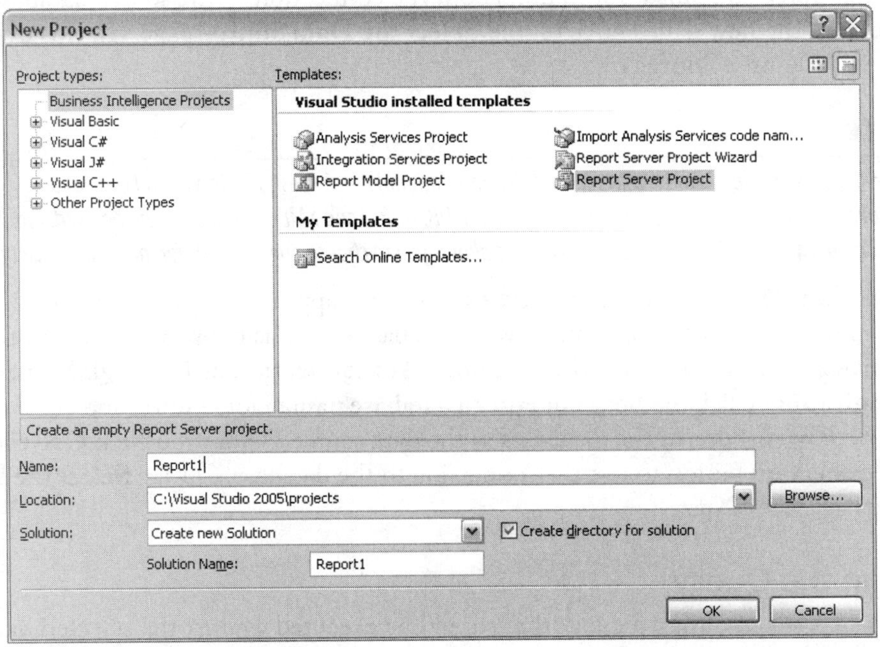

Figure 25-2   *The New Project dialog box*

Creating Reports with the Report Server Project Wizard

The Report Server Project Wizard welcome page introduces the steps it takes you through to create a report:

▶ Select the data source

▶ Design the query

▶ Select the report type

▶ Design the data in the table

▶ Specify the report layout

▶ Specify the report style

The following sections describe these steps as well as how to preview the created report.

Select the Data Source

The data source contains information about the connection to the source database. Type the name of the new data source on the **Select the Data Source** page. (In this example, call the data source **Source1**.)

NOTE

*Reporting Services can create reports from different relational databases (SQL Server and Oracle) or multidimensional databases (Analysis Services). OLE DB, ODBC, and XML data sources can be used, too. The **Type** drop-down list on the **Select Data Source** page allows you to choose one of the different data source types.*

Click **Edit**. The **Connection Properties** dialog box appears, as shown in Figure 25-3. Type either **localhost** or the name of your database server as the server name. In the same dialog box, choose either **Use Windows Authentication** or **Use SQL Server Authentication**. Click the **Select or enter a database name** radio button and choose from the drop-down list one of the databases as the data source. Before you click **OK**, click the **Test Connection** button to test the connection to the database. On the **Select the Data Source** page, click **Next**.

Design the Query

The next step is to design a query that should be executed against the selected data source. On the **Design the Query** page, you can either type (or paste) an existing query or use the Query Builder component to create a query from scratch.

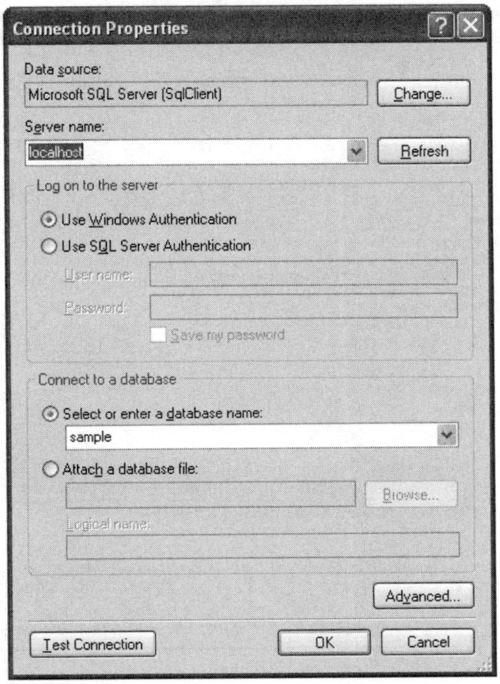

Figure 25-3 *The Connection Properties dialog box*

NOTE

Query Builder corresponds to the similar Access component that you can use to design queries without knowledge of the SQL language. This component is generally known as QBE (query by example).

For this first report, use the query given in Example 25.1.

EXAMPLE 25.1

```
SELECT dept_name, emp_lname, emp_fname, job, enter_date
    FROM department d JOIN employee e ON d.dept_no = e.dept_no
            JOIN works_on w ON w.emp_no = e.emp_no
    WHERE YEAR(enter_date) = 2007
    ORDER BY dept_name
```

The query in Example 25.1 selects data for employees who entered their job in 2007. The result set of the query is then sorted by department names. After that, click **Next**.

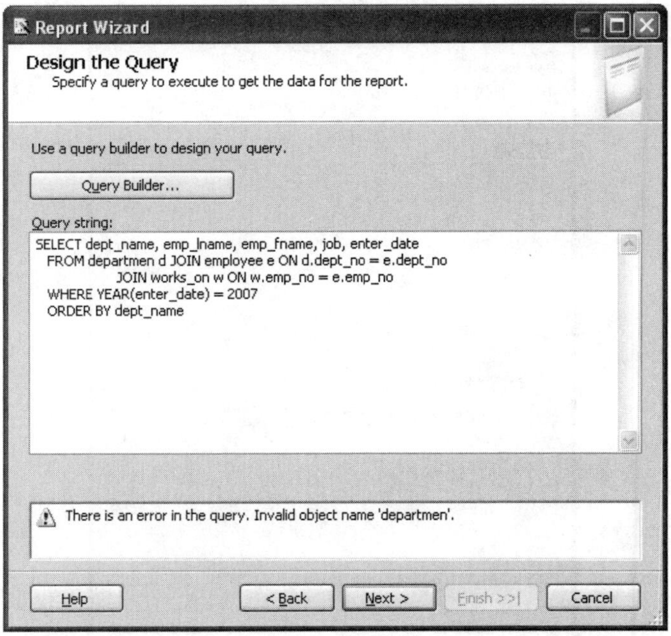

Figure 25-4   *The Design the Query page with an error message*

NOTE

Reporting Services checks the names of the tables and columns listed in the query. If the system finds any syntax or semantic errors, it displays the corresponding message in the lower part of the window (see Figure 25-4).

Select the Report Type

The next step in creating a report is to select the report type. You can choose between two report types:

▶ **Tabular**   Creates a report in tabular form. Columns of the table correspond to the columns from the SELECT list, while the number of rows in the table depends on the result set of the query.

▶ **Matrix**   Creates a report in matrix form, which is similar to table form but provides functionality of crosstabs. Unlike the tabular report type, which has a static set of columns, the matrix report type can be dynamic.

NOTE

You should use the matrix report type whenever you want to create queries that contain aggregate functions, such as AVG or SUM.

The query in Example 25.1 does not contain any aggregate functions. Therefore, choose the tabular report type.

Design the Data in the Table

After you click **Next**, the **Design the Table** page appears. This page allows you to decide where selected columns will be placed in your report. The **Design the Table** page contains two groups of fields:

▶ Available fields

▶ Displayed fields

The **Design the Table** page also has three views:

▶ Page

▶ Group

▶ Details

Available fields are the columns from the SELECT list of your query. Each column can be moved to one of the views. To move a field to the Page, Group, or Details view, select the field and then click the **Page**, **Group**, or **Details** button, respectively. A *displayed field* is an available field that is assigned to one of the existing views.

Page view lists all columns that appear at the page level, and Group view lists columns that are used to group the resulting set of the query. Details view is used to display columns that appear in the detail section of the table. Figure 25-5 shows the **Design the Table** page with the design of the tabular representation for the resulting set. In this example, the **dept_name** column will appear at the page level, while the **job** column will be used to group the selected rows. When you have chosen how to group the data in the table, click **Next**.

NOTE

The order of the columns can be important, especially for Group view. To change the order of the columns, select a column and click the up or down button to the right.

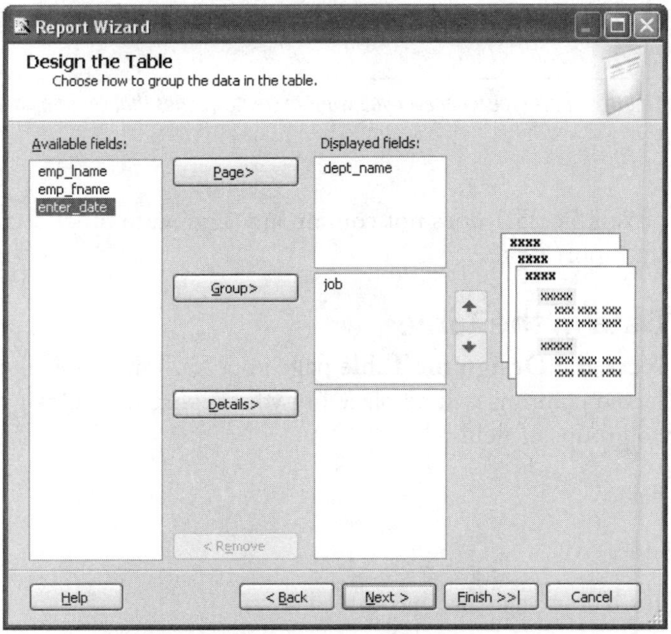

Figure 25-5   *The Design the Table page*

Specify the Report Layout

The next step is to specify the layout of your report. The **Choose the Table Layout** page has several options:

- ▶ Stepped
- ▶ Block
- ▶ Include subtotals
- ▶ Enable drilldown

If you choose **Stepped**, the report will contain one column for each field, with grouping fields appearing in headers to the left of columns from the detail field. In this case, the group footer will not be created. If you include subtotals with this layout type, the subtotal is placed in the group header rows.

The **Block** option creates a report that contains one column for each field, with group fields appearing in the first detail row for each group. This layout type has group footers only if the **Include subtotals** option is activated.

The **Enable drilldown** option hides the inner groups of the report and enables a visibility toggle. (You can choose **Enable drilldown** only if you select the **Stepped** option.) To continue, choose **Stepped** and **Include subtotals** and click **Next**.

Choose the Report Style

The next step is to choose a style for your report. The **Choose the Table Style** page allows you to select a template to apply styles such as font, color, and border style to the report. There are several different style templates, such as **Forest**, **Corporate**, and **Bold**. Chose **Bold** and click **Next**.

After choosing a report style, there is still one intermediate step if you are creating a report for the first time. In this step called Choose the Deployment location, you must choose the URL of the virtual directory of the report server and the deployment folder for your reports. For a report server running in native mode, use the path to the report server where the project is deployed, for example http://servername/ReportServer. For a report server running in Sharepoint integrated mode, use the URL of the Sharepoint site to which the project is deployed, for example http://servername.

NOTE

SQL Server 2008 Reporting Services support two modes of deployment for report server instances: native mode and Sharepoint integrated mode. In native mode, which is default, a report server is a stand-alone application server that provides all viewing, management, processing, and delivery of reports. In Sharepoint integrated mode, a report server becomes part of a SharePoint Web application deployment. Users of SharePoint Server can store reports in SharePoint libraries and access them from the same SharePoint sites they use to access other business documents.

Finally, you complete the wizard's work by providing a name for the report. Also, you can take a look at the report summary, where all your previous steps during the creation of the report are documented. Click **Finish** to finish the wizard.

Preview the Result Set

When you finish the creation of your report using the wizard, there are three tabs in the **Report Designer** pane that you can use to view the created report in different forms. (If the Report Designer pane isn't visible, click **View** and select **Designer**.) The tabs correspond to the following views:

► Layout
► Data
► Preview

The **Layout** tab allows you to view and modify the layout of your report. The **Layout** view consists of the following sections: body, page, header, and page footer. You can use the **Toolbox** and **Properties** windows to manipulate items in the report. To view these windows, select **Toolbox** or **Properties Window** in the **View** menu. Use the **Toolbox** window to select items to place them in one of the sections. Each item on the report design surface contains properties that can be managed using the **Properties** window.

Click the **Data** tab to view the query. You can use this view to display the query in two different forms: using the generic query designer or using the graphical query designer. The generic query designer consists of a toolbar and two panes: the **Query** pane shows the query you use to create the report, while the **Result** pane shows the result set of the query. The graphical query designer consists of a toolbar and four panes: the **Diagram** pane shows all tables that are used in the query, with corresponding referential constraints; the **Grid** pane uses the QBE component to display the query in tabular form; the **SQL** pane displays the SELECT statement; and the **Result** pane shows the result set of the statement.

To preview the report, click the **Preview** tab. The report runs automatically, using already specified properties. Figure 25-6 shows the preview for the report that was defined in the previous steps.

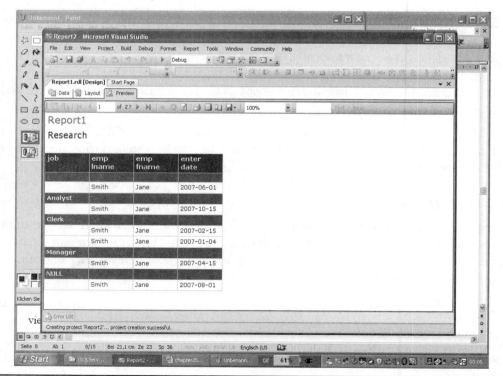

Figure 25-6   *The preview of the report*

Creating Parameterized Reports

A parameterized report is one that uses input parameters to complete report processing. The parameters are then used to execute a query that selects specific data for the report. If you design or deploy a parameterized report, you need to understand how parameter selections affect the report.

Parameters in Reporting Services are usually used to filter data. They are specified using the known syntax for variables (**@year**, for instance). If a parameter is specified in a query, a value must be provided to complete the SELECT statement or stored procedure that retrieves data for a report.

You can define a default value for a parameter. If all parameters have default values, the report will immediately display data when the report is executed. If at least one parameter does not have a default value, the report will display data after the user enters all parameter values.

When the report is run in a browser, the parameter is displayed in a box at the top of the report. When the report is run in the **Preview** mode, the value of the parameter is displayed in the corresponding box.

An example will be used to show you how to create a parameterized report. This example describes only those steps that are different from the steps already discussed in relation to Example 25.1. The query used in this example, shown in Example 25.2, selects data from the **AdventureWorksDW** database. For this reason, you have to select and define a new data source. The specification of the new source is identical to the specification of the source called **Source1**, except that you choose the **AdventureWorksDW** database instead of the **sample** database.

EXAMPLE 25.2

```
USE AdventureWorksDW;
SELECT t.MonthNumberOfYear AS month,
    t.CalendarYear      AS year,
    p.ProductKey        AS product_id,
    SUM(f.UnitPrice)    AS sum_of_sales,
    COUNT(f.UnitPrice)  AS total_sales
    FROM DimTime t, DimProduct p, FactInternetSales f
    WHERE t.TimeKey    = f.OrderDateKey AND
        p.ProductKey = f.ProductKey
        AND CalendarYear = @year
    GROUP BY t.CalendarYear, t.MonthNumberOfYear,  p.ProductKey
    ORDER BY 1;
```

The query in Example 25.2 calculates the number and the sum of unit product prices. It also groups the rows according to the list of column names in the GROUP BY clause. The expression

CalendarYear = @year

in the WHERE clause of the example specifies that the input parameter **@year** in this query is related to the calendar year for which you want to query data.

This report is a matrix type report. Values of the **year** column will be assigned to the **Page** view, values of the **month** column to the **Columns** view, and values of the **product_id** column to the **Rows** view. The **Detail** view displays the aggregate values SUM and COUNT.

To start the report in **Preview** mode, type the value of the **CalendarYear** parameter (2003, for instance) and click **ViewReport**.

Processing and Managing Reports

Report processing begins with a published report definition, which includes a query, layout information, and code. Report and data processing together create a dataset with layout information, which is stored as an intermediate format. After processing is complete, reports are compiled as a CLR assembly and executed on the report server.

The intermediate report format is used by the report server for the following report forms:

- ▶ Cached report
- ▶ Report snapshot

Caching means that a report is generated only for the first user who opens it, and thereafter is retrieved from the cache for all subsequent users who work with the same report. As you probably guessed, caching shortens the time to retrieve frequently accessed reports.

A report snapshot is one that contains data captured at a specific point in time. The main difference between a report snapshot and other reports is that other reports generally contain query information, while the snapshot report contains the result set of the executed query.

NOTE

A report snapshot is generally used if a report is based on a long-running query.

Generally, you use Report Manager to manage reports. Report Manager is a web-based report access and management tool that runs in Microsoft Internet Explorer or another browser. The following management functions, among others, can be performed using Report Manager:

▶ View or replace report definitions

▶ Manage data source connections

▶ View and configure report history

The description of all management functions provided by Report Manager can be found in Books Online.

Accessing and Delivering Reports

Before you can use or distribute a report, you have to deploy it. This can be done by right-clicking the created report and selecting **Deploy**. The deployment process contains several steps, which are shown in the **Output** pane:

```
------ Build started: Project: R1, Configuration: Debug ------
Build complete -- 0 errors, 0 warnings
------ Deploy started: Project: R1, Configuration: Debug ------
Deploying to http://localhost/ReportServer
Deploying data source '/R1/sample'.
Deploying report '/R1/Report1'.
Deploy complete -- 0 errors, 0 warnings
========== Build: 1 succeeded or up-to-date, 0 failed, 0 skipped ==========
========== Deploy: 1 succeeded, 0 failed, 0 skipped ==========
```

Reports can be accessed and delivered using two methods:

▶ On demand

▶ Subscription based

The following sections describe these two methods.

On-Demand Reports

On-demand access allows users to select the reports from a report-viewing tool. You can use Report Manager or a browser to view a report. This section explains how you can view on-demand reports using a browser.

Reporting Services is a web application. For this reason, all reports are organized in a hierarchical namespace and accessed through virtual directories in Report Server. Hence, within the browser, navigate to the home page for SQL Server Reporting Services (http://localhost/reportserver), which is the default virtual directory for Report Server. The default virtual directory for Report Manager is **http://localhost/Reports/**. (Both default values can be modified.)

To view a report on demand, select the report from the corresponding folder hierarchy. In this case, Report Server creates a temporary snapshot for the purpose of delivering the report. The snapshot is discarded after delivery.

There are several possibilities for running reports on demand. The first one is to specify that a report queries a corresponding data source each time a user runs the report. In this case, a new instance of the report is generated each time a new user executes the report.

If you want to enhance performance, cached reports should be your choice. As already stated, the system creates a cached copy of the report for the first user who opens it. All other users who work with the same report retrieve it from the cache.

Report Subscription

On-demand reporting requires report selection each time you want to view a report's result. On the other hand, subscription-based access automatically generates and delivers reports to a destination.

Reporting Services supports two kinds of subscriptions:

▶ Personal (standard) subscriptions

▶ Data-driven subscriptions

Personal Subscriptions

A personal subscription usually consists of specific parameters for parameterized reports as well as report presentation options and delivery options. You can use different tools to make personal subscriptions. As an example, here's how you can use SQL Server Management Studio to create a file share subscription:

1. In Object Explorer, expand the report to which you want to subscribe. To do this, you first have to connect to **Reporting Services**. Click the **Connect** button and select **Reporting Services**. Expand the corresponding instance, expand the folder where the report is stored, and expand the report.

2. Right-click the **Subscriptions** folder and click **New Subscription**.

3. Select **Report Server File Share** from the **Notify by** list box.

4. Type a filename for the report in the **File name** text box.

5. In the **Path** text box, type the path of the folder that contains the report.

6. Select a format and a mode from the **Render format** and **Write mode** list boxes, respectively.

7. Type a username and password in the corresponding text boxes.

NOTE

---

*The creation of an e-mail subscription with SQL Server Management Studio is similar, except for the following steps: from the **Notify by** list box, select **Report Server E-Mail**, and in the **To** text box, type the e-mail address.*

Data-Driven Subscriptions

A data-driven subscription delivers reports to a list of recipients determined at run time. This type of subscription differs from a personal subscription in the way it gets subscription information: some settings from a data source are provided at run time, and other settings are provided from the subscription definition. Static aspects of a data-driven subscription include the report that is delivered, the delivery extension, connection information to an external data source that contains subscriber data, and a query. Dynamic settings of the subscription are obtained from the row set produced by the query, including a subscriber list and user-specific delivery extension preferences or parameter values.

Conclusion

Reporting Services is the SQL Server–based enterprise reporting tool. To create a report, you can use the Report Server Project Wizard, Report Builder, or Report Designer. The definition of a report, which comprises the corresponding query, layout information, and code, is stored using the XML-based Report Definition Language (RDL). Reporting Services process the report definition into one of the standard formats, such as HTML or PDF.

Reports can be accessed on demand or delivered based on a subscription. When you execute a report on demand, a new instance of the report will usually be generated each time you run the report. Subscription-based reports can be either standard (personal) or data driven. Reports based on a personal subscription usually consist of specific parameters as well as report presentation options and delivery options. A data-driven subscription delivers reports to a list of recipients determined at run time.

The next chapter describes optimization techniques for business intelligence.

Exercises

E.25.1

Get the employee numbers and names for all clerks. Create a report in the matrix report type using this query. Use Report Manager to view a report.

E.25.2

Use the **sample** database and get the budgets of projects and project names being worked on by employees in the Research department that have an employee number < 25000. Create a report in the table report type using this query. Use a browser to view the report.

Chapter 26

Optimizing Techniques for Business Intelligence

In This Chapter

- ▶ Data Partitioning
- ▶ Star Schema Query Optimization

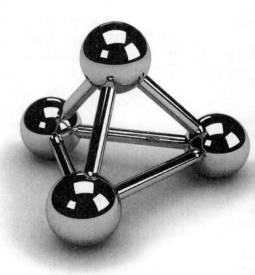

This chapter describes two optimizing techniques in relation to ROLAP. In other words, these techniques can be applied only to relational storage of multidimensional data. The first part of this chapter discusses when it is reasonable to store all entity instances in a single table and when it is better, because of performance reasons, to partition the table's data. After a general introduction, the ways how to partition data will be given. Besides guidelines for partitioning, this section describes the improvements in SQL Server 2008 concerning this technique.

In the second part of this chapter, the technique called star schema query optimization will be explained in detail. The advantages of the technique, as well as use of bitmap filters, will be given.

Data Partitioning

The easiest and most natural way to design an entity is to use a single table. Also, if all instances of an entity belong to a table, you don't need to decide where to store its rows physically, because the database system does this for you. For this reason there is no need for you to do any administrative tasks concerning storage of table data, if you don't want to.

On the other hand, one of the most frequent causes of poor performance in relational database systems is contention for data that resides on a single I/O device. This is especially true if you have one or more very large tables with several hundred thousands, or millions of rows. In that case, on a system with multiple CPUs, partitioning the table can lead to better performance through parallel operations.

Using data partitioning you can divide very large tables (and indices, too) into smaller parts that are easier to manage. If the partitioning is done, many operations can be done in parallel, such as loading data, backup and recovery, and query processing.

Partitioning also improves the availability of the entire table. By placing each partition on its own disk, you can still access data, even if one or more disks are unavailable. In that case all data in the available partitions can be used for read and write operations. The same is true for maintenance operations.

If a table is partitioned, the query optimizer can recognize when the search condition in a query references only rows in certain partitions and therefore limits its search to those partitions. That way, you can achieve significant performance gains.

Ways to Partition Your Data

A table can be partitioned using any column of the table. Such a column is called the *partition key*. (It is also possible to use a group of columns for the particular partition key.) The values of the partition key are used to partition table rows to different filegroups.

Beside partition key, there are two other important notions in relation to partitioning: partition scheme and partition function. The partition scheme maps the table rows to one or more filegroups. The way this mapping is done is described using the partitioning function. In other words, the partition function defines the algorithm that is used to direct the rows to their physical location.

Database Engine supports only one form of partitioning, which is range partitioning. *Range partitioning* divides table rows into different partitions based on the value of the partition key. Hence, by applying range partitioning you will always know in which partition a particular row will be stored.

NOTE

Besides range partitioning, there are several other partition forms. One of them is called hash partitioning. In contrast to range partitioning, hash partitioning places rows one after another in partitions by applying a hashing function to the partition key. This partition form is not supported by Database Engine.

Before we define range partitioning, we will look at the steps for creating partitioned tables.

Steps for Creating Partitioned Tables

Before you start to partition database tables, you have to complete the following steps:

► Set partition goals

► Determine partitioning key and number of partitions

► Create a filegroup for each partition

► Create partition function and partition scheme

► Create partitioned indices (if necessary)

All of these steps will be explained in the following sections.

Set Partition Goals

Partition goals depend on the type of applications that access the table that should be partitioned. There are many different goals, and each of them could be a single reason to partition a table:

► Improved performance for individual queries

► Reduced contention

► Improved data availability

If the primary goal of table partitioning is improved performance for individual queries, distribute all table rows evenly. The reason is that the database system doesn't have to wait for data retrieval from a partition that has more rows than other partitions. Also, if such queries access data by performing table scan against significant portions of a table, partition the table rows only. (The partition of the corresponding index will just make the overhead in such a case.)

Data partitioning can reduce contention when many simultaneous queries perform index scan to return just a few rows from a table. In this case, partition the table and index with a partition scheme that allows each query to eliminate unneeded partitions from its scan. To reach this goal, start by investigating which queries access which parts of the table. Then partition table rows so that different queries access different partitions.

Partitioning improves the availability of the database. By placing each partition on its own filegroup and locating each filegroup on its own disk, you can increase the data availability, because if one disk fails and is no longer accessible, only the data in that partition is unavailable. While the system administrator services the corrupted disk, other users can continue to access data from the other partitions of the table.

Determine Partitioning Key and Number of Partitions

A table can be partitioned using any table column. The values of the partition key are used to partition table rows to different filegroups. For the best performance, each partition should be stored in a separate filegroup, and each filegroup should be stored on one separate disk device. By spreading the data across several disk devices, you can balance the I/O and improve query performance, availability, and maintenance.

You should partition the data of a table using a column that does not frequently change. If the partitioning is done by a column that changes often, any update operation of that column can force the system to move the modified rows from one partition to the other, and this could be time consuming.

Create a Filegroup for Each Partition

To achieve better performance, higher data availability, and easier maintenance, you will use different filegroups to separate table data. The number of filegroups depends mostly on the hardware you have. When you have multiple CPUs, partition your data so that each CPU can access data on one disk device. If Database Engine can process multiple partitions in parallel, the processing time of your application will be significantly reduced.

Each data partition must map to a filegroup. To create a filegroup you use either the CREATE DATABASE or ALTER DATABASE statement. The following example shows the creation of a database called **test_partitioned** with one primary filegroup and two other filegroups.

NOTE

Before you create the test_partitioned database you have to change the physical addresses of all .mdf and .ndf files in Example 26.1 according to the file system you have on your computer.

EXAMPLE 26.1

```
USE master;
CREATE DATABASE test_partitioned
ON PRIMARY
  ( NAME='MyDB_Primary',
    FILENAME=
       'd:\mssql\PT_Test_Partitioned_Range_df.mdf',
    SIZE=2000,
    MAXSIZE=5000,
    FILEGROWTH=1 ),
FILEGROUP MyDB_FG1
  ( NAME = 'FirstFileGroup',
    FILENAME =
       'd:\mssql\MyDB_FG1.ndf',
    SIZE = 1000MB,
    MAXSIZE=2500,
    FILEGROWTH=1 ),
FILEGROUP MyDB_FG2
  ( NAME = 'SecondFileGroup',
    FILENAME =
       'f:\mssql\MyDB_FG2.ndf',
    SIZE = 1000MB,
    MAXSIZE=2500,
    FILEGROWTH=1 );
```

In Example 26.1 we create a database called **test_partitioned**, which contains a primary filegroup **MyDB_Primary** and two other filegroups: **MyDB_FG1** and **MyDB_FG2**. The **MyDB_FG1** filegroup is stored on the D drive, while the **MyDB_FG2** filegroup is stored on the F drive.

In case you want to add filegroups to an existing database, use the ALTER DATABASE statement. Example 26.2 shows how to create another filegroup for the **test_partitioned** database.

EXAMPLE 26.2

```
USE master;
ALTER DATABASE test_partitioned
  ADD FILEGROUP MyDB_FG3
GO
ALTER DATABASE test_partitioned
ADD FILE
  ( NAME = 'ThirdFileGroup',
  FILENAME =
    'G:\mssql\MyDB_FG3.ndf',
  SIZE = 1000MB,
  MAXSIZE=2500,
  FILEGROWTH=1)
TO FILEGROUP MyDB_FG3;
```

In Example 26.2 we use the ALTER DATABASE statement to create an additional filegroup called **MyDB_FG3**. With the second ALTER DATABASE statement we add a new file to the created filegroup. Notice that the TO FILEGROUP option specifies the name of the filegroup to which the new file will be added.

Create Partition Function and Partition Scheme

The next step after creating filegroups is to create the partition function. The partition function is created with the CREATE PARTITION FUNCTION statement. There are two forms of this statement, depending on the partitioning type. The syntax of the CREATE PARTITION FUNCTION concerning this range partitioning type is as follows:

```
CREATE PARTITION FUNCTION function_name(param_type)
  AS RANGE [ LEFT | RIGHT ]
    FOR VALUES ( [ boundary_value [ ,...n ] ] )
```

function_name defines the name of the partition function, while **param_type** specifies the data type of the partition key. **boundary_value** specifies one or more boundary values for each partition of a partitioned table or index that uses the partition function.

The CREATE PARTITION FUNCTION supports two forms of the RANGE option—RANGE LEFT and RANGE RIGHT. RANGE LEFT determines that the boundary condition is the upper boundary in the first partition. According to this, RANGE RIGHT specifies that the boundary condition is the lower boundary in the last partition. If not specified, RANGE LEFT is the default.

Before the partition function can be defined, you have to specify the table that will be used for partitioning. In this chapter's examples the **orders** table will be used. The following example creates the table. (Check first, whether your **sample** database already contains the **orders** table. If so, please drop it.)

EXAMPLE 26.3

```
USE sample;
CREATE TABLE orders
  (orderid INTEGER NOT NULL,
   orderdate DATE,
   shippeddate DATE,
   freight money);

GO
declare @i int , @order_id integer
        declare @orderdate datetime
        declare @shipped_date datetime
        declare @freight money
        set @i = 1
        set @orderdate = getdate()
        set @shipped_date = getdate()
        set @freight = 100.00
        while @i < 1000001
        begin
        insert into orders (orderid, orderdate, shippeddate, freight)
          values( @i, @orderdate, @shipped_date, @freight)
        set @i = @i+1
        end
```

The CREATE TABLE statement in Example 26.3 creates the **orders** table, while the subsequent batch loads one million rows in that table.

The following example shows the definition of the partition function for the **orders** table with 1000000 rows.

EXAMPLE 26.4

```
USE test_partitioned;
CREATE PARTITION FUNCTION myRangePF1 (int)
  AS RANGE LEFT FOR VALUES (500000) ;
```

The CREATE PARTITION FUNCTION **myRangePF1** specifies that there will be two partitions and that the boundary value is 500000. This means that all values of the partition key that are smaller than 500000 will be placed in the first partition, while all values greater than 500000 will be stored in the second partition. (Note that the boundary value is related to the values in the partition key, which in our example is the column **orderid** of the **orders** table. As you will see, we specify the name of the partition key in the corresponding CREATE TABLE statement.)

The created partition function is useless if we don't associate it with specific filegroups. This process is called partition scheme, and you use the CREATE PARTITION SCHEME statement to specify the association between a partition scheme and the corresponding filegroups. The following example shows the creation of the partition scheme for the partition function in Example 26.4.

EXAMPLE 26.5

```
USE test_partitioned;
CREATE PARTITION SCHEME myRangePS1
    AS PARTITION myRangePF1
    TO (MyDB_FG1, MyDB_FG2);
```

Example 26.5 creates the partition scheme called **myRangePS1**. According to this scheme all values to the left of the boundary value (i.e., all values < 500000) will be stored in the **MyDB_FG1** filegroup. Also, all values to the right of the boundary value will be stored in the **MyDB_FG2** filegroup.

NOTE

When you define a partition scheme, you must be sure to specify a filegroup for each partition, even if multiple partitions will be stored on the same filegroup.

The creation of a partitioned table is slightly different from the creation of a nonpartitioned one. As you might guess, the CREATE TABLE statement must contain the name of the partition scheme and the name of the table column, which will be used as partition key. The following example shows the enhanced form of the CREATE TABLE statement, which is used to define partitioning of the **orders** table.

EXAMPLE 26.6

```
USE test_partitioned;
CREATE TABLE orders
  (orderid INTEGER NOT NULL,
   orderdate DATETIME,
```

```
   shippeddate DATETIME,
   freight money)
ON myRangePS1 (orderid);
```

The ON clause at the end of the CREATE TABLE statement is used to specify the already-defined partition scheme (see Example 26.5). Using this scheme, the specified partition schema ties together the column of the table (**orderid**) with the partitioning function where the data type (int) of the partition key is specified (see Example 26.4).

Creation of Partitioned Index

When you partition table data, the indices that are associated with that table can be partitioned, too. You can partition table indices using the existing partition schema for that table or a different one. When both the indices and the table use the same partitioning function and the same partitioning columns (in the same order), the table and index are said to be aligned. When a table and its indices are aligned, the database system can move partitions in and out of partitioned tables very effectively, because the partitioning of both database objects is done with the same algorithm. For this reason, in the most practical cases it is recommended that you use aligned indices.

The following example shows the creation of a clustered index for the **orders** table. This index is aligned, i.e., it is partitioned using the partition scheme of the **orders** table.

EXAMPLE 26.7

```
USE test_partitioned;
CREATE UNIQUE CLUSTERED INDEX CI_orders
 ON orders(orderid)
 ON myRangePS1(orderid);
```

As you can see from Example 26.7, the creation of the partitioned index for the **orders** table is done using the enhanced form of the CREATE INDEX statement. This form of the CREATE INDEX statement contains an additional ON clause that specifies the partitioning scheme. If you want to align the index with the table, specify the same partition scheme as for the corresponding table. (The first ON clause is the part of the standard syntax of the CREATE INDEX statement and specifies the column for partitioning.)

Collocating Tables

Besides partitioning of a table together with the corresponding indices, Database Engine also supports the partitioning of two tables using the same partition function. This partition form means that rows of both tables that have the same value for the partitioning key are stored together on a specific location. This concept of data partitioning is called collocation.

Suppose that, besides the **orders** table, there is also the **order_details** table, which contains zero, one, or more rows with orders for each unique order number in the **orders** table. If you partition both the tables using the same partition function on the join columns **orders.orderid** and **order_details.orderid**, the rows of both tables with the same value for the **orderid** columns will be stored together on the disk. Suppose that there is a unique order with the identification number 49031 in the **orders** table and 5 corresponding rows in the **order_details** table. In the case of collocation, all six rows will be stored side by side on the disk. (The same procedure will be applied to all rows of these tables with the same value for the **orderid** column.)

SQL Server 2008 and Data Partitioning

SQL Server 2008 has the following improvements in relation to data partitioning:

▶ Performance benefits for many parallel query plans by changing how seek operations are executed

▶ Parallel execution for queries on partitioned tables using multiple threads

▶ Improved editing of information concerning partitioned tables

The following sections discuss these features.

New Partition-Aware Seek Operation

In SQL Server 2008, the internal representation of a partitioned table is changed so that the table appears to the query processor as a composite (multicolumn) index with the partitioned column as the leading column. (This column, called **partitionedID**, is a hidden computed column used internally to represent the ID of the partition containing a specific row.)

For example, suppose there is the **tab** table with three columns **col1**, **col2** and **col3**. (**col1** is used to partition the table, while the **col2** column has a clustered index.) In SQL Server 2008, such a table is treated internally as a non-partitioned table with the following schema:

tab (partitionID, col1, col2 col3)

and with a clustered index on the following composite key (partitioned, col2). This allows the query optimizer to perform seek operations based on the computed column **partitionID** on any partitioned table or index.

That way, the performance of a significant number of queries on partition tables can be improved because the partition elimination is done earlier.

Parallel Execution for Queries

In SQL Server 2005, one thread is allocated per partition when multiple partitions are queried. In other words, each query, which is used over partitioned tables cannot be parallelized. (For definition of parallel queries, see Chapter 15.) This can cause performance problems on systems with many CPUs, if the table schema has less partitions than there are CPUs. In that case not all the CPUs will be used to process the query.

SQL Server 2008 provides two query execution strategies for parallel query plans on partitioned objects: a single-thread-per-partition strategy and a multiple-thread-per-partition strategy.

In the single-thread-per-partition strategy, the query optimizer assigns one thread per partition to execute a parallel query plan that accesses multiple partitions. (This corresponds to the behavior in SQL Server 2005 and is the default in SQL Server 2008.) One partition is not shared between multiple threads, but multiple partitions can be processed in parallel.

The multiple-threads-per-partition strategy assigns multiple threads per partition regardless of the number of partitions to be accessed. In other words, all available threads start at the first partition to be accessed and scan forward. As each thread reaches the end of the partition, it moves to the next partition and begins scanning forward. The thread does not wait for the other threads to finish before moving to the next partition.

NOTE
The multiple-threads-per-partition strategy is enabled by using trace flag 2440. (Trace flags are used to temporarily set specific server characteristics or to switch off a particular behavior.) To set a trace flag, use the DBCC command with the TRACEON option. The following command enables the trace flag 2440: DBCC TRACEON (2440).

Which strategy to choose depends on your environment. The former strategy is recommended if queries are I/O-bound and include more partitions than the degree of parallelism. The latter strategy is recommended in the following cases:

► Partitions are striped evenly across many disks.

► Your queries use fewer partitions than the number of available threads.

► Partition sizes differ significantly within a single table.

Enhancements Concerning Partition Information

SQL Server 2008 provides the following enhanced partitioning information:

▶ An optional attribute called **Partitioned**, which indicates that an operator (seek, scan, insert, update or delete), is performed on a partitioned table.

▶ Enhanced information concerning the **partitionID** computed column.

▶ Summary information that provides a total count of the partitions accessed.

Guidelines for Partitioning Tables and Indices

The following suggestions are guidelines for partitioning tables and indices:

▶ Do not partition every table. Partition only those tables that are accessed most frequently.

▶ Think about partitioning a table if it is a huge one, i.e., if it contains at least several hundred thousands of rows.

▶ For best performance, use partitioned indices to reduce contention between sessions.

▶ Balance the number of partitions with the number of processors on your system. If it is not possible for you to establish the 1:1 relationship between the number of partitions and the number of processors, specify the number of partitions as a multiple factor of the number of processors.

▶ Do not partition the data of a table by a column that changes frequently. If the partitioning is done by a column that changes often, any update operation of that column can force the system to move the modified rows from one partition to another, and this could be very time consuming.

▶ For optimal performance, partition the tables to increase parallelism, but do not partition their indices. Place the indices in a separate filegroup.

Star Schema Query Optimization

As you already know from Chapter 22, the star and snowflake schemas are two general forms for structuring data in a data warehouse. Both the schemas have usually one fact table, which is connected with several dimension tables. The fact table can have 100 million rows or more, while dimension tables contain up to several million rows. Generally, in decision support queries, several dimension tables are joined with the corresponding fact table. Significant performance gains can be achieved, if the query optimizer can recognize such queries and apply special techniques to it. The use of these techniques by the query optimizer are generally called star schema query optimization.

> **NOTE**
> *Although star schema query optimization was supported by SQL Server 2005 the main enhancements are implemented in SQL Server 2008.*

Let us use an example to explain how star schema query optimization works.

EXAMPLE 26.8

```
USE AdventureWorksDW;
SELECT ProductAlternateKey
    FROM FactInternetSales f JOIN DimTime t ON f.OrderDateKey = t.TimeKey
JOIN DimProduct d ON d.ProductKey = f.ProductKey
WHERE CalendarYear BETWEEN 2003 AND 2004
AND ProductAlternateKey LIKE 'BK%'
GROUP BY ProductAlternateKey, CalendarYear;
```

> **NOTE**
> *Example 26.8 shows just a general form of a query, where star schema query optimization can be applied. (It is not said that the query optimizer will apply this mechanism to the query above.)*

The example above is a query based upon one of the star schemas of the **AdventureWorksDW** database. The query optimizer of SQL Server 2008 detects the star schema and identifies the fact table (**FactInternetSales**) and the corresponding dimension tables (**DimTime** and **DimProduct**). If the result sets of corresponding join operations between the fact table and each dimension table contain small or medium number of rows, the query optimizer applies so called bitmap filters to apply semi-join operation early on the query. (For the definition of semi-join, see Chapter 6.)

> **NOTE**
> *Do not mix bitmap filters with bitmap indices! Bitmap filters are an in-memory structure that is used for enhancing performance during the execution of a query. (Bitmap indices are persistent structures, which are used in BI as an alternative to B+-tree structures. SQL Server doesn't support bitmap indices.)*

The primary role of the bitmap filter is to speed up parallel plans by doing semi-join reduction, before rows are passed through the operator concerning parallel execution. (Bitmap filters are not used in serial plans.)

NOTE

Bitmap filters can be used with two processing techniques for join: Hash joins and Merge joins.

SQL Server 2008 supports the following enhancements in relation to bitmap filters:

▶ New query plans exist in relation to bitmap filters

▶ Query optimizer can dynamically change the position of bitmap filters

▶ Support of multiple bitmap filters

▶ Query optimizer decides, when and how to apply bitmap filters

Bitmap filters are visible in the XML form of the execution plan (see Chapter 20). In this case the XML attributes **PhysicalOP** and **LogicalOP** contains the values "Bitmap" and "Bitmap Create", respectively. (See Chapter 27 for the definition of XML attributes.)

In contrast to SQL Server 2005, the query optimizer of SQL Server 2008 can dynamically change the position of a bitmap filter. (Performance advantages can be achieved, if bitmap filters are pushed deeper into query tree.) Also, several bitmap filters can now be applied for a query.

Query optimizer's decisions in relation to join optimization cannot be influenced by users. In other words, there is no system procedure (or known trace flag), which can be used to deactivate (or reactivate) this feature.

NOTE

The decision of Microsoft to deliver star schema query optimization without the possibility for users to deactivate it, has its advantages and disadvantages. The main advantage is that the given solution does not enhance the complexity of the system. On the other hand, users should have the alternative to deactivate it for a query, which does not benefit from this feature.

Conclusion

Database Engine supports range partitioning of data and indices, which is entirely transparent to the application. Range partitioning partitions rows based on the value of the partition key. In other words, the data is divided using the values of the partition key.

If you want to partition your data, you must complete the following steps:

▶ Create a filegroup for each partition

▶ Create partition function and partition scheme

▶ Create partitioned indices (if necessary)

Using different filegroups to separate table data, you achieve better performance, higher data availability, and easier maintenance.

The partition function is used to map the rows of a table or index into partitions based on the values of a specified column. To create a partition function, use the CREATE PARTITION FUNCTION statement. To associate a partition function with specific filegroups, use partition scheme. When you partition table data, the indices that are associated with that table can be partitioned, too. You can partition table indices using the existing partition schema for that table or a different one.

Star schema query optimization is an index based optimization technique, which supports the optimal use of indices on the huge fact tables. The main advantages of this technique are the following:

▶ Significant performance improvements in case of high selective and medium selective star schema queries

▶ No additional storage cost. (The system does not create any new indices, but uses bitmap filters instead.)

This chapter is the last chapter of the book's part concerning business intelligence. The next chapter starts the last part of the book and gives you an introduction to XML.

Part V

Beyond Relational Data

Chapter 27

Overview of XML

In This Chapter

- ▶ World Wide Web
- ▶ XML-Related Languages
- ▶ XML—Basic Concepts

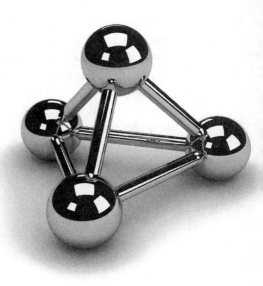

This chapter introduces the Extensible Markup Language (XML), which has become more and more important as a data storage format. The chapter first describes the World Wide Web. It then introduces the existing markup languages and the position of XML as a markup language. The chapter also explains the basic concepts of XML, such as elements, attributes, and namespaces. The end of the chapter discusses the document type definition (DTD) language and the XML Schema language.

World Wide Web

The World Wide Web has been gaining enormous importance as a medium, because it is used for many activities. The Web comprises of the most Internet services (under the same user interface) and is therefore the most powerful Internet service of all. Generally, the Web has four parts:

▶ Web server

▶ Web browser

▶ HTML (Hypertext Markup Language)

▶ HTTP (Hypertext Transfer Protocol)

The web server sends pages (usually HTML pages) to the network. A web browser receives the pages and displays them on the computer screen. (Microsoft Internet Explorer is an example of a web browser.)

You use HTML to create documents for the Web. This language allows you to format data that is shown using a web browser. The simplicity of HTML is one of the reasons that the Web has gained such importance. However, HTML has one main disadvantage: it can tell you only how the data should look. In other words, the language does not allow you to gain any meaning out of the data.

HTML documents are text files that contain tags, and each tag is written in angle brackets. The most important tags are hyperlinks. You use hyperlinks to reference documents that are managed by a web server. Those references build the network that spans the whole Internet. For this reason, it is called the "World Wide Web."

HTTP is a protocol that "connects" a web browser with a web server and sends the available pages from the former to the latter. If the pages contain another hyperlink, the protocol is used to connect to that web server, using the given address.

XML-Related Languages

XML is a language that is used for the digital representation of documents. This language is related to two other languages:

▶ SGML

▶ HTML

Standard General Markup Language (SGML) is a very powerful markup language that is used for the interchange of large and complex documents. (A markup language specifies special signs that are used either for formatting documents or to represent the logical structure of documents. LaTEX is an example of a formatting markup language.) SGML is used in many areas where there is a necessity for complex documents, such as airplane maintenance. As you will read in just a moment, XML is SGML lite—that is, it is a simplified subset of SGML that is primarily used for the Web.

HTML is the most important markup language used for the Web. Each HTML document is an SGML document with a fixed document type definition (DTD). (Fixed document types are described in the next section.) Therefore, HTML is just an instance of SGML.

HTML has two important features:

▶ It is used only to format a document.

▶ It is not an extensible language.

HTML is a markup language that you can use to describe how the data should look. (On the other hand, this language offers more than a simple formatted language such as LaTEX, because its elements are generalized and descriptive.)

HTML only uses a fixed number of elements. For this reason, you cannot use HTML suitably for particular document types.

XML—Basic Concepts

XML is an HTML-like language that is used for data exchange. In contrast to HTML, which has a fixed number of tags and where each tag has its own meaning, the repertoire of tags in XML is not set in advance, and semantic meaning is not set for any XML tag.

Example 27.1 helps to clarify these and other properties of XML. But before you look at the different parts of an XML document, consider the requirements of a well-formed XML document:

- ▶ It has a root element.

- ▶ Every opening tag is followed by a matching closing tag.

- ▶ The elements of the document are properly nested.

- ▶ An attribute must have a value, which is quoted.

EXAMPLE 27.1

```xml
<?xml version="1.0" encoding="UTF-8"?>
<PersonList Type="Employee">
   <Title> Value="Employee List"></Title>
   <Contents>
      <Employee>
         <Name>Ann Jones</Name>
         <No>10102</No>
         <Deptno>d3</Deptno>
         <Address>
            <City>Dallas</City>
            <Street>Main St</Street>
         </Address>
      </Employee>
      <Employee>
         <Name>John Barrimore</Name>
         <No>18316</No>
         <Deptno>d1</Deptno>
         <Address>
            <City>Seattle</City>
            <Street>Abbey Rd</Street>
         </Address>
      </Employee>
   </Contents>
</PersonList>
```

An XML document, as shown in Example 27.1, contains generally three parts:

▶ An optional first line that tells the program that receives the document, the version of XML it is dealing with (version 1.0 in Example 27.1)

▶ An optional schema (usually written using DTD or XSD; see the section "Document Type Definitions" later in this chapter)

▶ A root element—the element that contains all other elements

You use XML to digitally represent documents. To represent a document, you have to know its structure. For instance, if you consider a book as a document, it can first be broken into chapters (with titles). Each chapter comprises several sections (with their titles and corresponding figures), and each section has one or more paragraphs.

All parts of an XML document that belong to its logical structure are called *elements*. Therefore, in XML, each element represents a component of a document. In Example 27.1, **PersonList**, **Title**, and **Contents** are examples of XML elements. Also, each element can contain other elements. (The parts of an element that do not belong to the logical structure of a document are called character data. For instance, words or sentences in a book can be treated as character data.)

All elements of a document build a hierarchy of elements that is called the tree structure of the document. Each structure has an element on the top level that contains all other elements. This element is called the root element. All elements that do not contain any subelements are called leaves.

NOTE

In contrast to HTML, where valid tags are determined by the language specification, tag names in XML are chosen by the programmer.

The XML elements directly nested within other elements are called children. For instance, in Example 27.1, **Name**, **No**, and **Address** are children of **Employee**, which is a child of **Contents**, which is again a child of the root element **PersonList**. (The relationships **ancestor** and **descendant** are also defined in the XML language.)

Each element can have extra information that is attached to it. Such information is called an *attribute*, and it describes the element's properties. Attributes are used together with elements to represent objects (that is, document types). In the tag

```
<PersonList Type="Employee">
```

Type is the name of an attribute that belongs to the element **PersonList**, and **Employee** is the attribute value. The following section describes attributes in detail.

XML Attributes

Attributes are used to represent data. On the other hand, elements can also be used for the same purpose. For this reason, it is plausible to ask whether we need attributes at all, because almost everything you can do using attributes is possible to do with elements (and subelements). However, the following tasks can be accomplished only with attributes:

▶ Define a unique value

▶ Enforce a limited kind of referential constraint

NOTE

There is no general rule for how you should define data. The best rule of thumb is to use an attribute when a property of an element is general, and to use subelements for a specific property of an element.

An attribute can be specified to be an ID type attribute. The value of the ID attribute must be unique within the XML document. Therefore, the ID attribute is always used to define a unique value.

An attribute of type IDREF must refer to a valid ID declared in the same document. In other words, the value of the IDREF attribute must occur in the document as a value of the corresponding ID attribute.

An attribute of type IDREFS specifies a list of strings, separated by blanks, that are referenced by the values of the ID attribute. For instance, the following line shows the XML fragment of an IDREFS attribute:

```
<Department Members="10102 18316"/>
```

(This example assumes that the attribute No of the **Employee** element is the ID attribute, while the attribute **Members** of the **Department** element is of the type IDREFS.)

The pairs ID/IDREF and ID/IDREFS correspond to primary key/foreign key relationships in the database, with a few differences. In the XML document, the values of different ID type attributes must be distinct. For instance, if you have **CustomerID** and **SalesOrderID** attributes in an XML document, these values must be distinct.

NOTE

The types mentioned above (ID, IDREF, and IDREFS) are part of the document type definitions (DTDs), discussed later in this chapter.

XML Namespaces

When using XML, you build a vocabulary of terms that is appropriate for the domain in which you model your data. In this situation, different vocabularies for different domains can cause naming conflicts when you want to mix the domains together in an XML document. (This is usually the case when you want to integrate information obtained from different domains.) This problem can be solved using XML namespaces.

Generally, the name of every XML tag must be written in the form **namespace:name**, where **namespace** specifies an XML namespace and **name** is an XML tag.

A namespace is always represented by a worldwide unique URI (*uniform resource identifier*), which is usually a URL but can be an abstract identifier, too.

Example 27.2 shows the use of two namespaces.

EXAMPLE 27.2

```
<Faculty xmlns="http://www.fh-rosenheim.de/informatik"
        xmlns:lib="http:// www.fh-rosenheim.de/library">
    <Name>Book</Name>
    <Feature>
    <lib:Title>Introduction to Database Systems</lib:Title>
    <lib:Author>A. Finkelstein</lib:Author>
    </Feature>
</Faculty>
```

Namespaces are defined using the **xmlns** attribute. Example 27.2 specifies two namespaces. The first one is the *default namespace*, because it is specified only with the **xmlns** keyword. This namespace is the shorthand for the namespace http://www.fh-rosenheim.de/informatik. The second namespace is specified in the form **xmlns:lib**. The prefix **lib** serves as the shorthand for http://www.fh-rosenheim.de/library.

Tags belonging to the latter namespace should be prefixed with **lib:** Tags without any prefix belong to the default namespace. (In Example 27.2, two tags belong to the second namespace: **Title** and **Author**.)

Document Type Definitions

In contrast to HTML, which contains a set of fixed rules that you must follow when you create an HTML document, XML does not have such rules, because this language is intended for many different application areas. Hence, XML includes a language that is used to specify the document structure.

A set of rules for structuring an XML document is called a document type definition (DTD). A DTD can be specified as a part of the XML document, or the XML document can contain a uniform resource locator (URL) indicating where the DTD is stored. A document that conforms to the associated DTD is called a valid document.

NOTE

XML does not require that documents have corresponding DTDs, but it requires that documents be well formed.

Example 27.3 shows the DTD for the XML document in Example 27.1.

EXAMPLE 27.3

```
<?xml version="1.0" encoding="UTF-8"?>
<!DOCTYPE PersonList SYSTEM "C:\tmp\Unbenannt4.dtd">
<!ELEMENT EmployeeList (Title, Contents)>
<!ELEMENT Title EMPTY>
<!ELEMENT Contents (Employee*)>
<!ELEMENT Employee (Name, No, Deptno, Address)>
<!ELEMENT Name (Fname, Lname)>
<!ELEMENT Fname (#PCDATA)>
<!ELEMENT Lname (#PCDATA)>
<!ELEMENT No (#PCDATA)>
<!ELEMENT Deptno (#PCDATA)>
<!ELEMENT Address (City, Street) >
 <!ELEMENT City (#PCDATA)>
<!ELEMENT Street (#PCDATA)>
<!ATTLIST EmployeeList  Type CDATA #IMPLIED
            Date CDATA #IMPLIED>
 <!ATTLIST Title Value CDATA  #REQUIRED>
```

There are several common DTD components: a name (**EmployeeList** in Example 27.3) and a set of ELEMENT and ATTLIST statements. The name of a DTD must conform to the tag name of the root element of the XML document (see Example 27.1) that uses the DTD for validation.

Element type declarations must start with the ELEMENT statement, followed by the name of the element type being defined. (Every element in a valid XML document must conform to an element type declared in the DTD.) In Example 27.3, the first ELEMENT statement specifies that the element **EmployeeList** consists of **Title** and **Contents** elements, in that order. The **Title** element does not contain any subelements.

The * sign in the definition of the **Contents** element indicates that there are zero or more elements of the **Employee** type. The elements **Fname, Lname, No, Deptno, City,** and **Street** are declared to be alphanumerical—that is, of type #PCDATA.

NOTE

Elements can hold simple or complex types. In Example 27.3, **Address** *represents a complex type and* **City** *a simple type.*

Attributes are declared for specific element types using the ATTLIST statement. This means that each attribute declaration starts with the string <!ATTLIST. Immediately after that comes the attribute's name and its data type. In Example 27.3, the **EmployeeList** element is allowed to have the attributes **Type** and **Date**, while the **Title** element can only have the **Value** attribute. (All other elements do not have attributes.)

The #IMPLIED keyword specifies that the corresponding attribute is optional, while the #REQUIRED keyword determines the mandatory form of the attribute.

NOTE

Attributes can hold only simple data types.

Besides the definition of a document's structure, formatting a document can be an important issue for those of you who do not want the web browser, such as Microsoft Internet Explorer, to control the form of the document. For this task, XML supports another language called Extensible Stylesheet Language (XSL), which allows you to describe how the data of your document should be formatted or displayed.

NOTE

The style of a document is described as a separate unit. For this reason, each document without this additional unit will use the default formatting of the web browser.

XML Schema

XML Schema, or XML Schema Definition language (XSD), is a DDL for XML documents. It defines a standard set of base types that are supported as types in XML. XML Schema contains many advanced features and is therefore significantly more complex than the DTDs.

> **NOTE**
>
> *XML Schema is discussed only briefly in this book because of its complexity. (See also Chapter 28 for a discussion of XML Schema support in SQL Server.)*

The main features of XML Schema are the following:

▶ It uses the same syntax as that used for XML documents. (For this reason, schemas are themselves well-formed XML documents.)

▶ It is integrated with the namespace mechanism. (Although there can be more than one schema definition document for a namespace, a schema definition document defines type in only one namespace.)

▶ It provides a set of base types, the same way SQL provides CHAR, INTEGER, and other standard data types.

▶ It supports primary/foreign key integrity constraints.

Conclusion

XML is a data representation format based on SGML, and it is used more and more as a data storage format. An XML document contains several tags that are chosen by the person who implements the document. All parts of an XML document that belong to its logical structure are called elements. Elements can hold simple or complex data types. Each element can have extra information that is attached to it. Such information is called an attribute. Attributes can hold only simple data types.

A DTD is a set of rules that structure an XML document. An XML document that conforms to the associated DTD is called a valid document. Instead of DTDs, you can use XSD to validate an XML document. XSD comprises data definition statements for XML, in much the same way that the DDL (see Chapter 1), contains data definition statements for SQL.

The next chapter discusses XML in relation to the SQL Server system.

Chapter 28

SQL Server and XML

In This Chapter

- ▶ **Methods of Storing XML Documents in Relational Databases**
- ▶ **Storing XML Documents in SQL Server**
- ▶ **Retrieving Stored XML Documents and Fragments**
- ▶ **Presenting Relational Data as XML Documents**
- ▶ **SQL Server XQuery Methods**

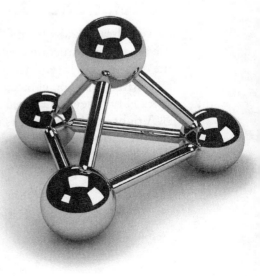

T his chapter discusses in detail three general topics that are important when XML and relational database systems are put together:

- ▶ Storing XML documents in relational databases
- ▶ Retrieving stored XML documents
- ▶ Presenting relational data in XML form

The first part of the chapter discusses the different ways in which XML documents can be stored in relational databases. The most important storage form, using the XML data type, is introduced after that. The retrieval of stored XML documents using system stored procedures and the standard INSERT statement is shown in the next part of the chapter. The other problem, the presentation of relational data in XML, is shown too. The end of the chapter briefly explains the XQuery language and the existing SQL Server XQuery methods.

NOTE

In this chapter, "XML" has two meanings. First, this term specifies the language, Extended Markup Language. Second, the same term is used to specify the XML data type in SQL Server. To keep the distinction clear, this chapter uses the term "XML" to specify the language and uses the phrase "XML data type" to specify the data type. (Also, "XML column" means a column of the XML data type.)

Methods of Storing XML Documents in Relational Databases

As you already know from Chapter 1, the relational data model is the best model to use if you have structured data with the corresponding schema. On the other hand, if the data you use is semistructured, you have to know how to model the data. In that case, XML is a good choice, because it is a platform-independent model, which ensures portability of semistructured data.

A tight relationship exists between relational database systems and XML documents, because the goal of modern database systems is to store any kind of data. There are three general techniques for storing XML documents in relational databases:

- ▶ As "raw" documents
- ▶ Decomposed into relational columns
- ▶ Using native storage

If you store an XML document as a large object (LOB), an exact copy of the data is stored. In this case, XML documents are stored "raw"—that is, in their character string form. The raw form allows you to insert documents very easily. The retrieval of such a document is very efficient if you retrieve the entire document.

To decompose an XML document into separate columns of one or more tables, you can use annotated XSD. (The XML Schema Definition language, described briefly in the previous chapter, defines a set of standard data types that are supported in XML documents.) In this case, the hierarchical structure of the document is preserved, while order among elements is ignored. (As you already know, the relational model does not support ordering of columns in a table, whereas elements of an XML documents are ordered.) Storing XML documents in decomposed form makes it much easier to index an element if it is placed in its own column.

> **NOTE**
>
> *The decomposition process of an XML document into separate columns is also known as "shredding."*

Native storage means that XML documents are stored in their parsed form. In other words, the document is stored in an internal representation (Infoset, for instance) that preserves the XML content of the data. (Infoset, or *XML Information Set*, is a World Wide Web Consortium [W3C; www.w3.org] specification that provides a set for use in other specifications that need to refer to the information in an XML document.)

Using native storage makes it easy to query information based on the structure of the XML document. On the other hand, reconstructing the original form of the XML document is difficult, because the created content may not be an exact copy of the document. (The detailed information about the significant white spaces, order of attributes, and namespace prefixes in XML documents is generally not retained.)

With this general introduction of storage models in mind, the following section describes how SQL Server supports these techniques.

Storing XML Documents in SQL Server

SQL Server supports all three general techniques for storing XML documents discussed in the previous section:

▶ **Raw documents**   SQL Server uses the VARCHAR(MAX) and VARBINARY(MAX) data types to store XML documents as raw documents. (This approach won't be discussed further in this book because of its complexity.)

NOTE

The implementation of XML in SQL Server (called SQLXML) is not part of SQL Server 2008. SQLXML is offered by Microsoft as a separate product.

▶ **Decomposition** SQL Server can decompose XML documents into separate columns of tables by using the **sp_xml_preparedocument** system procedure. This procedure parses the given document and represents its nodes as a tree. (The output tree can then be stored in columns of relational tables using the standard INSERT statement and the OpenXML function.)

▶ **Native storage** The XML data type enables you to store XML documents in the native way in a database managed by Database Engine. (Database systems, such as Database Engine, that store XML documents in a completely parsed form are called native XML database systems.)

The following sections discuss in detail the last two techniques. Because the use of the XML data type is the most important storage form, it is discussed first.

Storing XML Documents Using the XML Data Type

The XML data type is the base data type in Transact-SQL, meaning you can use the XML data type in the same way you use the standard data types, such as INTEGER or CHARACTER. On the other hand, the XML data type has some limitations, because an XML column cannot be declared using the UNIQUE, PRIMARY KEY, or FOREIGN KEY clauses.

Generally, you can use the XML data type to declare the following:

▶ Table columns
▶ Variables
▶ Input or output parameters (in stored procedures and user-defined functions)

NOTE

The following text describes the use of the XML data type to declare a table column. The use of this type to declare variables or parameters is similar.

Example 28.1 shows the use of the XML data type to declare a column of a table.

EXAMPLE 28.1

USE sample;
CREATE TABLE xmltab (id INTEGER NOT NULL PRIMARY KEY,
                xml_column XML);

The CREATE TABLE statement in Example 28.1 creates a table with two columns: **id** and **xml_column**. The **id** column is used to identify uniquely each row of the table. **xml_column** is an XML column that will be used in the following examples to show how XML documents can be stored, indexed, and retrieved.

As previously stated, XML documents can be stored in a native way in a column of the XML data type. Example 28.2 shows the use of the INSERT statement to store such a document.

EXAMPLE 28.2

```
USE sample;
INSERT INTO xmltab VALUES (1,
'<?xml version="1.0"?>
<PersonList Type="Employee">
    <Title> Value="Employee List"></Title>
    <Contents>
        <Employee>
            <Name>Ann Jones</Name>
            <No>10102</No>
            <Deptno>d3</Deptno>
            <Address>
                <City>Dallas</City>
                <Street>Main St</Street>
            </Address>
        </Employee>
        <Employee>
            <Name>John Barrimore</Name>
            <No>18316</No>
            <Deptno>d1</Deptno>
            <Address>
                <City>Seattle</City>
                <Street>Abbey Rd</Street>
            </Address>
        </Employee>
    </Contents>
</PersonList>');
```

The INSERT statement in Example 28.2 inserts two values: the value of the identifier and an XML document. (The inserted XML document is the same document used in the previous chapter; see Example 27.1.) Before the XML document is stored, it will be parsed using the XML parser, which checks its syntax. Actually, the parser checks whether or not the particular XML document is well formed. For instance, if you omit the last row of the XML document (</PersonList>), the XML parser displays the following error message:

```
Msg 9400, Level 16, State 1, Line 3
XML parsing: line 24, character 0, unexpected end of input
```

If you use the SELECT statement to see the content of the **xmltab** table, SQL Server Management Studio uses the XML editor to display XML documents. (To display the entire document in the editor, click the corresponding value in the result set.)

Indexing an XML Column

Database Engine stores XML values internally as binary large objects. Without an index, these objects are decomposed at run time to evaluate a query, which can be time-consuming. Therefore, the reason for indexing XML columns is to improve query performance.

NOTE

If you want to create any kind of XML indices, the corresponding table must include the explicit definition of the primary key.

The system supports a primary XML index and three types of secondary XML indices. The primary XML index indexes all tags, values, and paths within the XML instances of an XML column. Queries use the primary XML index to return scalar values or XML subtrees.

Example 28.3 creates a primary XML index.

EXAMPLE 28.3

```
USE sample;
GO
CREATE PRIMARY XML INDEX i_xmlcolumn ON xmltab(xml_column);
```

As you can see from Example 28.3, the creation of a primary XML index is similar to the creation of a "normal" index described in Chapter 10. A primary XML index uses an XML instance to generate the corresponding relational internal form out of it. That way, the repeated run-time generation of the internal form for queries and updates is omitted.

To further improve search performance, you can create secondary XML indices. A primary XML index must exist before secondary indices can be built. You can create three types of XML secondary indices using different keywords:

- ▶ **FOR PATH**   Creates a secondary XML index over the document structure
- ▶ **FOR VALUE**   Creates a secondary XML index over the element and attribute values of the XML column
- ▶ **FOR PROPERTY**   Creates a secondary XML index that searches for a property

The following list gives you some guidelines for creating secondary XML indices:

- ▶ If your queries use path expressions significantly on XML columns, the PATH index is likely to speed them up. The most common case is the use of the exist() method on XML columns in the WHERE clause of the Transact-SQL language. (The exist() method is discussed later in this chapter.)

- ▶ If your queries retrieve multiple values from individual XML instances by using path expressions, the use of the PROPERTY index may be helpful.

- ▶ If your queries involve retrieval of values within XML instances without knowing the element or attribute names that contain those values, you may want to create the VALUE index.

Example 28.4 shows the use of the FOR PATH keyword. (The syntax for creating all other secondary XML indices is analogous.)

EXAMPLE 28.4

```
USE sample;
GO
CREATE  XML INDEX i_xmlcolumn_path ON xmltab(xml_column)
    USING XML INDEX i_xmlcolumn FOR PATH;
```

Example 28.4 shows the creation of the secondary XML index with the FOR PATH keyword. You must specify the USING clause if you want to define any secondary XML index.

XML indices have some limitations in relation to "normal" indices:

- ▶ XML indices cannot be composite indices.
- ▶ There are no clustered XML indices.

NOTE

The reason for creating XML indices is different from the reason for creating convenient indices. XML indices enhance the performance of XQuery queries, while convenient indices enhance the performance of SQL queries.

SQL Server also supports the corresponding ALTER INDEX and DROP INDEX statements. The ALTER INDEX statement allows you to change the structure of an existing XML index, while the DROP INDEX statement deletes such an index.

There is also a catalog view for XML indices, called **sys.xml_indexes**. This view returns one row per each XML index. The most important columns of the view are **using_xml_index_id** and **secondary_type**. The former specifies whether the index is primary or secondary, while the latter determines the type of the secondary index ("P" for PATH, "V" for VALUE, and "R" for PROPERTY secondary index). (Besides that, this view inherits columns from the **sys.indexes** catalog view.)

Typed vs. Untyped XML

As you already know from Chapter 27, an XML document can be well formed and valid. (Only a well-formed document can be validated.) An XML document that conforms to one or more given schemas is said to be *schema valid* and is called an *instance document* of the schemas. The XML schemas are used to perform more precise type checks during compilation of queries.

XML data type columns, variables, and parameters may be typed (conform to a set of schemas) or untyped. In other words, whenever a typed XML instance is assigned to an XML column data type, variable, or parameter, the system validates the instance.

The following section explains the use of XML schemas, after which typed XML instances are discussed in more detail.

XML Schemas and SQL Server   An XML schema specifies a set of data types that exist in a particular namespace. XML Schema (or XML Schema Definition Language) is a data definition language for XML documents.

SQL Server uses the CREATE XML SCHEMA COLLECTION statement to import the schema components into the database. Example 28.5 shows the use of this statement.

EXAMPLE 28.5

USE sample;
CREATE XML SCHEMA COLLECTION EmployeeSchema AS
    N'<?xml version="1.0" encoding="UTF-16"?>
    <xsd:schema elementFormDefault="unqualified"

```
    attributeFormDefault="unqualified"
    xmlns:xsd="http://www.w3.org/2001/XMLSchema" >
     <xsd:element name="employees">
       <xsd:complexType mixed="false">
        <xsd:sequence>
          <xsd:element name="fname" type="xsd:string"/>
          <xsd:element name="lname" type="xsd:string"/>
          <xsd:element name="department" type="xsd:string"/>
          <xsd:element name="salary" type="xsd:integer"/>
          <xsd:element name="comments" type="xsd:string"/>
        </xsd:sequence>
       </xsd:complexType>
     </xsd:element>
    </xsd:schema>';
```

Example 28.5 shows how the CREATE XML SCHEMA COLLECTION statement can be used to catalog the **EmployeeSchema** schema as a database object. The XML schema for Example 28.5 includes attributes (elements) for employees, such as family name, last name, and salary. (A detailed discussion of XML schemas is outside the scope of this introductory book.)

Generally, an XML schema collection has a name, which can be qualified using the relational schema name (**dbo.EmployeeSchema**, for instance). The schema collection consists of one or more schemas that define the types in one or more XML namespaces. If the **targetNamespace** attribute is omitted from an XML schema, that schema does not have an associated namespace. (There is a maximum of one such schema inside an XML schema collection.)

SQL Server also supports the ALTER XML SCHEMA COLLECTION and DROP XML SCHEMA COLLECTION statements. The former allows you to add new schemas to an existing XML schema collection, while the latter deletes an entire schema collection.

Typed XML Columns, Variables, and Parameters   Each typed XML column, variable, or parameter must be specified with associated schemas. To do this, the name of the schema collection, which is created using the CREATE XML SCHEMA COLLECTION statement, must be written inside the pair of parentheses, after the instance name. Example 28.6 shows this.

EXAMPLE 28.6

```
USE sample;
CREATE TABLE xml_persontab (id INTEGER,
  xml_person XML(EmployeeSchema));
```

The **xml_person** column in Example 28.6 is associated with the XML schema collection **EmployeeSchema** (see Example 28.5). This means that all specifications from defined schemas are used to check whether the content of the **xml_person** column is valid. In other words, when you insert a new value in the typed XML column (or modify an existing value), all constraints specified in the schemas are checked.

The specification of an XML schema collection for the typed XML instance can be extended with two keywords:

▶ DOCUMENT

▶ CONTENT

The DOCUMENT keyword specifies that the XML column can contain only XML documents, while the CONTENT keyword, the default value, specifies that the XML column can contain either documents or fragments. (Remember, an XML document must have a single root element.)

Example 28.7 shows the use of the DOCUMENT keyword.

EXAMPLE 28.7

```
USE sample;
CREATE TABLE xml_persontab_doc (id INTEGER,
            xml_person XML(DOCUMENT EmployeeSchema));
```

XML Schema Catalog Views   SQL Server supports several catalog views in relation to XML Schema, the most important of which are the following:

▶ **sys.xml_schema_attributes**   Returns a row per XML schema component that is an attribute

▶ **sys.xml_schema_elements**   Returns a row per XML schema component that is an element

▶ **sys.xml_schema_components**   Returns a row per component of an XML schema

Storing XML Documents Using Decomposition

The **sp_xml_preparedocument** system procedure reads the XML text provided as input, parses the text, and represents the parsed document as a tree with the various nodes: elements, attributes, text, and comments.

Example 28.8 shows the use of the **sp_xml_preparedocument** system procedure.

EXAMPLE 28.8

```
USE sample;
DECLARE @hdoc int
DECLARE @doc varchar(1000)
SET @doc ='<ROOT>
     <Employee>
        <Name>Ann Jones</Name>
        <No>10102</No>
        <Deptno>d3</Deptno>
        <Address>Dallas</Address>
     </Employee>
     <Employee>
        <Name>John Barrimore</Name>
        <No>18316</No>
        <Deptno>d1</Deptno>
        <Address>Seattle</Address>
     </Employee>
</ROOT>'
EXEC sp_xml_preparedocument @hdoc OUTPUT, @doc
```

The XML document in Example 28.8 is stored as a string in the **@doc** variable.
This string is shredded by the **sp_xml_preparedocument** system procedure. The
procedure returns a handle (**@hdoc**) that can then be used to access the newly created
representation of the XML document.

The **sp_xml_removedocument** system procedure removes the internal representation
of the XML document specified by the document handle and invalidates the document
handle.

The next section shows how you can retrieve the stored XML data in the relational
form.

Retrieving Stored XML Documents and Fragments

You can generate a set of rows from XML documents and fragments, and query it by
using the Transact-SQL language. This is done using OpenXML, which lets you use
Transact-SQL statements to extract data from an XML document. Using OpenXML,
you can retrieve the data from an XML document as if it were in a relational table.
(OpenXML is an international standard for documents that can be freely implemented
by multiple applications on multiple platforms.)

Example 28.9 shows how you can query the XML document from Example 28.8 using OpenXML.

NOTE

The code in Example 28.9 must be appended to the code in Example 28.8 and executed together.

EXAMPLE 28.9

```
SELECT * FROM OPENXML (@hdoc, '/ROOT/Employee', 1)
    WITH (name VARCHAR(20)  'Name',
        no INT 'No',
        deptno VARCHAR(6) 'Deptno',
        address VARCHAR(50) 'Address');
```

The result is

Name	no	deptno	address
Ann Jones	10102	d3	Dallas
John Barrimore	18316	d1	Seattle

Presenting Relational Data as XML Documents

As you already know from Chapter 6, a SELECT statement queries one or more tables and displays the corresponding result set. The result set is displayed by default as a table. If you want to display the result set of a query as an XML document or fragment, you can use the FOR XML clause in your SELECT statement. With this clause, you can specify one of the four following modes:

▶ RAW

▶ AUTO

▶ EXPLICIT

▶ PATH

NOTE

The FOR XML clause must be specified at the end of the SELECT statement.

The following sections describe each of these modes.

RAW Mode

The FOR XML RAW option transforms each row of the result set into an XML element with the identifier <row>. Each column value is mapped to an attribute of the XML element in which the attribute name is the same as the column name. (This is true only for the non-null columns.)

Example 28.10 shows the use of the FOR XML RAW option specified for the join of the **employee** and **works_on** tables from the **sample** database.

EXAMPLE 28.10

```
USE sample;
SELECT  employee.emp_no, emp_lname, works_on.job
FROM employee, works_on
WHERE employee.emp_no <= 10000
AND employee.emp_no = works_on.emp_no
FOR XML RAW;
```

Example 28.10 displays the following XML document fragment:

```
<row emp_no="2581" emp_lname="Hansel    " job="Analyst   " />
<row emp_no="9031" emp_lname="Bertoni   " job="Manager   " />
<row emp_no="9031" emp_lname="Bertoni   " job="Clerk     " />
```

Without the FOR XML RAW option, the SELECT statement in Example 28.10 would retrieve the following rows:

emp_no	emp_lname	job
2581	Hansel	Analyst
9031	Bertoni	Manager
9031	Bertoni	Clerk

As you can see from both results, the first output produces one XML element for each row in the result set.

AUTO Mode

AUTO mode returns the result set of a query as a simple, nested XML tree. Each table in the FROM clause from which at least one column appears in the SELECT list is represented as an XML element. The columns in the SELECT list are mapped to the appropriate elements' attributes.

Example 28.11 shows the use of AUTO mode.

EXAMPLE 28.11

```
USE sample;
SELECT  employee.emp_no, emp_lname, works_on.job
FROM employee, works_on
WHERE employee.emp_no <= 10000
AND employee.emp_no = works_on.emp_no
FOR XML AUTO;
```

The result is

```
<employee emp_no="9031" emp_lname="Bertoni         ">
  <works_on job="Manager     " />
  <works_on job="Clerk        " />
</employee>
<employee emp_no="2581" emp_lname="Hansel          ">
  <works_on job="Analyst      " />
</employee>
```

The result in Example 28.11 is significantly different from the result in the previous example, although the SELECT statement for both examples is equivalent (except for the specification of AUTO mode instead of RAW mode). As you can see from Example 28.11, the result set is displayed as the hierarchy of the **employee** and **works_on** tables. This hierarchy is based on the primary key/foreign key relationship of both tables. For this reason, the data from the **employee** table is displayed first, and the corresponding data from the **works_on** table is displayed after that, at the lower hierarchy level.

The nesting of the elements in the resulting XML document or fragment is based on the order of tables identified by the columns specified in the SELECT clause; therefore, the order in which column names are specified in the SELECT clause is significant. For this reason, in Example 28.11 the values of the **emp_no** column of the **employee** table form the top element in the resulting XML fragment. The values of the **job** column of the **works_on** table form a subelement within the top element.

EXPLICIT Mode

As you can see from Example 28.11, the result set in AUTO mode is displayed as a simple, nested XML tree. The queries in AUTO mode are good if you want to generate simple hierarchies, because this mode provides little control over the shape of the XML document generated from a query result.

If you want to specify the extended form of the result set, you can use the FOR XML EXPLICIT option. With this option, the result set is displayed as a universal table that has all the information about the resulting XML tree. The data in the table is vertically partitioned into groups. Each group then becomes an XML element in the result set.

Example 28.12 shows the use of EXPLICIT mode.

EXAMPLE 28.12

```
USE sample;
SELECT 1 AS tag, NULL as parent,
emp_lname AS [employee!1!emp_lname],
NULL AS [works_on!2!job]
FROM employee
UNION
SELECT  2, 1, emp_lname, works_on.job
FROM employee, works_on
WHERE employee.emp_no <= 10000
AND employee.emp_no = works_on.emp_no
ORDER BY [employee!1!emp_lname]
FOR XML EXPLICIT;
```

The result is

```
<employee emp_lname="Barrimore         " />
<employee emp_lname="Bertoni           ">
  <works_on job="Clerk        " />
  <works_on job="Manager      " />
</employee>
<employee emp_lname="Hansel            ">
  <works_on job="Analyst      " />
</employee>
<employee emp_lname="James             " />
<employee emp_lname="Jones             " />
<employee emp_lname="Moser             " />
<employee emp_lname="Smith             " />
```

As you can see from the SELECT statement in Example 28.12, the FOR XML EXPLICIT option requires two additional metadata columns: **tag** and **parent**. (These two columns are used to determine the primary key/foreign key relationship in the XML tree.) The **tag** column stores the tag number of the current element, while the **parent** column stores the tag number of the parent element. (The parent table is the table with the primary key.) If the parent tag is NULL, the row is placed directly under the root element.

NOTE

Do not use EXPLICIT mode because of its complexity. Use PATH mode instead (discussed next).

PATH Mode

All of the three FOR XML options described above have different disadvantages and restrictions. The FOR XML RAW option supports only one level of nesting, while the FOR XML AUTO option requires that all columns selected from the same table occur at the same level. Also, both options do not allow mixing of elements and attributes in the same XML document. On the other hand, the FOR XML EXPLICIT option allows mixing of elements and attributes, but the syntax of this option is cumbersome, as you can see from the previous example.

The FOR XML PATH option allows you to implement in a very easy way almost all queries that require EXPLICIT mode. In PATH mode, column names or column aliases are treated as XPath expressions, which indicate how the values are being mapped to XML. (An XPath expression consists of a sequence of nodes, possibly separated by /. For each slash, the system creates another level of hierarchy in the resulting document.)

Example 28.13 shows the use of PATH mode.

EXAMPLE 28.13

```
USE sample;
SELECT d.dept_name "@Department",
    emp_fname   "EmpName/First",
    emp_lname   "EmpName/Last"
FROM   Employee e, department d
WHERE  e.dept_no = d.dept_no
AND    d.dept_no = 'd1'
FOR XML PATH;
```

The result is

```
<row Department="Research         ">
  <EmpName>
    <First>John          </First>
    <Last>Barrimore       </Last>
  </EmpName>
</row>
<row Department="Research         ">
  <EmpName>
    <First>Sybill        </First>
    <Last>Moser         </Last>
  </EmpName>
</row>
```

In PATH mode, the column names are used as the path in constructing an XML document. The column containing department names starts with @. This means that the **Department** attribute is added to the <row> element. All other columns include a / in the column name, indicating hierarchy. For this reason, the resulting XML document will have the <EmpName> child under the <row> element and <First> and <Last> elements at the next sublevel.

Directives

SQL Server supports several different directives that allow you to produce different results when you want to display XML documents and fragments. The following list shows several of these directives:

► TYPE

► ELEMENTS (with XSINIL)

► ROOT

The following subsections describe these directives.

TYPE Directive

SQL Server allows you to store the result of a relational query as an XML document or fragment in the XML data type by using the TYPE directive. When the TYPE directive is specified, a query with the FOR XML option returns a one-row, one-column result set. (This directive is a common directive, meaning you can use it in all four modes.) Example 28.14 shows the use of the TYPE directive with AUTO mode.

EXAMPLE 28.14

```
USE sample;
DECLARE @x xml;
SET @x = (SELECT * FROM department
            FOR XML AUTO, TYPE);
SELECT @x;
```

The result is

```
<department dept_no="d1  " dept_name="Research     " location="Dallas  " />
<department dept_no="d2  " dept_name="Accounting   " location="Seattle " />
<department dept_no="d3  " dept_name="Marketing    " location="Dallas  " />
```

Example 28.14 first declares the variable **@x** as a local variable of the XML data type and assigns the result of the SELECT statement to it. The last SELECT statement in the batch displays the content of the variable.

ELEMENTS Directive

As you already know from Chapter 3, Database Engine supports NULL values to specify unknown (or missing) values. In contrast to the relational model, XML does not support NULL values, and those values are omitted in the result sets of queries with the FOR XML option.

SQL Server allows you to display the missing values in an XML document by using the ELEMENTS directive with the XSINIL option. Generally, the ELEMENTS directive constructs the corresponding XML document so that each column value maps to an element. If the column value is NULL, no element is added by default. By specifying the additional XSINIL option, you can request that an element be created for the NULL value as well. In this case, an element with the XSINIL attribute set to true is returned for each NULL value in the column.

ROOT Directive

Generally, queries with the FOR XML option produce XML fragments—XML without a corresponding root element. This can be a problem if an API accepts only XML documents as input. SQL Server allows you to add the root element using the ROOT directive. By specifying the ROOT directive in the FOR XML query, you can request a single, top-level element for the resulting XML. (The argument specified for the directive provides the root element.)

Example 28.15 shows the use of the ROOT directive.

EXAMPLE 28.15

USE sample;
SELECT * FROM department
FOR XML AUTO, ROOT ('AllDepartments');

The result is

```
<AllDepartments>
 <department dept_no="d1 " dept_name="Research   " location="Dallas  " />
 <department dept_no="d2 " dept_name="Accounting " location="Seattle " />
 <department dept_no="d3 " dept_name="Marketing  " location="Dallas  " />
</AllDepartments>
```

The query in Example 28.15 displays the XML fragment with all rows from the **department** table. The ROOT directive adds the root specification in the result set with the **AllDepartments** parameter as the root name.

SQL Server XQuery Methods

XQuery is the new query language for XML. This language is much more complex than XPath (As a matter of fact, XQuery contains X Path as a sublanguage.) You can convert the data in relational and XML columns to an XML data type instance using FOR XML with the TYPE directive and query it by using XQuery. SQL Server supports five methods that can be used to query XML documents with XQuery:

▶ **query()**   Accepts an XQuery statement as input and returns an instance of the XML data type.

▶ **exist()**   Accepts an XQuery statement as input and returns 0, 1, or NULL, depending on the query result.

▶ **value()**   Accepts an XQuery statement as input and returns a single scalar value.

▶ **nodes()**   This method is useful when you want to shred an **XML** data type instance into relational data. It allows you to identify nodes that will be mapped into a new row.

▶ **modify()**   In contrast to the standardized version of XQuery, which in its Version 1.0 does not have the specifications for update statements, SQL Server supports insertion, modification, and deletion of XML documents using the **modify()** method.

NOTE

You can find detailed descriptions of XQuery in Books Online.

The following two examples show the use of two XQuery methods. Example 28.16 shows the use of the **query()** method.

EXAMPLE 28.16

```
USE sample;
SELECT xml_column.query('/PersonList/Title')
   FROM xmltab
   FOR XML AUTO, TYPE;
```

The result is

```
<xmltab>
    <Title> Value="Employee List"&gt;</Title>
</xmltab>
```

The SELECT list of the query in Example 28.16 contains the **query()** method with an XPath expression. (Note that the SQL Server XQuery methods are applied using dot notation.) The expression '/PersonList/Title' is an absolute expression, where the value of the **Title** element is retrieved. (Remember that XPath expressions are valid XQuery statements because XPath is a sublanguage of XQuery.)

As you already know, the **exist()** method accepts an XQuery statement as input and returns 0, 1, or NULL, depending on the query result. If the query result is an empty sequence, the return value is 0. A sequence with at least one item returns 1, and NULL is returned if the value of the column is NULL. Example 28.17 shows the use of the **exist()** method.

EXAMPLE 28.17

```
SELECT xml_column.exist('/PersonList/Title/@Value=EmployeeList') AS a
   FROM xmltab
   FOR XML AUTO, TYPE;
```

The result is

```
<xmltab a="1" />
```

The SELECT list of the query in Example 28.17 contains the **exist()** method with an XPath expression that tests whether the **Value** attribute of the XML document has the value **EmployeeList**. The test is evaluated to true, and therefore the return value of the query is 1.

SQL Server 2008 and XML Enhancements

SQL Server 2008 has the following minor changes in relation to the XML Schema support:

► Improved support for the **xs:dateTime, xs:date** and **xs:time** temporal functions. ("xs" is the namespace prefix associated with XML Schema)

► Improved support for the **xs:list** and **xs:union** functions.

As you already know from Chapter 4, SQL Server 2008 supports new data types DATE and TIME. The corresponding XML Schema data types are supported, too.

You can use XML schemas to define data types for your XML data that allow a limited set of values to be assigned to multi-value elements and attributes. One of them is **xs:list**, which is now supported. Also, SQL Server 2008 adds support for **union** types that contain **list** types, which you can use to merge multiple list type definitions and restrictions into a single type.

Besides these two enhancements, the system supports the **sql:variable** and **sql:column** functions on a parameter of the XML data type.

Conclusion

SQL Server has full support for XML. The most important feature is the existence of the XML data type, which allows the database system to store XML documents as first class objects.

The values of the XML data type can be schema validated if one or more schemas are associated with this type. You can determine the exact data types of elements and attributes only if the corresponding XML document contains types specified by XML schemas. Schema definitions are specified using the CREATE XML SCHEMA COLLECTION statement.

XML also has its own query languages, the most important of which is XQuery. SQL Server supports several non-standard methods that can be used to query XML documents with XQuery.

The next chapter describes spatial data.

Chapter 29

Introduction to Spatial Data

In This Chapter

I n the past few years, the need of businesses to incorporate geographic data into their databases and to manage it using a database system has grown significantly. The most important factor leading to this growth is the proliferation of geographical services and devices, such as Microsoft Virtual Earth and low-priced GPS devices.

Generally, the support of spatial data by a database vendor helps users to make better decisions in several scenarios, such as:

▶ Real-estate analysis ("Find a suitable property within 500m of an elementary school.")

▶ Consumer-based information ("Find the nearest shopping malls to a given ZIP code.")

▶ Market analysis ("Define geographic sales regions and ascertain whether there is a necessity for a new branch office.")

The first part of this chapter introduces two different spatial models. After that, the GEOMETRY data type and the corresponding methods are discussed in detail. Finally, the practical use of the methods in queries will be shown.

Presenting Spatial Data

Generally, there are two different groups of models for presenting spatial data:

▶ Geodetic spatial models

▶ Flat spatial models

The following sections describe these two groups.

Geodetic Spatial Models

Planets are complex objects that can be represented using a flattened sphere (called a *spheroid*). A good approximation for the representation of Earth (and other planets) is a globe, where locations on the surface are described using latitude and longitude. (Latitude gives the location of a place on Earth north or south of the equator, while longitude specifies the location in relation to a chosen meridian.) Models that use these measures are called *geodetic models*. Because these models provide a good approximation of spheroids, they provide the most accurate way to represent spatial data.

Flat Spatial Models

Flat spatial models (or planar models) use two-dimensional maps to represent Earth. In this case, the spheroid is flattened and projected in a plane. The flattening process results in some deformation of shape and size of the projected (geographic) objects. Flat spatial models work best for small surface areas, because the larger the surface area being represented, the more deformation that occurs.

Spatial Data Types

SQL Server 2008 provides two spatial data types:

▶ **GEOGRAPHY**   Represents spatial data in geodetic spatial models
▶ **GEOMETRY**   Represents spatial data in the flat spatial models

Both data types are implemented using CLR, and can be used to store different kinds of geographical elements such as points, lines, and polygons.

The following section describes the GEOMETRY data type in detail and gives some examples of how you can use it. Because the GEOGRAPHY data type is very similar to the GEOMETRY data type, only the GEOMETRY data type is described in detail, but a short section describing the differences between the two data types wraps up the chapter.

GEOMETRY Data Type

An example will help to explain the use of the GEOMETRY data type. Example 29.1 creates a table for nonalcoholic beverage markets in a given city (or state).

EXAMPLE 29.1

```
USE sample;
CREATE TABLE beverage_markets
    (id INTEGER IDENTITY(1,1),
     name VARCHAR(25),
     shape GEOMETRY);
INSERT INTO beverage_markets
        VALUES ('Coke', geometry::STGeomFromText
            ('POLYGON ((0 0, 150 0, 150 150, 0 150, 0 0))', 0));
INSERT INTO beverage_markets
        VALUES ('Pepsi', geometry::STGeomFromText
            ('POLYGON ((300 0, 150 0, 150 150, 300 150, 300 0))', 0));
```

```
INSERT INTO beverage_markets
        VALUES ('7UP', geometry::STGeomFromText
    ('POLYGON ((300 0, 150 0, 150 150, 300 150, 300 0))', 0));
INSERT INTO beverage_markets
        VALUES ('Almdudler', geometry::STGeomFromText
        ('POINT (50 0)', 0));
```

The beverage_markets table has three columns, of which the first one is just the **id** column, while the second, **name**, contains the beverage name. The third column, **shape**, specifies the shape of the market area in which the particular beverage is the most preferred one. The first three INSERT statements create three areas in which a particular beverage is most preferred. All three areas happen to be a polygon. The fourth INSERT statement inserts a point, because there is just one place where the particular beverage (Almdudler) can be bought.

As you can see from Example 29.1, the **STGeomFromText()** method is used to insert the coordinates of geometric figures, such as polygons and points. This method belongs to a group of static geography methods, discussed next. After that spatial indexing will be discussed in detail.

Static Geometry Methods

Using the GEOMETRY data type, you can specify spatial predicates on instances of spatial geometries within standard SQL statements. These predicates use special methods to perform spatial operations such as calculating distances between locations. (The same is true for the GEOGRAPHY data type.)

SQL Server 2008 supports the static geometry methods specified by the Open Geospatial Consortium (OGC). OGC is a nonprofit organization that is leading the development of standards for spatial data. The aim of the organization is to provide the necessary specification for features in relation to spatial data. The task of the software vendors is to implement the whole or part of the specification. (The vendors sometimes implement some nonstandard features, too.)

The list of static geometry methods specified by OGC and implemented by Microsoft is rather long. For this reason, just four methods that can be applied to the GEOMETRY data type are introduced here:

▶ **STGeomFromText()**   Returns an instance of the GEOMETRY data type from the Well-Known Text (WKT) representation, augmented with the corresponding elevation and measure values. (MKT specifies a text markup language for representing vector geometry objects.)

- ▶ **STPointFromText()** Returns the WKT representation of a POINT instance.
- ▶ **STLineFromText()** Returns the WKT representation of a LINESTRING instance augmented with the corresponding elevation and measure values.
- ▶ **STPolyFromText()** Returns the WKT representation of a MULTIPOLYGON instance augmented with the corresponding elevation and measure values.

NOTE
Besides static geometry methods, there are other geometry methods that are used with the DML statements; they are explained a bit later in the section "Querying the GEOMETRY Data."

Spatial Indexing

As you already know from Chapter 10, indexing is generally used to provide fast access to data. Therefore, spatial indices are necessary to speed up retrieval operations on spatial data.

A spatial index is defined on a table column of the GEOMETRY or GEOGRAPHY data type. In SQL Server 2008, spatial indices are built using B-trees, which means that the indices represent two dimensions in the linear order of B-trees. Therefore, before reading data into a spatial index, SQL Server 2008 implements a hierarchical uniform decomposition of space. The index-creation process decomposes the space into a four-level grid hierarchy.

NOTE
There are several types of indices that are used especially for spatial data. The most important one is called R-tree index. Hopefully this index type will be implemented by Microsoft in a subsequent version of SQL Server.

The CREATE SPATIAL INDEX statement is used to create a spatial index. The general form of this statement is similar to the convenient CREATE INDEX statement, but contains additional options and clauses, some of which are introduced here:

- ▶ **GEOMETRY_GRID clause** Specifies the geometry grid tessellation scheme that you are using. (Tessellation is a process that is performed after reading the data for a spatial object. During this process, the object is fitted into the grid hierarchy by associating it with a set of grid cells that it touches.) GEOMETRY_GRID can be specified only on a column of the GEOMETRY data type.

- ▶ **BOUNDING_BOX option**   Specifies a numeric four-tuple that defines the four coordinates of the bounding box: the x-min and y-min coordinates of the lower-left corner, and the x-max and y-max coordinates of the upper-right corner. This option applies only within the GEOMETRY_GRID clause.

- ▶ **GEOGRAPHY_GRID clause**   Specifies the geography grid tessellation scheme. This clause can be specified only on a column of the GEOGRAPHY data type.

Example 29.2 shows the creation of a spatial index for the **shape** column of the **beverage_markets** table.

EXAMPLE 29.2

```
USE sample;
GO
ALTER TABLE beverage_markets
 ADD CONSTRAINT prim_key PRIMARY KEY(id);
GO
CREATE SPATIAL INDEX i_spatial_shape
  ON beverage_markets(shape)
  USING GEOMETRY_GRID
  WITH (
  BOUNDING_BOX = ( xmin=0, ymin=0, xmax=500, ymax=200 ),
  GRIDS = (LOW, LOW, MEDIUM, HIGH),
  PAD_INDEX  = ON );
```

A spatial index can be created only if the primary key for the table with a spatial data column is explicitly defined. For this reason, the first statement in Example 29.2 is the ALTER TABLE statement, which defines this constraint.

The subsequent CREATE SPATIAL INDEX statement creates the index using the GEOMETRY_GRID clause. The BOUNDING_BOX option specifies the boundaries inside which the instance of the **shape** column will be placed. The GRIDS option specifies the density of the grid at each level of a tessellation scheme. (The PAD_INDEX option is described in Chapter 10.)

SQL Server 2008 supports, among others, two catalog views related to spatial data:

- ▶ sys.spatial_indexes
- ▶ sys.spatial_index_tessellations

The **sys.spatial indexes** view represents the main index information of the spatial indices. Using the **sys.spatial_index_tessellations** view, you can display the information about the tessellation scheme and parameters of each of the existing spatial indices. Example 29.3 shows the information that can be displayed using this view.

EXAMPLE 29.3

SELECT object_id, name, type_desc
    FROM sys.spatial_indexes

The result is

Object_id	name	type_desc
914102297	i_spatial_shape	SPATIAL

Querying the GEOMETRY Data

Spatial data can be queried the same way relational data is queried. SQL server supports many geometry methods for querying spatial data. The following examples show a sample of the information that can be found from the content of the **shape** column of the **beverage_markets** table.

Example 29.4 shows the use of the **STContains**() method.

EXAMPLE 29.4

Does the shop that sells Almdudler lie in the area where Coke is the preferred beverage?

DECLARE @g geometry;
DECLARE @h geometry;
SELECT @h = shape FROM beverage_markets WHERE name ='Almdudler';
SELECT @g = shape FROM beverage_markets WHERE name = 'Coke';
SELECT @g.STContains(@h);

The result is 0.

The **STContains**() method returns 1 if an instance of the GEOMETRY data type completely contains another instance of the same type. The result of Example 29.4 means that the shop that sells Almdudler does not belong to the area where the preferred beverage is Coke.

Example 29.5 shows the use of the **STLength**() method.

Find the length and the WKT representation of the **shape** column for the Almdudler shop:

```
SELECT id, shape.ToString() AS wkt, shape.STLength() AS length
    FROM beverage_markets
    WHERE name = 'Almdudler' ;
```

The result is

id	wkt	length
4	POINT (50 0)	0

The **STLength()** method in Example 29.5 returns the total length of the elements of the GEMOETRY data type. (The result is 0, because the displayed value is a point.) The **ToString()** method is the general method that loads an entire collection of variables with a single method call. In Example 29.5, this method is used to load all properties of the given point and to display it using the WKT representation.

Example 29.6 shows the use of the **STIntersects()** method.

Does the region that sells Coke intersect with the region that sells Pepsi?

```
USE sample;
DECLARE @g geometry;
DECLARE @h geometry;
SELECT @h = shape FROM beverage_markets WHERE name ='Coke';
SELECT @g = shape FROM beverage_markets WHERE name = 'Pepsi';
SELECT @g.STIntersects(@h);
```

The **STIntersects()** method in Example 29.6 is applied to both regions to find out whether the regions intersect. (The value 1 means that the regions intersect.)

NOTE

Besides the methods used in the preceding examples, there are many other nonstatic geometry methods, which are described in detail in Books Online.

Differences Between the GEOMETRY and GEOGRAPHY Data Types

As you already know, the GEOMETRY data type is used in flat spatial models, while the GEOGRAPHY data type is used in geodetic models. The main difference between these two groups of models is that with the GEOMETRY data type, distances and areas are given in the same unit of measurement as the coordinates of the instances. (Therefore, the distance between the points (0,0) and (3,4) will always be 5 units.) This is not the case with the GEOGRAPHY data type, which works with ellipsoidal coordinates that are expressed in degrees of latitude and longitude.

There are also some restrictions placed on the GEOGRAPHY data type. For example, each instance of the GEOGRAPHY data type must fit inside a single hemisphere. (Larger spatial objects are not allowed and will cause an error.)

Conclusion

SQL Server 2008 supports two spatial data types: GEOGRAPHY and GEOMETRY. The GEOGRAPHY data type is used to represent spatial data in geodetic models, while the GEOMETRY data type is used with flat spatial models. To work with these data types, you need a set of corresponding operations (i.e. methods). Microsoft implemented the static geometry methods specified by OGC. Besides the supported static geometry methods, there is another group of implemented methods that can be used to retrieve spatial data.

Index

C